The **Rough Guide** to

Vietnam

written and researched by

Jan Dodd, Ron Emmons, Mark Lewis and Martin Zatko

D1016191

ROUGH GUIDES

www.roughguides.com

Contents

Vietnam's natural wonders colour section following p.184

Vietnamese street food colour section following p.376

◀◀ Phu Quoc Island ◀ Exercisers at Hoan Kiem Lake

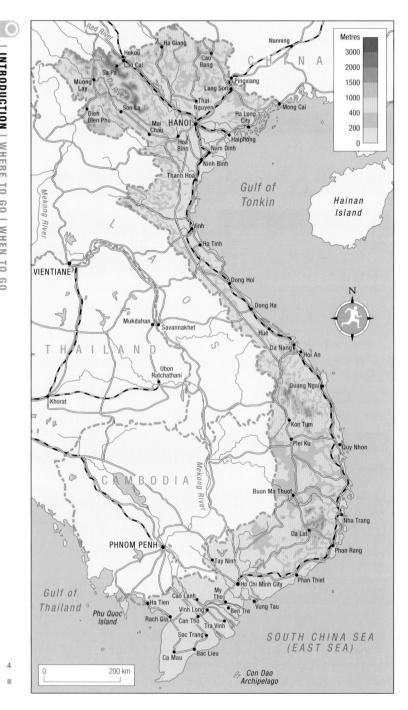

Metres
3000
2000
1500
1000
400
200
0

Introduction to
Vietnam

Few countries have changed so much over such a short time as Vietnam. Less than forty years since the savagery and slaughter of the American War, this resilient nation is buoyant with hope. It is a country on the move: access is now easier than ever, roads are being upgraded, hotels are springing up and Vietnam's raucous entrepreneurial spirit is once again alive and well as the old-style Communist system gives way to a socialist market economy. As the number of tourists finding their way here soars, the word is out that this is a land not of bomb craters and army ordnance but of shimmering paddy fields and sugar-white beaches, full-tilt cities and venerable pagodas – often overwhelming in its sheer beauty.

The speed with which Vietnam's population has been able to put the bitter events of its recent past behind it, and focus its gaze so steadfastly on the future, often surprises visitors expecting to encounter shell-shocked resentment of the West. It wasn't always like this, however. The reunification of North and South Vietnam in 1975, ending twenty years of bloody civil war, was followed by a decade or so of hardline centralist economic rule from which only the shake-up of **doi moi** – Vietnam's equivalent of *perestroika* – beginning in 1986, could awaken the country. This signalled a renaissance for Vietnam, and today a high fever of commerce grips the nation: from the flash new shopping malls and designer boutiques to the hustle and bustle of street markets and the booming cross-border trade with China. From a tourist's point of view, this is a great time to visit – not only to soak up the intoxicating sense of vitality and optimism, but also the chance to witness a country in profound flux. Inevitably, that's not the whole story. *Doi moi* is an economic policy, not a magic spell, and life, for much of the population, remains hard. Indeed, the move towards a market

Fact file

• The Socialist Republic of Vietnam, the **capital** of which is Hanoi, is one of the world's last surviving one-party **Communist states**. It shares land borders with China, Laos and Cambodia. Vietnam is a long, thin country comprising over 330,000 square kilometres, with more than 3400km of coastline. At its narrowest point it measures a mere 50km wide.

• Vietnam has a **population** of 86 million, of which 74 percent live in the countryside, giving Vietnam some of the highest rural population densities in Southeast Asia. Over half the people are under 25 years old and 13 percent belong to one of the many **ethnic minority groups**.

• Over half of the Vietnamese population earn their living from **agriculture**. The average per capita **income** hovers around $700 a year, though many people survive on less than $1 a day.

• During the last decade the Vietnamese **economy** has grown at over seven percent a year. Vietnam has transformed itself from being a rice-importer before 1986 to become the world's second largest rice-exporter after Thailand. The percentage of households living in poverty has fallen from seventy percent in the 1980s to under thirty percent today.

• Vietnam is home to a tremendous diversity of **plant and animal life**, including some of the world's rarest species, a number of which have only been discovered in the last few years. The Java rhino, Asiatic black bear, Sarus crane and golden-headed langur are just some of the endangered species maintaining a toehold in the forests and wetlands of Vietnam.

economy has predictably polarized the gap between rich and poor. Average monthly incomes for city-dwellers are around US$60, while in the poorest provinces workers may scrape by on as little as US$20 a month – a difference that amply illustrates the growing gulf between urban and rural Vietnam.

There is an equally marked difference between **north and south**, a deep psychological divide that was around long before the American War, and is engrained in Vietnamese culture. Northerners are considered reticent, thrifty, law-abiding and lacking the dynamism and entrepreneurial know-how of their more worldly-wise southern compatriots. Not surprisingly, this is mirrored in the broader economy: the south is Vietnam's growth engine, it boasts lower

◀ Sleeping cyclo driver

Tet

The biggest bash in Vietnam's festive calendar is the lunar New Year holiday known as **Tet Nguyen Dan**, or simply Tet. The date of the festival, which lasts for several days, varies from one year to the next, but falls somewhere between late January and the middle of February. Tet is the Vietnamese equivalent of Thanksgiving, New Year and a nationwide birthday celebration rolled into one – everyone becomes a year older at New Year. It is a time of forgiveness and fresh starts, when the trials and tribulations of the old year are left behind, to be replaced by renewed optimism for the year ahead. As the festival approaches, the streets fill with people buying new clothes, having their hair cut and stocking up on seasonal delicacies such as candied lotus seeds and sweetmeats made of sticky rice. Flower markets add to the colour with the first shy blossoms of peach, plum or apricot alongside miniature kumquat trees laden with their brash, golden fruit – the traditional symbols of Tet. The excitement culminates with municipal **fireworks displays** on New Year's Eve, after which the first few days of the year are traditionally devoted to renewing family ties – both with the living and with the ancestral spirits who come back to share in the feasting.

unemployment and higher average wages, and the increasingly glitzy Ho Chi Minh City looks more to Bangkok and Singapore than Hanoi.

Many visitors find more than enough to intrigue and excite them in Hanoi, Ho Chi Minh City and the other major centres; but despite the cities' allure, it's the country's striking **landscape** that most impresses. Vietnam occupies a narrow strip of land that hugs the eastern borders of Cambodia and Laos, hemmed in by rugged mountains to the west, and by the South China Sea – or the East Sea, as the Vietnamese call it. To the north and south of its narrow waist, it fantails out into the splendid deltas of the Red River and the Mekong, and it's in these regions that you'll encounter the paddy fields, dragonflies, buffaloes and conical-hatted farmers that constitute the classic image of Vietnam.

In stark contrast to the pancake-flat rice-land of the deltas, Ha Long Bay's labyrinthine network of **limestone outcrops** loom dramatically out of the Gulf of Tonkin – a magical spectacle in the early morning mist. Any trip to the remote upland regions of central and northern Vietnam is likely to focus upon the **ethnic minorities** who reside there. Elaborate tribal costumes, age-old customs and communal longhouses await those visitors game enough to trek into the sticks. As for **wildlife**, the discovery in recent years of several previously unknown species of plants, birds and animals speaks volumes for the wealth of Vietnam's biodiversity and makes the improving access to the country's several **national parks** all the more gratifying.

Where to go

The "Hanoi or bust" attitude, prompting new arrivals to doggedly labour between the country's two major cities, no matter how limited their time, blights many a trip to Vietnam. If you want to travel the length of the country at some leisure, see something of the highlands and the deltas and allow for a few rest days, you'll really need a month. With only two weeks at your disposal, the choice is either to hopscotch up the coast calling at only the most mainstream destinations or, perhaps better, to concentrate on one region and enjoy it at your own pace. However, if you *do* want to see both north and south in a fortnight, internal flights can speed up an itinerary substantially, and aren't too expensive.

For the majority of visitors, **Ho Chi Minh City** provides a head-spinning introduction to Vietnam. Set beside the broad swell of the Saigon River, the southern capital is rapidly being transformed into a Southeast Asian mover and shaker to compete with the best of them. The city's breakneck pace of life translates into a stew of bizarre characters and unlikely sights and sounds, and ensures that almost all who come here quickly fall for its singular charm. Furious commerce carries on cheek-by-jowl with age-old traditions; grandly indulgent colonial edifices peek out from under the shadows of looming office blocks and hotels; and cyclo drivers battle it out with late-model Japanese taxis in the chaotic boulevards.

Few tourists pass up the opportunity to take a day-trip out of the city to **Tay Ninh**, the nerve centre of the indigenous Cao Dai religion. The jury

◄ Hmong minority people

is still out on whether the ostentatious Cao Dai Holy See constitutes high art or dog's dinner, but either way it's one of Vietnam's most arresting sights, and is normally twinned with a stop-off at the Cu Chi Tunnels, where Vietnamese villagers dug themselves a warren stretching over two hundred kilometres, out of reach of US bombing.

Most tourists next venture southwest to explore the **Mekong Delta**, where one of the world's truly mighty rivers finally offloads into the South China Sea; its skein of brim-full tributaries and waterways has endowed the delta with a lush quilt of rice-rich flats and abundant orchards. You won't want to depart the delta without spending a day or more messing about on the water and visiting a floating market, which is easily arranged at **Cai Be** and **Can Tho**.

Da Lat, the "capital" of the central highlands, is chalk to Ho Chi Minh City's cheese.

> In the splendid deltas of the Red River and the Mekong you'll encounter the paddy fields, dragonflies, buffaloes and conical-hatted farmers that constitute the classic image of Vietnam.

Life passes by at a rather more dignified pace at this altitude, and the raw breezes that fan this oddly quaint hillside settlement provide the best air conditioning in Vietnam. **Minority peoples** inhabit the countryside around Da Lat, but to visit some really full-on montagnard villages you'll need to push north to the modest towns of **Buon Ma Thuot**, **Plei Ku** and **Kon Tum**, which are surrounded by E De, Jarai and Bahnar communities. Opt for Kon Tum, and you'll be able to visit minority villages independently or join treks that include river-rafting.

Northeast of Ho Chi Minh City, Highway 1, the country's jugular, girds its loins for the arduous journey up to Hanoi and the north. For many people, first stop is at the delightful beach and sand dunes of **Mui Ne**, fast becoming one of the country's top coastal resorts. Another popular spot is **Phan Rang**, which is blessed with some of the most splendid examples of the **Cham towers** that punctuate Vietnam's south-central coast. **Nha Trang** has grown into a crucial stepping stone on the Ho Chi Minh City –Hanoi run, and the tirelessly touted boat trips around the city's outlying islands are a must. North

▲ Burning incense at Quan Am pagoda

of Nha Trang, **Son My** village attained global notoriety when a company of American soldiers massacred some five hundred Vietnamese, including many women and children; unspeakable horrors continue to haunt the village's unnervingly idyllic rural setting.

Once a bustling seaport, the diminutive town of **Hoi An** perches beside an indolent backwater, its narrow streets of wooden-fronted shophouses and weathered roofs making it an enticing destination. Inland, the war-battered ruins of **My Son**, the greatest of the Cham temple sites, lie mouldering in a steamy, forest-filled valley. **Da Nang**, just up the coast, lacks Hoi An's charm, but good transport links make it a convenient base for the area. From Da Nang a corkscrew ride over clifftop Hai Van Pass, or a straight run through the new 6km-long tunnel, brings you to the aristocratic city of **Hué**, where the Nguyen emperors established their capital in the nineteenth century on the banks of the

> **Ha Long Bay provides the perfect antidote to urban exuberance, with its whimsically sculptured islands anchored in aquamarine waters**

languid Perfume River. The temples and palaces of this highly cultured city still testify to past splendours, while its Imperial mausoleums are master-pieces of architectural refinement, slumbering among pine-shrouded hills.

Only a hundred kilometres north of Hué, the tone changes as war-sites litter the Demilitarized Zone (**DMZ**), which cleaved the country in two from 1954 to 1975. More than three decades of peace have done much to heal the scars, but the monuments that pepper these windswept hills bear eloquent witness to a generation that lost their lives in the tragic struggle. The DMZ is most easily tackled as a day-trip from Hué, after which most people hop straight up to Hanoi. And there's little to detain you on the northward trek, save the glittering limestone caverns of **Phong Nha**, the entrance to a massive underground river system tunnelling under the Truong Son Mountains. Then, on the very fringes of the northern Red River Delta, lie the ancient incense-steeped temples of **Hoa Lu** and, nearby, the mystical landscapes of **Tam Coc** and **Van Long**, where paddy fields lap at the feet of limestone hummocks.

Anchored firmly in the Red River Delta, **Hanoi** has served as Vietnam's capital for close on a thousand years. It's a relatively small, decidedly proud city, a place of pagodas and dynastic temples, tamarisk-edged lakes and elegant boulevards of French-era villas, of national monuments and stately government edifices. But Hanoi is also being swept along on a tide of change as Vietnam forges its own shiny, high-rise capital. Though life proceeds at a slightly gentler pace than in Ho Chi Minh City, Hanoi is also throwing up new office blocks, hotels and restaurants.

From Hanoi most visitors strike out east to where northern Vietnam's premier natural attraction, **Ha Long Bay**, provides the perfect antidote to such urban exuberance, rewarding the traveller with a leisurely day or two drifting among the thousands of whimsically sculpted islands anchored in its aquamarine waters. Ha Long City, on the northern coast, is the usual embarkation point for Ha Long Bay, but a more appealing gateway is mountainous **Cat Ba Island**, which defines the bay's southwestern limits. The route to Cat Ba passes via the north's major port city, **Haiphong**, an unspectacular but genial place with an attractive core of faded colonial facades.

▲ Stilthouse around Mai Chau

Water-puppets

Vietnam's unique contribution to the world of marionettes, **water-puppetry** is a delightfully quirky form of theatre in which the action takes place on a stage of water. It was probably spawned in the murky rice paddies of the northern Red River Delta where performances still take place after the spring planting. Obscured by a split-bamboo screen, puppeteers standing waist-deep in water manipulate the wooden puppets, some weighing over 10kg, which are attached to the end of long poles concealed beneath the surface. Dragons, ducks, lions, unicorns, phoenixes and frogs spout smoke, throw balls and generally cavort on the watery stage – miraculously avoiding tangled poles. Brief scenes of rural life, such as water-buffalo fights, fishing or rice planting, take place alongside the legendary exploits of Vietnam's military heroes or perhaps a promenade of fairy-like immortals. In the more sophisticated productions staged for tourists in Hanoi and Ho Chi Minh City, even fireworks emerge to dance upon the water, which itself takes on different characters, from calm and placid to seething and furious during naval battles.

To the north and west of Hanoi mountain ranges rear up out of the Red River Delta. Vietnam's northern provinces aren't the easiest to get around, but these wild uplands are home to a patchwork of ethnic minorities and the country's most dramatic mountain landscapes. The bustling market town of **Sa Pa**, set in a spectacular location close to the Chinese border in the far northwest, makes a good base for exploring nearby minority villages, though a building boom has taken some of the shine off its laidback vibe. Further south, the stilthouse-filled valley of **Mai Chau** offers another opportunity to stay in a minority village. Though few people venture further inland, rough backroads heading upcountry link isolated outposts and give access to the northwest's only specific sight, where the French colonial dream expired in the dead-end valley of **Dien Bien Phu**. East of the Red River Valley lies an even less-frequented region, whose prime attraction is its varied scenery, from the vertigo-inducing valleys of **Ha Giang** to the limestone crags and multi-layered rainforest of **Ba Be National Park**, then east over immense, empty hill country to the remote valleys of **Cao Bang**, farmed by communities still practising their traditional ways of life.

When to go

Vietnam has a tropical monsoon **climate**, dominated by the south or southwesterly monsoon from May to September and the northeast monsoon from October to April. The southern summer monsoon brings rain to the two deltas and west-facing slopes, while the cold winter monsoon picks up moisture over the Gulf of Tonkin and dumps it along the central coast and the eastern edge of the central highlands. Within this basic pattern there are marked differences according to altitude and latitude; temperatures in the south remain equable all year round, while the north experiences distinct seasonal variations.

In **southern Vietnam** the dry season lasts from December to late April or May, and the rains from May through to November. Since most rain falls in brief afternoon downpours, this need not be off-putting, though flooding at this time of year can cause problems in the Mekong Delta. Daytime temperatures in the region rarely drop below 20°C, occasionally hitting 40°C during the hottest months (March, April and May). The climate of the central highlands generally follows the same pattern, though temperatures are cooler, especially at night. Again, the monsoon rains of May to October can make transport more complicated, sometimes washing out roads and cutting off remoter villages.

Along the **central coast** the rainfall pattern reverses under the influence of the northeast monsoon. Around Nha Trang the wet season starts with a flourish in November and continues to December. Further north, around Hué and Da Nang, the rains last a bit longer, from September to February, though even the dry season (March–Aug) brings a fair quantity of intermittent rain. If possible it pays to visit these two cities in the spring (Feb–May), just before the rains break in September or as they begin to fizzle out in November.

◀ The Old Quarter, Hanoi

13

Temperatures reach their maximum (often in the upper 30s) from June to August, when it's pleasant to escape into the hills. The northern stretches of this coastal region experience a more extreme climate, with a shorter rainy season (peaking in Sept and Oct) and a hot dry summer. The coast of central Vietnam is the zone most likely to be hit by **typhoons**, bringing torrential rain and hurricane-force winds. Though notoriously difficult to predict, in general the typhoon season lasts from August to November.

◀ Market vendor, Ho Chi Minh City

Northern Vietnam is generally warm and sunny from October to December, after which cold winter weather sets in, accompanied by fine persistent mists which can last for several days. Temperatures begin to rise again in March, building to summer maximums that occasionally reach 40°C between May and August, though average temperatures in Hanoi hover around a more reasonable 30°C. However, summer is also the rainy season, when heavy downpours render the low-lying delta area almost unbearably hot and sticky, and flooding is a regular hazard. The northern mountains share the same basic regime, though temperatures are considerably cooler and higher regions see ground frosts, or even a rare snowfall, during the winter (Dec–Feb).

With such a complicated weather picture, there's no one particular season to recommend as the **best time** for visiting Vietnam. Overall, autumn (Sept–Dec) and spring (March and April) are probably the most favourable seasons if you're covering the whole country.

Average daily temperatures (°C) and rainfall (mm)

	Jan	Feb	Mar	Apr	May	Jun	Jul	Aug	Sep	Oct	Nov	Dec
Ho Chi Minh City												
Temperature	27	28	29	30	29	29	28	28	27	27	27	27
Rainfall	15	3	13	43	221	330	315	269	335	269	114	56
Da Nang												
Temperature	22	23	24	27	29	30	30	30	28	26	25	23
Rainfall	102	31	12	18	47	42	99	117	447	530	221	209
Hanoi												
Temperature	17	18	20	24	28	30	30	29	28	26	22	19
Rainfall	18	28	38	81	196	239	323	343	254	99	43	20

31

things not to miss

It's not possible to see everything Vietnam has to offer in one trip – and we don't suggest you try. What follows is a selective taste of the country's highlights: outstanding architecture, classic landscapes and mouthwatering food and drink, arranged in five colour-coded categories which you can browse through to find the very best things to see, do and experience. All highlights have a page reference to take you straight into the Guide, where you can find out more.

01 Ethnic markets Pages **433** & **435** • Spectacular traditional dress and a lively atmosphere make the ethnic minority markets a must – especially those in Bac Ha and Can Cau.

02 **Nha Trang** Page **240** • Take a snorkelling trip in the emerald waters of the outlying islands around Nha Trang, or simply chill out on the beach.

04 **Traditional music** Pages **309** & **381** • Music is the most important of all Vietnam's performing arts and a traditional performance should feature on every itinerary.

03 **Snake wine** Page **53** • Partake of a glass of "snake wine", a snake-laced liquor that's supposedly imbued with all sorts of health-giving properties.

05 Water-puppets

Page **381** • Enjoy a performance of *mua roi nuoc* (puppets that dance on the water), an art form developed in the Red River Delta around Hanoi.

06 Express silk tailoring

Page **277** • Pick up a bargain at Hoi An market from one of the many tailors who can rustle up a made-to-measure silk dress, suit or even shoes for you in just a few hours.

07 Cu Chi tunnels

Page **122** • Look out for the spiked booby traps that Vietnamese guides reveal for visitors to the Cu Chi Tunnels.

09 Trekking around Sa Pa Page **431** • Go trekking in the northern mountains around Sa Pa – a small market town perched on a high plateau facing Fan Si Pan, Vietnam's highest peak.

08 Take a cyclo ride Page **85** • The quintessential Vietnamese mode of transport gives you an up-close view of street life.

10 Colonial architecture Page **363** • The legacy of French rule can be seen in the Vietnamese fondness for baguettes and, more impressively, the examples of colonial architecture, such as Hanoi's Opera House.

11 **Ride the Reunification Express** Pages **40** & **388** • Load your bike on, then sit back and relax as the train slowly chugs its way between Ho Chi Minh City and Hanoi.

12 **The northern mountains** Page **424** • Vietnam's most impressive mountainscapes offer not just scenic rewards but also the chance to visit an ethnic minority village.

13 **Hoi An** Page **266** • With its rich cultural heritage, beautifully preserved merchants' houses and slow pace of life, Hoi An is a captivating place to spend a few days.

15 **Street food** Pages **49**, **374** & *Vietnamese street food* colour section • Soak up the atmosphere at a street kitchen and have your plate piled as high with a selection of fresh food for next to nothing – but get there early for the best choice.

14 **Tet** Page **07** • The most important festival in the Vietnamese calendar, Tet sees the New Year ushered in with colourful flower markets, spectacular fireworks and exuberant dragon dances.

17 **Temples and pagodas** Page **245** • The Vietnamese architectural style is best represented by its temples and pagodas, which reflect the country's diverse range of religions: Long Son Pagoda in Nha Trang is a good example.

16 **Bahnar villages** Pages **211** & **212** • Spend the night in a communal house (*rong*) where timeless village ceremonies are performed and important decisions are made.

19 **The Mekong Delta** Page **131** • Putter through this fertile farming region, surrounded by classic Vietnamese scenery.

18 **Dambri Waterfalls** Page **190** • Even in the dry season you're guaranteed a drenching at these impressive fifty-metre falls near Da Lat.

20 **A boat trip in Ha Long Bay** Page **405** • Navigate the silent waters around the thousands of limestone islands jutting out of the water at Ha Long Bay, dubbed the eighth natural wonder of the world.

21 Hon Chong Peninsula

Page **173** • Enjoy the Mekong Delta's most attractive palm-fringed beaches, dramatic offshore isles and calm waters.

22 Bia hoi

Page **380** • Bia hoi bars are fun, friendly, cheap and a great way to mingle with the locals. Order a refreshing glass of bia hoi (lager-like beer) in any of the back lanes in the Old Quarter of Hanoi.

23 Browse the markets

Page **102** • Markets such as Binh Tay are good grazing grounds for snacks such as soups, spring rolls and sticky rice cakes. Try a banana-leaf filled with pâte to keep you going while you shop.

24 The citadel, Hué

Page **301** • The former capital's historic citadel, mausoleums and gardens are idiosyncratic enough to impress even the most jaded traveller.

25 **The Red River Delta** Page **387** • Slow the pace down with a trip to the countryside and experience a lifestyle little changed in centuries.

26 **Coffee** Page **378** • Vietnam's best coffee grows around the hills of Buon a Thuot. Drink it the Vietnamese way – strong and short, with a dollop of condensed milk – at one of the quirky cafés scattered all over town.

27 **My Son Cham towers** Page **280** • These battered but beautiful towers near Hoi An are all that remain of the once-powerful Champa kingdom.

28 **Cao Dai Cathedral** Page **124** • Vietnam's most charismatic indigenous religion goes in for exuberant architecture, with its Supreme Being symbolized by the all-seeing Eye.

29 **Lak Lake** Page **203** • Paddle around the serene waters of Lak Lake in a dug-out canoe, ride on an elephant, or take a guided trek into the surrounding forests and then feast at sunset whilst overlooking the sparkling water.

30 **Chill out on Phu Quoc** Page **177** • Unspoilt beaches lined with coconut trees circle the island. Feel the sand of Bai Sao between your toes or sail south to the unspoilt An Thoi islands for fine swimming in crystal-clear waters.

31 **Shopping** Page **381** • Browse the colourful shops lining the streets in Hanoi to pick up some unusual souvenirs.

Basics

Basics

Getting there

While the number of airlines offering non–stop services to Vietnam is gradually increasing, the majority of visitors take the cheaper option of an indirect flight routed through a carrier's domestic hub to one of Vietnam's three international airports: Hanoi, Ho Chi Minh City and Da Nang. With time in hand, you can generally build a stopover in Bangkok, Singapore or Hong Kong, for example, into your schedule, usually at no extra cost. It's also worth investigating the cost of buying a bargain–basement flight to Bangkok and a separate ticket through one of the region's low–cost carriers, such as Jetstar, Tiger Airways and Air Asia, for the Vietnam leg.

Airlines that fly in and out of both Hanoi and Ho Chi Minh City normally sell you an **open-jaw ticket**, which allows you to fly into one city and out of the other, leaving you to travel up or down the country under your own steam.

Airfares always depend on the **season**, with the highest generally being July to August, during the Christmas and New Year holidays and around Tet, the Vietnamese New Year; fares drop during the "shoulder" season – September to mid-December – and you'll get the best prices during the low season, January to June. Note also that flying at weekends is generally more expensive; price ranges quoted below assume midweek travel.

You can often cut costs by going through a **specialist flight agent** – either a consolidator, who buys up blocks of tickets from the airlines and sells them at a discount, or a **discount agent**, who in addition to dealing with discounted flights may also offer special student and youth fares and a range of other travel-related services such as travel insurance, rail passes, car rentals, tours and the like.

If Vietnam is only one stop on a longer journey, you might want to consider buying a **round-the-world** (RTW) ticket. Some travel agents can sell you an "off-the-shelf" RTW ticket that will have you touching down in about half a dozen cities; others will have to assemble one for you, which can be tailored to your needs but is apt to be more expensive. Although few off-the-shelf tickets take in Ho Chi Minh City or Hanoi, several

offer a stop in Bangkok, Singapore or Hong Kong, from where you can make a side-trip to Vietnam. The most comprehensive and flexible deals are offered by Sky Team, Star Alliance and One World, all of which allow you to take in a huge number of destinations around the globe. **Prices** vary enormously depending upon your itinerary, but tickets including Bangkok or Singapore – excluding taxes and surcharges – can be as low as £600 from the UK; $1300 from the US; CAN$2000 from Canada; AUS$2100 from Australia; and NZ$2700 from New Zealand; a side-trip to Vietnam can then usually be added for around $250.

Combining Vietnam with other **Southeast Asian countries** is becoming increasingly popular – and a lot cheaper and easier – thanks to some good-value regional air deals. Jetstar, for example, flies from Singapore to Ho Chi Minh City (from $40 one-way), while Tiger Airways flies from Singapore to Hanoi (from $100 one-way) and Ho Chi Minh City (from $55 one-way). Air Asia offers daily services from Bangkok and Kuala Lumpur to both Hanoi and Ho Chi Minh City, with fares starting at $50 one-way. As with all discount airlines, prices depend on availability, so the earlier you book the better, though you may also find last-minute promotional fares, seat giveaways and so forth at less busy times of the year.

From the UK and Ireland

There are as yet no non-stop flights to Vietnam from the UK or Ireland. Instead, most people fly with a Southeast Asian carrier such as Singapore Airlines, Thai Airways, Malaysia Airlines or Cathay Pacific from London via the airline's home city. Alternatively you can fly direct from Paris to Hanoi or Ho Chi Minh City with Air France, which has connecting flights to Paris from regional airports such as Dublin, Edinburgh and Manchester. Vietnam Airlines offers code-share flights from Paris with Air France or Frankfurt with Lufthansa. Scheduled low-season **fares** from London start at around £450, rising to £750 or more at peak periods.

A good place to look for the best deals is the travel sections of the weekend newspapers and in regional listings magazines. **Students** and **under-26s** can often get discounts through specialist agents such as STA (see p.34) or USIT in Ireland (ⓦwww .usit.ie). Whoever you buy your ticket through, check that the agency belongs to the travel industry bodies ABTA or IATA, so that you'll be covered if the agent goes bust before you get your ticket.

From the US and Canada

In 2004 United Airlines became the first American carrier to resume direct flights to Vietnam since 1975. The airline operates a daily service **from San Francisco** to Ho Chi Minh City via Hong Kong; standard return fares start at around $1100. As yet, no other American or Canadian carriers offer direct services, which means you'll either have to get a flight to San Francisco or catch one of the many flights to a regional hub, such as Bangkok, Singapore or Hong Kong, and continue on from there. Scheduled flights start at around $1300 **from New York**, $1100 **from Los Angeles**, CAN$2000 **from Vancouver** and CAN$2500 **from Toronto**.

Note that some routings require an **overnight stay** in another city such as Bangkok, Taipei, Hong Kong or Seoul, and often a hotel room will be included in your fare – ask the airline and shop around since travel agents' policies on this vary. Even when an overnight stay is not required, going to Vietnam can be a great excuse for a stopover: Most airlines will allow you one free stopover in either direction.

From Australia and New Zealand

A reasonable range of flights connects Australia and New Zealand with Vietnam, with Qantas, Vietnam Airlines and Jetstar offering direct services from Australia. The alternative is to fly to another Asian gateway, such as Bangkok, Kuala Lumpur, Singapore or Hong Kong, and then either get connecting flights or travel overland to Hanoi or Ho Chi Minh City.

By far the cheapest flight **from Australia** is the daily Jetstar service to Ho Chi Minh City from Sydney (AUS$390 one-way) via Darwin (AUS$240 one-way). Both Vietnam Airlines and Qantas operate direct flights to Ho Chi Minh City from Melbourne and Sydney; low-season scheduled fares start at around AUS$1300 with Vietnam Airlines, and slightly more with Qantas at AUS$1400. If you want to stop off on the way, there are good deals to Hanoi and Ho Chi Minh City with Malaysia Airlines via Kuala Lumpur, Singapore Airlines via Singapore, and Thai Airways via Bangkok, all costing around AUS$1100 to AUS$1500. Cheaper still are the fares offered by Tiger Airways, a discount airline operating daily **flights between Perth and Singapore**: one-way fares start as low as AUS$200. From Singapore you can get an onward flight to Hanoi (from around AUS$100 one-way) or Ho Chi Minh City (from around AUS$55 one-way).

From New Zealand, low-season fares with Malaysia Airlines, Thai, Qantas and Singapore Airlines are all around NZ$1500 to NZ$2200, with a change of plane in the carrier's home airport.

From neighbouring countries

It's increasingly popular to enter Vietnam overland from China, Laos or Cambodia, an option that means you can see more of the region than you would if you simply jetted in.

From China there are three possibilities. The Beijing–Hanoi train enters Vietnam at Dong Dang, north of Lang Son, where there's also a road crossing known as Huu Nghi Quan (see p.456). The border is also open to foot traffic at Lao Cai (see p.426) in the northwest and Mong Cai in the far northeast (see p.417).

Six steps to a better kind of travel

At Rough Guides we are passionately committed to travel. We feel strongly that only through travelling do we truly come to understand the world we live in and the people we share it with – plus tourism has brought a great deal of **benefit** to developing economies around the world over the last few decades. But the extraordinary growth in tourism has also damaged some places irreparably, and of course **climate change** is exacerbated by most forms of transport, especially flying. This means that now more than ever it's important to **travel thoughtfully** and **responsibly**, with respect for the cultures you're visiting – not only to derive the most benefit from your trip but also to preserve the best bits of the planet for everyone to enjoy. At Rough Guides we feel there are six main areas in which you can make a difference:

- Consider what you're contributing to the **local economy**, and how much the services you use do the same, whether it's through employing local workers and guides or sourcing locally grown produce and local services.
- Consider the **environment** on holiday as well as at home. Water is scarce in many developing destinations, and the biodiversity of local flora and fauna can be adversely affected by tourism. Try to patronize businesses that take account of this.
- Travel with a purpose, not just to tick off experiences. Consider **spending longer** in a place, and getting to know it and its people.
- Give thought to how often you **fly**. Try to avoid short hops by air and more harmful night flights.
- Consider **alternatives to flying**, travelling instead by bus, train, boat and even by bike or on foot where possible.
- Make your trips "**climate neutral**" via a reputable carbon offset scheme. All Rough Guide flights are offset, and every year we donate money to a variety of charities devoted to combating the effects of climate change.

From Laos, six border crossings are currently open to foreigners: Lao Bao (see p.325), the easiest and most popular, some 80km west of Dong Ha; Cau Treo and Nam Can, to the north and northwest of Vinh (see p.330); Na Meo, northwest of Thanh Hoa (see p.266); Bo Y, northwest of Kon Tum (see p.215); and Tay Trang, just west of Dien Bien Phu (see p.440). While it's perfectly possible – and cheaper – to use local buses to and from the borders, international bus services also run from Savannakhet and Vientiane to Hanoi, Dong Ha, Vinh, Da Nang and other destinations in Vietnam: these direct services are recommended, as regular reports of extortion continue to come in from those crossing independently.

From Cambodia you can travel by bus from Phnom Penh straight through to Ho Chi Minh City via Moc Bai (about 60km northwest of Ho Chi Minh City), or take a local bus to the border and continue by share taxi. The other option is to cross at Vinh Xuong or Tinh Bien (30km north and 25km west of Chau Doc in the Mekong Delta respectively). Vinh Xuong is the most popular crossing, as it entails a cheap boat ride (around $8) from Chau Doc to Phnom Penh, organized through Ho Chi Minh City's budget tour operators or through hotels in Chau Doc. There are also relatively new border crossings at Xa Xia near Ha Tien in the Mekong Delta, which is useful if you are coming from Kep or Sihanoukville on the Cambodian coast, and at Le Thanh in the Central Highlands, making it possible to go from Banlung in northeast Cambodia straight through to Plei Ku.

As long as you have a **valid visa**, crossing these borders is generally not a problem, though you may still find the odd Vietnamese immigration official who tries to charge a "processing fee", typically one dollar. Most border gates are open from around 7am to 5pm and may close for an hour over lunch.

small groups big adventures...

With an average group size of just 10 people, Intrepid journeys have more adventure to go around.

For more info, bookings & brochures...
www.intrepidtravel.com/rough
Call 0203 147 7777
or visit our travel store at
76 Upper Street, London N1 0NU

real life experiences...
Fun, affordable & sustainable travel since 1989

44911

Organized tours

If you want to cover a lot of ground in a short time in Vietnam or have a specific interest, an organized tour might be worth considering. **Specialist tour operators** offer packages that typically include flights, accommodation, day excursions and internal travel by plane, train or road. These are expensive compared to what you'd pay if you arranged everything independently, but the more intrepid tours often feature activities that would be difficult to set up yourself. There's a wide variety of all-inclusive **packages** available, as well as **organized tours** that cover everything from hill-tribe visits to trekking and biking. Tours range in length from a few days to several weeks, and you can choose to explore Vietnam only, or combine a tour with Laos and Cambodia.

Alternatively, you can make arrangements through **local tour operators** in Ho Chi Minh City, Hanoi and other tourist centres either before you arrive or on the ground; they'll arrange your entire trip or just the first few days to get you started. Fixing it up before you arrive saves time, though all local operators will also arrange an itinerary for you on the spot.

Prices will be generally cheaper with a local operator and they should have more in-depth local knowledge. However, you'll need to check carefully that they're financially sound, reliable and can deliver what they promise – *never* deal with a company that demands cash upfront or refuses to accept payment by credit card, and get references if you can. Also check carefully before booking to make sure you know exactly what's included in the price.

We've listed some of the bigger and better-established agents below with a solid reputation for organizing small-group and customized tours, and given details of others throughout the Guide.

Specialist tour operators abroad

Abercrombie & Kent UK ☎0845/070 0615, US☎1-800/554-7016, Australia ☎03/9536 1800, New Zealand ☎0800/441 638; ⓦwww .abercrombiekent.com. Specialist in luxury tours, many of which feature Vietnam as part of a greater trip through Indochina.
Active Travel Australia ☎1800/634 157, 02/6249 6122, ⓦwww.activetravel.com.au. Broad range of culture and adventure tours, plus customized itineraries.
Artisans of Leisure US ☎1-800/214-8144, ⓦwww.artisansofleisure.com. Luxury private and

20% DISCOUNT FOR ROUGH GUIDE READERS

Learn a language with

ROUTLEDGE COLLOQUIALS

The ideal way to get the most out of your holiday, year after year.

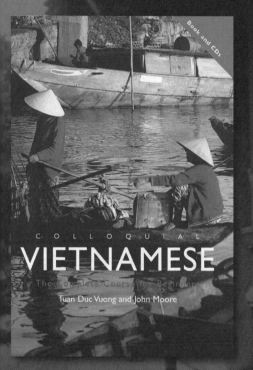

Book and CDs

COLLOQUIAL

VIETNAMESE

The Complete Course for Beginners

Tuan Duc Vuong and John Moore

'Undoubtedly the best series of... language courses on the market.'

– Waterstone's Booksellers

- self-taught courses for beginners - easy and fun to use
- over 70 languages from Afrikaans to Zulu
- learn the language the way it's spoken by native speakers
- communicate confidently by the end of each course

To claim your 20% discount on all Colloquial packs (containing a book and CD), just visit **www.routledge.com/colloquials**, search for your language of choice and enter the discount code **RG09**

For a full list of the 70 languages offered visit **www.routledge.com/colloquials** or email **colloquials@routledge.com** for a free catalogue.

Routledge
Taylor & Francis Group

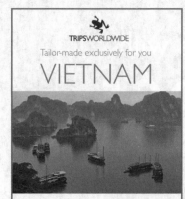

TRIPSWORLDWIDE

Tailor-made exclusively for you

VIETNAM

Our tailor-made trips to Vietnam offer you the chance to sample some beautiful contrasting scenery, fabulous cuisine and fascinating history dating back thousands of years. Vietnam is perfect for the adventure of a lifetime.

0117 311 6050
www.tripsworldwide.co.uk
info@tripsworldwide.co.uk

Latin America · Caribbean · Asia · Polar Regions

Vietnam specialist offering small-group, tailor-made itineraries.

Imaginative Traveller UK ☎01473/667 337, ⓦwww.imaginative-traveller.com. Small-group adventure tours to Vietnam from a responsible travel operator.

Intrepid Travel UK ☎020/8960 6333, Australia ☎1300/3670 887 or 03/9473 2626, New Zealand ☎0800/174 043; ⓦwww.intrepidtravel.com. Small-group tours with the emphasis on cross-cultural contact and low-impact tourism, and itineraries ranging from gourmet tours to cycling charity challenges.

Journeys International US ☎1-800/255-8735, ⓦwww.journeys.travel. Prestigious, award-winning operator focusing on eco-tourism and small-group trips.

Peregrine Adventures Australia ☎1300/854 444 or 03/8601 4444, ⓦwww.peregrine.net.au. Small-group adventure-travel specialist offering trekking, cycling and explorer tours to Vietnam.

Regent Holidays UK ☎0845/277 3317, ⓦwww.regent-holidays.co.uk. Well-established agent with a reputation for good-value, tailor-made travel arrangements. Off-the-shelf itineraries include a fourteen-day "Grand Indochina" tour, or the shorter nine-day "Classic Vietnam" option.

responsibletravel.com UK ☎01273/600030, ⓦwww.responsibletravel.com. UK-based online

individually tailored tours, including contemporary style, family and culinary tours.

Asian Pacific Adventures US ☎1-800/825-1680 or 818/881-2745, ⓦwww.asianpacificadventures.com. Tailor-made and small-group tours, including trekking and hill-tribe markets.

Backroads US ☎1-800/GO-ACTIVE or 510/527-1555, ⓦwww.backroads.com. Cycling, hiking and multi-sport tours, with the emphasis on going at your own pace.

Birding Worldwide Australia ☎03/9899 9303, ⓦwww.birdingworldwide.com.au. Prestigious company that organizes group trips to some of the world's best birdwatching destinations, including a combined Vietnam and Cambodia tour.

Common Ground Journeys US ☎503/307-7524, ⓦwww.commongroundjourney.com. Specialist, not-for-profit Vietnamese cycle-tour company.

Exodus UK ☎020/8675 5550, ⓦwww.exodus.co.uk. Adventure-tour operator taking small groups on specialist programmes that take in trekking, biking, kayaking and cultural trips.

Global Exchange US ☎415/648-8068, ⓦwww.globalexchange.org. A not-for-profit human rights organization that leads educational tours of Vietnam.

Griswalds Vietnamese Vacations Australia ☎02/9564 5040, ⓦwww.vietnamvacations.com.au.

TRANSINDUS
Journeys through Asia

Award-winning, cultural & tailor-made holidays through Asia

For expert advice or to request a brochure call the leading Asia specialist on

020 8566 3739
www.transindus.co.uk

travel agent listing pre-screened holidays from responsible tourism operators.

Velo Asia ☎1-888/833-4533 or 415/731-4311, ⓦ www.veloasia.com. Vietnam specialist with a range of organized and tailor-made cycling adventure tours.

World Expeditions UK ☎020/8545 9030, US & Canada 1-800/567-2216. Australia ☎1300/720 000, New Zealand ☎09/368 4161; ⓦwww .worldexpeditions.com.au, www .worldexpeditions.co.uk. Australian-owned adventure company with a programme ranging from sea-kayaking on Ha Long Bay to climbing Mount Fan Si Pan. Also offers community project trips, where participants help renovate a local school, for example, and arrange charity challenges.

Local tour operators

Ann Tours 58 Ton That Tung, Ho Chi Minh City ☎08/3833 2564, ⓦwww.anntours.com. A highly recommended, small-scale operation that offers personal service and good-value, tailor-made tours throughout the country.

Buffalo Tours 11 Hang Muoi, Hanoi ☎04/3828 0702; Satra House Suite 601, 58 Dong Khoi, Ho Chi Minh City ☎08/3827 9170; ⓦwww.buffalotours .com. Upmarket travel agency offering adventure trips (trekking, kayaking and cycling amongst other activities) and less rugged "discovery" tours. Prices are high but trips are well organized and can be individually tailored.

Explore Indochina ⓦwww.exploreindochina .com. Hanoi-based outfit that offers tailor-made, off-the-beaten-track adventure treks on Russian Minsk motorbikes organized by real enthusiasts. Options include the northern mountains or down the Ho Chi Minh Trail, with the possibility of looping through Laos.

Exotissimo Saigon Finance Centre, 9 Dinh Tien Hoan, Hu Chi Minh City ☎08/3825 1723, ⓦwww .exotissimo.com. Highly professional operation, aimed at the middle market and above, with a strong focus on adventure tours and responsible tourism.

Footprint 6 Le Thanh Tong, Hanoi ☎04/3933 2844, ⓦwww.footprintsvietnam.com. Specializes in customized, eco-friendly tours plus some off-the-shelf packages.

Handspan Adventure Travel 80 Ma May, Hanoi ☎04/3926 2828; F7 Titan Building, 18A Nam Quoc Cang, Ho Chi Minh City, ⓦwww.handspan .com. Environmentally conscientious adventure-tour specialist offering trips to the "hidden Vietnam". Highly professional and good service.

Queen Travel 65 Hang Bac, Hanoi ☎04/3826 0860, ⓦwww.queencafe.com.vn. Aims at the middle market and above with tailor-made and small-group tours, including Laos and Cambodia.

with

TENNYSON TRAVEL

award-winning specialist tour operators

Tel: 020 7736 4347
Fax: 020 7736 5672

30-32 Fulham High Street
London
SW6 3LQ

Web: www.visitasia.co.uk
Email: tennyson@visitasia.co.uk

Sinhbalo Adventures 283/20 Pham Ngu Lao, Ho Chi Minh City ☎08/3837 6766, ⓦwww.sinhbalo .com. A super-efficient setup that specializes in customized tours such as bicycle expeditions along the Ho Chi Minh Trail (see ⓦwww.cyclingvietnam.net), motorbike tours of the central highlands and kayaking in the Mekong Delta. They also have a wealth of reliable travel information.

Airlines, agents and operators

Many **airlines** and **discount travel websites** offer you the chance to book your tickets online, cutting out the costs of agents and middlemen. The websites listed below offer good deals and useful price comparisons.

Online booking

ⓦ www.expedia.co.uk (in UK), ⓦ www.expedia.com (in US), ⓦ www.expedia.ca (in Canada)
ⓦ www.lastminute.com (in UK)
ⓦ www.opodo.co.uk (in UK)
ⓦ www.orbitz.com (in US)
ⓦ www.travelocity.co.uk (in UK), ⓦ www.travelocity .com (in US), ⓦ www.travelocity.ca (in Canada)
ⓦ www.travelocity.co.nz (in New Zealand)
ⓦ www.zuji.com.au (in Australia),

Airlines

Air Asia Ⓦ www.airasia.com
Air China Ⓦ www.airchina.com.cn
Air France Ⓦ www.airfrance.com
Cathay Pacific Ⓦ www.cathaypacific.com
Jetstar Ⓦ www.jetstar.com
Lufthansa Ⓦ www.lufthansa.com
Malaysia Airlines Ⓦ www.malaysiaairlines.com
Qantas Airways Ⓦ www.qantas.com
Singapore Airlines Ⓦ www.singaporeair.com
Thai Airways Ⓦ www.thaiair.com
Tiger Airways Ⓦ www.tigerairways.com
United Airlines Ⓦ www.united.com
Vietnam Airlines Ⓦ www.vietnamairlines.com

Flight agents and tour operators

ebookers UK ☎ 0871/223 5000, Republic of Ireland ☎ 01/431 1311; Ⓦ www.ebookers.com, Ⓦ www.ebookers.ie. Low fares on an extensive selection of scheduled flights and package deals.
North South Travel UK ☎ 01245/608 291, Ⓦ www.northsouthtravel.co.uk. Friendly, competitive travel agency, offering discounted fares worldwide. Profits are used to support projects in the developing world, especially the promotion of sustainable tourism.
Trailfinders UK ☎ 0845/058 5858, Republic of Ireland ☎ 01/677 7888, Ⓦ www.trailfinders.com. One of the best informed and most efficient agents for independent travellers.
STA Travel UK ☎ 0871/230 0040, US ☎ 1-800/781-4040, Australia ☎ 134 782, New Zealand ☎ 0800/474 400, South Africa ☎ 0861/781 781; Ⓦ www.statravel.com. Worldwide specialists in independent travel; also student IDs, travel insurance, car rental, rail passes and more. Good discounts for students and under-26s.

Red tape and visas

All foreign nationals need a visa to enter Vietnam, with certain exceptions: citizens of Sweden, Denmark, Norway, Finland, Japan and South Korea do not need a visa if they are travelling to Vietnam for less than fifteen days, have a passport valid for three months following the date of entry and hold a return air ticket. Citizens of certain ASEAN–member countries, including Thailand, Malaysia and Singapore are also exempt for stays of up to thirty days. Tourist visas are generally valid for thirty days and for a single entry, though some embassies issue visas for three months or longer and may also issue multiple–entry visas. A standard thirty–day visa costs the local equivalent of US$30–100, depending on how quickly you want it processed.

The majority of visitors apply for a visa in their country of residence, either from the embassy direct, or through a specialist visa agent or tour agent. Processing normally takes around a week, though many embassies now also offer a more expensive "express" service. To be on the safe side, it's best to allow several weeks as delays and mistakes can occur (check the details carefully on receipt). For people travelling via neighbouring Asian countries, Bangkok is still the most popular place to apply for a Vietnamese visa, since it's relatively straightforward (1–5 working days; around US$55–80), though Cambodia has a reputation for being quick, helpful and cheap. At the time of writing, the embassy in Phnom Penh was issuing thirty-day tourist visas in two days for $30, while the consulate in Sihanoukville did them on the spot.

To apply for a tourist visa, you have to submit an **application form** with one or two passport-sized photographs (procedures vary) and the fee. The visa shows specific start and end **dates** indicating the period of validity within which you can enter and leave the country. The visa is valid for entry via

Hanoi, Ho Chi Minh City and Da Nang international airports and any of Vietnam's land borders open to foreigners (see p.28).

Business visas are valid for one month upwards and can be issued for multiple entry, though you'll need a sponsoring office in Vietnam to underwrite your application.

One-year **student visas** are relatively easy to get hold of if you enrol, for example, on a Vietnamese language course at one of the universities; you'll be required to attend a minimum number of classes per week to qualify. It's easiest to arrange it in advance, but you can enter Vietnam on a tourist visa and apply for student status later – the only downside is that you may have to leave the country in order to get the visa stamp.

Special circumstances affect **overseas Vietnamese** holding a foreign passport: check with the Vietnamese embassy in your country of residence for details.

Most major tour agents in Vietnam are now authorized to issue **visas on arrival** at Hanoi, Ho Chi Minh City and Da Nang international airports. It's not necessarily any more expensive (prices range from US$25 to US$90 for a one-month tourist visa, depending on your nationality and how quickly you need the application processed), but check carefully to make sure you're quoted a price including the visa and not just the handling fee. There's also an element of risk since you are reliant on the agency completing the paperwork in time for your arrival. However, it can be handy if there is no Vietnamese embassy in your home country. The agency will need a photocopy of your passport, your full name, date of birth, proposed dates of stay, flight details and a fax number or email address to which they will send an "invitation letter" saying you have approval to enter the country. While some agencies are able to process the application in one day, allow at least one week to be on the safe side. If you follow this route, look out for the Visa on Arrival desk at the airport before you pass through immigration.

On arrival In Vietnam, you'll need to fill in an Arrival and Departure Card, which has to be submitted when you leave the country, so it's a good idea to staple it into your passport while travelling.

Visa extensions

Thirty-day extensions are issued in Hanoi, Ho Chi Minh City, Nha Trang, Da Nang, Hué and Hoi An. Some people have managed to obtain second and even third extensions, usually in Hanoi and Ho Chi Minh City. Applications have to be made via a tour agent. In general they take three to five days to process and cost $25 for the first one-month extension.

Holders of **business visas** can apply for an extension only through the office that sponsored their original visa, backed up with reasons as to why an extension is necessary.

Incidentally, **overstaying** your visa will result in fines of between US$10 and US$50, depending how long you overstay and the mood of the immigration official, and is not recommended.

Vietnamese embassies and consulates

A full list of Vietnamese embassies and consulates is available at Ⓦ www .vietnamtourism.com.

Australia Embassy: 6 Timbarra Crescent, O'Malley, Canberra, ACT 2606 ☎ 02/6286 6059, Ⓦ www .au.vnembassy.org. Consulate: 202–233 New South Head Rd, Edgcliff, NSW 2027 ☎ 02/9327 1912.
Cambodia Embassy: 436 Blvd Preach, Monivong, Phnom Penh ☎ 023/726 273, Ⓔ vnembpnh @online.com.kh. Consulates: Sihanoukville ☎ 034/933 669, Ⓔ tlsqsiha@camintel.com; Road No.3, Batambang ☎ 053/952 894, Ⓦ www .vietnamembassy-cambodia.org
Canada 470 Wilbrod St, Ottawa K1N 6M8 ☎ 613/236-0772, Ⓦ www.vietnamembassy -canada.ca.
China Embassy: 32 Guang Hua Lu, Jian Guo Men Wai, PO Box 00600, Beijing ☎ 10/6532 1155, Ⓔ suquanbk@yahoo.com. Consulates: Jin Yanf Hotel, 92 Huanshi Western Rd, Guang Zhou ☎ 20/8652 7908; 15f Great Smart Tower, 230 Wanchai Rd, Hong Kong ☎ 852/2591 4510; 2f Kai Wah International Hotel, 157 Beijing Rd, Kunming 650011 ☎ 871/352 2669, Ⓔ tlsqcm @yahoo.com.
Ireland Contact UK office.
Lao PDR Embassy: 1 That Luang Rd, Vientiane ☎ 021/413 409, Ⓦ www.mofa.gov.vn. Consulates: 31 Ban Pha Bat, Pakse ☎ 031/212 058; 118 Sisavang Rd, Savannakhet ☎ 041/212418.
Malaysia 4 Persiaran Stonor, 50450 Kuala Lumpur ☎ 03/2148 4534, Ⓦ www.mofa.gov.vn.

New Zealand Level 21, Grand Plimmer Tower, 2 Gilmer Terrace, PO Box 8042, Welllington ☎04/473 5912, ⓦwww.vietnamembassy-newzealand.org Singapore 10 Leedon Park, Singapore 267887 ☎462 5938.
Thailand Embassy: 83/1 Wireless Rd, Bangkok 10330 ☎02/267 9602, Ⓔvnembassy@bkk.a-net .net.th. Consulate: 65/6 Chatapadung, Khonkaen 40000 ☎043/242190, ⓦwww.vietnamembassy -singapore.org

UK 12–14 Victoria Rd, London W8 5RD ☎020/7937 1912, ⓦwww.vietnamembassy.org.uk/consular.html. US Embassy: 1233 20th St NW, Suite 400, Washington DC 20036 ☎202/861-0737, ⓦwww.vietnamembassy-usa.org. Consulate: 1700 California St, Suite 430, San Francisco, CA 94109 ☎415/922-1577, ⓦwww .vietnamconsulate-sf.org.

Health

Vietnam's health problems read like a dictionary of tropical medicine. Diseases that are under control elsewhere in Southeast Asia have been sustained here by poverty, dietary deficiencies, poor healthcare and the disruption caused by half a century of war. The situation is improving, however, and by coming prepared and taking a few simple precautions while in the country, you're unlikely to come down with anything worse than a cold or a dose of travellers' diarrhoea.

Before you go

When planning your trip it's wise to visit a **doctor** as early as possible, preferably at least two months before you leave, to allow time to complete any recommended courses of **vaccinations**. It's also advisable to have a trouble-shooting **dental check-up** – and remember that you generally need to start taking **anti-malarial tablets** at least one week before your departure.

For up-to-the-minute information, it may be worth visiting a specialized **travel clinic**; most clinics also sell travel-associated accessories, including mosquito nets and first-aid kits.

Vaccinations

No **vaccinations** are required for Vietnam (except yellow fever if you're coming directly from an area where the disease is endemic), but typhoid and hepatitis A jabs are recommended; it's also worth ensuring you're up to date with boosters such as tetanus and polio. Additional injections to consider, depending on the season and risk of exposure, are hepatitis B, Japanese encephalitis, meningitis and rabies. All

these immunizations can be obtained at international clinics in Hanoi, Ho Chi Minh City and Da Nang, but it's less hassle and usually cheaper to get them done at home. Get all your shots recorded on an **International Certificate of Vaccination** and carry this with your passport when travelling abroad.

For protection against **hepatitis A**, which is spread by contaminated food and water, the vaccine is expensive but extremely effective – an initial injection followed by a booster after six to twelve months provides immunity for up to ten years. **Hepatitis B**, like the HIV virus, can be passed on through unprotected sexual contact, blood transfusions and dirty needles. The very effective vaccine (three injections over six months) is recommended for anyone in a high-risk category, including those travelling extensively in rural areas for prolonged periods, with access to only basic medical care. It's also now possible – and cheaper – to have a combined vaccination against both hepatitis A and B: the course comprises three injections over six months.

The risks of contracting **Japanese encephalitis** are extremely small, but, as

Avian flu

Avian flu or bird flu is a contagious disease normally limited to birds and, less commonly, pigs. However, the virus can spread to humans by direct contact with infected poultry or with contaminated surfaces. In the 2004–05 outbreak in Vietnam of the highly contagious H5N1 strain of the disease, there were around sixty confirmed cases involving humans, of which some forty were fatal, according to the World Health Organization. The vast majority of people infected had direct contact with diseased birds. Since the initial outbreak, a further forty or so cases have been reported, the most recent in February 2009.

Evidence of human-to-human transmission has yet to be confirmed but the indications are that, if it is possible, it is extremely rare and has so far been limited to close family members. The main fear among health experts is that the virus will mutate into a form that is highly infectious to and easily spread among humans.

At present the risk to travellers visiting infected areas remains low. As a precaution, however, you are advised to avoid contact with live poultry and pigs, including live animal markets, and to eat only well-cooked poultry and eggs. Check the latest with your doctor or travel health specialist prior to travel. You'll also find up-to-date information on the following websites: ⓦwww.avianinfluenza.com.au, ⓦwww.who.int/csr/disease/avian_influenza/en and ⓦwww.cdc.gov.

the disease is untreatable, those travelling for a month or more in the countryside, especially in the north during and soon after the summer rainy season (June–Nov), should consider immunization. The course consists of two or three injections over a month with the last dose administered at least ten days before departure. Note that it is not recommended for those with liver, heart or kidney disorders, or for multiple-allergy sufferers. If your plans include long stays in remote areas your doctor may also recommend vaccination against **meningitis** (a single shot) and **rabies**.

Mosquito-borne diseases

Both the Red River and Mekong deltas (including Hanoi and Ho Chi Minh City) have few incidences of **malaria**. The coastal plain north of Nha Trang is also considered relatively safe. Malaria occurs frequently in the highlands and rural areas, notably the central highlands, as well as the southern provinces of Ca Mau, Bac Lieu and Tay Ninh. The majority of cases involve the most dangerous strain, *Plasmodium falciparum*, which can be fatal if not treated promptly.

The key preventive measure is to avoid getting bitten by mosquitoes (which carry the disease), but if you're travelling in high-risk areas it's advisable to take **preventive tablets**.

Mosquitoes are also responsible for transmitting dengue fever and Japanese encephalitis. **Dengue** is carried by a variety of mosquitoes active in the daytime (particularly two hours after sunrise and several hours before sunset) and occurs mostly in the Mekong Delta, including Ho Chi Minh City, though the chances of being infected remain small. There is a more dangerous version called dengue haemorrhage fever, which primarily affects children but is extremely rare among foreign visitors to Vietnam. If you notice an unusual tendency to bleed or bruise, seek medical advice immediately.

There are several things you can do to avoid getting bitten. Mosquitoes are most active at dawn and dusk, so at these times wear long sleeves, trousers and socks, avoid dark colours and perfumes, which attract mosquitoes, and put **repellent** on all exposed skin. Sprays and lotions containing around thirty to forty percent DEET (diethyltoluamide) are effective and can also be used to treat clothes, but the chemical is toxic: keep it away from eyes and open wounds.

Many hotels and guesthouses provide mosquito nets over beds or meshing on windows and doors. Air-conditioning and fans also help keep mosquitoes at bay, as do mosquito coils and knockdown insecticide sprays (available locally), though none

What about the water?

The simple rule is don't drink tap **water** in Vietnam, with the exception of one or two top hotels which now offer filtered water, and never drink river water. It's wise also to avoid **ice** in your drinks except, again, in top hotels and other trustworthy places. Contaminated water is a major cause of sickness due to the presence of pathogenic organisms: bacteria, viruses and cysts. These micro-organisms cause ailments and diseases such as diarrhoea, gastroenteritis, typhoid, cholera, dysentery, poliomyelitis, hepatitis A and giardia – and can be present even when water looks clean and safe to drink.

Fortunately there are plenty of alternative drinks around: hot tea is always on offer, while cheap, **bottled water** and carbonated drinks are widely available. When buying bottled water check the seal is unbroken and the water is clear, as bottles are occasionally refilled from the tap. Tap water in Hanoi and Ho Chi Minh City is chlorinated and most travellers use it for brushing their teeth without problem, but this is not recommended in rural areas, where water is often untreated. Particular care should be taken anywhere where there is flooding as raw sewage may be washed into the water system. The only time you're likely to be out of reach of bottled water is trekking into remote areas, when you'll be relying on **boiled water**. Boiling for ten minutes gets rid of most bacteria in water but at least twenty minutes is needed to kill amoebic cysts, a cause of dysentery. Alternatively, you can use iodine purification tablets or solutions, which are more effective than chlorine compounds, though still leave a nasty aftertaste – using a filter afterwards makes the water slightly more palatable. Note that iodine products are unsuitable for pregnant women, babies and people with thyroid problems.

of these measures is as effective as a decent net.

Bites and creepy-crawlies

Bed bugs, fleas, lice or scabies can be picked up from dirty bedclothes, though this is relatively unusual in Vietnam. Try not to scratch bites, which easily become septic. Ticks picked up walking through scrub may carry a strain of typhus; carry out regular body inspections and remove ticks promptly.

Rabies is contracted by being bitten, or even licked on broken skin or the eyes, by an infected animal. The best strategy is to give all animals, especially dogs, cats and monkeys, a wide berth.

Vietnam has several poisonous **snakes** but in general snakes steer clear of humans and it's very rare to get bitten. Avoid walking through long grass or undergrowth, and wear boots when walking off-road. If bitten, immobilize the limb (most snake bites occur on the lower leg) to slow down absorption of the venom and remove any tight-fitting socks or other clothing from around the wound. It's important to seek medical assistance as

quickly as possible. It helps if you can take the (dead) snake to be identified, or at least remember what it looked like.

Leeches are more common and, though harmless, can be unpleasant. Long trousers, sleeves and socks help prevent them getting a grip. The best way to get rid of leeches is to burn them off with a lighted match or cigarette; alternatively rub alcohol or salt onto them.

Worms enter the body either via contaminated food, or through the skin, especially the soles of the feet. You may notice worms in your stools, or experience other indications such as mild abdominal pain leading, very rarely, to acute intestinal blockage (roundworm, the most common), an itchy anus (threadworm) or anaemia (hookworm). An infestation is easily treated with worming tablets from a pharmacy.

Heat trouble

Don't underestimate the strength of the tropical sun: **sunburn** can be avoided by restricting your exposure to the midday sun and liberal use of high-factor sunscreens. Drinking plenty of water will prevent dehydration, but if you do become dehydrated – signs are infrequent or irregular urination – drink a salt and sugar solution.

Heatstroke is more serious and may require hospital treatment. Indications are a high temperature, lack of sweating, a fast pulse and red skin. Reducing your body temperature with a lukewarm shower will provide initial relief.

High humidity often causes **heat rashes**, **prickly heat** and **fungal infections**. Prevention and cure are the same: wear loose clothes made of natural fibres, wash frequently and dry off thoroughly afterwards. Talcum powder helps, particularly zinc oxide-based products (prickly heat powder), as does the use of mild antiseptic soap.

Sexually transmitted diseases

Until recently Vietnam carried out very little screening for sex workers, injecting drug users and other high-risk groups. As a result, **sexually transmitted diseases** such as gonorrhoea and syphilis, both easily treated with antibiotics, and AIDS are flourishing. It is, therefore, extremely unwise to contemplate casual unprotected sex, and bear in mind that Vietnamese condoms (*bao cao su*) are often poor-quality (more reliable imported varieties are available in major cities).

Getting medical help

Pharmacies can generally help with minor injuries or ailments and in major towns you will usually find a pharmacist who speaks English. The selection of reliable Asian and Western products on the market is improving rapidly, and both Ho Chi Minh City and Hanoi now have well-stocked pharmacies. That said, drugs past their shelf life and even counterfeit medicines are rife, so inspect packaging carefully, check use-by dates – and bring anything you know you're likely to need from home, including **oral contraceptives**. **Tampons** and reliable, imported brands of **condoms** (*bao cao su*) are sold in Hanoi and Ho Chi Minh, but don't count on getting them easily elsewhere.

Local **hospitals** can also treat minor problems, but in a real emergency your best bet is to head for Hanoi or Ho Chi Minh City. Hospitals in both these cities can handle most eventualities and you also have the option of one of the excellent international medical centres. Addresses of clinics and hospitals can be found in our "Listings" sections for major towns throughout the book. Note that doctors and hospitals expect immediate cash payment for health services rendered; you will then have to seek reimbursement from your insurance company (make sure you get receipts for any payments you make).

Getting around

Vietnam's transport network has improved markedly in recent years. Massive infrastructure projects have seen the country's main thoroughfare, Highway 1 – which runs from Hanoi to Ho Chi Minh City, passing through Hué, Da Nang and Nha Trang en route – widened and resurfaced for much of its length, while the nation's first stretch of motorway was inaugurated early in the new millennium. State–run bus services are slowly being upgraded and there's an increasing number of relatively comfortable, privately owned minibuses in operation, while the introduction of new rolling stock, complete with air–conditioned carriages and restaurant cars, is slowly transforming train travel.

That said, there's plenty of room for improvement, particularly as regards road transport: buses are often packed to the gunnels; driving standards leave a lot to be desired; and passengers – not just foreigners – are sometimes overcharged or forced to change buses and pay a second time. It's therefore not surprising that an increasing number of tourists, and the more affluent Vietnamese, are opting for internal flights, privately operated "open-tour" buses or organized tours. Public transport shouldn't be rejected out of hand, though: many visitors have their warmest encounters with the Vietnamese within the chaos of a bus or train.

Security is an important consideration. Never fall asleep with your bag by your side, and never leave belongings unattended. On trains, be especially vigilant when the train stops at stations and ensure your money belt is safely tucked under your clothes before going to sleep and that your luggage is safely stowed.

By plane

Flying comes into its own on longer hauls, and can shave precious hours or even days off journeys – the two-hour journey **between Hanoi and Ho Chi Minh City**, for instance, compares favourably with the thirty to forty hours you would spend on the train, and costs from around 750,000đ with Jetstar. Other **useful services** from Hanoi and Ho Chi Minh City fly to Hué, Da Nang and Nha Trang, and Phu Quoc Island. Note that you'll need your passport with you when taking internal flights.

The Vietnamese national carrier, Vietnam Airlines (Ⓦwww.vietnamairlines .com), operates a reasonably cheap, efficient and comprehensive network of **domestic flights**. The company maintains booking offices in all towns and cities with an airport; addresses and phone numbers are listed throughout the Guide. If you're booking international flights with Vietnam Airlines, it's worth checking their domestic fares at the same time as they sometimes offer good discounts as part of a package; otherwise, it's generally cheaper to buy tickets in Vietnam. Two other airlines also operate domestic flights: Jetstar (Ⓦwww .jetstar.com), which flies from Hanoi to Ho Chi Minh City, Da Nang and Nha Trang, and from Ho Chi Minh City to Hanoi, Haiphong, Vinh and Da Nang; and Vasco (Ⓦwww .vasco.com.vn), from Ho Chi Minh City to Con Dao and Ca Mau.

By rail

Vietnam Railways (Ⓦwww.vr.com.vn) runs a single-track **train** network comprising more than 2500km of track, stretching from Ho Chi Minh City to the Chinese border. Much of it dates back to the colonial period, though it's gradually being upgraded. Most of the services are still relatively slow, but travelling by train can be far more pleasant than going by road – though prices on the coastal route can't compare with buses, you're away from the busy (and often dangerous) Highway 1, and get to see far more of the countryside.

The most **popular routes** with tourists are the shuttle from Da Nang to Hué (2–3hr), a picturesque sampler of Vietnamese rail travel, and the overnighters from Hué to Hanoi (11–16hr) and from Hanoi up to Lao Cai, for Sa Pa (8–9hr).

Services

The country's **main line** shadows Highway 1 on its way from Ho Chi Minh City to Hanoi, passing through Nha Trang, Da Nang and Hué en route. From Hanoi, three branch lines strike out towards the northern coast and into its hinterland. One line traces the Red River northwest to **Lao Cai**, site of a border crossing into **China**'s Yunnan Province, and just an hour by bus from Sa Pa. Another runs north to **Dong Dang**, and is the route taken by the trains from Hanoi **to Beijing**. The third branch, a shorter spur, links the capital with **Haiphong**.

Six **Reunification Express** services depart daily from Hanoi to Ho Chi Minh City and vice versa, a journey that takes somewhere between thirty and forty hours. On the **northern lines**, two trains per day make the run from Hanoi to Haiphong (2–3hr) and two to Dong Dang (6hr). There are also three night trains (7–8hr) and a day service (9hr) to Lao Cai.

Note that **departure times** change regularly – current times are displayed in stations and on the tickets themselves – and that trains generally leave pretty much on schedule. You'll also find timetables on the Vietnam Railway's website, though it's always wise to double-check at the station.

When it comes to choosing which **class** to travel in, it's essential to aim high. At the bottom of the scale is a **hard seat**, which is just as it sounds, though bearable for shorter journeys; the carriages, however, tend to be filthy and there are few views since the windows are caged. **Soft seats** offer slightly more comfort, especially in the new air-conditioned carriages, some of which are double-decker. On overnight journeys, you'd be well advised to invest in a **berth** of some description, though since the country's rolling stock is being upgraded it's not always possible to know exactly what you're getting. The new **hard-berth** compartments are now quite comfortable and have six bunks, three either side – the cramped top ones are the cheapest, and the bottom ones the priciest – though some of the old hard-as-nails relics remain in service. Roomier **soft-berth** compartments, containing only four bunks, are always comfortable.

All Reunification Express trains now have **air-conditioning**, as do the overnight Lao Cai trains which have been upgraded with soft-sleeper berths. All trains are theoretically **non-smoking**, though try telling the locals: in hard-seat class, even the guards will be puffing away.

Simple **meals** are often included in the price of the ticket, but you might want to stock up with goodies of your own. You'll also have plenty of opportunities to buy snacks when the train pulls into stations – and from carts that ply the aisles.

Tickets

Booking ahead is wise, and the further ahead the better, especially if you intend travelling at the weekend or a holiday period. Sleeping compartments should be booked at least three days before departure, and even further ahead for soft-sleeper berths on the Hanoi–Hué and Hanoi–Lao Cai routes. It's not possible to buy through tickets and break your journey en route; each journey requires you to buy a separate ticket from the point of departure.

Fares vary according to the class of travel and the train you take; as a rule of thumb, the faster the train, the more expensive it is. Prices (which are always quoted in dong) change regularly, but as an indication of the fare range, on the most expensive services from Hanoi to Ho Chi Minh City you'll pay

around 1,100,000đ for a soft-sleeper berth, and around 750,000đ for a hard sleeper in the slowest trains; the equivalent fares for Hanoi to Hué are 520,000đ and 250,000đ respectively. Prices to Lao Cai vary from 80,000đ for a hard seat on the day train to over 300,000đ for a soft sleeper.

By bus

Whilst Vietnam's national **bus** network offers daily services between all the major towns, the lion's share of tourist journeys are made on **privately-operated** services. These have air-conditioning, limited seating, fixed time-tables and don't pick up on route, making them infinitely more comfortable than the national services. Most travellers use buses to get around Vietnam but never actually see a bus station, since these companies operate from their own offices. Competition between the companies is so fierce that prices are as low as the national bus network. Though some operators are more reliable than others, on the whole these buses are reasonably comfortable (but don't expect much leg-room) and tend to run on time.

Most popular of all are the **"open-tour" buses** shuttling between the major tourist destinations. One-way through **tickets**, for example, from Ho Chi Minh City to Hué (around US$25) or Hanoi (US$35 and up), or vice versa, enable you to stop off at specified destinations en route: heading south to north, the main stops are Da Lat, Mui Ne, Nha Trang, Hoi An, Da Nang, Hué and Ninh Binh. On the way buses also call at the occasional tourist sight, such as the Marble Mountains and Lang Co. You can either make firm bookings at the outset or opt for an open-dated ticket for greater flexi-bility, in which case you may need to book your onward travel one or two days in advance to be sure of a seat. Alternatively, you can buy separate tickets as you go along, though this can work out slightly more expensive, depending on the operator. Each main town on the itinerary has an agent (one for each operator) where you can buy tickets and make onward reservations. To avoid being sold a fake ticket or paying over the odds, it's best to buy direct from the relevant agent rather than from hotels, restaurants or unrelated tour companies.

The downside of these open-tour buses is that you'll be encouraged to book into the company's own or affiliated hotels, though there's nothing to stop you staying elsewhere. You'll also have less choice when it comes to meal stops, which tend to be at rather mediocre and overpriced restaurants; it's worth taking a picnic. Finally, bear in mind that some buses run overnight – you may save on a night's accommodation, but don't expect to get much sleep.

On the national bus network, the government is slowly upgrading **state buses**, replacing the rickety old vehicles with swish air-conditioned models, particularly on the more popular routes. Don't necessarily expect a comfortable ride, however, since they still try to cram in as many people as possible, plus luggage, which could be anything from live pigs in baskets to scores of sacks of rice. Progress can be agonizingly slow as buses stop frequently to pick up passengers or for meal breaks. Among older vehicles, breakdowns are fairly common and can sometimes necessitate a roadside wait of several hours while driver, fare collector and mechanic roll up their sleeves and improvise a repair.

Tickets are best bought at bus stations, where **fares** should be clearly indicated above the ticket windows. At smaller and less organized stations, or if you join a bus mid-route, how much you pay depends very much upon luck and where you are: at certain tourist hot spots, especially in the south, you'll often be charged over the odds; elsewhere, you might pay the going price. Try to ascertain the correct price and have the exact money ready before boarding as fare collectors will often take advantage of your captive position. For long journeys, buy your ticket a day in advance since many routes are heavily oversubscribed.

Privately owned **minibuses** compete with public buses on most routes; they sometimes share the local bus station, or simply congregate on the roadside in the centre of a town. You can also flag them down on the road. If anything, they squeeze in even more people per square foot than ordinary buses, and often drive interminably around town, touting for passengers. On the other hand, they do at least run throughout the day and

serve routes not covered by public services. Again, try to find what the correct fare should be and agree a price before boarding. Even so, be prepared to find the price has suddenly increased once you've got going. You may also find yourself dumped at the side of the road before reaching your destination and having to cram onto the next passing service.

By ferry and boat

A boat-tour around Ha Long Bay is one of Vietnam's most enjoyable trips, while scheduled **ferries** sail year-round – weather permitting – to the major islands off Vietnam's coastline, including Phu Quoc, Cat Ba and Con Dao. In addition, ferry and hydrofoil services run from Haiphong to Cat Ba, and hydrofoils from Ho Chi Minh City to Vung Tau, and from Ha Long City (Bai Chay) to Mong Cai. Though they are gradually being replaced by bridges, a few river ferries still haul themselves from bank to bank of the various strands of the Mekong from morning until night. Numerous aged (and often less than seaworthy) cargo vessels also dawdle between towns, and some ply the route to Ho Chi Minh City, but they tend to be slow and basic; we've outlined a handful of the more do-able ones in the text.

By car and jeep

Self-drive in Vietnam is not yet an option for tourists and other short-term visitors. However, it's easy to rent a **car**, **jeep** or **minibus** with driver from the same companies, agencies and tourist offices that arrange tours. This can be quite an economical means of transport if you are travelling in a group. Moreover, it means you can plan a trip to your own tastes, rather than having to follow a tour company's itinerary.

Prices vary wildly so it pays to shop around, but expect to pay in the region of $35–50 per day for a car, and $60–100 per day for a jeep or other 4WD, depending on the vehicle's size, age and level of comfort. When negotiating the price, it's important to clarify exactly who is liable for what. Things to check include who pays for the driver's accommodation and meals, fuel, road and ferry tolls, parking fees and repairs and what happens in the case of a major breakdown. There should then be some sort of contract to sign showing all the details, including an agreed itinerary, especially if you are renting for more than a day; make sure the driver is given a copy in Vietnamese. In some cases you'll have to settle up in advance, though, if possible, it's best if you can arrange to pay roughly half before and the balance at the end.

Hitching

Although not really comparable to **hitching** in the Western sense, there is a tradition of drivers (especially truck drivers) picking up passengers from the roadside, in exchange for a small payment – and this system has been used to great effect by some travellers. However, in addition to the **risks** associated with hitching anywhere, you're also quite likely to be overcharged, due to the prevailing (and not unreasonable) assumption that all foreigners are wealthy. Set against the relatively low cost of other forms of transport, hitching is an ill-advised and unattractive proposition.

By motorbike

Motorbike rental is possible in most towns and cities regularly frequented by tourists, and pottering around on one can be a most enjoyable and time-efficient method of sightseeing. Lured by the prospect of independent travel at relatively low cost, some tourists cruise the countryside on motorbikes, but inexperienced bikers would do well to think very hard before undertaking any **long-distance biking** since Vietnam's roads can be distinctly dangerous (see "Rules of the road" box below).

The appalling road discipline of most Vietnamese drivers means that the risk of an accident is very real, with potentially dire consequences should it happen in a remote area. Well-equipped hospitals are few and far between outside the major centres, and there'll probably be no ambulance service.

On the other hand, many people ride around with no problems and thoroughly recommend it for both day-trips and touring. The best biking is to be found in the northern mountains, the central highlands and around the Mekong Delta, while the Ho Chi Minh Highway offers pristine tarmac plus wonderful scenery. Some also do the long haul up Highway 1 from Ho Chi Minh City to Hanoi (or vice versa), a journey of around two weeks, averaging a leisurely 150km per day.

There's no shortage of motorbikes **for rent** in Vietnam's major tourist centres; the

Rules of the road

There's no discernible method to the madness that passes as a **traffic** system in Vietnam so it's extremely important that you don't stray out onto the roads unless you feel a hundred percent confident about doing so. The theory is that you **drive on the right**, though in practice motorists and cyclists swoop, swerve and dodge wherever they want, using their **horn** as a surrogate indicator and brake. Unless otherwise stated, the **speed limit** is 60kph on highways and 40kph or less in towns.

Right of way invariably goes to the biggest vehicle on the road, which means that motorbikes and bicycles are regularly forced off the highway by thundering trucks or buses; note that overtaking vehicles assume you'll pull over onto the hard shoulder to avoid them. It's wise to use your horn to its maximum and also to avoid being on the road after dark, since many vehicles either don't have functioning headlights or simply don't bother to turn them on.

On the whole the **police** seem to leave foreign riders well alone, and the best policy at roadside checkpoints is just to drive by slowly. However, if you are involved in an **accident** and it was deemed to be your fault, the penalties can involve fairly major fines.

When **parking** your bike, it's advisable to leave it in a parking compound (*gui xe*) – the going rate is 2000đ to 5000đ for a motorbike and 1000đ to 2000đ for a bicycle – or paying someone to keep an eye on it. If not, you run the risk of it being tampered with.

average rate is around US$7 per day, with discounts for longer periods. You'll sometimes be asked to pay in advance, sign a rental contract and/or leave some form of ID (a photocopy of your passport should suffice). If you're renting for a week or so, you may be asked to leave a deposit, often the bike's value in dollars though it might also be your air ticket or departure card. In the vast majority of cases, this shouldn't be a problem.

Although it's technically illegal for non-residents to own a vehicle, there's a small trade in **secondhand motorbikes** in the two main cities – look at the noticeboards in hotels, travellers' cafés and tour agents for adverts. So far the police have ignored the practice, but check the latest situation before committing yourself. The bike of choice is usually a **Minsk 125cc**, particularly for the mountains; it's sturdy, not too expensive, and the easiest to get repaired outside the main cities.

Whether you're renting or buying, remember to check everything over carefully, especially brakes, lights and horn. Wearing a **helmet** is now a legal requirement, and most rental outlets have helmets you can borrow, sometimes for a small charge, though they may not be top-quality.

Note that international driving licences are not valid in Vietnam, but you will need your home **driving licence** and bike registration papers. You also need at least third-party **insurance**, which is available (with the afore-mentioned documentation) at Bao Viet insurance offices.

Though **road conditions** have improved remarkably in recent years, off the main highways they can still be highly erratic, with pristine asphalt followed by stretches of spine-jarring potholes, and plenty of loose gravel on the sides of the road. **Repair shops** are fairly ubiquitous – ask for *sua chua xe may* (motorbike repairs) – but you should still carry at least a puncture-repair kit, pump and spare spark plug. **Fuel** (*xang*) is cheap (18,000đ, around US$1 per litre, at the time of writing) and widely available. Finally, try to travel in the company of one or more other bikes in case one of you gets into trouble. And if you want to get off the main highways, it really pays to take a guide.

By bicycle

Cycling is an excellent way of sightseeing around towns, and you shouldn't have to pay more than 30,000đ per day for the privilege, even outside the main tourist centres.

While you can now buy decent Japanese-made bikes in Vietnam, if you decide on a **long-distance cycling** holiday, you should really bring your own bike with you, not forgetting all the necessary spares and tools. Hardy **mountain bikes** cope best with the country's variable surfaces, though tourers and hybrids are fine on the main roads. Bring your own helmet and a good loud bell; a rear-view mirror also comes in handy.

When it all gets too much, or you want to skip between towns, you can always put your bike on the train (though not on all services; check when buying your ticket) for a small fee; take it to the station well ahead of time, where it will be packed and placed in the luggage van. Some open-tour buses will also take bikes – free if it goes in the luggage hold (packed up), otherwise you'll have to pay for an extra seat.

If you want to see Vietnam from the saddle, there are several companies that offer specialist **cycling tours** – see details of specialist tour operators on p.33.

Organized tours

Ever-increasing numbers of tourists are seeing Vietnam through the window of a minibus, on **organized tours**. Ranging from one-day jaunts to two- or three-week trawls upcountry, tours are ideal if you want to acquaint yourself speedily with the highlights of Vietnam; they can also work out much cheaper than car rental. On the other hand, by relying upon tours you'll have little chance to really get to grips with the country and its people, or to enjoy things at your leisure.

Hordes of state-owned and private **tour companies** compete for business in Hanoi, Ho Chi Minh City and other major destinations (see p.33 for a list of well-established agents). While a few companies now put together more innovative itineraries, the vast majority offer similar tours. However, it pays to shop around since **prices** vary wildly depending, for example, on how many people there are in a group, the standard of transport, meals and accommodation, whether entry fees are included and so forth.

It's important to check exactly what is included in the price before handing over any cash. It's also a good idea to ask about the maximum number of people on the trip and whether your group will be amalgamated with others if you don't want to be travelling round in a great horde. Bear in mind, as well, that you're far better off dealing directly with the company organizing the tour, rather than going through a hotel or other intermediary. Not only are you more likely to get accurate information about the details of the tour, but you'll also be in a much stronger position should you have cause for complaint.

The other alternative is to set up your own **custom-made tour** by gathering together a group and renting a car, jeep or minibus plus driver (see "By car and jeep", p.42).

Local transport

In a country with a population so adept at making do with limited resources, it isn't surprising to see the diverse types of **local transport**. While taxis are increasingly common and a number of cities now boast reasonable **bus services**, elsewhere you'll be reliant on a host of two- and three-wheeled vehicles for getting around.

Most common by far are motorbike taxis known as **xe om**. In the cities you'll rarely be able to walk twenty yards without being offered a ride; prices tend to start at around 10,000đ for short runs, though this goes up after dark (as does the possibility of extortion). At all times the rules of bargaining apply: when haggling, ensure you know which currency you are dealing in (five fingers held up, for instance, could mean 5000đ or

US$5), and whether you're negotiating for a single or return trip, and for one passenger or two; it's always best to write the figures down. Should a difference of opinion emerge at the end of a ride, having the exact fare ready to press into an argumentative driver's hand can sometimes resolve matters.

Xe om have almost entirely replaced that quintessential Vietnamese mode of transport, the **cyclo**, which are becoming increasingly rare in city centres. These three-wheeled rickshaws comprising a "bucket" seat attached to the front of a bicycle can carry one person, or two people at a push, and are now only really found in tourist areas. Prices are a little lower than corresponding trips by xe om, though there are continuous stories of cyclo drivers charging outrageous sums for their services. To avoid getting badly ripped off, find out first what a reasonable fare might be – from your hotel or the like – and, if the first driver won't agree to your offer, simply walk on and try another.

Taxis are now a common sight on the streets of all major cities. The vast majority are metered (with prices in dong) and fares are not expensive; a short ride within central Hanoi, for example, should cost around 25,000đ (just over a dollar). Though standards have been improving with greater competition, some drivers need persuading to use their meters, while others dawdle along as the meter spins suspiciously fast, or take you on an unnecessarily long route. When arriving in a town, beware of drivers who insist the hotel you ask for is closed and want to take you elsewhere; this is usually a commission scam – be firm with your directions. In general, smarter-looking taxis and those waiting outside big hotels tend to be more reliable.

Accommodation

Vietnam's accommodation scene continues to improve – recent and ongoing booms in tourism and construction mean that rooms are generally becoming better value for money, and service standards are rising as a result of increased competition. An increase in the numbers of luxury resorts and boutique hotels has led to a decrease in the popularity of the country's state–owned monstrosities, while there's almost always plenty of choice for those travelling on a budget.

Another consequence of the number of new hotels springing up in recent years is that getting **a reservation** is no longer the nightmare it once was, and even among international-class hotels there are some bargains to be had, particularly at weekends; however, booking in advance is a must around the **Tet** festival in early spring.

Tourist booth staff at the airports in Ho Chi Minh City and Hanoi will phone to reserve a room for you, and it's increasingly simple to book online. Be wary of asking advice from **cyclo or taxi drivers**, as travellers are often told that their hotel of choice is full or closed. It's also important to note that Vietnam is full of copycat establishments – to avoid being taken to a similarly-named hotel, write down the street name and show it to your driver.

Once you've found a hotel, look at a range of rooms before opting for one, as standards can vary hugely within the same establishment. You'll also need to check the bed arrangement, since there are many permutations in Vietnam. A **"single"** room could have a single or twin beds in it, while a **"double"** room could have two, three or four single beds, a double, a single and a double, and so on.

When you **check in** at a Vietnamese hotel or guesthouse, you'll be asked for your **passport**, which is needed for registration with the local authorities. Depending on the establishment, these will be either returned to you the same night, or kept as security until you check out. If you're going to lose sleep over being separated from your passport, say you need it for the bank; many places will accept photocopies of your picture and visa pages. It's normally possible to pay your bill when you leave, although a few budget places ask for payment in advance.

Room **rates** fluctuate according to demand, so it's always worth bargaining – making sure, of course, that it's clear whether both parties are talking per person or per room. Your case will be that much stronger if you are staying several nights.

All hotels charge ten percent **government tax**, while top-class establishments also add a **service charge**. These taxes may or may not be included in the room rate, so check to be sure. (Our price codes – see box opposite – include all applicable taxes.) Increasingly, **breakfast** is included in the price of all but the cheapest rooms, though in budget places it will consist of little more than bread with jam or cheese and a cup of tea or coffee.

Although the situation is improving, hotel **security** can be a problem. Never leave valuables lying about in your room and keep documents, traveller's cheques and so forth with you at all times, in a money pouch. While top-end and many mid-range hotels provide safety deposit boxes, elsewhere you can sometimes leave things in a safe or locked drawer at reception; put everything in a sealed envelope and ask for a receipt. In the real cheapies, where the door may only be secured with a padlock, you can increase security by using your own lock.

In some older budget hotels, rooms are cleaned irregularly and badly, and **hygiene** can be a problem, with cockroaches and even rats roaming free; you can at least minimize health risks by not bringing foodstuffs or sugary drinks into your room.

Pretty much any guesthouse or hotel will offer a **laundry** service, and Western-style laundry and dry-cleaning services are widely available in Hanoi, Ho Chi Minh City and other major cities. Washing is often given a rigorous scrubbing by hand, so don't submit anything delicate.

Finally, **prostitution** is rife in Vietnam, and in less reputable hotels it's not unknown for Western men to be called upon, or even phoned from other rooms, during the night.

Types of accommodation

Grading accommodation isn't a simple matter in Vietnam. The names used (guesthouse, mini-hotel, hotel and so on) can rarely be relied upon to indicate what's on offer, and there are broad overlaps in standards. Vietnam's older hotels tend to be austere, state-owned edifices styled upon unlovely Eastern European models, while many private mini-hotels make a real effort. Some hotels cover all bases by having a range of rooms, from simple fan-cooled rooms with cold water, right up to cheerful air-conditioned accommodation with satellite TV, fridge and mini-bar. As a rule of thumb, the newer a place is, the better value it's likely to represent in terms of comfort, hygiene and all-round appeal.

Budget accommodation

The very cheapest form of accommodation in Vietnam is a bed in a **dormitory**. Dormitories are not a new concept in Vietnam: many bus and train stations have on-site dorms known as *nha tro*, but these practically never take foreigners – which is no loss, since they generally have appalling standards of cleanliness and little security.

However, there are a few "backpacker" dorms in Ho Chi Minh City and, to a lesser extent, Hanoi, where you can expect to pay US$3–8 for a bed or a mattress on the floor, sharing common facilities. You'll generally find these dorms in the budget **guesthouses** (*nha khach*) that proliferate around Ho Chi Minh City's De Tham enclave. In Hanoi, a couple of places in the Old Quarter offer dormitory accommodation. Details are given in the Guide.

Good news for single travellers is the recently established network of **youth hostels** fully accredited by Hostelling International (www.hihostels.com). You'll need a current Youth Hostel card, which is generally easiest and cheapest to obtain at home through your national youth hostel association; make sure it's a full member of Hostelling International. Alternatively, you can join Vietnam Hostelling International (VHI) at any of the hostels.

If you prefer your own privacy, you'll find simple fan rooms in either a guesthouse or **hotel** (*khach san*) costing anywhere between US$5 and $10 (❶); these are likely to be ensuite, although you might not get hot water at this price level in the warmer south. Add air-conditioning, satellite TV and slightly better furnishings, maybe even a window, and you'll be paying between $10 and $20 (❷). Upgrading to $20–30 (❸) will get you a larger room with better-standard fittings, usually including a fridge and bathtub, and possibly a balcony. Note that while many hotels advertise satellite TV, which channels you actually get varies wildly, let alone the quality of reception, so check first if it matters to you.

Accommodation price codes

All accommodation listed in this guide has been categorized according to the following scale:

❶ US$10 and under
❷ US$11–20
❸ US$21–30
❹ US$31–50
❺ US$51–75
❻ US$76–150
❼ US$151 and over

Rates are for the cheapest available **double** or twin **room**. During holiday periods, rates are liable to rise, and proprietors may be less amenable to bargaining. Although the law requires prices to be quoted in dong, most hotels give their rates in US$; payment can be made in either currency.

Mid- and upper-range accommodation

For upwards of US$30 per room per night, accommodation can begin to get quite rosy. Rooms at this level will be comfortable, reasonably spacious and well appointed with decent furniture, air-conditioning, hot water, fridge, phone and satellite TV in all but the most remote areas.

Paying US$30–75 (④–⑤) will get you a room in a **mid-range hotel** of some repute, with in-house restaurant and bar, booking office, room service and so on. At the **top of the range** (⑥–⑦) the sky's the limit. International-class hotels are for the most part confined to the two major cities, which also have some reasonably charismatic places to stay, such as the *Metropole* in Hanoi and Ho Chi Minh's *Continental*. However, in recent years developers have targeted Nha Trang, Hoi An, Da Nang and Ha Long City, all of which now boast upmarket resort hotels.

Village accommodation and camping

As Vietnam's minority communities have become more exposed to tourism, staying in stilthouses or other **village accommodation** has become more feasible.

In the north of the country, notably around Sa Pa, He Ho and in the Mai Chau Valley, you can either take one of the tours out of Hanoi which includes a home-stay in one of the **minority villages**, or make your own arrangements when you get there (see p.424 for details). In the central highlands, the Plei Ku and Kon Tum tourist offices can also arrange a stilthouse home-stay for you.

Accommodation usually consists of a mattress on the floor in a communal room. Those villages more used to tourists normally provide a blanket and mosquito net, but it's advisable to take your own net and sleeping bag to be on the safe side, particularly as nights get pretty cold in the mountains. Prices in the villages vary from US$5–15 per person per night, depending on the area and whether meals are included.

Where boat trips operate in the Mekong Delta, notably around Vinh Long, tour operators in Ho Chi Minh City or the local tourist board can arrange for visitors to stay with owners of **fruit orchards**, allowing a close-up view of rural life (see box, p.86).

Virtually no provisions exist in Vietnam for **camping** at the present time. The exceptions are at Nha Trang and Mui Ne, where some guesthouses offer tents for a few dollars a night when all rooms are full. Some tour companies also offer camping as an option when visiting Ha Long Bay (p.405).

Eating and drinking

At its best, Vietnamese food is light, subtle in flavour and astonishing in its variety. Though its cuisine is related to that of China, Vietnam has its own distinct culinary tradition, using herbs and seasoning rather than sauces, and favouring boiled or steamed dishes over stir–fries.

In the south, **Indian** and **Thai** influences add curries and spices to the menu, while other regions have evolved their own array of specialities, most notably the foods of Hué and Hoi An. Buddhism introduced a **vegetarian** tradition to Vietnam, while much later the **French** brought with them bread, dairy products, pastries and the whole café culture. Hanoi, Ho Chi Minh City and the major tourist centres are now well provided, with everything from street hawkers to hotel and Western-style restaurants, and even ice-cream parlours.

The quality and variety of food is generally better in the main towns than off the beaten track, where restaurants of any sort are few and far between. That said, you'll never go hungry; even in the back of beyond, there's always some stall selling a noodle soup or rice platter and plenty of fruit to fill up on.

Vietnam's national **drink** is green tea, which is the accompaniment to every social gathering or business meeting and is frequently drunk after meals. At the harder end of the spectrum, there's also **rice wine**, though some local **beer** is also excellent, and an increasingly wide range of imported **wines** and **spirits**.

For a glossary of **food and drink terms**, see Language, p.543.

Where to eat

Broadly speaking, there are two types of eating establishment to choose from. One step up from **hawkers** peddling their dish of the day from shoulder poles or handcarts are **street kitchens**, inexpensive joints aimed at locals. More formal, **Western-style restaurants** come in many shapes and sizes, from simple places serving unpretentious Vietnamese meals to top-class establishments offering high-quality Vietnamese specialities and international cuisine.

Throughout the Guide we've given phone numbers for those restaurants where it's advisable to make **reservations**. While most eating establishments stay open throughout the year, some close over Tet (see "Festivals and religious events", p.57 for more on Tet). The Vietnamese **eat early**: outside the major cities and tourist areas, food stalls and street kitchens rarely stay open beyond 8pm and may close even earlier, though they do stay open later in the south, especially in Ho Chi Minh City. You'll need to brush up your **chopstick**-handling skills, too, although other utensils are always available in places frequented by tourists – in Western-style restaurants you won't be expected to tackle your *steak-frites* with chopsticks.

When it comes to **paying**, the normal sign language will be readily understood in most restaurants. In street kitchens you pay as you leave – either proffer a few thousand dong to signal your intentions, or ask *bao nhieu tien?* ("how much is it?").

Street kitchens

Street kitchens range from makeshift food stalls, set up on the street round a cluster of pint-size stools, to eating houses where, as often as not, the cooking is still done on the street but you either sit in an open-fronted dining area or join the overspill outside. Like the food stall, these streetside restaurants offer few concessions to comfort, but they are permanent, with an address if not a name, and serve basic meals for next to nothing. Some places stay open all day (7am–8pm), while many close once they've run out of ingredients and others only open at lunchtime (10.30am–2pm). To be sure of the widest choice and freshest food, it pays to get there early (as early as 11.30am at lunchtime, and by 7pm in the evening), and note that the best places will be packed around noon.

Most specialize in one type of food, generally indicated on a signboard, or offer the ubiquitous com and pho rice dishes and noodle soups. *Com binh dan*, "people's meals", are also popular. Here you select from an array of prepared dishes displayed in a glass cabinet or on a buffet table, piling your plate with such things as stuffed tomatoes, fried fish, tofu, pickles or eggs, plus a helping of rice; expect to pay from around 20,000đ for a good plateful. Though it's not a major problem at these prices, some street kitchens overcharge, so double-check when ordering.

While regular restaurants in Vietnam are definitely improving, the food served at many street kitchens is often superior in quality and much cheaper; they're also a lot more fun. All you need is a bit of judicious selection – look for clean places with a fast turnover, where the ingredients are obviously fresh – plus a smattering of basic vocabulary (see p.543).

In a similar vein to street kitchens are **bia hoi outlets**. Though these are primarily drinking establishments, many provide good-value snacks or even main meals (see p.55 for more on bia hoi).

For more on street food, see the *Vietnamese street food* colour section.

Restaurants

If you're after more relaxed dining, where people aren't queuing for your seat, then head for a Western-style **Vietnamese restaurant** (*nha hang*), which will have chairs rather than stools, a name, a menu and will often be closed to the street. In general these places serve a more varied selection of Vietnamese dishes than the street kitchens, plus a smattering of international – generally European – dishes.

Menus at this level don't always show prices, and overcharging is a regular problem, making for tedious ordering as you check the cost of each dish or risk an astronomical bill at the end. Another thing to watch out for are the extras: peanuts, hot towels and packs of tissues on the table may be added to the bill even if untouched; ask for them to be taken away if you don't want them, and check the bill carefully. A modest meal for two should cost roughly 130,000–160,000d. **Opening hours** at such places are usually from 10.30am to 2pm for lunch, and in the evening from 5pm to no later than 9pm, or 8pm in the north.

In the main tourist haunts, you'll find cheap and cheerful **cafés** aimed at the backpacker market and serving often mediocre Western and Vietnamese dishes – from burgers and banana pancakes to spring rolls, noodles and other Vietnamese standards. They have the advantage, however, of **all-day opening**, usually from 7am to 11pm or midnight. And, should you crave a reasonably priced Western-style breakfast, fresh fruit salad or a mango-shake, these are the places to go.

As you move up the price scale, the decor and the cuisine become more sophisticated and the menu more varied. The more **expensive restaurants** (including the smarter hotel dining rooms) tend to stay open later in the evening, perhaps until 9.30pm or 10.30pm, have menus priced in dollars and accept credit cards. Usually menus indicate if there's a service charge, but watch out for an additional three to four percent on credit card payments. These restaurants can be relatively fancy places, with at least a nod towards decor and ambience, and correspondingly higher prices (a meal for two is likely to cost at least US$20 and often much more).

The most popular **foreign cuisine** on offer is French, though both Hanoi and Ho Chi Minh City boast some pretty good international restaurants, including Thai, Chinese, Tex Mex, Indian and Italian. As yet, high-class restaurants are scarce in the rest of Vietnam, though Hué, Da Nang, Hoi An and Nha Trang are beginning to get in on the act.

Vietnamese food

The staple of Vietnamese meals is **rice**, with noodles a popular alternative at breakfast or as a snack. Typically, rice will be accompanied by a fish or meat dish, a vegetable dish and soup, followed by a green tea digestive. **Seafood and fish** – from rivers, lakes, canals and paddy fields as well as the sea – are favoured throughout the country, either fresh or dried. The most commonly used **flavourings** are shallots, coriander and lemon grass, though ginger, saffron, mint, anise and a basil-type herb also feature strongly, and coconut milk gives some southern dishes a distinctive richness.

Even in the south, Vietnamese food tends not to be over-spicy; instead chilli sauces or

Breakfast

Vietnamese traditionally breakfast on pho or some other **noodle soup**. Alternatively, you might find early-morning hawkers peddling *xoi*, a wholesome mix of steamed **sticky rice** with soya bean, sweet corn or peanuts. Simple **Western breakfasts** (such as bread with jam, cheese or eggs and coffee) are usually available in the backpacker cafés or hotels. More upmarket places increasingly stretch to cereals and fresh milk, while some top-class hotels lay on the full works in their breakfast buffets. In towns, you could always buy jam and bread or croissants for a **do-it-yourself** breakfast; however, things get more difficult out in the sticks, where you may even develop a taste for starting the day on a pho.

fresh chillies are served separately. Vietnam's most famous seasoning is the ubiquitous **nuoc mam**, a nutrient-packed sauce which either is added during cooking or forms the base for various dipping sauces. *Nuoc mam* is made by fermenting huge quantities of fish in vats of salt for between six months and a year, after which the dark brown liquid is strained and graded according to its age and flavour. Foreigners usually find the smell of the sauce pretty rank, but most soon acquire a taste for its distinctive salty-sweetness.

The use of **monosodium glutamate** (MSG) can be excessive, especially in northern cooking, and some people are known to react badly to the seasoning. A few restaurants in the main cities have cottoned on to the foibles of foreigners and advertise MSG-free food; elsewhere, try saying *khong co my chinh* (without MSG), and keep your fingers crossed. Note that what looks like salt on the table is sometimes MSG, so taste it first.

The most famous Vietnamese dish has to be **spring rolls**, variously known as *cha gio*, *cha nem*, *nem ran* or just plain *nem*. Various combinations of minced pork, shrimp or crab, rice vermicelli, onions, bean sprouts and an edible fungus are rolled in rice-paper wrappers, and then eaten fresh or deep-fried. In some places they're served with a bowl of lettuce or mint, in which case you're supposed to wrap some leaves around each roll – using deft chopstick manoeuvres – before dipping it in the accompanying sauce. In addition, a southern variation has barbecued strips of pork wrapped in semi-transparent rice wrappers, along with raw ingredients such as green banana and star fruit, and then dunked in a rich peanut sauce.

Soups and noodles

Though it originated in the north, another dish you'll find throughout Vietnam is pho (pronounced "fur"), a noodle **soup** eaten at any time of day but primarily at breakfast. The basic bowl of pho consists of a light beef broth, flavoured with ginger, coriander and sometimes cinnamon, to which are added broad, flat rice-noodles, spring onions and slivers of chicken, pork or beef. At the table you add a squeeze of lime and a sprinkling of chilli flakes or a spoonful of chilli sauce.

Countless other types of soup are dished up at street restaurants. *Bun bo* is another substantial beef and noodle soup eaten countrywide, though most famous in Hué, while in the south, *hu tieu*, a soup of vermicelli, pork and seafood noodles, is best taken in My Tho. *Chao* (or *xhao*), on the other hand, is a thick rice gruel served piping hot, usually with shredded chicken or filleted fish, flavoured with dill and with perhaps a raw egg cooking at the bottom; it's often served with fried breadsticks (*quay*). Sour soups are a popular accompaniment for fish, while *lau*, a standard of most restaurant menus, is more of a main meal than a soup, where the vegetable broth arrives at the table in a steamboat (a ring-shaped metal dish on live coals or, nowadays, often electrically heated). You cook slivers of beef, prawns or similar in the simmering soup, and then drink the flavourful liquid that's left in the cooking pot.

Fish and meat

Among the highlights of Vietnamese cuisine are its succulent **seafood** and freshwater **fish**. *Cha ca* is a famous fish dish (sautéed in butter at the table with dill and spring onions, then served with rice noodles and a sprinkling of peanuts) invented in Hanoi but now found in most upmarket restaurants, while *ca kho to*, fish stew cooked in a clay pot, is a southern speciality. Another dish found in more expensive restaurants is *chao tom* (or *tom bao mia*), consisting of savoury shrimp pâté wrapped round sweet sugar cane and fried.

Every conceivable type of meat and part of the animal anatomy finds itself on the Vietnamese dining table, though the staples are straightforward beef, chicken and pork. **Ground meat**, especially pork, is a common constituent of stuffings, for example in spring rolls or the similar *banh cuon*, a steamed, rice-flour "ravioli" filled with minced pork, black mushrooms and bean sprouts; a popular variation uses prawns instead of meat. Pork is also used, with plenty of herbs, to make Hanoi's *bun cha*, small **hamburgers** barbecued on an open charcoal brazier and served on a bed of cold rice-noodles with greens and a slightly sweetish sauce. One famous southern dish is *bo bay mon* (often written *bo 7 mon*), meaning literally **beef** seven ways, consisting of a platter of beef cooked in different styles.

Roving gourmets may want to try some of the more unusual meats on offer. **Dog** meat (*thit cay* or *thit cho*) is a particular delicacy in the north, where "yellow dog" (sandy-haired varieties) is considered the tastiest. Winter is the season to eat dog meat – it's said to give extra body heat, and is also supposed to remove bad luck if consumed at the end of the lunar month. **Snake** (*thit con ran*), like dog, is supposed to improve male virility. Dining on snake is surrounded by a ritual, which, if you're guest of honour, requires you to swallow the still-beating heart. Another one strictly for the strong of stomach is *trung vit lon*, embryo-containing **duck eggs** boiled and eaten only five days before hatching – bill, webbed feet, feathers and all.

Vegetables – and vegetarian food

If all this has put you off meat for ever, it is possible to eat **vegetarian** food in Vietnam, though not always easy. The widest selection of vegetables is to be found in Da Lat where a staggering variety of tropical and temperate crops thrive. Elsewhere, most restaurants offer a smattering of meat-free dishes, from stewed spinach or similar greens, to a more appetizing mix of onion, tomato, bean sprouts, various mushrooms, peppers and so on; places used to foreigners may be able to oblige with vegetarian spring rolls (*nem an chay*, or *nem khong co thit*). At street kitchens you're likely to find tofu and one or two dishes of pickled vegetables, such as cabbage or cucumber, while occasionally they may also have aubergine, bamboo shoots or avocado, depending on the season.

However, unless you go to a **specialist** vegetarian outlet – of which there are some excellent examples in Ho Chi Minh City, Hanoi and Hué – it can be a problem finding genuine veggie food: soups are usually made with beef stock, morsels of pork fat sneak into otherwise innocuous-looking dishes and animal fat tends to be used for frying.

The phrase to remember is *an chay* (vegetarian), or seek out a vegetarian rice shop (*tiem com chay*). Otherwise, make the most of the first and fifteenth days of the lunar month when many Vietnamese Buddhists spurn meat and you're more likely to find vegetarian dishes on offer.

Snacks

Vietnam has a wide range of snacks and nibbles to fill any yawning gaps, from huge rice-flour **crackers** sprinkled with sesame seeds to all sorts of dried fish, nuts and seeds. The white steamed **dumpling** called *banh bao* is a Chinese import, filled with tasty titbits, such as pork, onions and tangy mushrooms or strands of sweet coconut. *Banh xeo*, meaning sizzling **pancake**, combines shrimp, pork, bean sprouts and egg, all fried and then wrapped in rice paper with a selection of greens before being dunked in a spicy sauce. A similar dish, originating from Hué – a city with a vast repertoire of snack foods – is *banh khoai*, in which the flat pancake is accompanied by a plate of star fruit, green banana and aromatic herbs, plus a rich peanut sauce.

Markets are often good snacking grounds, with stalls churning out soups and spring rolls or selling intriguing banana-leaf parcels of pâté (a favourite accompaniment for bia hoi), pickled pork sausage or perhaps a cake of sticky rice.

A relative newcomer on the culinary scene is French **bread**, made with wheat flour in the north and rice flour in the south. Baguettes – sometimes sold warm from streetside stoves – are sliced open and stuffed with pâté, soft cheese or ham and pickled vegetables.

Fruit and sweet things

Vietnam is not strong on desserts, and restaurants usually stick to ice cream and fruit, although fancier international places might venture into *tiramisu* territory. Those with a sweet tooth are better off browsing around street stalls where there are usually candied fruits and other Vietnamese **sweetmeats** on offer, as well as sugary displays of French-inspired cakes and pastries in the main tourist centres.

Green-coloured *banh com* is an eye-catching local delicacy made by wrapping pounded glutinous rice around sugary, green-bean paste. A similar confection, found only during the mid-autumn festival, is the "earth cake", *banh deo*, which melds the contrasting flavours of candied fruits, sesame and lotus seeds with a dice of savoury pork fat. **Fritters** are popular among children and you'll find opportunistic hawkers outside schools, selling banana fritters, *banh chuoi*, or mixed slices of banana and sweet potato, *banh chuoi khoai*.

Most cities now have **ice-cream** parlours selling tubs or sticks of the local, hard ices in chocolate, vanilla or green-tea flavours, though for health reasons it's safest to buy only from the larger, busier outlets and not from street hawkers. More exotic tastes can be satisfied at the European- and American-style ice-cream parlours of Hanoi and Ho Chi Minh City, while excellent yoghurts are also increasingly available at ice-cream parlours and some cafés.

With its diverse climate, Vietnam is blessed with both tropical and temperate **fruits**, including dozens of banana species. The richest orchards are in the south, where pineapple, coconut, papaya, mango, longan and mangosteen flourish. Da Lat is famous for its strawberries, while the region around Nha Trang produces the peculiar "dragon fruit" (*thanh long*). The size and shape of a small pineapple, the dragon fruit has a mauvish-pink skin, studded with small protuberances, and smooth, white flesh speckled with tiny black seeds. The slightly sweet, watery flesh is thirst-quenching, and so is often served as a drink, crushed with ice.

A fruit that is definitely an acquired taste is the durian, a spiky, yellow-green football-sized fruit with an unmistakably pungent odour reminiscent of mature cheese and caramel, but tasting like an onion-laced custard. Jackfruit looks worryingly similar to durian but is generally larger and has smaller spikes. Its yellow segments of flesh are deliciously sweet.

Drinks

Giai khat means "quench your thirst" and you'll see the signs everywhere, on stands selling fresh juices, bottled cold drinks or outside cafés and bia hoi (draught beer) outlets. Many drinks are served with ice: tempting though it may be, the only really safe policy is to avoid **ice** altogether – *dung bo da, cam on* ("no ice, thanks") should do the trick. That said, ice in the top hotels, bars and restaurants is generally reliable, and some people take the risk in far dodgier establishments with apparent impunity.

A traditional tipple

While beer and imported spirits are drunk throughout Vietnam, the traditional tipple is **ruou can**, or rice-distilled liquor. Until recently, *ruou can* was regarded as decidedly downmarket, the preserve of labourers, farmers and ethnic minorities. Nowadays, however, it's becoming popular among the middle class and especially young urban sophisticates – including a growing number of women – as city-centre bars and restaurants begin to offer better quality *ruou can*.

Recipes for *ruou can* are a closely guarded secret, but its basic constituents are regular or glutinous rice, the latter of which is said to be more aromatic and have a fuller, smoother taste. Selected herbs and fruits can then be steeped in the liquor to give it further flavour, not to mention all sorts of medicinal and health benefits. You'll also see jars containing snakes, geckos and even whole crows. Traditionally, the basic ingredients are heated together and buried in the ground for a month or more to ferment. Nowadays, more modern – and hygienic – techniques are used to produce *ruou can* for general consumption. Look out for the high-quality rice-distilled liquors marketed under the Son Tinh brand (⊛www.sontinh.com).

The **ethnic minorities** of the northwest (Thai and Muong) concoct their own home-distilled *ruou can*, sometimes known as stem alcohol. Visitors are often invited to gather round the communal jar to drink the liquor through thin, bamboo straws. In more traditional villages it's regarded as a sacred ritual, which it would be an insult to refuse. *Chuc suc khoe* (Your health)! Or, for more serious drinking sessions, *Tram phan tram* (down in one)!

Water and soft drinks

Bottled **water** is widely available at around 7000đ for a large bottle (1.5 litres); avoid any other water, and even drinks that may have been diluted with suspect water (see box on p.38 for more on this).

Locally made **soft drinks** are tooth-numbingly sweet, but are cheap and safe – as long as the bottle or carton appears well sealed – and on sale just about everywhere. The Coke, Sprite and Fanta hegemony also means you can find fizzy drinks in surprisingly remote areas. Oddly, canned drinks are usually more expensive than the equivalent-sized bottle, whether it's a soft drink or beer – apparently it's less chic to drink from the old-fashioned bottle.

A more effective thirst-quencher is fresh coconut juice, though this is more difficult to find in the north. Fresh juices such as orange and lime are also delicious – just make sure they haven't been mixed with tap water – or try sugar-cane juice (*mia da*) with a dash of lime. Pasteurized milk, produced by Vinamilk, is now sold in the main towns and cities.

Somewhere between a drink and a snack, **ché** is made from taro flour and green bean, and served over ice with chunks of fruit, coloured jellies and even sweet corn or potato. In hot weather it provides a refreshing sugar-fix.

Tea and coffee

Tea drinking is part of the social ritual in Vietnam. Small cups of refreshing, strong, green tea are presented to all guests or visitors: the well-boiled water is safe to drink, as long as the cup itself is clean, and it's considered rude not to take at least a sip. Although your cup will be continually replenished to show hospitality, you don't have to carry on drinking; the polite way to decline a refill is to place your hand over the cup when your host is about to replenish it. Green tea is also served at the end of every meal, particularly in the south, and is usually provided free in restaurants and at food stalls.

Vietnam's best tea is said to grow around Bao Loc, southwest of Da Lat in the central highlands, and the best **coffee** further north among the hills of Buon Me Thuot. Coffee production has boomed in recent years, largely for export, with serious environmental and social consequences. The Vietnamese drink coffee very strong and in small quantities, with a large dollop of condensed milk at the bottom of the cup. Traditionally, coffee is filtered at the table by means of a small dripper balanced over the cup or glass, which sometimes sits in a bowl of hot water to keep it warm. However, places accustomed to tourists increasingly run to fresh (pasteurized) milk, while in the main cities you'll now find fancy Western-style cafés turning out quite decent lattes and cappuccinos. Out in the sticks, look out for the Trung Nguyen chain of coffee houses – they're cheap and cheerful and the coffee isn't bad either.

Alcoholic drinks

Canned and **bottled beers** brewed under licence in Vietnam include Tiger, Heineken, Carlsberg and San Miguel, but there are also plenty of very drinkable – and cheaper – local beers around, such as Halida, 333 (Ba Ba Ba) and Bivina. Some connoisseurs rate Bière la Rue from Da Nang tops, though Saigon Export, Hanoi Beer and BGI are also fine brews. Many other towns boast their own local beers, such as Hué (where the main brand is Huda), Haiphong and Thanh Hoa (where it's simply named after the town) – all worth a try.

Roughly forty years ago technology for making **bia hoi** (draught beer) was introduced from Czechoslovakia and it is now quaffed in vast quantities, particularly in the north. Bia hoi may taste fairly weak, but it measures in at up to four percent alcohol. It's also cheap – between 2000đ and 4000đ a glass – and supposedly unadulterated with chemicals, so in theory you're less likely to get a hangover. Bia hoi has a 24-hour shelf life, which means the better places sell out by early evening and you're unlikely to be drinking it into the wee hours. In the south, you're more likely to be drinking **bia tuoi** ("fresh" beer), a close relation of bia hoi but served from pressurized barrels. Outlets are usually open at lunchtime and then again in the evening from 5pm to 9pm.

Wine made from grapes is becoming increasingly popular in Vietnam. Local production – dating from the French era and

Bia hoi know-how

There are countless **bia hoi** (draught beer) outlets in most major cities in Vietnam, ranging from a few ankle-high stools gathered round a barrel on the pavement to beer gardens. Quality tends to be more consistent at the larger outlets supplied by major breweries such as Hanoi Beer and Halida (under the name Viet Ha), rather than the smaller places which usually buy their beer from microbreweries. On the whole, the more expensive – and colder – the beer, the better it is.

Bia hoi culture is about enjoying a few beers with a group of friends – usually all male, though in the cities you see a few women these days. People almost never drink alone and rarely drink without eating, so many places serve a range of snacks and more extensive dishes.

To help you order food in a bia hoi outlet, we've listed a few classic dishes below. Menus, if they exist, will be in Vietnamese. They normally give a price range for each dish (meat dishes typically range between 30,000đ and 50,000đ), so you order a small, medium or large amount, for example, depending on the size of your group. To maximize the variety, it makes sense to order small quantities of several dishes and share. If no prices are indicated on the menu, be sure to ask when ordering. Usually a note with the running total is left on the table, so you can keep track of how much you're spending.

bo luc lac	cubed spicy beef and green pepper stir-fry	*khoai tay ran*	chips/French fries
		lac	peanuts
		muc chien bo	squid fried in butter
ca bo lo	oven-cooked fish	*muc kho*	dried squid
dau chien ron	fried tofu	*muc tam bot*	battered squid
dau tu xuyen	tofu in a Chinese pork and tomato sauce	*nem chua*	minced spicy cured pork wrapped in banana leaf
de tai chanh	lightly-cooked goat with green banana, pineapple and lemon	*nom du du*	papaya salad
		nom hoa chuoi	banana-flower salad
		nom ngo sen	lotus-stem salad
dua chuot che	sliced cucumber	*oc xao xa ot*	stir-fried snail, lemongrass and chilli
ech chien bo	deep-fried battered frogs' legs		
ech xao mang	frogs' legs with bamboo shoots	*rau bi xaoi bo/toi*	beef/pumpkin-leaf fried with garlic
ga xe phay	shredded chicken salad with bean sprouts, carrot, peanuts and basil	*tho quay*	roast rabbit
		tom hap bia	shrimps steamed in beer
		tom nuong	grilled shrimps

centred around Da Lat – has been ramped up in recent years and even in fairly small towns you'll find the odd bottle of imported wine for sale. Many bars and restaurants in the major tourist destinations now serve wine, though some of it is pretty disgusting. For a decent bottle that's been properly stored you'll be paying premium prices at one of the top restaurants or specialist shops in Hanoi and Ho Chi Minh City.

In Vietnam, drinking alcohol is a social activity to be shared with friends. You'll rarely see the Vietnamese drinking alone and never without eating. Be prepared for lots of toasts to health, wealth and happiness and no doubt to international understanding, too, and note that it's the custom to fill the glasses of your fellow guests; someone else will fill yours.

The media

Vietnam has several English–language newspapers and magazines, of which the daily *Viet Nam News* (Ⓦwww.vietnamnews.vnagency.com.vn) has the widest distribution. It provides a brief – and very select – run–down of local, regional and international news, as well as snippets on art and culture. Though short on general news, both the weekly *Vietnam Investment Review* (Ⓦwww.vir.com.vn) and the monthly *Vietnam Economic Times* (Ⓦwww.vneconomy.com.vn) cover issues in greater depth and are worth looking at for an insight into what makes the Vietnamese economy tick. Both also publish useful supplements (*Time Out* and *The Guide* respectively) with selective but up–to–date restaurant and nightlife listings mainly covering Hanoi and Ho Chi Minh City, plus feature articles on culture and tourist destinations.

All media in Vietnam are under tight government control. There is, however, a slight glimmer of less draconian censorship, with an increasing number of stories covering corruption at even quite senior levels and more criticism of government policies and ministers, albeit very mild by Western standards.

Specifically for tourists, the Vietnam National Administration of Tourism (Ⓦwww.vietnamtourism.com) puts out the excellent free monthly, *Vietnam Discovery*. In addition to travel articles and restaurant and shop reviews, the magazine includes a handy pull-out listings supplement covering the main tourist destinations. Lastly, *Vietnam Pathfinder* (Ⓦwww.pathfinder.com.vn), also published monthly, is usually worth a look for its travel features.

Foreign publications, such as the *International Herald Tribune*, *Time*, *Newsweek*, *The Financial Times* and the Bangkok papers are sold by street vendors and at some of the larger bookshops and in the newsstands of more upmarket hotels in Ho Chi Minh City and Hanoi (see p.118 & p.385 respectively).

The government **radio** station, Voice of Vietnam (Ⓦwww.vov.org.vn), began life in 1945 during the August Revolution. It became famous during the American War when "Hanoi Hannah" broadcast propaganda programmes to American GIs. Nowadays it maintains six channels, of which VOV5 broadcasts English-language programmes several times a day covering a whole range of subjects: news, weather, sport, entertainment and culture, even market prices. You can pick up the broadcasts on FM in and around Hanoi, Haiphong and Ho Chi Minh City.

To keep in touch with the full spectrum of international news, however, you'll need a short-wave radio to pick up one of the world service channels, such as **BBC** World Service (Ⓦwww.bbc.co.uk/worldservice), **Radio Canada** (Ⓦwww.rcinet.ca) and **Voice of America** (Ⓦwww.voa.gov); local frequencies are listed on the relevant website.

Vietnamese **television** (VTV, Ⓦwww.vtv.org.vn) is also government-run and airs a mix of films, music shows, news programmes, soaps, sport and foreign (mostly American, Korean and Japanese) imports. VTV1, the main domestic channel, presents the news in English once a day, usually at 2pm. However, hotels increasingly provide satellite TV, and even budget places in the main cities now offer CNN, MTV and HBO as standard.

Festivals and religious events

The Vietnamese year follows a rhythm of festivals and religious observances, ranging from solemn family gatherings at the ancestral altar to national celebrations culminating in Tet, the Vietnamese New Year. In between are countless local festivals, most notably in the Red River Delta, honouring the tutelary spirit of the village or community temple.

The majority of festivals take place in spring, with a second flurry in the autumn months. One festival you might want to make a note of, however, is **Tet**: not only does most of Vietnam close down for the week, but either side of the holiday local transport services are stretched to the limit and international flights are filled by returning overseas Vietnamese.

Many Vietnamese festivals are **Chinese** in origin, imbued with a distinctive flavour over the centuries, but minority groups also hold their own specific celebrations. The ethnic **minorities** continue to punctuate the year with rituals that govern sowing, harvest or hunting, as well as elaborate rites of passage surrounding birth and death. The **Cao Dai** religion has its own array of festivals, while **Christian** communities throughout Vietnam observe the major ceremonies. Christmas is marked as a religious ceremony only by the faithful, though it's becoming a major event for all Vietnamese as an excuse to shop and party, with sax-playing santas greeting shoppers in front of malls.

The ceremonies you're most likely to see are **weddings** and **funerals**. The tenth lunar month is the most auspicious time for weddings, though at other times you'll also encounter plenty of wedding cavalcades on the road, their lead vehicle draped in colourful ribbons. Funeral processions are recognizable from the white headbands worn by mourners, while close family members dress completely in white. Both weddings and funerals are characterized by streetside parties under makeshift marquees, and since both tend to be joyous occasions, it's often difficult to know what you're witnessing, unless you spot a bridal gown or portrait of the deceased on display.

Most festivals take place according to the **lunar calendar**, which is also closely linked to the Chinese system with a zodiac of twelve animal signs. The most important times during the lunar month (which lasts 29 or 30 days) are the full moon (day one) and the new moon (day fourteen or fifteen). Festivals are often held at these times, which also hold a special significance for Buddhists, who are supposed to pray at the pagoda and avoid eating meat during the two days. On the eve of each full moon, Hoi An now celebrates a **Full-Moon Festival**: traffic is barred from the town centre, where traditional games, dance and music performances take place under the light of silk lanterns.

All Vietnamese calendars show both the lunar and solar (Gregorian) months and dates, but to be sure of a festival date it's best to check locally.

Tet: the Vietnamese New Year

"Tet", simply meaning festival, is the accepted name for Vietnam's most important annual event, properly known as **Tet Nguyen Dan**, or festival of the first day. Tet lasts for seven days and falls sometime between the last week of January and the third week of

Public holidays

January 1 New Year's Day
Late January/mid-February (dates vary each year): Tet, Vietnamese New Year (four days, though increasingly offices tend to close down for a full week)
April 30 Liberation of Saigon, 1975
May 1 International Labour Day
September 2: National Day

February, on the night of the new moon. This is a time when families get together to celebrate renewal and hope for the new year, when ancestral spirits are welcomed back to the household and when everyone in Vietnam becomes a year older – age is reckoned by the new year and not by individual birthdays.

There's an almost tangible sense of excitement leading up to midnight on the eve of Tet, though the welcoming of the New Year is now a much more subdued – and less dangerous – affair since firecrackers were banned in 1995. Instead, all the major cities hold fireworks displays.

Tet kicks off seven days before the new moon with the **festival of Ong Tau**, the god of the hearth (23rd day of the twelfth month). Ong Tau keeps watch over the household throughout the year, wards off evil spirits and makes an annual report of family events, good or bad, to the Jade Emperor. In order to send Ong Tau off to heaven in a benevolent mood, the family cleans its house from top to bottom, and makes offerings to him, including pocket money and a new set of clothes. Ong Tau returns home at midnight on the first chime of the new year and it's this, together with welcoming the ancestral spirits back to share in the party, that warrants such a massive celebration.

Tet is all about **starting the year afresh**, with a clean slate and good intentions. Not only is the house scrubbed, but all debts

Vietnam's major festivals

Spring festivals (Jan–April)

Tet The most important date in the Vietnamese festival calendar is New Year (*Tet Nguyen Dan*). After an initial jamboree, Tet is largely a family occasion when offices are shut, and many shops and restaurants may close for the seven-day festival. Officially only the first four days are public holidays, though many people take the whole week. First to seventh days of first lunar month; late January to mid-Feb.

Tay Son Festival Martial arts demonstrations in Tay Son District, plus garlanded elephants on parade. Fifth day of first lunar month; late January to mid-Feb.

Water Puppet Festival As part of the Tet celebrations a festival of puppetry is held at Thay Pagoda, west of Hanoi. Fifth to seventh days of first lunar month; Feb.

Lim Singing Festival Two weeks after Tet, Lim village near Bac Ninh, in the Red River Delta, resounds to the harmonies of "alternate singing" (*quan ho*) as men and women fling improvised lyrics back and forth. Thirteenth to fifteenth days of the first lunar month; Febuary–March.

Hai Ba Trung Festival The two Trung sisters are honoured with a parade and dancing at Hanoi's Hai Ba Trung temple. Sixth day of the second lunar month; March.

Perfume Pagoda Vietnam's most famous pilgrimage site is Chua Huong, west of Hanoi. Thousands of Buddhist pilgrims flock to the pagoda for the festival, which climaxes on the full moon (fourteenth or fifteenth day) of the second month, though the pilgrimage continues for a month either side. March–April.

Den Ba Chua Kho The full moon of the second month sees Hanoians congregating at this temple near Bac Ninh, to petition the goddess for success in business. March–April.

Thanh Minh Ancestral graves are cleaned and offerings of food, flowers and paper votive objects made at the beginning of the third lunar month. April.

Summer festivals (May–Aug)

Phat Dan Lanterns are hung outside the pagodas and Buddhist homes to commemorate Buddha's birth, enlightenment and the attainment of Nirvana. Eighth day of the fourth lunar month; May.

are paid off and those who can afford it have a haircut and buy new clothes. To attract favourable spirits, good-luck charms are put in the house, most commonly cockerels or the trinity of male figures representing prosperity, happiness and longevity. The crucial moments are the first minutes and hours of the new year as these set the pattern for the whole of the following year. People strive to avoid arguments, swearing or breaking anything – at least during the first three days when a single ill word could tempt bad luck into the house for the whole year ahead. The first visitor on the morning of Tet is also vitally significant: the ideal is someone respected, wealthy and happily married who will bring good fortune to the family; the bereaved, unemployed, accident-prone and even pregnant, on the other hand, are considered ill-favoured. This honour carries with it an onerous responsibility, however: if the family has a bad year, it will be the first-footer's fault.

The week-long festival is marked by **feasting**: special foods are eaten at Tet, such as pickled vegetables, candied lotus seeds and sugared fruits, all of which are first offered at the family altar. The most famous delicacy is *banh chung* (*banh tet* in the south), a thick square or cylinder of sweet, sticky rice that is prepared only for Tet. The rice is wrapped round a mixture of green-bean paste, pork fat and meat marinated in *nuoc mam*, and then boiled in

Chua Xu Festival The stone statue of Chua Xu at Sam Mountain, Chau Doc, is bathed, and thousands flock to honour her. Twenty-third to twenty-fifth day of fourth lunar month; May.

Tet Doan Ngo The summer solstice (fifth day of the fifth moon) is marked by festivities aimed at warding off epidemics brought on by the summer heat. This is also the time of dragon-boat races. Late May to early June.

Trang Nguyen (or *Vu Lan*) The day of wandering souls is the second most important festival after Tet. Offerings of food and clothes are made to comfort and nourish the unfortunate souls without a home, and all graves are cleaned. This is also time for the forgiveness of faults, when the King of Hell judges everyone's spirits and metes out reward or punishment as appropriate. Until the fifteenth century prisoners were allowed to go home on this day. Fourteenth or fifteenth day of the seventh lunar month; August.

Autumn festivals (Sept–Dec)

Do Son Buffalo-fighting Festival Held in Do Son village, near Haiphong. Ninth and tenth days of the eighth lunar month.

Kate Festival The Cham New Year is celebrated in high style at Po Klong Garai and Po Re Me, both near Phan Rang. September–October.

Trung Thu The mid-autumn festival, also known as Children's Day, is when dragon dances take place and children are given lanterns in the shape of stars, carp or dragons. Special cakes, *banh trung thu*, are eaten at this time of year. These are sticky rice cakes filled with lotus seeds, nuts and candied fruits and are either square like the earth (*banh deo*), or round like the moon (*banh nuong*) and containing the yolk of an egg. Fourteenth or fifteenth day of the eighth lunar month; September–October.

Whale Festival Lang Ca Ong, Vung Tau. Crowds gather to make offerings to the whales. Sixteenth day of the eighth lunar month; September–October.

Oc Bom Boc Festival Boat-racing festival in Soc Trang. Tenth day of tenth lunar month; November–December.

Da Lat Flower Festival An annual extravaganza in which the city shows off the abundance of blooms grown locally. December.

Christmas Midnight services at the cathedrals in Hanoi and Ho Chi Minh City and much revelry in the streets. December 24.

banana leaves, which impart a pale green colour. According to legend, an impoverished prince of the Hung dynasty invented the cakes over two thousand years ago; his father was so impressed by the simplicity of his son's gift that he named the prince as his heir. Tet is an expensive time for Vietnamese families, many of whom save for months to get the new year off to a good start. Apart from special foods and new clothes, it's traditional to give children red envelopes containing *li xi*, or lucky money, and to decorate homes with spring blossoms. In the week before Tet, flower markets grace the larger cities: peach blossoms in the north, apricot in Hué and mandarin in the south. Plum and kumquat (symbolizing gold coins) are also popular, alongside the more showy, modern blooms of roses, dahlias or gladioli.

Sports and outdoor pursuits

Though Vietnam was slow to develop its huge potential as an outdoor adventure destination, things have really changed in the last few years. Apart from trekking in the mountainous north, visitors can now also go rock–climbing, canyoning, sea kayaking or kitesurfing, among other activities. Da Lat has emerged as Vietnam's adventure sports capital and Mui Ne its surf city, though some sports like mountain biking can be done throughout the country.

Trekking

The easiest and most popular area for trekking is in the northwest mountains around Sa Pa and, to a lesser extent, Mai Chau. Sa Pa is also the starting point for ascents of the country's highest peak, Fan Si Pan, a challenge to be undertaken only by experienced hikers. Other options include hiking around Kon Tum or Da Lat in the central highlands or in one of Vietnam's many national parks, including Cat Ba, Cuc Phuong, Bach Ma, Cat Tien and Yok Don. In Yok Don you can even go elephant trekking, though prices are rather steep.

There's no problem about striking out on your own for a day's hiking. However, for anything more adventurous, particularly if you want to overnight in the villages, you'll need to make arrangements in advance. This is easily done either before you arrive in Vietnam or through local tour agents, most of which offer organized tours and tailor-made packages. In most cases you can also make arrangements through guesthouses and guides on the spot. Note that it's essential to take a guide if you are keen to get off the beaten track: many areas are still sensitive about the presence of foreigners.

Biking

Mountainbiking is becoming increasingly popular in Vietnam. The classic ride is from Hanoi to Ho Chi Minh City, a journey of between two and three weeks. Previously, this would have taken you along Highway 1, battling with trucks and buses, but now the more switched-on tour companies are offering excursions down the Ho Chi Minh Highway which runs along the western Truong Son mountain chain, and is so far thankfully free of heavy traffic.

The area around Sa Pa is a focus for biking activity, with tour operators offering excursions to suit all levels of experience and fitness. You can choose from half-day excursions to multi-day outings including overnighting in minority villages. Other good areas for exploring by bike include Mai Chau, Bac Ha, Da Lat and the Mekong Delta.

North Vietnam is also popular among the **motorbiking** fraternity. Specialist outfits in Hanoi organize tailor-made itineraries taking you way off the beaten track.

Water sports

With its three-thousand-kilometre coastline, Vietnam should be a paradise for **water**

sports, but the options remain fairly limited at present, for a variety of reasons. One is simply a matter of access: the infrastructure is not yet in place. More crucial is the presence of potentially dangerous undercurrents along much of the coast, accompanied by strong winds at certain times of year. Many of the big beach resorts have guards or put out flags in season indicating where it's safe to swim. Elsewhere, check carefully before taking the plunge.

Whilst many of the beaches along the central and south-central coast are great for **swimming**, the best are those around Mui Ne, with Nha Trang, Hoi An and Da Nang close behind. Mui Ne is also the country's top venue for windsurfing and kitesurfing, both of which are currently hugely popular. Phu Quoc Island, off Vietnam's southern coast, is also famed not only for its fabulous beaches but also as the country's top spot for **snorkelling** and **scuba-diving**. The Con Dao Islands and Nha Trang are other popular places to don a snorkel or wet suit, but wherever you dive, it's worth noting that standards of maintenance aren't always great, so check equipment carefully and only go out with a properly qualified and registered operator that you trust.

Heading inland, the rivers and waterfalls around Da Lat provide good possibilities for **canyoning** and **rock-climbing**.

Both Mui Ne and Non Nuoc beach near Da Nang have a good reputation for **windsurfing**. Mui Ne even hosts an international **kitesurfing** competition each spring (usually February).

In north Vietnam Ha Long Bay is the watersports centre. Most boat tours of the bay allow time for swimming – weather permitting – while there are decent beaches on Cat Ba and better still on remote Quan Lan Island. For those in search of more strenuous exercise, a number of tour agents offer **sea-kayaking** trips on the bay – not recommended in the heat of summer.

Other activities

Vietnam has over 850 species of birds, including several that have only been identified in the past few years. The best places for **birdwatching** are the national parks, including Cuc Phuong (famous also for its springtime butterfly displays), Bach Ma and Cat Tien. The rare Sarus crane, amongst many other species, spends the dry season in and around the Tram Chim National Park in the Mekong Delta. For more information check out Ⓦwww.vietnambirding.com or Ⓦwww.birdwatchinigvietnam.net.

Finally, there are now dozens of excellent **golf** courses in Vietnam – around Ho Chi Minh City, Hanoi, Phan Thiet and Da Lat amongst others – all with much cheaper green fees than in the West.

Crime and personal safety

Vietnam is a relatively safe country for visitors, including women travelling alone. In fact, given the country's recent history, many tourists, particularly Americans, are pleasantly surprised at the warm reception that foreign travellers receive. That said, petty crime is on the rise – though it's still relatively small–scale and shouldn't be a problem if you take common–sense precautions. Generally, the hassles you'll encounter will be the milder sort of coping with pushy vendors and over–enthusiastic touts and beggars.

Petty crime

As a tourist, you're an obvious target for thieves (who may include your fellow travellers): carry your passport, traveller's cheques and other valuables in a concealed **money belt**. Don't leave anything important lying about in your room: use a safe, if you have one. A cable lock, or **padlock** and chain, comes in handy for doors and windows in cheap hotels, and is useful for securing your pack on trains and buses. It's not a bad idea to keep US$100 or so separately from the rest of your cash, along with your traveller's cheques receipts, insurance policy details and photocopies of important documents, such as the relevant pages of your passport including your visa stamp, and departure card.

At street level it's best not to be ostentatious: forego eye-catching jewellery and flashy watches, try to be discreet when taking out your cash, and be particularly wary in **crowds** and on **public transport**. If your pack is on the top of the bus, make sure it's attached securely (usually everything is tied down with ropes) and keep an eye on it during the most vulnerable times – before departure, at meal stops and on arrival at your destination. On trains, either cable-lock your pack or put it under the bottom bench-seat, out of public view. The odd instance has been reported of travellers being drugged and then robbed, so it's best not to accept food or drink from anyone you don't know and trust. Bear in mind that when walking or riding in a cyclo you are vulnerable to moped-borne **snatch-thieves**; don't wear cameras or expensive sunglasses hanging round your neck and keep a firm grip on your bags. If you do become a target, however, it's best to let go rather than risk being pulled into the traffic and suffering serious injury.

The place you are most likely to encounter street crime is in Ho Chi Minh City, which has a fairly bad reputation for bag-snatchers, pickpockets and con artists. Be wary of innocent-looking kids and grannies who may be acting as decoys for thieves – especially in the bar districts and other popular tourist hangouts. It's best to avoid taking a cyclo at night, and you'd be unwise to walk alone at any time outside Districts One, Three and Five.

Petty crime, much of it drug- and prostitution-related, is also a problem in Nha Trang, where you should watch your belongings at all times on the beach. Again, be wary of taking a cyclo after dark and women should avoid walking alone at night. Single males, on the other hand, are a particular target for "taxi girls", many of whom also double as thieves.

It's important not to get paranoid, however: crime levels in Vietnam are still a long way behind those of Western countries, and violent crime against tourists is extremely rare.

If you do have anything stolen, you'll need to go to the nearest **police** station for a report in order to claim on your insurance. Try to recruit an English-speaker to come along with you – someone at your hotel should be able to help.

"Social evils" and serious crime

Since liberalization and *doi moi*, Vietnamese society has seen an increase in prostitution, drugs – including hard drugs – and more serious crimes. These so-called "**social evils**" are viewed as a direct consequence of reduced controls on society and ensuing westernization. The police have imposed midnight closing on bars and clubs for several years now, mainly because of drugs, but also to curb general rowdiness, although you'll always find the occasional bar that somehow manages to keep serving. That apart, the campaign against social evils should have little effect on most foreign tourists.

Single Western males tend to get solicited by **prostitutes** in cheap provincial and seaside hotels, though more commonly by women cruising on motorbikes. Quite apart from any higher moral considerations, bear in mind that AIDS is on the increase in Vietnam.

Finally, having anything to do with **drugs** in Vietnam is extremely unwise. At night there's a fair amount of drug selling on the streets of Ho Chi Minh City, Hanoi, Nha Trang and even Sa Pa, and it's not unknown for dealers

Emergency phone numbers

The following numbers apply throughout Vietnam. If possible, get a Vietnamese-speaker to phone on your behalf.
Police ☎113
Fire ☎114
Ambulance ☎115

to turn buyers in to the police. Fines and jail sentences are imposed for lesser offences, while the death penalty is regularly imposed for possessing, trading or smuggling larger quantities.

Military and political hazards

Not surprisingly, the Vietnamese authorities are sensitive about **military installations** and strategic areas – including border regions, military camps (of which there are many), bridges, airports, naval dockyards and even train stations. Anyone taking photographs in the vicinity of such sites risks having the memory card removed from their camera or being fined.

Unexploded ordnance from past conflicts still poses a threat in some areas: the problem is most acute in the Demilitarized Zone, where each year a number of local farmers, scrap-metal scavengers or children are killed or injured. Wherever you are, stick to well-trodden paths and never touch any shells or half-buried chunks of metal.

Needless to say, **political activists** aren't exactly welcome in Vietnam and anyone carrying political literature or in contact with known activists will be treated with suspicion, possibly tailed and even deported. Their Vietnamese contacts will be treated less leniently. The same goes for **religious activists**, too.

Beggars, hassle and scams

Given the number of disabled, war-wounded and unemployed in Vietnam, there are surprisingly few **beggars** around. Most people are actually trying hard to earn a living somehow, and in the circumstances it doesn't seem unreasonable to have your shoes cleaned more times than they might need, or buy a couple of extra postcards.

At many tourist spots, you may well be swamped by a gaggle of children or teenagers selling cold drinks, fruit and chewing gum. Although they can sometimes be a bit overwhelming, as often as not they're just out to practise their English and

be entertained for a while. They may even turn out to be excellent guides, in which case it's only fair that you buy something from them in return.

A common **scam** among taxi drivers is to tell new arrivals in a town that the hotel they ask for is closed or has moved or changed its name. Instead, they head for a hotel that pays commission. This may work out fine (new hotels often use this method to become known), but more often than not it's a substandard hotel and you will in any case pay over the odds since the room rate will include the driver's commission. To avoid being ripped off, always insist on being taken to your chosen hotel, at least just to check the story.

Another common complaint is that organized tours don't live up to what was promised. There are more people on the tour than stated, for example, or the room doesn't have air-conditioning, or the guide's English is limited. If it's a group tour and you've paid up front, unfortunately there's very little you can do beyond complaining to the agent on your return; you may be lucky and get some form of compensation, but it's very unlikely. As always, you tend to get what you pay for, so avoid signing up for dirt-cheap tours.

Women travellers

Vietnam is generally a safe country for women to travel around alone. Most Vietnamese will simply be curious as to why you are on your own and the chances of encountering any threatening behaviour are extremely rare. That said, it pays to take the normal precautions, especially **late at night** when there are few people on the streets and you should avoid taking a cyclo by yourself; use a taxi instead – metered taxis are generally considered safest.

Most Vietnamese women **dress** modestly, keeping covered from top to toe. It helps to do the same and to avoid skimpy shorts and vests, which are considered offensive. Topless sunbathing, even beside a hotel pool, is a complete no-no.

Culture and etiquette

With its blend of Confucianism and Buddhism, Vietnamese society tends to be both conservative and, at the same time, fairly tolerant. This means you will rarely be remonstrated with for your dress or behaviour. Furthermore, by following a few simple rules, you can minimize the risk of causing offence. This is particularly important in rural areas and small towns where people are less used to the eccentric habits of foreigners.

As a visitor, it's recommended that you err on the side of caution. Shorts and sleeveless shirts are fine for the beach, but are not welcome in pagodas, temples and other religious sites. When dealing with officialdom, it also pays to look as neat and tidy as possible. Anything else may be taken as a mark of disrespect.

Women in particular should dress modestly, especially in the countryside and ethnic minority areas, where revealing too much flesh – no shorts or sleeveless shirts – is regarded as offensive. (See p.63 for more advice for women travellers.)

It's also worth noting that **nudity**, either male or female, on the beach is absolutely beyond the pale.

When entering a Cao Dai temple, the main building of a pagoda or a private home it's the custom to remove your **shoes**. In some pagodas nowadays this may only be required when stepping onto the prayer mats – ask or watch what other people do. In a pagoda or temple you are also expected to leave a small donation.

Officially, **homosexuality** is regarded as a "social evil", alongside drugs and prostitution. However, there is no law explicitly banning homosexual activity and, as long as it is not practised openly, it is largely ignored. Indeed, the number of openly gay men has increased noticeably in recent years, particularly in Ho Chi Minh City and

Hanoi, and homosexuality is discussed more frequently in the media, although the lesbian scene remains very low-key. Although outward discrimination is rare, this is still a very traditional society and it pays to be discreet in Vietnam. For more information, consult the excellent Utopia Asia website, ⓦ www.utopia-asia.com.

As in most Asian countries, it's not done to get angry, and it certainly won't get things moving any quicker. Passing round cigarettes (to men only) is always appreciated and is widely used as a social gambit aimed at progressing tricky negotiations, bargaining and so forth.

Tipping, while not expected, is always appreciated. In general, a few thousand dong should suffice. Smart restaurants and hotels normally add a service charge, but if not ten percent is the norm in a restaurant, while the amount in a hotel will depend on the grade of hotel and what services they've provided. If you're pleased with the service, you should also tip the guide, and the driver where appropriate, at the end of a tour.

Other social conventions worth noting are that you shouldn't touch **children** on the head and, unlike in the West, it's best to ignore a young baby rather than praise it, since it's believed that this attracts the attention of jealous spirits who will cause the baby to fall ill.

Shopping

Souvenir–hunters will find rich pickings in Vietnam, whose eye–catching handicrafts and mementos range from colonial currency and stamps to fabrics and basketware crafted by the country's ethnic minorities, and from limpet–like conical hats to fake US Army–issue Zippo lighters.

Throughout the Guide, we've highlighted places to shop, but in general you'll find the best quality, choice and prices in Ho Chi Minh City, Hanoi and Hoi An. Though you'll find more shops now have fixed **prices**, particularly those catering to tourists, in markets and rural areas prices are almost always open to negotiation (see the box below for some tips on successful bargaining).

Clothing, arts and crafts

Few Western tourists leave Vietnam without the obligatory **conical hat**, or *non la*, sewn from rain- and sun-proof palm fronds; at around 25,000đ for a basic version, they're definitely an affordable keepsake. From the city of Hué comes a more elaborate version, the **poem hat,** or *non bai tho*, in whose brim are inlays which, when held up to the light, reveal lines of poetry or scenes from Vietnamese legend. Vietnamese women traditionally wear the **ao dai** – baggy silk trousers under a knee-length silk tunic slit up

both sides. Extraordinarily elegant, *ao dai* can be bought off the peg anywhere in the country for around US$20; or, if you can spare a few days for fitting, you can have one tailor-made for US$30 or so, depending on the material.

Local **silk** is sold by the metre in Vietnam's more sizeable markets and in countless outlets in Hoi An, along Dong Khoi in Ho Chi Minh City and on Hanoi's Hang Gai. These same shops also sell ready-made clothes and accessories, including embroidered silk handbags and shoes, and most also offer tailoring. In general, Hoi An's tailors have the best reputation, either working from a pattern book or copying an item you take along. Just make sure you allow plenty of time for fittings.

Embroidered **cotton**, in the form of table-cloths, sheets and pillowcases, also makes a popular souvenir. Meanwhile, the sartorial needs of backpackers are well catered for in major tourist destinations, where **T-shirt** sellers do brisk business. Predictably

The art of bargaining

The Vietnamese, not unreasonably, see tourists as wildly rich – how else could they afford to stop working and travel the world – and a **first quoted price** is usually pitched accordingly. It makes sense, therefore, to be prepared.

First of all, do your homework. Find out the approximate going rate, either from your hotel or fellow tourists, or from one of the increasing number of fixed-price shops – remembering to take into account the difference in quality, for example, between mass-produced and hand-crafted goods.

The trick then is to remain **friendly** and amused, but also to be realistic: traders will quickly lose interest in a sale if they think you aren't playing the game fairly. Any show of aggression, and you've lost it in more ways than one. If you feel you're on the verge of agreement, **moving away** often pays dividends – it's amazing how often you'll be called back.

Keep a sense of **perspective**. If a session of bargaining is becoming very protracted, step back and remind yourself that you're often arguing the toss over mere pennies – nothing to you, but a lot to the average Vietnamese.

popular designs include a portrait of Uncle Ho, and the yellow Communist star on a red background.

Traditional handicrafts

Of the many types of traditional handicrafts on offer in Vietnam, **lacquerware** (*son mai*) is among the most beautiful. Made by applying multiple layers of resin onto an article and then polishing vigorously to achieve a deep, lustrous sheen, lacquer is used to decorate furniture, boxes, chopsticks and bangles and is sometimes embellished with eggshell or inlays of **mother-of-pearl** (which is also used in its own right, on screens and pictures) – common motifs are animals, fish and elaborate scrolling. More recently, the lacquerware tradition has been hijacked by more contemporary icons, and it's now possible to buy colourful lacquerware paintings of Mickey Mouse, Tin Tin and Batman. Imported synthetic lacquer has also made an appearance. These brightly coloured, almost metallic, finishes may not be for the purist, but they make for eye-catching bowls, vases and all sorts of household items.

Bronze, **brass** and **jade** are also put to good use, appearing in various forms such as carvings, figurines and jewellery. In Hué, brass and copper **teapots** are popular. Of the earthenware, porcelain and ceramics available across the country, thigh-high **ceramic elephants** and other animal figurines are the quirkiest buys – though decidedly tricky to carry home. Look out, too, for boxes and other knick-knacks made from wonderfully aromatic **cinnamon** and **camphor wood**. For something a little more culturally elevated, you could invest in a **water puppet** or a traditional **musical instrument** (for more on both of these, see "Music and theatre", p.512).

Vietnam's **ethnic minorities** are producing increasingly sophisticated fare for the tourist market. Fabrics – sometimes shot through with shimmering gold braid – are their main asset, sold in lengths and also made into **purses**, **shoulder bags** and other accoutrements. The minorities of the central highlands are adept at **basketwork**, fashioning backpacks, baskets and mats, and **bamboo pipes**. Hanoi probably has the greatest variety of **minority handicrafts** on sale. In the far north, Sa Pa is a popular place to buy Hmong clothes, bags and **skull-caps**, and you'll find lengths of woven fabrics or embroidery in markets throughout the northern mountains.

Paintings

A healthy fine arts scene exists in Vietnam, and **painting** in particular is thriving. In the galleries of Hanoi, Ho Chi Minh City and Hoi An you'll find exquisite works in oil, watercolour, lacquer, charcoal and silk weaving by the country's leading artists. Hanoi is the best single place to look for contemporary art.

For the top names you can expect to pay hundreds or even thousands of dollars. Buyer beware, however: many artists find it lucrative to knock out multiple copies of their own or other people's work. You'll need to know what you're doing, or to buy from a reputable gallery.

A cheap alternative is to snap up some of the charming hand-painted silk **greetings cards** sold in most tourist centres. A recent innovation is the sale of old Communist-era **propaganda posters**, both genuine and copies.

Books, stamps and coins

You can buy photocopied editions of almost all the **books** ever published on Vietnam from strolling vendors in Hanoi and Ho Chi Minh City. There are also an increasing number of locally published coffee-table books, histories and guides available from bona-fide bookshops and the more upmarket hotels. However, if all you want is some general reading matter, both Hanoi and Ho Chi Minh City now have secondhand bookshops where you can exchange or buy used books.

Philatelists meanwhile will enjoy browsing through the old Indochinese **stamps** sold in the souvenir shops of Hanoi and Ho Chi Minh City. Similarly, old **notes** and **coins**, including French-issue piastres and US Army credits, are available.

Memorabilia, trinkets and food

Army surplus gear is still a money-spinner, though fatigues, belts, canteens and dog tags purportedly stolen from a dead or wounded GI aren't the most tasteful of souvenirs – and the vast majority are fakes anyway. The green **pith helmets** with a red star on the front, worn first by the NVA during the American War and now by the regular Vietnamese Army, find more takers. Other items that sell like hot cakes, especially in the south, are fake **Zippo lighters** bearing such pithy adages as "When I die bury me face down, so the whole damn army can kiss my ass" and "We are the unwilling, led by the unqualified, doin' the unnecessary for the ungrateful", though again they're very unlikely to be authentic GI issue. In Ho Chi Minh City, extravagant wooden **model ships** are sold in a string of shops on Hai Ba Trung, at the east side of Lam Son Square.

Finally, **foodstuffs** that may tempt you include coffee from the central highlands, candied strawberries and artichoke tea from Da Lat, coconut candies from the Mekong Delta, preserved miniature tangerines from Hoi An and packets of tea and dried herbs and spices from the northern highlands. As for **drinks**, most of the concoctions itemized on p.54 are securely bottled. The Soc Tinh range of rice-distilled liquor makes an attractively packaged souvenir.

Travel essentials

Addresses

Locating an **address** is rarely a problem in Vietnam, but there are a couple of conventions it helps to know about. Where two numbers are separated by a slash, such as 110/5, you simply make for no. 110, where an alley will lead off to a further batch of buildings – you want the fifth one. Where a number is followed by a letter, as in 117a, you're looking for a single block encompassing several addresses, of which one will be 117a. Vietnamese cite addresses without the words for street, avenue and so on; we've followed this practice throughout the Guide except where ambiguity would result.

Admission charges

Admission charges are usually levied at museums, historic sights, national parks and any place that attracts tourists – sometimes even beaches. Charges at some **major sights** range from a dollar or two up to around US$4–5 for the Cham ruins at My Son or Hué's citadel and royal mausoleums. Elsewhere, however, the amount is usually just a few thousand dong. Note that there's often a hefty additional fee for **cameras** and **videos** at major sights.

Apart from those with some historical significance, **pagodas and temples** are usually free, though it's customary to leave a donation of a few thousand dong in the collecting box or on one of the altar plates.

Costs

With the average Vietnamese annual income hovering around US$500–600, daily expenses are low, and if you come prepared to do as the locals do, then food, drink and transport can all be incredibly cheap – and even accommodation needn't be too great an expense. **Bargaining** is very much a part of everyday life, and almost everything is negotiable, from fruit in the market to a room for the night: see box on p.65 for some tips.

By eating at simple com (rice) and pho (noodle soup) stalls, picking up local buses and opting for the simplest accommodation there's no reason why you shouldn't be able to adhere to a **daily budget** in the region of US$15–20. Upgrading to more salubrious lodgings with a few mod cons, eating good food followed by a couple of beers in a bar and signing up for the odd minibus tour and visiting a few sights could bounce your expenditure up to a more realistic US$30–35. A fair mid-level budget, treating yourself to three-star hotels and more upmarket restaurants, would lie in the US$50–100 range, depending on the number and type of tours you took. And if you stay at the ritziest city hotels, dine at the swankiest restaurants and rent cars with drivers wherever you go, then the sky's the limit.

Electricity

The **electricity** supply in Vietnam is 220 volts. Plugs generally have two round pins, though you may come across sockets requiring two flat pins and even some requiring three pins. Power supplies are erratic, so be prepared for cuts and surges.

Ethical tourism and the environment

The **expansion of tourism** in Vietnam has been spectacular, growing from just ten thousand foreign visitors in 1993 to more than four million in 2008. In addition, at least fifteen million Vietnamese now take holidays within the country each year. While this has undoubtedly been a boon for the economy, tourism has brought with it serious and potentially disruptive effects environmentally, socially, culturally, and economically. Some of the most distressing examples are to be found in Vietnam's ethnic minority areas. Sa Pa's famous "love market" attracted so much tourist attention it eventually relocated to a more remote location. Many families in the area have sold off their antique jewellery, while Hmong children beg for sweets, pens and money, and some even sell drugs.

Insurance

It is essential to have a good **travel insurance policy** to cover against theft, loss and illness or injury. It's also advisable to have medical cover that includes evacuation in the event of serious illness, as the local hospitals aren't that great. Most policies exclude so-called dangerous sports unless an extra premium is paid: in Vietnam this can include scuba-diving, whitewater-rafting, windsurfing and trekking. If you're doing any motorbike touring, you are strongly advised to take out full medical insurance including emergency evacuation; make sure the policy specifically covers you for biking in Vietnam, and ascertain whether benefits will be paid as treatment proceeds or only after return home, and whether there is a 24-hour medical emergency number. If you need to make a claim, you should keep receipts for medicines and medical treatment, and in the event that you have anything stolen, you must obtain an official statement from the police.

Internet and email

Accessing the **internet** in Vietnam has become a great deal easier, though it is still monitored and controlled by a government fearful of this potentially subversive means of communication.

Pricing policy

Although Vietnamese law requires that all **prices** are quoted in dong, you'll find many hotels, the more upmarket restaurants, tour agents and so forth still use US dollars and, occasionally, euros. To reflect this and to avoid exchange-rate fluctuations, throughout the Guide we quote prices in the currency used on the spot.

Incidentally, don't be alarmed if you notice that Vietnamese pay less than you for plane tickets, at some hotels and at certain sights: Vietnam maintains a **two-tier pricing system**, with foreigners sometimes paying many times more than locals. The good news for tourists is that the system is being phased out, with prices for foreigners being adjusted downwards while those for Vietnamese rise to meet them. A single price system now applies on the trains, for example, while the gap has gradually been narrowing for air travel. It will take several more years before the practice disappears completely, however, and for the moment it remains something of a grey area, particularly as regards hotels and bus tickets, where the amount you pay may well depend on the person you happen to be dealing with.

There's no problem about logging on in the major cities and tourist centres in Vietnam, where you'll find dozens of **internet cafés,** while many hotels also offer internet access. Many upmarket and even some budget hotels offer wi-fi broadband access in your room – sometimes free to attract custom. Even remote regions are wired to the web these days, though the service may be slower and more expensive. Rates in the big cities currently stand at around 100đ per minute, with some places charging by the hour (about 6000đ).

Laundry

Most top- and mid-range hotels provide a **laundry service**, and many budget hotels too, but rates can vary wildly, so it's worth checking first. In the bigger cities, especially in tourist areas, you'll find laundry shops on the street, where the rate is usually around 5000đ per kilo.

Mail

Mail can take anything from four days to four weeks in or out of Vietnam, depending largely where you are. Services are quickest and most reliable from the major towns, where eight to ten days is the norm. **Overseas postal rates** are reasonable: a postcard costs 7000–8000đ, while the price of a letter is in the region of 10,000đ for the minimum weight. **Express Mail Service** (EMS) operates to most countries and certain destinations within Vietnam; the service cuts down delivery times substantially and the letter or parcel is automatically registered. For a minimum-weight dispatch by EMS (under 250g), you'll pay around US$30 to the UK, US$32 to the US, US$35 to Canada and US$27 to Australia.

Poste restante services are available at all main post offices. You'll need to show your passport to collect mail and will be charged a small amount per item. Mail is held for two months before being returned. To avoid misfiling, your name should be printed clearly, with the surname in capitals and underlined, and it's still worth checking under all your names, just in case. Have letters addressed to you c/o Poste Restante, GPO, town or city, province.

When **sending parcels** out of Vietnam, take everything to the post office unwrapped since it will be inspected for any customs liability and wrapped for you, and the whole process, including wrapping and customs inspection, will cost you upwards of 30,000đ. Pirated CDs and DVDs and any other suspect items will be seized. Surface mail is the cheapest option, with parcels taking between one and four months.

Receiving parcels is not such a good idea. Some parcels simply go astray; those that do make it are subject to thorough customs inspections, import duty and even confiscation of suspicious items – particularly printed matter, videos or cassettes. However, if you do need to collect a parcel, remember to take your passport.

Maps

The most accurate and reliable map of Vietnam is the **Rough Guides** Map of Vietnam, Laos and Cambodia (1:1,200,000). Other decent maps are the International Travel Map of Vietnam (1:1,000,000) or Nelles (1:1,500,000) map of Vietnam, Laos and Cambodia: both feature plans of Ho Chi Minh City and Hanoi. Alternatively, the locally produced maps you'll find on sale in all the major towns and tourist destinations in Vietnam aren't bad.

If you need more detailed coverage, if you're cycling or motorbike touring for example, there's no beating the book of maps entitled Giao Thong Duong Bo Vietnam (1:500,000) published by Ban Do Cartographic Publishing House and available in bigger bookshops in Hanoi and Ho Chi Minh City. Trouble is, it weighs about a kilo. Another good option for cyclists and bikers is the Vietnam Administrative Atlas by the same publisher, with a map of each province per page. Look out, too, for Fauna and Flora International's Vietnam Ecotourism Map (1:1,000,000). Not only is it pretty accurate, but also includes information on visiting the national parks and other areas of environmental interest.

Money

Vietnam's unit of currency is the **dong**, which you'll see abbreviated as "đ", "d" or "VND" after an amount. Notes come in denominations of 500đ, 1000đ, 2000đ, 5000đ, 10,000đ, 20,000đ, 50,000đ, 100,000đ, 200,000đ and 500,000đ, coins in 200đ, 500đ, 1000đ, 2000đ and 5000đ. In addition to the dong, the **American dollar** operates as a parallel, unofficial currency and most travellers carry some dollars as a back-up to pay large bills. On the whole, though, it's more convenient to operate in dong, and you'll often find dong prices are slightly lower than the equivalent in dollars.

At the time of writing, the **exchange rate** was around 25,000đ to £1; 17,000đ to US$1; 21,000đ to 1 Euro; 14,000đ to CA$1; 11,000đ to AUS$1; and 9,000đ to NZ$1. Recently the country has been plagued by high inflation rates, so these exchange rates are liable to fluctuate. For the latest exchange rates go to ⑩www.xe.com.

Dong are not available outside Vietnam at present, so take in some small-denomination American dollars to use until you reach a bank. Most **banks** and **exchange bureaux** don't charge for changing foreign currency into dong; banks in major cities will accept euros and other major currencies, but elsewhere may only accept dollars. Some tour agents and hotels will also change money, and most jewellery shops in Vietnam will exchange dollars at a slightly better rate than the banks, but watch out for scams. Wherever you change money, ask for a mix of denominations (in remote places, bigger bills can be hard to split), and refuse really tatty banknotes, as you'll have difficulty getting anyone else to accept them.

There's also a comprehensive network of **ATMs**, many open 24 hours: most accept Visa, MasterCard and American Express cards issued abroad. The maximum withdrawal is two million dong at a time, with a flat-rate charge of 20,000đ per transaction (in addition to whatever surcharges your own bank levies). In Hanoi and Ho Chi Minh City you'll also find ATMs operated by ANZ and HSBC. These accept a wider range of cards, including those in the Cirrus and Plus networks.

Major **credit cards** – Visa, MasterCard and, to a lesser extent, American Express – are accepted in Vietnam's main cities and major tourist spots. All top-level and many mid-level hotels will accept them, as will a growing number of restaurants, though some places levy surcharges of three to four percent.

Traveller's cheques are less common now that ATMs are so widespread, but can be cashed at major banks (you need your passport as ID), for a commission of up to two percent. Vietinbank generally charges the lowest rates: at the time of writing these were 0.55 percent (minimum US$1.1) when changing into dong and 1.1 percent (minimum US$2.2) into dollars or other foreign currencies. Vietcombank waives commission on American Express traveller's cheques.

Having **money wired** from home via MoneyGram (UK ☎0800/8971 8971, US ☎1-800/☎666-3947, ⑩www.moneygram.com) or Western Union (US ☎1-800/325 6000, ⑩www.westernunion.com) is never cheap, and should be considered a last resort. It's also possible to have money wired directly from a bank or post office in your home country to a bank in Vietnam, although this has the added complication of involving two separate institutions; money wired this way normally takes two working days to arrive, and charges vary according to the amount sent.

Opening hours

Basic **hours of business** are 7.30–11.30am and 1.30–4.30pm, though after lunch nothing really gets going again before 2pm. The standard closing day for offices is Sunday, and many now also close on Saturdays, including most state-run banks and government offices.

Most **banks** tend to work Monday to Friday 8–11.30am and 1–4pm, though some stay open later in the afternoon or may forego a lunch break. In tourist centres you'll even find branches open evenings and weekends. **Post offices** keep much longer hours, in general staying open from 6.30am through to 9pm with no closing day. Some sub-post offices work shorter hours and close at weekends.

Shops and **markets** open seven days a week and in theory keep going all day, though in practice most stallholders and many private shopkeepers will take a siesta. Shops mostly stay open late into the evenings, perhaps until 8pm or beyond in the big cities.

Museums tend to close one day a week, generally on Mondays, and their core opening hours are 8–11am and 2–4pm. **Temples** and **pagodas** occasionally close for lunch but are otherwise open all week and don't close until late evening.

Telephones

Rates for **international calls** are very reasonable, with international direct dialling (IDD) costing around 3,500đ per minute (depending where you are calling). Using the prefix 171 routes calls through the internet and reduces rates by a further 10–20 percent. The 171 service can be used from any phone, except for operator-assisted calls, mobile phones, cardphones or faxes: post offices will charge a small fee for using it.

Nearly all post offices have IDD (international direct dialling) facilities, and most hotels offer IDD from your room, but you'll usually be charged at least ten percent above the norm and a minimum charge of one minute even if the call goes unanswered.

If you're running short of funds, you can almost always get a **"call-back"** at post offices. Ask to make a minimum (1min) call abroad and remember to get the phone number of the booth you're calling from. You can then be called back directly, at a total cost to you of a one-minute international call plus a small charge for the service. It's also possible to make **collect calls** to certain countries; ask at the post office or call the international operator on ℡110.

Local calls are easy to make and are often free, though you may be charged a small fee of a few thousand dong for the service. As in many countries, public phones are turning into battered monuments to outdated technology as mobile phones become ubiquitous (over 30 million users in Vietnam and numbers rising daily). However, transport centres like airports and bus stations still maintain a few functioning machines, which accept only pre-paid phone cards, not coins. All post offices also operate a public phone service, where the cost is displayed as you speak and you pay the cashier afterwards.

In late 2008, all phone numbers in Vietnam acquired an extra digit after the area code and before the actual number, so phone numbers in Hanoi and Ho Chi Minh City now have eleven digits and other towns have ten

Dialling codes

All phone numbers in Vietnam consist of 10 or 11 digits, with the first 2–4 digits representing the area code and the remaining digits the specific number. The complete number must be dialled whether you are phoning locally or long-distance.

To **call Vietnam from abroad**, dial your international access code, then ℡84 + number minus the first 0.

To **call abroad from Vietnam**, dial either ℡171 00 or just ℡00 followed by the country code (see below) + area code minus first 0 + number.

Australia ℡61
Canada ℡1
Ireland ℡353
New Zealand ℡64
UK ℡44
US ℡1

digits. For subscribers to Vietnam Post and Telecommunications (VNPT), which is over 95 percent of the country, the extra digit is 3, though subscribers to smaller service providers have added a 2, 4, 5 or 6. We have included the new digits in this Guide, though you may still see some old numbers in Vietnam itself.

Mobile phones

If you want to use your own **mobile phone** in Vietnam, the simplest – and cheapest – thing to do is to buy a SIM card and a prepaid phone card locally. Both the big phone companies, Vinaphone (Ⓦwww .vinaphone.com.vn) and Mobiphone (Ⓦwww .mobiphone.com.vn), offer English-language support and similar prices, though Vinaphone perhaps has the edge for geographical coverage (which extends pretty much nationwide). At the time of writing, Vinaphone starter kits including a SIM card cost 120,000đ (with 100,000đ worth of calls credited to your account). Further prepaid cards are available in various sizes from 100,000đ to 500,000đ. Phone calls cost slightly more than from a land line, while sending an SMS message costs 350–400đ in Vietnam and about 2,500đ internationally.

However, rates are falling rapidly as more competitors enter the increasingly deregulated market.

The other, far more expensive, option is to stick with your home service-provider – though you'll need to check beforehand whether they offer international roaming services.

Time

Vietnam is seven hours ahead of London, twelve hours ahead of New York, fifteen hours ahead of Los Angeles, one hour behind Perth and three hours behind Sydney – give or take an hour or two when summer time is in operation.

Tourist information

Tourist information on Vietnam is at a premium. The Vietnamese government maintains a handful of **tourist promotion offices** and a smattering of accredited travel agencies around the globe, most of which can supply you with only the most general information. A better source of information, much of it based on firsthand experiences, is the internet, with numerous **websites** around to help you plan your visit. Some of the more useful and interesting sites are ⓦwww.travelfish.org, a regularly-updated online guide to Southeast Asia; ⓦwww.worldtravelguide.net, a viewer-friendly source of information on Vietnam and other countries; ⓦwww.activetravelvietnam.com, with helpful information about national parks and beaches; and ⓦwww.thingsasian.com, which consists mostly of features on Asian destinations and culture.

In Vietnam itself there's a frustrating dearth of free and impartial advice. The **state-run tourist offices** – under the auspices of either the Vietnam National Administration of Tourism (ⓦwww.vietnamtourism.com) or the local provincial organization – are thinly disguised tour agents, profit-making concerns which don't take kindly to being treated as information bureaux, though the official website has a lot of useful information about destinations and practicalities such as visas. In any case, Western concepts of information don't necessarily apply here – bus timetables, for example, simply don't exist. The most you're likely to get is a glossy brochure detailing their tours and affiliated hotels.

You'll generally have more luck approaching one of the many **private tour agencies** operating in all the major tourist spots (see "Listings" for individual cities in the Guide), where staff have become accustomed to Westerners' demands for advice.

Another useful source of information, including restaurant and hotel listings as well as feature articles, is the growing number of **English-language magazines**, such as *Vietnam Discovery*, *Time Out*, *The Guide* and *Vietnam Pathfinder* (see p.352). There's also a government-run **telephone information service** (☎1080; 300đ per minute) with some English-speaking staff who will answer all manner of questions – if you can get through, since the lines are often busy.

Travellers with special needs

Despite the fact that Vietnam is home to so many war-wounded, few provisions are made for the disabled. This means you'll have to be pretty self-reliant. It's important to contact airlines, hotels and tour companies as far in advance as possible to make sure they can accommodate your requirements.

Getting about can be made a little easier by taking internal flights, or by renting a private car or minibus with a driver. Taxis are widely available in Hanoi, Ho Chi Minh City and other major cities. Even so, trying to cross roads with speeding traffic and negotiating the cluttered and uneven pavements – where pavements exist – pose real problems. Furthermore, few buildings are equipped with ramps and lifts.

When it comes to **accommodation**, Vietnam's new luxury hotels usually offer one or two specially adapted rooms. Elsewhere, the best you can hope for is a ground-floor room, or a hotel with a lift.

One, albeit expensive, option is to ask a tour agent to arrange a **customized tour**. Saigontourist (ⓦwww.saigontourist.com) has experience of running tours specifically for disabled visitors. For general **information**, post a question on the Vietnamese-run Disability Forum ⓦhttp://forum.wso.net.

Travelling with children

Travelling through Vietnam with children can be challenging and fun. The Vietnamese adore kids and make a huge fuss of them, with fair-haired kids coming in for even more manhandling. The main concern will probably be **hygiene**: Vietnam can be distinctly unsanitary, and children's stomachs tend to be more sensitive to bacteria. Avoiding spicy foods will help while their stomachs adjust, but if children do become sick it's crucial to keep up their fluid intake, so as to avoid dehydration. Bear in mind, too, that **healthcare facilities** are fairly basic outside Hanoi and Ho Chi Minh City, so make sure your travel insurance includes full medical evacuation.

Long bus journeys are tough on young children, so wherever possible, take the train – at least the kids can get up and move about in safety. There are reduced fares for children on domestic flights, trains and open-tour buses. On trains, for example, it's free for under-fives (as long as they sit on your lap) and half-price for children aged five to ten. Open-tour buses follow roughly the same policy, though children paying a reduced fare are not entitled to a seat; if you don't want them on your lap you'll have to pay full fare. Tours are usually either free or half-price for children.

Many budget **hotels** have rooms with three or even four single beds in them. At more expensive hotels under-twelves can normally stay free of charge in their parents' rooms and baby cots are becoming more widely available.

Working and studying in Vietnam

Without a prearranged job and work permit, don't bank on finding work in Vietnam. With specific skills to offer, you could try approaching some of the Western companies now operating in Hanoi and Ho Chi Minh City.

Otherwise, **English-language teaching** is probably the easiest job to land, especially if you have a TEFL (Teaching English as a Foreign Language), TESOL (Teacher of English to Speakers of Other Languages) or

CELTA (Certificate in English Language Teaching to Adults) qualification. Universities are worth approaching, though pay is better at private schools, where qualified teachers earn upwards of $15–20 an hour. In either case, you'll need to apply for a work permit, sponsored by your employer, and then a working visa. Private tutoring is an unwieldy way of earning a crust, as you'll have to pop out of the country every few months to procure a new visa. Furthermore, the authorities are clamping down on people working without the proper authorizations.

The main English-language teaching operations recruiting in Vietnam include the British Council (ⓦwww.britishcouncil.org /Vietnam.htm), ILA Vietnam (ⓦwww .ilavietnam.com), Language Link Vietnam (ⓦwww.languagelink.edu.vn) and RMIT International University (ⓦwww.rmit.edu.vn). The TEFL website (ⓦwww.tefl.com) and Dave's ESL Café (ⓦwww.eslcafe.com) also have lists of English-teaching vacancies in addition to lots of other useful information.

There are also opportunities for **volunteer work.** Try contacting the organizations listed below, or look on the websites of the NGO Resource Centre Vietnam (ⓦwww .ngocentre.org.vn) and Volunteer Abroad (ⓦwww.volunteerabroad.com).

Study, work and volunteer programmes

Australian Volunteers International Australia ☏03/9279 1788, ⓦwww.australianvolunteers .com. Postings for up to two years, focusing on rural development, vocational education and capacity building.
British Council UK ☏0161/957 7755, ⓦwww .britishcouncil.org. TEFL vacancies are posted at ⓦwww.britishcouncil.org/teacherrecruitment, or call ☏020/7389 4931. Information on teacher exchange and development programmes abroad can be found at ⓦwww.britishcouncil.org/learning-ie-teaching-exchange.htm.
Brockport Vietnam Project US ☏1-800/ 298-7869, ⓦwww.brockportabroad.com. Opportunities for American undergraduates and graduates to study in Da Nang, and to participate in community service activities.
Council on International Educational Exchange (CIEE) US ☏1-800/40-STUDY, ⓦwww .ciee.org. The non-profit parent organization of Council Travel, CIEE runs semester and academic-year programmes in Vietnam.

Earthwatch Institute UK ☎01865/318 838,
US & Canada ☎1-800/776-0188, Australia
☎03/9682 6828; ⊛www.earthwatch.org. Long-
established international charity with environmental
and archeological research projects worldwide,
including Vietnam. Participation mainly as a paying
volunteer but fellowships for teachers and students
are available.

Global Volunteer Network UK ☎0800/032 5035,
US ☎1-800/963-1198, Australia ☎1800/203 012,
New Zealand ☎04/569 9080; ⊛www.volunteer
.org.nz. Non-governmental organization that supports
the work of local communities through the placement
of international volunteers.

Voluntary Service Overseas (VSO) UK
☎020/8780 7500, ⊛www.vso.org.uk. A British
government-funded organization that places
volunteers on various projects around the world.

Volunteers for Peace US ☎802/259-2759,
⊛www.vfp.org. Non-profit organization with links to
a huge international network of "workcamps", two- to
four-week programmes that bring volunteers together
from many countries to carry out needed community
projects. Most workcamps are in summer, with
registration by April/May.

Guide

Guide

1

Ho Chi Minh City and around

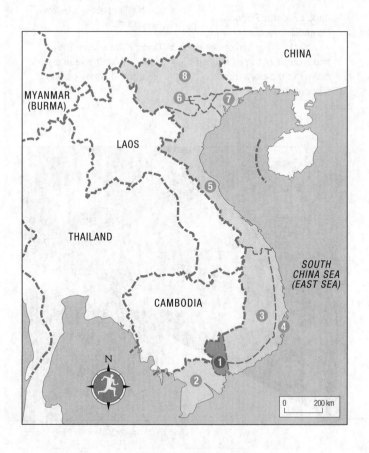

CHAPTER 1 # Highlights

✳ **War Remnants Museum**
The city's most moving
museum, a stark reminder
of man's inhumanity to man.
See p.97

✳ **Ben Thanh Market** Check
the city's pulse here on an
early-morning stroll. See p.98

✳ **Jade Emperor Pagoda**
Beautiful carved woodwork,
an eclectic collection of deities
and a constant fog of incense
make this the city's most
fascinating temple. See p.101

✳ **Saigon's restaurants**
Several stylish locations
offer the ideal ambience in
which to savour the
delights of Vietnamese
cuisine. See p.107

✳ **Bars with great views** Sip a
sundowner while gazing over
the bustling activity below.
See p.115

✳ **Dong Khoi shops** The
boutiques in this area are
great for silks and paintings.
See p.118

▲ US plane at the War Remnants Museum

Ho Chi Minh City
and around

Ho Chi Minh City (HCMC for short), still known as Saigon to its seven million or so inhabitants, is Vietnam's centre of commerce and the country's biggest city by far, though not its administrative capital – an honour that rests with Hanoi. As a result of the sweeping economic changes wrought by *doi moi* in 1986, this effervescent city, perched on the west bank of the Saigon River, has changed its image from that of a war-torn city to one of a thriving metropolis, challenging Singapore, Bangkok and the other traditional Southeast Asian powerhouses.

All the accoutrements of economic success – fine restaurants, flash hotels, glitzy bars and clubs, and shops selling imported luxury goods – are here, adding a glossy veneer to the city's hotch-potch landscape of French stones of empire, venerable pagodas and austere, Soviet-style housing blocks. Sadly, however, Ho Chi Minh City is still full of people for whom economic progress has not yet translated into food, housing and jobs. Street children range through tourist enclaves hawking books, postcards, lottery tickets and cigarette lighters; limbless mendicants haul themselves about on crude trolleys; and watchful pickpockets prowl crowded streets on the lookout for unguarded wallets. Though the number of beggars is gradually declining, tourists must quickly come to accept them as a hassle that goes with the territory. In addition, the arrival, en masse, of wealthy Westerners has lured many women into prostitution, for which the go-go bars of Dong Khoi became famous during the American War.

If Hanoi is a city of romance and mellow charms, then Ho Chi Minh City is its antithesis, a fury of sights and sounds, and the crucible in which Vietnam's rallying fortunes are boiling. Few corners of the city afford respite from the cacophony of **construction work** casting up new office blocks and hotels with logic-defying speed. An increasing number of cars and minibuses jostle with an organic mass of state-of-the-art SUVs, Hondas and cyclo, choking the tree-lined streets and boulevards. Amid this melee, the local people go about their daily life: smartly-dressed schoolkids wander past streetside baguette-sellers; women shoppers ride Hondas clad in gangster-style bandanas and shoulder-length gloves to protect their skin from the sun and dust; while teenagers in designer jeans chirrup into mobile phones. Much of the fun of being in Ho Chi Minh City derives from the simple pleasure of absorbing its flurry of activity – something best done from the seat of a cyclo or a roadside café. To blink is to miss some new and singular sight, be it a

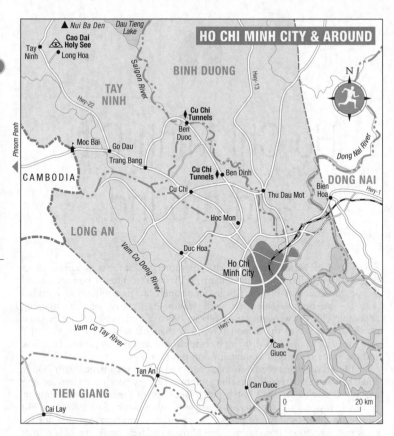

motorbike stacked high with piglets bound for the market, or a boy on a bicycle rapping out a staccato tattoo on pieces of bamboo to advertise noodles for sale.

It's one of Ho Chi Minh City's many charms that once you've exhausted, or been exhausted by, all it has to offer, paddy fields, beaches and wide-open countryside are not far away. The most popular trip **out of the city** is to the **Cu Chi tunnels**, where villagers dug themselves out of the range of American shelling. The tunnels are often twinned with a tour around the fanciful Great Temple of the indigenous Cao Dai religion at **Tay Ninh**. A brief taster of the Mekong Delta at **My Tho** or a dip in the South China Sea at **Ho Coc** are also eminently possible in a long day's excursion (see p.134 & p.229 respectively).

The **best time to visit** tropical Ho Chi Minh City is in the dry season, which runs from December through to April. During the wet season, May to November, there are frequent tropical storms, though these won't disrupt your travels too much. Average temperatures, year-round, hover between 26 and 29°C; March, April and May are the hottest months.

Some history

Knowledge of Ho Chi Minh City's early history is sketchy, at best. Between the first and sixth centuries, the territory on which it lies fell under the nominal rule of the **Funan Empire** to the west. Funan was subsequently absorbed by the Kambuja peoples of the pre-Angkor **Chen La Empire**, but it is unlikely that these imperial machinations had much bearing upon the sleepy fishing backwater that would later develop into Ho Chi Minh City.

Khmer fishermen eked out a living here, building their huts on the stable ground just north of the delta wetlands, which made it ideal for human settlement. Originally named **Prei Nokor**, it flourished as an entrepôt for Cambodian boats pushing down the Mekong River, and by the seventeenth century it boasted a garrison and a mercantile community that embraced Malay, Indian and Chinese traders.

Such a dynamic settlement was bound to draw attention from the north. By the eighteenth century, the **Viets** had subdued the kingdom of Champa, and this area was swallowed up by Hué's **Nguyen Dynasty**. With new ownership came a new name, **Saigon**, thought to be derived from the Vietnamese word for the kapok tree. Upon the outbreak of the **Tay Son Rebellion**, in 1772, Nguyen Anh bricked the whole settlement into a walled fortress, the eight-sided **Gia Dinh Citadel**. The army that put down the Tay Son brothers included an assisting **French** military force, who grappled for several decades to undermine Vietnamese control in the region and develop a trading post in Asia. Finally, in 1861, they seized Saigon, using Emperor Tu Duc's persecution of French missionaries as a pretext. The 1862 **Treaty of Saigon** declared the city the capital of French Cochinchina.

Ho Chi Minh City owes much of its form and character to the French colonists: channels were filled in, marshlands drained and steam tramways set to work along its regimental grid of tamarind-shaded boulevards, which by the 1930s sported names like Boulevard de la Somme and Rue Rousseau. Flashy examples of European architecture were erected, cafés and boutiques sprang up to cater for its new, Vermouth-sipping, baguette-munching citizens, and the city was imbued with such an all-round Gallic air that Somerset Maugham, visiting in the 1930s, found it reminiscent of "a little provincial town in the south of France… a blithe and smiling little place". The French *colons* (colonials) bankrolled improvements to Saigon with the vast profits they were able to cream from exporting Vietnam's **rubber** and **rice** out of the city's rapidly expanding seaport.

On a human level, however, French rule was invariably harsh; dissent crystallized in the form of strikes through the 1920s and 1930s, but the nationalist movement hadn't gathered any real head of steam before **World War II**'s tendrils spread to Southeast Asia. At its close, the **Potsdam Conference** of 1945 set the British Army the task of disarming Japanese troops in southern Vietnam. Arriving in Saigon two months later, they promptly returned power to the French, and so began thirty years of war. Saigon saw little action during the anti-French war, which was fought mostly in the countryside and resulted in the French capitulation at Dien Bien Phu in 1954.

Designated the capital of the **Republic of South Vietnam** by President Diem in 1955, Saigon was soon both the nerve centre of the American war effort, and its R&R capital, with a slough of sleazy bars along Dong Khoi (known then as Tu Do) catering to GIs on leave from duty. Despite the Communist bomb attacks and demonstrations by students and monks that periodically disturbed the peace, these were good times for Saigon, whose entrepreneurs prospered on the back of the tens of thousands of Americans posted here. The gravy train ran out of steam with the withdrawal of American troops in 1973, and two years later the **Ho Chi Minh Campaign** rolled into the city and through the gates of the presidential palace and the

Communists were in control. Within a year, Saigon had been renamed **Ho Chi Minh City**.

The **war years** extracted a heavy toll: American carpet-bombing of the Vietnamese countryside forced millions of refugees into the relative safety of the city, and ill-advised, post-reunification policies triggered a social and economic stagnation whose ramifications are still evident. To make matters worse, persecution of southerners with links to the Americans saw

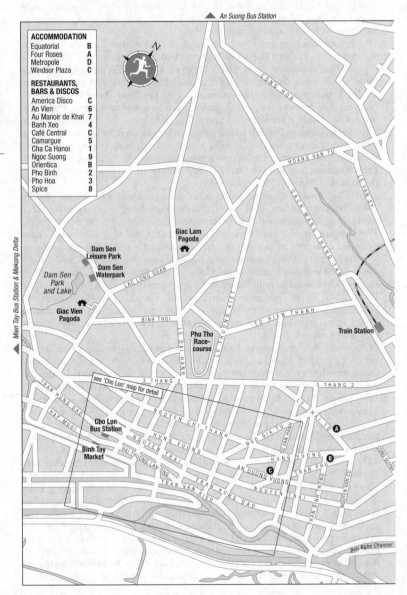

▲ An Suong Bus Station

ACCOMMODATION

Equatorial	**B**
Four Roses	**A**
Metropole	**D**
Windsor Plaza	**C**

RESTAURANTS, BARS & DISCOS

America Disco	**C**
An Vien	**6**
Au Manoir de Khai	**7**
Banh Xeo	**4**
Café Central	**C**
Camargue	**5**
Cha Ca Hanoi	**1**
Ngoc Suong	**9**
Orientica	**B**
Pho Binh	**2**
Pho Hoa	**3**
Spice	**8**

N

Giac Lam Pagoda

Dam Sen Leisure Park

Dam Sen Waterpark

Dam Sen Park and Lake

Giac Vien Pagoda

CONG HOA

HOANG VAN TU

LE VAN SY

CACH MANG THANG TAM

LAC LONG QUAN

BINH THOI

LE DAI HANH

LY THUONG KIET

TO HIEN THANH

Phu Tho Race-course

Train Station

◀ Mien Tay Bus Station & Mekong Delta

3 THANG 2

3 THANG 2

see 'Cho Lon' map for detail

TRAN HUNG DAO

HAP MUOI

Cho Lon Bus Station

Binh Tay Market

NGUYEN CHI THANH

HUNG VUONG

NGUYEN TRAI

HAI THUONG LAN ONG

NGO GIA TU

SU VAN HANH

LY THAI TO

AN DUONG VUONG

HUNG VUONG

TRAN PHU

NGUYEN TRAI

TRAN BINH TRONG

NGUYEN VAN CU

CONG QUYNH

TRAN VAN KIEU

TRAN HUNG DAO

Ben Nghe Channel

Ⓐ Ⓑ Ⓒ

many thousands sent to re-education camps, and millions more flee the country by boat.

Only in 1986, when the **economic liberalization** of *doi moi* was established, and a market economy reintroduced, did the fortunes of the city show signs of taking an upturn. Today, more than two decades later, the city's resurgence is well advanced, and its inhabitants are eyeing the future with unprecedented optimism.

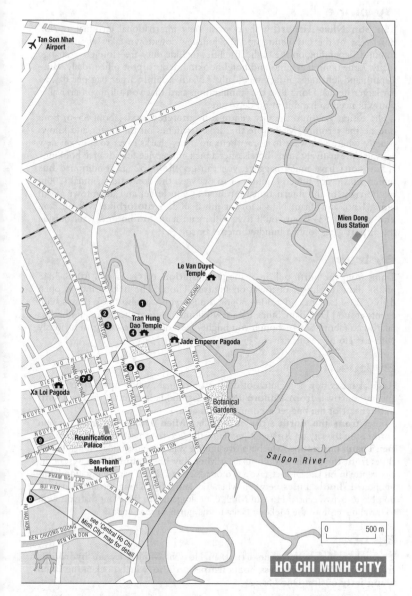

HO CHI MINH CITY

Arrival

The lion's share of new **arrivals** to Vietnam fly into Ho Chi Minh City's Tan Son Nhat Airport, which is also the terminus for all internal flights. Arriving overland, you'll end up either at the train station, a short distance north of the downtown area, or at one of a handful of bus terminals scattered across the city.

By plane

Tan Son Nhat Airport, with its swish new international terminal, is 7km northwest of the city centre and the journey downtown takes about 30–45 minutes, depending on the traffic. Facilities include duty-free; foreign exchange (daily 7am–1am); taxi, limo and hotel booking desks; a post office (daily 9am–10pm); and left-luggage facilities (daily 7.30am–10pm; $3 per bag per day, $4 for larger items). Don't lose the immigration card that you fill in on arrival as you will need to hand it in on departure.

The easiest way into the city centre is by **metered taxi** (about $5–6) from outside the terminal. Make sure the driver switches on the meter and knows exactly where you want to go, as there are many sharks eager to prey on new arrivals. Alternatively, many hotels offer a pick-up service for advance bookings. If you don't have much baggage, you can get the #152 air-conditioned **bus** which runs every fifteen minutes or so between the domestic terminal (200m to the right of the international terminal as you leave) and downtown (both Dong Khoi and Pham Ngu Lao) for just 3000đ. A **motorbike** will run you into town for $3–4, but you'll have to bargain hard: to find one, walk outside the airport gates (only a hundred metres or so).

By train

Trains from the north pull in at the **train station**, or Ga Saigon (☎08/3843 6528), 3km northwest of town, on Nguyen Thong. The ticket office is open daily 7.30–11.30am and 1.30–4.30pm, though you can also book tickets with agents around De Tham. Since it's a few kilometres from the centre, it's best to take a taxi (about $3–4), though you might save a dollar if you bargain furiously with a cyclo or xe om driver.

By bus

Regular buses stop at a clutch of different terminals, while **open-tour buses** and most arrivals **from Phnom Penh** in Cambodia terminate on **De Tham** in the heart of the budget accommodation area.

Buses **from the north** arrive at sprawling **Mien Dong bus station**, 5km northeast of the city on Xo Viet Nghe Tinh; the #26 bus shuttles between here and **Ben Thanh bus station**, which is a five-minute walk from the budget hotel district. Buses **from the southwest** terminate at **Mien Tay bus station**, 10km west of the city centre in An Lac District; take a taxi or a #2 bus to Ben Thanh bus station. Well-signposted **shuttle buses** between Mien Tay and Mien Dong terminals make it possible to bypass central Ho Chi Minh City altogether in the event that you want to travel direct from the Mekong Delta to the north, or vice versa.

By boat

The only regular waterborne arrivals in Ho Chi Minh City are **hydrofoils from Vung Tau** and **express boats from Can Tho**, which dock at the **Bach Dang jetty** on Ton Duc Thang.

Information

For practical information with no strings attached, enquire at your **guesthouse** or **hotel**, or at one of the **tour agents** along Pham Ngu Lao and De Tham. These should also be able to provide you with a basic **map** of the city centre, while a more detailed map is available from bookshops and street hawkers.

For information about **what's on** in Ho Chi Minh City, you'll find in many hotels and restaurants the free magazines, *The Word* or *Asia Life*, which are aimed at expats. Another useful source of info is *The Guide*, which covers the whole country and is sold in bookstores for 30,000đ. All are published monthly.

City transport

Faint-hearted visitors to Ho Chi Minh City will blanch upon first encountering the chaos that passes for its **traffic system**. Thousands of motorcycles, bicycles and cyclo fill the city's streets and boulevards in an insectile swarm that is now supplemented by a burgeoning number of cars and minibuses, most with their horns constantly blaring.

Despite the city's massive sprawl, most of its attractions are conveniently clustered so that it is quite feasible to explore many of them **on foot**. But first you have to learn to cross the streets where the traffic never stops. There's an art to crossing the street in Vietnam: besides nerves of steel, a steady pace is required – motorbike riders are used to dodging pedestrians, but you'll confuse them if you stop in your tracks.

To get from A to B when you don't fancy walking, the **xe om** is the most prevalent and practical mode of transport, though **taxis** are also inexpensive and worth considering if only to avoid interminable haggling over fares. **Cyclo** routes are sadly limited, being prohibited from several central streets, though for many visitors a leisurely ride around some of the city's main sights adds a uniquely Vietnamese touch to the experience.

Cyclo

Cyclo are a dying breed in Ho Chi Minh City, since the local government plans to phase them out. Already they are forbidden to enter many key streets in the city centre, so if your rider seems to be taking a circuitous route, he is probably not doing so to bump up the fare. Despite these difficulties, a ride in a cyclo is usually a memorable experience, if only for the close encounter with the city's crazy traffic; about $3 an hour is the normal rate, though initially they will ask more than double this. Though it's feasible to ride two (very small) passengers to a cyclo, the corresponding rise in cost and lessening of comfort make this a false economy.

Taxis and xe om

Taxis are easy to flag down on the street, though it's just as easy to call for a pick-up wherever you are (see "Listings" on p.122 for numbers). The flag fare of 12,000đ goes up after dark but you can still traverse a decent chunk of the city for 30,000đ, so they are well worth considering, especially given the horrifying pollution levels of the city's streets.

Tour agents

There are hundreds of tour agents in Ho Chi Minh City, but many of them are fly-by-night set-ups, and we receive numerous reports of inefficient and unscrupulous companies, so it's worth choosing your agent carefully. Those listed below have good reputations for consistent, reliable services.

Ann Tours 58 Ton That Tung ⊤08/3833 2564, ⓦwww.anntours.com. Highly recommended, it offers good-value, tailor-made tours.

Atlas Tours 267 Ben Chuong Duong ⊤08/3838 5033, ⓕ08/3920 0261. Organizes tailor-made tours for niche groups such as gourmets or divorcees.

Buffalo Tours Satra House, Suite 601, 58 Dong Khoi ⊤08/3828 0702. This Western-managed set-up specializes in customized tours throughout Indochina.

Delta Adventure Tours 267 De Tham ⊤08/3920 2112, ⓦwww.deltaadventuretours.com. Highly recommended for its boat tours to the Cu Chi tunnels, the Mekong Delta or all the way to Phnom Penh.

Exotissimo Travel Saigon Finance Centre, 9 Dinh Tien Hoang ⊤08/3825 1723, ⓦwww.exotissimo.com. Has an extensive tour programme that includes special interests, Laos and Cambodia add-ons.

Innoviet 158 Bui Ven ⊤08/3295 8840, ⓦwww.innoviet.com. This newish company runs popular bike and boat tours of the Delta as well as half-day city tours.

Kim Travel 270 De Tham ⊤&ⓕ08/3920 5552, ⓦwww.kimtravel.com. A veteran of the independent travel scene, it offers open-tour buses, flight and rail bookings, car and minibus rental and guides.

Saigontourist 49 Le Thanh Ton ⊤08/3829 8914, ⓦwww.saigontourist.net. A state-run operation that tends to guide tourists to its own hotels but offers a wide range of tour possibilities.

Sinh Café 246–248 De Tham ⊤08/3836 7338, ⓦwww.sinhcafe.com. Offers cut-price organized tours of Vietnam, open-bus tours, guides, visa services, buses and boats to Cambodia and vehicle rental.

Sinhbalo Adventure Travel 283/20 Pham Ngu Lao ⊤08/3837 6766, ⓦwww.sinhbalo.com. A super-efficient set-up that specializes in customized tours such as bicycle expeditions along the Ho Chi Minh trail (see ⓦwww.cyclingvietnam.net), motorbike tours, long-distance boat cruises and kayaking in the Mekong Delta. They also have a wealth of reliable travel info.

TNK Travel 216 De Tham ⊤08/3920 5847, ⓦwww.tnktravelvietnam.com. One of the newer tour operators, which gets good feedback from those who take its tours.

The motorbike taxi or **xe om** is a faster alternative to both taxi and cyclo. Translated, it means "motorbike embrace": passengers ride pillion on a motorbike, hanging on for dear life. Wearing helmets is compulsory for passengers as well as riders. Xe om are much more prevalent than cyclo, so you'll probably find yourself using them at some stage, but beware of riders who double up as pimps and drug dealers, of which there are many. If you find a reliable driver, take his phone number so you can call him again. Prices are about 10,000đ for a short ride, or $2 an hour.

Buses

Few visitors ever take a public bus, though it's relatively easy to hop on one to **Cho Lon** from the backpacker district. When leaving the city, **Ben Thanh bus station** is a useful point of departure, linking other long-distance bus stations in Ho Chi Minh City, as well as offering direct services to Vung Tau and other places.

Sample fares around town

Costs of local transport are quite reasonable. For example, you can expect to pay about 10,000đ for a short **cyclo** or **xe om** ride within central Ho Chi Minh City, while the standard fare for **bus services** is 3000–5000đ. Fares for cyclo and xe om are negotiable, though the list below provides a guideline. Note that cyclo drivers charge more for extra passengers or luggage, and that by "centre" we mean Dong Khoi.

Pham Ngu Lao to GPO: 15,000đ
Train station to centre: 15–20,000đ
Pham Ngu Lao to Cho Lon: 20–25,000đ
Centre to Jade Emperor Pagoda: 20,000đ
Mien Dong bus station to centre: 40,000đ

Motorbikes, bicycles and car rental

Motorbike and bicycle rental in Ho Chi Minh City is very cheap – just $5–6 and $1.50 per day respectively, though you'll need bravery far beyond that necessary to cross the street to survive in the traffic. Most hotels and guest-houses can arrange a motorbike for you, though bicycles are a bit more difficult to track down. Self-drive car rental isn't an option yet in Ho Chi Minh City, but **Budget** and many **tour operators** offer **car rental plus driver** (see opposite and "Listings" on p.119) for $50–100 per day, depending on the vehicle and driver's proficiency in English.

Accommodation

There are thousands of **hotel** rooms in Ho Chi Minh City, ranging from budget windowless cupboards to top-end sumptuous suites, yet the city is so popular that rooms can be difficult to find, especially in December and January. If you make an **advance booking**, you will save hauling your bags round the streets and may also be picked up at the airport or station, making a smooth start to your stay.

The best hotels in town are located around **Dong Khoi** in the city centre, and there are some smart mini-hotels on nearby **Mac Thi Buoi**. Ho Chi Minh City's budget enclave centres around **Pham Ngu Lao**, **De Tham** and **Bui Vien**, which lies 1km west of the city centre but is still convenient for visiting most city attractions. Besides having over a hundred accommodation options, there are also travel agencies, restaurants, bars and shops catering for travellers. By staying in this area, you'll save not only on accommodation, but on food and drinks as well, since most restaurants here are significantly cheaper than those downtown. Hotels, mini-hotels, guesthouses and rooms for rent are ten-a-penny here, ranging from dormitories costing a few dollars to luxurious rooms for around $150. If the De Tham region is too much for you, there's a smaller clutch of budget hotels in an alley a few blocks south off Co Giang. Most places that charge more than $15 a night include breakfast in the price.

Dong Khoi and around

All the following hotels and guest-houses are marked on the map on p.88.
Asian 150 Dong Khoi ☎08/3829 6979, ✉asianhotel@hcm.fpt.vn. Centrally located mid-range hotel, but compact and intimate enough not to overwhelm. All rooms have satellite TV, IDD, bathtubs and mini-bars. ⑤–⑥
Bong Sen 117–123 Dong Khoi ☎08/3829 1516, ⓦwww.hotelbongsen.com. Stylish yet personable upmarket hotel right at the heart of Dong Khoi with an in-house business centre. The *Bong Sen II*

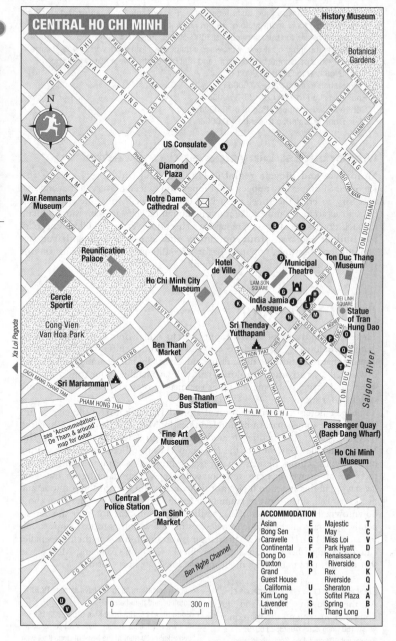

CENTRAL HO CHI MINH

History Museum

Botanical Gardens

US Consulate Ⓐ

Diamond Plaza

War Remnants Museum

Notre Dame Cathedral

Ⓑ

Ⓒ

Reunification Palace

Hotel de Ville

Ⓓ **Municipal Theatre**

Ton Duc Thang Museum

Ho Chi Minh City Museum

Ⓔ
Ⓕ

LAM SON SQUARE

Cercle Sportif

Ⓖ Ⓗ
Ⓙ Ⓛ
Ⓘ Ⓜ

MEI LINH SQUARE

Cong Vien Van Hoa Park

Ⓚ **India Jamia Mosque**

Ⓝ

Statue of Tran Hung Dao

Sri Thenday Yutthapani

Ⓟ
Ⓞ

Ben Thanh Market

Ⓢ

Sri Mariamman

Ⓡ

Ⓣ

Ben Thanh Bus Station

Saigon River

Xa Loi Pagoda

see 'Accommodation: De Tham & around' map for detail

Passenger Quay (Bach Dang Wharf)

Fine Art Museum

Ho Chi Minh Museum

Central Police Station

Dan Sinh Market

Ⓤ Ⓥ

Ben Nghe Channel

0   300 m

ACCOMMODATION			
Asian	**E**	Majestic	**T**
Bong Sen	**N**	May	**C**
Caravelle	**G**	Miss Loi	**V**
Continental	**F**	Park Hyatt	**D**
Dong Do	**M**	Renaissance	
Duxton	**R**	Riverside	**O**
Grand	**P**	Rex	**K**
Guest House		Riverside	**Q**
California	**U**	Sheraton	**J**
Kim Long	**L**	Sofitel Plaza	**A**
Lavender	**S**	Spring	**B**
Linh	**H**	Thang Long	**I**

(☎08/3823 5818), around the corner at 61 Hai Ba Trung, has newer rooms at slightly cheaper rates, but without the Dong Khoi address. **6**

Caravelle 19 Lam Son Square ☎08/3823 4999, ⓦwww.caravellehotel.com. A grandiose entrance leads to the city's most prestigious hotel, featuring luxurious rooms and suites with all conceivable comforts and dizzying views across the city. **7**

Continental 132–134 Dong Khoi ☎08/3829 9201, ⓦwww.continentalvietnam.com. The grandly carpeted staircases, marbled floors and dark-wood doors of this venerable address's halls and corridors convey a colonial splendour that doesn't quite extend to its rooms, though some do boast commanding views down Dong Khoi. **7**

Dong Do 35 Mac Thi Buoi ☎08/3827 3637, ⓔdongdohotel@hcm.vnn.vn. Nicely furnished mini-hotel with all facilities and a restaurant with a view on the sixth floor. **4–5**

Duxton 63 Nguyen Hué ☎08/3822 2999. Nearly two hundred rooms in this luxurious place with a restaurant and business centre. **7**

Grand 8 Dong Khoi ☎08/823 0163, ⓦwww.grandhotel.vn. Painstakingly restored 1930s hotel, whose spacious suites and friendly staff lend an old-world charm. Attractive furnishings and polished wooden floors add to the effect, while modern facilities include a swimming pool and jacuzzi. **6–7**

Kim Long 58 Mac Thi Buoi ☎08/3822 8558, ⓦwww.kimlonghotel.com. Another good mini-hotel right in the centre, with bathtubs in some rooms and cable TV. **4**

Lavender 208–210 Le Thanh Ton ☎08/2222 8888, ⓦwww.lavenderhotel.com.vn. This place occupies a great location for shoppers, just beside the Ben Thanh market, and features smallish but cosy, carpeted rooms with all facilities. **6–7**

Linh 16 Mac Thi Buoi ☎08/3824 3954, ⓦwww.linhhotelvn.com. The most appealing of the mini hotels on Mac Thi Buoi, this place has 22 bright, well-appointed rooms with attractive bamboo furnishings. **4–5**

Majestic 1 Dong Khoi ☎08/3829 5517, ⓦwww.majesticsaigon.com.vn. Historic 1920s riverfront hotel, still oozing character. All the rooms are charming (especially those with a river view) and the staff fall over themselves to be helpful. There's a first-floor pool and rooftop bar too. **7**

May 28–30 Thi Sach ☎08/38234501, ⓦwww.mayhotel.com.vn. With a good downtown location, this new place features a pool, spa and fitness centre. Rooms are bright with solid furnishings and ADSL connections. **6**

Park Hyatt 2 Lam Son ☎08/38241 234, ⓦwww.saigon.park.hyatt.com. Enjoying a prime spot on Lam Son Square with over 250 classically elegant rooms, three stylish restaurants, a pool and spa, the *Park Hyatt* rivals the *Caravelle*, which it eyes over the Municipal Theatre, for the title of top spot in town. **7**

Renaissance Riverside 8–15 Ton Duc Thang ☎08/3822 0033, ⓦwww.renaissance-saigon.com. This smart hotel in a modern building down by the river offers a challenge to other top-line hotels in the vicinity with its immaculate rooms and personalized, friendly service. **7**

Rex 141 Nguyen Hué ☎08/3829 2185, ⓦwww.rexhotelvietnam.com. A recent make-over has re-established the *Rex* as one of the most appealing options on the Ho Chi Minh City hotel scene, with plush, comfortable rooms, and an excellent central location. A sundowner on the fifth-floor terrace is one of the city's treats. **7**

Riverside 18–20 Ton Duc Thang ☎08/3822 4038, ⓦwww.riversidehotelsg.com. This modernized grand colonial pile proudly eyes the river from the base of Dong Khoi, and offers much cheaper rooms than its famous neighbours like the *Majestic* and *Grand*. Rooms are spacious and cosy, making them good value. **4–6**

Sheraton 88 Dong Khoi ☎08/3827 2828, ⓦwww.sheraton.com/saigon. Monolith on Dong Khoi, ideally located for shopping and sights. Sumptuous rooms, but sky-high prices. **7**

Sofitel Plaza 17 Le Duan ☎08/3824 1555, ⓦwww.accorhotels.com/asia. One of the jewels in Ho Chi Minh City's crown, firmly established as a favourite with business travellers. The hi-tech, open-plan lobby is a masterpiece and the rooftop pool is simply stunning. The rooms and facilities boast luxurious elegance with the most modern trimmings. **7**

Spring 44–46 Le Thanh Ton ☎08/3829 7362, ⓦwww.springhotelvietnam.com. An excellent mid-range hotel with top-quality services, conveniently located just north of the centre. All the rooms are carpeted with cable TV and bathtubs. **4–5**

Thang Long 48 Mac Thi Buoi ☎08/3822 2595, ⓔthanglonghotel@hcm.fpt.vn. With similar facilities as *Dong Do* and *Kim Long*, this offers a reasonably priced base in the centre. **3**

De Tham and around

All the following hotels and guesthouses are marked on the map on p.90, except *Guest House California* and *Miss Loi* on p.88.

An An 40 Bui Vien ☎08/3837 8087, ⓦwww.ananhotel.com. This welcoming mini-hotel has 22 bright and airy rooms, all with

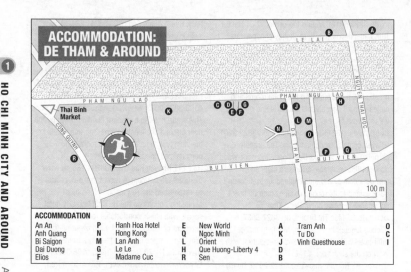

**ACCOMMODATION:
DE THAM & AROUND**

Thai Binh Market

PHAM NGU LAO

PHAM NGU LAO

LE LAI

BUI VIEN

BUI VIEN

0   100 m

ACCOMMODATION

An An	**P**	Hanh Hoa Hotel	**E**	New World	**A**	Tram Anh	**O**
Anh Quang	**N**	Hong Kong	**Q**	Ngoc Minh	**K**	Tu Do	**C**
Bi Saigon	**M**	Lan Anh	**L**	Orient	**J**	Vinh Guesthouse	**I**
Dai Duong	**G**	Le Le	**H**	Que Huong-Liberty 4	**D**		
Elios	**F**	Madame Cuc	**R**	Sen	**B**		

a/c, bathtubs and internet connections. There's a second branch with slightly smaller and cheaper rooms at 216 De Tham. ❹

Anh Quang 217/12 De Tham ☎08/3836 9906. One of several private homes offering bargain lodgings down the Dickensian alleyway between 217 and 219 De Tham. ❶

Bi Saigon 185/16 & 185/26 Pham Ngu Lao ☎08/3836 0678, ⓦwww.bisaigon.com. Gloomy corridors, but clean and comfortable, if rather chintzy, rooms with hot water and cable TV, as well as four expensive suites with balconies. Both locations have more than adequate restaurants. ❸–❹

Dai Duong 217 Pham Ngu Lao ☎08/3836 8231. Also known as *Ocean Hotel*, this mini-hotel has nineteen smallish rooms, all with hot water and a choice of a/c or fan, plus a lift to all six floors. A good-value budget option. ❷

Elios 231–235 Pham Ngu Lao ☎08/3838 5584, ⓦwww.elioshotel.vn. This swish place, with ninety cosy, compact rooms, could be the shape of things to come for the budget district. Efficient, helpful staff, a rooftop restaurant and wi-fi in all rooms. ❺–❻

Guest House California 171A Co Bac ☎08/3837 8885, ⓔguesthousecaliforniasaigon @yahoo.com. Away from the backpacker scene of De Tham, this friendly place has some good-sized rooms and some smaller ones, some with fan and others with a/c. ❷

Hanh Hoa Hotel 237 Pham Ngu Lao ☎08/3836 0245. This smart place has some spacious rooms with flat-screen TVs and bamboo furnishings at a very reasonable price. ❸–❹

Hong Kong 22 Bui Vien ☎08/3836 4904, ⓕ08/3836 8757. Long-running and popular mini-hotel, offering a selection of clean, comfortable rooms with a/c; the friendly staff will also help with tour bookings. ❷

Lan Anh 252 De Tham ☎08/3836 5197, ⓔlan-anh-hotel@hcm.vnn.vn. In a prime location, this friendly, family-run mini-hotel in the heart of De Tham has 23 bright, clean rooms with a/c. Ask for a room at the back to escape the street noise. ❷–❸

Le Le 171 Pham Ngu Lao ☎08/3836 8686, ⓔlelehotel@hcm.fpt.vn. Ageing but popular mini-hotel. Rooms all have hot water, cable TV and IDD, and breakfast is included. ❷

Madam Cuc 127 Cong Quynh ☎08/3836 8761, ⓦwww.madamcuchotels.com. The genial Madam Cuc pays more attention to detail than most, resulting in a range of wholesome rooms, some sleeping up to four. Staff are informative and helpful and there's free breakfast, fruit, tea and coffee. They will also collect from the airport. If this place is full, they have two more branches at 184 Cong Quynh and 64 Bui Vien. ❷–❸

Miss Loi 178/20 Co Giang ☎08/3837 9589, ⓔmissloi@hcm.fpt.vn. Located out of sight of the De Tham activity, this spotlessly clean and cosy guesthouse has a range of rooms in a quiet backstreet community. ❷

New World 76 Le Lai ☎08/3822 8888, ⓦwww .newworldvietnam.com. A benchmark on the Ho Chi Minh City hotel scene since its opening in 1993 – over five hundred luxurious rooms complemented by impressive sports and leisure facilities and a business centre. **⑦**

Ngoc Minh 283/11-13 Pham Ngu Lao ☎08/3837 6407, ✉ngocminh.hcm@gmail.com. Located in a narrow alley and tucked away from the honking horns on Pham Ngu Lao, this place has a range of competitively-priced rooms, all with a/c, cable TV and wi-fi. **②**

Orient 274-276 De Tham ☎08/3920 3993, ⓦwww.orienthotel.vn. Decent mini-hotel with small but comfy rooms and friendly, helpful staff, right in the heart of the budget district. **②**

Que Huong–Liberty 4 265 Pham Ngu Lao ☎08/3836 4556, ⓦwww.libertyhotels.com.vn. Run by the reliable Liberty group, this place offers stylish, well-equipped rooms in the budget district, with a decent buffet breakfast served in its ninth-floor restaurant. **⑥–⑦**

Sen 82 Le Lai ☎08/3925 3873, ✉senhotel82 @yahoo.com. This recently-renovated place has bright, spacious rooms equipped with a/c, cable TV and wi-fi. **③–④**

Tram Anh 185/24 Pham Ngu Lao ☎08/3837 1004, ✉ tramanhhotel@yahoo.com. Located in a narrow alley away from traffic noise, this place has twenty decent-sized rooms, all with a/c and cable TV, plus there's free internet access. **②**

Tu Do 267–269 Pham Ngu Lao ☎08/3836 7345, ⓕ08/3836 8171. This mini-hotel with thirty rooms is an attractive mid-range choice; all rooms have a/c and cable TV; some rooms have bathtubs. **②**

Vinh Guesthouse 269 De Tham ☎08/3836 8585, ⓕ08/3920 8127. Located at the heart of the action on De Tham, this tiny place has just a few fan and a/c rooms, plus a $4 dorm at the top of a seemingly endless staircase. **①**

West of De Tham

All the following hotels and guesthouses are marked on the map on pp.82–83.

Equatorial 242 Tran Binh Trong ☎08/3839 7777, ⓦwww.equatorial.com. This palatial hotel offers very comfortable rooms with the full gamut of facilities. It has a pool on the 4th floor as well as a gym, sauna and beauty salon, plus an excellent restaurant (*Orientica*, see p.112). **⑦**

Four Roses 790/5 Nguyen Dinh Chieu ☎08/3832 5895, ✉roseminne@hcm.vnn.vn. Located in no-man's-land between Cho Lon and the city centre, the *Four Roses* is hard to find. Set in a tranquil garden bordered by bougainvillea, it has just six immaculately clean, pleasantly furnished rooms all with balconies. Family-run with a distinctly French flavour, it offers the perfect antidote to hectic Ho Chi Minh City; there's a beauty salon in the basement (the owner is a beautician) and meals can also be rustled up on request. **②–③**

Metropole 148 Tran Hung Dao ☎08/6295 8944, ⓦwww.metropolesaigon.com. This is a sedate and friendly 74-room hotel, worth considering for its business facilities, modest pool and well-turned-out rooms with 24hr room service. **⑥–⑦**

Windsor Plaza 18 An Duong Vuong ☎08/3833 6688, ⓦwww.windsorplazahotel.com. It may be a short distance from the city centre in district 5, but the *Windsor* has a lot going for it. The rooms are luxurious and most have fantastic views, and there are good shopping, entertainment and dining options in the same building (see *Cafe Central*, p.112). **⑦**

The City

Ho Chi Minh City – or Thanh Pho Ho Chi Minh, to give it its full Vietnamese title – is divided into 24 districts, though tourists rarely travel beyond districts One, Three and Five. In addition, an increasing number of expats reside in **Phu My Hung**, aka South Saigon, in district Seven – a squeaky-clean suburb that wouldn't look out of place in Singapore, making quite a contrast to the rest of this seething metropolis. The city proper hugs the west bank of the **Saigon River**, and its central area, District One, nestles in the hinge formed by the confluence of the river with the silty ooze of the **Ben Nghe Channel**; traditionally the French Quarter of the city, this area is still widely known as Saigon. **Dong Khoi** is its delicate backbone, and around the T-shape it forms with **Le Duan Boulevard** are located several of the city's museums and colonial remnants. However, many of the city's other sights are scattered further afield, so visitors have to effect a dot-to-dot of the sights that appeal most. These invariably include one or more of the museums that pander to the West's fixation with the American War, the pick of the bunch being the **War Remnants Museum** and **Ho Chi Minh City Museum**.

For some visitors, the war is their primary frame of reference, and such historical hot spots as the **Reunification Palace** rank highly on their itineraries. Yet the city pre-dates American involvement by several centuries, and not all of its sights revolve around planes, tanks and rusting ordnance. Ostentatious reminders of French rule abound, among them such memorable buildings as **Notre Dame Cathedral** and the grandiose **Hotel de Ville** – but even these look spanking-new when compared to gloriously musty edifices like **Quan Am Pagoda** and the **Jade Emperor Pagoda**, just a couple of the many captivating places of worship across the city. And if the chaos becomes too much, you can escape to the relative calm of the **Botanical Gardens** – also home to the city's **History Museum** and **zoo**.

Dong Khoi

Slender **Dong Khoi**, running for just over 1km from Le Duan to the Saigon River, has long mirrored Ho Chi Minh City's changing fortunes. The French knew the road as Rue Catinat, a tamarind-shaded thoroughfare that constituted the heart of French colonial life. Here the *colons* would promenade, stopping at chic boutiques and perfumeries, and gathering at noon and dusk at cafés such as the *Rotonde* and the *Taverne Alsacienne* for a Vermouth or Dubonnet, before hailing a *pousse-pousse* (a hand-pulled variation on the cyclo) to run them home. With the departure of the French in 1954, President Diem saw fit to change the street's name to Tu Do, "Freedom", and it was under this guise that a generation of young American GIs came to know it, as they toured the glut of bars – *Wild West*, *Uncle Sam's*, *Playboy* – that sprang up to pander to their more lascivious needs. After Saigon fell in 1975, the more politically correct moniker of Dong Khoi, or "Uprising", was adopted, but the street quickly went to seed in the dark, pre-*doi moi* years, and by the seventies had gone, in the words of Le Ly Hayslip, from "bejewelled, jaded dowager to shabby, grasping bag lady".

Today, however, Dong Khoi is enjoying a renaissance. Its eclectic melange of buildings – from grand colonial facades and slender shophouses to unlovely concrete-slab buildings – is crammed with **souvenir shops** and **designer boutiques** catering for the current wave of tourism, with a massive development called "Times Square", half-way down the street, set to transform the street's image yet again in the near future.

Notre Dame Cathedral

Straddling the northern reach of Dong Khoi is the pleasing redbrick bulk of the late nineteenth-century **Notre Dame Cathedral**. Aside from the few stained-glass windows above and behind its altar, and its marble relief *Stations of the Cross*, the interior boasts only scanty decoration, but there's plenty of scope for people-watching, as a steady trickle of Catholics pass through in their best silk tunics and black pants, fingering rosary beads, their whispered prayers merging with the insistent murmur of the traffic outside. A statue of the Virgin Mary provides the centrepiece to the small **park** fronting the cathedral, where cyclo drivers loiter and kids hawk postcards and maps. Take a close look at her face, as on occasion locals swear they have seen her shed tears.

The cathedral's twin compass-point spires were, for decades, one of Saigon's handiest landmarks, but they're now dwarfed by the glass facade of **Diamond Plaza**, one of the city's gleaming **shopping malls**, and by the telecom tower above the **General Post Office**, east of the park. A classic colonial edifice

▲ Notre Dame Cathedral with the modern Diamond Plaza shopping mall behind

unchanged since its completion in the 1880s, the GPO is worth a peek inside for its nave-like foyer, lent character by two huge map-murals, one charting Saigon and its environs in 1892, the other the telegraphic lines of southern Vietnam and Cambodia in 1936. Further in, a huge portrait of Uncle Ho sporting a healthy tan and warm smile gazes down at the aged wooden benches and tables of the cavernous main hall.

Lam Son Square

Dong Khoi briefly widens a couple of hundred metres south of the cathedral, where the smart, white walls of the **Hotel Continental** (see p.89) announce your arrival in **Lam Son Square**. Once a bastion of French high society, and still one of the city's premier addresses, the hotel front terrace was *the* place to see and be seen earlier last century. Little wonder, then, that Somerset Maugham's nose for a story led him here in the mid-twenties: "Outside the hotels are terraces," he recounted, "and at the hour of the aperitif, they are crowded with bearded, gesticulating Frenchmen drinking the sweet and sickly beverages…which they drink in France and they talk nineteen to the dozen in the rolling accent of the Midi… It is very agreeable to sit under the awning on the terrace of the *Hotel Continental*, with an innocent drink before you, [and] read in the local newspaper heated controversies upon the affairs of the colony." Sadly the terrace no longer exists, so if you want to tap into the history of the place, the best you can do is to ensconce yourself in the hotel's café.

Standing grandly on the eastern side of Lam Son Square, its cyclopean, domed entrance peering southwestwards down Le Loi, is the century-old **Municipal Theatre**. The National Assembly was temporarily housed here in 1955, but today, lovingly restored to its former glory, it once again embraces programmes that include fashion shows, drama and dance. Just below the theatre, the 1958-built and now grandiosely revamped **Caravelle Hotel** (see p.89) gazes down across the square at the more diminutive *Continental*. In its former incarnation, the *Caravelle* found favour with those Western journalists assigned to cover the war, and its terrace bar saw many a report drafted over a stiff drink.

Down towards the riverbank

Though glitzy boutiques predominate along Dong Khoi below the *Caravelle*, they haven't yet managed entirely to eradicate the past, and it's still possible to winkle out relics of old Saigon. Wander south of Lam Son and you'll soon meet Dong Du, where a left turn reveals the white and blue-washed walls of the 1930s **Indian Jamia Mosque**, now towered over by the *Sheraton* (see p.89). The rounded curves of its arches and its slender minarets make a stark contrast to the utilitarian design of the hotel next door, and there's a reassuring sense of peace that's enhanced by the slumbering worshippers lazing around the complex. If you're feeling peckish, check out the simple restaurant that is tucked round the back of the mosque, serving cheap and tasty dishes, many of which are vegetarian. Continuing down Dong Khoi to the river takes you past two of the city's more venerable hotels, the lovingly restored *Grand* (see p.89) on the left, followed 30m later on the right by the lavish, riverfront *Majestic* (see p.89).

Along the waterfront

In colonial days, the **quay** hugging the confluence of the Saigon River and Ben Nghe Channel provided new arrivals with their first real glimpse of Indochina – scores of coolie-hatted dock-workers lugging sacks of rice off ships, shrimp farmers dredging the oozy shallows, and junks and sampans bobbing on the tide under the vigilant gaze of *colons* imbibing at nearby cafés. Arriving by steamer in 1910, Gabrielle Vassal felt as if "all Saigon had turned out… Some expected friends, others came in the hope of meeting acquaintances or as mere spectators. One was reminded of a fashionable garden party, for the dresses and equipages were worthy of Paris itself." These days the only river traffic consists of hydrofoils bound for Vung Tau, a few tourist boats and a ferry linking Districts one and two, though a tunnel currently being built beneath the river will soon render this obsolete.

At the bottom of Dong Khoi, take a left onto Ton Duc Thang, and it's only a short skip to **Me Linh Square**, where a statue of Tran Hung Dao points across the river: it's a striking image when framed by the towering *Renaissance Hotel* (see p.89) and the Me Linh Point Tower. Ton Duc Thang draws its name from a former president of the Democratic Republic of Vietnam, whose life is celebrated at the nearby **Ton Duc Thang Museum** (Tues–Sun 7.30–11.30am & 1.30–5pm; free). Don't expect any fireworks here: besides some grim photographs highlighting the many years he spent de-husking rice on the prison island of Poulo Condore (now known as Con Dao, see p.221), a few evocative photos of old Saigon and some of the bric-a-brac of the man's life comprise the museum's principal highlights.

The Ho Chi Minh Museum

Where the Ben Nghe Channel enters the Saigon River, a bridge crosses it to an imposing mansion that was erected in the 1860s. Known as the *Nha Rong*, or Dragon House, this former headquarters of a French shipping company is now home to the **Ho Chi Minh Museum** (1 Nguyen Tat Thanh; Tues–Sun

7.30–11.30am & 1.30–5pm; 10,000₫) – an apposite venue, given that it was from the abutting wharf that Ho left for Europe in 1911. Sadly, the collection within fails to capture the spirit of this man whose life was dedicated to liberating his homeland from colonialism. If you decide to visit, you'll need to wring all the interest you can out of personal effects such as Ho's walking stick, rattan suitcase, sandals made from tyres and watering can, a map of his itinerant wanderings, and a few blurred photographs of him at official receptions. If all the Ho Chi Minh museums in Vietnam are to be believed, Ho was evidently a compulsive hoarder.

The days when the Ben Nghe Channel was choked with sampans are long gone, and now its pitch-black waters are eerily calm. An effort is under way to clean up this pungent part of the city; already parts of it are being built over and the rotting shacks on its banks have been cleared. However, the fetid stench of the canal still lingers.

Around Nguyen Hué

When Saigon's French administrators laid the 750-metre sweep of Charner Boulevard over a filled-in canal and down to the Saigon River, their brief was to replicate the elegance of a tree-lined Parisian boulevard, and in its day this broad avenue was known as the Champs Elysées of the East. These days, however, **Nguyen Hué**, as it is now known, has little character except on Sundays and at festival time. Each Sunday evening, the city's trendsetting youth converge here and on nearby Dong Khoi on their motorbikes, to circle round and round, girlfriends riding pillion, in a strange ritual that recreates the traffic jams that they suffer through on weekdays. At Tet the street also bursts into life, hosting a vast, riotously colourful flower market which draws Vietnamese belles in their thousands to pose in their best *ao dai* among the roses, sunflowers, chrysanthemums and conical orange trees.

The stately edifice that stands at Nguyen Hué's northern extent is the former **Hotel de Ville**, the city's most photographed icon and an ostentatious reminder of colonial Europe's stubborn resolve to stamp its imprint on the countries it subjugated, no matter how incongruous. Built in 1908 as the city's administrative hub, this wedding cake of a building today houses the People's Committee behind its showy jumble of Corinthian columns, classical figures and shuttered windows. A **statue of Uncle Ho** cradling a small child in his lap watches over the tiny **park** fronting the building, where flower beds add a splash of colour.

Though the **Rex Hotel** (see p.89), at the junction of Nguyen Hué and Le Loi, may give the impression of being venerable, in fact it has only operated as a hotel since 1976. Having started out as a garage for the Renaults and Peugeots of the city's French expat community, during the 1960s it billeted American officers, and hosted regular press briefing sessions that came to be known by jaded members of the press as the "Five O'Clock Follies". From its fifth-floor *Rooftop Garden* bar, the hotel yields a superb view of the whirl of life on the street below, best enjoyed over a fruit juice or cool glass of beer. At night, the hotel's emblem, a giant **crown**, lights up on the terrace, providing the city with one of its best-known landmarks.

The southern face of the block south of the *Rex* hides peaceful **Sri Thendayyutthapani Temple**, whose *gopuram* (sculpted gate tower) stands at 66 Ton That Thiep. The place manages a certain rag-tag charisma, the lavish murals normally associated with Hindu temples replaced by faded paintings of Jawaharlal Nehru, Mahatma Gandhi and various deities from the Hindu pantheon, plus a ceiling gaily studded with coloured baubles and lamps. Steps beyond the topiary to the right of the main sanctuary lead to a roof terrace that's dominated by a weather-beaten tower of deities, whose ranks have been infiltrated by two incongruous characters dressed like public schoolboys in braces, shorts and striped ties, and waving merrily.

The Ho Chi Minh City Museum

Of all the stones of empire thrown up in Vietnam by the French, few are more eye-catching than the former **Gia Long Palace**, a block west of the Hotel de Ville at 65 Ly Tu Trong, built in 1886 as a splendid residence for the governor of Cochinchina. Homeless after the air attack that smashed his own palace, Diem decamped here in 1962, and it was in the tunnels beneath the building that he spent his last hours of office, before fleeing to the church in Cho Lon where he finally surrendered (see p.104). Ironically, it now houses the **Ho Chi Minh City Museum** (daily 8am–5pm; 15,000đ), which makes use of photographs, documents and artefacts to trace the struggle of the Vietnamese people against France and America. Even if you're not desperate to learn more about the country's war-torn past, you're likely to be enchanted by the grandeur of the building, and you might even witness couples posing for wedding photographs, as the regal structure and well-tended gardens are a favourite backdrop for photographers.

The downstairs area is a hotchpotch of ancient artefacts and antique collections, along with a section on nature and another featuring ethnic clothing and implements. The museum shifts into higher gear upstairs, where the focus turns to the war with America. The best exhibits are those showcasing the ingenuity of the Vietnamese – bicycle parts made into mortars, a Suzuki motorbike in whose inner tubes documents were smuggled into Saigon, a false-floored boat in which guns were secreted, and so on. Look out, too, for sweaters knitted by female prisoners on Con Dao Island bearing the Vietnamese words for "peace" and "freedom". Elsewhere, there's a cross-sectional model of the Cu Chi tunnels, and a rewarding gallery of photographs of the Ho Chi Minh Campaign and the fall of Saigon.

As with many of Vietnam's museums, the hardware of war is on display in the **gardens**. Tucked away behind the frangipanis and well-groomed hedges out back are a Soviet tank, an American helicopter and an anti-aircraft gun, while out front are two sleek but idle jets.

The Reunification Palace and around

Five minutes' stroll north up Nam Ky Khoi Nghia from the Ho Chi Minh City Museum, a red flag billows proudly above the **Reunification Palace** (daily 7.30–11am & 1–4pm; 15,000đ including guided tour). A whitewashed concrete edifice with all the charm of a municipal library, the palace occupies the site of the former Norodom Palace, a colonial mansion erected in 1871 to house the governor-general of Indochina. After the French departure in 1954, Ngo Dinh Diem commandeered this extravagant monument as his presidential palace, but after sustaining extensive damage in a February 1962 assassination attempt by two disaffected Southern pilots, the place was condemned and pulled down. The present building was named the Independence Palace upon completion in 1966, only to be retitled the Reunification Hall when the South fell in 1975 (see box opposite). The reversion to the label "Palace" was doubtless made for tourist appeal.

Spookily unchanged from its working days, much of the building's **interior** is a time capsule of sixties and seventies kitsch: pacing its airy banqueting rooms,

The taking of the presidential palace

The Reunification Palace is so significant to the Vietnamese because it was the storming **of its gates** by a tank belonging to the Northern Army, on April 30, 1975, that became the defining moment of the fall of Saigon and the South. These days two tanks stand in the grounds as a reminder of the incident.

Of the many Western journalists on hand to witness the spectacle, none was better placed than English journalist and poet James Fenton, who conspired to hitch a ride on the tank that first crashed through the gates: "The tank speeded up, and rammed the left side of the palace gate. Wrought iron flew into the air, but the whole structure refused to give. I nearly fell off. The tank backed again, and I observed a man with a nervous smile opening the centre portion of the gate. We drove into the grounds of the palace, and fired a salute. An NLF soldier took the flag and, waving it above his head, ran into the palace. A few moments later, he emerged on the terrace, waving the flag round and round. Later still, there he was on the roof. The red and yellow stripes of the Saigon regime were lowered at last."

Inside the palace, Duong Van Minh ("Big Minh"), sworn in as president only two days before, readied to perform his last presidential duty. "I have been waiting since early this morning to transfer power to you," he said to General Bui Tin, to which the general replied: "Your power has crumbled. You cannot give up what you do not have."

conference halls and reception areas, it's hard not to think you've strayed into the arch-criminal's lair in a James Bond movie. Before the tour you enter a **movie room**, where a potted account of Vietnamese history and the American War is screened half-hourly. Then guides usher you through the hall's many chambers, proudly pointing out every piece of porcelain, lacquerwork, rosewood and silk on display. Most interesting is the **third floor**, where, as well as the presidential library (with works by Laurens van der Post and Graham Greene alongside heavyweight political tomes), there's a curtained projection room, and an entertainment lounge complete with tacky circular sofa and barrel-shaped bar. Nearby, a set of sawn-off elephant's feet add an eerie touch to the decor. Perhaps the most atmospheric part of the building is the **basement** and former command centre, where wood-panelled combat staff quarters yield archaic radio equipment and vast wall maps.

Adjoining the western edge of the Reunification Palace's grounds is **Cong Vien Van Hoa Park**, a municipal park whose tree-shaded lawns are pleasant for a stroll and heave with life each Sunday. During the colonial era, the park's northernmost corner was home to one of the linchpins of French expat society, the **Cercle Sportif**, a Westerners-only sports club where the *colons* gathered to swim and play tennis before sinking an aperitif and discussing the day's events. Today it functions as the Workers' Sports Club.

The War Remnants Museum

A block above the park, at 28 Vo Van Tan, the **War Remnants Museum** (daily 7.30–noon & 1.30–5pm; 15,000đ) is the city's most popular attraction but not for the faint-hearted. Unlike at the Ho Chi Minh City Museum, you are unlikely to be distracted here by the building that houses the heart-rending exhibits – a distressing compendium of the horrors of modern warfare. Some of the instruments of destruction are on display in the courtyard outside, including a 28-tonne howitzer and a ghoulish collection of bomb parts. There's also a guillotine that harvested heads at the Central Prison on Ly Tu Trong, first for the French and later for Diem.

Inside, a series of halls present a grisly portfolio of **photographs** of mutilation, napalm burns and torture. Most shocking is the gallery detailing the effects of the 75 million litres of defoliant sprays dumped across the country: beside the expected images of bald terrain, hideously malformed foetuses are preserved in pickling jars. A gallery that looks at international opposition to the war as well as the American peace movement adds a sense of balance, and makes a change from the self-glorifying tone of most Vietnamese museums. Accounts of servicemen – such as veteran B52 pilot Michael Heck – who attempted to discharge themselves from the war on ethical grounds are also featured. Artefacts donated to the museum by returned US servicemen add to the reconciliatory tone.

At the back of the museum is a grisly mock-up of the **tiger cages**, the godless prison cells of Con Son Island (see p.221), which could have been borrowed from the movie set of *Papillon*. The **souvenir shop**, hidden between the tanks and planes in the courtyard, sells Zippo lighters, penknives, dog tags and models crafted from spent bullets.

Xa Loi Pagoda

Vapid **Xa Loi Pagoda** (daily 6–11.30am & 2–9pm), a short walk west of the museum at 89 Ba Huyen Thanh Quan, became a hotbed of Buddhist opposition to Diem in 1963. The austere, 1956-built complex is unspectacular, its most striking component a tall **tower** whose unlovely beige blocks lend it a drabness even six tiers of Oriental roofs can't quite dispel. The main **sanctuary**, accessed by a dual staircase (men scale the left-hand flight, women the right), is similarly dull: beyond a vast joss-stick urn inventively decorated with marbles and shards of broken china, it's a lofty hall featuring a huge gilt Buddha and fourteen murals that narrate his life. Turn left and around the back of the Buddha, and you'll come across a shrine commemorating Thich Quang Duc and the other monks who set fire to themselves in Saigon in 1963 (see box opposite). Quang Duc's is the ghostly figure holding a set of beads, to the left of the shrine.

Ben Thanh Market and around

There's much more beneath the pillbox-style clock tower of **Ben Thanh Market** than just the cattle and seafood pictured on its front wall. The city's busiest market for almost a century, and known to the French as the *Halles Centrales*, Ben Thanh's dense knot of trade has caused it to burst at the seams, disgorging stalls onto the surrounding pavements. Inside the main body of the market, a tight grid of aisles, demarcated according to produce, teems with shoppers, and, if it's souvenirs you're after, a reconnaissance here will reveal conical hats, basketware, bags, shoes, Da Lat coffee and Vietnam T-shirts. All this, though, is tame stuff compared with the wet market along the back of the complex, where you'll find buckets of eels, clutches of live frogs tied together at the legs, heaps of pigs' ears and snouts, and baskets wedged full of hens, among other gruesome sights. If you can countenance the thought of eating after seeing – and smelling – this patch of the market, com, pho and baguette stalls proliferate towards the back of the main hall. In the evenings, foodstalls specializing in seafood set up along the sides of the market, attracting a mixed crowd of locals and tourists.

The aroma of jasmine and incense replaces the stench of butchery a block northwest of Ben Thanh, at Truong Dinh's **Sri Mariamman Hindu Temple**. Less engaging than Sri Thendayyutthapani (see p.95), Sri Mariamman's imposing walls are sometimes lined with vendors selling oil, incense and jasmine

The self-immolation of Thich Quang Duc

In the early morning of June 11, 1963, a column of Buddhist monks left the **Xa Loi Pagoda** and processed to the intersection of Cach Mang Thang Tam and Nguyen Dinh Chieu. There, **Thich Quang Duc**, a 66-year-old monk from Hué, sat down in the lotus position and meditated as fellow monks doused him in petrol, and then set light to him in protest at the repression of Buddhists by President Diem, who was a Catholic. As flames engulfed the impassive monk and passers-by prostrated themselves before him, the cameras of the Western press corps rolled, and by the next morning the grisly event had grabbed the world's headlines. More self-immolations followed, and Diem's heavy-handed responses at Xa Loi – some four hundred monks and nuns were arrested and others cast from the top of the tower – led to massed popular demonstrations against the government. Diem, it was clear, had become a liability. On November 2, he and his brother were assassinated after taking refuge in Cho Lon's Cha Tam Church (see p.104), the victims of a military coup.

petals. The walls are topped by a colourful *gopuram*, or bank of sculpted gods. Inside, the gods Mariamman, Maduraiveeran and Pechiamman reside in stone sanctuaries reminiscent of the Cham towers upcountry, and there are more deities set into the walls around the courtyard.

South of Ben Thanh

A short stroll from Ben Thanh Market down Pho Duc Chinh, in a grand colonial mansion, Ho Chi Minh City's **Fine Art Museum** (Tues–Sun 9am–5pm; 10,000đ) is worth a visit to view some of the country's best Cham and Oc Eo relics on the third floor. The first floor hosts temporary exhibitions, while the courtyard out back is given over to commerce in the form of art works on sale by various city galleries. If you're in the market for a piece of Vietnamese art, it's worth checking these places out as standards are high and some prices are affordable. Revolutionary art dominates the second floor, relying heavily on hackneyed images of soldiers, war zones and Uncle Ho, though a few offerings capture the anguish and turmoil of the conflicts. Things get better on the third floor where there's an impressive collection of Oc Eo and Cham statues, gilt Buddhas and other antiquities.

Across the road from the museum, **Le Cong Kieu** is lined with antique shops selling Oriental and colonial bric-a-brac. Memorabilia reflecting Vietnam's more recent history are available at the army surplus stalls at the back of **Dan Sinh Market**, behind the Phung Son Tu Pagoda on Yersin; here you can pick up khaki gear, Viet Cong pith helmets, old compasses and Zippo lighters embossed with saucy pearls of wisdom coined by GIs.

Along Le Duan Boulevard to the Botanical Gardens

Above Notre Dame Cathedral, **Le Duan Boulevard** runs between the Botanical Gardens and the grounds of the Reunification Palace. Known as Norodom Boulevard to the French, who lined it with tamarind trees to imitate a Gallic thoroughfare, it soon became a residential and diplomatic enclave with a crop of fine pastel-hued colonial villas to boot. Its present name doffs a cap to Le Duan, the secretary-general of the *Lao Dong*, or Workers Party, from 1959. Turn northeast from the top of Dong Khoi and the sense of harmony created by Le Duan's graceful colonial piles ends abruptly with a number of brand-new edifices.

One of these, the nondescript building that is the US Consulate, was built right on top of the site of the infamous former **American Embassy**, where a commemorative plaque is now the only reminder of its existence and significance in the American War. Two events immortalized the former building on this site, in operation from 1967 to 1975 and left standing half-derelict until 1999 as a sobering legacy. The first came in the pre-dawn hours of January 31, 1968, when a small band of Viet Cong commandos breached the embassy compound during the nationwide **Tet Offensive**. That the North could mount such an effective attack on the hub of US power in Vietnam was shocking to the American public. In the six hours of close-range fire that followed, five US guards died, and with them the popular misconception that the US Army had the Vietnam conflict under control.

Worse followed seven years later, during "Operation Frequent Wind", the chaotic **helicopter evacuation** that marked the United States' final undignified withdrawal from Vietnam. The embassy building was one of thirteen designated landing zones where all foreigners were to gather upon hearing the words, "It is 112 degrees and rising" on the radio followed by Bing Crosby singing *White Christmas*. At noon on April 29, 1975, the signal was broadcast, and for the next eighteen hours scores of helicopters shuttled passengers out to the US Navy's Seventh Fleet off Vung Tau. Around two thousand evacuees were lifted from the roof of the embassy alone, before Ambassador Graham Martin finally left with the Stars and Stripes in the early hours of the following morning. In a tragic postscript to US involvement, as the last helicopter lifted off, many of the Vietnamese civilians who for hours had been clamouring at the gates were left to suffer the Communists' reprisals.

The Botanical Gardens and zoo

The pace of life slows down considerably – and the odours of cut grass and frangipani blooms replace the smell of exhaust fumes – when you duck into the city's **Botanical Gardens** (daily 7am–9pm; 8000đ), accessed by a gate at the far eastern end of Le Duan, and bounded to the east by the Thi Nghe Channel. Established in 1864 by the Frenchmen Germain and Pierre (respectively a vet and a botanist), the gardens' social function has remained unchanged in decades, and their tree-shaded paths still attract as many courting couples and promenaders as when Norman Lewis followed the "clusters of Vietnamese beauties on bicycles" and headed there one Sunday morning in 1950 to find the gardens "full of these ethereal creatures, gliding in decorous groups...sometimes accompanied by gallants". In its day, the gardens harboured an impressive collection of tropical flora, including many species of orchid. Post-liberation, the place went to seed but nowadays a bevy of gardeners keep it reasonably well tended again, and portrait photographers are once again lurking to take snaps of you framed by flowers.

Stray right inside and you'll soon reach the **zoo**, home to camels, elephants, crocodiles and big cats, also komodo dragons – a gift from the government of Indonesia. There's also an **amusement park** that is sometimes open, and you can get an ice cream or a coconut from one of the several **cafés** sprinkled around the grounds.

The History Museum

A pleasing, pagoda-style roof crowns the city's **History Museum** (Tues–Sun 8–11am & 1.30–4.30pm; 15,000đ), at 2 Nguyen Binh Khiem, next to the Botanical Gardens. It houses fifteen galleries illuminating Vietnam's past from primitive times to the end of French rule by means of a decent if unastonishing array of artefacts and pictures. Dioramas of defining moments in Vietnamese military history lend the collection some cohesion – included are Ngo Quyen's 938 AD victory at Bach Dang (see p.406), and the sinking of the *Esperance*. Should you tire of Vietnamese history, you might explore halls focusing on such disparate subjects as Buddha images from around Asia; seventh- and eighth-century Champa art; and the customs and crafts of the ethnic minorities of Vietnam. There's also a room jam-packed with exquisite ceramics from Japan, Thailand and Vietnam, and you could round off your visit at the **water puppetry theatre** (shows are performed on the hour from 10am to 4pm, except 1pm; $2).

Jade Emperor Pagoda

A few blocks northwest of the Botanical Gardens, on Mai Thi Luu, stands the **Jade Emperor Pagoda**, or Chua Phuoc Hai (daily 5am–7pm; free), built by the city's Cantonese community around 1900. If you visit just one temple in town, make it this one, with its exquisite panels of carved gilt woodwork, and its panoply of weird and wonderful deities, both Taoist and Buddhist, beneath a roof that groans under the weight of dragons, birds and animals.

To the right of the tree-lined **courtyard** out front is a grubby pond whose occupants have earned the temple its alternative moniker of Tortoise Pagoda. Once over the threshold, look up and you'll see Chinese characters announcing: "the only enlightenment is in Heaven" – though only after your eyes have adjusted to the fug of joss-stick smoke. A statue of the **Jade Emperor** lords it over the main hall's central altar, sporting an impressive moustache, and he's surrounded by a retinue of similarly moustached followers.

A rickety flight of steps in the chamber to the right of the main hall runs up to a **balcony** looking out over the pagoda's elaborate **roof**. Set behind the balcony, a neon-haloed statue of Quan Am (see p.104) stands on an altar. Left out of the main hall, meanwhile, you're confronted by Kim Hua, to whom women pray for fertility; judging by the number of babies weighing down the female statues around her, her success rate is high. The Chief of Hell resides in the larger chamber behind Kim Hua's niche. Given his job description, he doesn't look particularly demonic, though his attendants, in sinister black garb, are certainly equipped to administer the sorts of punishments depicted in the ten dark-wood reliefs on the walls before them.

Le Van Duyet Temple

A national hero is commemorated at the **Temple of Marshal Le Van Duyet**, known locally as Lang Ong and sited at the top of Dinh Tien Hoang, in the region of the city where the **Gia Dinh Citadel** once stood. A military mandarin and eunuch who lived around the turn of the nineteenth century, Le Van Duyet succeeded in putting down the Tay Son Rebellion, and later became military governor of Gia Dinh. Strolling around the grounds reveals the two unmarked oval mounds under which the marshal and his wife are buried. The temple itself, which stretches through three halls behind a facade decorated with unicorns assembled from shards of chinaware, is quite atmospheric. Inside, a portrait of the marshal stands on an altar, in front of which is a massive and ancient pair of tusks. The temple receives a steady stream of visitors paying their respects with burning incense, and the ringing of a brass bell adds to the pious mood. On the first day of the eighth lunar month, to coincide with the marshal's birthday, a **theatre** troupe dramatizes his life; and there's more activity around Tet, when crowds of pilgrims gather to ask for safekeeping in the forthcoming year.

Cho Lon

The dense cluster of streets comprising the Chinese ghetto of **CHO LON** was once distinct from Saigon, though linked to it by the five-kilometre-long umbilical cord of Tran Hung Dao. The distinction was already somewhat blurred by 1950, when Norman Lewis found the city's Chinatown "swollen so enormously as to become its grotesque Siamese twin", and the steady influx of refugees into the city during the war years saw to it that the two districts eventually became joined by a swathe of urban development. Even so, a short stroll around Cho Lon (whose name, meaning "**big market**", couldn't be more apposite) will make clear that, even by this city's standards, the mercantile mania here is breathtaking. The largest of Cho Lon's many covered markets are Tran Phu's An Dong, built in 1991, and the more recent but equally vast An Dong II. If you're looking to sightsee rather than shop, then historic Binh Tay (see p.102) is of far more interest. You'll get most out of Cho Lon simply by losing yourself in its amorphous mass of life: amid the melee, streetside barbers clip away briskly, bird-sellers squat outside tumbledown **pagodas and temples**, heaving markets ring to fishwives' chatter, and stores display mushrooms, dried shrimps and rice paper.

The **ethnic Chinese**, or **Hoa**, first began to settle here around 1900; many came from existing enclaves in My Tho and Bien Hoa. The area soon became the largest Hoa community in the country, a title it still holds, with a population of over half a million. Residents gravitated towards others from their region of China, with each congregation commissioning its own places of worship and clawing out its own commercial niche – thus the Cantonese handled retailing and groceries, the Teochew dealt in tea and fish, the Fukien were in charge of rice, and so on.

The great wealth that Cho Lon generated had to be spent somewhere. By the early twentieth century, sassy restaurants, casinos and brothels existed to facilitate this. Also prevalent were **fumeries**, where nuggets of opium were quietly smoked from the cool comfort of a wooden opium bed. Among the expats and wealthy Asians who frequented them was Graham Greene, and he recorded his experiences in *Ways of Escape*. By the 1950s, Cho Lon was a potentially dangerous place to be, its vice industries controlled by the **Binh Xuyen** gang. First the French and then the Americans trod carefully here, while Viet Minh and Viet Cong **activists** hid out in its cramped backstreets – as Frank Palmos found to his cost, when the jeep he and four other correspondents were riding in was ambushed in 1968.

Post-reunification, Cho Lon saw hard times. As Hanoi aligned itself increasingly with the Soviet Union, Sino-Vietnamese tensions became strained. Economic **persecution** of the Hoa made matters worse, and, when Vietnam invaded Chinese-backed Cambodia, Beijing launched a punitive **border war**. Hundreds of thousands of ethnic Chinese, many of them from Cho Lon, fled the country in unseaworthy vessels, fearing recriminations. Today, the business acumen of the Chinese is valued by the local authorities, and the distemper that gripped Cho Lon for over a decade is a memory.

Binh Tay Market and around

First impressions of **Binh Tay Market**, with its multi-tiered, mustard-coloured roofs stalked by serpentine dragons, are of a huge temple complex. Once inside, however, it quickly becomes obvious that only mammon is deified here. If any one place epitomizes Cho Lon's vibrant commercialism, it's Binh Tay, its well-regimented corridors abuzz with stalls offering products of all kinds, from dried fish, pickled vegetables and chilli paste to pottery piled up to the rafters, and the

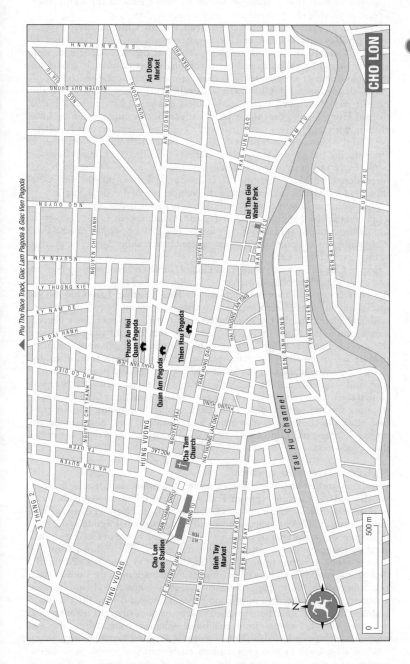

Phu Tho Race Track; Giac Lam Pagoda & Giac Vien Pagoda

SU VAN HANH
TRAN PHU
GIA TU
NGUYEN DUY DUONG
An Dong Market
HUNG VUONG
AN DUONG VUONG
TRAN HUNG DAO
HAM TU
NGO QUYEN
NGUYEN CHI THANH
NGUYEN TRAI
TRAN VAN KIEU
Dai The Gioi Water Park
HUNG PHU
BEN BA DINH
NGUYEN KIM
LY THUONG KIET
KY NAM DE
LA DAI HANH
PHO CO DIEU
HAI THUONG LAN ONG
Phuoc An Hoi Quan Pagoda
CHAU VAN LIEM
Thien Hau Pagoda
TRAN HUNG DAO
BEN BINH DONG
TUNG THIEN VUONG
THIEN VUONG
Quan Am Pagoda
TRAN HUNG DAO
PHUNG HUNG
Tau Hu Channel
NGUYEN CHI THANH
HUNG VUONG
HOC LAC
NGUYEN TRAI
Cha Tam Church
HAI THUONG LAN ONG
3 THANG 2
TA UYEN
HA TON QUYEN
TRAN CHANH CHIEU
TRANG TU
HT YEN
LE QUANG SUNG
Cho Lon Bus Station
PHAN VAN KHOE
Binh Tay Market
THAP MUOI
BEN BAI SAY
HUNG VUONG

N

0   500 m

103

colourful bonnets that Vietnamese women so favour. Beyond Binh Tay's south side, stalls provide cheap snacks for shoppers and traders.

A few steps north of the market lies **Tran Chanh Chieu**, a street clogged by a **poultry market** full of chickens, geese and ducks tied together in bundles. **Cereals and pulses** are the speciality at the street's east end, with weighty sacks of rice, lentils and beans forming a sort of obstacle course for the cyclo that try to negotiate the narrow strip of roadway still visible.

The slender spire of **Cha Tam Church** peers down from above the eastern end of cramped Tran Chanh Chieu, but you'll have to walk round to Tran Hung Dao to find the entrance. It was in this unprepossessing little church, with its Oriental outer gate and cheery yellow walls, that President Ngo Dinh Diem and his brother Ngo Dinh Nhu holed up on November 1, 1963, during the coup that saw them chased out of the Gia Long Palace (see p.96). Early the next morning, Diem phoned the leaders of the coup and surrendered. An M-113 armoured car duly picked them up, but they were shot dead by ARVN soldiers before the vehicle reached central Saigon.

With clearance from the janitor (who's usually somewhere around hoping for a tip) you can clamber up into the **belfry** and under the bells, Quasimodo-style, to join the statue of St Francis Xavier for the fine views he enjoys of Cho Lon. The janitor can also point out the pew where Diem and his brother sat praying as they awaited their fate.

Exiting Cha Tam Church along Tran Hung Dao, you're swallowed up by Cho Lon's vast and colourful cloth market, while a further five minutes' walk towards the river brings you to the eastern end of **Hai Thuong Lan Ong**. Shops specializing in Chinese and Vietnamese traditional medicine have long proliferated here, identifiable by the sickly-sweet aroma that hangs over them. Named after a famous herbalist who practised and studied in Hanoi two centuries ago, the street is lined by dingy shophouses banked with cabinets whose wooden drawers are crammed full of herbs. Step over the sliced roots laid out to dry along the pavement and peer inside any one of the shops, and you'll see rheumy men and women weighing out prescriptions on ancient balances. Steepled around them are boxes, jars and paper bags containing anything from dried bark to antler fur and tortoise glue. Predictably popular is **ginseng**, the Oriental cure-all said to combat everything from heart disease to acne. Also available are monkey-, tiger- and rhino-based medicines – despite a government ban on these products.

Nguyen Trai and around

Cho Lon's greatest architectural treasures are its temples and pagodas, many of which stand on or around **Nguyen Trai**, whose four-kilometre sweep northeast to Pham Ngu Lao starts just north of Cha Tam Church. North of Nguyen Trai's junction with Chau Van Liem, on tiny Lao Tu, **Quan Am Pagoda** is the pick of the pagodas in this part of town. Set back from the bustle of Cho Lon, it has an almost tangible air of antiquity, enhanced by the film of dust left by the incense spirals hanging from its rafters. Don't be too quick to dive inside, though: the pagoda's ridged roofs are impressive enough from the outside, their colourful crust of "glove-puppet" figurines, teetering houses and temples from a distance creating the illusion of a gingerbread house. Framing the two door gods and the pair of stone lions assigned to keeping out evil spirits are gilt panels depicting petrified scenes from traditional Chinese court life – dancers, musicians, noblemen in sedan chairs, a game of chequers being played.

When Cho Lon's Fukien congregation established this pagoda well over a century ago, they dedicated it to the Goddess of Mercy, but it's **A Pho**, the

▲ Quan Am Pagoda

Queen of Heaven, who stands in the centre of the main hall, beyond an altar tiled like a mortuary slab. A pantheon of deities throngs the open courtyard behind her, decked out in sumptuous apparel and attracting a steady traffic of worshippers. Twin ovens, flanking the main chamber, burn a steady supply of fake money offerings and incense sticks.

Phuoc An Hoi Quan Pagoda (aka Minh Huong Pagoda), three minutes' walk north on Hung Vuong, is a disarming place. Beyond the menacing dragons and sea monsters patrolling its roof, and the superb wood carving depicting a king being entertained by jousters and minstrels hanging over the entrance, is the temple's **sanctuary**, in which stately Quan Cong sits, instantly recognizable by his blood-red face, and fronted by two storks standing on top of turtles fashioned from countless plectrum-shaped ceramic shards.

Along Nguyen Trai, at **Thien Hau Pagoda** local women come in numbers to make offerings to Me Sanh, Goddess of Fertility, and to Long Mau, Goddess of Mothers and Newborn Babies. When Cantonese immigrants established the temple towards the middle of the nineteenth century, they named it after Thien Hau, Goddess of Seafarers. New arrivals from China would have hastened here to express their gratitude for a safe passage across the South China Sea. Three statues of her stand on the altar, one behind the other, while a large mural on the inside of the front wall depicts her guiding wildly pitching ships across a storm-tossed sea. The temple's most attractive aspect is its roof, bristling with so many figurines you wonder how those at the edge can keep their balance.

North of Cho Lon

Two of Ho Chi Minh City's oldest and most atmospheric places of worship, the **Giac Lam** and **Giac Vien Pagodas**, are tucked away in the hinterland to the north of Cho Lon – as is the thriving **Phu Tho Racecourse**, if you fancy a flutter. Also nearby is **Dam Sen leisure park**. The best way to get to these destinations is by xe om or cyclo, as they are hidden away in the backstreets.

Giac Lam Pagoda

You'll see the gate leading up to **Giac Lam Pagoda** (daily 5am–noon &
2–8pm) on Lac Long Quan, a couple of hundred metres northeast of its intersection with Le Dai Hanh. From there, a short track passes a new tower (its
seven levels are scaleable and afford good city views) and a cluster of monks'
tombs on its way to the actual pagoda. Built in 1744, rambling Giac Lam is
draped over 98 hardwood pillars, each inscribed with traditional *chu nom*
characters (Vietnamese script, based on Chinese ideograms). From its
terracotta floor-tiles and extravagant chandeliers to the antique tables at
which monks sit to take tea, Giac Lam is characterized by a clutter that
imbues it with an appealingly fusty feel, and a reassuring sense of age.

Access is through an **entrance** at the rear of the right-hand wall, which leads
into a **funerary chamber** flanked by row upon row of gilt tablets above photos
of the deceased. The many-armed goddess that stands in the centre of the
chamber is Chuan De, a manifestation of Quan Am. A right turn leads to a
courtyard-garden, around which runs a roof studded with blue and white
porcelain saucers. Monks would once have sat studying on the huge wooden
benches in the peaceful old **classroom** at the back of the complex, still in use
as a study centre today. The panels in this chamber depict the ten Buddhist hells;
study them carefully, and you'll see sinners being variously minced, fed to dogs,
dismembered and disembowelled by fanged demons.

To the left of the funerary chamber as you enter the pagoda is the **main
sanctuary**, whose multi-tiered altar dais groans under the weight of the many
Buddhist and Taoist statues it supports (remember to take off your shoes before
entering). Elsewhere in this chamber you'll spot an ensemble of oil lamps
balanced on a Christmas-tree-shaped wooden frame. Worshippers pen prayers
on pieces of paper, which they affix to the tree and then feed the lamps with
an offering of oil. A similar ritual is attached to the bell across the chamber,
though in this case people believe that their prayers are hastened to the gods by
the ringing of the bell.

Giac Vien Pagoda

Hidden away in a maze of backstreets, **Giac Vien Pagoda** was founded in the
late eighteenth century, and said to have been frequented by Emperor Gia Long.
Like Giac Lam, it has a dark live in atmosphere. Upon entering its red doors
daubed with yellow *chu nom* characters, visitors are confronted by banks of old
photos and funerary tablets flanking long refectory-style tables. The two rows
of black pillars lend an arresting sense of depth to this first chamber, which is
dominated by a panel depicting a ferocious-looking red lion. Continue around
the stone walls (crafted, incongruously, in classical Greek style) and into the
main sanctuary, and you'll find a sizeable congregation of deities, as well as a
tree of lamps similar to the one at Giac Lam. The monks residing in Giac Vien
are hospitable to a fault, and you'll probably be invited for a cup of tea before
you leave.

Phu Tho Racecourse and Dam Sen leisure park

There's no more potent symbol of the Vietnamese love of gambling than
Phu Tho Racecourse (☎08/3855 1205), located at 2 Le Dai Hanh, just
north of Cho Lon. Apart from a 14-year spell between 1975 and 1989, when
gambling was seen as an example of bourgeois decadence and outlawed, the
track resounds every weekend to the roar of the crowd urging on their
favourite. **Meetings** take place on Saturday and Sunday afternoons (noon–
4.30pm; 10,000đ entry), and spending a few hours here is a great antidote to

trudging round pagodas, though try not to get swept too deep into the crowd as pickpockets are rife. If you feel like a flutter, the minimum bet is 10,000đ and there's no upper limit. However, be warned that there are frequent allegations of horses being doped and races being fixed, so the form card is not to be relied on.

Also out this way is **Dam Sen Leisure Park** at 3 Hoa Binh (Mon–Fri 9am–6pm, Sat & Sun 8am–7.30pm; 25,000đ, children 15,000đ). Its kitsch diversions – fountains, themed gardens and fairground rides – won't appeal to everyone, but it's a welcome retreat from the frenetic pace of the city. Next door, the **Dam Sen Water Park** (Mon–Sat 9am–6pm, Sun 8.30am–6pm; 80,000đ, children 50,000đ) is a great place to cool down, and easy to get to; take a number 11 bus from Ben Thanh bus station.

Eating

Hanoi may be Vietnam's administrative capital, but Saigon is without doubt its culinary capital. Besides **Vietnamese cuisine**, which these days enjoys global popularity, just about every other type of food you could imagine is served here, including Indian, Italian, Brazilian, Japanese, Mexican, Lebanese and German, though perhaps predictably **French** restaurants comprise the most formidable foreign contingent in town. The French legacy is also evident in the city's abundance of **cafés**, which are scattered throughout the city.

Though you'll probably be tempted by a pizza or burrito at some time during your stay, it would be a crime to ignore the fabulous variety of indigenous food on offer, both in sophisticated **restaurants** and at **streetside stalls**. Owing to the transitory nature of foodstalls, it's impossible to make specific recommendations, but there are plenty to choose from (see p.49 for more on how to spot a good one). One area well worth checking out in the evening is around Ben Thanh Market, where a cluster of foodstalls offer a bewildering variety of dishes, many specializing in seafood.

Restaurants

One step up from street stalls are **eating houses**, where good, filling rice and noodle dishes are served from buffet-style tin trays and vast soup urns. If you chance upon such a place displaying something that catches your eye, just point, sit down and eat, then pay a pittance later.

Cheap **restaurants**, concentrated around De Tham, Pham Ngu Lao and Bui Ven, which cater exclusively for travellers, are fine if you want an inexpensive steak and chips or some fried noodles, but hardly in the league of the city's heavyweights, its **specialist restaurants**. Of course, by Vietnamese standards, these restaurants are incredibly expensive – eat at one and you'll probably spend enough to feed a Vietnamese family for a month – but by Western standards many of them are low-priced, and the quality of cooking is consistently high. What's more, ingredients are fresh, with vegetables transported from Da Lat, and meat often flown in from Australia.

Many of the upmarket hotels run lunch buffets, which at around $15 for as much as you can eat are excellent value. Some of the swankier restaurants lay on reasonably-priced **set menus** and also live **traditional music** in order to lure diners – we've mentioned a few such places in our listings. Though there are many delectable dishes to discover in Ho Chi Minh City, keep an eye open for *chao bo*, slithers of beef grilled on sticks of lemon grass, which can be superb when the beef is well marinated. You'll find it on the menu of a few of the places listed below, such as *Vietnam House* and *Blue Ginger*.

Central Ho Chi Minh City

The following are all marked on the map on p.109.

Al Fresco's 27 Dong Du. Huge portions of everything here – pizzas, steaks, burgers and barbecued ribs – keep customers coming back for more. There's an upstairs room if downstairs is full. 10am–11pm.

Amigo 55 Nguyen Hué. Recommended for its T-bone steaks and seafood prepared on an open grill, plus a good salad bar. 11am–11pm.

Ashoka 17/a10 Le Thanh Ton. Smart Indian restaurant offering authentic Moghul Indian dishes – some, such as *cho cho tikka* (chicken marinated in yoghurt), cooked in the tandoor – and a satisfying range of veggie dishes. 11.30am–2pm & 5–10pm.

Augustin's 10 Nguyen Thiep. Secreted down a narrow lane linking Dong Khoi and Nguyen Hué, an intimate bistro serving well-cooked but pricey French dishes. 11.30am–2pm & 6–10.30pm. Closed Sun.

Au Parc 23 Han Thuyen ☎08/3829 2772. Stylish place between Notre Dame Cathedral and Reunification Palace serving great breakfasts and salads, with a good deli counter and home delivery too. 7am–10.30pm.

Bi Bi 17/a6 Le Thanh Ton. This cosy French restaurant serving Mediterranean specialities is popular with expats. Set lunch $12. 11.30am–2pm & 6.30–10pm.

Blue Ginger 37 Nam Ky Khoi Nghia. Refined, low-ceilinged dining room with eye-catching artwork on the walls and traditional live evening music as you tuck into quality Vietnamese dishes (main courses around $5, excellent menus at $12–27). Popular with tour groups but still worth checking out for its agreeable ambience and great food. 7am–2.30pm & 5–10pm.

Bun Ta 136 Nam Ky Khoi Nghia. Hoping that the runaway success of its neighbour, *Ngon*, will rub off, this new place offers noodles every which way, with a pleasant streetside and indoor ambience. 6am–11pm.

Chu 158 Dong Khoi. American-style café, popular with well-off locals who enjoy the eclectic menu, including beef pie, spaghetti, Asian dishes and ice creams, as well as the nightly live music. 9am–midnight.

Ciao Café 40 Ngo Duc Khe & 74–76 Nguyen Hué. These smartly decorated, popular venues serve steaks, spaghetti and Asian food, and a kids' menu too. 7am–11pm.

Cung Dinh *Rex Hotel*, 141 Nguyen Hué ☎08/3829 2185. Some may find the lavish Oriental decor oppressive but there's no knocking the food: try the pork ribs with chilli and lemongrass or one of the ten different set menus, ranging from $20–40. There are nightly traditional music performances; prior bookings are sometimes necessary. 11am–2pm & 6–10pm.

Dong Du 57 Dong Du. Sharing an entrance with *Le Mekong*, as well as a reputation for high-quality Vietnamese dishes. 11am–2pm & 5–10pm.

Gartenstadt 34 Dong Khoi. High-quality German bar-restaurant; generous portions, imported sausages and a good selection of German beers, some on draught. 10.30am–midnight.

Givral 169 Dong Khoi. A local institution, with an extensive light Western and Asian menu. It boasts a prime position facing the *Continental* on Lam Son Square, and there's a newer, second branch at 56–66 Nguyen Hue . 6.30am–10pm.

Hoi An 11 Le Thanh Ton ☎08/3823 7694. Refined, traditional Vietnamese food is served in a sumptuous wooden house, run by the owners of *Mandarine*. Set menus start at $30. Book ahead to reserve a table. 5.30–10.45pm.

Jaspa's 33 Dong Khoi. Under the same management as *Al Fresco's* and *Pepperoni*, this place is a bit classier, featuring international fusion cuisine such as salt and pepper steak with wasabe mash. 7.30am–late.

La Fourchette 9 Ngo Duc Ke. Varnished light-wood panelling creates an old-world feel; the compact menu features melt-in-your-mouth imported steaks (around $15) and a well-stocked cheeseboard. 11.30am–2.30pm & 6.30–10pm.

Le Jardin 31 Thai Van Lung. ☎08/3825 8465. Excellent French food at very reasonable prices served in a pleasant garden setting. Very popular so advance booking is advisable. 11am–2pm & 6–11pm.

Le Mekong 57 Dong Du. This established French favourite still draws the crowds with tempting French cuisine such as roasted duck with orange and pepper sauce and hot chocolate soufflé with Grand Marnier; set menus from around $15. Guitarists meander between the tables during dinner. 11am–2pm & 5–10pm.

Lemongrass 4 Nguyen Thiep. Traditional upmarket establishment, where the highly rated Vietnamese food is eaten to the strains of serenading players during dinner. 11am–2pm & 5–10pm.

EATING AND DRINKING: CENTRAL HO CHI MINH

0   150 m

US Consulate

Notre Dame Cathedral

Reunification Palace

Ho Chi Minh City Museum

LAM SON SQUARE

Ben Thanh Market

MEI LINH SQUARE

Statue of Tran Hung Dao

Saigon River

Fine Art Museum

Passenger Quay (Bach Dang Wharf)

RESTAURANTS			
Al Fresco's	36	Mali Thai	39
Amigo	67	Mandarine	7
Ashoka	8	Miss Saigon	37
Augustin's	46	Mogambo	73
Au Parc	16	Nam Giao	60
Bi Bi	15	Nam Kha	52
Blue Ginger	76	Ngon	27
Bun Ta	28	Pho 24	47
Chu	19	Pho 2000	72
Ciao Café	43 & 63	Refinery	21
Cung Dinh	38	Restaurant 13	59
Dong Du	42	Santa Lucia	68
Gartenstadt	51	Seoul House	71
Givral	32	Skewers	14
Hoi An	6	Sushi Bar	3
Jaspa's	61	Tandoor	22
La Fourchette	58	Temple Club	70
Le Jardin	9	Tin Nghia	74
Le Mekong	42	Underground	55
Lemongrass	40	Vietnam House	48
Liberty	45	Warda	54
		Wrap & Roll	23

PUBS, BARS & CLUBS	
17 Saloon	75
Apocolypse Now	24
Bia Hoi – Bia Chai	25
Blue Gekko	10
Bop Club	13
Café Latin	35
Cage	18
Crystal Club	66
Fashion TV	65
Ice Blue	49
La Habana	17
Le Caprice	30
Liquid	2
Maxim's	20
O'Briens Factory	69
Pacharan	26
Panorama	1
Q Bar	33
Qing	41
Rooftop Garden	38
Saigon-Saigon Rooftop Bar	34

Sax n' Art	57
Sheridan's Irish House	11
Vascos	21
Wild Horse	12

CAFÉS	
Fanny's Ice Cream	64
Gloria Jean's	44
Java Coffee Bar	31
Kem Bach Dang	50 & 53
La Dolce Vita Bar	29
La Fenetre Soleil	56
Napoli Café	4
On the 6	62
Sao Café	5

Liberty 80 Dong Khoi. Popular place – with musicians playing romantic tunes from 7– 9.30pm – which serves well-prepared Vietnamese dishes. 10am–midnight.

Mali Thai 37 Dong Du. Most central of the few Thai restaurants in town, with spicy curries and *tom yam* soup that are sure to bring tears to your eyes. Set lunches under $4. 11am–10pm.

Mandarine 11a Ngo Van Nam ☎08/3822 9783. This established upmarket restaurant, beautifully decorated in traditional Vietnamese style, serves well-prepared Vietnamese standards. It's not cheap, though a range of set menus starts from $30. Live traditional music in evenings; reservations essential. 11.30am–2pm & 5–10pm.

Miss Saigon 86 Le Thanh Ton. This establishment offers reasonably priced Vietnamese and seafood specialities in a pleasant garden restaurant backing onto the grounds of the Ho Chi Minh City Museum. Noon–11pm.

Mogambo 50 Pasteur. Fish and chips, bangers and mash and big burgers are the attractions of this small but cosy place. 10am–10.30pm.

Nam Giao 136/15 Le Thanh Ton. Excellent Hué food served in this hugely popular but simple place tucked away down an alley behind Ben Thanh Market. 7.45am–10pm.

Nam Kha 46–50 Dong Khoi ☎08/823 8309. Probably Dong Khoi's swankiest spot to eat, with a sunken pond bordered by columns. Emphasis is on Imperial cuisine, and customers are made to feel special. Main dishes cost around $15–25. 10.30am–2pm & 5.30–10pm.

Ngon 138 Nam Ky Khoi Nghia ☎08/3825 7179. An experience not to be missed – delicious regional specialities served in and around a delightful colonial building at very reasonable prices. It's extremely popular, so book or be prepared to wait for a table at peak eating times. 7am–11pm.

Pho 24 5 Nguyen Thiep. If the thought of eating from a street stall makes you shudder, sample your first bowl of pho, the nation's signature dish, in this spotless café. It has several other branches near the centre, including 89 Mac Thi Buoi and the third floor of Diamond Plaza. 6.30am–10pm.

Refinery 74/7c. This cute little bistro set back from busy Hai Ba Trung has a relaxing vibe and serves an appealing range of dishes such as barbecued lamb ($12) as well as beers and cocktails. Occasional live music in the evenings. 10am–late.

Restaurant 13 15 Ngo Duc Ke. Simple but clean and air-conditioned spot which serves some of the cheapest food downtown – a seafood or meat and rice dish will set you back around $3, and the beers are relatively cheap too. 6.30am–11.30pm.

Santa Lucia 14 Nguyen Hué. Classic and stylish Italian venue, serving traditional pizzas and pasta; two can dine for around $25. 9.30am–11pm.

Seoul House 37 Ngo Duc Ke. *Bulgogi* (marinated beef, barbecued at the table), pork with *kimchi* (vegetables in chilli sauce) and other good-value, authentic Korean dishes, can be eaten sitting on the floor or, if you prefer, Western-style in utilitarian but friendly surroundings. 7am–10pm.

Skewers 9a Thai Van Lung. Mediterranean cuisine using simple and healthy ingredients. Try the pan-fried salmon with nicoise salad ($15). 11am–2pm & 5–10pm.

Sushi Bar 2 Le Thanh Ton. Highly rated sushi or sashimi mix for around $16, plus Japanese beer and sake. Delivery service too. 10am–11.30pm.

Tandoor 74/6 Hai Ba Trung. An excellent range of Indian dishes, from biriyani to vindaloo, with several vegetarian options, in a convenient central location. Set lunches from around $6. 10am–11pm.

Temple Club 29 Ton That Thiep. Excellent Vietnamese food at around $20 a dish is served in a wonderful, relaxed atmosphere with tasteful decor. There's also a comfy lounge bar out back. 11.30am–10.30pm.

Underground Basement of Lucky Plaza, 69 Dong Khoi. Better known as a night spot (see "Bars and pubs"), it also turns out some of the tastiest and most imaginative Western food in town. Try the succulent New Zealand grilled steaks, as thick as your fist, for around $12.

Vietnam House 93–95 Dong Khoi. Occupying a splendid louvred colonial building, this is a cracking introduction to Vietnamese food, featuring staff in traditional garb. There's a pianist on the ground floor and traditional folk music upstairs; set lunches and dinners from $13. 10am–10pm.

Warda 71/7 Mac Thi Buoi. Middle-eastern dishes such as kefta kebab and duck with apricot tajine for around $10, with shisha pipes on hand as well. 11am–midnight.

Wrap & Roll 62 Hai Ba Trung. Handy outlet of a chain doing for spring rolls what *Pho 24* does for pho – serving street food in a sanitized, a/c environment. Choose from a host of ingredients, peel off a rice wrapper and get rolling. 10am–11pm.

De Tham and around

The following are all marked on the map opposite, except Ngoc Suong, on p.83, and Tin Nghia and Pho 2000 on p.109.

Akbar Ali 240 Bui Ven. Delicious Indian food served up in a simple, shophouse setting, where you can get a meal and beer for around $5. Try the Chicken Jalfrezi. 10am–11pm.

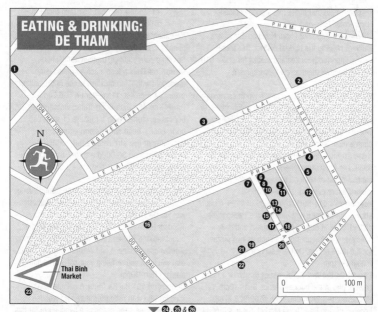

EATING & DRINKING:
DE THAM

N

Thai Binh
Market

0   100 m

▼ ㉔, ㉕ & ㉖

RESTAURANTS, CAFÉS & BARS							
Akbar Ali	26	Coriander	24	Good Morning Vietnam	17	Milwaukee	16
Allez Boo	7	Cyclo Bar	4	Highlands Coffee	6	Minh Duc	1
Asian Kitchen	9	Dinh Y	23	Kim Café	8	Pepperoni's	22
Bia Hoi bar	21	Dynasty	2	Lac Thien	25	Pho 94	19
Café Sinh To	15	Eden Bar	14	Le Pub	12	Sasa Café	13
Cappuccino	10	Go 2	20	Lucky Café	18	Sawasdee	3
				Margherita	5	Zen	11

Allez Boo 195 Pham Ngu Lao. It may be better known as a watering hole (see "Bars and pubs"), but this place also turns out very acceptable Vietnamese, Thai and Western dishes at about $5 each. 6am–late.

Asian Kitchen 185/22 Pham Ngu Lao. Tucked away down the alley east of De Tham, this laidback place features well-priced Vietnamese, Japanese and vegetarian dishes. 7am–midnight.

Cappuccino 258 De Tham ☏08/3887 5701. Serves up good pizzas at around $5 as well as reasonable Mexican and Vietnamese fare and wines by the glass too. There's another branch at 86 Bui Ven, and delivery service too. 6am–11.30pm.

Coriander 185 Bui Ven. Great Thai food at reasonable prices. 7am–11pm.

Dinh Y 171B Cong Quynh. Cheap but tasty vegetarian food prepared by Cao Dai adherents in a convenient location by Thai Binh market. 6.30am–9pm.

Dynasty *New World Hotel*, 76 Le Lai. Overlooking the lobby of the hotel. The noise may irritate but there's no faulting the elegant decor (porcelain and

bonsai), nor the splendid food, featuring delicious *dim sum* every lunchtime. Set menus start at around $20 and two can dine well for $30, but the sky's the limit if you plump for delicacies like bird's-nest soup or shark's fin. 11am–2pm & 6–10pm.

Good Morning Vietnam 197 De Tham. Part of an Italian-run chain of restaurants that serves dependably good pizza and pasta in a cosy environment. 9am–midnight.

Kim Café 268 De Tham. Besides breakfasts and veggie meals galore, there's guacamole, garlic bread, mashed potatoes and a fantastic chicken curry ($4). 7am–late.

Lac Thien 207 Bui Vien. An opportunity to try Hué Imperial food at this unassuming, reasonably priced restaurant. 7am–11pm.

Lucky Café 224 De Tham. A choice of Western, Thai or Japanese food in this popular, a/c restaurant. Sports on satellite TV too. 7am–late.

Margherita 175/1 Pham Ngu Lao. Some of the cheapest and tastiest pizzas and pasta dishes in town ($3–4), not to mention the burritos and shepherd's pie that make this a good choice for cheap eats. 7am–midnight.

Milwaukee 275–279 Pham Ngu Lao. Bringing a touch of class to the budget district, this place serves imported New Zealand steaks for under $10 in an attractive, plant-strewn environment. 7am–midnight.

Minh Duc 100 Ton That Tung. It's worth escaping the tourist enclave around De Tham at lunchtime to join the scrum of locals at this point-and-eat place, where great food is served up for a few thousand dong a dish. 6am–9pm.

Ngoc Suong 106 Suong Nguyet Anh ☏08/3925 6939. The most atmospheric branch of this hugely popular chain of seafood restaurants, drawing big crowds every evening. 10am–10.30pm.

Pepperoni's 111 Bui Ven ☏08/3920 4989. A cut above your average restaurant in the backpacker district, serving pizzas, pasta, steaks and daily specials, with frequent offers such as two pizzas for the price of one. Delivery service too. 8.30am–11pm.

Pho 94 94 Bui Ven. Reliable spot to savour a tasty bowl of pho in the budget district. 6am–10pm.

Pho 2000 1–3 Phan Chu Trinh ☏08/822 2788. Located next to Ben Thanh Market. Clean surroundings and big bowls of delicious noodle soup and other Vietnamese staples for around $2. 6.30am–11pm.

Sasa Café 242 De Tham. Not exactly gourmet food, but it has a huge menu of international dishes at cheap prices, with internet access upstairs. 6.30am–midnight.

Sawasdee 102–104 Le Lai. Authentic Thai food in this classy restaurant just a few steps away from the budget district. Relaxing ambience, friendly staff and yummy curries at around $5–8. 10am–11pm.

Tin Nghia 9 Tran Hung Dao. Mushrooms and tofu provide the backbone to the inventive menu in this friendly vegetarian restaurant. 7am–2pm & 4–8.30pm.

Zen 185/30 Pham Ngu Lao. One of the few really authentic vegetarian options around De Tham. Cheap and tasty dishes such as burritos, wild red rice and Chinese mushrooms; delicious fruit shakes too. 6.30am–10.30pm.

Greater Ho Chi Minh City

The following are all marked on the map on pp.82–83.

An Vien 178a Hai Ba Trung. Tucked away from the main road, this place is extremely intimate, with many different alcoves and corners on three floors, all sumptuously decorated, and with high-quality food to match. 11am–11pm.

Au Manoir de Khai 251 Dien Bien Phu ☏08/3930 3394. This is the nearest you're ever likely to get to feeling like a colonial of consequence, though the experience isn't cheap. Stunning surroundings, tranquil atmosphere, sensational French food, such as grilled lamb tenderloin with Dijon mustard sauce ($29), and an extensive wine list. 11am–2pm & 6–9.30pm.

Banh Xeo 46a Dinh Cong Trang. Vietnamese pancakes, stuffed with a mixture of shrimps, pork, beans, bean sprouts and egg are the speciality at this streetside eatery off Hai Ba Trung. At around 30,000đ a throw, they'll fill you up for most of the day, and there's also an English menu. 9am–9pm.

Café Central 4th floor, 18 An Duong Vuong. Located in district 5 a couple of kilometres west of De Tham (in the same building as the *Windsor Plaza Hotel*). Fantastic lunch and dinner buffet (around $10 and $20 respectively), featuring Vietnamese, Japanese and Western culinary treats that will have you re-filling your plate time and again. 11am–10pm

Camargue 191 Hai Ba Trung. A colonial-style modern villa with rattan furniture and wooden ceiling fans, sets the scene of a bygone era for this expensive French restaurant. It's set back from the main road down a narrow lane. 6–11pm.

Cha Ca Hanoi 5a Tran Nhat Duat ☏08/3848 4240. Very smart cafe-style restaurant serving a variety of tasty Hanoi specialities, including grilled, marinated fish with noodles. 11am–2pm & 4–10pm.

Orientica *Equatorial Hotel*, 242 Tran Binh Trong, District 5. Super-stylish restaurant on the second floor of the *Equatorial*, specializing in seafood prepared in a variety of ways, plus steaks and hotpots. Main dishes cost between $15–30. 11.30am–2.30pm & 6.30–10.30pm.

Pho Binh 7 Ly Chinh Thang. A must-see for all war buffs: a wartime safe house for Communists, it was from here that the command was given to kick off the 1968 Tet Offensive. Don't make the trip for the soup alone, though. 6am–10pm.

Pho Hoa 260c Pasteur. High-quality pho shops proliferate along Pasteur, none better than *Pho Hoa*. On offer are huge bowlfuls of soup complemented with chunks of chicken or beef and plenty of fresh greens on the tables to add yourself. You'll pay more than the usual but it's well worth it. 6am–midnight.

Spice 27c Le Quy Don ☏08/3930 7873. Stylishly furnished Thai restaurant with menu that looks like a magazine, featuring classics like *tom yam* and *som tam*, but also some unusual dishes such as "volcano chicken". 11am–2pm & 5.30–10.30pm.

Buying your own food: markets and supermarkets

With baguettes, cheese and fruit in such abundant supply in Vietnam, making up a picnic is easy. All the basics can be found at any of the city's **markets**, though if you're homesick for peanut butter, Vegemite or other such exotica, you'll need to head for a specialist **supermarket** or **provisions store**.

Markets

The handiest market for De Tham is **Thai Binh Market**, down at the southwestern end of Pham Ngu Lao. Just about as near, and larger, is **Ben Thanh Market** (see p.98), the central market in the city centre. Cho Lon is served by **Binh Tay Market** (see p.102) on its southwestern border and by **An Dong Market**, northeast of it at the junction of Tran Phu and An Duong Vuong.

Supermarkets and provisions stores

Annam Gourmet Shop 16–18 Hai Ba Trung. Huge deli located downtown, pandering to the whims of expats and visitors alike.

Co-op Mart 189c Cong Quynh. Huge Western-style supermarket within easy walking distance of De Tham, selling clothes, toys, household goods, cosmetics and a good selection of Western foods. There's also a large branch at 168 Nguyen Dinh Chieu.

Minimart 250 De Tham. Snacks, drinks and basic toiletries on sale in the budget district.

Parkson Plaza 39–45 Le Thanh Ton. On the fourth floor of this shopping mall is a supermarket selling a good range of imported goods.

Nhu Lan Bakery 66–68 Ham Nghi. Famed bakery selling bread, croissants and cakes.

Thuong Xa Supermarket 135 Nguyen Hué. On the first floor of this centrally located shopping plaza, this large supermarket sells, amongst other things, Western tinned and dairy products.

Veggy's 15 Thai Van Lung. Well-stocked with imported meats, cheeses and cereals, this place is a popular shopping spot for local expats.

Cafés, ice cream and desserts

Café culture, introduced by the French, is still very much alive in Ho Chi Minh City, and there are numerous places at which to round dinner off with an ice cream, crêpe or sundae. Earlier in the day, the same venues offer the chance to linger over a coffee and watch the world go by.

The following are all marked on the map on p.109 except Café Sinh To and Highlands Coffee on p.111.

Café Sinh To 231 De Tham. A no-frills but remarkably good-value juice bar bang in the centre of De Tham. Serves sandwiches too. 6am–10pm.

Fanny's Ice Cream 29–31 Ton Thap Thiep. With its mustard-coloured walls, wrought-iron chairs and magazines to read, this is an ideal spot to enjoy a peach melba or maybe even a cocktail. 8am–11pm.

Gloria Jean's 131 Dong Khoi. Formerly known as *Brodard's*, this popular spot on Dong Khoi serves coffee, sandwiches and pastries. 7am–11pm.

Highlands Coffee 187 Pham Ngu Lao. Located at the hectic junction of De Tham and Pham Ngu Lao, this cool, a/c place has comfy armchairs and a flashy internet terminal, and serves cakes, sandwiches, smoothies and coffee. 7.30am–11pm.

Java Coffee Bar 38–42 Dong Du. Cosy coffee bar in the heart of the downtown area, serving a few main dishes plus sandwiches and smoothies. 7.30am–11.30pm.

Kem Bach Dang 26 & 28 Le Loi. Twin open-fronted ice-cream parlours, revered for extravagant creations, some of which feature fruits from Da Lat; unfortunately, it's a magnet for beggars who periodically stray inside. 9am–midnight.

La Dolce Vita Bar *Hotel Continental*, 132–134 Dong Khoi. Café, restaurant, bar and *gelateria* rolled into one, set in the refined courtyard surroundings of this Saigon institution. 7am–10pm.

La Fenetre Soleil 1st floor, 135 Le Thanh Ton (entrance at 125 Nam Ky Khoi Nghia). Don't be put off by the dingy stairwell that leads up to this quirky café. An odd collection of chairs and tables, sofas and even a four-poster bed give the place a wonderfully offbeat feel. Order coffee or tea, a juice or a shake, a pudding or a jelly, and kick back. Functions as a bar (see "Bars and pubs", below) in the evening. 11.30am–midnight.

Napoli Café 7 Pham Ngoc Thach. Terracotta tiles and al fresco tables breathe a rustic sigh through

the *Napoli*, a short stroll above the cathedral; choose from a modest selection of main dishes, cakes, pastries and sundaes or indulge in the *mangia e bevi* – a sensational blend of ice cream, orange juice and fresh fruit. 7.30am–11pm.

On the 6 6 Dong Khoi. Spacious and serene coffee lounge set among the boutiques on Dong Khoi, with a fine-dining restaurant upstairs. 8am–midnight.

Sao Café 5 Pham Ngoc Thach. If you're curious about how the well-off youth of the city spend their days, this is the place to find out. Enjoy ear-splitting Vietnamese pop music while sipping a coffee or cocktail. 7am–late.

Drinking, nightlife and entertainment

Ho Chi Minh City boasts a good range of nightlife, so there's no need to head back to your hotel once dinner is through, although an ongoing crackdown on late opening means you'll probably be tucked up in bed by midnight unless you're in the De Tham area. **Bars** and **pubs** abound, and an increasing number of them now feature live music to pull the crowds. It isn't unheard-of for big showbiz names from the West to make appearances, so check out the local press for details. Later at night, a number of **clubs** and **discos** get going, though they often have short lifespans unless they are under the protection of a major hotel.

The free monthly magazines *The Word* and *Asia Life* carry up-to-the-minute listings of the city's latest bars, plus the hottest new clubs and any more highbrow entertainment on offer.

Traditional entertainment

Few places cater for Westerners wanting an insight into Vietnamese culture, though there is the odd exception. About 8km north of the city, **Binh Quoi Village** (℡08/3556 5891, ⓦwww.binhquoiresort.com.vn) features Tuesday, Thursday and Saturday evening programmes of dinner followed by folk music and traditional dancing, organized by Saigontourist (tickets for meal and show around $25). For Western and Vietnamese **classical music**, ask the Conservatory of Music (℡08/3824 3774) at 112 Nguyen Du about the HCMC Youth Chamber Music Club's performances, which can be scheduled on demand. It's also worth checking out what's on at Lam Son Square's Municipal Theatre (℡08/3829 9976), which frequently hosts fashion shows, traditional **drama** and **dance**. Water puppetry isn't as big in Ho Chi Minh City as it is in Hanoi, though if you aren't going to the north you might want to attend one of the shows laid on at the History Museum, Le Duan (hourly 10am–4pm, except 1pm; $2).

Bars and pubs

Bars and pubs in Ho Chi Minh City range from hole-in-the-wall dives to elegant venues that would not be out of place in a European capital. The area around Dong Khoi is predictably well endowed, and another boozy enclave exists around Le Thanh Ton, Hai Ba Trung and Thi Sach, where a glut of places ranging from slick yuppie haunts to watering holes which hark back to the raunchy GI bars of the 1960s has developed to cater for expats renting apartments nearby. At the other end of the scale, all the cheap restaurants and cafés around De Tham turn their hand to drink at night – fine if you're willing to forego atmosphere in order to save a dollar or two on a beer, and great for meeting like-minded tourists. For more of a bar atmosphere, head for somewhere like *Allez-Boo* or *Cyclo Bar*.

For some years now, a police crackdown has led to the city being strangely silent after midnight, with the notable exception of several bars around De Tham, which seem to be spared the blitz. **Prices** vary wildly: a Saigon beer at a streetside café in De Tham will cost you less than $1, but you can multiply that by four or five in a more upmarket bar on Dong Khoi. One way to economize while downtown is to take advantage of early-evening **happy hours**, or check out the surprisingly cheap and tasty **bia hoi** (see box, p.117). Several of the pricier bars, such as *Saigon-Saigon*, *Le Caprice* and *Panorama*, offer sweeping **views** across the city, best enjoyed as the sun sets.

Central Ho Chi Minh City

The following are all marked on the map on p.109.

Blue Gekko 31 Ly Tu Trong. Expat hangout offering pub atmosphere with pool, darts and sports TV. Happy hour is 5–7.30pm, but at other times drinks are pricey. 5pm–late.

Café Latin 25 Dong Du. Trendy (and pricey) bar-restaurant with stylish metallic decor and designer furniture. Its international menu and screenings of worldwide sports and films makes this an expats' favourite. Latin music on Fri nights. 10am–midnight.

Fashion TV 21–27 Ton Thap Thiep. You'll have to dress up to look the part at this cavernous place on trendy Ton That Thiep. Wide range of cocktails and wines, plus several international dishes on the menu that looks like a fashion magazine. 10am–midnight.

Ice Blue 54 Dong Khoi. Traditional English pub-style bar, with a dartboard, a friendly atmosphere and a range of international beers; 4–8pm is happy hour. 4pm–late.

La Fenetre Soleil 1st floor, 135 Le Thanh Ton (entrance at 125 Nam Ky Khoi Nghia). Once you've solved the puzzle of how to enter this place, it's happily worth discovering. Functioning as a chill-out café (see opposite) during the day, this little gem turns its hand to mixing cocktails in the evenings. Wed is swing dancing night. 11.30am–midnight.

La Habana 6 Cao Ba Quat. A touch of Cuba in Saigon in the form of a cosy bar serving a good range of beers and cocktails as well as Spanish food and tapas. Good Latin music too. 11am–late.

Le Caprice 15th floor, Landmark Building, 5b Ton Duc Thang. A pricey and stylish restaurant, but it's worth splashing out on an expensive cocktail to enjoy the view along the river. 11am–2pm & 3–10.30pm.

O'Briens Factory 74 a2 Hai Ba Trung. *O'Briens Factory* isn't a world away from a smart London pub, and is popular with expats for its good atmosphere, well-stocked bar and comforting Western menu. Happy hour 3–7pm (except Sun). 11am–late.

Pacharan 97 Hai Ba Trung. Smart, three-floored Spanish place just behind the Municpal Theatre, serving tapas and a wide range of drinks. Live music some nights. 10am–late.

Panorama Level 32–33, Saigon Trade Centre, 37 Ton Duc Thang. An aptly named bar worth visiting for the view alone. Look down on the tiny Notre Dame Cathedral and *Caravelle Hotel*, and a sweeping bend in the Saigon River while enjoying a predictably high-priced drink. 9am–midnight.

Q Bar 7 Cong Tuong, Lam Son Square. Located under the Municipal Theatre, facing the *Caravelle Hotel*, this leading bar attracts the city's fashion-conscious to its stylish bars and alcoves. Cocktails around 90,000đ, beers around 50,000đ. 5pm–late.

Qing 31 Dong Du. Stylish wine bar just across from the *Sheraton* with relaxing ambience, several types of wine by the glass, fusion food and Asian tapas. 8am–late.

Rooftop Garden *Rex Hotel*, 141 Nguyen Hué. A drink amidst the fairy-lit topiary and clumsy model animals of the *Rex* terrace is still *de rigueur* on a trip to the city. 7am–late.

Saigon–Saigon Rooftop Bar *Caravelle Hotel*, 19 Lam Son Square. Romantic views of the city and nightly live music in a stylish ambience more than compensate for the pricey drinks list in this lofty (10th floor) hotel bar. Popular with local expats. 9am–midnight.

Sax n' Art 28 Le Loi. Slick jazz club with mellow sounds from various performers, neat decor and pricey drinks. 5pm–midnight.

Sheridan's Irish House 17/13 Le Thanh Ton. DJs spin tunes every night in this cosy bar which also has an extensive menu. 8am–late.

Underground Basement of Lucky Plaza, 69 Dong Khoi. The ideal location, along with 20,000đ happy-hour beers (9am–9pm), a pool table and a good range of Western food on the menu, makes this place perpetually busy. 9am–midnight.

Vascos 74/7d Hai Ba Trung. Live bands on Fri and DJs on Sat, plus a good range of food at this hip bar set back from the main road. 11am–midnight.

Wild Horse 8a1/d1 Thai Van Lung. Saloon-type place specializing in steaks and international dishes. Live music too. 10am–2pm & 4pm–midnight.

De Tham and around

The following are all marked on the map on p.111, except for 17 Saloon, on p.109.

17 Saloon 103A Pham Ngu Lao. Wild West-style bar occupying two floors near the budget hotel district. Its competent Filipino band draws a mixed and enthusiastic audience. 7pm–1am.

Allez–Boo 187 Pham Ngu Lao. Bamboo and thatch decor, loud music, great food (see p.111) and a good selection of cocktails make this place hugely popular and it's heaving most nights. Open 24hr.

Cyclo Bar 163 Pham Ngu Lao. This congenial place with dartboard and pool table offers draught beer and cocktails as well as comfort food such as bangers and mash and a roast on Sun. Three floors and sports on TV. 9am–late.

Eden 236 De Tham. Dim-lit and noisy, popular spot where you can find a drink and someone to talk to almost 24hr a day. 6am–late.

Go 2 187 De Tham. The winning formula from the owners of *Allez Boo* is packing them in at this large, two-storey bar and restaurant on the corner of Bui Ven. 7am–late.

Le Pub 175/22 Pham Ngu Lao. Tucked away down a lane off Pham Ngu Lao, this place stands out for its attractive decor, cheap beer, good selection of food and cool sounds played by the resident DJ. 7am–late.

Discos and clubs

Ho Chi Minh City's **disco and club scene** has been floundering for the last few years as midnight closing is enforced throughout the city. Apart from regular discos, there are more traditional nightclubs, where the practice of employing hostesses in slit gowns is still prevalent. In addition, some establishments continue to cater for the locals' love of **ballroom dancing** – a tradition

▲ Sax 'n Art

Bia hoi bars

If you can't afford the price of a bottle of Saigon beer, you might try a **bia hoi bar**, where locals glug cheap local draught beer at around 5000đ a litre. These spit-and-sawdust bars tend to open in the morning and close early in the evening, though some stay open later. They crop up all over the city, but the two listed below are convenient for Dong Khoi and De Tham.

Bia Hoi – Bia Chai 20 Dong Du. See map, p.109. If the restaurants and bars around Dong Khoi seem too expensive, duck in here and drown your sorrows in a jug of the local special.

Bia Hoi Bar 102 Bui Ven. See map, p.111. Tiny place but an excellent spot to watch the world wander by while chilling out with a cool beer.

which is fading out as MTV turns local youngsters on to Viet pop and the latest Western sounds. Most clubs and discos levy a **cover charge** (normally $4–5), though some just charge higher prices for drinks. Again, see local listings magazines for the hottest new clubs. All the clubs below are marked on the map on p.109, except *America* on p.82.

America 3rd Floor, 18 An Duong Vuong, District 5. Located in the same building as the *Windsor Hotel*, this swish disco attracts an upmarket clientele with its big dance floor, nightly DJs and impressive light show. 7pm–1am.

Apocalypse Now 2c Thi Sach. A pioneer of the city's nightlife scene, always rowdy and sweaty at weekends with an eclectic crowd, though can be rather dull during the week. Dark and cavernous, with two dance floors and a compact garden. 7pm–late.

Bop Club 8a1/d1 Thai Van Lung. Second-floor bar with small dance floor and dance music. 5pm–1am.

Cage 3a Ton Duc Thang. The city's newest and hippest nightclub is located in a converted warehouse in an alley down near the river, and

features live bands and DJs with special events at weekends. 6pm–1am.

Crystal Club 138 Ton That Dam. This downtown disco gets packed with locals at weekends but is often quiet in the week. 9pm–1am.

Liberty 80 Dong Khoi. A largely Vietnamese crowd waltzes along to the smoochy live music in this dark upstairs club above the smart restaurant (see p.108); disco music takes over later. 8.30pm–late.

Liquid 104 Hai Ba Trung. Western and local pop both feature at this venue that draws a lively local crowd. 8pm–late.

Maxim's 13–17 Dong Khoi. Sedate dancing at this classic downtown location. The dance hall is upstairs from the restaurant of the same name 8pm–midnight.

Markets and shopping

Ho Chi Minh City can be a dangerous place to go **shopping**, as you'll likely buy more than you intended once you see the prices. Paintings on rice paper, silk *ao dai*, lacquerware, embroidered cloth, musical instruments and ethnic garments are all popular gifts and souvenirs, as are **curios** such as opium pipes, antique watches, French colonial stamps and banknotes, and US Army-issue cigarette lighters, while the cheapest items are the ubiquitous T-shirts and conical hats. Visitors interested in Vietnam's history will find a wealth of copied **books** on the subject, sold in tourist areas by wandering vendors with a metre-high stack on their hip. Sadly the range of English-language books available in regular bookshops is very limited. For cheap and cheerful **souvenirs**, head for Ben Thanh Market, Le Loi or De Tham; for something precious and pricey, browse the upmarket boutiques along Dong Khoi and its tentacles, such as Dong Du and Mac Thi Buoi. **Bargaining** is an essential skill to cultivate if you're going to be doing much shopping – see Basics, box on p.65, for some tips.

Shopping malls attract curious crowds with their glitz and glamour; some offer distractions other than shopping in the form of cinemas and bowling alleys. The local **markets** are also well worth checking out, both as a source of bargains and as a window on Vietnamese culture. The biggest is **Ben Thanh Market** (see p.98), at the junction of Tran Hung Dao, Le Loi and Ham Nghi, which has a huge variety of cheap clothes (*ao dai* under $30) and all kinds of souvenirs like chopstick sets and carved seals. **Dan Sinh Market**, 104 Yersin (p.99), has a section specializing in army surplus, both American and Vietnamese. For other smaller souvenirs, check out the shops along Le Loi and Dong Khoi for old **coins**, **stamps**, notes and **greetings cards** featuring typical Vietnamese scenes hand-painted onto silk. **Antiques and curios** are available in several stores along Le Cong Kieu (see p.199), while intriguing **model ships** are sold on Cao Ba Quat, north of the Municipal Theatre, just east of the *Caravelle Hotel*.

Generally speaking, shops **open** daily 10am to dusk, while larger stores often stay open beyond 8pm.

Department stores and shopping malls

An Dong Plaza 18 An Duong Vuong, District 5. Occupying three floors below the *Windsor Plaza Hotel* and infrequently visited by tourists, this place has several outlets selling jewellery, clothes and handicrafts.

Diamond Plaza 34 Le Duan. Probably the city's most diverse mall, featuring department store, supermarket, fitness centre, hospital, swimming pool, bowling alley, cinemas and serviced apartments.

Parkson Department Store 39–45 Le Thanh Ton. Upmarket department store in the heart of the hotel district, selling expensive handicrafts, jewellery and cosmetics among other things. There are other branches at Hung Vuong Plaza (District 5) and beside the airport.

Saigon Centre 65 Le Loi. Cafés, souvenir shops, boutiques, small department store and supermarket in convenient location between downtown and budgetsville.

Thuong Xa Tax Shopping 135 Nguyen Hué. Known locally as the Russian Market and located opposite the *Rex*, this is a sprawling department store selling electronic goods, cameras, watches, pirate cassettes and videos, jewellery, leather goods and lacquerware.

Zen Plaza 54–56 Nguyen Trai. Black and white eight-storey shopping complex, packed with cosmetics, toys, electrical and household goods and video games. A cafeteria on the top floor has stunning views of the city.

Books, newspapers and magazines

Bookazine 28 Dong Khoi. Stocks a range of newspapers and magazines, as well as detailed maps of Vietnamese provinces and an intriguing hotch-potch of second-hand books, some of which look like collectors' items.

Fahasa 40 Nguyen Hué, 185 Dong Khoi and 60 Le Loi. Probably the best-stocked bookshops in town, with a range of titles, including some novels, and magazines.

Lao Dong 104 Nguyen Hué, opposite the entrance to the Rex. Stocks a wide range of magazines and newspapers.

NV Tours 179 Pham Ngu Lao. A wide selection of second-hand books on sale, tucked away behind the tour desk.

Handicrafts, fabrics and antiques

A.M. Lacquerware 185 Pham Ngu Lao. Lacquerware, ceramic, stone, bamboo, shell and horn products at affordable prices.

Art Arcade 151 Dong Khoi. Paintings, lacquerware and ceramics, plus Buddha statues, old watches and trinkets.

Bich Lien 125 Dong Khoi. General souvenirs-cum-handicrafts, plus a good range of Tin Tin paintings on lacquer.

Khai Silk 81 Dong Khoi. One of several downtown outlets for the creations of one of the city's top designers, selling exclusive outfits at high prices.

Nhat Uyen 237 De Tham. Striking designs on bags, scarves, cushion covers and silks.

Nhu Y 257 De Tham. Tasteful pieces of lacquerware, Buddha images and reproduction art.

Phuong Tam 153 Dong Khoi. Tin Tin lacquerware, copies of old French advertisements, antique watches and handicrafts.

Saigon Kitsch 43 Ton That Thiep. Mao T-shirts, propaganda posters, gaudy tea trays and retro bags.

Sapa 223 De Tham & 7 Ton That Thiep. Attractive garments and artefacts from Vietnamese ethnic minority groups.

Song 76D Le Thanh Ton. Beautifully designed garments made with natural materials and organic dyes but big prices.

Tay Son 198 Vo Thi Sau. Frequented by tourist groups, since you can watch processes such as making lacquerware as well as browse their large warehouse of furniture, wooden carvings and lacquered art.

Paintings

Apricot Gallery 50–52 Mac Thi Buoi. One of the city's most exclusive galleries, with intriguing, original oils by local artists from $650 upwards.

Nam Phuong 105 Bui Vien. One of many artists making a living by reproducing classic images in the travellers' quarter; good work and reasonable prices.

Nguyen Thanh Gallery 53 Bui Ven. Original paintings and reproductions.

Van Gogh Art Gallery 114b Nguyen Hué. Reproductions of classic paintings.

Tailors

Chuong 270 Hai Ba Trung. A long-established and reliable tailor located a few blocks north of downtown.

Nhut Van 107 Bui Ven. Reports of good work by this tailor in the budget district.

T&V 39 Dong Du. Slightly more expensive than other places but worth it for the fresh and original designs.

Zakka 134 Pasteur. High-quality tailor, also sells divine ready-to-wear silk creations.

Listings

Airlines Air France, 130 Dong Khoi ☏08/3829 0981; British Airways, 170–172 Nam Ky Khoi Nghia ☏08/3930 2933; Cathay Pacific, ground floor, Sun Wah Tower, 115 Nguyen Hué ☏08/3822 3203; China Airlines, 132–134 Dong Khoi ☏08/3825 1388; China Southern Airlines, 52b Pham Hong Thai ☏08/3829 1172; Emirates, 170–172 Nam Ky Khoi Nghia ☏08/3930 2939; Garuda, 170–172 Nam Ky Khoi Nghia ☏08/3930 3033; Japan Air Lines, 88 Dong Khoi ☏08/3821 9098; Jetstar, 112 Hong Ha, Tan Binh District ☏08/3955 0550; Lufthansa, 14th floor, Bitexco Building, 19–25 Nguyen Hué ☏08/3829 8529; Malaysia Airlines, 235 Dong Khoi ☏08/3829 2529; Philippine Airlines, 229 Dong Khoi ☏08/3822 2241; Qantas, PetroVietnam Tower, 1–5 Ton Duc Thang ☏08/3827 3888; Singapore Airlines, Saigon Tower, 29 Le Duan ☏08/3823 1588; Thai Airways, 29 Le Duan ☏08/3822 3365; United Airlines, 17 Le Duan ☏08/3823 4755; Vietnam Airlines, 116 Nguyen Hué ☏08/3832 0320.

Banks and exchange Most banks now have ATMs and exchange cash or traveller's cheques. Sacombank at 211–213 Pham Ngu Lao (Mon–Fri 7.30–11.30am & 1–4.30pm, Sat 7.30–11am) is convenient for those staying around Pham Ngu Lao. Otherwise, foreign exchange kiosks on Nguyen Hué and Le Loi have extended daily opening times. Also, most gold and jewellery shops will exchange dollars for dong at a slightly better rate than the bank.

Bike and motorbike rental Most rental operations are in Pham Ngu Lao and De Tham, such as Mrs Chin at 211 Pham Ngu Lao (☏0903 939126);

average daily costs are $1–2 for a bicycle and $5–6 for a motorbike.

Car and minibus rental Car and minibus rental with driver can be arranged through tour agents (see box, p.86), and Budget have now opened an office at Tan Son Nhat Airport (☏08/3930 1118, ⓦwww.budget.com.vn), though self-drive is still not an option, as yet.

Cinema Diamond Cinema complex on the 13th floor of Diamond Plaza (see opposite; ☏08/3822 7897); Galaxy Cinema, 116 Nguyen Du (☏08/3822 8533); Bobby Brewer's Movie Lounge, 45 Bui Ven (☏08/3610 2220, ⓦwww.bobbybrewers.com).

Consulates Australia, Landmark Building, 5b Ton Duc Thanh ☏08/3829 6035; Cambodia, 41 Phung Khac Khoan ☏08/3829 2751; Canada, 235 Dong Khoi ☏08/3854 5025; China, 39 Nguyen Thi Minh Khai ☏08/3829 2457; Indonesia, 18 Phung Khac Khoan ☏08/3825 1888; Laos, 93 Pasteur ☏08/3829 7667; Malaysia, 2 Ngo Duc Ke ☏08/3829 9023; New Zealand, 41 Nguyen Thi Minh Khai ☏08/3822 6907; Singapore, Saigon Centre, 65 Le Loi ☏08/3822 5173; Thailand, 77 Tran Quoc Thao ☏08/3932 7637; UK (& British Council), 25 Le Duan ☏08/3829 8433; US, 4 Le Duan ☏08/3822 9433.

Courier services DHL, 4 Phan Thuc Duyen, Tan Binh District ☏08/3844 6203; FedEx, 146 Pasteur, close to the Rex Hotel ☏08/3829 0995.

Dentists Grand Dentistry, 183 Le Thanh Ton (☏08/3821 9446), is an international-standard dental clinic. Also conveniently situated in the centre is the Family Dental Practice HCMC

(☏08/3822 4771) on the ground floor of Diamond Plaza. The International SOS Dental Clinic (☏08/3829 8520) at 65 Nguyen Du has a 24hr emergency centre.

Emergencies Dial ☏113 for the police, ☏114 in case of fire or ☏115 for an ambulance; if possible, get a Vietnamese speaker to call on your behalf.

Hairdressers Trong, 143 Bui Ven. Haircut, highlights, manicure, pedicure, etc.

Hospitals and clinics International SOS Clinic, 65 Nguyen Du (☏08/3829 8424), has international doctors, can arrange emergency evacuation and has a 24hr emergency service (☏08/3829 8520). Columbia Saigon, 8 Alexandrae De Rhodes (☏08/3823 8888), and Columbia Gia Dinh at 1 No Trang Long, Binh Thanh (☏08/3803 0678), have multinational doctors with 24hr emergency cover and evacuation. HCM City Family Medical Practice, Diamond Plaza, 34 Le Duan (☏08/3822 7848), is an international clinic with multinational doctors and specialist knowledge of vaccinations, as well as 24hr emergency cover and evacuation. International Medical Centre, 1 Han Thuyen (☏08/3827 2366), is a French-run, non-profit, 24hr hospitalization centre with in-patient wards, intensive care and emergency surgery. Cho Lon's Cho Ray Hospital, at 201 Nguyen Chi Thanh (☏08/3855 4137) has an out-patients' room for foreigners and a foreigners' ward. The Hospital of Traditional Medicine, 187 Nam Ky Khoi Nghia (☏08/3932 6579), has acupuncture treatment.

Internet access Most hotels now provide free wi-fi or internet access, but there are still a few shops offering internet access for around 6–8,000đ an hour, such as at 273 Pham Ngu Lao.

Laundry Most hotels and guesthouses will wash clothes for you, but rates vary wildly so check first; upmarket hotels can do dry-cleaning; there are also a number of laundry and dry-clean operators around Pham Ngu Lao such as at 203 Bui Vien, where rates are 5,000đ per kilo.

Massage To ease aches and pains, head for the Traditional Vietnamese Massage Institute at 185

Moving on from Ho Chi Minh City

For addresses and telephone numbers of airlines and foreign consulates in Ho Chi Minh City, see "Listings", p.119.

By plane

The easiest way to get to Tan Son Nhat is by taxi ($5–6; see p.84). If you don't have much baggage, you could consider hopping on an xe om (around $3–4), or taking the #152 bus, which stops on Dong Khoi and Pham Ngu Lao. **Flight enquiries** should be made at the office of the relevant carrier (see "Airlines", p.119).

By train

Vietnamese trains are oversubscribed, so book as far ahead as possible – particularly for a sleeping berth (see p.40 for details). Most tour operators, as well as some guesthouses and hotels can reserve tickets for a small fee. The official agent for the railways is Saigon Railways Tourist Service Company, 275c Pham Ngu Lao (☏08/3836 7640), which has computerized reservations and doesn't charge any extra commission. Otherwise, go along in person to the ticket office at the main station, Ga Saigon (daily 7.30–11.30am & 1.30–4.30pm; ☏08/3846 6528) for reservations and timetables.

By bus

To the Mekong Delta The easiest way of making a journey round the delta is to sign up for a tour (see tour agents box on p.86). If you want to strike out alone, make your way to **Mien Tay bus station**, where several buses a day leave for all the delta's major towns.

North of HCMC Buses to all points north depart from Xo Viet Nghe Tinh's **Mien Dong bus station**. Shuttle buses run from **Ben Thanh bus station** to Mien Dong (#26), Mien Tay (#2) and Cho Lon (#1).

By open–tour bus

Many of the tour operators concentrated around De Tham sell tickets for **open-tour buses** that criss-cross the country. One-way tickets from Ho Chi Minh

Cong Quynh (☎08/3839 6697; 9am–9pm), where blind masseurs and masseuses will pummel you for 40,000đ/hr (fan room) or 50,000đ/hr (a/c).

Pharmacies There are several pharmacies in and around the De Tham area, such as 65 Bui Vien. Downtown is a large pharmacy at 197–199 Dong Khoi, while the one at 389 Hai Ba Trung is reputed to be the best stocked in the city.

Police Main police station is at 73 Yersin ☎08/3829 7073. You must first go to the police station in the ward where the crime took place to obtain an initial report before coming here; try to avoid lunchtime visits, as there's likely to be nobody on duty.

Post offices The GPO (daily 6am–10pm) is beside the cathedral at the head of Dong Khoi; poste restante is kept here. There are several sub post offices around town, such as one at 137 Cong Quynh (daily 7.30am–10pm).

Spas If you need to pamper yourself, check out ⓦwww.spasvietnam.com for a complete listing of the city's many spas and treatments on offer.

Sports Many upmarket hotels have excellent sport and leisure facilities which non-residents can generally use – at a price – but it's wise to check ahead first. The Lan Anh Country Club, 291 Cach Mang Thang (☎08/3862 7144), has international-standard tennis courts, squash courts and a gym. There are also tennis courts at the Workers' Club, in the northern corner of the Cong Vien Van Hoa Park, on Nguyen Thi Minh Khai. California Wow has a branch of its fitness centres at the Queen Ann Building, 28–32 La Lai (☎08/6222 0355). For runners and walkers, the Hash House Harriers (ⓦwww.saigonh3.com) meet every Sun at the *Caravelle Hotel* at 2.30pm. For golf, the Vietnam Golf and Country Club, Long Thanh My Village, District 9 (☎08/3733 0126), has two high-quality courses and a driving range.

Swimming There are inexpensive but extremely busy pools at the Workers' Club, Cong Vien Van Hoa Park, and at Lam Son, 242 Tran Binh Trong. For a little more peace and quiet, try the relatively cheap pool favoured by expats at the Lan Anh Country

to Hanoi (around $35) or Hué (about $24) allow you to break your journey at various points along the way, including Da Lat and Nha Trang. Tickets for shorter, in-between trips are also available, such as Ho Chi Minh City to: Nha Trang ($9); Da Lat ($8) and Hoi An ($20). There are also daily departures to Phnom Penh in Cambodia ($14). Tickets, information and departing buses, which leave daily in the early morning or evening, can be found at the various companies' offices around De Tham and Pham Ngu Lao.

By boat

Hydrofoils to Vung Tau make several daily departures from the **Passenger Quay of Ho Chi Minh City** (Bach Dang Wharf), opposite the end of Ham Nghi at 2 Ton Duc Thang. For tickets ($10) and further information, contact the Vina Express booth at the jetty (daily 6.30–11am & 1.30–4.30pm; ☎08/3829 7892). There's also a daily **express boat** from here to **Can Tho** operated by Thanh Nhan (☎08/3914 7979; tickets 250,000đ), which usually leaves at 8am but call to check.

One of the most popular boat trips from Ho Chi Minh City is to **Phnom Penh**, with a stop-over in **Chau Doc** in the delta. Visas can be organized by tour agents, and if you book with a company like Delta Adventure Travel, you won't have to change boats half-way. Prices start at around $30 per person.

By organized tour

Tour agencies abound in Ho Chi Minh City and offer a range of itineraries, from one-day whistle-stop tours around the region to lengthy trips upcountry including accommodation. Operators like Delta Adventure Travel and TNK offer efficiently run and amazingly cheap tours to the Mekong Delta and the Cu Chi tunnels, while smaller, more personal set-ups like Sinhbalo Tours can custom-build a cycling or motorbike tour in many parts of the country. Most of the recommended tour operators listed on p.86 can lay on **tailor-made itineraries**, **private cars** and personal **guides** for you. See Basics, p.44, for provisos and tips on signing up for a tour in Vietnam.

Club (see Sports), or the more luxurious hotel pools at the *Park Hyatt, Renaissance and Sofitel* for a daily fee of between $5 and $10 (some include use of sauna and steam bath). Some shopping malls like Diamond Plaza also have pools.

Taxis Several companies operate in the city centre, but the most reliable are Mai Linh ☎08/3826 2626 and Vinasun ☎08/3827 2727.

Telephone services Several places, such as the post office at 137 Cong Quynh, offer phone services from which you can call the US or UK for under 20 cents a minute. There are IDD, fax and telex facilities at the GPO (see above) and numerous IDD telephone kiosks around De Tham;

otherwise, IDD calls can be made (more expensively) from most hotels.

Tour agents See box, p.86.

Visas Visa extensions and re-entry visas must be organized through an agent or tour operator; the process takes about four days and costs $25.

Water parks Dai The Gioi (Mon–Fri 8am–9pm, Sat & Sun 10am–6pm; 55,000đ, children 40,000đ) has pools and slides and is conveniently located at 600 Ham Tu in Cho Lon, while a little further north, the water park at Dam Sen (see p.107; Mon–Fri 9am–6pm, Sat & Sun 8.30am–6pm; 80,000đ, children 50,000đ) has 25 different types of water games.

Around Ho Chi Minh City

When Ho Chi Minh City's blaring horns and pushy vendors become too much for you, you'll find you can get quite a long way **out of the city** in a day. With public transport slow and erratic, day-trips are best arranged through a tour operator (see box, p.86). The single most popular trip out of the city takes in one or both of Vietnam's most memorable sights: the **Cu Chi tunnels**, for twenty years a bolt hole, first for Viet Minh agents, and later for Viet Cong cadres; and the weird and wonderful **Cao Dai Holy See** at Tay Ninh, the fulcrum of the country's most charismatic indigenous religion. While it's possible to see both places in a day (indeed, most people do), be prepared to spend most of the day on the road.

Another enjoyable day (or half-day) out can be had at one of the **water parks** that are located on the fringe of the city and make a great antidote to the dust and heat of Ho Chi Minh City (see Listings above). Southwest of the city, Highway 1 runs down to **My Tho** (see p.134), where you can catch a glimpse of the Mekong River; while to the northeast, it breezes up to the dreary orbital city of **Bien Hoa**, from where Highway 51 drops down to the beaches around **Vung Tau** (see p.224).

The Cu Chi tunnels

During the American War, the villages around the district of **Cu Chi** supported a substantial **Viet Cong** (VC) presence. Faced with American attempts to neutralize them, they quite literally dug themselves out of harm's way, and the legendary **Cu Chi tunnels** were the result (see box, pp.124–125). Today, tourists can visit a short stretch of the tunnels, drop to their hands and knees and squeeze underground for an insight into life as a tunnel-dwelling resistance fighter. Some sections of the tunnels have been widened to allow passage for the fuller frame of Westerners but it's still a dark, sweaty, claustrophobic experience, and not one you should rush into unless you're confident you won't suffer a subterranean freak-out.

There are two sites where the tunnels can be seen – **Ben Dinh** and, 15km beyond, **Ben Duoc** (both daily 7am–5pm; about $5 entrance, not generally included in tour price), though most foreigners get taken to Ben Dinh. If you don't want to join a crowd in a bus (around $8 per person), four people will pay around $50 for a **taxi** following the same itinerary. Another option is to go by boat and return by bus ($14) – contact Delta Adventure Tours (see box, p.86) for details.

The **guided tour** of Ben Dinh kicks off in a thatched hut, where a map of the region, a cross-section of the tunnels and a black and white movie bristling with national pride fill you in on the background. From there, you head out into the bush, where your guide will point out lethal booby-traps, concealed trap doors and an abandoned tank. There are several models showing how unexploded ordnance was ingeniously converted into lethal mines and traps, and a demonstration of how smoke from underground fires was cleverly dispersed far from its source.

When you reach the shooting range, you have the chance to shoulder an M16 or AK47 and shoot off a few rounds (about $15 per clip of bullets, depending which rifle you choose), or stop at the adjacent souvenir and snack stalls. Finally, you get the chance to stoop, crawl and drag yourself through a section of the tunnels about 140 metres long (with frequent escape routes for anyone who can't hack it). It only takes 10–15 minutes to scramble through, but the pitch blackness and intense humidity can be discomforting, so when you emerge, you'll be glad you don't have to live down there for weeks on end as the VC did (see box, pp.124–125).

The Cao Dai Holy See at Tay Ninh

Above Cu Chi, Highway 22 pushes on northwestward through idyllic paddy flatlands. After several kilometres the highway runs through **TRANG BANG**, where the photographer Nick Ut captured one of the war's most horrific and enduring images – that of a naked girl with her back in flames running along the highway, fleeing a napalm attack. The girl, Phan Thi Kim Phuc, now married and living in Canada, was named in 1997 as a goodwill ambassador for UNESCO. Despite third-degree burns covering half of her body, she remains remarkably unembittered, stating "I am happy because I am living without hatred."

A few kilometres off the highway lies **LONG HOA**, the site of the enigmatic **Cao Dai Great Temple**, or Cathedral, of the Holy See of Tay Ninh District. **Joss-stick factories** line the road into Long Hoa, their produce bundled into

▲ Worshippers at the Cao Dai Temple

A history of the tunnels

When the first spades sank into the earth around Cu Chi, the region was covered by a rubber plantation tied to a French tyre company. Anti-colonial **Viet Minh** dug the first tunnels here in the late 1940s; intended primarily for storing arms, they soon became valuable hiding places for the resistance fighters themselves. Over a decade later, VC activists controlling this staunchly anti-government area, many of them local villagers, followed suit and went to ground. By 1965, 250km of tunnels criss-crossed Cu Chi and surrounding areas – just across the Saigon River was the notorious guerrilla power base known as the **Iron Triangle** – making it possible for the VC guerrilla cells in the area to link up with each other and to infiltrate Saigon at will. One section daringly ran underneath the Americans' Cu Chi Army Base.

Though the region's compacted red clay was perfectly suited to tunnelling, and lay above the water level of the Saigon River, the **digging parties** faced a multitude of problems. Quite apart from the snakes and scorpions they encountered as they laboured with their hoes and crowbars, there was the problem of inconspicuously disposing of the soil by spreading it in bomb craters or scattering it in the river under cover of darkness. With a tunnel dug, ceilings had to be shored up, and as American bombing made timber scarce the tunnellers had to resort to stealing iron fence posts from enemy bases. Tunnels could be as small as 80cm wide and 80cm high, and were sometimes four levels deep; **vent shafts** (to disperse smoke and aromas from underground ovens) were camouflaged by thick grass and termites' nests. In order to throw the Americans' dogs off the scent, pepper was sprinkled around vents, and sometimes the VC even washed with the same scented soap used by GIs.

Tunnel life

Living conditions below ground were appalling for these "human moles". Tunnels were foul-smelling, and became so hot by the afternoon that inhabitants had to lie on the floor in order to get enough oxygen to breathe. The darkness was absolute, and some long-term dwellers suffered temporary blindness when they emerged into the light. At times it was necessary to stay below ground for weeks on end, alongside bats, rats, snakes, scorpions, centipedes and fire ants. Some of these unwelcome guests were co-opted to the cause: boxes full of scorpions and hollow bamboo sticks containing vipers were secreted in tunnels, where GIs might unwittingly knock them over.

Within the multi-level tunnel complexes, there were latrines, wells, meeting rooms and dorms. Rudimentary **hospitals** were also scratched out of the soil. Operations were carried out by torchlight using instruments fashioned from shards of ordnance, and a patient's own blood was caught in bottles and then pumped straight back using a bicycle pump and a length of rubber hosing. Such medical supplies as existed were secured by bribing ARVN soldiers in Saigon. Doctors also administered herbs and acupuncture – even honey was used for its antiseptic properties. **Kitchens**

mini-haystacks by the roadside to dry. Around 4km later you reach Long Hoa's **market**, from where the cathedral itself is another 2km. Most people go on a **tour** (see p.121), but if you'd rather go it alone, infrequent **buses** to Tay Ninh depart from Ho Chi Minh City's An Suong station; ask the driver to drop you off at the front gates of the temple.

The Great Temple

A grand gateway marks the entrance to the grounds of the 1927-built Cao Dai Great Temple. Beyond it, a wide boulevard escorts you past a swathe of grassland used on ceremonial occasions, to the wildly exotic temple itself, over whose left shoulder rises distant **Nui Ba Den**, Black Lady Mountain.

cooked whatever the tunnellers could get their hands on. With rice and fruit crops destroyed, the diet consisted largely of tapioca, leaves and roots, at least until enough bomb fragments could be transported to Saigon and sold as scrap to buy food. Morale was maintained in part by **performing troupes** that toured the tunnels, though songs like "He who comes to Cu Chi, the Bronze Fortress in the Land of Iron, will count the crimes accumulated by the Enemy" were not quite up to the standard set by Bob Hope as he entertained the US troops.

The end of the line

American attempts to **flush out** the tunnels proved ineffective. Operating out of huge bases erected around Saigon in the mid-Sixties, they evacuated villagers into strategic hamlets and then used defoliant sprays and bulldozers to rob the VC of cover, in "scorched earth" operations such as January 1967's **Cedar Falls**. Even then, tunnels were rarely effectively destroyed – one soldier at the time compared the task to "fill[ing] the Grand Canyon with a pitchfork". GIs would lob down gas or grenades or else go down themselves, armed only with a torch, a knife and a pistol. Die-hard soldiers who specialized in these underground raids came to be known as **tunnel rats**, their unofficial insignia *Insigni Non Gratum Anus Rodentum*, meaning "not worth a rat's arse". Booby-traps made of sharpened bamboo stakes awaited them in the dark, as well as "bombs" made from Coke cans and dud bullets found on the surface. Tunnels were low and narrow, and entrances so small that GIs often couldn't get down them, even if they could locate them. Maverick war correspondent Wilfred Burchett, travelling with the NLF in 1964, found his Western girth a distinct impediment: "On another occasion I got stuck passing from one tunnel section to another. In what seemed a dead end, a rectangular plug was pulled out from the other side, and, with some ahead pulling my arms and some pushing my buttocks from behind, I managed to get through...I was transferred to another tunnel entrance built especially to accommodate a bulky unit cook."

Another American tactic aimed at weakening the resolve of the VC guerrillas involved dropping leaflets and broadcasting bulletins that played on the fighters' fears and loneliness. Although this prompted numerous desertions, the tunnellers were still able to mastermind the **Tet Offensive** of 1968. Ultimately, the Americans resorted to more strong-arm tactics to neutralize the tunnels, sending in the B52s freed by the cessation of bombing of the North in 1968 to level the district with **carpet bombing**. The VC's infrastructure was decimated by Tet, and further weakened by the **Phoenix Programme**. By this time, though, the tunnels had played their part in proving to America that the war was unwinnable. At least 12,000 Vietnamese guerrillas and sympathizers are thought to have perished here during the American War, and the terrain was laid waste – pockmarked by bomb craters, devoid of vegetation, the air poisoned by lingering fumes.

On first sighting, the **Great Temple** seems to be subsiding, an optical illusion created by the rising steps inside it, but your first impressions are more likely to be dominated by what Graham Greene described as a "Walt Disney fantasia of the East, dragons and snakes in Technicolor". Despite its Day-Glo hues and rococo clutter, this gaudy construction somehow manages to bypass tackiness. Two square, pagoda-style **towers** bookend the front facade, whose central portico is topped by a bowed, first-floor balcony and a **Divine Eye**. The most recurrent motif in the temple, the eye, is surrounded by a triangle, as it is on the American one-dollar bill. A figure in semi-relief emerges from each tower: on the left is Cao Dai's first female cardinal, Lam Huong Thanh, and on the right, Le Van Trung, its first pope.

The eclectic ideology of Cao Dai is mirrored in the **interior**. Part cathedral and part pagoda, it draws together a potpourri of icons and elements under a vaulted ceiling, and daubs them all with the primary colours of a Hindu

Cao Dai

The basic tenets of **Cao Dai** were first revealed to **Ngo Van Chieu**, a civil servant working in the criminal investigation department of the French administration on Phu Quoc Island, at the beginning of the 1920s. A spiritualist, Ngo was contacted during a seance by a superior spirit calling itself Cao Dai, or "high place". This spirit communicated to him the basics of the Cao Dai creed, and instructed him to adopt the Divine Eye as a tangible representation of its existence. Posted back to Saigon soon afterwards, Ngo set about evangelizing, though according to French convert and chronicler Gabriel Gobron the religion didn't gather steam until late in 1925, when Ngo was contacted by a group of mediums sent his way by the Cao Dai.

At this stage, **revelations** from the Cao Dai began to add further meat to the bones of the religion. Twice already, it informed its mediums, it had revealed itself to mankind, using such vehicles as Lao-tzu, Christ, Mohammed, Moses, Sakyamuni and Confucius to propagate systems of belief tailored to suit localized cultures. Such religious intolerance had resulted from this multiplicity, that for the **third alliance** it would do away with earthly messengers and convey a universal religion via spirit intermediaries, including Louis Pasteur, William Shakespeare, Joan of Arc, Sir Winston Churchill and Napoleon Bonaparte. The revelations of these "saints" were received using a *planchette* (a pencil secured to a wooden board on castors, on which the medium rests his hand, sometimes known as a *corbeille à bec*).

Though a fusion of Oriental and occidental religions, propounding the concept of a **universal god**, Cao Dai is primarily entrenched in Buddhism, Taoism and Confucianism, to which cause-and-effect creeds, elements of Christianity, Islam and spirituality are added. By following its five commandments – Cao Dai followers must avoid killing living beings, high living, covetousness, verbal deceit and the temptations of the flesh – adherents look to hasten the evolution of the soul through reincarnation.

The religion was effectively **founded** in October 1926, when it was also officially recognized by the French colonial administration. Borrowing the structure and terminology of the Catholic Church, Cao Dai began to grow rapidly, its emphasis upon simplicity appealing to disaffected peasants, and by 1930 there were 500,000 followers. In 1927, Tay Ninh became the religion's Holy See; Ngo opted out of the papacy, and the first pope was **Le Van Trung**, a decadent mandarin from Cho Lon who saw the error of his ways after being visited by the Cao Dai during a seance.

Inevitably in such uncertain times, Cao Dai developed a **political agenda**. Strongly anti-French during World War II, subsequently the Cao Dai militia turned against the Viet Minh, with whom they fought, using French arms, in the French War. By the mid-Fifties, the area around Tay Ninh was a virtual fiefdom of Cao Dai followers. In *The Quiet American*, Graham Greene describes the Cao Dai militia as a "private army of 25,000 men, armed with mortars made out of the exhaust-pipes of old cars, allies of the French who turned neutral at the moment of danger". Even then, however, they were feuding with the rival Hoa Hao sect, and in a few years their power had waned.

Post-liberation, the Communist government confiscated all Cao Dai land, though it was returned ten years later. Today, the religion continues to thrive in its twin power bases of Tay Ninh District and the Mekong Delta.

temple. Men enter the cathedral through an entrance in the right wall, women by a door to the left, and all must take off their shoes. Inside the lobby, a **mural** shows the three "signatories of the 3rd Alliance between God and Mankind": French poet Victor Hugo and the fifteenth-century Vietnamese poet, Nguyen Binh Khiem, are writing the Cao Dai principles of "God and humanity, love and justice" in French and Chinese onto a shining celestial tablet. Beside them, the Chinese nationalist leader Sun Yat Sen holds an inkstone, a symbol of "Chinese civilization allied to Christian civilization giving birth to Cao Dai doctrine", according to a nearby sign.

Tourists are welcome to wander through the **nave** of the cathedral, as long as they remain in the aisles, and don't stray between the rows of **pink pillars**, entwined by green dragons, that march up the chamber. Cut-away windows punctuate the outer walls, their grillework consisting of the Divine Eye, surrounded by bright pink lotus blooms. Walk up the shallow steps that lend the nave its litheness, and you'll reach an **altar** that groans under the weight of assorted vases, fruit, paintings and slender statues of storks. The **papal chair** stands at the head of the chamber, its arms carved into dragons. Below it are six more chairs, three with eagle arms, and three with lion arms, for the cardinals. Dominating the chamber, though, and guarded by eight scary silver dragons, a vast, duck-egg-blue **sphere**, speckled with stars, rests on a polished, eight-sided dais. The ubiquitous Divine Eye peers through clouds painted on the front. You'll see more spangly stars and fluffy clouds if you look up at the sky-blue **ceiling**, with mouldings of lions and turtles.

Services

Services are held daily at 6am, noon, 6pm and midnight. Tours usually arrange their visit to coincide with the midday one. Though other times are inconvenient, they do offer the opportunity to concentrate on what's happening without the accompanying roadshow of hundreds of flashing cameras. Visitors are shepherded upstairs and past the traditional **band** that plays behind the front balcony, and on into the gods, from where they can look down on proceedings and take photographs. Most worshippers dress in white robes, though some dress in yellow, blue and red, to signify the Buddhist, Taoist and Confucian elements of Cao Dai. Priests don square hats emblazoned with the Divine Eye. At the start of a service, worshippers' heads nod, like a field of corn in the breeze, in time to the clanging of a gong. Then a haunting, measured chanting begins, against the insect whine of the string band playing its own time. As prayers and hymns continue, incense, flowers, alcohol and tea are offered up to the Supreme Being.

Travel details

Trains

Ho Chi Minh City to: Da Nang (7 daily; 15–22hr); Dieu Tri (7 daily; 11–13hr); Hanoi (6 daily; 30–41hr); Hué (7 daily; 21–23hr); Muong Man (10 daily; 4–5hr); Nha Trang (9 daily; 9–10hr); Ninh Binh (4daily; 34–37hr); Quang Ngai (5 daily; 13–16hr); Thap Cham (6 daily; 6–7hr); Vinh (6 daily; 29–33hr).

Buses

Bus stations are gradually becoming more organized, with ticket desks and scheduled departures. However, it is still almost impossible to give the **frequency** with which buses run because of the large number of private minibuses that ply more popular routes, and depart only when they have enough passengers to make the journey worthwhile. It's advisable to start your journey early – most long-distance departures are between 5am and 9am, and few run after midday. **Journey times** can also vary; figures below show the normal length of time you can expect to take by public bus. **Ho Chi Minh City** to: Buon Ma Thuot (7hr); Ca Mau (8hr 30min); Can Tho (4hr); Chau Doc (6hr); Da Lat (7hr); Da Nang (21hr); Hanoi (41hr); Ha Tien (9hr); Hué (25hr); My Tho (2hr); Nha Trang (10hr); Phan Thiet (4–5hr); Qui Nhon (13hr); Vung Tau (2hr).

Hydrofoils and boats

Ho Chi Minh City to: Can Tho (1 daily; 4hr); Vung Tau (about 12 daily; 1hr 15min).

Flights

Ho Chi Minh City to: Buon Ma Thuot (1–2 daily; 1hr); Con Dao (1–2 daily; 1hr); Da Lat (2 daily; 50min); Da Nang (5 daily; 1hr 10min); Haiphong (2 daily; 2hr); Hanoi (12–14 daily; 2hr); Hué (3–4 daily; 1hr 40min); Nha Trang (3 daily; 1hr 10min); Phu Quoc (5–6 daily; 1hr); Plei Ku (1 daily; 1hr 15min); Qui Nhon (1–2 daily; 1hr 10min).

2

The Mekong Delta

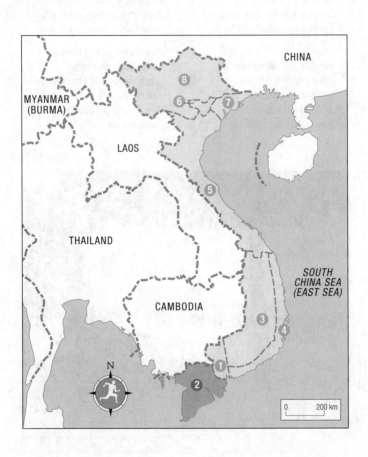

CHAPTER 2 # Highlights

✻ **Boat trips** Drift along narrow canals, visiting floating markets and fruit orchards around Vinh Long and Can Tho. See p.145 & p.153

✻ **Home-stays** Stay in rural communities, observing daily aspects of Vietnamese culture, and getting to know your hosts. See p.146

✻ **Khmer pagodas** Marvel over the rich colours of temples around Tra Vinh and Soc Trang. See p.147 & p.155

✻ **Bird sanctuaries** Watch flocks of storks and migrating cranes wheeling in the sky at Bang Lang near Long Xuyen and Tram Chim near Cao Lanh. See p.163

✻ **Chau Doc** Visit a Cham village and fish farms on the river, and explore nearby Sam Mountain. See p.164

✻ **Phu Quoc Island** Sprawl on its gorgeous beaches, ride a motorbike through its mountainous interior and dive or snorkel around the coastline. See p.177

▲ Chill out on one of Phu Quoc Island's stunning beaches

2

The Mekong Delta

ouring the orchards, paddy fields and swamplands of the **Mekong Delta**, you could be forgiven for thinking you've stepped into the pages of a geography textbook. A comma-shaped flatland stretching from Ho Chi Minh's city limits southwest to the Gulf of Thailand, the delta is Vietnam's **rice bowl**, an agricultural miracle that pumps out more than a third of the country's annual food crop from just ten percent of its total land mass. Rice may be the delta's staple crop, but coconut palms, fruit orchards and sugar-cane groves also thrive in its nutrient-rich soil, and the sight of conical-hatted farmers tending their land is one of Vietnam's most enduring images.

To the Vietnamese, the region is known as *Cuu Long*, "Nine Dragons", a reference to the nine tributaries of the **Mekong River** which dovetail across plains fashioned by millennia of flood-borne alluvial sediment. By the time it reaches Vietnam, the Mekong has already covered more than four thousand kilometres from its source high on the Tibetan Plateau; en route it traverses southern China, skirts Burma (Myanmar), then hugs the Laos–Thailand border before cutting down through Cambodia and into Vietnam – a journey that ranks it as Asia's third-longest river, after the Yangtse and Yellow rivers. **Flooding** has always blighted the delta; ever since Indian traders imported their advanced methods of irrigation more than eighteen centuries ago, networks of canals have been used to channel the excess water, but the rainy season still claims lives from time to time.

Surprisingly, agriculture gripped the delta only relatively recently. Under **Cambodian** sway until the close of the seventeenth century, the region was sparsely inhabited by the *Khmer krom*, or "downstream Khmers", whose settlements were framed by swathes of marshland. The eighteenth century saw the Viet **Nguyen** lords steadily broaden their sphere of influence to encompass the delta, though by the 1860s **France** had taken over the reins of government. Sensing the huge profits to be gleaned from such fertile land, French *colons* spurred Vietnamese peasants to tame and till tracts of the boggy delta; the peasants, realizing their colonial governors would pay well for rice harvests, were quick to comply. Ironically, the same landscape that had served the French so well also provided valuable cover for the Viet Minh resistance fighters who sought to overthrow them; later it did the same for the Viet Cong, who had well-hidden cells here – inciting the Americans to strafe the area with bombs and defoliants.

A visit to the Mekong Delta is so memorable because of the region's **diversity**. Everyday scenes include schoolgirls clad in white *ao dai* cycling along country lanes; children riding on the backs of water buffalo; rice workers stooping in a sea of emerald; market vendors grinning behind stacks of fruit;

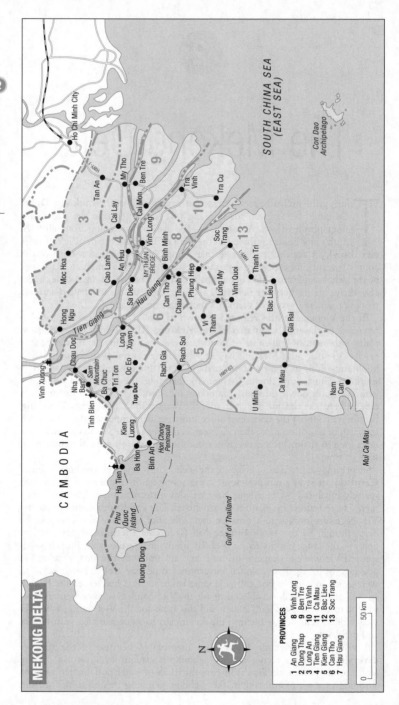

MEKONG DELTA

THE MEKONG DELTA

SOUTH CHINA SEA
(EAST SEA)

Con Dao
Archipelago

CAMBODIA

Gulf of Thailand

Phu Quoc
Island

Hon Chong
Peninsula

Mui Ca Mau

Ho Chi Minh City

My Tho
Ben Tre
Tan An
Cai Lay
Cai Mon
Vinh Long
Tra Vinh
Tra Cu

Moc Hoa
Cao Lanh
An Huu
Binh Minh
Soc Trang
Thanh Tri

Hong Ngu
Sa Dec
Hau Giang
Can Tho
Chau Thanh
Phung Hiep
Long My
Vinh Quoi
Bac Lieu

Chau Doc
Long Xuyen
Vi Thanh
Gia Rai

Vinh Xuong
Nha Ban
Sam Mountain
Ba Chuc
Tri Ton
Oc Eo
Rach Gia
Rach Soi
U Minh
Ca Mau
Nam Can

Tinh Bien
Tuc Duc

Ha Tien
Kien Luong
Ba Hon
Binh An

Duong Dong

MY THUAN BRIDGE

QL 1A / HWY 1A

HWY 63

Tien Giang

N

0   50 km

PROVINCES

1 An Giang
2 Dong Thap
3 Long An
4 Tien Giang
5 Kien Giang
6 Can Tho
7 Hau Giang
8 Vinh Long
9 Ben Tre
10 Tra Vinh
11 Ca Mau
12 Bac Lieu
13 Soc Trang

bright yellow incense sticks drying at the roadside; flocks of storks circling over a sanctuary at dusk; Khmer monks walking mindfully in the shadow of pastel pagodas; locals scampering over monkey bridges or rowing boats on the Delta's maze of channels.

It's difficult to overstate the influence of the river: the lifeblood of the rice and fruit crops grown here, it also teems with craft that range in size from delicate rowing boats to hulking sampans, and it forms a backdrop to everyday activities – some of the region's biggest markets are waterborne. Inevitably the best way to experience riverine life is on a **boat trip**. Day trips can be organized in Ho Chi Minh City, My Tho, Vinh Long, Can Tho or Chau Doc, while some tour operators offer 2–3 day live-aboard trips (see box below). Since most day tours follow a similar itinerary (a visit to a floating market and stops at cottage industries on the shore), you'll probably want to choose just one. Though Can Tho is most popular for its good range of hotels and restaurants, you're likely to see more tourists than locals in the nearby floating markets. A good alternative is Vinh Long, from where boats head out in many different directions through the canals of An Binh Island to the floating market at Cai Be.

There are over a dozen towns in the delta with facilities for tourists, though some are rarely visited as they are not on the way to anywhere. **My Tho** is well geared up for boat trips, and near enough to Ho Chi Minh City to be seen on a day-trip: it affords an appetizing glimpse of the delta's northernmost tributary, the Tien Giang. From My Tho, laidback **Ben Tre** and the bounteous fruit orchards besieging it are only a hop and a skip away. **Cao Lanh** is strictly for bird enthusiasts, but **Sa Dec**, with its timeless river scenes and riotously colourful flower nurseries, has a more universal appeal, while just down the road, **Vinh Long** is another jumping-off point for boat trips.

Many visitors spend a day or two in **Can Tho**, the Delta's biggest settlement, to take advantage of its decent hotels and restaurants and to recharge batteries before venturing out to the **floating markets** nearby. From Can Tho, there's something to be said for dropping down to the foot of the delta, where the

Getting around the delta

Most visitors hurtle around on a **tour bus** out of Ho Chi Minh City, denying themselves the chance to sink into the languid life of the delta. With time in hand, it's far more satisfying to **hire a vehicle** or take **local transport** – not nearly as daunting a prospect as it is up the coast, since the number of settlements with hotels means journeys can be kept relatively short. Traffic has to stop occasionally at the **ferries** that make road travel in the delta possible, though construction of some long-awaited bridges is speeding up travel times. The enforced halts at the ferries are at least enlivened by strolling hawkers. Locals used to do much of their travelling on the **passenger and cargo boats** that crawl around the delta's waterways, but the increased prevalence of motorbikes has led to many routes being cut, so this is no longer a viable way of getting around for visitors.

If you really want to do the delta in style, Trans Mekong (℡071/382 9540, ⓦwww .transmekong.com) offers a two-day, one-night trip aboard a **traditional rice barge** converted into a floating hotel. The barge makes its way from Cai Be to Can Tho, stopping at villages and fruit orchards on the way. Prices begin at around $250 per person. Another luxury option, with similar itinerary and rates, is the Song Xanh **sampan** cruise (℡091 227 0058, ⓦwww.vietnamluxurytravel.com). If these rates sound a bit steep, Saigon-based Delta Adventure Tours (℡08/3920 2112, ⓦwww .deltaadventuretours.com) offer a more basic 3-day, 2-night Mekong cruise, taking in Cai Be, Sa Dec, Long Xuyen and Chau Doc for just $55 per person.

swampland that surrounds **Ca Mau** can be explored by boat. Pulling up, en route, at the Khmer stronghold of **Soc Trang** is especially rewarding if your trip coincides with the colourful Oc Om Bok festival, during which the local Khmer community takes to the river to stage spectacular longboat races. Northwest of Can Tho meanwhile, and a stone's throw from the Cambodian border, is the ebullient town of **Chau Doc**, south of which **Sam Mountain** provides a welcome undulation in the surrounding plains. The opening of the border here has brought a steady stream of travellers going on to Phnom Penh by boat, and several of them rest up a few days here before leaving the country.

A bustling fishing port due south of Chau Doc on the Gulf of Thailand, **Rach Gia** is a convenient place to catch a boat or short flight to **Phu Quoc Island**, whose splendid beaches are a big draw for tourists. Northwest of Rach Gia, **Ha Tien**, a remote border town surrounded by Khmer villages, now also has daily boats to Phu Quoc. The town has recently become popular for its **international border crossing**, which allows beach bums to slide along the coast from Phu Quoc Island to Sihanoukville in Cambodia or vice versa.

Given its seasonal flooding, **the best time to visit** the delta is, predictably enough, in the dry season, which runs from December to May.

My Tho and around

Southwest of Ho Chi Minh City, buses plying Highway 1 eventually emerge from the city's unkempt urban sprawl and into the pastoral surrounds of the Mekong Delta's upper plains. The delta is too modest to flaunt its full beauty so soon, but glimpses of rice fields behind the scruffy settlements draped along the highway hint at things to come, their burnished golds and brilliant greens interspersed with the occasional white ancestral grave. Seventy kilometres out of Ho Chi Minh City, a left fork marks the turning to **MY THO**, an amiable market town that nestles on the north bank of the Mekong River's northernmost strand, the Tien Giang, or Upper River.

My Tho's proximity to Ho Chi Minh City means that it receives the lion's share of day-trippers to the delta, resulting in a scrum of pushy vendors crowding round each tour bus that arrives. Nevertheless, the town comes as a great relief after the onslaught of Ho Chi Minh City, its uncrowded boulevards belying a population of around 200,000, and you can easily escape the melee by hopping onto a boat or wandering into the backstreets.

This daily influx of visitors seems appropriate, given the town's **history**. Chinese immigrants fleeing Formosa (modern-day Taiwan) after the collapse of the Ming dynasty established the town in the late seventeenth century, along with a Vietnamese population keen to make inroads into this traditionally Khmer-dominated region. Two centuries later the French, wooed by the district's abundant rice and fruit crops, rated it highly enough to post a garrison here and to lay a (now-defunct) rail line to Saigon; while the American War saw a consistent military presence in town. Today My Tho's commercial importance is as pronounced as ever, something a walk through the busy town market amply illustrates.

Arrival and information

Buses terminate at Tien Giang station, 3km northwest of town, from where xe om shuttle into the centre (about 15,000đ). Two state-run companies offer **boat trips** from My Tho to the islands in the Mekong: Tien Giang

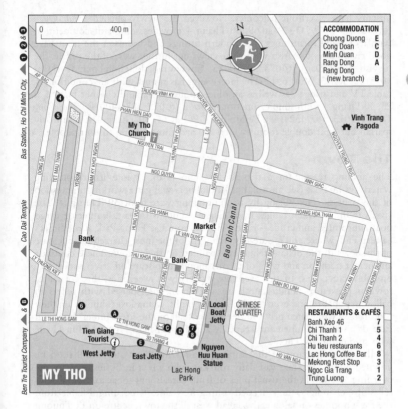

ACCOMMODATION

Chuong Duong	E
Cong Doan	C
Minh Quan	D
Rang Dong	A
Rang Dong	
(new branch)	B

RESTAURANTS & CAFÉS

Banh Xeo 46	7
Chi Thanh 1	5
Chi Thanh 2	4
Hu tieu restaurants	6
Lac Hong Coffee Bar	8
Mekong Rest Stop	3
Ngoc Gia Trang	1
Trung Luong	2

MY THO

Tourist Company has its main office located next to the western tour boat jetty at 8, 30 Thang 4 (☎073/387 3184, ⓦwww.tiengiangtourist.com), while Ben Tre Tourist Company is at 4/1 Le Thi Hong Gam (☎073/387 9103, ⓔmekongtourbentre@hcm.vnn.vn), down a lane to the left just before the new bridge over the river. Both charge $20–50 per boat, depending on how long you want to hire it for. Local boats, which you can find at the small jetty on Trung Trac, are much cheaper, and $15 should get you a two- to three-hour trip – time enough to explore the waterways along the coast of Ben Tre Province, and to land on an island in the river. However, bear in mind that the owners of these boats are not licensed or insured to carry tourists, so it's a bit of a risky business.

There's an **ATM** opposite the jetties (next to the *Cong Doan* hotel) and another at Vietinbank, at the western end of Thu Khoa Huan. The Agribank at the opposite end of Thu Khoa Huan on the corner of Le Loi will change dollars for dong. The **post office** is conveniently located opposite the boat jetties on Le Thi Hong Gam, where you can also find **internet** access.

Accommodation

The *Chuong Duong* (☎073/387 0875; ❸–❹), opposite the GPO at 10, 30 Thang 4, with prime views of the river, has long been the town's smartest place to stay; its tidy rooms all have air-conditioning, hot water and TVs, and those upstairs have riverfront balconies. However, the newly-opened *Minh Quan* (☎073/397 9979; ❸–❹) at 69, 30 Thang 4 provides some stiff competition with its tasteful furnishings and modern fittings, and rooms at the front have good river views too. Also with river views but further west of the centre, the newish *Rang Dong* (☎073/397 0085; ⓦwww.rangdonghotel.net; ❷–❸) at 40/5 Section 3, Ward 6, Le Thi Hon Gam, has rooms with air conditioners, cable TV and fridges, as well as an older, more central and cheaper branch at 25, 30 Thang 4, with simple, functional rooms (☎073/387 4400; ❶). The *Cong Doan* (☎073/387 4324; ❶), beside the GPO at 61, 30 Thang 4, has similarly spartan but light double rooms which can accommodate up to four people.

The Town

The abiding reason for a trip to My Tho is to explore its surrounding waterways by boat (see above), but landlubbers will get a working impression of the majestic Tien Giang by strolling along waterfront **30 Thang 4**. The river's traffic – which ranges from elegant sampans to vast, lumbering cargo boats, unpainted and crude – is best viewed from Lac Hong Park at the street's eastern end, where you're sure to catch sight of the most characteristic feature of the boats in the delta – feline eyes painted on their prows. These continue an ancient tradition and were originally intended to scare off "river monsters", probably crocodiles. In the evenings, especially at weekends, this corner of town is packed as families stroll up and down, interspersed with sellers of balloons, popcorn and even tropical fish. At night, young lovers huddle on their motorbikes, while men play shuttlecock football on the street under the intent gaze of a statue of nineteenth-century anti-French hero Nguyen Huu Huan, who studied in My Tho.

Follow the direction of the canal up past Trung Trac and you'll soon be gobbled up by My Tho's vast daily **market**, which is at its busiest early in the morning. As well as the usual piles of fruit, cereals and tobacco, several stalls sell ships' chandlery, their heaped fishing nets almost indistinguishable from the fresh noodles on sale nearby. Head west of the town centre on Ly Thuong Kiet, for the **Cao Dai Temple**, which is worth a look for its colourful architecture.

East of the canal

The southernmost of the bridges spanning the canal deposits you at the start of waterfront Phan Thanh Gian, home to My Tho's modest **Chinese Quarter**, though there's little to betray its existence other than a feverish sense of commerce. Shopfronts here are piled to the rafters with sugar-cane poles, watermelons and fish awaiting transportation to Ho Chi Minh City, as well as half-hatched eggs (containing chick embryos), prized as the perfect complement to a bia hoi.

A short walk or cyclo journey (about 10,000đ) northeast of Phan Thanh Gian to Nguyen Trung Truc's attractive **Vinh Trang Pagoda**, with its rajah's palace-style front facade, is a worthwhile side-trip. Since its construction in 1849, it has been renovated several times, most recently in 2002. The entrance, round to the right, leads into the heart of the temple, where a tiny courtyard is flanked by the cubicles where the monks sleep. The main chamber, beyond the miniature mountain to your left, is characterized by dark-wood pillars and tons of gilt woodwork, but of more interest are the eclectic influences at play in the pagoda's decor – classical pillars, Grecian-style mouldings of urns and bowls of fruit, and glazed tiles similar to Portuguese *azulejos*. Outside, the tombs of several monks stand near a pond patrolled by huge elephant-ear fish, while a tall, standing Buddha image watches over the front gate.

Eating and drinking

Though there's nowhere to get very excited about in town, there are three places just out of town that cater mostly to tour groups but turn out consistently good dishes, including the locally-famous elephant-ear fish. The first, the *Ngoc Gia Trang*, is at 196A Ap Bac, about 2km northwest of the centre, while the *Trung Luong* is a couple of kilometres beyond, to the right where the road forks for Ho Chi Minh City and Can Tho. The third, and newest, is the *Mekong Rest Stop*, about 4km further on the road to Saigon. This one is set in a beautifully-landscaped garden with lotus ponds and offers set menus for two people at around $5–7.

Back in town, the *Chuong Duong* hotel restaurant, which specializes in seafood, is the best bet, with large reasonably-priced portions. For simple but tasty local dishes, the *Chi Thanh 1* and *2*, the first of which is at 279 Tet Mau Than, and the second around the corner at 19 Ap Bac, are generally reliable, drawing plenty of locals each evening. Down by the riverside, at 11 Trung Trac, the *Banh Xeo 46* serves up tasty shrimp pancakes. There are also several cheap but popular restaurants at the southern end of Nam Ky Khoi Nghia, including a couple at numbers 24 and 44 that serve *hu tieu* (noodles with seafood and meat), the local speciality.

There's little **nightlife** in My Tho, though the recently-opened *Lac Hong Coffee Bar* at 63, 30 Thang 4, adds a touch of class to the town with its colonial-style shuttered windows, comfy armchairs and good selection of coffee and cocktails. The bar features live jazz and blues on Thursday evenings.

Around My Tho

Day-trippers tend to see little of My Tho as they disgorge from tour buses and embark on a **boat trip** round two or three of the **islands** in the Tien Giang branch of the Mekong River. Upstream at **Cai Be** it's a similar story, with fleets of buses from Ho Chi Minh City descending on the village at around 11am for boat tours of the **floating market**. Arranging trips locally tends to lead to a more relaxed and enjoyable experience, but you'd probably need to sleep over at least one night. In contrast to Cai Be, the quirky **snake farm** at Dong Tham sees few foreign visitors.

The islands

Beyond its chaotic shoreline of stilthouses and boatyards, **Tan Long** ("Dragon Island"), the least frequently visited, boasts bounteous sapodilla, coconut and banana plantations, as well as highly regarded longan orchards. As with the other islands, Dragon Island is sparsely inhabited, by small communities of farmers and boat-builders. **Thoi Son** ("Unicorn Island") is the largest of the four islands and many of the organized tours out of Ho Chi Minh City stop here for lunch and fruit sampling. Local tours do not always include lunch in the price, but all tours will stop somewhere you can get refreshment. Narrow canals allow boats to weave through its interior. Gliding along these slender waterways, overhung by handsome water-palm fronds which interlock to form a cathedral-like roof, it's easy to feel you're charting new territory. Swooping, electric-blue kingfishers and sumptuously coloured butterflies add to the romance.

Qui ("Turtle") **Island** is the newest of the group, having been formed by sediment in the river, then stabilized by planting mangroves, and is overflowing

Ong Dao Dua, the Coconut Monk

Ong Dao Dua, the **Coconut Monk**, was born Nguyen Thanh Nam in the Mekong Delta, in 1909. Aged 19, he travelled to France where he studied chemistry until 1935, when he returned home, married and fathered a child. During a lengthy period of meditation at Chau Doc's Sam Mountain (see p.168) he devised a new religion, a fusion of Buddhism and Christianity known as **Tinh Do Cu Si**. By the Sixties, this new sect had established a community on Phung Island, where the monk lorded it over his followers from a throne set into a man-made grotto modelled on Sam Mountain. The monk became as famous for his idiosyncrasies as for his doctrine: his name, for instance, was coined after it was alleged he spent three years meditating and eating nothing but coconuts.

Unfortunately, the Coconut Monk never got to enjoy his "kingdom" for long: his belief in a peaceful reunification of North and South Vietnam (symbolized by the map of the country behind his grotto, on which pillars representing Hanoi and Saigon are joined by a bridge) landed him in the jails of successive South Vietnamese governments and the Communists were no more sympathetic to his beliefs after 1975. Ong Dao Dua died in 1990.

with longans, dragon fruit, mango, papaya, pineapple and jackfruit. A small, family-run coconut candy factory is located just opposite on the Ben Tre coastline. Here you can watch the coconut being pressed, and the extracted juice being mixed with sugar and heated, then dried and cut into bite-size pieces. After tasting, many visitors buy a box to take home.

Phung ("Phoenix") **Island** is famed as the home of an offbeat religious sect set up three decades ago by the eccentric **Coconut Monk**, Ong Dao Dua (see box above), although there's not much left to see from his era, and only the skeleton of the open-air **complex** he established remains. Among its mesh of rusting staircases and platforms, you'll spot the rocket-shaped elevator the monk had built to whisk him up to his private meditation platform. Elsewhere are nine dragon-entwined pillars, said to symbolize the Mekong's nine tributaries and betraying a Cao Daist influence. The Coconut Monk's story is told (in Vietnamese) on a magnificent **urn** which he is said to have crafted himself out of shards of porcelain from France, Japan and China.

Dong Tam Snake Farm

Located 10km west of My Tho and run by the military, the **Dong Tam Snake Farm** (daily 7am–5pm; 20,000đ) breeds snakes for their meat and skins. Watching the sluggish pythons and cobras sleeping in cages is not a pretty sight, though there are several other animals on display in a small zoo, including porcupines, monitor lizards, otters, monkeys, eagles, peacocks and an enormous albino turtle. One of the farm's most popular products is Cobratox – a cream that includes cobra venom and stings on application, but is rated by many as an effective cure for rheumatism. A xe om to the farm costs around 20,000đ.

Cai Be Floating Market

Cai Be's floating market is one of the most popular in the delta, and also the most distinctive because of its backdrop of a slender cathedral spire. Throughout the day boats of all sizes throng in the waters of the Tien Giang, with fruit vendors displaying a sample of their produce suspended from a stick. The market reaches its busiest at around midday when busloads of visitors on organized tours roll in to Cai Be village from Ho Chi Minh City, 110km away. They are shepherded on to boats for a few hours to explore the market and fruit orchards on nearby islands before zipping back to the city. While this may be convenient for those who are short of time, it's all a bit rushed, and the midday heat can be oppressive. If you have a more relaxed schedule, meandering through the picturesque channels of An Binh Island between Vinh Long and Cai Be market, or overnighting in a home-stay (see p.146) before visiting the market in the morning, offers a more rewarding experience. Cai Be is about 40km west of My Tho and lies just south of Highway 1.

Ben Tre

The few travellers who push on beyond My Tho into **Ben Tre Province** are rewarded with some of the Mekong Delta's most breathtaking scenery. Until recently this province was isolated by the Mekong's wide arms around it, but the new bridge from My Tho (opened in early 2009) is likely to bring a rush of visitors. Famed for its fruit orchards and coconut groves (Vietnamese call it the "coconut island"), the province has proved just as fertile a breeding ground for revolutionaries, first plotting against the French, and later against the Americans, and was one of the areas seized by the Viet Cong during the Tet Offensive of 1968.

Of the US bombing campaign on the provincial capital of **BEN TRE**, a US major was quoted as saying, "It became necessary to destroy the town in order to save it." Today, Ben Tre is a pleasant and industrious town displaying none of the wounds of its past, and makes an agreeable contrast to the tourist bustle of nearby My Tho. Though rather short on sights, it's still a relaxing and friendly place to hole up for a couple of days, with a buzzing **town market** and a new **riverside promenade**, which makes a pleasant place to stroll in the morning or evening. You might also be tempted to pass over the quaint bridge leading to the Ben Tre River's more rustic south bank, where scores of cross-eyed boats moor in front of a jumble of simple houses. With a bicycle or motorbike, you can explore the maze of dirt tracks on this side of the river. Before striking off, though, duck into the riverside **wine factory**, 450m west of the bridge, where fermenting *ruou trang* (Vietnamese rice wine) fizzes away in vast earthenware jars. A mountain of rice husks indicates the factory's location, though you'll find it easily if you follow your nose.

For more of an adventure, head out of town on a boat trip along the **Ben Tre coastline**, where labyrinthine creeks afford marvellous scope for exploring, and sometimes include stops at apiaries, rice-wine and sugar-processing workshops. Such an outing can be organized through the Ben Tre Tourist Company (see below), or try the *Thao Nhi Guest House* (see below), which has a good reputation for cheap and enjoyable boat trips to watch a sunrise or sunset over the Mekong River.

Thao Nhi Guest House & ▲ My Tho

BEN TRE

Dong Khoi ◉

HAI BA TRUNG

ⓘ Truc Giang Lake

30 THANG 4

DONG KHOI

N

Floating Restaurant & Bus Station

Bank 🏠

NGUYEN DINH CHIEU

LE LOI

Hung Vuong ◉

LE DUI HANH

✉

Market

HUNG VUONG

Wine Factory ◀

0   200 m

Practicalities

The opening of the new bridge to Ben Tre means that most visitors arrive by road: **buses** terminate on Doan Hoang Minh about a kilometre west of the town centre. Located at 65 Dong Khoi to the north of the centre, Ben Tre Tourist Company (daily 7–11am & 1–5pm; ☎075/382 9618) can organize car rental, bicycles and some tours; for motorbikes, contact the *Hung Vuong Hotel*. The Vietinbank on Nguyen Dinh Chieu exchanges dollars.

The riverside *Hung Vuong Hotel* (☎075/382 2408; ❹) at 166 Hung Vuong has easily the best location and facilities of Ben Tre's hotels. Its large, well-equipped rooms all have air-conditioning and TVs, and some have bathtubs and river views. On the north bank of Truc Giang Lake, the state-run *Dong Khoi* (☎075/3822501; ❶–❷) at 16 Hai Ba Trung has well-equipped rooms at very cheap rates, but it can get rowdy when they host a wedding, as they often do. Another cheap but adventurous option is the ⚘ *Thao Nhi Guest House* (☎075/386 0009; ✉ thaonhitours@yahoo.com; ❶–❷), set in the grounds of a longan orchard. It has a range of rooms, including small ones with fans and larger ones with air-conditioning, and the staff are friendly and helpful. The atmosphere is very relaxing – the kind of place to settle in for a few days – and its restaurant has a good menu that features elephant-ear fish and huge prawns. It's about 11km north of Ben Tre town, near the former ferry terminal: to get there, take the right turn just before the old ferry terminal and look for a sign after a few hundred metres pointing down a narrow lane to the right. From here it's another 150m.

There's not a great deal of choice for **places to eat** in Ben Tre; the restaurant at the *Hung Vuong Hotel* serves up decent food in an uninspiring environment, while the *Ben Tre Floating Restaurant*, moored on the riverbank about 3km west of the centre, is a fine venue for a sunset drink or dinner, with main courses costing around 60,000đ. Failing that, there are plenty of **food stalls** around the market.

Cao Lanh and around

West of My Tho, and Cai Be, Highway 1 crosses the My Thuan Bridge on its way to Vinh Long and Can Tho. Just before the bridge, however, at An Huu, Highway 30 branches north, rolling into modest **CAO LANH** 34km later. The town is no oil painting, and offers little unless you're charmed by **wading birds**; its location beside the western edge of the **Plain of Reeds** makes Cao Lanh an ideal launching pad for trips out to the storks and cranes that nest in the nearby swamplands. Coming from Ho Chi Minh City, you'll pass the two great concrete tusks (intended to resemble lotus petals) of the **war memorial** as you veer onto the main drag, Nguyen Hué. One tusk bears a hammer and sickle, the other a Vietnamese red star. Way across on the southwestern outskirts of town, another concrete edifice, shaped like an open clam, marks the burial place of Ho Chi Minh's father, **Nguyen Sinh Sac** (daily 7–11.30am & 1.30–5pm), which is set in attractive gardens.

The only other place worth visiting in town is the **Dong Thap Museum** (daily 7–11.30am & 1.30–5pm; free), also located to the southwest of town, just to the left beyond the first bridge. Though there are no English signs, the well-organized display of fossils, skulls, farming tools, fishtraps, basketware and textiles, as well as the inevitable paintings of heroic Vietnamese forces repelling French and American troops, is worth a look.

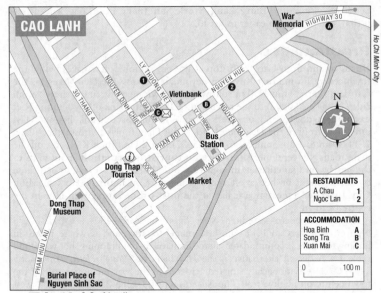

Ferry station, Sa Dec & Long Xuyen

And that's about it, unless you're here for the birds. Of the 220 species nesting 45km northwest of Cao Lanh at the **Tram Chim National Park** (previously called the Tam Nong Bird Sanctuary), it's the sarus cranes, with their distinctive red heads, that most visitors come to see, though numbers have sadly declined drastically in recent years, and there's not much to be seen outside the months of December to May. In flight above the marshland of the sanctuary, the slender grey birds reveal spectacular black-tipped wings. **Cranes** feed not from the water but from the land, so when the spate season (July–November) waterlogs the delta, they migrate to Cambodia. Visiting the park, however, can be very expensive, so this is a trip for committed bird enthusiasts only: if you're keen, ask at the office of Dong Thap Tourist in Cao Lanh for details (see p.142).

You'll also need to approach the tourist office if you want to take a trip out to **Xeo Quyt Relic Area**, deep in the cajeput forest 20km southeast of Cao Lanh. The district's dense cover provided the perfect bolt-hole for Viet Cong guerrillas during the American War, and from 1960 to 1975 the struggle against America and the ARVN was masterminded from here. The boggy nature of the terrain made a tunnel system similar to that of Cu Chi (see p.122) unfeasible, so they made do with six submerged metal chambers sealed with tar and resin. Suspecting the base's existence, Americans bombed the area regularly, and even broadcast propaganda from the air to demoralize its occupants, but by developing a policy of "going without trace, cooking without smoke, speaking without noise", the cadres residing here escaped discovery throughout the war. The **boat trip** there involves a charming glide along eucalyptus-shaded canals teeming with freshwater fish and shrimps.

There are further birdwatching opportunities at the **Gao Giong Stork Sanctuary**, where storks can be seen any day of the year. It's located just 23km from Cao Lanh, though getting there involves an expensive boat ride, so you're better off visiting the **Bang Lang Stork Sanctuary** near Long Xuyen (see p.163), which is much easier to get to.

Practicalities

Buses to and from Cao Lanh stop at the bus station, a few paces below the town centre. From Long Xuyen or beyond, buses cross the Tien Giang via the Cao Lanh ferry, around 4km southwest of town, necessitating a short xe om ride (15,000–20,000đ) to the town centre. The Vietinbank on Ly Thuong Kiet **exchanges** dollars and traveller's cheques, while Sacombank has an ATM directly in front of the *Hoa Binh Hotel*. Dong Thap Tourist, whose office (daily 7–11.30am & 1.30–5pm; ☎067/385 5637) is at 2 Doc Binh Kieu, just off the main road, Nguyen Hué, is the place for **tourist information** about visits to the nearby bird sanctuaries, though very little English is spoken, so dedicated twitchers might be better off approaching tour operators in Ho Chi Minh City. **Internet access** is available at the **post office** on Nguyen Hué in the centre of town.

The tourist board-accredited *Song Tra* (☎067/385 2504; ❸–❹), at 178 Nguyen Hué, is Cao Lanh's poshest **place to stay**, and is where those on birding tours are accommodated; all rooms have air-conditioning, hot water and cable TV. A decent alternative is the *Hoa Binh*, or "*Peace*" *Hotel*, (☎067/385 1469; ❸–❹) – symbolically situated across from the war memorial, east of the town centre on Highway 30. The *Xuan Mai* (☎067/385 2852; ❷–❸), just west of the post office at 33 Le Qui Don, has been recently renovated: its larger rooms have bathtubs and breakfast is included in the price.

As for **eating**, there are several options along Nguyen Hué, of which the best is the *Ngoc Lan*, at no. 210, which is very popular with locals. The *A Chau*, at 42 Ly Thuong Kiet, also has a good range of dishes such as rice with fried pork and vegetables for around 30,000đ, or there's the in-house restaurant at the *Song Tra*, though it's a rather uncharismatic affair

▲ Boat trip on the River Mekong

Vinh Long

Ringed by water and besieged by boats and tumbledown stilthouses, the island that forms the heart of **VINH LONG** has the feel of a medieval fortress. However, if you find yourself yearning for a peaceful backwater, first impressions will be a let-down; central Vinh Long is hectic and noisy, its streets a blur of buses and motorbikes. Make for the waterfront, though, and it's a different story, with hotels, restaurants and cafés conjuring up something of a riviera atmosphere. From here you can watch the **Co Chien River** roll by, dotted with sampans, houseboats and the odd raft of river-weed. Though there's little to see or do in town, Vinh Long offers some of the most interesting **boat trips** in the delta – to the Cai Be floating market, coconut candy workshops, fruit orchards or even overnighting in home-stays.

Arrival and information

State-run **buses** pull into the bus station on 3 Thang 2 in the centre of town, while private buses use another bus station a couple of kilometres southwest of town on Nguyen Hué; from here take a xe om (about 10,000đ) into the centre. For information about boat trips or home-stays, check the state-run **Cuu Long Tourist** (T070/382 3616), whose main office is in the *Cuu Long 'B' Hotel*, or the private **Mekong Travel** 8, 1 Thang 5 (T070/383 6252): both charge around $25–30 for a 4–5 hour tour of Cai Be floating market, fruit orchards and the narrow waterways of An Binh Island.

Vietinbank at 143 Le Thai To **exchanges** traveller's cheques and cash and has an ATM. The **post office** is in the middle of town at 12C Hoang Thai Hieu, and **internet access** is available at the *Cuu Long 'B' Hotel*.

Accommodation

Most of Vinh Long's **accommodation** options are located near the boat jetty on the northern edge of town. Where boat trips operate in the Mekong Delta, notably around Vinh Long, the local tourist board can also arrange for visitors to stay with the owners of fruit orchards, allowing a close-up view of rural life (see box on home-stays on p.146).

Cuu Long 'A' 1, 1 Thang 5 T070/382 2494. This ageing edifice offers great views of the river, and has a/c, hot water and the like, but its grimy rooms are long overdue a make-over. ❶–❷
Cuu Long 'B' Phan Boi Chau T070/382 3656. Much newer and better maintained than its older sister, with higher prices to match. Some rooms have fine views of the Vinh Long riviera and all include satellite TV, a/c, hot water and breakfast. ❸–❹
Nam Phuong 11 Le Loi T070/382 2226. A smart mini-hotel near the town centre, where all rooms come with a/c, hot water and cable TV, and breakfast is included. ❷–❸

Phung Hoang 2h Hung Vuong T070/382 5185. This mini-hotel represents some of the best value in town. It has a dozen or so rooms with varying sizes and facilities, all with chintzy furnishings, and the staff are very friendly. ❶–❷
Phuong Hoang 2r Hung Vuong T070/382 2156. Just twenty metres south of its almost-namesake, this place has slightly less fancy rooms at marginally cheaper prices. ❶–❷
Van Tram Boarding House 4, 1 Thang 5 T070/382 3820. Just five rooms here, but all are a good size and well equipped with TVs, fridges, hot water and a/c. Add in its prime location and cheap prices, and the result is great value. ❷

The Town

Vinh Long has few specific sights, though the **Vinh Long Museum** (Tues–Thurs 8–11am & 1.30–4.30pm, Fri & Sat 6–9pm; free), facing the waterfront

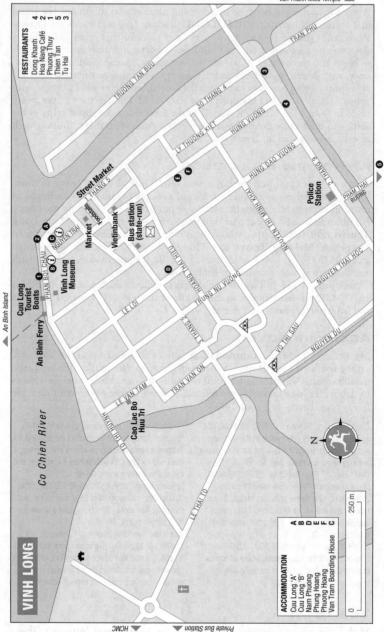

VINH LONG

Van Thanh Mieu Temple ▲

Co Chien River

▲ An Binh Island

RESTAURANTS
Dong Khanh   4
Hoa Nang Café   2
Phuong Thuy   1
Thien Tan   5
Tu Hai   3

TRAN PHU

TRUONG TAN BUU

30 THANG 4

LY THUONG KIET

HUNG VUONG

HUNG DAO VUONG

2 THANG 9

PHAM THAI BUONG

Police Station

NGUYEN THI MINH KHAI

NGUYEN THAI HOC

HOANG THAI HIEU

TRUNG NU VUONG

VO THI SAU

NGUYEN DU

Street Market
1 THANG 5

Foodstalls

Market

Vietinbank

Bus station (state-run)

Cuu Long Tourist Boats

An Binh Ferry

PHAN BOI CHAU

NGUYEN TRAI

Vinh Long Museum

LE LOI

3 THANG 2

LE VAN TAM

TRAN VAN ON

Cao Lac Bo Huu Tri

TO THI HUYNH

LE THAI TO

HCMC ▼

Private Bus Station ▼

N

250 m
0

ACCOMMODATION
Cuu Long 'A'   A
Cuu Long 'B'   B
Nam Phuong   D
Phung Hoang   E
Phuong Hoang   F
Van Tram Boarding House   C

on Phan Boi Chau, is worth a look if you haven't already visited war museums elsewhere. Displays in various buildings include historical finds from the region, farming implements and musical instruments, as well as a gruesome photographic catalogue of the province's pummelling during the American War. In the gardens around are tanks, a helicopter and planes from the war. Further west, on Le Van Tam, look out for the impressive French colonial building, **Cau Lac Bo Huu Tri**. This oddly shaped mansion, with its red-tiled roof and shuttered windows topped by mouldings of garlands, recalls the ghosts of French *colons* and rice merchants.

Thereafter, you'll have to journey 2km down the bumpy road that runs parallel to the Rach Long Canal and southeast of town, to the **Van Thanh Mieu Temple** (daily 5–11am & 1–7pm), in search of diversion. If you wander into the tiny lanes that back onto the river along the way, you can watch tiles and coffins being made in the simplest of surroundings, and you might even be invited to take a tea with the friendly locals. The temple itself is dedicated to Confucius – unusually for southern Vietnam – and a heavily bearded portrait of him watches over proceedings. Another temple at the front of the compound honours local mandarin Phan Thanh Gian (see box below), who is pictured in red robes, flanked by slender storks. Fronting the temple are two cannons that rained fire on the French in 1860. Unfortunately, both temples are often kept locked, though the gardener or caretaker may be able to open them for you.

Boat trips from Vinh Long

The cheapest and simplest way to see the river is to hop on the An Binh Ferry on Phan Boi Chau, and cross the Co Chien River (5min; 3000đ) to reach **AN BINH ISLAND**. Sometimes called Minh Island, it's a jigsaw of bite-sized pockets of land, skeined by a fine web of channels and gullies, eventually merging, to the east, with the province of Ben Tre. This idyllic landscape is criss-crossed by a network of dirt paths, making it ideal for a morning's rambling, though you'll need to take your own refreshments.

Phan Thanh Gian

Born in Vinh Long Province in 1796, the mandarin diplomat **Phan Thanh Gian** was destined to be involved in a chain of events that was to shape over a century of Vietnamese history.

On August 31, 1858, French naval forces attacked Da Nang, citing persecution of Catholic missionaries as their justification. The French colonial land-grab, that would culminate, in 1885, in the total conquest of Vietnam, had begun. By 1861, the three eastern provinces of Cochinchina had been conquered by the **French Expeditionary Corps**, and although there were popular anti-French uprisings Emperor Tu Duc sold out the following year, when the three provinces were formally ceded to the French by the **Treaty of Saigon**, which was signed by Phan Thanh Gian. A year later he had the opportunity to redress the situation, when he journeyed to Paris as ambassador to Emperor Napoleon III, to thrash out a long-term peace – the first Vietnamese ambassador ever to be despatched to Europe.

However, efforts to reclaim territory given up under the terms of the treaty failed, and by 1867 France moved to take over the rest of Cochinchina. Unable to persuade the spineless Tu Duc to sanction popular uprisings, Phan Thanh Gian embarked on a hunger strike in protest at French incursions and Hué's ineffectuality. When, after fifteen days, he had still not died, he swallowed **poison**, and his place among the massed ranks of Vietnamese heroes was assured.

However, most people fork out for a day or half-day boat trip to see several aspects of delta life, organized either through Cuu Long Tourist or Mekong Travel (see Arrival and information above), or through local boatmen always on the look-out for customers near the tourist jetty. These tours often include the option of overnighting in a **home-stay** (see box below) in a totally rural environment, though as they increase in popularity, some start to resemble guest houses rather than home-stays, with visitors put up in custom-built bamboo huts separated from the family home.

Most tour itineraries head upriver to the floating market at **CAI BE** (see p.138), stopping to visit fruit orchards, rice-paper making and candy factories en route; some tours also stop for a fish lunch at a rural outpost. Watching the river traffic, from the tiny rowing boats to huge sampans loaded with rice husks (fuel for the nearby brick kilns), is fascinating, and stepping ashore from time to time reveals insights into the lifestyles of the locals.

Eating and drinking

The Cuu Long Tourist-owned *Phuong Thuy*, built out over the river, boasts the best location of the town's **restaurants**, though the Vietnamese food is only average. The *Hoa Nang Café*, next to the *Cuu Long 'A'*, is a perfect place to sip a cool drink while watching the sun sink into the Mekong. South of town, at 56/1 Pham Thai Buong, the *Thien Tan* serves up delicious barbecued dishes, while on 2 Thang 9, *Tu Hai* (at no 29) and *Dong Khanh* (at no 49) produce standard Vietnamese stir-fries, soups and grilled dishes, with menus in English.

Tra Vinh and around

It's only another 65km southeast through some classic delta scenery – vivid green rice paddies, backed by coconut and water palms – to **TRA VINH**, an outback market town whose broad, tree-lined streets and smattering of colonial piles have yet to see tourists in any numbers. Even if you don't plan to stay here, it makes an interesting day out from Vinh Long. This region of the delta is Khmer country; as you get nearer to Tra Vinh, distinctive pagodas begin to appear beside the road, painted in rich pastel shades of lilac, orange and

---

Home-stays in the delta

While the Vietnamese are generally gregarious people, it's unusual for foreigners to be invited into their homes. However, most visitors are curious about local culture, so it's not surprising that home-stays are becoming ever more popular and widely available. Though there are **home-stays** all around the country, those located on tranquil islands of the delta, surrounded by acres of orchards, are particularly attractive.

For around $20 a head, you are transported by boat to your host's (usually isolated) abode, shown around the gardens, given a tasty dinner (most likely including the delicious elephant-ear fish – a delta speciality) and lodgings for the night, either in a bed or hammock in a spare room. Bathroom facilities are basic, with squat toilets and bucket baths, but generally clean. If you book your home-stay with a tour operator like Sinhbalo Adventures (see p.86), you can also spend the day kayaking between water palms along narrow canals, or cycling along narrow lanes between coconut, mango and papaya trees.

turquoise, their steep horned roofs puncturing the sky. Altogether there are over 140 Khmer pagodas scattered around the province.

Most visitors come here to visit the storks at nearby Hang Pagoda (see p.148), although the town's low-key charm makes it an intriguing place to spend a day or two. Unusually, Tra Vinh isn't ostensibly dominated by a branch of the Mekong – you'll have to journey a couple of hundred metres east of the 800-metre-square grid forming the town centre to find the river. A hike through the **market** to riverside Bach Dang makes the most engaging approach. The bridge 100m north of the fish market commands great views of the **Tra Vinh River**, whose eddying waters run canal-straight to the north. In places the river is almost corked by boats moored seven or eight deep.

Just south of the market, at the junction of Pham Thai Buong and Tran Quoc Tuan, the Chinese **Ong Pagoda** is worth a visit as it's a very active place of worship and there's always something interesting going on. North of the town centre up Le Loi, the **Ong Met Pagoda** is very different, with a Khmer-style roof above colonial arches and shutters: you're assured of a friendly reception here from the monks studying at its English school. Immediately north is the pretty **Tra Vinh Church**, an imposing buttressed construction, fronted by a statue of Christ above the entrance, with waves of stonework rippling up its spire.

Practicalities

Buses from Vinh Long and beyond hit the southwest corner of Tra Vinh, terminating about 800m from the centre of town at the bus station on Nguyen Dang, off Dien Bien Phu. The extremely helpful Tra Vinh Tourist Company at 64–66 Le Loi (℡074/385 8556, ℱ074/385 8768) can provide local **information**, while the Agribank, one block west of the market at 70–72 Le Loi, will change US dollars, and has an **ATM**. The **post office** is located on Hung Vuong, just opposite the *Thanh Tra Hotel*.

The *Cuu Long Hotel* (℡074/386 2615, ℱ074/386 6027; ➋–➍), at 999 Nguyen Thi Minh Khai (on the main road just before entering town), is one of the best **places to stay**, and brings an aura of prosperity to the small town with its surprisingly well-equipped rooms that have a touch of elegance. Almost opposite, the mini-hotel *Hoan My* (℡074/386 2211, ℱ074/386 6600; ➋–➌), at 105a Nguyen Thi Minh Khai, has tastefully furnished rooms, some with massage showers. The smartest places in the town centre are the *Palace* (℡074/386 4999; ➋), at 3 Le Thanh Ton, with fancy furnishings and all facilities, and the recently refurbished *Thanh Tra* (℡074/385 3626, ℱ074/625 0658; ➋–➌) at 1 Pham Thai Buo, which is more of a business-style hotel. For a decent budget choice, the *Duy Tung* (℡074/385 8567; ➊–➋), just opposite the market at 6 Dien Bien Phu, has clean and functional rooms with cable TV.

Eating options include the popular *Ben Co*, which serves up huge bowls of delicious *banh canh* – a noodle soup with pork; it's located about 5km from the town centre, on the right-hand side of Highway 53 (the road to Vinh Long) about half a kilometre after the turning for Ba Om. Other reliable places are the thatched bar-restaurant behind the *Cuu Long Hotel*, on the same road heading out of town, and the top-floor restaurant of the *Thanh Tra Hotel*. For a little more ambience, try the *Tuy Huong*, opposite the front of the market, whose friendly owners offer a range of Chinese and Vietnamese dishes, or the *Viet Hoa*, at 80 Tran Phu, which specializes in seafood; to get there walk south of the front of the market along Dien Bien Phu and turn right on to Tran Phu. Be warned that some places, including *Viet Hoa* close around 8pm. Finally, **stalls** around the western edge of the market hawk pho and com throughout the evening.

Ba Om Pond

Five kilometres southwest of town, a signposted road on the left runs down to **Ba Om Pond**, beloved of Tra Vinh picnickers and courting couples. Buses to and from Vinh Long pass the short approach road here, or a xe om from the centre of Tra Vinh costs around 20,000đ. Around the pond, drinks and snack vendors lie in wait for visitors. Though it can get crowded at weekends, on weekdays it is usually restful. Bordered by grassy banks, and shaded by towering, aged trees whose roots clutch the ground, Ba Om is cloaked with plants that attract flocks of birds in the late afternoon.

The area across the far side of the pond has been a Khmer place of worship since the eleventh century, and today it's occupied by **Ang Pagoda**. Steep-roofed and stained with age, the pagoda makes an affecting sight, especially when it echoes with the chants of its resident monks. Fronting it is a nest of stupas guarded by stone lions, while murals inside depict scenes from the Buddha's life. In season, rice from the pagoda's paddy fields is heaped next to the altar, where it's guarded by an impressive golden Sakyamuni image and a host of smaller ones. Several Cambodian monks are resident here, who are eager to practise their English with visitors.

Also worth a look is the **Khmer Minority People's Museum** (daily 7–11am & 1–5pm; free), just in front of the pagoda. The display includes musical instruments, a depiction of Khmer daily life, Buddha statues and samples of traditional dress.

Hang Pagoda

The sight of the hundreds of **storks** that nest in the grounds of **Hang Pagoda**, a Khmer pagoda around 6km south of town along Dien Bien Phu, is one that will linger in the memory. Timing, however, is all-important, and you should aim to catch these magnificent creatures before dusk, when they wheel and hover over the treetops, their snowy wings catching the evening's sunlight. It's a stirring sight, though you might find yourself distracted by the saffron-robed monks who clamour to practise their English. They may also show you their wood-carving workshop, where there's usually someone at work on a wooden rat or tiger. Hang Pagoda itself – an arched stone gate to the left of the main road betrays the entrance to the compound – is nothing to write home about. Dominating it is a **Sakyamuni statue**, hooped by a halo of fairy lights and flanked by murals depicting scenes from his life. There's no public transport to the pagoda, so you'll have to take a xe om: about 40,000đ for the return trip.

Sa Dec

A cluster of brick and tile kilns on the riverbank announces your arrival in the charming town of **SA DEC**, a little over 20km upriver of Vinh Long. French novelist Marguerite Duras lived here as a child (see box opposite), and decades later the town's stuccoed shophouse terraces, riverside mansions and remarkably busy stretch of the rumbling Mekong provided the backdrop for the movie adaptation of her novel *The Lover*.

As you come in from the bus station, the town's three main arteries – Nguyen Hué, Tran Hung Dao and Hung Vuong – branch off to your right. It's worth wandering along Nguyen Hué, whose umbrella-choked lanes hide Sa Dec's extensive riverside market. Waterfront comings and goings are observed by

Marguerite Duras

Marguerite Duras (1914–96) was born to French parents in a suburb of Saigon, and lived in various locations in Vietnam and Cambodia before going, aged 18, to study at the Sorbonne in France. She wrote many novels, plays and film scripts including the autobiographical novel *The Lover* (1984) which sold over three million copies and was translated into forty languages. Its subject is an interracial affair between a 15-year-old French girl and her middle-aged Chinese lover, set in 1930s' Indochina. Duras had little sympathy for her peers, of whom she wrote "I look at the (French) women in the streets of Saigon. They don't do anything, just save themselves up… Some of them go mad…some are deserted for a young maid." Duras clearly had no intention of letting life pass her by in this way, even if it meant becoming the subject of the town's gossip.

Though her novels are principally about the inner thoughts of her characters, she also describes the landscape around Sa Dec as it still appears today: "In the surrounding flatness, stretching as far as the eye can see, the rivers flow as if the earth slopes downward."

rheumy old men playing chequers, and women squat on their haunches, selling fruit from wicker baskets. From about halfway down Nguyen Hué, ferries cross to the childhood **home of Marguerite Duras**, which now belongs to the People's Committee, and is not open to the public. It's an elegant old colonial villa that's been reasonably maintained, and its pale blue shutters and red-tiled roof still give off a refined aura.

A few kilometres north of town by the river, Sa Dec's famed **flower nurseries** consist of more than a hundred farms cultivating a host of ferns, fruit trees, shrubs and flowers. The expansive grounds of **Tu Ton Rose Garden** (daily 8–11am & 1–5pm) get the lion's share of tourists visiting the area. In addition to the varieties of roses cultivated here (among them the *Brigitte Bardot*, the *Jolie Madame* and the *Marseille*), over 580 species of plants are grown, ranging from orchids, carnations and chrysanthemums, through to medicinal herbs and pines grown for export around Asia. Bear in mind that the nurseries are overrun on Sundays by tourists from Ho Chi Minh City, who come to pose for photos among the blooms; and that things get particularly busy and colourful in the run-up to Tet, as farms prepare to transport their stocks to the city's flower markets.

Practicalities

Buses terminate 300m southeast of the town centre. The town's **post office**, at the corner of Nguyen Sinh Sac and Hung Vuong, also has **internet access**.

Accommodation in Sa Dec is pretty limited. The best value in town is the family-run, mini-hotel *Huong Thuy* (☎067/386 8963; ❶–❷) at 58 Le Thanh Ton: it's centrally located with immaculately clean, air-conditioned rooms which all have hot water, TVs and fridges. Alternatively, there's little to choose between the *Bong Hong* at 251a Nguyen Sinh Sac (☎067/386 8287; ❷–❸) and the *Sa Dec*, 108/5a Hung Vuong (☎067/386 1430; ❷–❸), at the northern end of the street: both are reasonable if uninspiring places to stay. **Eating** options are also fairly limited: the *Com Thuy* at 439 Hung Vuong, serves up Vietnamese staples and has an English menu, while the family-run *Chanh Ky*, at 193 Nguyen Sinh Sac, doles out Chinese noodles and rice dishes for under $2 that you can wash down with cold beer. The *Bong Hong* and *Sa Dec* hotels also have their own, rather soulless, attached restaurants.

Can Tho and around

A population of around half a million makes **CAN THO** the delta's biggest city, and losing yourself in its commercial thrum for a few days is the perfect antidote to time spent in quiet backwaters of the delta. However, first impressions are rather less than encouraging: Can Tho is a hefty settlement but, once the oppressive urban sprawl encasing the town has been negotiated, its breezy waterfront comes as a pleasant surprise.

At the confluence of the Can Tho and Hau Giang rivers, the city is a major mercantile centre and transport interchange. But Can Tho is no mere staging post. Some of the best restaurants in the delta are located here; what's more, the abundant rice fields of Can Tho Province are never far away, and at the intersections of the canals and rivers that thread between them are some of the delta's best-known floating markets. Can Tho was the last city to succumb to the North Vietnamese Army, a day after the fall of Saigon, on May 1, 1975 – the date that has come to represent the reunification of the country.

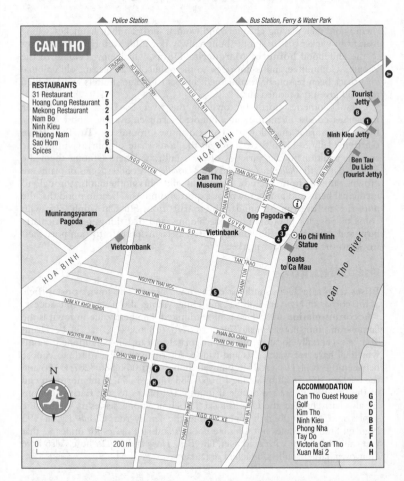

CAN THO

RESTAURANTS
31 Restaurant	7
Hoang Cung Restaurant	5
Mekong Restaurant	2
Nam Bo	4
Ninh Kieu	1
Phuong Nam	3
Sao Hom	6
Spices	A

Police Station

Bus Station, Ferry & Water Park

Tourist Jetty

Ninh Kieu Jetty

Ben Tau Du Lich (Tourist Jetty)

Can Tho Museum

Munirangsyaram Pagoda

Ong Pagoda

Vietinbank

Ho Chi Minh Statue

Vietcombank

Boats to Ca Mau

Can Tho River

N

0   200 m

ACCOMMODATION
Can Tho Guest House	G
Golf	C
Kim Tho	D
Ninh Kieu	B
Phong Nha	E
Tay Do	F
Victoria Can Tho	A
Xuan Mai 2	H

Bridging the Delta

The Mekong River deposits tons of fertile earth on the delta each year, making the region's produce so abundant, but it also provides a barrier to swift travel, forcing drivers to queue for hours to cross its countless channels by slow, lumbering ferries. In the late 1990s a plan was hatched to build huge bridges at three key points in the delta –My Thuan, My Tho and Can Tho – in order to cut down journey times. The first of these, at My Thuan, crossing the Tien Giang, opened in 2000 and immediately slashed hours off journey times. The second, linking My Tho and Ben Tre, suffered delays but finally opened in early 2009. The third and biggest project, crossing the widest of the Mekong's nine arms (the Hau Giang) at Can Tho, was the scene of a tragic accident in September 2007 when a 90-metre section of an approach ramp collapsed, killing more than 50 workers. Construction was delayed for a while but is now in full swing again and this most important of the delta's bridges should finally be complete by 2010.

Arrival, information and city transport

Construction began in 2005 on the much-touted **bridge** across the Hau Giang River to Can Tho (see box above), but until its completion, probably in 2010, all visitors have to approach the city by ferry. Buses from all destinations currently roll off the ferry and into Can Tho's **bus station**, 1200m northwest of town at the junction of Nguyen Trai and Hung Vuong; a xe om into town costs around 10,000đ.

For **information** about boat trips and other local attractions, drop in at the helpful Can Tho Tourist at 20 Hai Ba Trung (℗0710/382 1852, ⓔcanthotour @hcm.vnn.vn). Can Tho Tourist tour **boats** along the river and to the markets depart from the tourist jetty ("Ben Tau Du Lich"), as do evening river **cruises** (daily 8–9.30pm; 10,000đ), which feature Vietnamese music.

Accommodation

Hai Ba Trung and Chau Van Liem together form the axis of Can Tho's healthy **hotel** scene, with the more expensive and mid-range properties clustered around the northern end of Hai Ba Trung, and budget places located around Chau Van Liem and streets further south. If you'd rather stay in a rural setting than amid the downtown bustle, consider the *Victoria* or the more affordable *My Khanh Village* (see p.154). Xe om drivers at the bus station will try to take you to a hotel of their choice (thus receiving a small commission), so be firm if you know where you want to go.

Can Tho Guest House 41 Chau Van Liem ℗0710/381 1773, ℗0710/3820 356. A good-value, budget place. Some rooms are large, with carpets, bathtubs and all facilities. ❷

Golf 2 Hai Ba Trung ℗0710/381 2210, ⓦwww .vinagolf.vn. With over a hundred rooms, a pool and all facilities, not to mention fabulous river views, this place stands at the head of the pack in Can Tho, even though it's all a bit soulless and international. ❻–❼

Kim Tho 1A Ngo Gia Tu ℗0710/322 2228, ⓦwww.kimtho.com. Squeezing in beside the established hotels along the riverfront, this new

place promises stiff competition with its state-of-the-art fixtures and fittings, plus sweeping river views. ❹

Ninh Kieu 2 Hai Ba Trung ℗0710/382 4583. Attractive place offering good-value, well-appointed rooms off coolly tiled halls; all rates include breakfast. A new extension has more expensive rooms that enjoy great river views. ❹–❺

Phong Nha 70 Nguyen An Ninh ℗0710/382 1615. Recently relocated in a smart new building, this represents one of Can Tho's best budget options. All rooms have a/c and bathrooms are spotless. ❷

Tay Do 61 Chau Van Liem ☎0710/382 1009. Possibly the best mid-range option in town, with over forty cosy rooms boasting all mod cons, including cable TV. ❹

🏃 **Victoria Can Tho** Cai Khe Ward ☎0710/381 0111, ⓦ www.victoriahotels .asia. Built and furnished in classic French-colonial style but with all the modern facilities you'd expect

from the delta's first international standard hotel. It's set in a grand riverside location opposite the town and surrounded by lush tropical growth. ❼

Xuan Mai 2 17 Dien Bien Phu ☎0710/382 3578. Tucked away down a side street off Chau Van Liem, this is a decent budget option, with large, bright rooms, some with fan and others with a/c. ❶–❷

The City

Though its boat trips (see opposite) are the main reason for visiting Can Tho, a handful of lesser diversions on dry land will help keep you amused in the meantime. Broad Hoa Binh is the city's backbone, and the site of the impressive **Can Tho Museum**, 1 Hoa Binh (Tues–Thurs 8–11am & 2–5pm, Sat & Sun 8–11am & 6.30–9pm; free), which presents "the history of the resistance against foreign aggression of Can Tho people", as well as local economic and social achievements.

The 1946-built **Munirangsyaram Pagoda**, 250m southwest of the museum, warrants examination only if the more impressive Khmer pagodas around Tra Vinh or Soc Trang aren't on your itinerary. Entrance into the pagoda compound is through a top-heavy stone gate weighed down with masonry reminiscent of Angkor Wat, but there is little to see inside apart from a few plaster Buddha images.

The waterfront

Walking east of Munirangsyaram Pagoda for five minutes, along Nguyen Thai Hoc, deposits you bang in the middle of the city's **riverside promenade**, which extends along Hai Ba Trung. The whole riverfront has been cleaned up in recent years, and the promenade is now lined by beds of plants and stone seats: the old market has also been replaced by a covered area with souvenir stalls and an excellent restaurant. As with most delta towns, this riverside area gets crowded in the evenings as locals come out for a stroll in the cooler air.

Heading north along Hai Ba Trung, an imposing silver statue of a waving Uncle Ho greets you on the promenade. Just north of this is **Ong Pagoda**, a prosperous place built in the late nineteenth century by wealthy Chinese townsman Huynh An Thai. Inside, a ruddy-faced Quan Cong presides, flaunting Rio Carnival-style headgear. On his left is Than Tai, to whom a string of families come on the first day of every month, asking for money and good fortune. On his right is Thien Hau, Goddess of the Sea. There's also a small chamber dedicated to Quan Am to the left of the main hall. Waterfront **cafés** will rustle up a fresh coconut or a pot of green tea to clear the incense smoke out of your lungs, and from your seat you can watch the relentless sampan traffic of the Can Tho River.

Eating

Can Tho is well endowed with good, affordable **restaurants**, most serving Vietnamese food, though there are plenty that also offer international dishes. Those along Hai Ba Trung target a primarily foreign market, while locals tend to patronize places around the market and along Nam Ky Khoi Nghia.

31 Restaurant 31 Ngo Duc Ke. Simple café serving up tasty and cheap Vietnamese dishes enjoyed by tourists and locals alike. 8am–11pm.

Hoang Cung Restaurant 55 Phan Dinh Phung. Located on the ground floor of the *Saigon Can Tho* hotel, this place serves decent Western and Vietnamese dishes in a stylish environment at reasonable prices. 6am–11pm.

Mekong Restaurant 38 Hai Ba Trung. This long-established favourite is still hard to top for its cheap, flavoursome Vietnamese and Chinese meals, as well as succulent chateaubriand steaks for around 70,000đ. There is also a good vegetarian selection. 8am–2pm & 4–10pm.

Nam Bo 50 Hai Ba Trung ☎0710/382 3908. French café-inspired place with attractive furnishings and an intimate atmosphere; dining on the first-floor balcony gives a bird's-eye view of waterfront activities. Tempting salads, sandwiches and desserts cost around 40,000–90,000đ. It gets crowded in the evening when reserving a table is recommended. 9am–11pm.

Ninh Kieu 2 Hai Ba Trung. Stylish riverside venue with a terrace that takes full advantage of its location. Seafood is the speciality here, though they serve steaks too. 6am–10pm.

Phuong Nam 48 Hai Ba Trung. A good range of cheap and tasty Western and Vietnamese dishes, with an upstairs balcony too. 9am–2pm & 5–11pm

Sao Hom Hai Ba Trung. This tastefully decorated, open-sided riverfront place serves an appealing menu of Vietnamese and Western dishes that features items such as sauteed pumpkin flowers with garlic. Draft beer, wines, cocktails, coffee and ice cream too. 5am–11pm.

Spices *Victoria Can Tho* hotel, Cai Khe Ward. Fine dining in a tasteful ethnic interior, or outside on the romantic riverside terrace; this and the extensive menu, with appetizers such as *banh cuon* (rice pancakes stuffed with pork, shrimp and salmon eggs ($7) and main courses for $12–25, make the detour to this hotel restaurant worth the effort. 6am–10pm.

Listings

Airlines Vietnam Airlines has a branch at Can Tho Tourist, 20 Hai Ba Trung.

Banks Vietcombank, 7 Hoa Binh (Mon–Fri 7–11am & 1–5pm), changes cash and traveller's cheques and has an ATM. Vietinbank at 9 Phan Dinh Phung (Mon–Fri 7.30–noon & 1–6pm) changes traveller's cheques and cash for similar rates.

Bicycle and motorbike rental Enquire at the Huy Hoang hotel, 35 Ngo Duc Ke. Rates are around $4 a day for a bicycle, $6 a day for a motorbike.

Hospital The general hospital is located 3km west of the centre on Highway 91B.

Internet access Most hotels offer internet access, and there is an independent operator at 9 Chau Van Liem.

Pharmacy 31b Chau Van Liem; and 78 Hai Ba Trung.

Police 67–69 Hung Vuong, just down from the bus station.

Post office 2 Hoa Binh (daily 6am–9pm). IDD, internet, poste restante, fax and express mail service.

Sports Non-residents can use the swimming pool and tennis courts at *Victoria Can Tho* hotel (floodlit in the evening) for a few dollars.

Supermarket There is a huge Co-op Mart at the junction of Hoa Binh and Ngo Quyen.

Waterpark Can Tho Water Park (☎0710/376 3343; Mon–Fri 9am–6pm, Sat & Sun 8am–7pm; 40,000đ), in Cai Khe Ward to the north of town, has several pools, water chutes and slides in a large, landscaped area.

Boat trips and floating markets

Every morning an armada of boats takes to the web of waterways spun across Can Tho Province and makes for one of its **floating markets**. Everything your average villager could ever need is on sale, from haircuts to coffins, though predictably fruit and vegetables make up most of what's on offer. Each boat's produce is identifiable by a sample hanging off a bamboo mast in its bow, but it's difficult to get colourful pictures as the produce is stored below. Among the flotilla of craft are ancient luggers piled so high they seem sure to sink, and sampans whose oarsmen and women stand up to strain against their scissor-oars. Few boats are painted, so photographers will have to rely on the glimpses of fruit for splashes of colour.

Of the three major nearby markets, two are west of the city. The most commonly visited, 7km out of Can Tho, is **Cai Rang**, but you'll have to be prepared to queue up with all the other tourist boats before you can weave among the fervent waterborne activity, with drinks vendors clamouring to make a sale. This market is particularly active on Sundays.

Another 10km west and you're at modest **Phong Dien**, whose appeal is that it sees relatively few tourists and so the locals are correspondingly friendly. If you wish to stay longer here, the purpose-built *My Khanh Village* (T0710/384 6260, W www.mykhanh.com; 3–4), is nearby at 335 Lo Vong Cung, with wooden bungalows in a shady setting and a good-sized pool. Its attractions include an ancient house, a pond full of crocodiles, caged monkeys and a pig-racing track, plus a pony and trap to take visitors round the site. There are also demonstrations on making rice cakes and brewing wine, and traditional musicians perform in the evenings.

To get to **Phung Hiep** market, 32km south of Can Tho, on the road to Soc Trang, it's better to go by car or motorbike to arrive early and take a walk through the narrow lanes of the colourful street market, where you'll see mounds of longans and custard apples, squid and crab, paper flowers, baguettes and chillies, before making your way to the river. Here, dozens of boats jostle and bump along the water's edge, their owners shouting out to advertise their wares. There is a good view of the maelstrom from Phung Hiep Bridge, which carries the main road across the river. This was once a main centre for buying and selling snakes, but dwindling numbers have forced the government to ban this trade.

Practicalities

Most organized tours take you to Cai Rang or Phong Dien early in the morning, then make a leisurely return to the city, via the maze of picturesque canals and orchards that surround it, usually stopping to sample star fruit and sapodilla, longan and rambutan along the way. Can Tho Tourist (see p.151) charges between 150,000–250,000đ per person for such a tour, depending on the itinerary and type of boat. As usual, unofficial boat operators are cheaper, charging about 50,000đ per hour for a simple sampan: women prowl for customers along Hai Ba Trung, and some can be friendly and informative, but be on the lookout for scams. Phong Dien and Phung Hiep are more easily reached by **hiring an xe om** (about 80,000đ and 150,000đ return respectively), then renting a sampan for an hour's rowing (about 50,000–60,000đ) among the buyers and sellers.

Around Can Tho: Binh Tuy Temple and The Duong Home

Just six kilometres north of Can Tho along the road to Long Xuyen (about 40,000đ return by xe om) is the **Binh Tuy Temple** (daily 7.30–10.30am & 1.30–5.30pm; free), which began life in the nineteenth century as a *dinh*, or communal house for travellers to rest in. The present building dates back to 1909, and immediately catches the eye with its green-tiled eaves framed by frangipani trees. Though it appears small from outside, the cool interior runs very deep, and the walls are decorated with images of Chinese gods and Vietnamese heroes. Between the sturdy wooden pillars are several altars, with some ghoulish characters guarding one of them with axes raised.

Down a side street opposite Binh Tuy Temple, at 26/1a Bui Huu Nghia, is the beautiful **Duong Home**, which was used in the 1992 filming of *The Lover* (see p.535). A classic example of French colonial architecture, its shuttered windows and elaborate stucco decorations conceal a spacious living room featuring

Moving on from Can Tho

Onward routes from Can Tho either veer up to Long Xuyen, Chau Doc and the Cambodian border, or follow Highway 1 to Soc Trang and on to Ca Mau. There's a speedboat to Ca Mau (see p.157), which departs from the jetty just below the Ho Chi Minh statue (4hr; about 100,000đ) with several departures each morning. Speedboats to Ho Chi Minh City (4hr; about 250,000đ) leave from the Ninh Kieu jetty at the northern end of Hai Ba Trung.

period furnishings with mother-of-pearl inlay. The affable owner is often on hand to show visitors round, and the adjacent orchid garden contains what is thought to be the tallest cactus in the country.

Soc Trang

Straddled across an oily branch of the Mekong, **SOC TRANG** lacks the panache of other delta towns, though on the fifteenth day of the tenth lunar month (Nov–Dec) the town springs to life as thousands converge to see traditional Khmer boats (*thuyen dua*) racing each other during the **Oc Om Boc festival**.

Khmer pagodas are ten-a-penny in this region of the delta, with one of the most impressive, the **Khleang Pagoda**, located right in the middle of town on Nguyen Chi Thanh. It is surrounded by a two-tiered terrace, and the doors and windows are adorned with traditional Khmer motifs in greens, reds and golds. Inside is a wonderfully reposeful golden Sakyamuni statue, though unfortunately, the doors are often locked. Directly opposite the pagoda at 23 Nguyen Chi Thanh, the **Khmer Museum** (Mon–Sat 7–11am & 1–5pm; free), houses some low-key exhibits including stringed instruments made of snakeskin and coconut husks, and some wonderfully colourful food covers, shaped like conical hats, but with a stippled surface.

▲ Soc Trang's Khleang Pagoda

Head north from here along Mau Than 68 for a few minutes, and on the right you'll see **Dat Set Pagoda**, aka Buu Son Tu Pagoda. Constructed almost entirely from clay, with a smart sheet-metal roof to keep the rain off, Dat Set makes a welcome change from the more numerous Khmer pagodas in this region of the delta. Chinese visitors flock here to see the pagoda's impressive and highly colourful collection of clay statues; many are life-size, with animals and figures from Chinese mythology being the most popular subjects. The pagoda is also home to some truly gargantuan candles that look like pillars, weigh around 200kg each and are said to last for seventy years of continuous burning.

Located a short way south of the town centre, **Mahatup Pagoda**, aka Bat Pagoda, is famed for its vast community of golden-bodied fruit bats, which spectacularly take to the skies at dusk. Plan to get here around 5.30pm and as the drop in temperature wakes them you'll see the bats spinning, preening and flapping their matt-black wings – some have a span of 1.5m. Khmer monks have worshipped at this site for four hundred years, though the present pagoda is only a hundred years old. Inside, bright murals bearing the names of the Khmer communities around the world that financed them recount the life of the Buddha. Outside, look out for the graves of four pigs behind the large hall to the right opposite the pagoda, each of which had five toenails (pigs usually have four). Since such animals are believed to bring bad luck, they are honoured with well-tended resting places to ward off any evil tendencies. The tombstones are painted with their likenesses and the dates of their passing on. To get to the pagoda, go 2km south of town along Le Hong Phong, then turn right at a fork beside a small market and continue another 800m. Cars are not allowed on the last few hundred metres, so you'll have to walk or hop on one of many waiting xe om.

Practicalities

The waterway running roughly west to east splits Soc Trang in two, with most of the town nestling on its south bank. The town's spine is Hai Ba Trung, which runs across the water, before becoming Tran Hung Dao on the southern outskirts. The **bus station** is at the northern end of town on Nguyen Chi Thanh. Soc Trang Tourist, at 104 Le Loi (daily 7–11am & 1–5pm; ☎079/382 2024), can usually help with local **information**. The **post office** is in the centre of town at 1 Tran Hung Dao, and has **internet** access. There's an **ATM** in front of the *Khanh Hung Hotel*.

If you have your own transport, the best **place to stay** is a few kilometres out of town at km2127 on Highway 1 – the *Ngoc Suong* (☎079/361 3108; Ⓦwww.ngocsuonghotel.com; ❸–❹) has a range of comfortable rooms, with a pool and tennis court; the cheaper rooms at the back are particularly good value. At 89 Highway 1, just on the northern fringe of town, the *Vinh Thong* (☎079/326 2111; ❷) is a smart new, six-storey mini-hotel with wi-fi, cable TV and a top-floor café. In the centre of town, the *Khanh Hung Hotel* (☎079/382 1026; ❶–❷), at 15 Tran Hung Dao, has 55 rooms ranging from basic and cheap to carpeted suites that have seen better days. A block west, at 128 Nguyen Trung Truc, the *Que Huong* (☎079/361 6122; ❷) is a newer place with spacious, well-equipped rooms and wi-fi in the lobby.

Eating options are limited, as the town is not really geared up for independent travellers. One very popular place among locals is *Hung*, north of the river at 24 Hung Vuong (down a small lane), which serves various dishes with rice, although its speciality is steamboat. Alternatively, *Hang Ky*, at 67 Hung Vuong in the northwest corner of town, turns out tasty Vietnamese staple dishes on rice. For a snack, *Lap Hung*, at 134 Ly Thuong Kiet, serves the local speciality *banh bia*, a round cake with a filling made from sweetened beans or durian – something of an acquired taste.

Bac Lieu

Beyond Soc Trang the landscape becomes progressively more waterlogged and water palms hug the banks of the waterways that criss-cross it. A little over 40km southwest of Soc Trang, Highway 1 dips south towards the crown of **BAC LIEU**, before veering off west to Ca Mau. It may be the back end of nowhere, but Bac Lieu's prosperity is evident in new shopping complexes and upmarket homes around the centre. The source of this prosperity is overseas Vietnamese, many of whom hail from this region. The town may not boast sights to set the pulse racing, but it's got the only accommodation between Soc Trang and Ca Mau, and the **Bac Lieu Bird Sanctuary** (daily 7.30am–5pm; 15,000đ), 6km southwest of town towards the coast, is well worth the visit. There is an observation tower and paths among the cajeput forest, along which local guides can lead you. Lots of birds can be seen here from July to December, but there is little to see from January to June. Guides will appreciate a tip, even if their English skills are limited.

Practicalities

The Bac Lieu Tourist Company, at 2 Hoang Van Thu (daily 7–11am & 1–5pm; ☎0781/392 2922, ☏0781/382 4273), is conveniently situated next to the *Bac Lieu* hotel, and the staff are reasonably helpful with local **information**. The **post office** is in the centre of town at 20 Tran Phu, and a little further along the road at no. 82 is Sacombank, where you can **exchange money**. There's an ATM conveniently located in front of the *Bac Lieu*. The **bus station** is 1.5km west of town, and xe om shuttle back and forth to the centre. Moving on, it's best to get back on Highway 1 and flag down express buses passing through.

The town's main **hotel**, *Bac Lieu* (☎0781/395 9697; ❷–❸), in the centre of town at 4–6 Hoang Van Thu, has clean but dull rooms, complete with air-conditioning, cable TV and hot water. For more character, head next door to the *Cong Tu* (☎0781/395 3304; ❷–❸), whose main entrance is on the riverside at 13 Dien Bien Phu: this palatial colonial villa has just ten rooms with fancy furnishings and high ceilings. *Kieu Hoi*, 8 Ly Tu Trong (☎0781/☎395 8080; ❷), is slightly cheaper though its surroundings are distinctly drab.

The *Bac Lieu*'s ground-floor **restaurant** offers set menus as well as a la carte dishes at around $3–4, while the cafe at the *Cong Tu* is much more atmospheric, though its menu is long on drinks and short on food. Your best option for **nightlife** is to join the overseas Vietnamese at *Kitty*, on the corner of Ba Trieu and Tran Phu: this first-floor bar wouldn't look out of place in Ho Chi Minh City and serves expensive cocktails, beers and coffee, as well as a reasonable range of Vietnamese dishes.

Ca Mau and around

With its left shoulder braced against the Bac Lieu Canal, Highway 1 now heads westwards from Bac Lieu towards the **Ca Mau Peninsula**, which constitutes not only the end of mainland Vietnam but of Southeast Asia as well. In this part of the country, waterways are the most efficient means of travel – a point pressed home by the slender ferries moored in all the villages the road passes. Much of this pancake-flat region of the delta is composed of silt deposited by the Mekong, and the swamplands covering portions of it are home to a variety of wading birds. In addition to rice cultivation, shrimp farming is a major local concern – along the way you're sure to spot shrimp ponds, demarcated by mud banks that have been baked and cracked crazily by the sun.

CA MAU itself, Vietnam's southernmost town of any size, has a frontier feel to it, though rapid development is changing that fast. Things have changed since 1989 when travel writer Justin Wintle described it as a "scrappy clutter…a backyard town in a backyard province", though there are still pockets of squalor between the glitzy new buildings. Ca Mau sprawls across a vast area, with broad

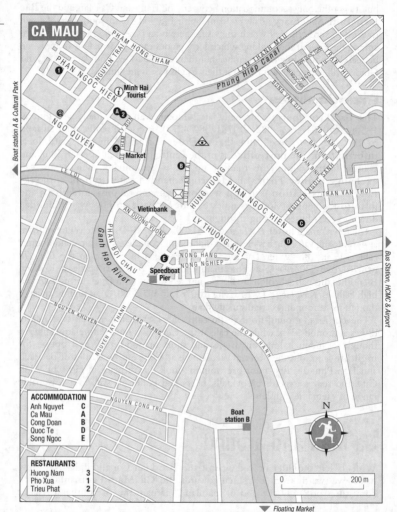

CA MAU

◄ Boat station A & Cultural Park

► Bus Station, HCMC & Airport

ACCOMMODATION
Anh Nguyet	C
Ca Mau	A
Cong Doan	B
Quoc Te	D
Song Ngoc	E

RESTAURANTS
Huong Nam	3
Pho Xua	1
Trieu Phat	2

0   200 m

N

▼ Floating Market

boulevards connected by pot-holed lanes and a couple of busy bridges spanning the canal that splits the town in two.

As yet, few Western travellers visit Ca Mau, which is hardly surprising; it is nearly 350km from Saigon and until recently was a dead-end destination. However, there are now speedboats to Rach Gia that cover the journey in less than three hours, and improvements to Highway 63 make the journey by road less arduous, so incorporating Ca Mau in a circular tour of the delta is now a possibility.

Arrival and information

Vasco Airlines (@www.vasco.com.vn) operates a daily **flight** from Ho Chi Minh City to Ca Mau airport, a few kilometres southeast of town on Highway 1. Almost next door is the **bus station**, where buses from Ho Chi Minh City, Can Tho and other destinations pull up: a xe om into town will cost about 20,000đ. Minh Hai Tourist (☎0780/383 1828, ⓕ0780/383 7022), at 91–93 Phan Dinh Phung, has helpful staff for local **information** and can arrange a **tour** of the region, as well as **car** and **speedboat rental** for trips to outlying areas. You'll need a sizeable group to make hiring a boat economical, as rates are quite high (at least $100 per day).

To **exchange** traveller's cheques or cash, Vietinbank is at 94 Ly Thuong Kiet (Mon–Fri 7.30–11am & 1.30–4.30pm); it also has an ATM. The main **post office** (daily 6am–10pm) is opposite Vietinbank, on Luu Tan Tai; **internet** is available here, as well as at 68 Nguyen Trai.

Accommodation

Ca Mau's hotel scene has improved in recent years and there are now plenty of options, including a cluster of long-standing places along Phan Ngoc Hien in the centre, and some smart new alternatives on the south side of town.

Anh Nguyet (Moonlight) 207 Phan Ngoc Hien ☎0780/356 7666, ⓕ0780/356 7547. The exterior may not look much, but the plush, carpeted rooms with stylish furnishings and excellent facilities make this Ca Mau's most luxurious place to stay. ❸–❺

Ca Mau 20 Phan Ngoc Hien ☎0780/383 1165. A recent renovation has smartened up the rooms at this conveniently located hotel, making it a reasonable choice. ❷–❸

Cong Doan (Trade Union) 9 Luu Tan Tai ☎0780/383 3245. Top-priced rooms here are excellent value; big and bright with all facilities,

though the cheaper rooms are smaller and gloomier. ❶–❷

Quoc Te (International) 179 Phan Ngoc Hien ☎0780/382 6745, ⓔquoctehotel@yahoo.com.vn. Top-end rooms here are big, clean and comfy with all facilities, while cheaper rooms are a bit smaller. ❸–❹

Song Ngoc 2b Hung Vuong ☎0780/381 7303, ⓕ0780/381 7307. All rooms in this mini-hotel situated near the roundabout south of the canal have bathtubs as well as a/c, hot water, TVs and mini-bars. Rooms on the upper floors have a good view of the town. ❷

The Town

The town is bordered by the Ganh Hao River, which snakes past as though trying to wriggle free before the encroaching stilthouses squeeze the life from it. Lurking along the north bank of the Phung Hiep Canal, which divides the town, is the rag-tag squall of the **market**, a shantytown of corrugated iron, canvas and sacking. There is little to see in town itself, though the **Cao Dai Temple** on Phan Ngoc Hien near the canal, is worth a look for its ornate towers, and a couple of parks opposite the temple offer shady areas to escape the bustle of town.

Just a couple of kilometres west of the centre (about 20,000đ for a xe om) lies the town's most intriguing attraction, at least during the rainy season (July–Nov). The **Cultural Park** on Ly Van Lam (daily dawn–dusk; 4000đ) is something of a misnomer; it is, in fact, a bird sanctuary teeming with storks and many other birds that nest in the trees in easily observed fenced-off areas. The huge park also has a mini zoo featuring elephants, monkeys, deer and other animals, as well as lots of pavilions and picnic spots.

Owners of small boats at Boat Station B will take you a couple of kilometres downstream to see Ca Mau's small **floating markets** for around 30,000đ a person. The two-kilometre journey gives a taste of riverine life, passing factories, a fish market and warehouses, plus lots of flotsam and jetsam, on the way to see a string of boats advertising their produce by suspending a sample from sticks above their bows. A definite risk on this trip is getting splashed by the wake of huge ferries speeding by. The round trip takes around thirty to forty minutes.

Eating

The restaurant at the *Anh Nguyet Hotel* has tasty food and a relaxing ambience. On the north side of town, *Pho Xua* at 126d Phan Ngoc Hien is set in traditional pavilions with wooden pillars around a shady garden. It has a fairly extensive menu in English and plenty of seafood options. For basic and cheap rice and noodle dishes, it's difficult to beat the central *Trieu Phat*, 22 Phan Ngoc Hien, though you'll need your phrasebook to understand the menu. If you're looking for a snack in town, head for *Huong Nam*, at 21 De Tham, where you can get a sandwich or cake to take away, then drop into the nearby coffeeshop at 17 De Tham and wash it down with a strong coffee or soft drink.

Around Ca Mau

The **marshes** circling Ca Mau form one of the largest areas of swampland in the world, covering about 150,000 hectares. The Ca Mau Peninsula was a stronghold of resistance against France and America, and for this it paid a heavy price, as US planes dumped millions of gallons of Agent Orange over it to rob guerrillas of jungle cover. Further damage has been done by the shrimp-farm industry, but pockets of mangrove and cajeput forests remain, inhabited by sea birds, wading birds, waterfowl and also honey bees, attracted by the mangrove blossoms.

Minh Hai Tourist (see p.159) can arrange boat trips to several destinations around town, but with prices beginning at well over $100 per boat, travelling

Boats from Ca Mau

The most useful **boat services** are to be found at the speedboat jetty, located on the south side of town at 162 Phan Boi Chau. From here you can get to Rach Gia in under three hours for about $6, to Nam Can in 1 hour 15 minutes for around $3, or to Dat Mui (for Cape Ca Mau) in 3 hours for about $5. Regular ferries heading north (apart from Rach Gia) leave from Boat Station A ("Ben Tau A"), a few kilometres west of the centre, while vessels heading south and for Rach Gia depart from Boat Station B, 2km south of the town, on the west bank of the Ganh Hao River. This is also the spot to take a boat to the floating market, and is worth a look for its constant bustle even if you're not going anywhere. For Can Tho (3hr; $6), you'll need to go to Cong Ca Mau jetty, about 3km east of town.

in a group makes it much more feasible. A much cheaper way of going about is to hop on a **public ferry or speedboat** to an outlying settlement, and **rent a boat** there. You will need some basic language skills for this, and must be prepared for intense haggling over prices. Local boatmen begin by asking sky-high prices, though most will accept 100,000–150,000đ per hour, depending on the size of the boat.

Mui Ca Mau

This voyage to the end of the earth may not quite be a Jules Verne epic, but it's a fun and satisfying way to pass a day, as you get to visit not only the southern-most point of Vietnam but also the end of mainland Southeast Asia. Take a speedboat from the speedboat jetty in Ca Mau to **Dat Mui** and join in the throng of life in the delta. The boats can get pretty crowded, but if you're lucky you might get a window seat to look out on the houses, shacks and boats that line the river. On arrival in Dat Mui, either rent a local boat or hop on a xe om (about 30,000đ return) to **Mui Ca Mau** (Cape Ca Mau) through a mangrove swamp for the last few kilometres.

Once at the cape, you have to pay 10,000đ to enter the **national park**, after which you can take a photo of yourself standing beside a boat-shaped monument marking the latitude (8 degrees north) and longitude (104 degrees east) of this remote location, then gaze out over the endless ocean and the mountainous Khoai Island just off the coast. There's even a look-out tower from where you can get good views over the mangrove forests, and a restaurant on stilts over the water.

U Minh Forest

Heading northwest from Ca Mau, ferries leave Boat Station A regularly throughout the day to **U Minh**, famous for its cajeput forests. Lining the ferry route are water palms, modest groves of cajeput and fish traps consisting of triangles of bamboo sticks driven into the riverbed. From U Minh's jetty it is about 5km further to the forest. Ask a boatman to take you to "Rung U Minh Ha" or tell them you want to see the cajeput forest, "rung tram". About an hour or two should be sufficient, as the boats are uncovered (take a hat and brolly for the sun or rain) and the landscape doesn't vary. The slender white trunks of the cajeput thrive in U Minh's marshy, coffee-coloured waters, and gliding through them in a boat would be a truly tranquil experience if it were not for the racket of the boat engine. Along the way, you may spot bright blue birds flitting over the water, or, depending on the season, apiarists collecting honeycombs from the trees, which attract bees in huge numbers when they are in flower.

Long Xuyen and around

Some 60km (an hour's drive) northwest of Can Tho, **LONG XUYEN** attracts few foreign visitors, though the unusual cathedral, the well-organized museum, Tiger Island and the nearby stork garden are all worth a look. Dominating the town is the spire of the concrete **cathedral**, on Nguyen Hué, shaped in the form of two upstretched arms whose hands clasp a cross. Unfortunately the church is often locked, but if you can get inside check out the numerous tiny portals that shed light on the dim-lit interior, illuminating gilt Stations of the Cross, and another giant pair of hands over the altar, clutching a globe.

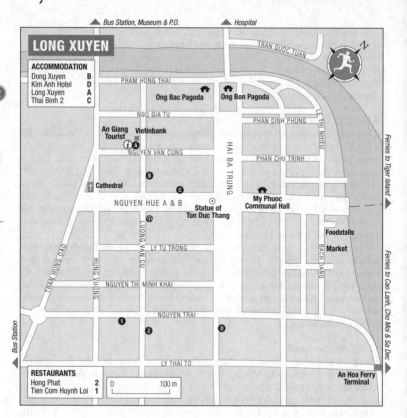

At the other end of Nguyen Hué, you'll find the dragon-stalked roofs of the grandest building in town, the **My Phuoc Communal Hall**, which has carved pillars and embroidered banners in its temple-like interior. Nearby is a very large statue of a meek-looking **Ton Duc Thang**: born locally, he was successor to Ho Chi Minh as president of the Democratic Republic of Vietnam, giving the town its main claim to fame. You can visit his birthplace and childhood home at **My Hoa Hung Village** on **Tiger Island**, accessible by ferry (2000đ) from the eastern end of Nguyen Hué. Here you will find the **Ton Duc Thang Exhibition House** (daily 7–11am & 1–5pm; free), which displays well-presented photos and memorabilia such as the leg irons he wore in Con Dao prison, the prime-ministerial bicycle and the plane that took him from Hanoi to Saigon in 1975 to celebrate victory. The island is very tranquil and unspoilt, and home-stays here can be arranged through An Giang Tourist (see opposite).

Also worth a look, particularly for its display of Oc Eo relics (see box, p.164), is the **An Giang Museum** (Tues–Sun 7.30–11am & 1.30–5pm; about 15,000đ) housed in a grand edifice at 11 Ton Duc Thang on the corner of Ly Thuong Kiet in the northern part of town. On the first floor the focus is on the different religions practised in the region – Catholicism, Buddhism and Hoa Hao. On the second floor is a treasure trove of remnants of Oc Eo culture. Among the exhibits are a large lingam and a wooden Buddha that is so decayed it is now almost unrecognizable, as well as delicate items of gold jewellery. Other displays focus on minority culture, particularly the Cham, and the inevitable documenting of the local revolutionary movement and battles against the French and Americans. Unfortunately, there are no signs in English.

South of Long Xuyen is one of the Mekong Delta's best stork sanctuaries, the **Bang Lang Stork Garden** (daily 6am–6pm; 6000đ), with thousands of birds wheeling, swooping and squabbling over nesting places. Wearing a hat might help as the site is smothered with their droppings. To get there, head about 15km along Highway 91 towards Can Tho, then just before a small bridge, take a lane on the right marked "Ap Van Hoa Thoi An", which leads through a few kilometres of idyllic countryside to the sanctuary: a xe om from Long Xuyen will cost around 80,000–100,000đ for the round-trip.

A few kilometres north of Long Xuyen on Highway 91 to Chau Doc, look out for the **incense factories**, where the sticks are spread out to dry along the roadside, often arranged in photogenic circles.

Practicalities

Most **buses** stop on Tran Hung Dao about a kilometre to the south of town, though local buses, including some from Chau Doc, pull up at the bus station about 2km to the north of town, also on Tran Hung Dao. Travelling to and from Cao Lanh by **ferry**, you'll come via Choi Moi Isle – to the east – and the An Hoa Ferry terminal, at the end of Ly Thai To in the centre of town.

The main office of An Giang Tourist is at 17 Nguyen Van Cung (daily 7–11am & 1–5pm; ☎076/384 1036, ✉angiangtour@hcm.vnn.vn), and the staff are helpful with local **information**. Vietnam Airlines' office is located in the *Dong Xuyen* hotel, which also has an **ATM**. Vietinbank, just north of the *Long Xuyen* hotel on Luong Van Cu, can **exchange** money and also has an ATM. There is **internet access** at 81 Nguyen Huế, though the entrance is round the corner on Luong Van Cu. Long Xuyen's **post office** (daily 6am–10pm) is at 106 Tran Hung Dao, to the north of the centre. The town's **hospital** is also north of the centre on Le Loi.

Accommodation

The fanciest-looking **place to stay** is the *Dong Xuyen* (☎076/394 2260, ✉dongxuyenag@hcm.vnn.vn; ❸–❹), at 9a Luong Van Cu. It occupies almost an entire block and boasts sauna, jacuzzi and carpeted rooms with all facilities, though the service is rather sloppy. A reasonable alternative, at 5–9 Thi Sach, is the *Kim Anh Hotel* (☎076/394 2551, ✉kimanh-hotel@hcm.vnn.vn; ❷), an eight-storey block with comfy rooms and a palatial suite on the top floor. There are cheaper, well-maintained rooms in the ageing *Long Xuyen*, 19 Nguyen Van Cung (☎076/384 1927, ✉longxuyenhotel@hcm.vnn.vn; ❷), and even cheaper ones (some with fan) at the *Thai Binh 2*, 4–8 Nguyen Huế (☎076/384 1859, ☏076/384 6451; ❶–❷), but try not to get put near the karaoke rooms here.

Eating

The most reliable **restaurant** in town is at the *Long Xuyen* hotel, which serves specialities such as snake, turtle, pigeon and eel, as well as more familiar items like chicken and pork. On Nguyen Trai, *Tien Com Huynh Loi*, at no. 252/1, has delicious, cheap, rice dishes and *bun bo Huế* served in clean surroundings. Round the corner, at 242/4 Luong Van Cu, the smart *Hong Phat* has tasty Chinese and Vietnamese fish and meat dishes.

Oc Eo and the Funan Empire

Between the first and sixth centuries AD, the western side of the Mekong Delta, southern Cambodia and much of the Gulf of Siam's seaboard came under the sway of the Indianized **Funan Empire**, an early forerunner of the great Angkor civilization. The heavily romanticized annals of contemporary Chinese diplomats describe how the Funan Empire was forged when an Indian Brahmin visiting the region married the daughter of a local serpent-god, and how the serpent rendered the region suitable for cultivation by drinking down the waters of the flood plains. Such fables are grounded in truth: Indian traders would have halted here to pick up victuals en route from India to China, and would have disseminated not only their Hindu beliefs, but also their advanced irrigation and wet-rice cultivation methods.

One of Funan's major trading ports, **Oc Eo**, was located between Long Xuyen and Rach Gia. In common with other Funan cities, Oc Eo was ringed by a moat and consisted of wooden dwellings raised off the ground on piles. Given the discovery of Persian, Egyptian, Indian and Chinese artefacts (and even a gold coin depicting the Roman emperor Marcus Aurelius) at Oc Eo sites, the port must have played host to a fair number of traders from around the world. The **ancient ruins** of Oc Eo lie about 30km southwest of Long Xuyen, but there's nothing left to see there: even the provincial tourist office advises against visiting the site, but if you are really determined, contact An Giang Tourist (see p.163). To view **artefacts** from the site, visit the museums at Long Xuyen and Rach Gia, or the Fine Arts Museum in Ho Chi Minh City (see p.99).

The Funan Empire finally disappeared in the seventh century, when it was absorbed into the adjacent **Chen La** Empire (see p.81).

Chau Doc and around

Since the opening of the border to Cambodia a few kilometres north of town, **CHAU DOC** has boomed in popularity, and is the only place apart from Can Tho where you are likely to see foreigners in any numbers. Snuggled against the west bank of the Hau Giang River, the town came under Cambodian rule until it was awarded to the Nguyen lords in the mid-eighteenth century for their help in putting down a localized rebellion. The area sustains a large Khmer community, which combines with local Cham and Chinese to form a diverse social melting pot. Just as diverse is Chau Doc's religious make-up: as well as Buddhists, Catholics and Muslims, the region supports an estimated 1.5 million devotees of the indigenous Hoa Hao religion (see box, p.166). Forays by Pol Pot's genocidal Khmer Rouge into this corner of the delta led to the Vietnamese invasion of Cambodia in 1978.

Arrival, information and town transport

Buses offload 2km southeast of town at the bus station on Le Loi, from where xe om run into town (about 10,000đ). Chau Giang is reached by ferry from the jetty opposite the church on Le Loi.

The state-run An Giang Tourist does not have an office in Chau Doc, but most hotel and guesthouse owners can help out with local **information**, as well as arrange **local excursions** and **onward travel**, including boat services to and from Phnom Penh. Both Mekong Tours (☎076/386 8222, ⓦwww .mekongvietnam.com), 14 Nguyen Huu Canh, and Delta Adventure (☎076/356 3810, ⓦwww.deltaadventuretours.com) at 53 Le Loi offer half-day trips to a fish farm and Cham village (about $12 per person), and day-trips to Tuc Dup (about $25 per person). They also sell minibus tickets to Ho Chi Minh City ($10) or Can Tho ($6), as does the tour desk at *Vinh Phuoc* hotel, another useful source of local information.

Accommodation

As one of the Delta's most popular destinations, Chau Doc has a range of **accommodation** ranging from windowless hovels up to luxury quarters with river views, air-conditioning and TV. It's even possible to sleep on the river at the *Delta Floating Hotel*.

Chau Pho Trung Nu Vuong ℡076/356 4139, ⓔchauphohotel@vnn.vn. Spacious, well-maintained rooms with expansive views, though it is several blocks from the riverside action. ❸–❹

Delta Floating Hotel beside the tourist jetty, just south of the *Victoria* hotel ℡076/356 3810, ⓦwww.deltaadventuretours.com. Neat rooms over the river (fixed, in fact, not floating), all with en-suite bathrooms and a ringside view of the watery action. Can be a bit noisy though. ❸–❹

Ngoc Phu 17 Doc Phu Thu ℡076/386 6484. The lobby looks a bit desolate but this no-frills establishment is perfectly habitable, and even the cheapest fan rooms have hot water. ❶

Song Sao 12–13 Nguyen Huu Canh ℡076/356 1777. Smart rooms, all fully equipped with hot water, a/c and so on. ❷

Thuan Loi 18 Tran Hung Dao ℡076/386 6134. This riverside mini-hotel near the market offers some of the best value in town. Both fan and a/c

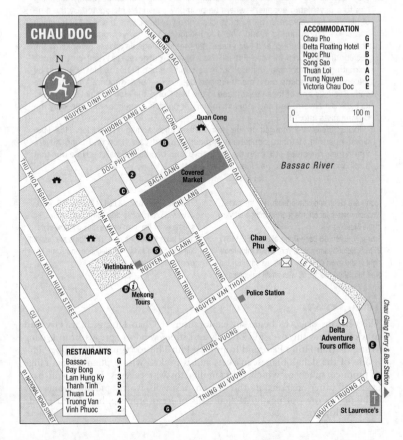

CHAU DOC

N

Bassac River

0   100 m

Quan Cong

Covered Market

Chau Phu

Vietinbank

Mekong Tours

Police Station

Delta Adventure Tours office

Chau Giang Ferry & Bus Station

St Laurence's

165

The Hoa Hao religion

Sited 20km east of Chau Doc, the diminutive village of Hoa Hao lent its name to a unique religious movement at the end of the 1930s. The **Hoa Hao Buddhist sect** was founded by the village's most famous son, Huynh Phu So. A sickly child, Huynh was placed in the care of a hermitic monk under whom he explored both conventional Buddhism and more arcane spiritual disciplines. In 1939, at the age of 20, a new brand of Buddhism was revealed to him in a trance. Upon waking, Huynh found he was cured of his congenital illness, and began publicly to expound his breakaway theories, which advocated purging worship of all the clutter of votives, priests and pagodas, and paring it down to simple unmediated communication betwen the individual and the Supreme Being. The faith has a fairly strong **ascetic** element, with alcohol, drugs and gambling all discouraged. Peasants were drawn to the simplicity of the sect, and by rumours that Huynh was a faith healer in possession of prophetic powers.

Almost immediately, the Hoa Hao developed a **political agenda**, and established a **militia** to uphold its fervently nationalist, anti-French and anti-Communist beliefs. The Japanese army of occupation, happy to keep the puppet French administration it had allowed to remain nominally in charge of Vietnam on its toes, provided the sect with arms. For themselves, the French regarded the Hoa Hao with suspicion: Huynh they labelled the "Mad Monk", imprisoning him in 1941 and subsequently confining him to a psychiatric hospital – where he promptly converted his doctor. By the time of his eventual release in 1945, the sect's uneasy alliance with the Viet Minh, which had been forged during World War II in recognition of their common anti-colonial objectives, was souring, and two years later Viet Minh agents assassinated him. The sect battled on until the mid-Fifties when **Diem's purge** of dissident groups took hold; its guerrilla commander, Ba Cut, was captured and beheaded in 1956, and by the end of the decade most members had been driven underground. Though in the early Sixties some of these resurfaced in the Viet Cong, the Hoa Hao never regained its early dynamism, and any lingering military or political presence was erased by the Communists after 1975.

Today there are thought to be somewhere approaching 1.5 million Hoa Hao worshippers in Vietnam, concentrated mostly around Chau Doc and Long Xuyen. Some male devotees still sport the distinctive long beards and hair tied in a bun that traditionally distinguished a Hoa Hao adherent.

rooms are clean and comfortable, and the stilted wooden restaurant affords a great front-seat view of the Mekong. ❶

Trung Nguyen 86 Bach Dang ☏076/356 1561, ✉trunghotel@yahoo.com. Very smart mini-hotel, right in the town centre, with fifteen smallish but well-furnished rooms, all with small balconies. ❷

Victoria Chau Doc 32 Le Loi ☏076/386 5010, ⓦwww.victoriahotels-asia.com. Just 300m southeast of the town centre, this colonial-style hotel lords it over the river. The rooms are tastefully furnished with *Indochine* elegance and some have glorious river views. ❼

The Town

The obvious place to begin an exploration of Chau Doc is at its **covered market**, where the overspill of stalls and street vendors spreads from Quang Trung to Tran Hung Dao, and from Doc Phu Thu to Nguyen Van Thoai. This is one of the delta's biggest markets and is packed with a phenomenal range of produce, much of which is unfamiliar to Western eyes. Even if you have explored other markets in the region, it's well worth picking your way through the rows of neatly stacked stalls of fresh produce, household goods, fish and flowers.

To the east of the covered market, stalls are crammed into narrow alleyways which run towards the river, where you're greeted by a multitude of bobbing boats and waterside activities. On Doc Phu Thu and a few other streets in town, colonial relics are still evident, but their grand shophouse terraces, flaunting arched upper-floor windows and awnings propped up by decorous wrought-iron struts, are interspersed with characterless new edifices.

A four-tiered gateway deep in the belly of the open market announces **Quan Cong Temple**. Beyond the courtyard, two rooftop dragons oversee its entrance and the outer walls' vivid murals. Inside the temple is the red visage of Quan Cong, sporting green robe and bejewelled crown, and surrounded by a sequin-studded red velvet canopy. A few steps southeast through the market stalls along Tran Hung Dao, the lofty chambers of **Chau Phu Temple** offer a cool respite from the heat outside, and fans of gilt woodwork will find much to divert them. From this temple down to the *Victoria Chau Doc*, a narrow park borders the river. It features a tall statue celebrating the local catfish, and makes a pleasant place for a breezy stroll in the morning or evening. Just south of the *Victoria* is the tourist jetty where most boat tours leave from, and about 1km beyond on the opposite side of Le Loi, is **St Laurence's Church**, built over the site of its previous namesake, which was established by a French missionary in the late nineteenth century. A small statue of the saint stands in the garden, while a bust of him peers out from behind a glass panel set in the spire, and statues of two local Catholic martyrs oversee the courtyard.

Eating

Chau Doc has more **places to eat** than most Mekong Delta towns, with a further selection of places at the base of Sam Mountain (see p.168), though none is particularly outstanding and their prices are over the odds. A snack at one of the **food stalls** around the market, particularly on Tran Hung Dao, Chi Lang and Le Cong Thanh, is a good option if you're strapped for cash.

Bassac *Victoria Chau Doc*, 32 Le Loi. Imaginative Western and Asian dishes, such as rack of lamb and roasted duck breast, served in a romantic riverside dining terrace overlooking the Mekong, with dishes averaging around $12–15. There's also an attractive adjoining bar with pool table and backgammon, ideal for a sundowner.

Bay Bong 22 Thuong Dang Le. Delicious pork cooked in a clay pot and sweet-and-sour fish at reasonable prices.

Lam Hung Ky 71 Chi Lang. Friendly, family-run eatery opposite the market, whose imaginative Chinese-influenced menu features beef with bitter melon and black beans; a full meal, including a beer, will come to around 60,000đ.

Thanh Tinh 13 Quang Trung. Reliable vegetarian outlet next door to the *Truong Van*, serving cheap and cheerful dishes.

Thuan Loi 18 Tran Hung Dao. Enjoy the riverside action and choose from a huge range of dishes, most of which cost around 30,000–40,000đ.

Truong Van 15 Quang Trung. Above-average com shop, a stone's throw from the market and usually busy, serving Chinese and Vietnamese staples.

Vinh Phuoc 14 Quang Trung. Smart place with appealing dishes such as chicken with chilli and lemongrass for just over 20,000đ.

Listings

Banks Vietinbank, 68–70 Nguyen Huu Canh, can exchange foreign currency and traveller's cheques, and also has an ATM.

Bicycle and motorbike rental Available at *Trung Nguyen* hotel ($3 & $8 per day respectively).

Hospital Opposite the *Victoria Chau Doc* on Le Loi.

Pharmacy 14 Nguyen Huu Canh.

Post office On the corner of Le Loi and Nguyen Van Thoai (daily 6am–10pm); it also has **internet** access.

▲ Khmer cyclists near Chau Doc

Around Chau Doc

There are a few places of interest to visit in the area **around Chau Doc**, including a **Cham community** and the brooding **Sam Mountain** with its kitsch pagodas.

Con Tien Island and Chau Giang District

Two settlements a stone's throw away from Chau Doc across the Hau Giang River are worth venturing out to, and most people visit both on a half-day tour (see p.164 for details). One is the cluster of **fish-farm houses** floating on the river next to **Con Tien Island**, above cages of catfish that are fed through a hatch in the floor. Fish farming is big business in the delta, and some of these cages can be over 1000 cubic metres in size.

The other settlement is a **Cham community** in **Chau Giang District**, which you can visit independently via a ferry from a jetty south of the tourist jetty on Le Loi. Here you'll discover kampung-style wooden houses, sarongs and white prayer caps that betray the influence of Islam, as do the twin domes and pretty white minaret of the **Mubarak Mosque**.

Sam Mountain

Arid, brooding **Sam Mountain** rises dramatically from an ocean of paddy fields 5km southwest of Chau Doc. It's known as *Nui Sam* to Vietnamese tourists, who flock here in their thousands to worship at its clutch of pagodas and shrines. There are lots of hotels near the base of the mountain, of which the *Long Chau Resort* on Sam Mountain Road, about 4km from Chau Doc (☏076/386 1249, ✉longchauresort@vamcotravel.com; ❶–❷) is a cosy option, with small, brick and thatch rooms with fan or air conditioning around a central pond with good views of the mountain. Many Western visitors, however, find the temples here distinctly tacky, and prefer to be based in Chau Doc itself, just hiring a motorbike or xe om (about $5) to ride to the top of the hill.

At the foot of the mountain the first pagoda you'll see is kitsch, 1847-built **Tay An Pagoda**, the pick of the bunch, its frontage awash with portrait photographers, beggars, incense-stick vendors and bird-sellers (releasing one from captivity accrues merit). Guarding the pagoda are two elephants, one black, one white, and a shaven-headed Quan Am Thi Kinh. The number of gaudy statues inside exceeds two hundred: most are of deities and Buddhas, but an alarmingly lifelike rendering of an honoured monk sits at one of the highly varnished tables in the rear chamber. To the right of this room an annexe houses a goddess with a thousand eyes and a thousand hands, on whose mound of heads teeters a tiny Quan Am.

Chua Xu Temple, 50m to the right beyond Tay An, honours Her Holiness Lady of the Country, a stone statue said to have been found on Sam's slopes in the early nineteenth century, though the present building, with its four-tiered, glazed green-tile roof, dates only from 1972. Inside, the Lady sits in state in a marbled chamber, resplendent in colourful gown and headdress. Glass cases in corridors either side of her are crammed to bursting with splendid garb and other offerings from worshippers, who flood here between the 23rd and 25th of the fourth lunar month, to see her ceremonially bathed and dressed. Shops in front of the temple sell colourful baskets of fruit that locals buy to offer to Her Holiness. Multi-storey **Chua Hang** (Cave Pagoda), a few hundred metres further along, is a popular stopping-off point for local tourists, although the tiny grotto after which the pagoda is named is rather a let-down after the sweaty ascent.

Even if the temples don't appeal, it's fun to walk (approx 30min) or take a xe om **up the mountain** itself. Turn left at the base of the mountain, then take the first turning on the right after about 300m. As you climb, you'll pass massive boulders that seem embedded in the hillside, as well as some plaster statues of rhinos, elephants, zebras and a Tyrannosaurus rex near the top. From the top, the **view** of the surrounding, pancake-flat terrain is breath-taking, though the hill is, in fact, only 230 metres high. In the rainy season, the view is particularly spectacular, with lush paddy fields scored by hundreds of waterways, though in the dry season the barren landscape is hazy and less inspiring. There's a tiny military outpost at the summit, from where you can gaze into Cambodia, and from the other side you can also look back over Chau Doc. A small refreshment stall at the top sells cool drinks in case you forgot to bring water.

Southwest to Ba Chuc and Tup Duc

With your own transport, by joining a tour (about $25; see p.164) or by hiring the services of a xe om driver (about $15–20), it's possible to explore both Ba Chuc and Tup Duc, located in a sweep of staggeringly beautiful countryside southwest of Chau Doc. Refugees fleeing Pol Pot's Cambodia boosted the Khmer population here in the late 1970s, and pursuit by the Khmer Rouge ended in numerous indiscriminate massacres; a grisly memorial to one of these, at the village of Ba Chuc (see p.170), lends a tragic focus to a trip through the region. It's about 40km from Chau Doc to Tri Ton and another 10km or so to Ba Chuc.

After rounding Sam Mountain, the road is raised up above paddy fields that are etched by an intricate canal system. Beyond a left fork at **Nha Bang**, the variable road chicanes through gently sloping hills. There's a timeless grandeur to the scenery here: distant waterways are lined by spiky *thot not* (sugar palm) trees, whose fronds are clustered like firework flashes, and whose fruits, reminiscent of coconuts roasted in a fire, yield a handful of translucent, edible seeds. What transport there is consists of cattle- and pony-drawn carts as well as cars and trucks. On the right the road passes a turning for Cam Mountain, the highest peak in the region at 716m. In this area, darker skins, red-and-white checked turbans and horned temples indicate you're in Khmer territory. As you hit **TRI TON**, a road to your right just past the bus station signals the way to Ba Chuc.

You'll know you're upon **BA CHUC** when you pass beneath graceful glades of bamboo flanking the road. Bear right, and you'll quickly spot the **memorial** to the thousands massacred in twelve days in April 1978. An unattractive concrete canopy fails to lessen the impact of the eight-sided memorial: behind its glass enclosure, the bleached skulls of the dead of Vietnam's own "killing fields" are piled in ghoulish heaps, grouped according to age to highlight the youth and innocence of many of the dead.

Beside the memorial is a small room, where a horrific set of black-and-white photos taken just after the massacre shows buckled, abused corpses scattered around the countryside. Some of the images on display are extremely disturbing and you should not enter if you are a sensitive type. There are also a few food stalls set up to cater to visitors to the site.

Another possible side-trip from Tri Ton is to visit the former Viet Cong base at **TUP DUC** (daily 6am–5pm; 7000đ), a 10km drive from Tri Ton – take the right turn at the end of town. During the American war, Tup Duc gained the rather ignominious moniker "Two Million Dollar Hill", a reference to the amount the US military is said to have spent trying to dislodge the enemy from its slopes.

Now the Vietnamese government has ploughed in money of its own in an attempt to turn it into a tourist resort, by installing pedal boats on a lake, an ostrich-breeding farm, a flower garden, a shooting range, a restaurant and refreshment kiosks at the foot of the boulder-strewn hill. There is also a small museum here, an electronic mock-up of the battle (daily 7–11am & 1–5pm) and dummies in a cave on the hill, re-creating a Viet Cong briefing scene. Kids will probably latch onto you and lead you up a stairway past the massive boulders that provided such effective cover to the Viet Cong. Squeezing through the narrow passageways formed by the jumble of boulders, it is easy to see how it made such a perfect hide-out.

It is possible to head on from here to the coast, by taking a turn to the left just before re-entering Tri Ton. The road follows a canal for about 30km with views of rice paddies and eucalyptus plantations. After crossing a big new bridge at Vam Ray, the route joins Highway 80, the main coast road, from where it is about 47km northwest to Ha Tien, or the same distance southeast to Rach Gia.

Ha Tien and around

Of all the Delta towns, **HA TIEN**, at the extreme northwest on the border with Cambodia, is changing the fastest: where once it received only a trickle of visitors, it now buzzes with Western travellers. In addition to the ongoing construction boom, two major factors have caused this: first, is the **opening of the border** to foreigners at Xa Xia, just north of Ha Tien, meaning that it's now possible to head directly to Cambodia's coastal towns of Kep and Sihanoukville without passing through Phnom Penh; and the second factor

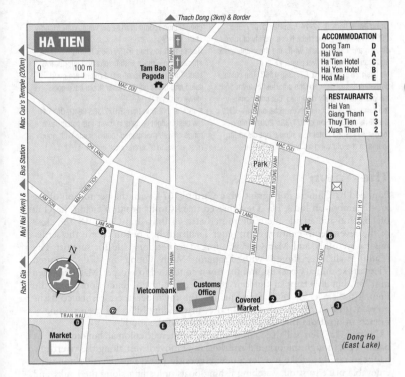

is the beginning of **hydrofoil services to Phu Quoc**, offering a shorter and cheaper route to the island than from Rach Gia. Thus this town, which until recently had an end-of-the-line feel, is coming to terms with its newfound popularity.

Arrival and information

Buses terminate at the new bus station on Highway 80 a couple of kilometres north of town and just a few kilometres from the Cambodian border post at Xa Xia: to get into town from here take a xe om (about 10,000đ). **Hydrofoils** to and from Ham Ninh on **Phu Quoc's** east coast (1hr 30min) dock on the south bank of the To Chau River, and tickets (190,000đ) can be bought at the office at 11 Tran Hau (☎077/395 9060). For local **information**, you'll have to rely on staff at your hotel, most of whom should have at least a smattering of English. The **post office** (daily 6.30am–9pm) is on To Chau a short walk north of the river and has **internet** access, as does the shop at 54 Tran Hau. The Vietcombank at 4 Phuong Thanh can **exchange** cash or traveller's cheques, and also has an ATM. If you're heading onto Cambodia, **visas** are available at the border at Xa Xia ($25), but it's better to get one in Ho Chi Minh City to avoid any overcharging, which is a common occurrence.

Accommodation

As part of Ha Tien's construction boom, several new hotels have opened recently, giving visitors plenty of options.

Dong Tam Block 5, 12-14 Tran Hau ☏077/395 0555. This smart new place has a variety of rooms, all with a/c, cable TV and wi-fi, and the enthusiastic staff can help with travel plans. ❷

Ha Tien 36 Tran Hau ☏077/385 1563. The plush, carpeted rooms here are the smartest in town and the place is tastefully designed, but unfortunately the service does not match expectations. ❷–❸

Hai Van 55 Lam Son ☏077/385 2001. This long-established hotel has simple but clean fan rooms in the old wing as well as smart air-conditioned rooms in the new wing, with friendly staff. ❶–❷

Hai Yen 15 To Chau ☏077/385 1580. An efficiently-run place with helpful and informative staff. The bright, decent-sized rooms are good value and those on the upper floors have good views of Dong Ho. ❶–❷

Hoa Mai 1-3 Tran Hau ☏077/385 0849. One of the best budget options in town, this place has a range of well-maintained rooms, some with good river views, in a central location. ❶–❷

The Town

Founded by Chinese immigrant **Mac Cuu** in 1674, with the permission of the local Cambodian lords, **Ha Tien** thrived thanks to its position facing the Gulf of Thailand and astride the trade route between India and China. By the close of the seventeenth century, Siam (later Thailand) had begun to eye the settlement covetously, and Mac Cuu was forced to petition Hué for support. The resulting alliance, forged with Emperor Minh Vuong in 1708, ensured Vietnamese military backup, and the town continued to prosper. Mac Cuu died in 1735, but the familial fiefdom continued for seven generations, until the French took over in 1867. Subsequently, the town became a resistance flashpoint, with Viet Minh holing up in the surrounding hills, and even sniping at French troops from the **To Chau Mountain**, to the south.

Central Ha Tien still has a few quaint, shuttered, colonial buildings in its backstreets, though the original **market**, now moved west along the riverbank, has been razed to make way for a new **riverside park**. The riverside is now an enjoyable place to stroll, watching fishing boats unloading along the banks, and by following Tran Hau eastwards and then continuing north on Dong Ho, you can enjoy pleasant views and often an agreeable breeze blowing off the so-called East Lake (Dong Ho). In fact, it is not a lake but a large inlet where the To Chau River flows out to the sea.

Alternatively, take a walk up Mac Thien Tich and west along Mac Cuu, to where a **temple dedicated to Mac Cuu** stands at the foot of the hill where he and his relatives lie buried in semicircular Chinese graves. Inside the temple, electric "incense" sticks glow constantly before Mac Cuu's funerary tablet, keeping the memory of Ha Tien's founding father alive. Mac Cuu's actual **grave** is uppermost on the hill, guarded by two swordsmen, a white tiger and a blue dragon. From this vantage point, there are good views from the hill over the mop-tops of the coconut trees below and down to the sea.

Further up Mac Thien Tich is the colourful **Tam Bao Pagoda**, set in tree-lined grounds dominated by an attractive lotus pond, a huge statue of Quan Am and a large reclining Buddha. Out the back of the pagoda, said to have been founded by Mac Cuu himself, is a pretty garden tended by the resident nuns, its colourful flowers interspersed with tombs. In the rear chamber of the pagoda, a statue of the goddess with a thousand hands and a thousand eyes sits on a lurid pink lotus, while behind her are photos and funerary tablets remembering the local dead.

Eating

The waterfront *Hai Van*, at 4 Tran Hau, is a good choice for **eating**: run by the hotel of the same name, it serves up decent breakfasts and an extensive menu of

Vietnamese dishes. Further along the front at 20 Tran Hau, the *Xuan Thanh* serves cheap Vietnamese dishes in clean surroundings, and is often busy; try the stir-fried squid with pineapple or the fried fish with lemon. For something a bit classier, the *Giang Thanh*, in front of the *Ha Tien Hotel*, serves Vietnamese and Chinese dishes in a traditional, open-sided building. Conveniently located for people-watching, the *Thuy Tien*, a café right by the pontoon bridge, offers coffee, soft drinks and snacks. In the evening, a **night market** sets up along Tran Hau, some stalls selling souvenirs and others selling seafood, attracting crowds of locals and visitors alike.

Around Ha Tien

A pleasant half or full day can be spent exploring the countryside around Ha Tien, with a convenient circular route northwest of town meaning you won't need to backtrack. This makes an ideal bike ride and, though nowhere officially rents vehicles, most hotels can help out. Rates should be around $3 for a bike and $8 for a motorbike. Failing that, hire the services of a xe om (about 150,000đ for a half-day trip).

Strike off west along Lam Son. At the end of the road, turn left and continue straight at a small roundabout. Endless rice fields and coconut groves border the road as it kinks gently around low-lying hills towards the Cambodian border. A **war cemetery** serves as a landmark on the right 2.5km from town, and from here it's another 1.5km to a left turn to **Mui Nai** – "Stag's Head Peninsula" – though you'd be hard-pressed to see the silhouette of a stag's head in of any of the surrounding hills. Take this turning, follow it to the coast and along a winding stretch of road with some beautiful views until you reach the entrance to the beach (2000đ).

A pleasant – if not idyllic – four-hundred-metre curve of sand, shaded by coconut palms and backed by lush green hills, Mui Nai beach offers reasonable swimming in clean, shallow waters. The beach is very popular among Vietnamese, and there's even a small resort here, the *Hai Dang* (☎077/385 2878; ❷), with reasonable air-conditioned rooms and a restaurant too. There are a few other restaurants and beachside cafés, so you can kick back and crack open a few crabs while enjoying a fresh coconut juice or a refreshing slice of watermelon.

On leaving the beach, turn left and continue up the coast. You'll see the 48-metre-high granite outcrop housing **Thach Dong**, or Stone Cave, long before you reach it; 3–4km past Mui Nai the road reaches a junction, where a left turn leads to the Cambodian border. Turn right at this junction and very shortly the road passes a cluster of food stalls that mark the entrance to the cave. A **monument** shaped like a defiant clenched fist stands as a memorial to 130 people killed by Khmer Rouge forces near here in 1978. Beyond this, steps lead up to a **cave pagoda** that's home to a colony of bats. Its shrines to Quan Am and Buddha are unremarkable, but balconies hewn from the side of the rock afford great views over the hills, paddy fields and sea below. Look to your right and you're peering into Cambodia. From here, continue along the circular road which brings you after a few kilometres back into Ha Tien.

Hon Chong Peninsula

Just 30km south of Ha Tien lies the **Hon Chong Peninsula**. A string of offshore isles has earned this region the moniker "mini-Ha Long", but it's as a coastal resort that it draws throngs of Vietnamese and a smattering of foreigners.

The approach to the peninsula is blighted by unsightly cement factories belching out clouds of smoke, and while Hon Chong has yet to suffer any significant environmental degradation as a result of these factories, their ugly presence looms over the area and certainly detracts from its appeal. For the moment, Hon Chong's calm waters and beaches fringed with palms and casuarinas remain among the most attractive in the delta, though they cannot compare with the beaches on Phu Quoc.

The sweep of **beach** in front of most of the resorts is fine for sunbathing and enjoys a decidedly unspoilt feel with few signs of tourist trappings, but is too shallow and spongy for swimming. Things are better nearer the *Hon Trem Resort* (see below), though the most picturesque beach, Bai Duong (admission 2000đ), lies 1.5km further south. After passing pandanus, tamarind and sugar-palm trees, the coastal track ends at a towering cliff, in front of which stands **Sea and Mountain Pagoda** ("Chua Hai Son") and a cluster of souvenir and food stalls. After passing through the temple grounds, an opening in the rock leads into **Cave Pagoda** ("Chua Hong"). A low doorway leads from its outer chamber to a grotto in the cliff's belly, where statues of Quan Am and several Buddhas are lit by coloured lights. The cramped stone corridor that runs on from here makes as romantic an approach to a beach as you could imagine, though the stench of the resident bats somewhat spoils the atmosphere.

As you hit the sand, the rugged rocks out to sea in front of you constitute **Father and Son Isle** ("Hon Phu Tu"), though it is now rather a misnomer as "Father", the biggger of the two pillars of rock, fell crashing in to the sea in 2006. The beach here is reasonably attractive, though still too shallow for swimming. For a small fee (9000đ) you can join a short (45min) boat tour out to Hon Phu Tu and the nearby **Hang Tien Grotto**, which has some attractive stalactites and stalagmites. Nguyen Anh (later to become Gia Long) hid here while on the run after the Tay Son Rebellion, and locals have dubbed its stone plateaux as his throne, sofa, bed and so on. If there's no-one else around, you can rent the entire boat for about 180,000đ for this short trip.

For a more luxurious boat trip around local islands, the *Hon Trem Resort* (see below) can organize a full day-trip, including fishing and lunch as well as a visit to **Nghe Island** and the **Ba Lua Archipelago**, for about \$150 per person.

Practicalities

Irregular **buses** ply the route between Hon Chong and Rach Gia (about 30,000đ). Check with Kien Giang Tourist (see p.176) for times. Coming from Ha Tien, you'll have to take a Rach Gia-bound bus and get off at Ba Hon, then take a xe om (about 100,000đ) the last few kilometres.

All the **accommodation** at Hon Chong is a few steps from the beach, though the shallow bays make them unsuitable for swimming. Perched on the hillside at the top end of the strip, the friendly *Green Hill Guesthouse* (☎077/385 4369; ❷–❸) lives up to its billing, its handful of beautifully furnished rooms all commanding sweeping views of the bay and probably representing the best deal around here. Alternatively, the *An Hai Son* (☎077/375 9226; ❷) and the *My Lan* (☎077/375 9044; ❷) are both well-managed and have smart rooms with air-conditioning, TVs and fridges, as well as decent restaurants. The *Binh An Hotel* (☎077/385 4332; ❶–❷) has dingy fan rooms in billet-style quarters for just 80,000đ and much smarter air-conditioned doubles in a newer wing, while the *Hon Trem Resort* (☎077/385 4331; ❹–❺) boasts a prime location with all its compact villas enjoying great views from a steep hillside, as well as all facilities.

Even if you choose not to stay here, it's worth visiting the ⚓ *Hon Trem Resort*'s smart **restaurant**, both for its fantastic view of the islands in the bay and for its wide range of dishes priced at 60,000–80,000đ each. For something simpler, the *Tan Phat*, at the southern end of Binh An Village, about half a kilometre north of the *Green Hill Guesthouse*, serves up tasty seafood dishes on a deck overlooking a fishing harbour.

Rach Gia and around

About 100km southwest of Ha Tien, though also easily accessible from Long Xuyen, Can Tho or Ca Mau, the thriving port of **RACH GIA** teeters precariously over the Gulf of Thailand. The capital of Kien Giang Province, it's home to a community of nearly 200,000 people, who eke out a living through rice cultivation in the surrounding fields, or by tapping the gulf's rich vein of seafood. A small islet in the mouth of the Cai Lon River forms the hub of the town, but the urban sprawl spills over bridges to the north and south of it and onto the mainland. The town has little in the way of historical and cultural attractions, and for most foreign visitors it is simply a place to overnight en route to Phu Quoc Island.

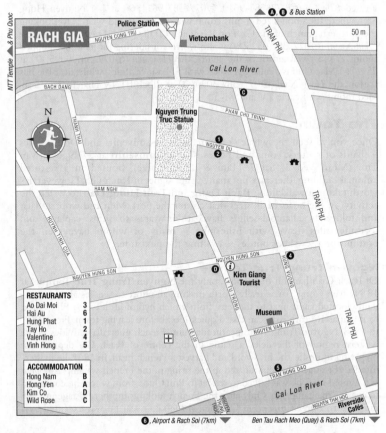

RACH GIA

RESTAURANTS

Ao Dai Moi	3
Hai Au	6
Hung Phat	1
Tay Ho	2
Valentine	4
Vinh Hong	5

ACCOMMODATION

Hong Nam	B
Hong Yen	A
Kim Co	D
Wild Rose	C

Arrival and information

Buses from points north pull up 500m above town, at Rach Gia's local bus station on Nguyen Binh Kiem. Arrivals from Long Xuyen and Can Tho hit the coast at Rach Soi, 7km southeast of Rach Gia. Arriving at the **airport** (flights from Ho Chi Minh City or Phu Quoc), call a taxi (☎077/391 9191). Arriving **boats** dock at the same jetties used for departures (see box opposite), where you can pick up a xe om into town.

Kien Giang Tourist at 137 Nguyen Hung Son (7.30–11.30am & 1–5pm; ☎077/386 2103) can arrange **boat rental** and **tours** around Kien Giang Province. You can exchange **traveller's cheques** and cash at Vietcombank, which also has an ATM, north of the river on Mac Cuu. Just north of here on Mau Than is the **post office** (daily 6.30am–10pm), which also has **internet** access The **hospital** is at 46 Le Loi, and there's a **pharmacy**, north of the centre, at 14a Tran Phu.

Accommodation

As far as **accommodation** goes, there's nowhere outstanding, nor any good budget options, but few people spend more than a night here, anyway, on their way to or from Phu Quoc Island. Probably the most convenient is the centrally-located *Kim Co* (☎077/387 9610, ℱ077/387 9611; ❷) at 141 Nguyen Hung Son, where the good-sized rooms come with cable TV and wi-fi. Overlooking the northern branch of the Cai Lon River at 19 Tran Quang Dieu, the *Wild Rose (Tam Xuan)* (☎077/392 0325; ❷) is also worth considering for its well-equipped rooms. A short way north of the centre, the *Hong Yen* (☎077/387 9095; ❷) at 259–261 Mac Cuu is a reliable choice with all basic facilities, while, near the bus station, the *Hong Nam* (☎077/387 3090; ❷) at Block B1, Ly Thai To, has clean, tiled rooms with cable TV and wi-fi.

The Town

Once you've seen the whale skeleton, wartime souvenirs and Oc Eo relics – shards of pottery, coins and bones – of the **museum** at 27 Nguyen Van Troi (Mon–Wed & Sat 7–11am & 1–5pm; free), housed in a restored colonial building, there are not many other sights in Rach Gia. However, it's worth taking a walk along **Bach Dang** and **Tran Hung Dao** to watch the activity on the boats of all sizes that clutter the port. Men and women darn and fold nets, charcoal-sellers hawk their wares to ships' captains and roadside cafés heave with fishermen – many of whom have seen the bottoms of a few beer bottles – awaiting the next tide.

Nguyen Trung Truc Temple

Of Rach Gia's handful of pagodas, only the **Nguyen Trung Truc Temple**, at 18 Nguyen Cong Tru, is really worth making an effort to see. It's also conveniently located right next to the jetty from which hydrofoils leave to Phu Quoc, so if you arrive early, you can take a quick look before leaving town. From 1861 to 1868, Nguyen Trung Truc spearheaded anti-French guerrilla activities in the western region of the delta: a statue in the centre of Rach Gia depicts him preparing to unsheathe his sword and harvest a French head. In 1861, he masterminded the attack that culminated in the firing of the French warship *Esperance*; as a wanted man, he was forced to retreat to Phu Quoc, from where he continued to oversee the campaign. Only after the French took his mother hostage in 1868 did he turn himself in, and in October of the same year he was executed by a

Moving on from Rach Gia

Most buses leave from Rach Soi though some destinations, such as Hon Chong and Ha Tien, are served by buses from Nguyen Binh Khiem: a taxi or xe om from the town centre to Rach Soi costs about 50,000–80,000đ, and about 10,000–20,000đ to Nguyen Binh Khiem.

Boats out of Rach Gia depart from one of two sites. Several companies operate express boats to Phu Quoc Island (see below), at around 8am and 1pm (2hr 30min; $13-15) from **Phu Quoc quay**, 200m west of the Nguyen Trung Truc Temple. It's better to buy a ticket for the speedboat in advance; the Superdong office at 14 Tu Do (☎077/387 7742, ☎077/387 7741) is just round the corner from the pier. From **Rach Meo quay**, 5km south of town on Ngo Quyen, express boats and regular boats leave for Ca Mau and other destinations in the delta.

If you're heading to Phu Quoc, it's worth considering the daily **flight** (9.30am; about $36), which saves the journey from Vong Beach to Duong Dong on the island, as well as a bumpy trip when the weather is rough. The same flight continues to Ho Chi Minh City ($36). For tickets or information, contact Vietnam Airlines at 16 Nguyen Trung Truc (☎077/392 4320). A taxi or xe om to the airport costs 50,000–80,000đ.

firing squad in the centre of Rach Gia. Defiant to the last, his final words could have been lifted from a Ho Chi Minh speech: "So long as grass still grows on the soil of this land, people will continue to resist the invaders."

The temple roof, with its red and green tiles stalked by dragons made of porcelain shards, is plainly visible from a distance. In front of the temple is a statue of the hero drawing his sword. Inside, a portrait of Nguyen in black robe and hat provides the main chamber with its centrepiece. Up at the main altar, a brass urn labelled "Anh hung dan toc Nguyen Trung Truc" and flanked by slender storks standing on turtles, is said to hold the ashes of Nguyen Trung Truc himself.

Eating

When it's time to **eat**, seafood is the obvious choice in this bustling port. However, there are no outstanding restaurants. The best of the bunch is probably the *Hai Au*, 2 Nguyen Trung Truc, which serves steamboat and fish specialities in a prime open-terraced riverside location, just across the bridge to the southeast of town. Also facing the river, at 31 Tran Hung Dao, is the *Vinh Hong*, where the staples of its seafood dishes eye you warily from tanks mounted on the walls. In the town centre, a couple of reasonable places stand opposite each other on Nguyen Du: the *Tay Ho*, at no. 6, and the *Hung Phat*, no. 7, both have English menus and are popular with locals, though the surroundings are none too inspiring. The *Ao Dai Moi*, 26 Ly Tu Trong, has a few cheap and tasty dishes, but closes at 1pm, while the stylish bar/café *Valentine*, at 35–39 Hung Vuong, serves a good range of food, as well as coffee and beer, and the staff speak some English.

Phu Quoc Island

Located just 15km off the coast of Cambodia in the Gulf of Thailand, **PHU QUOC ISLAND** rises from its slender southern tip like a genie released from a bottle. Virtually unknown by outsiders a decade ago, it has now cast a spell on enough visitors, with its soft-sand beaches, swaying palms and limpid waters, to challenge Nha Trang as Vietnam's top beach destination. Spanning 46km from north to south, it's Vietnam's largest offshore island (593 square kilometres), though Cambodia also claims Phu Quoc, calling it Ko Tral. Phu Quoc is just 45km from Ha Tien, and a little under 120km from Rach Gia.

The topography and vegetation are quite unlike the rest of the delta, and give the place a totally different feel. Phu Quoc's isolation made it an attractive hiding place for two of the more famous figures from Vietnam's past. **Nguyen Anh** holed up here while on the run from the Tay Son brothers in the late eighteenth century (see p.463), and so too, in the 1860s, did **Nguyen Trung Truc** (see p.76). Today, over 80,000 people – and a sizeable population of indigenous dogs (recognizable by a line of hair running up the spine instead of down) – dwell on the island, famous throughout Vietnam for its black pepper and its fish sauce (*nuoc mam*), which is graded like olive oil.

Until the turn of the century, Phu Quoc had almost no facilities for tourists, but now development is in full swing and visitors are spoiled for choice of accommodation, restaurants and activities, such as **snorkelling** and **diving**. There are a few corals just off Ong Lang Beach, but the best locations are around the **An Thoi Islands** to the south or **Turtle Island** off the northwest coast, both of which can be visited by boat trip from Phu Quoc. At these reefs – the former of which is rated by some as the best dive site in Vietnam – you can float above brain and fan corals, watching parrot fish, scorpion fish, butterfly fish, huge sea urchins and a host of other marine life.

Like Mui Ne, Phu Quoc is a favourite bolt-hole for expats living in Ho Chi Minh City and, with work already begun on an international airport in the centre of the island, its future looks rosy. Yet while resorts and bars are springing up fast, for the moment Phu Quoc retains a pioneer outpost feel. Many places can only be reached via dirt tracks and the beaches are largely free of vendors. In the rainy season (May–Oct) Phu Quoc is relatively quiet, and room rates become more easily negotiable, though in peak season (Dec–Jan), accommodation prices can increase sharply and advance booking is necessary.

Arrival

Whether you arrive by air or by sea, you will be besieged by touts trying to drag you off to their favoured hotel or guesthouse, so it's a good idea to have somewhere in mind before arrival. If you have made a prior booking, you will be met and will save yourself a lot of hassle and expense.

Flights from Ho Chi Minh City (several daily; 1hr) land at Phu Quoc Airport, on the edge of Duong Dong town, from where it is a short trip to the resorts on Long Beach, or a seven-kilometre ride to those at Ong Lang Beach.

Speedboats from Rach Gia (several daily; 2hr 30min) dock at Vong Beach, while those from Ha Tien (1 daily; 1hr 30min) dock at Ham Ninh, a little further north. There is currently no organized bus service so you'll have to take a **taxi** or **xe om** to your chosen resort. Be prepared for some hard bargaining, as some drivers take new arrivals to the cleaners. From both ports, a taxi to Long Beach should cost no more than 100,000đ and around 200,000đ to Ong Lang Beach, while a xe om should be about half these prices.

Information, tours and trips

The Vietcombank at 20, 30 Thang 4 in Duong Dong will **exchange** money and cash traveller's cheques; it also has an ATM. The **post office** (6.30am–9pm) is also on 30 Thang 4, where **internet** access is available. There is a **hospital**

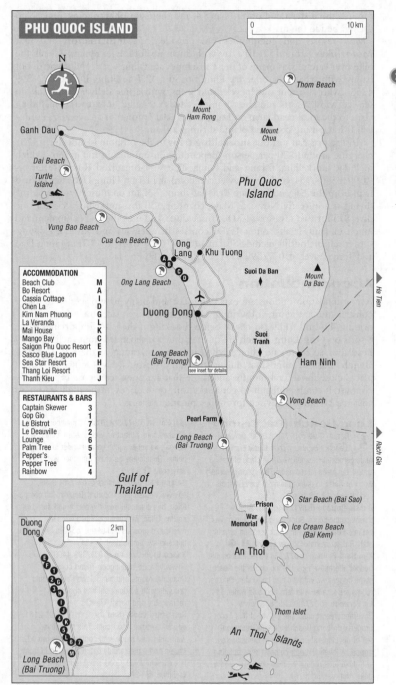

PHU QUOC ISLAND

0   10 km

N

Thom Beach

Mount Ham Rong

Mount Chua

Ganh Dau

Dai Beach

Turtle Island

Phu Quoc Island

Vung Bao Beach

Cua Can Beach

Ong Lang

Khu Tuong

A B

C D

Ong Lang Beach

Suoi Da Ban

Mount Da Bac

Ha Tien

ACCOMMODATION

Beach Club	**M**
Bo Resort	**A**
Cassia Cottage	**I**
Chen La	**D**
Kim Nam Phuong	**G**
La Veranda	**L**
Mai House	**K**
Mango Bay	**C**
Saigon Phu Quoc Resort	**E**
Sasco Blue Lagoon	**F**
Sea Star Resort	**H**
Thang Loi Resort	**B**
Thanh Kieu	**J**

Duong Dong

Long Beach (Bai Truong)

see inset for details

Suoi Tranh

Ham Ninh

Rach Gia

RESTAURANTS & BARS

Captain Skewer	**3**
Gop Gio	**1**
Le Bistrot	**7**
Le Deauville	**2**
Lounge	**6**
Palm Tree	**5**
Pepper's	**1**
Pepper Tree	**L**
Rainbow	**4**

Vong Beach

Pearl Farm

Long Beach (Bai Truong)

Gulf of Thailand

Star Beach (Bai Sao)

Prison

War Memorial

Ice Cream Beach (Bai Kem)

An Thoi

Duong Dong

0   2 km

E F

1

2 **G**

3 **H**

I J

4 **K**

5 L 6 **7**

M

Long Beach (Bai Truong)

Thom Islet

An Thoi Islands

towards the eastern end of 30 Thang 4, and there are **pharmacies** along Ngo Quyen beside the market.

Most resorts and guesthouses can provide local **information** and rent **motorbikes** (around $7–10 a day, with discounts for longer rentals). Check the bike over carefully, as many of these machines are falling apart, and if you're not happy with what they offer, try PhuQuocSun, 42 Tran Hung Dao, ☏077/399 4266), who also rent out bicycles and jeeps, with a free delivery and pick-up service. Most resorts and guest houses can also arrange **boat tours**, including visits to the local pearl farm on Long Beach (Bai Truong) or an evening's cuttle-fish fishing, using coloured plastic shrimps as bait.

Most resorts can sort out **snorkelling trips** to the offshore islands (see p.178), charging around $20 per person (depending on number in the group), which includes snorkelling, fishing and lunch. The well-organized Rainbow Divers (☏091/340 0964, ⓦwww.divevietnam.com) at 11 Tran Hung Dao runs **diving** trips from the *Saigon Phu Quoc Resort* at about 7.30am on most days during the diving season (early Nov–late May), charging $30 for snorkelling, $50 for one dive, $75 for two dives or $100 for three dives, and including all equipment and lunch or fruit. It also offers PADI courses in open-sea and advanced diving. Other reliable outfits include Searama (☏077/329 1679) at 14 Tran Hung Dao and Tony Travel (☏077/399 6277) at 100 Tran Hung Dao.

Accommodation

Accommodation options are expanding fast and many new places were under construction at the time of writing. Not all mid-range places include air conditioning, TV and fridge, so check before booking if these are important. While resorts on **Ong Lang Beach** are quieter, they are separated from each other by headlands, so there's no choice when it comes to eating, as there is on **Long Beach**. Bear in mind that during the rainy season (May–Oct), many small places close for several months and those that are open reduce their prices. By contrast, it can be difficult to get a room in some places in the high season, so advance booking is advised for more upmarket places.

Long Beach (Bai Truong)

Beach Club ☏077/398 0998, ⓦwww .beachclubvietnam.com. Under English management, this small, well-run place offers simple but pleasant rooms and bungalows, some with hot water, in one of the most tranquil spots on Long Beach. ②–③

Cassia Cottage ☏077/384 8395, ⓦwww .cassiacottage.com. Brick bungalows and rooms set in a lush garden with small pool and helpful staff. Rates can halve in low season. ⑤–⑥

Kim Nam Phuong ☏077/384 6319. Reasonable budget alternative near the top end of the beach; some bungalows with a/c and hot water; cheaper rooms are smaller with fans and cold water. ①

La Veranda ☏077/398 2988, ⓦwww .laverandaresort.com. The arrival of this Accor property on Long Beach is the clearest sign yet of developers' confidence in the island's appeal. A lovely, French-colonial style building with luxurious rooms, a small pool, spa, and a delightful restaurant. ⑦

Mai House ☏077/384 7003, ⓔmaihouseresort @yahoo.com. Attractive, well-spaced, thatched bungalows set in a lush garden under towering palms. Rooms are tastefully furnished and feel very cosy. ⑤

Saigon Phu Quoc Resort ☏077/384 6999, ⓦwww.vietnamphuquoc.com. Despite stiff competition, this place still sets the benchmark for luxury on Phu Quoc, with well-equipped villas in manicured grounds and useful facilities like shuttle bus and swimming pool. ⑥–⑦

Sasco Blue Lagoon ☏077/399 4499, ⓦwww.sasco-bluelagoon-resort.com. Spacious rooms and bungalows set in ample grounds with a huge pool and choice of restaurants and bars. ⑥–⑦

Sea Star Resort (Sao Bien) ☏077/398 2161, ⓦwww.seastarresort.com. This attractive, well-managed place with competitively priced rooms and a nice shady patch of beach in front is excellent value. Good-sized rooms with all facilities. ④–⑤

Thanh Kieu (Coco Beach) ☎077/384 8394. One of the cheapest options along this stretch of beach with basic but clean rooms, though it is set back a bit from the beach. ❸–❹

Ong Lang Beach (Bai Ong Lang)

Bo Resort ☎077/398 6142, ⓦwww.boresort .com. Simple but tastefully furnished bungalows on a steep hill overlooking a gorgeous stretch of beach, with a well-appointed restaurant too. ❹–❺

Chen La ☎077/399 5895, ⓦwww.chenla-resort .com. The southernmost and most expensive resort on Ong Lang Beach, featuring luxurious rooms in a mixed traditional and modern style, some with private pool. ❼

Mango Bay ☎0903/382207, ⓦwww .mangobayphuquoc.com. This place enjoys a lovely tranquil location and offers spacious, stylish bungalows, made with local soil using eco-friendly techniques, with fans and large verandas (no a/c or TV). The coast is rocky in front but there are deserted sandy bays on each side. ❺–❻

Thang Loi Resort ☎077/398 5002. A remote setting, with simple bamboo and wood huts nestled on a hillside. Facilities are basic, with no hot water or fans and electricity in the evening only, but it's a great place to get away from it all; the snorkelling is excellent too. ❷–❹

Duong Dong

Though you'll probably want at some time to go into the main town of **Duong Dong**, the island's only settlement of any size, for the **post office**, **internet** or to buy supplies in the market, there's not a lot else to see. There is a small **lighthouse** and **temple** (Dinh Cau) situated on a promontory at the entrance to the harbour, which is of no great consequence but does provide good **views** up and down the coast. The town's **market**, on Ngo Quyen, to the left across the bridge in the centre of town, is always bustling and photogenic with its displays of fruit and flowers, and it's well worth joining the throng of shoppers, especially early in the morning. There's also a **night market** that sets up each evening along Vo Thi Sau near the lighthouse, where you can pick up a few souvenirs and check out the good value Vietnamese food stalls. Alternatively, you could visit one of the **fish sauce factories** in town. Phu Quoc is famed throughout the country for producing top-quality fish sauce – a key ingredient in many Vietnamese dishes. Hung Thanh factory (daily 8–11am & 1–5pm; free), located on Nguyen Van Troi, to the left just beyond the market, welcomes visitors, though you might need a peg for your nose as the aroma is rather pungent.

The west coast

The main attraction of Phu Quoc is its fabulous beaches, and the **west coast** has some of the best. The majority of resorts and guesthouses are strung out to the south of Duong Dong, on **Long Beach** (Bai Truong) – an appropriate name, as it stretches almost to the southern tip of the island some 20km away. Most resorts have fine stretches of soft yellow sand and swaying coconut palms right in front, and the beach is ideal for sunbathing, sunset-watching and swimming. Beyond the first few kilometres south of town the beach is completely deserted, and the road which runs behind the palm trees provides some classic tropical beach views. About halfway down the beach, the **Phu Quoc Pearl Farm** (daily 8am–5pm) is worth a look to see how pearls are cultured or to pick up a souvenir. If you're here for rest and relaxation, you need do nothing more than saunter back and forth between your room, the resort's restaurant and the beach. If you get restless, you can always rent a motorbike to explore the island or sign up for a boat trip.

The west coast north of town is a bit more rugged, but the beautiful bays tucked along **Ong Lang Beach** (Bai Ong Lang) are certainly worth visiting, and a few cosy resorts offer the chance to really get away from it all. Ong Lang

Beach is much quieter than Long Beach, and has the added attraction of coral reefs teeming with tropical fish just off the coast, which makes it good for snorkelling. North of Ong Lang, there are a few more attractive beaches called **Cua Can**, **Vung Bao** and **Dai**. They have basic restaurants and can be reached by motorbike on a dirt road that follows the coast to the northwest corner.

The east coast

The **east coast** is, so far, largely undeveloped, though it does have a good surfaced road behind it that makes a pleasant change from the constant dust kicked up off the dirt roads around the rest of the island. The most impressive beach here is **Star Beach** (Bai Sao), which is signposted just north of the T-junction where the road from Duong Dong meets the road up the east coast. Its dazzling white sand and pale blue water are a great attraction for local people at weekends, and a couple of beach restaurants, the *My Lan* and *Ai Xim*, do a healthy trade. A little south of Bai Sao, **Ice Cream Beach** (Bai Kem) is also a blinding white colour, but there is no shade, the beach is full of rubbish washed in by the tide, and in any case, the military generally prohibit entry to foreigners.

Inland Phu Quoc

Inland Phu Quoc is the kind of island that is ideal for exploration, and there is very little traffic, making it easy to ride a motorbike around, though until the roads are surfaced, you are likely to return at the end of day covered in a film of red dust. Wearing a helmet is compulsory and a face-mask is a good idea too. Over seventy percent of the island is forested at present, and the hills of the north are particularly verdant.

All over the island, and especially in the north, you will pass by **pepper plantations**, the plants easily identifiable as climbers on three-metre-high poles – at places like **Khu Tuong**, they welcome visitors to look around. There are also two cleansing **streams** in the centre of Phu Quoc: **Suoi Da Ban** and **Suoi Tranh**. A walk beside them reveals moss-covered boulders, tangled vines and small cascades, though they tend to dry up between January and May, when the trip is not worth it.

In the south of the island, two unusual attractions are located almost opposite each other, the **war memorial** and the former **prison** (Nha Tu Phu Quoc; Tues–Sun 7.30–11am & 1.30–5pm; 3000đ). The war memorial, perched on a slight rise beside the main road, consists of three abstract forms, in one of which is cut the shape of a human form, while the prison's small museum chronicles its use to detain enemies of the state, though there is no English signage.

Eating and drinking

Duong Dong's **night market** (see p.181) is a great place to sample authentic Vietnamese dishes at very cheap prices. Not surprisingly, every beach resort, apart from the cheapest guesthouses, has its own **restaurant**; most have reasonable menus and some have sea views, but the quality is erratic and prices are often inflated. Bear in mind if you stay at Ong Lang Beach, you'll be limited to the restaurant at your resort unless you have a rented motorbike. Long Beach may be busier, but you do get several choices in a small area. Most places listed below operate only as restaurants and bars, and they're all on or around Long Beach.

Moving on from Phu Quoc

Speedboats to Rach Gia leave from the jetty at Vong Beach ($13–15, 2hr 30min), while those bound for Ha Tien ($11; 1hr 30min) leave from Ham Ninh. It's certainly advisable to book in advance: either ask your hotel or guesthouse to help you, or visit the offices at the top of Tran Hung Dao, just behind the northern end of Long Beach.

Flights to Ho Chi Minh City (several daily; 1hr) leave from Phu Quoc Airport. Reservations can be made at the Vietnam Airlines office at 122 Nguyen Trung Truc (℡077/398 2320), in front of the airport gate, or at the branch office at the Saigon-Phu Quoc resort.

Captain Skewer In front of *Kim Nam Phuong* guesthouse. Set in an attractive building with huge wooden pillars, this place specializes in barbecued skewers of beef and bell pepper, or chicken, onion and grape (about 110,000đ each), though it also has a good range of salads and fillings for rice-paper wrappers.

Gop Gio 78 Tran Hung Dao. Not on the beach, but within walking distance of many resorts, this place serves up tasty Vietnamese dishes (around 30,000–50,000đ) in a no-frills environment.

Le Bistrot On the lane leading to *La Veranda* resort. Relaxing place with pool table offering French and international dishes (100,000–120,000đ), and with a children's playground in the garden.

Le Deauville In front of *Kim Nam Phuong* guesthouse, next to *Captain Skewer*. French-style preparation of many dishes, such as cassolette of stuffed squid and barbecued chicken Deauville-style. Good prices, around 70,000–85,000đ for a main course, and some wines on offer too.

Lounge On the lane leading to *La Veranda* resort. Fancy restaurant serving a range of Vietnamese dishes at around 80,000–90,000đ, and a good choice of cocktails too.

Palm Tree On the beach, just north of *La Veranda* resort. Heavenly, open-sided spot where you can wriggle your toes in the sand while devouring seafood noodles and an ice-cold beer at dirt-cheap prices.

Pepper's 89 Tran Hung Dao, on the main road near the north end of Long Beach, ℡077/384 8773. The

▲ Coracles on Phu Quoc island

place to go for pizzas, grills and jumbo salads, with a delivery service too. Most dishes are around 80,000–100,000đ.

Pepper Tree *La Veranda* resort. The ideal place for a splurge is at this classy, first-floor restaurant in a colonial-style building. Plenty of seafood on offer, such as smoked salmon and lobster, in a refined atmosphere.

Rainbow In front of *Thanh Kieu* resort. Classic beach bar, serving up burgers and steaks, at around 80,000–100,000đ, as well as beers and cool sounds.

Travel details

Buses

Bus stations are gradually becoming more organized, with ticket desks and scheduled departures. However, it is still almost impossible to give the frequency with which buses run because of the large number of private minibuses that ply more popular routes, and depart only when they have enough passengers to make the journey worthwhile. Off the main highway, to be sure of a bus it's advisable to start your journey early – most long-distance departures are between 5am and 9am, and few run after midday. Journey times can also vary; figures below show the normal length of time you can expect to take by public bus.

Ca Mau to: Bac Lieu (2hr); Can Tho (5hr); Ho Chi Minh City (7hr); Long Xuyen (6hr); Soc Trang (3hr).
Can Tho to: Bac Lieu (3hr); Ca Mau (5hr); Chau Doc (2hr 30min); Ha Tien (5hr); Ho Chi Minh City (4hr); Long Xuyen (1hr 30min); My Tho (2hr 30min).
Chau Doc to: Ca Mau (7hr); Can Tho (2hr 30min); Ha Tien (4hr); Ho Chi Minh City (6hr); Long Xuyen (1hr).
Ha Tien to: Can Tho (5hr); Chau Doc (4hr); Ho Chi Minh City (8hr); Long Xuyen (6hr); Rach Gia (2hr 30min).

Long Xuyen to: Ca Mau (5hr); Chau Doc (1hr) Ha Tien (6hr); Ho Chi Minh City (5hr).
My Tho to: Can Tho (2hr 30min); Cao Lanh (2hr); Ho Chi Minh City (2hr).
Vinh Long to: Sa Dec (50min); Tra Vinh (1hr 30min).

Boats

Ca Mau to: Rach Gia (daily; 3hr).
Can Tho to: Ho Chi Minh City (daily; 4hr)
Chau Doc to Phnom Penh (daily; 4hr).
Ha Tien to: Phu Quoc (daily; 1hr 30min)
Phu Quoc to: Ha Tien (daily; 1hr 30min); Rach Gia (several daily; 2hr 30min).
Rach Gia to: Ca Mau (daily; 3hr); Phu Quoc (several daily; 2hr 30min).

Flights

Ca Mau to: Ho Chi Minh City (daily; 1hr).
Phu Quoc to: Ho Chi Minh City (several daily; 1hr).
Rach Gia to: Ho Chi Minh City (daily; 2hr); Phu Quoc (daily; 25min).

Vietnam's natural wonders

With vertiginous valleys smothered by lush forest and a rice paddy patchwork of vibrant emerald, Vietnam is a country blessed with breathtaking natural beauty. Chunky mountains rifle down much of her western flank, offering wonderful opportunities to trek through colourful minority villages. From the highlands, a succession of rivers head towards a coastline dotted with innumerable beaches, and a tantalizing selection of islands. Whether you're lazing on the beach, charging through the jungle or floating along the Mekong, be sure to keep your camera handy.

Beach at Nha Trang ▲

Mui Ne beach ▼

Beaches

With a tropical coastline of well over three thousand kilometres, Vietnam has plenty of beaches to choose from; largely at their best in the south of the country, these idyllic stretches of sand cater to everyone from party-goers to solitude-seekers. The city of **Nha Trang** sits firmly in the "party" corner, though there are more strings to its bow; after clubbing all night, the day can be spent snorkelling, diving, island-hopping, visiting ancient Cham ruins, or simply lazing on the beach. Equally lively is **Mui Ne**, a lengthy curl of white sand hemmed in by sand dunes of baked Saharan red; in addition to climbing and sliding down the dunes, activities here include windsurfing and kitesurfing.

At the opposite end of the spectrum is **Jungle Beach**; located on a peninsula just north of Nha Trang, it's made up of little more than the constituent parts of its name, plus a few ramshackle wooden huts. **Ho Coc** beach also has its moments of tranquillity, while there are pockets of quiet on the shores at **Ca Na**.

Islands

Vietnam's principal offshore attractions are found at the extremes of her S-shaped coastline. To the north lie the fairytale shapes of **Ha Long Bay**, a maze of contorted limestone bluffs that are deservedly at the forefront of many travellers' itineraries. Many visitors overnight here on a traditionally-styled junk to view the undulating horizon at sunset dissolving into wave after wave of improbably-shaped karst islets. It's also worth spending a night on **Cat Ba**; by far the largest island in the bay, it makes a great base for rock-climbing, beach-lazing or jungle treks, and its laid-back air persuades many visitors to miss their boat and stay longer.

A densely forested full-stop at the southern end of the Vietnamese coast, **Phu Quoc Island** is blessed with pristine white-sand beaches, tree-cloaked peaks and cute fishing villages; during the dry season it's one of Vietnam's best dive-spots, while its meandering dirt roads appeal to motorbike fans. Also becoming popular are the islands of the **Con Dao Archipelago**, which offer the rare opportunity to see turtles laying eggs on the beach.

▲ Boats in Cat Ba harbour

▼ Mountain landscape around Sa Pa

Mountains

Vietnam's lofty peaks exert a magnetic draw for trekkers, climbers and lovers of nature; the jagged scenery toggles between karst, highland and alpine, and reaches its summit in the 3143m-high form of **Mount Fan Si Pan**. However, even more appealing than the scenery itself is a rich mosaic of **hill tribes** – Vietnam boasts the most complex ethnic make-up in Southeast Asia, with 52 offical minority groups, most living in highland areas.

Cleaved neatly in two by the Red River, the **northern mountains** include Vietnam's highest peaks. The most interesting region is between Muong Lai and **Sa Pa**, a once obscure village-with-a-view which has blossomed into Vietnam's trekking capital. Here minority people still generally dress in **traditional costume** – especially the women – and colourful groups you are likely to encounter include Red Dao, White Thai and Black Hmong. On the other side of the Red River, **Bac Ha** is surrounded by Flower Hmong folk who participate in a vibrant Sunday market. The **central highlands** also feature hugely photogenic scenery and

▼ Red Dao minority people

ethnic groups; foremost among the natural attractions are the Dambri Waterfalls and canoe-friendly Lak Lake, while hill tribes include the E De, Koho and Bahnar, with their fascinating traditional houses.

Rivers

Though the Ben Hai once divided the nation, and the Red River feeds Hanoi, the mighty **Mekong** is the undisputed star of Vietnam's waterways. Having tumbled over four thousand kilometres from its Tibetan source, the world's eleventh-longest river fans out into a **delta region** wide and fertile enough to provide the country with a weighty rice surplus, before emptying into the South China Sea. You can take **boat trips** through its lush landscape of green fields and dirt-brown tributaries to see fish farms, floating markets, orchid gardens and wooden homes that remain an integral part of river life. The main draw for many, though, is the chance to stay overnight at a **riverside guesthouse** – friendly locals, hammock beds, homecooked meals and homebrewed drinks all make for a memorable stay.

Floating market on the Mekong ▲

Delacour's langur at the Cuc Phuong centre for endangered primates ▼

National parks

Many of Vietnam's more pristine corners have been protected as national parks. Some of the most notable are:

▶▶ **Ba Be** (p.452), centred around the country's largest natural lake.

▶▶ **Cuc Phuong** (p.339), containing a centre for endangered primates.

▶▶ **Bach Ma** (p.294), a haven for ornithologists and botanists.

▶▶ **Cat Tien** (p.190), where you'll find elephants, rhinos and crocodiles.

▶▶ **Cat Ba** (p.411), the largest of Ha Long Bay's enchanting islands.

▶▶ **Yok Don** (p.208), home to more than a dozen ethnic groups.

The central highlands

CHAPTER 3 # Highlights

* **Trekking** Trek along forest trails in a national park at Cat Tien or Yok Don. See p.190 & p.208

* **Dambri Waterfalls** The most impressive waterfalls in the highlands – stand right below them and feel the spray on your face. See p.190

* **Da Lat** Abseil down a waterfall or pose for pictures on a pony in the capital of adventure sports and kitsch. See p.191

* **Lak Lake** Paddle around Lak Lake in a dug-out canoe at dawn and watch the sunrise shimmer across its surface. See p.203

* **Coffee country** Enjoy a cup of fresh coffee in one of Buon Ma Thuot's cool cafés. See p.207

* **Bahnar villages** Overnight in a dramatically tall communal *rong* in a Bahnar village near Kon Tum. See p.215

▲ Café in Buon Ma Thuot

3

The central highlands

Vietnam's mountainous midriff isn't the first region of the country that most tourists think to visit. And yet, after a hot and sticky stint labouring across the coastal plains, the central highlands, with their host of ethnic minorities, mist-laden mountains and thundering waterfalls, can provide an enjoyable contrast to the tropics. Getting around is at times a challenge: travel can be slow with some roads impassable after a downpour. In addition, local tourist authorities may raise a fuss about tourists travelling independently, and there are no really heart-stopping sights. But the highlands' allure lies in such simple pleasures as inhaling their invigoratingly chill airs, and walking or cycling with a spray of mist on your face. And, cocooned in woolly jumpers, scarves and bobble hats, the highlanders exude a warmth unsurpassed elsewhere in the country, making a trip here doubly appealing.

Bounded to the west by the Cambodian border, and spreading out over the lofty peaks and broad plateaux of the **Truong Son Mountains**, the central highlands stretch from the base of Highway 1 right up to the bottleneck of land that squeezes past Da Nang towards Hanoi and the north. The region's fertile red soils yield considerable **natural resources** – among them coffee, tea, rubber, silk and hardwood. Not all of the highlands, though, have been sacrificed to plantation-style economies of scale – pockets of primeval forest still thrive, where **wildlife** including elephants, bears and gibbons somehow survived the days when the region was a hunting ground for Saigon's idle rich and Hué's idle royalty.

For most visitors who ascend to these altitudes, the main target is **Da Lat**, an erstwhile French mountain retreat that can appear very romantic when the mists roll over its pine-crested hilltops, though some find it disappointing close-up, with its dreary architecture and tacky tourist trappings. Yet the city is not without its charms, among them a bracing climate, some beguiling colonial buildings, picturesque bike rides and a market overflowing with delectable fruits and vegetables.

It's a picturesque journey from Ho Chi Minh City to Da Lat by road, though it takes about six hours and buses can be cramped, so it's worth considering taking a plane. From Da Lat, it's possible to drop down to the coast at Phan Rang or Nha Trang, or continue northwards over the hills, passing pretty **Lak Lake** on the way to a series of gritty highland towns whose reputations rest less on tourist sights than on the villages and open terrain that ring them. Sensitive to the minority rights issue, the Vietnamese authorities only opened this region to foreigners in 1993, and still few visitors venture to its main towns, **Buon Ma Thuot**, **Plei Ku** and **Kon Tum**. North of Buon Ma Thuot, Highway 14 makes a beeline across the Dac Lac Plateau to Plei Ku, and then continues to Kon Tum, a journey of less than an hour. Since restrictions on independent travel are less stringent in Kon Tum than around Plei Ku or Buon Ma Thuot, and as there are

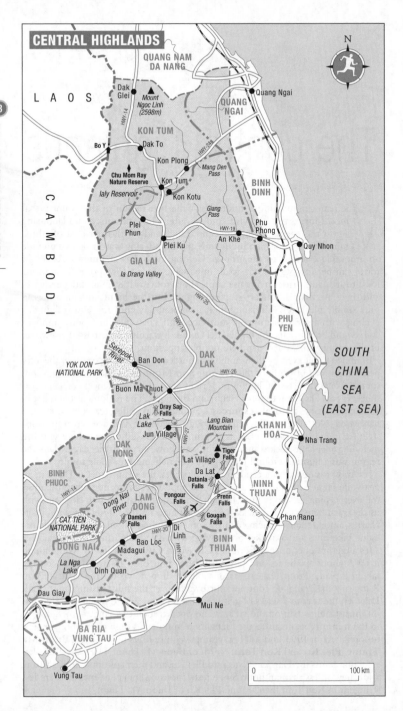

several nearby minority villages that feature towering *rong* where home-stays are possible, the town has started to attract adventurous travellers. From Kon Tum you can travel 80km northwest to **Bo Y** and cross the new international border to Laos, or head straight for the coast at Quang Ngai, or even go north along the route of the new **Ho Chi Minh Highway**.

Many of the highlands' inhabitants belong to **ethnic minorities** who are struggling to maintain their identities in the face of persistent pressure from Hanoi to assimilate (for more on the background of the ethnic minorities, see p.492). Apart from around Kon Tum, visiting one of the highlands' many minority villages independently can be difficult: in most cases you'll need to go through a local tourist office (and pay handsomely for the privilege), but in each area it's best to double-check the current regulations, especially concerning overnight stays in villages.

Your highland experience will vary enormously depending upon **when you visit**. The dry season runs from November through to April. To see the region at its atmospheric best, it's better to go in the wet season, May to October, although at this time the rain can make some outlying villages inaccessible.

Into the highlands

The route to the central highlands from Ho Chi Minh City follows Highway 1 for about 70km before branching northeast on **Highway 20**, which starts a steady climb. The rubber trees corralling its traffic occasionally reveal tantalizing views of the valleys below. Buses sometimes screech to a brief halt on the causeway traversing **La Nga Lake**, from where the **houseboats** cast adrift on its waters are only a zoom lens away. Locals use foot-powered rowing boats to access their homes, beneath which lie fish farms. East of La Nga, Highway 20 passes wooded slopes whose verdant greens are flecked occasionally by the red-tiled roofs of farmsteads and the roving figures of grazing cattle. Look out for unusual rock formations at the roadside in **Dinh Quan**, 112km from Ho Chi Minh City, where enormous smooth boulders are scattered beside the highway in the southern part of town, and volcanoes with symmetrical slopes and flat tops are visible from the road both south and north of town.

In time the hills yield to the tea, coffee and mulberry plantations of the **Bao Loc Plateau**. The town of **Bao Loc** is the best place for a pit stop between Ho Chi Minh City and Da Lat, and it's also a jumping-off point for visits to nearby **Cat Tien National Park** and **Dambri Waterfalls**. Another 100km further northeast, Highway 20 switchbacks up the considerable climb to **Da Lat** at an altitude of just under 1500 metres.

Bao Loc and around

The undulating hills around **BAO LOC** provide fertile soil for the cultivation of **tea** and **coffee**, while locals also cultivate the mulberry bushes whose leaves **silkworms** eat. There are no sights of interest in the town itself, but it offers a convenient place to break the long journey between Ho Chi Minh City and Da Lat, and the surrounding countryside is very attractive.

Accommodation in Bao Loc is rather unexciting, with the *Seri Bank Hotel* (T063/386 4150; ❹), set back from the main highway behind a small lake, being the most comfortable place in town. Of several smaller hotels on the main road (Highway 20), the *Bao Loc* (T063/386 4107; ❶–❷), south of the town centre at 795 Tran Phu, has reasonable rooms; those at the back have nice views over the countryside. For a decent meal, try the *Nam Hue*, at 821 Tran Phu, a few steps away from the *Bao Loc Hotel*.

Cat Tien National Park

The area's outstanding attraction is **Cat Tien National Park** (T061/366 9228, Wwww.cattienpark.com.vn; 50,000đ), a protected area situated 150km north of Ho Chi Minh City and about 50km west of Bao Loc, covering the largest lowland tropical rainforest in south Vietnam. The park hosts nearly 350 species of birds, over 450 species of butterflies and over 100 mammals, including wild cats, elephants, monkeys and the rare Javan rhinoceros. Don't bank on seeing a rhino, though, as the few residing here are in a secluded reserve closed to visitors. If you're coming by public transport, take a bus for Da Lat from Mien Dong station in Ho Chi Minh City; tell the driver you want "Vuon Quoc Gia Cat Tien" (Cat Tien National Park), and he will drop you at the km125 junction at Tan Phu town. From here, xe om (about 60,000đ) cover the final 24km to the park along a narrow surfaced road. If you're arriving from the north, a signposted road (also surfaced) to the park branches right just before the small town of Madagui. You need to pay the entrance fee at a park office on stilts about 100m before the ferry across the Dong Nai River to park headquarters.

As the park can only accommodate about a hundred visitors at a time, it's important to book ahead. **Accommodation** here (❷–❸) consists of simple rooms with air-conditioning, and a campsite with two-person tents for $8 a day. You can also hire vehicles and boats for travel to the park's more remote areas, but there are few English-speaking guides. Though a dozen walking trails exist, the catch is that you need to hire a jeep or pick-up to get to the start of most of them ($10–25), plus a guide to go with you ($15–25), so a day out can easily cost $40–50. There's also a night safari ($10), though few people spot more than a flash of deer eyes before the panicked creatures flee. Some tour operators in Ho Chi Minh City (such as Sinhbalo tours; see p.86) and Da Lat (such as Phat Tire Ventures; see p.200) can organize tours that include a visit to the park.

Dambri Waterfalls and north to Da Lat

Another interesting attraction of the area is the impressive drop (about 80m) of **Dambri Waterfalls** (daily 7am–5pm; small entrance fee), some 18km north of Bao Loc; a xe om should cost around 100,000đ return. The road to the falls, which branches north from Highway 20 just east of Bao Loc, bisects rolling countryside carpeted by coffee, tea and pineapple plantations. Once you arrive, there are two paths leading to the falls. The main one to the right leads to the top of the falls, where some ugly fencing stands between you and a precipice over which a torrent tumbles in the rainy season. From here, you can descend to the base of the falls by steep steps, or if you're feeling lazy, there's a lift available for 5000đ. A second path, to the left by a restaurant, leads down a steep stairway among towering trees to a superb view of the falls from in front. The two paths are linked by a bridge over the river, where you're likely to get drenched in spray even during the dry season. The path continues downstream to a smaller cascade, Dasara Falls, but the trail can be slippery after rain. Surrounded as they are by dense forest, Dambri Falls are much more attractive than any of those in the vicinity of Da Lat, and the only ones worth visiting in the dry season.

More hummocky tea plantations abound along the road around **Di Linh**, the biggest town between Bao Loc and Da Lat. From here, Highway 28 branches right and heads down to Phan Thiet. Around 25km beyond Di Linh on Highway 20, pine trees begin to feature in the landscape. At this point you'll see signs for two more of the region's most impressive waterfalls, **Pongour** to the left, and **Gougah** to the right. The former are about 7km to the left off the main road, but the latter are just 400m to the right of the road, and are well worth stopping for a look in the wet season, when a thundering torrent pours over them. From here it's about 40km to **Da Lat**, of which the final ten-kilometre stretch cuts steeply through heavily wooded slopes.

Da Lat and around

Hinged by the Cam Ly River, and nestled at an elevation of just under 1500m among the pitching hills of the **Lang Bian Plateau**, the city of **DA LAT** is Vietnam's premier hill station, a beguiling amalgam of squiggly streets, picturesque churches, bounteous vegetable gardens and crashing waterfalls, all suffused with the intoxicating scents of pine trees and wood-smoke.

It was Dr Alexander Yersin who first divined the therapeutic properties of Da Lat's temperate climate on an exploratory mission into Vietnam's southern highlands, in 1893. His subsequent report on the area must have struck a chord: four years later Governor-General Paul Doumer of Indochina ordered the founding of a convalescent hill station, where Saigon's hot-under-the-collar *colons* could recharge their batteries, and perhaps even take part in a day's game-hunting. The city's Gallic contingent had to pack up their winter coats after 1954's Treaty of Geneva, but by then the cathedral, train station, villas and hotels had been erected, and the French connection well and truly forged. By tacit agreement during the American War, both Hanoi and Saigon refrained from bombing the city and it remains much as it was half a century ago.

It's important to come to Da Lat with no illusions, though. With a population of around 200,000, the city is anything but an idyllic backwater: sighting its forlorn architecture for the first time in the 1950s, Norman Lewis found the place "a drab little resort", and today its colonial relics and pagodas stand cheek by jowl with some of the dingiest examples of East European construction anywhere in Vietnam. Moreover, attractions here pander to the domestic tourist's predilection for swan-shaped pedal-boats and pony-trek guides in full cowboy gear, while at night the city can be as bleak as an off-season ski resort.

Despite all this, Da Lat remains a quaint colonial curio, and a welcome tonic to heat-worn tourists – all in all, a great place to chill out, literally and metaphorically. If the cool air gets you in the mood for action, you could try trekking to minority villages, mountain-biking or rock-climbing, but you'll need a permit and a guide. Contact one of Da Lat's tour operators for more details of what's on offer (see "Listings", p.200). Horticultural enthusiasts might like to time their visit to coincide with the annual **Flower Festival**, which takes place each December (see ⓦ www.vietnamtourism.com for exact dates).

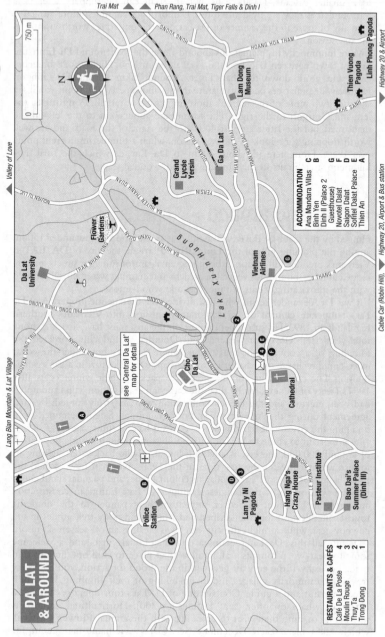

DA LAT
& AROUND

RESTAURANTS & CAFÉS
Café De La Poste   4
Moulin Rouge   3
Thuy Ta   2
Trong Dong   1

ACCOMMODATION
Ana Mandara Villas   C
Binh Yen   B
Dinh II (Palace 2   G
  Guesthouse)
Novotel Dalat   F
Saigon Dalat   D
Sofitel Dalat Palace   E
Thien An   A

Trai Mat   Phan Rang, Trai Mat, Tiger Falls & Dinh I

Valley of Love

Lang Bian Mountain & Lat Village

Cable Car (Robin Hill),   Highway 20, Airport & Bus station

Highway 20 & Airport

Linh Phong Pagoda
Thien Vuong Pagoda
KHE SANH
Lam Dong Museum
HOANG HOA THAM
HUNG VUONG

Ga Da Lat
Grand Lycée Yersin
YERSIN
PHAM HONG THAI
QUANG TRUNG

Flower Gardens
Da Lat University
NGUYEN TU LUC
TRAN NHAN TONG
PHU DONG THIEN VUONG
BUI THI XUAN
NGUYEN CONG TRU
DINH TIEN HOANG
BA HUYEN THANH QUAN

Lake Xuan Huong

Vietnam Airlines
3 THANG 4

PHAN DINH PHUNG
HAI BA TRUNG

see 'Central Da Lat' map for detail

Cho Da Lat

YERSIN
ANH SANG
TRAN PHU
Cathedral

Police Station

Lam Ty Ni Pagoda
Hang Nga's Crazy House
Pasteur Institute
Bao Dai's Summer Palace (Dinh III)
LE HONG PHONG

750 m
0

N

Arrival and information

Buses from Ho Chi Minh City, Nha Trang and elsewhere arrive at Da Lat bus station, located about a kilometre south of the city centre on 3 Thang 4, from where it is a short xe om or taxi ride into town (20,000–30,000đ). Modest **Lien Khuong Airport** (☏063/384 3373) is 29km south of the city, off the road to Ho Chi Minh City: Vietnam Airlines buses (20,000đ) shuttle from the airport to their offices in town (see p.200), or you can take a xe om for about $3–5, or a taxi for around $10–12. The handful of **tourist offices** in Da Lat can all arrange guides, bus tickets, car hire and tours; the main one is Da Lat Travel Services, though *Sinh Café* and TM Brothers have offices here too. If you plan to go trekking to minority villages, you may need to get a permit from the police and be accompanied by a certified guide. You can skirt around the red tape by signing up for a tour of one or several days with one of Da Lat's adventure sports operators which also offer mountain-biking, rock-climbing and abseiling outings. Phat Tire Ventures is a reliable outfit; see "Listings", p.200, for details.

City transport

Da Lat is too hilly for cyclo, and the horse-drawn carts that were once one of the city's more attractive features are pretty much a thing of the past (apart from trots around the lake in high season), so for journeys of any distance you'll have to rely on **xe om** and **taxis**. If you're fit, you might consider **renting a bicycle** or tandem (about $2 a day), though with all the steep hills, a **motorbike** makes more sense (around $5–6 a day): both are available from hotels and tour operators. Renting a **car and driver** for the day (also easily arranged through hotels or tour operators) costs around $40. Alternatively, take a customized tour of the highlands or even the whole country with the Da Lat-based **Easy Riders** (ⓦwww.dalat-easyrider.com.vn), who ride late-model big bikes and speak good English. The tours are highly recommended, with prices ranging from around $15 a day for a tour of the main sights in the city to around $75 a day for a longer trip, usually including accommodation and entrance fees to sights. Many hotels and tour operators offer 'Easy Rider' tours with inferior guides at inflated prices, so make sure you get the real thing by booking via their website or approaching them where they hang out in the early evening in front of the *Hoa Binh I (Peace) Hotel*. All riders wear blue jackets and waistcoats stamped with the group's insignia, but to be doubly sure your rider is genuine, ask to see his badge with name and number, as well as his tour guide licence.

Accommodation

Enduringly popular with both Western and domestic tourists, Da Lat has a wide range of places to stay, from cheap, windowless rooms to luxury, international-standard hotels. However, if your visit coincides with a **public holiday**, especially Tet, be warned that prices increase by up to fifty percent, and you'll need either to arrive early or book ahead.

The densest concentrations of **budget hotels** lie on Phan Dinh Phung; ask for a room at the back, as the main road can be noisy. Several classy hotels operate downtown, but there are many more out in the open spaces south and west of the city centre. Check that prices include hot water – a luxury in much of southern Vietnam, but a necessity in Da Lat. Air-conditioning is neither necessary nor usually provided in Da Lat.

Central Da Lat

The following are all marked on the map opposite.

9$ Hotel 4c Bui Thi Xong ☏ 063/382 2883 @ brothermoon48@yahoo.com. Decent-sized rooms at budget prices – $9 for a single, $12.50 for a double, just a few steps from the lake. **②**

Cam Do 81 Phan Dinh Phung ☏ 063/382 2732 ⓦ www.camdohotel.com.vn. A good mid-range choice located near the centre, featuring spacious rooms, all with bathtubs. **④**

Chau Au–Europa 76 Nguyen Chi Thanh ☏ 063/382 2870, @ europa@hcm.vnn.vn. Professionally run place with a range of rooms. All are dazzlingly clean with homely touches – an extra $5 secures a front room with view. Staff are extremely helpful and there's free internet and wi-fi. **②**

Dreams 1 & 2 151 and 164b Phan Dinh Phung ☏ 063/383 3748, @ dreams@hcm.vnn.vn. Superbly maintained mini-hotels; rooms are well equipped, clean, with modern bathrooms. Windows have double glazing and there's free use of the jacuzzi and sauna; free internet access 7am–10pm, generous buffet breakfasts and extremely helpful staff. **③**

Empress 5 Nguyen Thai Hoc ☏ 063/383 3888 ⓦ www.empresshotelvn.com. Small but attractive colonial-style building overlooking the lake with tastefully furnished rooms and all facilities. **⑤–⑥**

Golf 3 4 Nguyen Thi Minh Khai ☏ 063/382 6042, ⓦ www.vinagolf.vn. Part of the *Golf* empire, in an upmarket tower-block hotel situated slap-bang in the centre of town. Choose from a selection of comfortable suites or cheaper standard rooms. **⑤–⑥**

Hoa Binh I 64 Truong Cong Dinh ☏ 063/382 2787. Budget hotel that's reliably popular with backpackers. All rooms have hot water and private bathrooms, and some have balconies with views of the busy street below – or opt for quieter rooms with a terrace at the back. There's also a cheap and popular café downstairs. **①–②**

Hoa Binh II 67 Truong Cong Dinh ☏ 063/382 2982. Small, cosy auberge-style hotel just around the corner from its sister hotel, with the same good-value rooms, all with hot water and generous-sized bathrooms and, as before, friendly staff. **①–②**

Hoang Hau Villa 8a Ho Tung Mau ☏ 063/382 1431. Just below the GPO, this appealing mini-hotel has an art gallery and café in the lobby, and well-appointed rooms, some with balconies; breakfast is included. **②–③**

Ngoc Lan 42 Nguyen Chi Thanh ☏ 063/382 2136 ⓦ www.ngoclanhotel.vn. Spacious, well-equipped rooms with good views over the lake at this newly refurbished four-star hotel. **⑥–⑦**

Outer Da Lat

The following are all marked on the map on p.192.

Ana Mandara Villas Le Lai ☏ 063/355 5888, ⓦ www.anamandararesortdalat.com. This new complex of luxury villas located in spacious grounds just outside the city centre and boasting every conceivable comfort vies with the *Sofitel Dalat Palace* for the title of fanciest place to stay in Da Lat. **⑦**

Binh Yen 7 Hai Thuong ☏ 063/382 3631. Tucked away at the top of Hai Thuong and overlooking parts of the city, there's much to like about the *Binh Yen*'s location and helpful staff. Rooms are nothing special, but all have hot water and TVs, and there's free wi-fi too. **②**

Dinh II (Palace 2 Guest House) 12 Tran Hung Dao ☏ 063/382 2092. If you fancy living like a colonial but can't afford the rates at the *Dalat Palace* or *Ana Mandara*, then this is your spot. The huge rooms in the main house, once home to the French governor, are beautifully furnished and the complex is surrounded by pines. **③–⑤**

Novotel Dalat 7 Tran Phu ☏ 063/382 5777, ⓦ www.accorhotels.com. A sympathetically restored colonial edifice that plays second fiddle to the more expensive *Sofitel Dalat Palace* nearby. Pleasing, well-ventilated rooms with elegant interiors and polished wooden floors. **⑤–⑥**

Saigon Dalat 2 Hoang Van Thu ☏ 063/355 6789 ⓦ www.saigondalathotel.com. This new four-star hotel makes a reasonable attempt at capturing a bygone era with its traditional furnishings, though it includes modern touches like flat-screen TVs. **⑥–⑦**

Sofitel Dalat Palace 12 Tran Phu ☏ 063/382 5444, ⓦ www.sofitel.com/asia. Da Lat's most magnificent colonial pile sits in manicured grounds, still radiating its 1920s splendour. All rooms are lavishly appointed and decked out with period furnishings, including clunky telephones and massive bathtubs. **⑦**

Thien An 272a Phan Dinh Phung ☏ 063/352 0607. Run by the owner of *Dreams*, this place offers the same benefits of smart rooms, big breakfasts and internet use a few steps further from the town centre. **②**

The City

Central Da Lat forms a rough crescent around the western side of man-made **Lake Xuan Huong**, created in 1919 when the Cam Ly River was dammed by the French, who named it the "Grand Lac". The city escaped bomb damage,

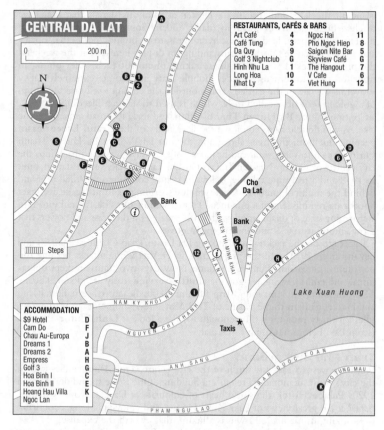

CENTRAL DA LAT

0   200 m

N

RESTAURANTS, CAFÉS & BARS			
Art Café	4	Ngoc Hai	11
Café Tung	3	Pho Ngoc Hiep	8
Da Quy	9	Saigon Nite Bar	5
Golf 3 Nightclub	G	Skyview Café	G
Hinh Nhu La	1	The Hangout	7
Long Hoa	10	V Cafe	6
Nhat Ly	2	Viet Hung	12

Cho
Da Lat

Bank

Bank

Steps

Lake Xuan Huong

ACCOMMODATION	
$9 Hotel	D
Cam Do	F
Chau Au-Europa	J
Dreams 1	B
Dreams 2	A
Empress	H
Golf 3	G
Hoa Binh I	C
Hoa Binh II	E
Hoang Hau Villa	K
Ngoc Lan	I

Taxis

and a French influence is still evident in its central area, whose twisting streets and steps, lined with stone buildings rising to red-tiled roofs, cover a hillock located between the streets of Bui Thi Xuan and Phan Dinh Phung. Your first stop should be at the market, **Cho Da Lat**, which stands on top of the hill, a charmless reinforced-concrete structure housing a staggering range of fruit and vegetables. Strawberries, beetroot, fennel, artichokes, avocados, blackberries and cherries grown in the market gardens surrounding the city are all sold here, along with a riot of flowers. Artichoke teabags, with their diuretic properties, make quirky **souvenirs**, and candied Da Lat strawberries are also sold at many stalls. **Montagnards** carrying their chattels in backpacks are a fairly common sight at the market, especially early in the morning when they come to trade with stallholders.

Around Lake Xuan Huong

It's a pleasant 7km cycle or walk around glassy **Lake Xuan Huong**, or if you're feeling lazy, go by electric car from the western end of the lake (10,000đ). Head eastwards around the north side of the lake along **Nguyen Thai Hoc**, and you'll soon leave the bustle of the city behind as you pass between the lake and the extensive grounds of Da Lat's **golf club**. A small island in the lake and (usually) a cluster of minivans signals that you have reached Da Lat's **flower gardens** (daily 7.30am–5pm; small entrance fee) on the left. Inside, paths lead you past hydrangeas, roses, orchids, poinsettia, topiary and a nursery. There's nothing outstanding on display here, but at the weekend the place is packed with Vietnamese taking photos of each other posing in front of the flowerbeds. Besides bobble hats and some extremely tacky souvenirs on sale in the gardens, **stalls** outside the entrance sell knotted lumps of a golden fern fibre called *cu ly*, which is used to staunch bleeding.

Continue along **Ba Huyen Thanh Quan**, and trace its broad arc around the lake. As you double back, you'll see the slate belfry of the **Grand Lycée Yersin** peeping out from the trees above and to your left. Where Ba Huyen Thanh Quan turns into Yersin, you can head one of two ways: west, and back into the city centre; or east up Nguyen Trai to **Ga Da Lat**, the city's train station, built in 1938 and a real time capsule. Below its gently contoured red-tiled roof and behind the multicoloured Art Deco windows striping its front facade, its ticket booths are reminiscent of a provincial French station. Outside, the rail yard is in a charming state of dilapidation, with cattle grazing on the grass and flowers that grow among its tracks and ancient locomotives.

Trains ran on the rack railway linking Da Lat to Thap Cham (see p.237) and beyond from 1933 until the mid-Sixties, when Viet Cong attacks became too persistent a threat for them to continue. Nowadays two trains are kept operational, and enthusiasts may enjoy the **shuttle service** (daily at 7.45am, 9.50am, 11.55am, 2pm, 4.05pm; round trip 90min; 80,000đ) across horticultural land and market gardens to the village of **Trai Mat**, a few kilometres away; the train idles for thirty minutes – time enough to take a look at **Linh Phuoc Pagoda** (see p.199) before returning to Da Lat.

Tran Phu and around

Running west to east just south of the city centre, **Tran Phu**, cradles two of the city's most memorable French-era buildings. One is the splendidly restored 1920s **Palace Hotel**, the social heart of colonial-era Da Lat. Now owned by *Sofitel*, it has great views of Lake Xuan Huong, and enjoying a long, cool drink overlooking its manicured lawns is a luxury that's worth the expense.

Across the road and a few steps west along Tran Phu, Da Lat's dusty pink **cathedral**, consecrated in 1931 and completed eleven years later, is dedicated to St Nicholas, protector of the poor; a statue of him stands at the opposite end of the nave to the simple altar, with three tiny children loitering at his feet. Light streaming in from the cathedral's seventy stained-glass windows, mostly crafted in Grenoble, teases a warm, sunny glow from the mellow pink of the interior walls, and picks out the flamboyant colours of the fresh-cut flowers adorning the nave. A tiny metal cockerel perched almost invisibly at the top of the steeple has earned the cathedral its rather unglamorous moniker, "Chicken Church".

Bao Dai's Summer Palace (Dinh III) and the Crazy House

The nautical portholes punched into its walls, and the mast-like pole sprouting from its roof, give **Dinh III** (daily 7.30–11.30am & 1.30–4.30pm; small admission fee), erstwhile summer palace of Emperor Bao Dai, the distinct look of a ship's bridge. Reached by bearing left onto Le Hong Phong 500m west of the cathedral, the building is indeed palatial, though not in a traditional style. Erected between 1933 and 1938 to provide Bao Dai with a bolt-hole between elephant-slaughtering sessions, its mustard-coloured bulk, etched with stark white grouting, is set amid rose and pine **gardens**.

▲ Inside Bao Dai's Summer Palace

Past the two large blue metal lanterns flanking the front entrance, the first room to your right is Bao Dai's **working room**, dominated by a bust of the man himself, and home both to the imperial motorbike helmet, and to a small book collection. Buffalo horns in the **reception room** come from animals bagged by Bao Dai himself on one of his hunting forays into the forests around Da Lat. His queen preferred more sedate pastimes, and would have tinkled on the piano here. The palace's most elegant common room is its **festivities room** or dining room, though catching a whiff of furniture polish in this dark, echoing chamber, it's hard to imagine the royal revelries that once went on here.

Royal ghosts are far easier to summon upstairs, where the musty **imperial bedrooms** seem just to have had the dustsheets whipped back for another royal season. Princes and princesses all had their quarters, as did the queen, whose chamber features a chaise longue that looks unnervingly like a dentist's chair. But the finest room, predictably enough, went to Bao Dai, who enjoyed the luxury of a balcony for his "breeze-getting and his moon-watching". Out on the landing, look out for a bizarre mini-sauna, labelled a *Rouathermique*. The place is surrounded by the usual attractions – pony rides and dressing up in minority costume, and the exit forces you to pass through a gauntlet of souvenir stalls.

On the way back into town at 3 Huynh Thuc Khang, **Hang Nga's Crazy House** (small admission fee) is perennially popular with tourists, though the citizens of Da Lat are more divided over the merits of this unusual building, shaped to resemble the knotted trunks of huge trees. It functions as a guest-house, but cannot be recommended as the experience is akin to paying to be an exhibit in a zoo. Day-visitors are welcome to look around any unoccupied rooms, most of which have entertaining *Alice in Wonderland*-style interiors with mirrors and mushrooms in abundance. A selection of photographs on the walls inside the entrance provide clues as to how such a bizarre construction got planning permission. As the daughter of former president Truong Chinh, its owner, Hang Nga, is above the usual planning constraints.

Lam Ty Ni Pagoda

Dropping in at **Lam Ty Ni Pagoda**, north of Le Hong Phong on Thien My, represents one of the oddest attractions of a stay in Da Lat. The focus of interest here is not the pagoda itself but its sole occupant. It is home to Vien Thuc, the so-called "mad monk" of Da Lat, who lives there with his dogs and paintings. You may find the gate locked on arrival, but if he is not away travelling he will sense your presence and admit you, though his moods vary from friendly to indifferent to aggressive, so be prepared for any kind of reception. Poet, gardener, builder and artist, Vien Thuc is a monk of all trades, but his proudest achievements are his paintings and poetry.

His normal outfit, a dark-brown monk's habit with a pointed woolly hat, is often spattered with paint. His studio, a warren of lean-tos behind the pagoda, is stacked to the rafters with over 100,000 paintings, some in watercolour and others in oil; the paint of the latter is spread so thick on the canvas they look almost three-dimensional. The paintings have names like "Golden Dragon Swimming in the River Milky Way" and "Blue Music in the Bosom of a Human World", though most are self-portraits, and all are for sale.

Tran Hung Dao and beyond

The movers and shakers who once maintained **villas** in Da Lat preferred to site their homes on a hill to the southeast of the city centre, rather than in the maw of its central area. The villas that they built along Tran Hung Dao survive today, some renovated and others in a sad state of disrepair, but they evoke the feel of the colonial era more than anywhere else in Da Lat.

Set on a hill beyond the eastern end of Tran Hung Dao near the beginning of Hung Vuong, the **Lam Dong Museum**, 4 Hung Vuong (Mon–Sat 7.30–11.30am & 1.30–4.30pm; small admission fee), is the best museum in the central highlands and well worth visiting. Located in a new building, the displays are thoughtfully laid out and give a tantalizing taste of the region's rich history. Exhibits include Cham artefacts from recent archeological digs as well as a collection of rice jars, ceramics and jewellery found in tombs, and some vicious-looking spears. The museum also gives a thorough introduction to the lifestyles of the local minority groups such as the Ma, Koho and Churu, along with a map showing their distribution in the province and many of their handicrafts and household implements. There's also a display covering the French and American Wars, though it is little different to similar displays around the rest of the country.

Continuing east along Hung Vuong, a small lane to the right leads to **Dinh I**, 1 Tran Quang Dieu (daily 7.30–11.30am & 1.30–4.30pm; small admission fee) one of Bao Dai's many palaces in the region. If you visit Bao Dai's Summer Palace, which features strongly on many tours of the city, you might want to give this a miss, as the layout and furnishings are rather similar. However, Dinh I enjoys better views over the city, is in a more peaceful setting and receives fewer visitors, so you can wander round without hordes of other tourists to disturb you. This building was used as Bao Dai's workplace, and the conference room upstairs, with its large map of the country, has a business-like air to it. There are several interesting photos on the walls of the other rooms, including one of Bao Dai in a racing car, and another of his concubines. As at Dinh III, the furnishings are classic 1930s; other points of interest are a doorway to a secret tunnel and an archaic phone switchboard at the entrance to the building.

Thien Vuong and Linh Phong Pagodas

From Tran Hung Dao two roads wiggle south, offering pleasant detours out into the countryside. **Khe Sanh** branches south off Tran Hung Dao, opposite

Pham Hong Thai, and further south leads back to Highway 20. The focus of this detour is **Thien Vuong Pagoda**, remarkable for its trio of four-metre-tall, sandalwood statues (Sakyamuni, in the centre, rubs shoulders with the Goddess of Mercy and the God of Power), imported from Hong Kong in 1958, and for the huge **statue of Buddha** seated on a lotus, 100m up the hill above the pagoda. Stalls in front of Thien Vuong hawk the usual candied strawberries, artichoke tea and *cu ly* to the Vietnamese tourists who flock here, many of whom are young girls who come from all over Vietnam to pray for good fortune and a successful marriage.

Further east, **Hoang Hoa Tham** leads to colourful **Linh Phong Pagoda**, which is fronted by a gateway bearing a fierce, panting dragon face with protruding eyes. Behind its gaudy yellow doors, the pagoda exudes a peaceful aura. Its resident nuns are very friendly, and the remote location affords peerless views of the cultivated and wooded valley below.

Eating, drinking and nightlife

Da Lat has a broad range of **restaurants** serving Vietnamese, Chinese and international cuisines, as well as abundant **food stalls**. Head to the central market for pho, com and the like, as well as one or two vegetarian stalls, signed as *com chay*. It's also the place to make up a **picnic** of bread, cheese and cake, complemented by fresh local berries.

For most locals, **nightlife** means a cup of coffee in one of the city's atmospheric **cafés**. For visitors, there's not much more unless you fancy a game of pool or a dance at one of the hotel discos. All the places listed below are marked on the Central Da Lat map on p.195, unless otherwise stated.

Restaurants

Art Café 70 Truong Cong Dinh. Located in the heart of the budget hotel district, this place has stylish, bamboo-themed decor, and appealing dishes, such as capsicum stuffed with pork and minced beef wrapped in a herbal leaf, for around 50,000đ each. Spaghetti and vegetarian dishes are served too, plus cheap cocktails. 10am–9.30pm.

Da Quy 49 Truong Cong Dinh. Serves up very acceptable Western and Vietnamese fare in smart surroundings at competitive prices. 6.30am–11pm.

Hinh Nhu La (HNL) 94 Phan Dinh Phung. Convenient for the budget hotels, this place is smartly furnished and offers pizzas as well as a good range of Vietnamese dishes. 11.30am–11pm.

Le Rabelais 12 Tran Phu. Da Lat's premier French restaurant enjoys a superb location on the ground floor of the *Sofitel Dalat Palace*, and offers delectable dishes like lobster with vanilla perfume and turnip cooked in soya ($39) 6am–10pm

Long Hoa 3 Thang 2. With a French-café ambience and attentive staff, *Long Hoa* serves tasty and filling Vietnamese dishes – kick off with a strawberry wine aperitif, while for dessert, the homemade yoghurt takes some beating. Two can dine for 150,000–200,000đ. 11am–9pm.

Moulin Rouge 83, 3 Thang 2. See map, p.192. On a chilly day in Da Lat, the ideal meal is a hotpot, which is the speciality at this place with smart furnishings and well-dressed staff. For 220,000đ you get a host of ingredients to cook at your table to your taste – enough food for four. 6am–10pm.

Nhat Ly 88 Phan Dinh Phung. A hugely popular place with Vietnamese and foreigners alike for its wide menu of dishes at very reasonable prices. There's a back room, if it's full in front. 9am–9pm.

Ngoc Hai 6 Nguyen Thi Minh Khai. Tasty Vietnamese dishes, such as fried deer with curry, in a convenient location between the market and the lake. 9am–10pm.

Pho Ngoc Hiep 58 Tang Bat Ho. The speciality here is steamy bowls of tasty pho that fill a gap. 7am–10pm.

Thuy Ta 1 Yersin. See map, p.192. Set on a tiny island on the south side of the lake, this is an ideal spot for breakfast or an evening cocktail while listening to live sax and piano (Tues, Thurs & Sat 7.30–10pm). 6.30am–11pm.

Trong Dong 220 Phan Dinh Phung. See map, p.192. Impressive service and menu at this three-floored restaurant, with tasty sugar-cane prawns and a Vietnamese special salad (shrimps, peanuts, lotus gourd, pork and herbs), in a refined setting. 9.30am–9.30pm.

V Cafe 1/1 Bui Thi Xuan. A bit removed from the budget hotel district, but worth tracking down for its cosy atmosphere and good cooking, including some great homemade pies and cakes, at affordable prices. 7am–10.30pm.

Viet Hung 7 Nguyen Chi Thanh. One of a clutch of cafés offering partial views across the lake. Vietnamese and fast food that caters to Western tastes (fruit shakes, soups, pizzas and pancakes), with internet and wi-fi too. 6.30am–11pm.

Villa 9 Le Lai. Refined and expensive dining in one of the beautiful villas at the Ana Mandara complex west of the city centre. Treat yourself to the slow-cooked New Zealand lamb ($23) or the sweet and sour tiger prawns ($16). 6am–10pm.

Cafés, bars and discos

Café De La Poste 12 Tran Phu. See map, p.192. Modern, French-style café opposite the post office on Tran Phu; part of the *Sofitel* empire, so smart but pricey (buffet breakfast $8, set lunch or dinner $13.50). There's also a smart Vietnamese restaurant, *Y Nho Y*, upstairs. 6am–10pm.

Café Tung 6 Khu Hoa Binh. Leather upholstery, dark varnished wood and 1950s French crooners on the sound system: truly a café lost in time. 6am–10pm.

Golf 3 Nightclub 4 Nguyen Thi Minh Khai. Situated beneath the hotel, this is one of the few places in town where you can party. 6pm–1am.

Larry's Bar *Sofitel Dalat Palace*. Wood-panelled bar in the hotel basement that tries a little too hard for a rustic European look; its casual ambience belies the relatively high prices. 4pm–midnight.

Saigon Nite Bar 11a/1 Hai Ba Trung. Da Lat's long-standing Western-style bar, with friendly, welcoming staff, pool table, darts and a reasonable selection of CDs. The guest books chronicle a stream of drunk but contented customers. 3pm–late.

Skyview Café *Golf 3 Hotel*. Perched on the hotel's top floor, this is a fine venue for relaxing over a beer and watching the city unfurl below. 1–11pm.

The Hangout 71 Truong Cong Dinh. A new place aimed at travellers, with a pool table, cheap beers and motorbikes for rent. 9am–midnight.

Listings

Adventure tours Phat Tire Ventures, 73 Truong Cong Dinh (T&F 063/382 9422, W www .phattireventures.com) is located in the budget district and offers treks of one or several days, beginning at around $20 per day including permit, guide and food, as well as mountain-biking, rock-climbing, abseiling and canyoning trips.

Airlines Vietnam Airlines Booking Office, 40 Ho Tung Mau (daily 7.30–11.30am & 1–4.30pm; T 063/383 3499).

Banks Vietcombank, 6 Nguyen Thi Minh Khai, and Sacombank on Hoa Binh Square change traveller's cheques and cash, and have ATMs.

Hospital Lam Dong Hospital, 4 Pham Ngoc Thach T 063/383 4158.

Internet access Many hotels and guesthouses provide internet access and wi-fi, sometimes free

to guests, while NM Net at 9 Truong Cong Dinh charges 4000đ per hour.

Police 9 Tran Binh Trong T 063/382 2032.

Post office 14 Tran Phu (daily 7.30am–5.30pm), with poste restante, IDD, fax and DHL courier services.

Sports There's an eighteen-hole golf course at Da Lat Palace Golf Club, Phu Dong Thien Vuong, T 063/3821201. The *Sofitel Dalat Palace* and *Novotel Dalat* have tennis courts.

Tourist offices Da Lat Travel Service, 34 Hoa Binh Square T 063/351 0993, W www .welcome-to-vietnam.com; Dalattoserco, 7, 3 Thang 2 T 063/382 2125, W www.dalattoserco .com.vn; Dalat Travel Bureau, 1 Nguyen Thi Minh Khai T 063/351 0104, W www.dalattourist.com.vn; Sinh Café, 4a Bui Thi Xuan T 063/382 2633; TM Brothers, 58 Truong Cong Dinh T 063/382 8383, E tmbrother_dalat@yahoo.com.

Around Da Lat

There is some spectacular scenery in the vicinity of Da Lat, which lends itself to challenging **treks**, **bike rides** and other **adventure activities.** None of the local waterfalls is worth visiting in the dry season (Dec–May), with the possible exception of **Tiger Falls**, though you might enjoy a **boat ride** on one of the local lakes or a **cable-car ride** from Robin Hill to Lake Tuyen Lam, where kayaks are available for rent. Another popular jaunt is by **train** to **Trai Mat**, taking time out to admire the adornments on the **Linh Phuoc Pagoda**. If you want to visit one of the few remaining **traditional minority villages**, that have yet to be assimilated into mainstream Vietnamese culture, contact Phat Tire Ventures (see "Listings" opposite), and be prepared for some tough trekking.

North of Da Lat

Thung Lung Tinh Yeu, or the **Valley of Love** (daily 7am–5pm; small admission charge), located 5km north of town, offers typical kitsch diversions such as pony rides round the lake escorted by a cowboy. The valley's still waters and wooded hills are actually quite enticing, though the music blasting from souvenir stalls and the buzzing of rented motorboats do not enhance the aura of romance. Bao Dai and his courtiers used to hunt here in the 1950s, though a dam project in 1972 flooded part of the valley and created **Lake Da Thien**.

Opposite the Valley of Love is the **XQ Historical Village** (daily 8am–5pm; small admission charge), where several traditional houses display the process and product of silk embroidery picture-making. You can watch the girls painstakingly producing images thread by thread, then walk through an exhibition of landscapes, still lifes, portraits and more surreal compositions, all woven from silk.

If you bother to travel up this way, you'll be aware of the highest peak (2169m) of **Lang Bian Mountain** looming above you to the north. Inevitably, a schmaltzy legend has been concocted to explain the mountain's formation. The story tells of two ill-starred lovers, a Lat man called Lang and a Chill girl named Bian, who were unable to marry because of tribal enmity. Broken-hearted, Bian passed away, and the peaks of Lang Bian are said to represent her breast heaving its dying breath. Bian's death seems not to have been wholly in vain: so racked with guilt was her father, that he called a halt to tribal unrest by unifying all of the local factions into the Koho.

It's possible to drive up to the canopy of pines on the lower peak of Lang Bian Mountain from where you can see the coast on a clear day. Alternatively, you can make the four-hour ascent on foot, beginning just beyond **Lat Village**, 14km north of Da Lat along Xo Viet Nghe Tinh. The village's thatch-roofed bamboo stilthouses are occupied by Chill and Ma, but mostly Lat, groups of Koho peoples eking out a living growing rice, pulses and vegetables. The path is quite easy to follow so a guide is not essential, though one can be easily arranged through any of Da Lat's tour operators. If you go it alone and hire a motorbike for the day, you could combine a visit to Lat Village with a jaunt out to **Ankroet lakes and falls**, signposted 8km along the road to Lat. The falls are more secluded and attractive than most in the area but there is little water during the dry season.

South of Da Lat

As you leave town to the south on Highway 20, a slip road to the right leads to the top of **Robin Hill**, crowned by a huge **cable-car** terminus. Cable-car rides (daily 7.30–11.30am & 1.30–5pm; 75,000đ return, children 50,000đ) are available here, and offer fantastic views over the pine-clad slopes around the city. The trip takes about twelve minutes to cover the 2km down to **Lake Tuyen Lam**, a placid and attractive expanse of water. There are a few **refreshment kiosks** on the shore of the lake, and **boat trips** ($10–20 per boat) round the lake are also possible. Just beside the cable-car terminal at the lake is **Truc Lam Pagoda**, a modern, Chinese-style temple that houses a meditation centre. The lake can also be approached by road; look for a turning to the right off Highway 20 about 5km from the centre of Da Lat as you go down the hill.

Just a couple of hundred metres further south is a turning for **Datanla Falls** (daily 7am–5pm; small entrance fee), signposted on the right of the road as

"Thac Datanla". In Koho, *datanla* means "water under leaves", and that pretty much sums up the place: from the car park, it's a steep fifteen-minute clamber down to the falls, probing some splendidly lush forest. The falls themselves are unthrilling, their muddy waters cascading onto a plateau spanned by a wooden footbridge that provides a hackneyed photo opportunity.

The **Prenn Waterfall** (daily 6.30am–5.30pm; small entrance fee) is about another 6km down Highway 20 on the left. A major attraction for Vietnamese tourists, the fall sees a convoy of buses roll into its car park, harried by a stampede of cigarette and chewing-gum vendors. Unlike Datanla, the attraction here is the waterfall itself, which thunders (or trickles, depending on the season) over a wide overhang and into a broad pool below. By following the path that circles the pool, you can walk right behind the fall. Surrounding Prenn Waterfall are a host of tacky diversions: mock-up rope bridges and tree houses, souvenir shops and the chance to take a photo with an elephant or camel. If you're too lazy to walk down the few steps to the base of the falls, you can hop in a cable car for 5000đ. Back up at the car park, the *Prenn Restaurant* is on hand to cater for hungry visitors, overlooked by a modern, octagonal pagoda.

Chicken Village (ask for Lang Con Ga), 18km south of Da Lat and just west of Highway 20, is just like any other Vietnamese village, apart from the bizarre, five-metre-high cement cockerel that stands proudly on a plinth in the centre, its mouth open in mid-squawk. The local Koho women can be found weaving in many makeshift stalls around. Whether you're a potential buyer of textiles or not, it's interesting to take a look at the rudimentary looms that the women need to strap themselves into to operate. It's also possible to go rambling through the nearby fields and foothills without a permit.

East of Da Lat

Seven kilometres east of Da Lat and accessible by road or by rail (see p.196), the orbital village of **TRAI MAT** is ideally placed for a short excursion. The journey there takes you past a sweep of some of the region's most splendid countryside. Terraced fields crammed full of crops and immaculately tended market gardens escort you for most of the way, and the elevated road provides an excellent vantage point.

The highlight of Trai Mat is **Linh Phuoc Pagoda**, an incredibly ornate building which showcases the art of tessellation, whereby small pieces of broken china or glass are painstakingly arranged in cement. The first thing to catch the eye is the huge dragon in the courtyard to the right of the main building, constructed from over 12,000 carefully broken beer bottles. Artwork inside the pagoda is more intricate, with mosaic dragons entwined around the main hall's pillars, while stairs lead up on the left to colourfully inlaid galleries, shrines and good views. The main hall is very atmospheric, with the deep sound of bells rung by devotees resonating around.

About 4km beyond Trai Mat, a left turn points the way to **Tiger Falls** (daily 7.30am–5pm; small entrance fee), though you still need to descend a few more kilometres on a precarious switchback road to reach them. Above the falls are a couple of restaurants, as well as a statue of a primitive hunter and another of a huge hollow tiger, whose mouth you can climb into for a photo. A steep concrete stairway leads down to the base of the falls, which tumble from a great height and offer good photo opportunities. The falls are a very popular destination for Vietnamese, so you're unlikely to be able to enjoy the place alone. Pools and boulders around the base of the falls make ideal spots for a picnic.

Through the highlands

North of Da Lat, the yawning plateaux of the **central highlands** are worth visiting for their scenery and minority peoples. After heading south from Da Lat on Highway 20 for about 20km turn right onto **Highway 27**, which snakes its way northwards over the hills. First stop is usually **Lak Lake**, an attractive body of water surrounded by minority villages, about 60km south of **Buon Ma Thuot**, which can also be approached directly from Ho Chi Minh City on Highway 14, bypassing Da Lat. The town itself is an unlovely place, but it is the gateway to E De longhouses, elephant-back rides and treks into **Yok Don National Park**.

From Buon Ma Thuot, Highway 14 probes further north to **Plei Ku**, where it's possible (with a guide) to visit Jarai villages. From Plei Ku it's little over an hour's journey straight north on Highway 14 to the likeable town of **Kon Tum**, where you don't need a permit to visit villages of minority groups like the Bahnar, with their towering tribal **rong**, or communal halls. From Kon Tum you can follow Highway 24 eastwards over a high pass to the coast at Quang Ngai, or get into high-adventure gear and continue north through the highlands along Highway 14, the **Ho Chi Minh Highway**. A further option is to head into Southern Laos via the new border crossing at **Bo Y**.

Lak Lake

Some 150km north of Da Lat, Highway 27 passes serene **LAK LAKE**, a charming spot that has become very popular with tourists, aided by the upgrading of the highway between Da Lat and Buon Ma Thuot. Emperor Bao Dai grabbed some of the best sites in southern Vietnam for his many palaces, so it comes as no surprise to learn that he had one here, in a prime spot on a small hill overlooking the lake. The palace is long gone, but the site is now home to a small hotel, the *Bao Dai Residence* (☎0500/385 6767; ❸–❹), with a few well-equipped rooms enjoying fabulous views over the lake. With intriguing snaps of Vietnam's last emperor adorning the walls and a decent restaurant, it's far and away the best place to stay hereabouts. Alternatively, snuggled into a protected bay east of the hill, the *Lak Resort* (☎0500/358 6184; ❸) consists of smart, brick bungalows with air-conditioning, TV and fridge in the rooms, as well as two longhouses ($5) beneath a grove of tall, shady trees. There's also a floating **restaurant** where the food is reasonable and Mnong staff wear traditional dress.

If you're intent on getting the whole minority village experience, complete with grunting pigs and squawking chickens waking you in the morning, head on round to **Jun Village**, a thriving Mnong community on the west side of the hill, whose longhouses crowd together near the shore. Dak Lak Tourist (see p.204) has a branch office here (☎0500/358 6268) and a longhouse where it's possible to overnight ($5, $7 including American breakfast); mosquito nets and mattresses are provided, and there are outside toilet facilities. They can also organize a show with gong-playing, dancing and rice-wine tasting ($60 per group); elephant rides around the lake ($30 for two for an hour); a dug-out canoe trip on the lake with one of the locals ($10 per hour for two); and guided treks into the surrounding forested hills.

Although Lak Lake is mostly geared towards organized tour groups, it's possible to arrive here independently, either by xe om or by the local bus from Buon Ma Thuot. For bookings and enquiries, contact Dak Lak Tourist Office (℡0500/385 2108).

Buon Ma Thuot and around

The town of **BUON MA THUOT** itself has little to offer, its central sprawl of modern buildings being splayed across a grid of characterless streets. The main incentive to visit is the nearby minority villages and waterfalls, with **longhouses** and traditional **minority communities** – of which most around these parts comprise E De people – at **Ako Dhong**, on the northern outskirts of town, and in the surrounding countryside at **Ban Don** near **Yok Don National Park**. Although Dak Lak Province is fairly relaxed about visits to these villages, some, particularly those near the Cambodian border, are still theoretically off limits, while others are not permitted to take foreign overnight guests. Check with the Dak Lak or Dam San Tourist Office (see below), before heading out.

Sited around 200km north of Da Lat and the same distance south of Plei Ku, Buon Ma Thuot is both administrative centre to Dak Lak Province, and the western highlands' unofficial capital. During French colonial times, the town developed on the back of the coffee, tea, rubber and hardwood crops that grew in its fertile red soil, and was the focal point for the **plantations** that smothered the surrounding countryside: plantation-owners and other *colons* would amuse themselves by picking off the elephants, leopards and tigers once prevalent in the area. In later years Americans superseded the French, but they were long gone by the time the North Vietnamese Army (NVA) swept through in March 1975, making Buon Ma Thuot the first "domino" to fall in the Ho Chi Minh Campaign. More recently, natural resources and coffee in particular have made the town a comparatively affluent community, as evidenced by the number of building projects and flash cars that buzz around its streets.

Arrival and information

Buon Ma Thuot's **bus station** (℡0500/387 6833) is 3km above town on Nguyen Tat Thanh; several air-conditioned express buses arrive daily from Nha Trang ($6–7) and from Ho Chi Minh City ($10–12). A private bus company, Rang Dong (℡0500/395 6956) offers hotel pick-up for rides to Ho Chi Minh City for 150,000đ. The **airport** is a few kilometres back off the road towards Da Lat, while Vietnam Airlines (℡0500/395 4442) is at 67 Nguyen Tat Thanh; a taxi into town costs around $7.

Dak Lak Tourist (℡0500/385 2108, ⓦwww.daklaktourist.com.vn), temporarily based at 51 Ly Thuong Kiet, is very helpful and can arrange car rental, guides, visa extensions and **tours**. Dam San Tourist (℡0500/385 0123, ⓔdamsantour@dng.vnn.vn), a small, private tour operator based at the *Dam San Hotel* (see p.206) is also good for local exploration, and rents out motorbikes at around $7 a day. Vietcombank, 6 Tran Hung Dao, changes traveller's cheques and foreign currency and has an **ATM** – there are several more around the town centre. The **post office** (daily 7am–8.30pm) is on Le Duan just south of Victory Monument, and also has **internet** access, or try the cheap internet shop at 36 Ly Thuong Kiet.

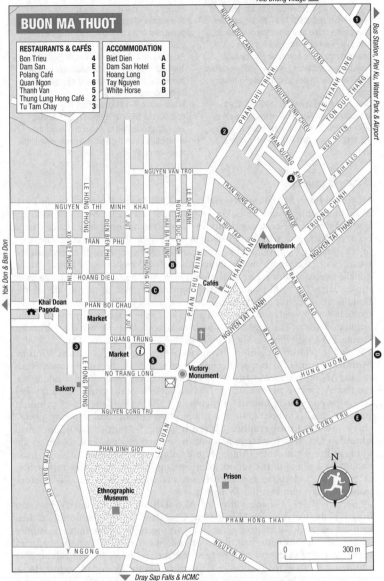

BUON MA THUOT

RESTAURANTS & CAFÉS		ACCOMMODATION	
Bon Trieu	4	Biet Dien	A
Dam San	E	Dam San Hotel	E
Polang Café	1	Hoang Long	D
Quan Ngon	6	Tay Nguyen	C
Thanh Van	5	White Horse	B
Thung Lung Hong Café	2		
Tu Tam Chay	3		

Ako Dhong Village

Bus Station, Plei Ku, Water Park & Airport

Yok Don & Ban Don

Vietcombank

Cafés

Khai Doan Pagoda

Market

Market

Bakery

Victory Monument

Ethnographic Museum

Prison

N

0   300 m

Dray Sap Falls & HCMC

Accommodation

There are plenty of **places to stay** in Buon Ma Thuot, catering for most budgets, though few of them have much character. Most of the cheaper places are clustered along Ly Thuong Kiet, while mid-range hotels are scattered around town.

Dam San Hotel 212–214 Nguyen Cong Tru ☎0500/385 1234, ✉damsanhotel @dng.vnn.vn. The best place to stay in town, though it is about a kilometre from the centre. Its smart rooms are furnished with tasteful local textiles and most have lovely views across a lush hillside. There's also a pool and tennis courts. **④**

Biet Dien 1 Ngo Quyen ☎0500/395 4299 ✉bietdienhotel@vnn.vn. A newish, five-storey block just northeast of the town centre with big, bright rooms that have desks and free wi-fi. **②–④**

Hoang Long 168 Hung Vuong ☎0500/384 1841 ⊛www.hoanglonghotel.vn. A nondescript building to the east of the centre, with some of the best-value rooms in town. **②**

Tay Nguyen 110 Ly Thuong Kiet ☎0500/385 1009, ℻0500/385 2250. Located near the town centre, this place has a range of ageing but functional rooms. **②–③**

White Horse 7–13 Nguyen Duc Canh ☎0500/381 5656, ℻0500/381 5588. Tucked away in a backstreet to the north of town, this smart place offers the best mid-range value in the town centre. **③–④**

The Town

Of central Buon Ma Thuot's few sights, the **Khai Doan Pagoda**, built in 1951, is an interesting fusion of E De longhouse and Hué Imperial architecture. Located west of the centre on Phan Boi Chau, it stands on a slope beside a large bo tree, underneath which sits a Buddha image in meditation posture. The front of the building, approached by steps, is made of huge slabs of glossy, painted wood, with the approximate dimensions of a longhouse, but the ornate, double-layered roof is classic Hué architecture. Just below the roof at the front runs a frieze of gold-painted panels depicting scenes from the life of the Buddha. A more recent extension of brick and cement at the back houses the altar with several more Buddha images, while the bright pillars have dragons leaping off them. The pagoda was built to honour Emperor Khai Dinh's wife, Hoang Thi Cuc, who was also mother of the last emperor, Bao Dai.

With a jeep protruding from its central column, the town's dramatic **Victory Monument** on Le Duan is the hub from which all the town's main roads radiate. About half a kilometre south of here, tucked away down a side street, the town's former **prison** (daily 7–11am & 1.30–5pm; small admission fee) seems frozen in time, and the cells contain a few realistic models of prisoners and wardens. To find out more about the cultures of the local minority groups, check out the **Ethnographic Museum** (daily 7–11am & 1.30–5pm; small admission fee), which is set in a crumbling edifice in a peaceful garden to the south of the town centre. Among the exhibits are a waistcoat made of bark, traditional clothing of the various ethnic groups of the region, funerary statues of peacocks and tusks, and instruments for taming elephants, like vicious mahouts' spikes and two thorny harnesses.

The tidy E De weaving village of **Ako Dhong**, on the town's northern fringes, is also worth a visit. Follow Phan Chu Trinh towards the northeast, then turn left on Tran Nhat Duat, which leads you into the community. The sturdy longhouses on stilts with their tiled roofs spaced out evenly down the road, and the clean-swept yards and trim hedges give the feel of an affluent suburb. The tantalizing aroma of roasting coffee beans often fills the air, and the gentle clack-clack emanating from the buildings signals the weavers at work. The locals are welcoming and are likely to invite you in to watch the process and perhaps to buy a sample of their work, which is generally good quality.

If you're in need of coolling down, head for **Dak Lak Water Park** (☎0500/395 0381; 30,000đ), 4km northeast of town on Nguyen Chi Thanh. Finally, if you're in town in March, don't miss the **Elephant Race Festival**, which takes place on the banks of the Serepok River near Ban Don: ask at Dak Lak Tourist for dates and details.

Eating and drinking

All the big hotels have **restaurants**, of which the *Dam San* is probably the best. The *Thanh Van* at 20 Ly Thuong Kiet is famed locally for its fine *nem* (spring rolls). Hai Ba Trung's *Bon Trieu* cooks up tasty beef dishes that are perennially popular as well as a very passable *cari de* (goat curry), for around 25,000đ a dish. Although the food on display at *Tu Tam Chay*, 103 Quang Trang, looks meaty and fishy, all the dishes here are one hundred percent vegetarian; point, sit and eat. For a bit of ambience and some adventurous eating, head to the *Quan Ngon* at 72–74 Ba Trieu, where you'll be greeted by a veritable zoo of animals floating in huge jars of exotic wine. Java mouse deer, weasel and conger eel all feature in various preparations, and if you're having trouble deciding, try the grilled porcupine and pigeon rice soup, washed down with a BGI beer. Back in the centre of town, a big **bakery** called Banh Mi Hanoi at 123–127 Le Hong Phong can provide all your picnic needs.

Cafés

It would be a crime to visit the heart of Vietnam's coffee industry without tasting the product itself, and there are plenty of opportunities in Buon Ma Thuot's **cafés**. They're scattered all over town, so you need never suffer from caffeine withdrawal, but there's a particular concentration along the south end of Le Thanh Tong, known to locals as "Coffee Street". These cafés are packed in the evenings and surrounded by a sea of motorbikes, whose owners sip their drinks in the dim-lit interiors. For the most atmospheric places, however, head north of town, where the 🍴 *Thung Lung Hong Café*, Hem 153 Phan Chu Trinh, is snuggled at the base of a steep valley at the end of a sidestreet off Phan Chu Trinh. It's hugely popular among locals and, given the dearth of nightlife in Buon Ma Thuot, a godsend for visitors too. Over at G26 Tran Khanh Du, the *Polang Café* has a striking facade, which resembles a longhouse entrance, and inside the decor utilizes minority patterns and motifs, while the bases of some tables and chairs are made of the gnarled stumps of coffee bushes – an inspired use of the plant. The menu includes coffee, tea and cocktails at very reasonable prices; there's often live music here at the weekend.

Around Buon Ma Thuot

Once you've exhausted Buon Ma Thuot's urban attractions, which doesn't take long, it's time to get out and explore the highlands. There are some impressive **waterfalls** southwest of town, while the northwest route out of town leads to **Yok Don National Park** and the touristy village of **Ban Don**.

The waterfalls

About 30km southwest of Buon Ma Thuot are several waterfalls (small admission and parking fee at each one) that are worth visiting, especially in the wet season, though unless you're a real waterfall fan, there's no real point in seeing them all. **Dray Sap** and **Dray Nur**, situated side by side, are the most impressive and most popular.

To get to the falls, follow Highway 14 for 20km southwest of town, then turn left at the village of **Ea Ting**. Just a kilometre down this road, a left turn leads to **Trinh Nu Falls**, a narrow chute of water approached by a steep path. At the top of the falls is a **restaurant** with small, inviting pavilions overlooking the river – a good spot to rest up for refreshment or lunch.

The crescent-shaped **Dray Sap** and neighbouring **Dray Nur Falls** are about 10km down the road from Ea Ting. After a short descent down steps from the car park, a wooden **suspension bridge** to the left leads to Dray Nur Falls, which, though not as wide as Dray Sap, carry more water in the dry season. On the other hand, at the end of the wet season, in September, water levels are usually too high for the short walk to the falls to be accessible. Almost 15m high and over 100m wide, Dray Sap doesn't mean "waterfall of smoke" for nothing: a fug of invigorating spray sags the air around. The area round the falls can get very crowded at weekends and on public holidays, but midweek a trip here makes a pleasant outing for a half or full day. Just after passing the ticket office at the approach to Dray Sap Falls, a road branching to the right leads another 7km to **Gia Long Falls**, yet another waterfall in the region, where there's also the chance of **camping**.

Yok Don National Park

Exit west out of Buon Ma Thuot along Phan Boi Chau, and 45km later you'll arrive at the entrance to Vietnam's largest wildlife preserve, the **Yok Don National Park**, whose 115,000 hectares lie nestled into the hinge of the Cambodian border and the **Serepok River**. The surfaced road to the park makes a pleasant journey, and if you start off early in the morning you might see the minority peoples leaving their split-bamboo thatch houses lined along the route for work in the fields, carrying their tools in raffia backpacks.

Over sixty species of animals, including tigers, leopards and bears, and more than 450 types of birds, from peacocks to hornbills, populate Yok Don Park. Most of them, however, reside deep in the park's interior, which stretches to the Cambodian border. Of all its exotic animals, **elephants** are what the park is best known for. Elephant-hunters found rich pickings in the region's lush forest for centuries, and today an elephant-back ride is the park's main attraction, though the prices are a bit steep. For $30 for an hour (maybe cheaper if you haggle), two can lumber around the park's eastern edge by elephant.

In the dry season, the park's wildlife makes for **Yok Don Mountain** in search of food and water, and your chances of seeing something interesting improve. Longer safaris can be arranged by the park HQ. If you're only here for the day, the park can arrange elephant trekking tours (around $60) or one-day walking tours (around $20) into the forest. There's a handful of twin-bedded cabin-style rooms with attached bathrooms ($10), should you wish to overnight; for **bookings**, prices and enquiries, contact the park HQ (☎0500/378 3049). From Buon Ma Thuot, hourly public buses go to the park via Phan Boi Chau (about $1), or a xe om costs around $12–15.

Ban Don

The three sub-hamlets that comprise **BAN DON** lie a few kilometres beyond Yok Don's park HQ on the bank of the crocodile-infested Serepok. Khmer, Thai, Lao, Jarai and Mnong live in the vicinity, though it's the **E De** who are in the majority. They adhere to a matriarchal social system, whereby a groom takes his bride's name, lives with her family and, should his wife die subsequently, marries one of her sisters so that her family retains a male workforce. Houses around the village, a few of which are longhouses, are built on stilts, and some are decorated with ornate woodwork.

Village life in Ban Don has become ridiculously commercial with the Ban Don Tourist Centre (☎0500/378 3019) organizing its residents into a tourist-welcoming taskforce. Though constantly visited by busloads of Vietnamese, the rampant consumerism and fees charged for low-grade attractions will make most Westerners want to turn round and get out straight away. If you linger, you can pay a dollar to walk on a rickety bamboo suspension bridge through a tangle of banyan roots, or to look around the village's oldest house, which seems to be under constant repair. The village's other attractions include expensive elephant rides and a glut of souvenir stalls.

Ban Don village has a long and distinguished tradition of **elephant-taming**; indeed, elephants were still caught and trained until recently, though dwindling numbers of wild elephants make it a vanishing art. (If you're lucky you may get a chance to see the annual elephant festival in March). Beyond its final sub-hamlet stands an elephant trainers' graveyard, which includes the tomb of the legendary Y Thu Knu (1850–1924), the greatest elephant-catcher of them all. His lifetime tally of 244 included an auspicious white elephant which he presented to the King of Siam, from whom he received the honorary title **khusunop**, meaning something like "great elephant catcher". Y Thu Knu's is the square tomb, and the pointed one in front is his nephew's, also a prodigious elephant-hunter. Other tombs nearby are adorned with paintings of elephants and wooden carvings of peacocks standing on tusks – the latter being considered expensive items to take into the next life.

Most people visit Ban Don on an organized tour; to go it alone, take the bus to Yok Don National Park (see above), then a xe om (about 30,000đ) for the last few kilometres.

Plei Ku and around

North of Buon Ma Thuot, Highway 14 rocks and rolls over the hills and plains of the **Dak Lak Plateau**, passing rubber plantations, hardwood forests and the corrugated leaves of coffee plants on its way to **PLEI KU**. The band of peaks to the west of the highway, and the rugged terrain buttressing them, constituted one of the American War's major combat theatres. It was an NVA (North Vietnamese Army) attack on Plei Ku, in February 1965, that elicited the "Rolling Thunder" campaign (see p.472); the war's first conventional battle of any size was fought in the **Ia Drang Valley**, southwest of Plei Ku, eight months later. Hundreds of Americans died at Ia Drang, but many times more Communists perished, spurring America to claim victory by dint of a higher body count. A decade later, in March 1975, Plei Ku was abandoned when NVA troops overran Buon Ma Thuot. As the South's commanding officers flew by helicopter to safety, 200,000 Southern soldiers and civilians were left to make their own way down to the coast, hounded at every step by NVA shells.

So little of the town was left standing by the last days of the war that a near-total reconstruction was required. The 1980s reincarnation that you'll see, stacked up the side of a gentle slope, lacks any charm. Indeed, you'd be hard-pushed to find any real reason for spending time here, as you need a permit and guide to visit the few minority villages that are open to foreigners, and there's little to see in any case. If you're keen to explore minority villages without a government chaperone, it makes sense to push on 50km north, just an hour's journey, to Kon Tum, where there are fewer restrictions.

Barring an early morning stroll along central, east–west **Tran Phu**, where hawkers sell aubergines, shallots, parsnips and garlic, and into the adjacent town market, there's little to do in Plei Ku. Should you get stalled by the weather, you could check out the two museums in town, though they are not always open. The **Ho Chi Minh Museum** (Mon–Fri 7.30–11am & 1–5pm; free), to the north of the town centre at 1 Phan Dinh Phuong, features swords, crossbows, bamboo xylophones, a weaving loom and a pair of Uncle Ho's sandals, but no

English signs. The **Gia Lai Museum** (Mon–Fri 7.30–11am & 1–5pm; small admission fee), at 28 Quang Trung, is a little better, with a gong and rice-wine jar collection in one gallery and, in another, replicas of a Bahnar grave and longhouse are displayed.

This far north in the highlands, the **Jarai** and, to a lesser extent, the **Bahnar** outnumber the E De, though many of them have been assimilated into mainstream Vietnamese culture. Also, Plei Ku's tourist board, Gia Lai Tourist, is notoriously defensive of the region's few remaining traditional settlements and doesn't approve of individuals making forays into the wilds, insisting that you should always be with a licensed guide when visiting villages. If you try to by-pass this regulation and just turn up in villages, you'll get little cooperation from the locals, who receive a cut from the fees for "official" visitors.

Practicalities

Plei Ku's **airport** (☏059/382 5097) lies 7km northeast of the city, from where taxis (about 60,000đ) and xe om (about 40,000đ) make the journey to the centre; Vietnam Airlines, at 55 Quang Trung (Mon–Sat; ☏059/382 4680), can arrange onward flight reservations. From Plei Ku's long-distance **bus station**, below the three-way crossroads 600m southeast of the centre, it's a short xe om ride into the city along Hung Vuong, Plei Ku's southern limit, from which its main roads shoot north.

The **Vietcombank** at 62 Phan Boi Chau can change traveller's cheques and has an ATM. Gia Lai Tourist (☏059/387 4571, ⓦwww.gialaitourist.com) is inside the *Hung Vuong Hotel* at 215 Hung Vuong, and can provide **information** as well as arrange expensive, tailor-made trekking and battlefield tours and overnight stays in minority villages. **Internet access** is available at many places in town, including the shop at 80 Nguyen Van Troi.

Accommodation

Accommodation in Plei Ku is decidedly uninspiring. The *HAGL Hotel*, about half a kilometre east of the town centre at 1 Phu Dong (☏059/371 8459, ⓦwww .hagl.com.vn; ❹), is the most comfortable: its rooms are spacious and well-equipped with desks and bathtubs, and those on the upper floors have good views across the countryside. The best budget option is the *Duc Long* (☏059/387 6303, ☏059/387 6305; ❷) at 95–97 Hai Ba Trung, a couple of blocks west of the market, where the big, carpeted rooms with pine furnishings are good value.

Eating

There are no outstanding places to **eat** in Plei Ku, though the *Acacia Restaurant* at the *HAGL Hotel* serves up a good range of Vietnamese and a few Western dishes. The basic *My Tam* at 3 Quang Trung produces tasty staple rice dishes, though you'll need your phrasebook, while the tiny *Nem Ninh Hoa* at 66 Nguyen Van Troi churns out delicious *nem*. *Thien Thanh* is a pleasant garden restaurant about a kilometre north of the town centre, at the end of a steep lane off Le Loi: look for the sign on the right. This attractive place has a landscaped garden with small ponds and sweeping views over rice fields, as well as a good range of Vietnamese food. For a decent coffee, the *Café Tennis* at 61 Quang Trang is a reasonable spot.

The Jarai and Bahnar villages

North of Plei Ku, Highway 14 probes the coffee, tea and rice crops that hem the road to Kon Tum. A right turning at a roundabout 7km north of town will take you after just 500m to **Bien Ho**, a volcanic lake which is also the town's reservoir; it's pretty enough viewed from the observation point, but doesn't warrant much more than a five-minute stop. About 16km north of Plei Ku, a left turn leads through some pretty countryside and some **Jarai** villages and continues for 23km to the hydroelectric dam at **Ialy**.

To visit the Jarai village of **PLEI PHUN**, you'll need to be with an official guide from Gia Lai Tourist, who will show you around the headman's house, the local graveyard and village spring. The only real interest is in the graveyard, where roughly hewn **hardwood statues** depicting figures in a range of moods are placed around each family grave. In the past the Jarai would stick bamboo poles through the earth and into a fresh grave, through which to "feed" the dead, though now they tend to leave fruit and bowls of rice on top of the grave. If you're interested in the workings of the hydroelectric dam, it's possible to take a tour, lasting an hour and a half, for a small fee at the **Ialy Hydro Electric Plant**, which marks the end of the road. The reservoir created by the dam covers 650 hectares and produces 720 megawatts of electricity, making this the second-largest plant in the country (after Hoa Binh). It took nine years to build and was completed in 2001.

There's also a group of four secluded but easily accessible **Bahnar** settlements, lying 38km east of Plei Ku, en route to Quy Nhon. The villages of **DEK TU**, **DE COP**, **DE DOA** and **DEK ROL** all rub shoulders with one another across a small area of forests and streams. Small split-bamboo and straw houses on stilts proliferate through these orderly communities, and each one boasts an impressive, steeply thatched *rong*, or communal house, where ceremonies are performed, local disputes are resolved and decisions taken.

At Dek Tu, there's a good example of a Bahnar cemetery where the practice of feeding the dead is prevalent. Curiously, unlike the Jarai, each of the deceased has his own individual grave complete with a small sloping roof. Ladders made out of bamboo poles leaning against the graves will aid the journey to a new life. As at Plei Phun, you need to be accompanied by a guide, and it is also possible to arrange a **home-stay** in the largest village of the four, De Cop. Gia Lai Tourist have commandeered a house on stilts here, from where you can visit each village on a one-day hike. A two-day programme visiting both Plei Phun and these villages works out about $30–35 a head for a group of five people. Further afield, to the southeast of Plei Ku, there are even more remote settlements, such as **AN KHE** and **AYUNPA**, which can be incorporated into a longer trek.

Phu Phong and around

As recently as five decades ago, tigers stalked the upper reaches of **Highway 19** from Plei Ku down to Quy Nhon, known as the **Giang Pass**. Norman Lewis, travelling here in the 1950s, found a French military outpost commanded by "a slap-happy sergeant from Perpignan, a cabaret-Provençal, who roared with laughter at the thought of his isolation, and poured us out half-tumblers of Chartreuse". The fort may have gone, but scores of **Bahnar settlements** (see p.215) speckle the route, as it snakes its way through a majestic blister of hills and down to the coast.

For the most spectacular panoramas, you'll need to wait until you're 65km out of Plei Ku, when the countryside slowly begins to level out. Shortly after scruffy An Khe, a kink in the highway leads you to the **An Khe Pass**, from where you can see the coastal plain yawning magnificently below you, embroidered by the Ha Giao River. By the time you've passed through **Vinh Son**, and traversed the bridge that crosses to more sizeable **PHU PHONG**, 50km from Quy Nhon, you're down in the paddy of the coastal plain.

Phu Phong lies under the jurisdiction of **Tay Son District** whose most famous sons, the Tay Son brothers, engineered a popular uprising that succeeded in unifying Vietnam for the first time in the 1770s. Sickened by the land-grabbing and hunger afflicting their countrymen, Nguyen Nhac, Nguyen Lu and Nguyen Hué in 1771 mustered a peasant army, in order more volubly to express their anger. The army exceeded all expectations: by 1788 it had defeated the Trinh dynasty to the north and the Nguyen dynasty to the south, and Nguyen Hué had proclaimed himself Emperor Quang Trung of Vietnam – a situation he buttressed further a year later when he booted the Chinese out of northern Vietnam at the battle of Dong Da. Quang Trung's death in 1792 deprived the Tay Son dynasty of his charismatic leadership, and ten years later French-backed Nguyen Anh of the Nguyen dynasty snatched power once more. Despite its brevity, the Tay Son period is recalled as a prosperous one, when economic reforms were established and education encouraged.

The brothers' escapades are celebrated at the **Quang Trung Museum** (Mon–Fri 8–11.30am & 1–4.30pm; small admission fee), a three-kilometre ride by xe om from Phu Phong. Its exhibits include costumes, weapons, gongs and drums, and there are often demonstrations of **martial arts**, which are very popular in this region.

Beyond Phu Phong, countless brick kilns pepper the landscape, their rippling roofs seeming to melt in the heat. Quy Nhon itself is covered in Chapter Four, p.253.

Kon Tum and the minority villages

Some 49km north of Plei Ku, Highway 14 crosses the Dakbla River and runs into **KON TUM**, a sleepy, friendly town which serves as a springboard for onward travel to **Laos** as well as jaunts to outlying villages of the **Bahnar** and other minority groups such as the **Sedang**, **Gieh Trieng** and **Rongao**. There are about 650 minority villages in the province, of which only a few have been visited by foreigners, so the scope for adventure here is broad indeed. Unlike other provinces in the central highlands, local authorities in Kon Tum do not insist that visitors obtain permits and guides to visit most minority villages, so you are more or less free to explore as you like. However, you're strongly advised to discuss your travel plans with the local tourist office to check on their feasibility, especially if you plan to head west towards the Cambodian border, which is still considered a sensitive area.

Known here as Phan Dinh Phung, Highway 14 forms the western edge of Kon Tum; running east above the river is Nguyen Hué, and between these two axes lies the town centre. Just south of Nguyen Hué is an attractive **riverside promenade**, which makes for a pleasant stroll in the morning or evening. At the junction of Nguyen Hué and Tran Phu stands the grand bulk of **Tan Huong Church**, with colourful bas reliefs in pastel shades on its facade. Further east is the **Wooden Church**, built by the French in 1913, and frequently restored since then. A statue of Christ stands over the front entrance; below him, a stained-glass window neatly fuses the classic Christian symbol of the dove with images of local resonance – a Bahnar village and an elephant. In the grounds is a statue of the nineteenth-century French bishop who established the diocese of Kon Tum.

Behind the church, a Bahnar orphanage looks after children of all ages in spartan but well-cared-for surroundings. Visitors are welcome to look around. There is another branch of the orphanage tucked away down by the river off Ly Thai To, which receives fewer visitors, so you're likely to get a warm welcome. At 56 Tran Hung Dao is a **Catholic seminary** and **minorities museum** (Mon–Fri 8–11am & 2–4pm; free) that is worth a look for its impressive architecture and small museum, which contains examples of minority wood carvings, work implements and clothes, as well as a history of Christianity in the hills of Vietnam. It doesn't stick rigidly to its opening hours, so if you can't find anyone around, contact staff at Kon Tum Tourist (see below) to arrange a visit.

One good thing about Kon Tum is that you don't have to go far to get a feel of a minority village, as there are a couple of Bahnar villages on the eastern fringe of town. Following Nguyen Hué to its eastern end brings you to **Kon Tum Konam**, while following Tran Hung Dao to the east takes you directly to **Kon Tum Kopong**, where there is a wonderful example of a *rong*, or communal house, which is such a striking feature of Bahnar villages. Built on sturdy stilts with a platform and entrance at either end (or in the middle, as is the case here); the interior is generally made of split bamboo and protected by a towering thatched roof, usually about 15m high. The *rong* is used as a venue for festivals and village meetings, and as a village court at which anyone found guilty of a tribal offence has to ritually kill a pig and a chicken, and must apologize in front of the village. Villagers at Kon Tum Kopong are big on basket-weaving, and you might chance upon locals cutting bamboo into thin strips and crafting them into sturdy baskets, which they sell very cheaply in the local market.

Practicalities

Kon Tum's **bus station** is to the northwest of town on Phan Dinh Phung. From here, it's best to take a xe om to the town centre, which is about 3km

▲ The Bahnar minority people live in villages around Kon Tum

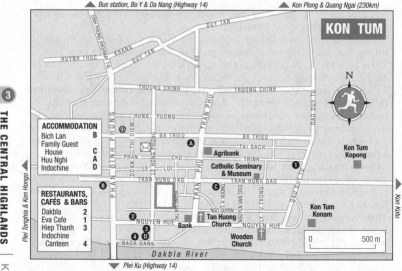

away. **Currency exchange** is possible at the BIDV Bank at 1 Tran Phu, and there's an ATM at the Agribank at 88 Tran Phu. The **post office** is at 205 Le Hong Phong. There are several places offering **internet access**, including an outlet at 202 Ba Trieu.

Kon Tum Tourist (℡060/386 2703, ✉ktourist@dng.vnn.vn) is at 2 Phan Dinh Phung, just north of the bridge over the river, on the ground floor of the *Dakbla Hotel*. They can organize a wide range of **tours**, including trekking, river trips and traditional dance performances, and offer **information** on new areas opening up in the surrounding region. Even if you don't book a tour through them, they're happy to give independent advice. Most hotels rent **bicycles** and **motorbikes**.

Accommodation

The town's fanciest **hotel** is the *Indochine* (℡060/386 3334, ℻060/386 3961; ❹–❺), at 30 Bach Dang, which enjoys a prime riverside location. The carpeted rooms are very cosy and those facing the river have great views. On a quiet street near the town centre, the *Bich Lan*, at 233 Tran Hung Dao (℡060/391 3913, ⟐www.hotelkontum.com; ❷), is a newish place that has good-sized, well-equipped rooms (some with computers) and friendly staff. Probably the best deal in town, however, is the *Huu Nghi*, 69 Ba Trieu (℡060/391 1560, ℻060/391 1556; ❷), whose huge rooms are fitted with beautiful furnishings, though breakfast is not included in the price. A good budget option is the ⚘ *Family Guest House* (℡ & ℻060/386 5748; ❶), which has two places, at 55 and 61 Tran Hung Dao: the rooms are clean and brightly decorated, there's an attractive garden at number 61, and the friendly owners are very helpful.

Eating and drinking

There are several **eating** options along Nguyen Hué: the *Hiep Thanh*, at no. 129, specializes in chicken dishes but also serves up good sautéed beef and tasty soups. The *Dakbla*, at no. 168, is very popular with foreign visitors, offering a range of Vietnamese and Western dishes, as well as selling a selection of ethnic souvenirs. Next to the *Indochine Hotel* on Bach Dang, the huge *Indochine Canteen* can be a bit daunting when it's empty, but serves a wide range of Vietnamese dishes in a prime riverfront location. The place to savour the excellent local coffee is the *Eva Café*, 1 Phan Chu Trinh, run by a local sculptor, whose work is also displayed here; the three-storey café has been built to resemble a stilt-house, and its surrounding garden yields fountains, wooden sculptures of distorted faces and a waterfall trickling down the back wall.

Around Kon Tum

There are dozens of Bahnar villages encircling Kon Tum. As most are free from the official restrictions that hang over Plei Ku, you're at liberty to explore this area at will, although for overnight stays it's best to check first with the local tourist office. West of Le Loi, the village of **PLEI TONGHIA**, just a kilometre away, and **KON HONGO**, a few kilometers further, are inhabited by members of the Rongao, one of the smaller minority groups in the region. Women are often busy weaving in the shade of their simple, wooden huts, ox carts trundle along the dusty road, and children splash about in the Dakbla River.

About 5km to the east of town is the most frequently visited of Bahnar villages, **KON KOTU**. Though now linked to Kon Tum by a surfaced road, it makes a pleasant walk to go there by country paths (contact the local tourist office for details) and it's possible to overnight in the village *rong*. To get there by road, follow Tran Hung Dao east out of town for a couple of kilometres until you reach a suspension bridge over the river at **KON KLOR**. On the right here is a very impressive *rong* with attractive patterning along the peak of the roof. A couple of hundred metres beyond the bridge, turn left and follow the road to Kon Kotu. Most of the dwellings here are made of bamboo and secured with rattan string, although some houses now are made of timber and sport tiled or aluminium roofs, and the schoolhouse is built of brick. However, it's the village's immaculate *rong* that commands the most attention. No nails were used in the construction of the bamboo walls, floor, and the impossibly tall thatch roof of this lofty communal hall. It also doubles as an occasional overnight stop for local trekking tours organized by Kon Tum Tourist.

There are plenty of other villages of interest on the road northeast to **KON PLONG**, the only town of any size between Kon Tum and the coast at Quang Ngai. About 36km from Kon Tum, there's a **Sodra** village on the left, while a kilometre further on the right is a **Jolong** village with a very different type of *rong*, without the towering roof favoured by other groups. Beyond Kon Plong, Highway 24 climbs up to the **Mang Den Pass** at 1200 metres, where there is a lovely stand of pine trees. This is also the starting point for one of the many treks organized by Kon Tum Tourist in the area.

About 17km southwest of Kon Tum is the village of **Ya Chim**, where there are a few Jarai cemeteries that can be visited, though it's best to go with a guide from

---

Moving on to Laos

The **international border crossing** from the central highlands to Laos, open at Bo Y 80km northwest of Kon Tum, provides access to the rarely-visited region of southern Laos. Heading on west it takes you to Isaan, in the forgotten northeast of Thailand. Though in theory you can obtain a fifteen-day Lao visa at the border ($30; two passport photos required), it's best to get your visa in advance at the Lao consulate in either Ho Chi Minh City or Da Nang or their Hanoi embassy (see p.119, p.288 & p.386 respectively), as border officials are notorious for extorting unscheduled payments from travellers in order to prevent administrative delays. There are irregular bus departures from Kon Tum to Attapeu and Pakse in Laos: check at the bus station for times.

Kon Tum Tourist as they are tricky to find. Wooden posts, some of them carved in the form of mourning figures, surround the graves and personal possessions such as a bicycle or TV are placed inside. The graves are carefully tended for a period of three to five years after death and offerings are brought to the site daily. At the end of this period a buffalo is sacrificed to make a feast for the villagers and the grave is abandoned in the belief that the spirit of the deceased has now departed.

North of Kon Tum

From Kon Tum, travellers have the choice of heading for the **Laos** border at Bo Y (see box, p.215), down to the coast at **Quang Ngai** on Highway 24, or continuing north on the picturesque Highway 14, also know as the **Ho Chi Minh Highway**, which is a pleasure to travel on.

Around 42km north of Kon Tum is the district of **DAK TO**, which witnessed some of the most sustained fighting of the American War; to the west of the road to Dak To is Rocket Ridge, a brow of hills that earned its name from the heavy bombing – napalm and conventional – it received during this time. To the south of town is Charlie Hill, which was the scene of one of the fiercest battles of the war, ending in a VC victory over Southern troops. There's a *rong* right in the middle of Dak To, where the inhabitants are mostly Sedang, and with a little exploration you should be able to find more Sedang longhouses in the settlements surrounding Dak To.

Heading north along the route from Dak To, the road passes through **DAK GLEI**, where there's another spectacular *rong*. Directly east is virgin jungle surrounding Mount Ngoc Linh (2598m), the highest peak in the central highlands. Beyond here, the route takes you through wonderfully verdant and unpopulated countryside before Highway 14B branches off to the right at **Nam Giang**, taking you down to the coast at Hoi An or Da Nang.

Travel details

Trains

Da Lat to: Trai Mat (5 daily; 40min).

Buses

Bus stations are gradually becoming more organized, with ticket desks and scheduled departures. However, it is still almost impossible to give the frequency with which buses run because of the large number of private minibuses that ply more popular routes, and depart only when they have enough passengers to make the journey worthwhile. Off the main highway, to be sure of a bus it's advisable to start your journey early – most long-distance departures are between 5am and 9am, and few run after midday. Journey times can also vary; figures below show the normal length of time you can expect to take by public bus.

Buon Ma Thuot to: Da Nang (12hr); Ho Chi Minh City (7hr); Nha Trang (4hr); Plei Ku (4hr).
Da Lat to: Buon Ma Thuot (4hr); Da Nang (16hr); Ho Chi Minh City (6hr); Nha Trang (3hr); Phan Rang (3hr).
Kon Tum to: Da Nang (5hr); Hanoi (20hr); Ho Chi Minh City (12hr); Attapeu, Laos (8hr).
Plei Ku to: Buon Ma Thuot (4hr); Da Nang (10hr); Kon Tum (1hr); Quy Nhon (4hr).

Flights

Buon Ma Thuot to: Da Nang (daily; 1hr 10min); Hanoi (daily; 2hr); Ho Chi Minh City (daily; 1hr).
Da Lat to: Hanoi (daily; 2hr 40min); Ho Chi Minh City (daily; 40min).
Plei Ku to: Da Nang (daily; 50min); Hanoi (daily; 5–7hr, via Danang or Ho Chi Minh City); Ho Chi Minh City (daily; 1hr 10min).

The south-central coast

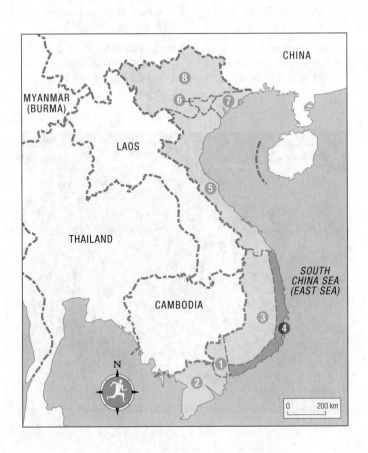

CHAPTER 4   # Highlights

✳ **Con Dao Islands** Discover
the site of Vietnam's most
feared prison, which now
welcomes divers, trekkers and
beach bums. See p.221

✳ **Deserted beaches** Explore
some fantastic off-the-
beaten-track beaches, such
as those at Ho Coc or Ca Na.
See p.229 & p.236

✳ **Mui Ne** Stay in a fancy
resort at Mui Ne and go kitesurfing in the breezy bay.
See p.232

✳ **Cham monuments** Get up
close to the impressive Po
Klong Garai towers, just
outside Phan Rang, and other
other Cham towers in the
region. See p.238

✳ **Underwater activities**
Snorkel or dive in the clear
waters off the islands near
Nha Trang. See p.246

✳ **Mud baths** Wallow in a
mud bath at the Thap Ba
Hot Springs near Nha Trang.
See p.251

▲ Taking a mud bath at the Thap Ba Hot Springs

4

The south–central
coast

A side from Phu Quoc Island (see p.177), the south central Coast is the best region for good **beaches** in Vietnam. **Nha Trang** is still the country's premier beach resort, though up-and-coming **Mui Ne** edges it out for trendiness and surfer cool. Besides these options, there are half a dozen other barely-developed beaches where you might actually get some rest, including **Ho Coc**, **Ninh Chu**, **Ca Na** and **Doc Let**.

Sea-fishing provides a living for a considerable percentage of the region's population. Fleets of fishing boats jostle for space in the cramped ports and estuaries of the coastal towns, awaiting the turn of the tide; and fish and seafood drying along the road are a common sight. The fertile soil blesses the coastal plains with coconut palms, rice paddies, cashew orchards, sugar cane fields, vineyards and shrimp farms. One of the most commonly seen fruits here, especially around Phan Thiet, is the dragon fruit, which grows on plants with distinctive, octopus-like tentacles. Another striking sight is the blinding white rectangles of the salt flats that occasionally border the road.

Historically, this region of Vietnam was the domain of the Indianized trading empire of **Champa**. Courted in its prime by seafaring merchants from around the globe, Champa was steadily marginalized from the tenth century onwards by the march south of the Vietnamese. These days a few enclaves around Phan Thiet and Phan Rang are all that remain of the Cham people, but the remnants of the towers that punctuate the countryside – many of which have recently been restored – recall Champa's former magnificence.

On leaving Ho Chi Minh City, there's an early choice to be made: Highway 1 runs inland until it reaches Phan Thiet (near Mui Ne); while, from Bien Hoa, Highway 51drops down to the coast at **Vung Tau**, once a French seaside resort, and now a smart, oil-rich coastal town with average beaches, though much better beaches can be found further up the coast at places like **Ho Coc.** Few beaches in this region have been developed as yet, so with your own transport and an adventurous spirit, you'll find somewhere to pace out a solitary set of footprints in the pristine sand. While in exploring mode, consider a trip to the former French prison islands of **Con Dao**, which can be reached by plane from Ho Chi Minh City or an irregular boat service from Vung Tau.

You'll never be alone at **Mui Ne**, which is perhaps a sign of things to come for Vietnamese tourism – slick resorts rubbing shoulders along a fine sweep of

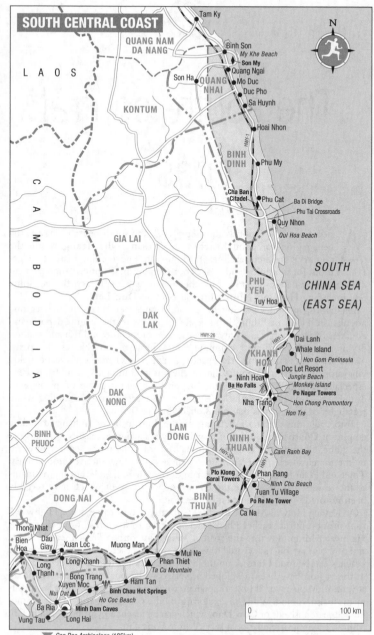

SOUTH CENTRAL COAST

N

Tam Ky

QUANG NAM
DA NANG

Binh Son
My Khe Beach
Son My
Quang Ngai
Son Ha
QUANG
NHAI
Mo Duc
Duc Pho
Sa Huynh

LAOS

KONTUM

Hoai Nhon

BINH
DINH

Phu My

**Cha Ban
Citadel**
Phu Cat
Ba Di Bridge
Phu Tai Crossroads
Quy Nhon

GIA LAI

Qui Hoa Beach

C
A
M
B
O
D
I
A

SOUTH

CHINA SEA
(EAST SEA)

PHU
YEN
Tuy Hoa

DAK
LAK

HWY-26

HWY-1
Dai Lanh
Whale Island
Hon Gom Peninsula
KHANH
HOA
Doc Let Resort
Jungle Beach
Ninh Hoa
Ba Ho Falls
Monkey Island
Po Nagar Towers
Nha Trang
Hon Chong Promontory
Hon Tre

DAK
NONG

LAM
DONG

BINH
PHUOC

NINH
THUAN

Cam Ranh Bay

HWY-20
HWY-1
**Plo Klong
Garai Towers**
Phan Rang
Ninh Chu Beach
Tuan Tu Village
Po Re Me Tower
Ca Na

DONG NAI

BINH
THUAN

Thong Nhat
Bien
Hoa
Dau
Giay
Xuan Loc
Muong Man
Mui Ne
Long
Thanh
Long Khanh
Phan Thiet
Ta Cu Mountain
Bong Trang
Ham Tan
Xuyen Moc
Binh Chau Hot Springs
Nui Dat
Ho Coc Beach
Ba Ria
Minh Dam Caves
Vung Tau
Long Hai

0   100 km

Con Dao Archipelago (185km)

soft sand, looking out over aquamarine waters. This tourist enclave attracts a steady stream of overseas visitors as well as expats from Ho Chi Minh City on a short break. Those for whom a day sunbathing is a day wasted will prefer to make a little more headway, and rest up around **Phan Rang**, site of the most impressive of the many **tower complexes** erected by the once-mighty empire of **Champa** (see box, p.238). The nearby beaches at **Ninh Chu** and **Ca Na** aren't quite in the same league as Mui Ne, but both make appealing options for a bit of peace and quiet.

If you press on to **Nha Trang**, however, you can enjoy a combination of Cham towers, the attractive municipal beach and diving and snorkelling trips. Other, more secluded, beaches that warrant an expedition further north include **Doc Let** and **Sa Huynh**, while for a little more civilization, **Quy Nhon** makes a useful halt above Nha Trang. The scars of war tend not to intrude too much along this stretch of the country, though many visitors make time to visit **Quang Ngai**, where Vietnam's south-central arc of coastline culminates, and view the sombre site of the notorious **My Lai** massacre perpetrated by US forces in 1968.

The Con Dao Archipelago

Cast adrift in the South China Sea some 185km south of Vung Tau, the sixteen islands of the **Con Dao Archipelago** are emerging as one of Vietnam's hottest new destinations. Once home to the most feared prison in the country, Con Dao is now metamorphosing into a laidback island get-away with some striking colonial buildings, alluring beaches and challenging treks in the rugged hills of the national park. Since regular flights began to Con Son Island early this century, it has taken its first steps to welcoming tourists, and fortunately there is more to see than the abandoned prisons. **Trekking** in the national park, **diving** at the surrounding islands, watching **sea turtles** laying eggs and lounging on the uncrowded **beaches** are some of the alternative activities.

Con Son Island

Had the **fortified outpost** established here by the British East India Company in 1703 flourished, **CON SON**, by far the largest of the islands, could by now have been a more diminutive Hong Kong or Singapore, given its strategic position on the route to China. But within three years, the Bugis mercenaries (from Sulawesi) drafted in to construct and garrison the base had murdered their British commanders, putting paid to this early experiment in colonization. Known then as Poulo Condore, Con Son was still treading water when the American sailor John White spied its "lofty summits" a little over a century later, in 1819. White deemed it a decent natural harbour, though blighted by "noxious reptiles, and affording no good fresh water".

The island finally found its calling when decades later the French chose it as the site of a **penal colony** for anti-colonial activists. Con Son's savage regime soon earned it the nickname "Devil's Island". Prisoners languished in squalid pits called "tiger cages", which featured metal grilles instead of roofs, from which guards sprinkled powdered lime and dirty water on the inmates. As the twentieth century progressed the colony developed into a sort of unofficial "revolutionary university". Older hands instructed their greener cell-mates in the finer points of Marxist-Leninist theory, while the dire conditions they endured helped reinforce the lessons.

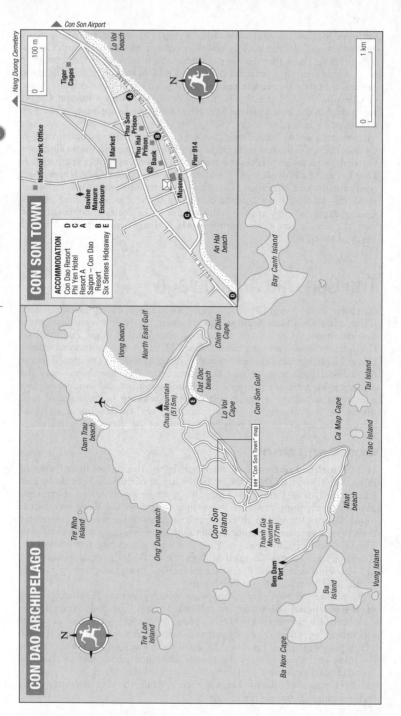

CON DAO ARCHIPELAGO

Tre Nho Island
Tre Lon Island
Ba Non Cape
Vung Island
Ba Island
Ben Dam Port
Thanh Gia Mountain (577m)
Con Son Island
Nhat beach
Trac Island
Ca Map Cape
 Tai Island
Con Son Gulf
Lo Voi Cape
Bay Canh Island
Dat Doc beach
Chim Chim Cape
Chua Mountain (515m)
North East Gulf
Vong beach
Dam Trau beach
Ong Dung beach

see "Con Son Town" map

N
0   1 km

CON SON TOWN

Con Son Airport
Hang Duong Cemetery
Lo Voi beach
Tiger Cages
Phu Son Prison
Phu Hai Prison
Market
National Park Office
Bovine Manure Enclosure
@ Bank
Museum
Pier 914
An Hai beach

N
0   100 m

ACCOMMODATION
Con Dao Resort   D
Phi Yen Hotel   C
Resort A   A
Saigon – Con Dao Resort B
Six Senses Hideaway   E

Arrival and information

The easiest way to visit Con Son is to take a Vietnam Air Services Company (VASCO; ☎08/3842 2790; ⓦwww.vasco.com.vn) **flight** from Ho Chi Minh City, which takes just an hour (about $80 return). There's at least one flight a day, sometimes more. You'll arrive at the **airport**, about 15km northeast of town, and all hotels operate a pick-up service; the ride into town gives a tantalizing glimpse of the island's rugged beauty and windswept, deserted beaches. For more of an adventure in getting to the archipelago, contact Vung Tau Tourist in Vung Tau (☎064/351 1043, ⓔvungtautour@hcm.vnn.vn; see p.226) and ask about the irregular overnight **ferries**; they take 12–15 hours and cost about $25 per person.

There's an **ATM** outside the Vietinbank at the junction of Le Duan and Le Van Viet, with **internet access** a few doors further up Le Duan. The **post office** is on Nguyen Thi Minh Khai. Rainbow Divers (☎091/340 8146, ⓦwww.divevietnam.com) organize **dives** in the area.

Con Son Town

The most popular activity in Con Son, particularly for Vietnamese visitors, is a tour of the island's **historic monuments**. A 35,000đ ticket from the **Revolutionary Museum** (Mon–Sat 7–11.30am & 1.30–5pm), located directly behind Pier 914, allows entry to the prisons, the so-called "tiger cages" and the cemetery, with a guide. It's all rather depressing, beginning with the poorly stuffed black squirrel, the island's most distinctive animal, in the dingy museum. Emaciated statues in the prison show how the Vietnamese inmates spent their days shackled and crowded together, unless they were selected for the "tiger cages" or the "solariums", where they were exposed to the elements in roofless rooms.

The unmarked graves in the **Hang Duong Cemetery** continue the tragic theme, though bright-coloured combs deposited on the grave of revolutionary heroine Vo Thi Sau add a poignant touch. She was the first woman to be executed here, in 1952, aged 19, and clearly loved combing her long black hair. If the morbid mood gets you, you could even visit the **bovine manure enclosure**, located just off Vo Thi Sau on the way to the national park headquarters. The prison warders used to march prisoners into this windowless room, then pump it full of manure as a form of torture or execution, depending on their whim. Oh, and if you're wondering where Pier 914 got its name, that's one estimate (others being 915, 917 & 871) of the number of prisoners who died during its construction.

Inland Con Son

A hike along one of the island's many trails in the National Park may be more appealing than a tour of the prisons. Some trails, such as one heading straight north to Ong Dung Beach, are well marked and can be followed independently, while others, such as to Thanh Gia Mountain, the island's highest peak at 577m, require the services of a guide. Birdwatchers might be lucky enough to spot rare species such as the Red-billed Tropicbird or the Pied Imperial Pigeon. Make sure to take plenty of water and food, as there is nothing available outside the town. The **Con Dao National Park** headquarters are located north of the town centre at 29 Vo Thi Sau, and are worth dropping by for information about hiking trails.

If trekking in the hills seems too much like hard work, a stroll along the seafront of Con Son Town is pleasant enough; on your way you can admire the huge gnarled trunks of the unusual malabar almond trees that line the promenade and watch the colourful fishing boats bobbing in the bay.

Beaches and islands

After visiting the historic monuments and trekking across the island you may want to focus on some serious relaxation. **Lo Voi** and **An Hai** beaches, which front the town, are not bad, though the bay is often cluttered with fishing boats. Other good beaches around the island are **Dam Trau** and **Bai Ong Dung** in the north and **Bai Dat Doc** to the east of town, but you'll need to trek or rent a motorbike (ask your hotel; about 120,000đ per day) to get there. If you fancy a trip to the offshore islands, where there are plenty of deserted beaches and healthy coral reefs, try to get a group together as boats, available for hire through hotels or the national park, cost around four million dong a day. The best **diving** months are April and May, when visibility can be over twenty metres. From June to October it is possible to watch sea turtles laying eggs at night on nearby **Bay Canh Island**; less predictable are occasional sightings of dugongs, which are endearing mammals (also known as sea cows) that feed only on seagrass, grow up to three metres long and weigh up to four hundred kilos. There are a few basic **rooms** on Bay Canh Island operated by the national park.

Accommodation and eating

Accommodation options reflect strong confidence in the island's potential as a slice of paradise, with the opening of one luxury resort and a smart new mid-range place in 2009. The new *Six Senses Hideaway* (W www.sixsenses.com; **7**) at Dat Doc Beach, a few minutes' drive up the coast from Con Son Town, has super-modern, timber-framed villas, and a private butler to take care of guests' every need. For those on a more moderate budget, the new *Saigon – Con Dao Resort*, 18–24 Ton Duc Thang (T 064/383 0336, W www.saigoncondao.com; **4**), is the best of the rest, with a small pool and most rooms offering good views of the beach. The nearby *Resort A*, 16b Ton Duc Thang (T 064/383 0456, F 064/383 0111; **4**), has a few rooms in thatched, wooden, stilt-houses and others in brick bungalows, though the bungalows are a bit cramped together. The *Con Dao Resort* (T 064/383 0939, W www.condaoresort.vn; **4**), 8 Nguyen Duc Thuan, has a swimming pool and probably the best beach location in Con Son, plus they can arrange boat trips. The only budget option is the *Phi Yen Hotel* (T 064/383 0168, F 064/383 0428; **2**) at 34 Ton Duc Thang, which has simple but clean rooms, all with hot water. All the resorts have **restaurants**, and there are a few basic eateries around the market, but you'll need your phrase book.

Vung Tau and the coast road

From **Bien Hoa**, just outside Ho Chi Minh City, Highway 51 heads southward via modest **Long Thanh** (famed locally for its impressive **fruit market**) to **Ba Ria**. From there, a dog-legged road ventures out across the swampland and shrimp farms of the **Vung Tau Peninsula** to Vung Tau itself, home of the most southerly beaches on the eastern Vietnamese coast.

VUNG TAU, "The Bay of Boats", is located some 125km southeast of Ho Chi Minh City on a hammerheaded spit of land jutting into the mouth of the Saigon River. Once a thriving riviera-style beach resort, the city's **offshore oil** industry and steadily growing port have transformed it into a more business-oriented conurbation, though residents of Ho Chi Minh City still flock here on weekends, when hotel rates rise. However, despite a recent effort to clean them up, the town's **beaches – Bai Dau**, **Bai Truoc**, **Bai Dua** and **Bai Sau** – are all second-rate.

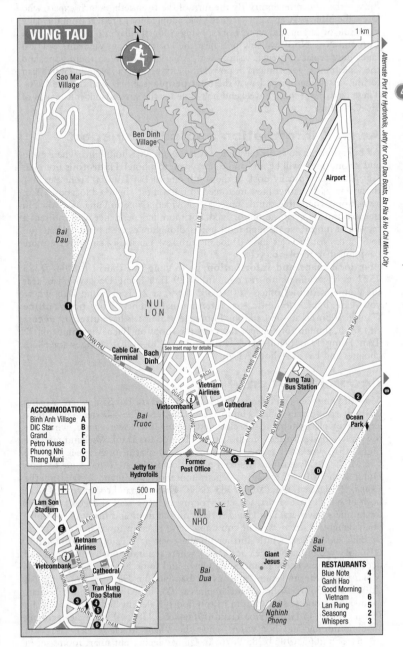

VUNG TAU

N

0   1 km

Alternate Port for Hydrofoils; Jetty for Con Dao Boats; Ba Ria & Ho Chi Minh City

Sao Mai
Village

Ben Dinh
Village

Airport

Bai
Dau

NUI
LON

Cable Car
Terminal   Bach
       Dinh

See Inset map for details

TRAN PHU

Vung Tau
Bus Station

Vietnam
Airlines

Vietcombank   Cathedral

Ocean
Park

Bai
Truoc

ACCOMMODATION
Binh Anh Village   A
DIC Star   B
Grand   F
Petro House   E
Phuong Nhi   C
Thang Muoi   D

Jetty for
Hydrofoils

Former
Post Office

NUI
NHO

Lam Son
Stadium

0   500 m

Vietnam
Airlines

Vietcombank

Cathedral

Tran Hung
Dao Statue

Bai
Dua

Giant
Jesus

Bai
Sau

RESTAURANTS
Blue Note   4
Ganh Hao   1
Good Morning
   Vietnam   6
Lan Rung   5
Seasong   2
Whispers   3

Bai
Nghinh
Phong

Portuguese ships are thought to have exploited the city's deep anchorage as early as the fifteenth century. By the turn of the twentieth, French expats, who knew the place as "Cap Saint-Jacques", had adopted it as a retreat from the daily rigmarole of Saigon, and set to work carving colonial villas into the sides of **Nui Lon** and **Nui Nho**, two low hills near the coast. Shifts in Vietnam's political sands duly replaced French visitors with American GIs. With them gone, and the Communist government in power, the city became a favoured launch pad for the vessels that spirited away the **boat people** (see p.477) in the late 1970s. These days, it's become a weekend bolt-hole for the stressed-out inhabitants of Ho Chi Minh City.

Arrival, information and city transport

All **buses** terminate at the bus station at 192 Nam Ky Khoi Nghia, where cyclo and xe om riders will be on hand to ferry you to a hotel. **Hydrofoils** from Ho Chi Minh City usually dock at the south end of Bai Truoc ("Front Beach"), though in bad weather they are forced to use a more sheltered location 12km away, from where free shuttle buses are provided. Once in Vung Tau, you can **get around** by cyclo, xe om or taxi. For more independence, you can rent a bicycle or motorbike through most hotels, though rates are a bit steep here (up to $5 a day for bicycles and $10 for motorbikes). Curiously, tandems are more common than regular bicycles.

For local **maps and information**, go to Vung Tau Tourist (☎064/🖷385 7527, ⓦwww.vungtautourist.com.vn) at 29 Tran Hung Dao, which is near the Vietnam Airlines office (☎064/385 6099) at 21 Tran Hung Dao, where you can book domestic or international flights. The **post office** (7am–8.30pm) is at 408 Le Hong Phong; several hotels have **internet access** and wi-fi, though for cheaper rates, try the shops on Bacu. Vietcombank, 27 Tran Hung Dao (Mon–Fri 7–11.30am & 1.30–4pm), changes traveller's cheques and has a 24-hour ATM.

Accommodation

Most of Vung Tau's mid-range **hotels** are located on Bai Sau, where a string of high-rise places offer comfortable facilities. The classier (and more expensive) places tend to be clustered around the town centre, while the town's few budget places are mostly on Hoang Hoa Tram. Weekend rates are higher than weekdays, as the town is invaded by swarms of escapees from Ho Chi Minh City. Two of the swankier places downtown are *Petro House*, 63 Tran Hung Dao (☎064/385 2014, 🖷petrohousehotel@vnn.vn; ➍–➎), and the *Grand*, 2 Nguyen Du (☎064/385 6888, ⓦwww.grand.oscvn.com; ➎–➏), both of which have smart, attractive rooms, attentive staff and good facilities for business travellers. The *Grand* is right on the front and many of its rooms boast delightful sea views. The most appealing place in town, however, is the 🛈 *Binh Anh Village*, a little further up the coast at 1 Tran Phu (☎064/351 0016, ⓦwww.binhanvillage.com; ➏–➐), where ten individually furnished and decorated rooms enjoy fabulous sea views, and some have private gardens as well. Among the mid-range options on Bai Sau, the *Dic Star*, 169 Thuy Van (☎064/358 5537, 🖷dicstarhotel@vnn.vn; ➏), has over a hundred smart rooms with good sea views from its top floors. A decent budget option is the *Phuong Nhi* at 46 Hoang Hoa Tham (☎064/352 4382; ➋), with clean rooms, air-conditioning and hot water, while the *Thang Muoi*, at 151 Thuy Van (☎064/385 2665, 🖷064/385 9876; ➋–➌), has ageing but smart rooms set in a quiet, single-storey compound opposite the beach.

The City

For Vung Tau's most interesting sights and views, head for **Nui Nho** ("Small Mountain"), to the south of town. The town's **lighthouse**, built in 1910, seems to have been based on a child's sketch of a space-rocket, and is a popular place for locals to walk or jog to in the morning and evening. To get there, turn up a small lane called Hai Dang, just north of the hydrofoil jetty. The views from here out to sea and across town make for good photos, as do those from Vung Tau's own little touch of Rio, the 28-metre-high **Giant Jesus** (daily 7.30–11.30am & 1.30–5pm; free), which sits on a lower peak a few hundred metres further south: it's approached by a stairway from the southern end of Ha Long. Cherubs wielding harps and trumpets herald your approach to the outstretched arms of the city's most famous landmark. Climb the steps inside the wind-buffeted statue and you can perch, parrot-like, on Jesus's shoulder, from where you'll enjoy giddying views of the surrounding seascape. A new **cable car** is currently being built on the slopes of Nui Lon, to the north of Nui Nho, which will take tourists to the top of Vung Tau's highest peak for yet more sweeping views.

One of the few remaining colonial structures worth a look is the imposing **Bach Dinh** at 12 Tran Phu (daily 7am–5pm; small admission fee), peeping out from behind a vanguard of frangipani and bougainvillea. Built at the end of the nineteenth century, it served as a holiday home to Vietnam's political players, hosting such luminaries as Paul Doumer, governor-general of Indochina (for whom it was originally erected), emperors Thanh Thai and Bao Dai, and President Thieu. Inside you can see the building's collection of "valuable antique items", excavated from a seventeenth-century shipwreck off Con Dao; among the exhibits are such unmissables as "dry burned fruits", "beard-tweezers" and "pieces of stone in the ship". Upstairs is a display of Cambodian Buddhist statuary and shards of old pottery, but they are eclipsed by the commanding views of the bay.

If swimming and sun-seeking brought you to Vung Tau, your best bet is to head for the sands of **Bai Sau** ("Back Beach"), far and away Vung Tau's widest, longest (5km) and best, which is not saying much. Backed by high-rise hotels, it's not exactly a tropical paradise, though on weekends, when it's cluttered with

▲ The views from Vung Tau's Giant Jesus are stunning

kids, deckchairs and umbrellas, and the fruit- and seafood-vendors are out in force, it's pleasant enough. **Ocean Park** (daily 6.30am-5.30pm; free), which occupies a seven-hundred-metre beach frontage, rents out watersports equipment, offers beach games, lifeguards, showers and a smart restaurant.

Finally, if you enjoy a flutter and are in town on a Saturday night, head for the **Lam Son Stadium** at 15 Le Loi, Vietnam's only venue for greyhound racing (daily 7am–10.30pm; admission 20,000đ).

Eating, drinking and nightlife

With a large number of resident expats, Vung Tau supports a more cosmopolitan span of **restaurants** than your average Vietnamese town; French cuisine weighs in heavily, but it's also possible to find spaghetti and burgers as well as delicious Vietnamese seafood. In addition, there are a number of **bars** in the town centre catering to the expat community.

For something special, try the restaurant at *Binh An Village*, where you can enjoy seafood or steaks in a sumptuous setting for around $20, accompanied by live jazz on Saturday night and Sunday lunchtime. Just north of here, the *Ganh Hao* at 3 Tran Phu is Vung Tau's top seafood restaurant, with dining tables looking out to sea. The area around the huge statue of Tran Hung Dao, at the southern end of the street with the same name, is peppered with appealing restaurants and bars, including *Lan Rung* at 2 Tran Hung Dao, a cavernous place specializing in seafood that is very popular with locals, as well as a branch of *Good Morning Vietnam* at 6 Hoang Hoa Tham, which serves up tasty pizzas and pasta. Also in this area, *Whispers*, 15 Nguyen Trai, is one of the most popular haunts for resident expats, with traditional roasts and good-quality Western fare, while *Seasong*, on the fourth floor of the flash new Imperial Shopping Mall at 163 Thuy Van, has a refined atmosphere and serves up dishes like wok-fried tiger prawn with hazelnut for around $6.

Several bars along Nguyen Trai, as well as in other streets around the Tran Hung Dao statue provide the epicentre of what **nightlife** exists in Vung Tao. While some are intent on persuading lonesome males to buy the hostesses drinks, others, like *Blue Note* on the corner of Tran Hung Dao and Truong Cong Dinh, simply provide an appealing ambience in which to enjoy a drink and chat.

The northeast coast road

As you move up the coast northeast of Vung Tau, the beaches gradually get more enticing. Since the region is near to Ho Chi Minh City, you have to go quite a way before you escape the hordes of domestic tourists who head for the area at weekends and on public holidays, though weekdays can be blissfully quiet. If you're travelling by bus, you'll need to backtrack to Ba Ria to get a connection, but if you have a rented vehicle, you can explore a new road that hugs the coast much of the way from Vung Tau to Mui Ne, throwing up glimpses of rural life as well as the salty tang of the nearby sea.

Long Hai and around

The first town along the coast, some 20km from Vung Tau, is **LONG HAI**, set below a wall of impressive mountains. It's very popular with Vietnamese, many of who find its wide beach and fishing-village atmosphere more appealing than Vung Tau. Dunes fringe the town's eastern extreme; to the west stands a fishing village, complete with a huge flotilla of fishing boats and assorted coracles sporting brightly coloured flags. Long Hai is served by **buses** from Ho Chi

Minh City's Mien Dong station; coming from Vung Tau, you'll need to take a bus to Ba Ria and then change, or take a xe om direct for about $5. Few foreigners stay here, though there are some **hotels**, of which the best is probably the *Military Guest House* (☎064/386 8316; ❷), located at the end of the road that runs into the village. It has basic rooms with a choice of fan or air-conditioned rooms, and looks out over a wide expanse of beach shaded by casuarinas. There are a few **food stalls** by the road leading up to the guesthouse.

Most foreign visitors bypass the town altogether and head straight along to the **resort area** east of town, where the aptly named 🏠 *Anoasis Beach Resort* (☎064/386 8227, ⓦwww.anoasisresort.com.vn; ❻) is a lovingly restored former residence of Emperor Bao Dai overlooking a deserted coastline. The thatch-roofed individual bungalows discreetly set amongst pine-studded hills are very special, with gorgeous bamboo furnishings and fittings and huge bathtubs. Facilities also run to a business centre, swimming pool and charming open-air terraced restaurant. The resort has won many awards, and non-residents can enjoy its facilities for $10 a day at weekends or $6 a day on weekdays. Just east of here, the new *Long Hai Beach Resort* (☎064/366 1355, ⓦwww.longhaibeachresort .com; ❻–❻) has tastefully furnished rooms, a large swimming pool, a casino and fitness centre, but is mostly geared towards large groups. A little further along, the *Thuy Duong Resort* (☎064/886 215; ☏064/388 6180; ❹–❺) is a good mid-range option, standing behind a fine beach lined with casuarinas: its accommodation ranges from pleasant beach huts to luxurious suites in the main hotel, and there's a pool and tennis courts too.

Trace the road eastwards hugging the coast and just beyond *Thuy Duong Resort* you'll find a signposted left turn that runs up to the elevated **Minh Dam caves**, a Communist bolt-hole from 1948, from where you can enjoy prodigious views of the rice fields that quilt the coastal plain stretching to the horizon to the northeast, and of the boulder-strewn coastline below. The caves are not much more than gaps between piled boulders, yet with a little imagination it's still possible to picture Viet Minh and Viet Cong soldiers lounging, cooking and sleeping here. Bullets have left pockmarks on some of the rocks, and joss sticks are still lodged in crevices in memory of those who fell here. Since there are many forks in the path, however, you really need a guide to find your way around.

From here, the coast road continues eastwards through the village of **Phuoc Hai**, then after a couple of kilometres passes the brand-new *Tropicana Beach Resort* (☎064/367 8888, ⓦwww.tropicanabeachresort.com; ❻), with a spa and pool, though its rooms hardly justify the high price tag. About 8km later, the road passes the isolated *Loc An Resort* (☎064/388 6377, ⓦwww.locanresort .com; ❹), nestled beside a lagoon cut off from the sea by a line of sand dunes: it has cosy rooms with all facilities, and bicycles and tandems are available for guests' use. The pick of the bunch on this remote stretch of beach, however, lies 4km west of **Ho Tram**, the 🏠 *Ho Tram Beach Resort* (☎064/3781525, ⓦwww .hotramresort.com; ❻–❼), where all the rooms ooze character with elegant furnishings and fittings. As all these resorts are just a couple of hours' drive from Ho Chi Minh City, they are very popular with urbanites at the weekend when rates rise and reservations are often necessary.

Ho Coc Beach

The new road continues to wind along the coast, fringed by casuarinas and sand dunes, until it reaches **Ho Coc Beach**. Ho Coc is a spellbinding, five-kilometre stretch of wonderfully golden sand, dotted with coracles and large boulders, lapped by clear waters and backed by fine dunes. As with most places around here, it gets crowded with day-trippers at the weekend but is practically deserted during the week. There are a couple of decent accommodation choices here, including the *Saigon-Ho Coc Resort* (☎064/379 1036, ℗064/387 8175; ❻), on the beach itself, with good-sized and well-furnished brick bungalows; guests get free entry to the nearby Binh Chau Hot Springs. Set back from the beach, but better-value, the *Ven Ven* (☎064/379 1121, ✉info@kimsabai.com; ❸) has so-so rooms in the main building, but the villas out back are good value, and there's a cosy restaurant. **Buses** from Ho Chi Minh City, Vung Tau and Ba Ria trundle as far as Xuyen Moc, about 10km north of here, from where you'll need to take a motorbike taxi.

Binh Chau Hot Springs

Binh Chau Hot Springs (☎064/387 1131, ⊛www.saigonbinhchauecoresort .com; 20,000đ) are 15km northeast of Ho Coc Beach, and the springs have been developed into a kind of theme park with the addition of a golf-driving range, tennis courts, sand volleyball court, billiards and ox-cart rides around the site. The sulphurous waters bubbling hellishly in the streams and wells here vary greatly in temperature. Old people soothe their aching limbs in the foot-soaking stream, while elsewhere visitors boil eggs sold on site to make up ad hoc picnics. For 30,000đ, you can bathe in the mineral waters of the "Dreaming Lake", a communal **swimming pool**, but renting your own **mini-pool** (about 50,000đ per person per hour) is a more tempting option. There are also a sauna, massage and mud baths in the main complex, which features a range of accommodation (❹–❻) in villas and bungalows and a large **restaurant**. There's no public transport to Binh Chau Hot Springs, but if you fancy spending a night or two there, call their Ho Chi Minh City office (☎08/3997 0677), and they will arrange a pick-up.

On to Mui Ne

Beyond Binh Chau, **Highway 55** follows the windswept coast to **Ham Tan**, passing through cashew orchards with glimpses of huge sand dunes to your right. This route is so far off the beaten track that ox carts are almost as common as motorized vehicles. Occasional dirt tracks lead down to some fantastic stretches of deserted beach, where a few coracles pulled up beyond the tide level hint at human habitation. After passing Ham Tan, the coast road continues eastward; the landscape is beautiful, with remote fishing villages sheltered by coconut palms, and dragon-fruit orchards lining the road, which eventually veers away from the coast in the form of Highway 712 to join the unrelenting traffic of Highway 1 about 30km before Phan Thiet.

If you're enjoying the coast road, however, it's possible to branch off Highway 712 about 15km after Ham Tan and follow the coast all the way to **Cape Ke Ga**, where a lighthouse stands that was built by the French over 100 years ago. Tucked away in this unknown corner of the country, the 🏠 *Princess D'Annam* (☎062/368 2222, ⊛www.princessannam.com; ❼) comes as something of a surprise, with its fabulously-furnished villas and calming, minimalist decor: facilities include four pools, a spa, two restaurants and 24-hour butler service

Back on Highway 712, about 2km south of its junction with Highway 1 at **Thuan Nam**, is **Ta Cu Mountain**, home to Vietnam's largest reclining Buddha (49m). It makes an interesting trek to climb the mountain, probably in the company of Buddhists on pilgrimage, though there is also a cable car (60,000đ return) that stops near the summit, leaving just a short climb. Resorts in Mui Ne can also arrange visits to the mountain.

The coastal road to Nha Trang

In reality, few travellers have time to meander along the beaches between Vung Tau and Mui Ne, and most hop straight on a bus from Ho Chi Minh City to **Mui Ne**, taking just a few hours to whizz across the coastal plain with the Truong Song mountain range looming on the left. By this route, the first whiff of the seaside comes at **Phan Thiet**, where brightly-painted fishing boats bob on the Ca Ty River, and from here it's just 20km to the sands of **Mui Ne**, one of the country's fastest-growing beach resorts. There's another chance to take a dip in the South China Sea a little further north at **Ca Na**, and some superb Cham towers, the impressive **Po Klong Garai Towers**, near **Phan Rang**, where you can also enjoy a long sweep of often-deserted beach at **Ninh Chu**. North of Phan Rang, Highway 1 ploughs through sugar-cane plantations, salt flats and shrimp farms on its way into **Nha Trang**.

Phan Thiet

The unassuming capital of Binh Thuan Province, **PHAN THIET** has little of interest for foreigners, though the reasonably attractive Doi Duong beach just east of town is very popular with the Vietnamese. In the centre of town, Highway 1 crosses **Tran Hung Dao Bridge**, beside which lies a fleet of fishing boats looking like they come straight off a postcard. Turn left off the bridge's southwestern end and stroll along Trung Trac, and you'll soon plunge into the thick of things at the wharfside **fish market**. In the other direction, Trung Trac skirts the city centre en route to the sedate riverside **Ho Chi Minh Museum** (Tues–Sun 7.30–11.30am & 1.30–4.30pm; small admission fee). Currently undergoing renovation, its exhibits include memorabilia of Ho's life from his early days abroad up to his death in 1969, such as his white tunic, walking stick, sandals and metal helmet. The rows of varnished wooden desks and tables in the evocative **Duc Thanh School** (same hours) next door have remained unchanged since Ho's brief spell as a teacher here, and effortlessly conjure up another age.

Over Tran Hung Dao Bridge, beside the Victory Monument, Nguyen That Thanh strikes off to the right and to the city **beach**. The scruffy patch of sand it hits first doesn't look too promising, but 700m northeast it opens out into a more wholesome casuarina-shaded spot, backed up by some smart hotels. There's also a string of restaurants and bars along here that do a good trade at the weekend.

Practicalities

The **bus station** is a couple of kilometres north of the centre on Tu Van Tu, while Binh Thuan Tourist, 82 Trung Truc (℡062/381 6821, Ⓦwww .binhthuan-tourist.com), can provide **information** and a map of the region around Phan Thiet. There's an **ATM** at the Vietinbank on Nguyen Tat Thanh, with the **post office** a few steps further down the same road, while several places offer **internet access** along Tran Hung Dao.

There are plenty of **places to stay** in Phan Thiet, though there's nothing exciting about any of them. The best place in town is the ageing *Phan Thiet* at 364 Tran Hung Dao (℡062/381 5830; ❷), where the spacious rooms are reasonable value. Down on the beach are a few fancier places, including the *Doi Duong* (℡062/382 1579, Ⓕ062/382 5858; ❸–❹), a smart high-rise that has over seventy well-equipped rooms, a swimming pool, tennis courts and two restaurants. Bigger still is the mammoth *Novotel Ocean Dunes Resort* (℡062/382 2393,

ⓦ www.novotel.com; ⑥–⑦), a little further along, which has an eighteen-hole golf course, two swimming pools and free use of bicycles.

There are few appealing **eating** options in town, though on the southwestern side of the square below the city's central bridge, the *Nam Thanh Lau*, at 5 Nguyen Thi Minh Khai, has great seafood and the generous portions are good value. Upmarket dining can be found at the *Sea Horse*, at the *Novotel Ocean Dunes Resort*, where dishes such as stuffed prawn with crab meat and sesame seeds cost around $10.

Mui Ne

From being a sleepy backwater ignored by domestic and international tourists alike, **MUI NE** has become the country's hottest beach destination, thanks largely to an eclipse of the sun in the mid-1990s that had its optimum viewing spot at this pretty beach. Now it's popular as a weekend retreat for expats living in Ho Chi Minh City as well as a favourite with upmarket visitors happy to pay $50–100 a day to lounge around in a luxurious resort.

The village of Mui Ne lies just 22km east along the coast road from Phan Thiet, and most resorts are located along the 10km crescent of sand that leads up to it. After about 8km, a turning on the right leads to the **Po Shanu Towers** (daily 7am–5pm; small admission fee), which date from the eighth century. While they can't compare with monuments like Po Klong Garai near Phan Rang (see p.238), they are worth a look as the two big towers and one small one are in reasonable repair, and the site occupies a pretty hilltop location with good views. As the road dips down to the coast, it passes the entrance to a massive new development, the **Sealinks Golf and Country Club** (ⓦ www .sealinksvietnam.com), which sprawls across the hills with fabulous ocean views, a challenging 72-par golf course (green fees around $50), 300 villas and a five-star hotel.

Arrival and information

Daily **open-tour buses** operated by companies such as Sinh Café and Hanh Café arrive at their offices in central Mui Ne from Nha Trang and Ho Chi

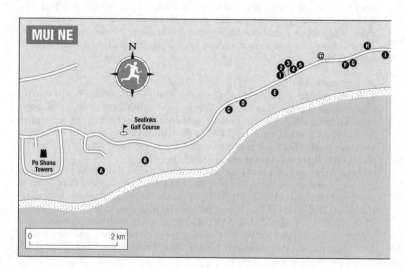

Minh City, usually at around lunchtime. For **getting around**, the best bet is to rent a bicycle (about $2 a day) or motorbike ($6–7 a day) from your resort or guesthouse, but first check details like the brakes to avoid unnecessary accidents. Alternatively, there's a **shuttle bus** that trundles back and forth between Mui Ne and Phan Thiet, supposedly every 15 minutes (8000đ). **Internet access** and wi-fi is available at many resorts, though rates can be high: try the *Coco Café*, at 121 Nguyen Dinh Chu, which currently charges 7000đ per hour. There are several **ATMs** along the strip, including in front of the big resorts.

With a seemingly-captive audience sprawled on the beach and lounging in cafes, local **tour operators** offer day tours of the region taking in the sand dunes, Fairy Spring, the Po Shanu Towers, and Ta Cu Mountain (see p.230). However, it has to be said that Mui Ne's local attractions are limited, and these tours often include missable destinations such as the guide's uncle's dragon fruit orchard. For more in-depth **information** on the local area, visit Ⓦ www.muinebeach.net.

Accommodation

Since the main activity in Mui Ne is lazing on the beach, choosing where to stay is the biggest decision to make while here. Budget options are limited, as the resort's upmarket image means that many places which previously offered cheap rooms have now upgraded their facilities and prices, though this means more choice in the moderate and expensive categories. Bear in mind that many places bump their prices up at weekends. Not all places along the beach have street numbers; in these cases places are identified by kilometre distance along the road from Phan Thiet.

Budget

Hiep Hoa 80 Nguyen Dinh Chieu ☏ 062/384 7262, Ⓦ www.muinebeach.net/hiephoa. Just fifteen basic but smart rooms, some with fans and others a/c, in this tiny, friendly compound facing a fine stretch of beach. ❷–❸
Small Garden 48 Nguyen Dinh Chieu ☏ 062/384 7012. The small, thatched bungalows here are

nothing fancy but are quite adequate and set in a quiet compound. ❷–❸
Thai Hoa 56 Huynh Thuc Khang ☏ 062/384 7320, Ⓦ www.thaihoaresort.com. The simple, concrete rooms lack character, but are clean and offer a choice of fan or a/c: all have small balconies and are set around a well-tended garden. ❷–❸

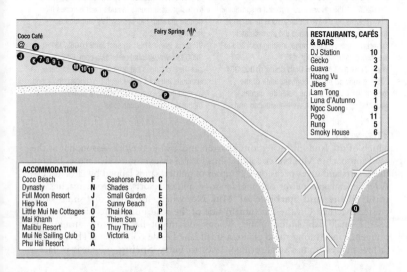

RESTAURANTS, CAFÉS & BARS	
DJ Station	10
Gecko	3
Guava	2
Hoang Vu	4
Jibes	7
Lam Tong	8
Luna d'Autunno	1
Ngoc Suong	9
Pogo	11
Rung	5
Smoky House	6

ACCOMMODATION			
Coco Beach	F	Seahorse Resort	C
Dynasty	N	Shades	L
Full Moon Resort	J	Small Garden	G
Hiep Hoa	I	Sunny Beach	G
Little Mui Ne Cottages	O	Thai Hoa	P
Mai Khanh	K	Thien Son	M
Malibu Resort	Q	Thuy Thuy	H
Mui Ne Sailing Club	D	Victoria	B
Phu Hai Resort	A		

Thien Son 102 Nguyen Dinh Chieu ⊕062/384 7187. Just half a dozen rooms in one of the few remaining havens for budget travellers. There are no sea views from the rooms, but the beach is just a few steps away. ❷

Moderate

Dynasty 140A Nguyen Dinh Chieu ⊕062/384 7816, ⓦwww.dynastyresorts.com. The elegantly furnished rooms, attentive staff and filling buffet breakfasts make this a comfortable place to stay. ❺–❻

Full Moon Resort 84 Nguyen Dinh Chieu ⊕062/384 7008, ⓔfullmoon@windsurf-vietnam .com. Attractive and sturdy, thatched bamboo huts with verandas and spacious rooms, some on stilts and with attached bathrooms; rates include breakfast. ❹–❻

Little Mui Ne Cottages 10b Huynh Thuc Khang ⊕062/384 7550-1, ⓦwww.littlemuine.com. Large bungalows and cosy rooms with bamboo furnishings in a tidy compound with a good-size pool, free internet access and bikes. The attention to detail makes this place very appealing. ❺–❻

Mai Khanh 86 Nguyen Dinh Chieu ⊕062/384 7177. The attractively designed rooms, each with its own balcony, are very comfortable, and the garden here has a laidback feel to it, making this place good value for money. ❸–❹

Malibu Resort Ward 5 ⊕062/384 9669, ⓦwww .malibu-resort.com. Located to the east of the main bay at Mui Ne, this place with smartly furnished and spacious rooms has an "away-from-it-all" feeling. ❹–❺

Sunny Beach 64–66 Nguyen Dinh Chieu ⊕062/374 1355, ⓦwww.sunnybeachresortmuine .com. Rooms here have natural wood furnishings and are quite spacious, while the immaculately manicured grounds and huge, inviting pool add to the resort's attractions. ❹–❺

Thuy Thuy 123 Nguyen Dinh Chieu ⊕062/384 7357. It may be on the opposite side of the road to the beach, but the beautiful garden, pool and spa, along with well-positioned and

tastefully-equipped bungalows, make this an appealing place to stay. ❺

Expensive

Coco Beach 58 Nguyen Dinh Chieu ⊕062/384 7111, ⓦwww.cocobeach.net. This French-run resort has 28 tasteful, thatched wooden bungalows and some family-size villas, complete with verandas, Cham-style fabrics, a/c and all modern comforts, set among tropical gardens off the beach. The relaxed style and friendly staff have made this an established favourite. ❻–❼

Mui Ne Sailing Club 24 Nguyen Dinh Chieu ⊕062/384 7440, ⓦwww .sailingclubvietnam.com/scmuine.php. Delightfully landscaped resort, featuring rooms and bungalows with thatched roofs and mustard-coloured walls, plus imaginative interiors with good use of local textiles. Swimming pool, popular bar and restaurant too. ❻–❼

Phu Hai Resort km8 ⊕062/381 2799, ⓦwww .phuhairesort.com. One of the biggest resorts at Mui Ne, with over eighty villas snuggled away behind lush tropical growth. Large pool with waterfall, tennis courts, fitness club and stylish restaurant. ❻–❼

Seahorse Resort km11 ⊕062/384 7507, ⓦwww.seahorseresortvn.com. Spacious bungalows with traditionally tiled roofs and elegant furnishings in a well-landscaped garden, plus pool, spa and restaurant overlooking the beach. ❻–❼

Shades 98A Nguyen Dinh Chieu ⊕062/374 3237, ⓦwww.shadesmuine.com. This collection of just seven individual apartments is super-hip in design, and rooms include neat touches like double glazing, flat-screen TVs and kitchen facilities. ❻–❼

Victoria Phan Thiet Resort km9 ⊕062/381 3000, ⓦwww.victoriahotels-asia.com. Fifty nine sea-view cottages set amongst tropical gardens; spacious interiors with tasteful European decor and all mod cons. Excursions arranged and free use of mountain bikes for guests. ❼

The village

Much of the land in this region is barren and arid in the dry season, but as the road approaches Mui Ne, coconut palms form a shady avenue that passes behind the resorts and gives occasional glimpses of golden sands lapped by clear waters. After several kilometres of shoulder-to-shoulder resorts, the road reaches the small **village and harbour of Mui Ne**, where hundreds of fishing boats cluster together. On the left (north) side of the road just before the village are several small **fish sauce** plants, where you might like to nose around the pungent vats. Among these plants, a small lane beside 63b Huynh Thuc Khang (a few metres from a small bridge) leads to **Fairy Spring**, which is in fact a narrow stream running through a psychedelic landscape of white and red **sand dunes**, which are also accessible via a left turn at the village of Mui Ne. The softness of the sand makes the dunes difficult to climb, but the resulting views are ample reward. The sand can also get very hot, so it makes sense to go early or late in the day.

Though the number one activity at Mui Ne is **relaxing on the beach**, the place also attracts **wind- and kitesurfers** when the wind is up between August and April, and Mui Ne even hosts an event in the Asian Windsurf Tour each February. If you'd like a crack at **windsurfing** or **kitesurfing**, head on down to *Jibes*, more or less at the centre of the bay at 90 Nguyen Dinh Chieu, or to *Storm* (Ⓦwww.stormkiteboarding.com), based at the *Mui Ne Sailing Club*, where an hour's instruction costs around $40 for windsurfing and around $60 for kitesurfing.

There's no doubt that its laidback atmosphere is one of its best features, but Mui Ne is also something of a tourist enclave, separated as it is from any Vietnamese community. If you're just here to chill out on the beach, that probably won't bother you, but if you crave interaction with locals or dancing at night, you'd be better off heading on up to Nha Trang. Another potential problem at Mui Ne is that the strong winds and surf tend to erode parts of the beach from August to December, so you might just find the waves lapping onto the garden of your chosen resort. However, there are always good stretches of soft sand along most of this enormous bay.

Eating, drinking and nightlife

Whilst budget **restaurants** are thin on the ground in Mui Ne, gourmets will find plenty of variety. As well as the resorts and hotels, all of which have their own restaurants, there's no shortage of independent eating joints and bars along the strip, so what Mui Ne lacks in terms of cultural attractions, it makes up for with gastronomic diversity. **Nightlife** is also improving in direct proportion to the number of visitors looking for action, with a surfing crowd at *Jibes*, 90 Nguyen Dinh Chieu, where spontaneous parties have been known to happen.

▲ Sunset on Mui Ne beach

Gecko and *Guava*, located almost next to each other at 53b and 53 Nguyen Dinh Chieu, are also cool places to hang out: both offer food and have super-comfortable lounging areas and a huge menu of cocktails. Another popular spot is *Pogo*, at 138 Nguyen Dinh Chieu, an atmospheric bar with seats on the sand, a pool table and cool sounds. *DJ Station*, at 120c Nguyen Dinh Chieu, provides food, drink and dancing under one roof, while a more sedate yachting crowd gathers round the bar at the *Mui Ne Sailing Club*.

Restaurants

Champa *Coco Beach Resort* 58 Nguyen Dinh Chieu. On a delightful terrace, Champa serves up top-class French cuisine (dinner only) with impeccable service and prices from about 200,000đ for a main dish.

Hoang Vu 121 Nguyen Dinh Chieu. The dark-panelled room is more enticing than the bright, new place next door, but both turn out delicious Vietnamese cuisine – try the red snapper in pepper sauce (57,000đ).

Lam Tong 92 Nguyen Dinh Chieu. This no-frills place is right on the beach and has some of the lowest prices on the strip for decent Vietnamese and international food, plus cheap wine.

Luna d'Autunno 51A Nguyen Dinh Chieu. Beautiful bamboo decor sets the scene for devouring a wood-fired pizza (around 110,000đ)

and washing it down with a bottle of wine from the extensive list.

Ngoc Suong 94 Nguyen Dinh Chieu. Part of a nationwide chain that specializes in seafood and has a solid reputation. It is in a good seaside location, with an extensive menu at reasonable prices.

Rung 65B Nguyen Dinh Chieu. "Rung" means forest, which is exactly what it feels like inside this cavernous eatery which is decorated to look like a forest. A grilled fish will set you back 100,000đ, while a dish of snake or crocodile costs about 150,000đ.

Smoky House 125 Nguyen Dinh Chieu. Order one of their barbecue specials (70,000–100,000đ), and when it's grilled by the table you'll realise why it's called *Smoky House*. They also serve breakfasts and international dishes, and the owner is a mine of knowledge about the local area.

Ca Na

Highway 1 ducks inland above Phan Thiet, which is how Mui Ne remained a secret so long. Now, however, a new road cuts up the coast from Mui Ne, rejoining Highway 1 near Phan Ri. By the time you coast down into **CA NA**, a little over 100km northeast of Phan Thiet as the crow flies, you're tightly sandwiched between hills and the choppy, turquoise waters of the South China Sea. Hardly more than a wide spot in the road, Ca Na is nevertheless reasonably well equipped for feeding and watering passing tourists and, with time in hand, you might consider an overnight stay in this area. Given its proximity to the highway, Ca Na is a more relaxing place than it has any right to be. Beyond the coracles parked along the beach the water is invitingly clear, and snorkelling is a possibility, though you'd be wise to ask locals where to wade in as the coral here is razor sharp. If you crave a little more solitude, a spine of decent dunes back up another good stretch of sand a couple of kilometres south; a fifteen-minute walk north of the resort area is Ca Na village itself, characterized by the blue fishing boats typical of coastal Vietnam. Just 3km before reaching the town, on the right, the Korean-operated *Vietnam Scuba* (☎062/385 3917, ⓕ062/385 3918) offers **dive trips** for $100 to join a day's dive, with all equipment provided. It also has smart, well-equipped bungalows with balconies looking over the sea and jetty, plus two pools (❺–❻): a package of room, diving and all meals costs $170 per day.

There are a few other **places to stay** at Ca Na, with the best being the *Hon Co Ca Na Motel*, right beside Highway 1 (☎068/386 0999, ⓔhoncocana @hcm.vnn.vn; ❹), where small but smartly furnished rooms with balconies are scattered across a promontory: its facilities include internet access, karaoke, massage, billiards and a large restaurant. A little south of here, the *Hai Son*

(☎068/376 1322; ❷) is showing signs of age, but has clean and simple air conditioned rooms with doors straight onto the beach. The *Ca Na* (☎068/376 1320; ❶–❷), between the two, is very run-down and best avoided. All these places have their own **restaurants**, and there's a smart new eatery, the *Mai Linh*, just south of town where, unsurprisingly, fresh seafood is the order of the day.

Phan Rang and around

The numerous vine trellises that abut the highway are the biggest surprise of the journey between Ca Na and Phan Rang. Grapes are a speciality of **Ninh Thuan Province** (of which Phan Rang is the capital) and the vineyards in which they grow lend the area a faintly Mediterranean tang. **PHAN RANG** itself is an unlovely place, with the main thoroughfare, Thong Nhat, dissecting the centre of town. Its western limits have fused with the neighbouring town of **THAP CHAM**, whose name, meaning "Cham Towers", gives a clue to the real reason for stopping here. This region of Vietnam once comprised the Cham kingdom of Panduranga, and of the nearby Cham remnants none is better preserved than those at **Po Klong Garai**. Another nearby attraction is **Ninh Chu Beach**, a glorious sweep of wide sand that is sometimes deliciously quiet on weekdays, but often overrun with Vietnamese at weekends. There are a few resorts along the beach, which make better **accommodation** alternatives than staying in Phan Rang's drab hotels, though they are mostly geared towards Vietnamese visitors. Even if beaches and Cham ruins aren't on your agenda, you may have to overnight in the area if you're heading into the hills around Da Lat (see p.191).

Arrival, information and accommodation

Arriving in Phan Rang by **bus** you'll be dropped at the bus station 300m north of the town centre; **trains** pull in 7km northwest of town at Ga Thap Cham. The Agribank at 540–544 Thong Nhat exchanges foreign currency. The **post office** is at the northern end of town at 217a Thong Nhat, where there is also **internet access**.

Accommodation in **Phan Rang** itself is limited; your best bet is the *Huu Nghi* (☎068/392 0434, ✉huunghihotel@hcm.vnn.vn; ❷–❸) at 398 Thong Nhat, which has smartly furnished, carpeted rooms with bathtubs, and excellent value suites. Alternatively, try the *Ho Phong* (☎068/392 0333, ✉hophonghotel @yahoo.com), south of the town centre at 363 Ngo Gia Tu, with surprisingly stylish high-ceilinged rooms.

However, you're better off avoiding the town completely and heading for **Ninh Chu Beach**, where the options are much more appealing. At the far north, quieter, end of the bay, the new *Saigon-Ninh Chu* (☎068/387 6000, ⓦwww.saigonninhchuhotel.com.vn; ❻–❼) has beautifully furnished, thick-carpeted, spacious rooms, and the executive suites even have beach views from the bath: there's also a big pool, tennis courts and a classy restaurant. In the centre of the beach, the *Den Gion Resort* (☎068/387 4047-8, ⓦwww.dengion-resort.com; ❸) draws heavily on the region's Cham heritage for its design, and the rooms are smartly decorated if rather small. Next door, the *Hoang Cau* (☎068/389 0600, ⓦwww.hoancautourist .com.vn; ❷–❸) is rather bizarre with rooms made to look like old tree stumps, and though they're ugly and cramped together, inside they are spacious and good value, and very popular with the Vietnamese. The resort also features life-size statues of Snow White and the seven dwarfs as well as traditional Vietnamese characters.

The Town

There's really nothing of interest in Phan Rang itself, unless you fancy wandering round the 150-year-old **Quan Cong Temple**, situated in the centre of town on Thong Nhat. Its faded, pink-wash walls rise to three consecutive roofs, each draped upon huge red wooden piles imported from China, and laden with fanciful figurines and dragons. Quan Cong is at the head of the third and final chamber, framed by ornate gilt woodwork and rows of pikes. Cham people sometimes come to shop at the **market** immediately below the pagoda, but for closer encounters you'll need to venture out to Tuan Tu (see below).

The Cham towers and Tuan Tu Village

Elevated with fitting grandeur on a granite mound known as Trau Hill, the **Po Klong Garai Cham towers** (daily 7.30am–6pm; small admission fee) are far worthier of your time than anything in the town centre. Dating back to around 1400 and the rule of King Jaya Simharvarman III, the complex comprises a *kalan*, or sanctuary, a smaller gate tower and a repository, under whose boat-shaped roof offerings would have been placed. It's the 25-metre-high *kalan*, though, that's of most interest. From a distance its stippled body impresses; up close, you see a bas-relief of six-armed Shiva cavorting above doorposts etched with Cham inscriptions and ringed by arches crackling with stonework flames, while other gods sit cross-legged in niches elsewhere around the exterior walls. Push deeper into the *kalan*'s belly and there's a

The kingdom of Champa

The weathered but beguiling **towers** that punctuate the scenery upcountry from Phan Thiet to Da Nang are the only remaining legacy of **Champa**, an Indianized kingdom that ruled parts of central and southern Vietnam for over fourteen centuries. In 192 AD, Chinese annals reported that a man named Khu Lien (later to be titled King Sri Mara) had gathered a chain of coastal chiefdoms in the region around Quang Tri in defiance of the expansionism of the Han Chinese to the north, and established an independent state which the Chinese referred to as **Lin Yi**. Subsequently, Champa unified an elongated strip from Phan Thiet to Dong Hoi, and by the end of the fourth century Champa comprised four provinces: **Amaravati**, around Hué and Da Nang; **Vijaya**, centred around Quy Nhon; **Kauthara**, in the Nha Trang region; and **Panduranga**, which corresponds to present-day Phan Thiet and up to Phan Rang. The unified kingdom's first capital, established in the fourth century in Amaravati, was **Simhapura** ("Lion City"); nearby, just outside present-day Hoi An, **My Son**, Champa's holiest site, was established (see p.280).

Concertinaed between the Khmers to the south and the clans of the Vietnamese (initially under Chinese rule) to the north, Champa's history was characterized by consistent **feuding with the neighbours**. Between the third and fifth centuries, relations with the **Chinese** followed a cyclical pattern of antagonism and tribute, culminating in the 446 AD sacking of Simhapura when the Chinese made off with a fifty-tonne, solid gold Buddha statue. Wars raged with the **Khmers** in the twelfth and thirteenth centuries, one fateful retaliatory Cham offensive culminating in the destruction of Angkor. With the installation on Champa's throne of warmongering **Binasuor** in 1361, three decades of Cham expansionism ensued; upon his death in 1390, though, the Viets regained all lost ground, and soon secured the region around Indrapura. In a decisive push south, the Viets, led by **Le Thanh Tong**, overran Vijaya in 1471; Champa shifted its capital south again, but by now it was becoming profoundly marginalized. For a few centuries more, the Cham kings still claimed nominal rule of the area around Phan Rang and Phan Thiet, but in 1697 the last *mukha* lingam fashioned in a likeness of the Cham king, Po Klong Garai, after whom the complex is named. In days gone by, the statue of Shiva's bull (Nandi) that stands in the vestibule would have been "fed" by farmers wishing for good harvests; nowadays it gets a feed only at the annual **Kate Festival** (the Cham New Year), a great spectacle if you're here around October. On the eve of the festival, there's traditional Cham music and dance at the complex, followed, the next morning, by a lively procession bearing the king's raiment to the tower.

To reach the complex, take the road to Da Lat for 7km, then veer north for a further 500m (about $5 return by xe om from Phan Rang). Even if you don't plan to visit the towers, you may find yourself taking a break here, as all open-tour buses pull in for a short stop.

If Po Klong Garai inspires further interest in Cham towers, you could make the trickier journey out to **Po Re Me Tower**. Like its near-neighbour, the tower (which draws its name from the last Cham king) enjoys a fine hilltop location, though its four storeys tapering to a lingam are sturdier and less finished than Po Klong Garai. Its high point is the splendid bas-relief in the *kalan*'s entrance, depicting Shiva manifest in the image of mustachioed King Po Re Me waggling his arms, and watched over by two Nandis. Po Re Me is also a focus of Cham festivities during the Kate Festival. To reach the tower, follow Highway 1 south for 8km and then bear west at Hau Sanh; the track is hard to find, so a xe om (about $6 return from Phan Rang) is a wise option.

independent Cham king died, and what little remained of the kingdom became a Vietnamese vassal state. **Minh Mang** dissolved even this in the 1820s, and the last Cham king fled to Cambodia. Most of the estimated 100,000 **descendants** of the Cham kingdom reside around Phan Rang and Phan Thiet, though there are also tiny pockets in Tay Ninh and Chau Doc.

Champa's **economy** hinged around agriculture, wet-rice cultivation, fishing and maritime trade, which it carried out with Indians, Chinese, Japanese and Arabs through **ports** at Hoi An and Quy Nhon. Exposure to Indian traders in the fourth century had a particularly strong influence upon the kingdom's culture, agriculture and religion. Though Buddhism flourished for a time in the ninth century, **Hinduism** was the dominant religion in Champa until Islam started to make inroads in the second half of the fourteenth century. Orthodox Hindu gods, and in particular Shiva, were fused with past kings, in accordance with the belief that kings were *devaraja* – reincarnations of deities.

To honour their gods, Cham kings sponsored the construction of the **religious edifices** that still stand today. The typical Cham **temple complex** is centred around the **kalan**, or sanctuary, normally pyramidal inside, and containing a lingam, or phallic representation of Shiva, set on a dais that was grooved to channel off water used in purification rituals. Having first cleansed themselves and prayed in the **mandapa**, or meditation hall, worshippers would then have proceeded under a **gate tower** and below the *kalan*'s (normally) east-facing vestibule into the sanctuary. Any ritual objects pertaining to worship were kept in a nearby repository room, which normally sported a boat-shaped roof.

Cham towers crop up at regular intervals all the way up the coast from Phan Thiet to Da Nang, and many of them have been restored in recent years. A handful of sites representing the **highlights** of what remains of Champa civilization would include: Po Klong Garai towers (see above); Thap Doi towers (see p.256); Po Re Me Tower (see p.239); My Son (see p.280); Po Nagar towers (see p.249).

There's still a Cham presence around Phan Rang. **Tuan Tu Village** is home to more than a thousand Cham people, whom you'll recognize by the headcloths that they favour over conical hats. Largely Muslim, they maintain an unpretentious, 1966-built mosque free of any trappings, not even a minaret. Tuan Tu is 3–4km along a track that veers east 350m below the bridge at the bottom of town; a xe om shouldn't be more than 70,000đ for the round trip. Finally, about 15km north of Phan Rang, directly beside Highway 1, look out for two recently-restored Cham towers called **Ho Lai**.

Ninh Chu Beach

A more indolent alternative to trekking around Phan Rang's Cham towers is to visit **Ninh Chu Beach**, a reasonably clean and wide crescent of sand that's at least soft, if not exactly golden. Ninh Chu doesn't have the same pulling power for foreigners as Mui Ne or Nha Trang, but its beach is good for swimming, sunbathing, beach games and jogging too. With several resorts located here, it's worth considering as a place to rest up, particularly midweek, when it can be very quiet. If you're here at a weekend, be prepared for crowds of noisy teenagers. To reach Ninh Chu, turn east onto 16 Thang 4 just south of the *Huu Nghi Hotel* and keep going straight for about 5km.

Eating and drinking

Eating out in Phan Rang is a bit tricky, as nowhere has an English menu: *Quan 172* at 376 Thong Nhat serves cheap and tasty rice and noodle dishes, but you'll need your phrasebook. Things are a bit easier on Ninh Chu Beach, as the restaurants at both the *Saigon-Ninh Chu* and the *Den Gion Resort* feature some Western as well as Vietnamese dishes on their menus, as well as offering good views out to sea.

Nha Trang and around

From Phan Rang, Highway 1 pushes on against a backdrop of first sugar-cane plantations, then toothpaste-white salt flats and shrimp farms around **Cam Ranh Bay** on its way to the city of **NHA TRANG**. Nestled below the bottom lip of the Cai River, some 260km north of Phan Thiet, Nha Trang has earned its place as Vietnam's top beach destination, despite stiff competition from places like Phu Quoc and Mui Ne.

Much has changed here since the days when the Cham people knew the area as Eatrang, the "river of reeds", and the city now supports a population of over 300,000. By the time the Nguyen lords wrested this patch of the country from Champa in the mid-seventeenth century, the intriguing **Po Nagar Cham towers** had already stood, stacked impressively on a hillside above the Cai, for over 700 years. They remain Nha Trang's most famous image, yet it's the **coastline** that brings tourists flocking: boasting the finest municipal **beach** in Vietnam, Nha Trang offers splendid scope for mellowing out on the sand, with hawkers on hand to supply paperbacks, fresh pineapple and massages. **Scuba-diving** classes and all kinds of **water sports**, such as **windsurfing**, **kayaking** and **parasailing**, are available here, and local companies offer popular day-trips to Nha Trang's outlying **islands** that combine island visits and **snorkelling** with an onboard feast of seafood. Bear in mind that there is a rainy season in Nha Trang, around November and December, when the sea gets choppy and the beach loses its appeal.

Nha Trang is much more than a pretty strip of sand, however. The southern streets around **Biet Thu** are packed with great-value budget hotels and restaurants, plus some stylish boutiques and bars that are actually worth hanging out in. The **downtown** area, which swirls aound **Cho Dam** ("central market"), its colourful epicentre, heaves with life; while the route up to the Po Nagar towers escorts you past the city's huge and photogenic fishing fleet.

Arrival and city transport

Nha Trang's **long-distance bus station** (☎058/382 2192) sits 1km west of the city centre at 58, 23 Thang 10; the **train station** (ticket office daily 7.30–11am & 1.30–9pm; ☎058/382 2113) is a few hundred metres east along Thai Nguyen, a continuation of the same road. Flights into the city land at the **airport** (☎058/398 9918), at Cam Ranh, 35km south of the city. From here take a bus (25,000đ) or taxi (around 200,000đ, depending on where you're staying) to Nha Trang, and enjoy the superb coastal views along the way.

Nha Trang isn't a very large city, so **walking** may well be your means of covering the ground – especially if a daily pilgrimage to the municipal beach marks the extent of your travels. Should you plan to stray a little further afield, **bicycle rental** is the most efficient and enjoyable way to go. Bicycles are available for around 20,000đ per day at most of the city's hotels, though less active souls will always find **cyclo** and **xe om** aplenty. Fully fledged **car tours** of the region (around $40–50 per day) can be arranged by tour operators (see "Listings", p.248), who also offer day-trips to the islands off Nha Trang and minibus tours of the central highlands.

Accommodation

The fact that Nha Trang is chock-full of hotels doesn't seem to be discouraging developers, and the city's already wide choice of **accommodation** just keeps on growing. Beachfront monoliths are gradually blocking out any sea view from the mini-hotels on backstreets of the town. Even so, it's worth bearing in mind that the city draws Vietnamese as well as foreign tourists, and that there can be difficulties finding a room over public holidays, when prices rise. The good news is that Nha Trang offers some of the best accommodation options outside Ho Chi Minh City or Hanoi, with great deals hidden away in the backstreets. Budget travellers, in particular, should head straight for "Hotel Alley", beside 64 Tran Phu, where a clutch of newish mini-hotels vie for custom.

Budget

Chi Thanh 17b Hoang Hoa Tham ☎058/352 1092, ✉chi_thanh_Hotel@yahoo.com. This mini-hotel with clean, decent-sized rooms, all with a/c, is one of Nha Trang's longest-standing budget options. ❷

Dong Phuong 1 101–103 Nguyen Thien Thuat ☎058/352 6896, ✉dongphuongnt@dng.vnn.vn. Hugely popular family-run hotel, and one of many budget options clustered around this area. Functional but spacious rooms, ranging from small fan rooms to the enormous, a/c penthouse. ❶–❸

Golden Dragon 78/36 Tue Tinh ☎058/352 7117, ✇www.goldendragonhotel.com.vn. A cosy and welcoming mini-hotel tucked away down a quiet

backstreet in the south of town, just 5min from the beach, with good-value a/c rooms. The latest proud addition is a tiny pool and sundeck on the fourth floor. ❷–❸

Hoang Long 30/12 Hoang Hoa Tham ☎058/352 5316. Tucked away down an alley opposite the *Chi Thanh*, this place offers compact fan or a/c rooms at very good prices. ❶–❷

My Hoa 7 Hang Ca ☎058/381 0111, ✉myhoahotel@dng.vnn.vn. This smart, family-run mini-hotel in a central location is a decent budget option. The tidy rooms all have satellite TV, hot water and en-suite showers. ❶–❷

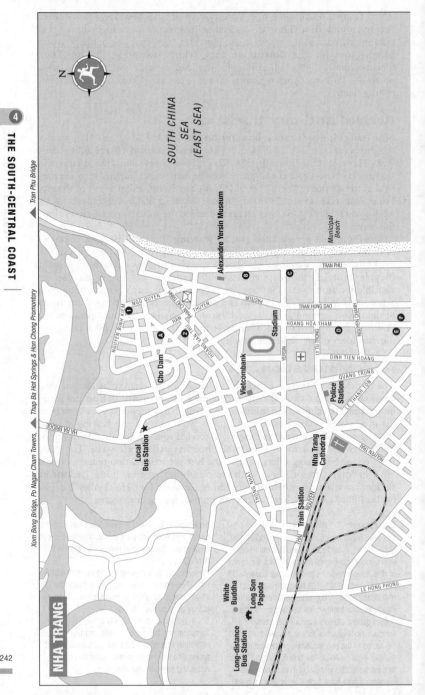

NHA TRANG

SOUTH CHINA SEA
(EAST SEA)

Municipal Beach

Alexandre Yersin Museum

TRAN PHU

TRAN HUNG DAO

HOANG HOA THAM

DINH TIEN HOANG

QUANG TRUNG

Stadium

Vietcombank

Cho Dam

NGO QUYEN

NGUYEN BINH KIEM

HAN

HOANG VAN THU

THONG NHAT

PHAN CHU TRINH

THUYEN

PASTEUR

YERSIN

LY TU TRONG

NGUYEN CHANH

LE THANH TON

Police Station

Local Bus Station

HA RA BRIDGE

Nha Trang Cathedral

Train Station

THAI NGUYEN

NGUYEN TRAI

LE HONG PHONG

White Buddha

Long Son Pagoda

Long-distance Bus Station

N

A B C D E F

1 2

Tran Phu Bridge

Xom Bong Bridge, Po Nagar Cham Towers, Thap Ba Hot Springs & Hon Chong Promontory

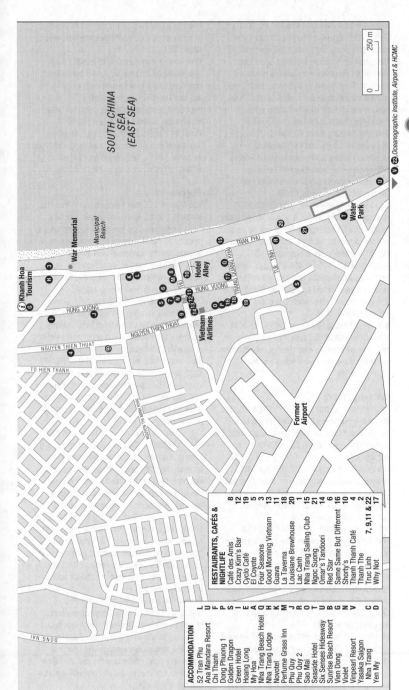

SOUTH CHINA
SEA
(EAST SEA)

War Memorial

Municipal
Beach

Khanh Hoa
Tourism

HUNG VUONG

NGUYEN THIEN THUAT

NGUYEN THIEN THUAT

TO HIEN THANH

HUNG VUONG

TRAN PHU

Hotel
Alley

TRAN QUANG KHAI

Vietnam
Airlines

LE THANH TON

LE TINH

Former
Airport

Water
Park

0   250 m

V. ❷❷ Oceanographic Institute, Airport & HCMC

ACCOMMODATION
52 Tran Phu L
Ana Mandara Resort .... U
Chi Thanh .... F
Dong Phuong 1 .... P
Golden Dragon .... S
Green Hotel I
Hoang Long .... E
My Hoa .... A
Nha Trang Beach Hotel ..... Q
Nha Trang Lodge .... H
Novotel .... K
Perfume Grass Inn .... M
Phu Quy .... J
Phu Quy 2 .... R
Sao Mai .... O
Seaside Hotel .... T
Six Senses Hideaway .... U
Sunrise Beach Resort ...... B
Vien Dong .... G
Violet .... N
Vinpearl Resort V
Yasaka Saigon
Nha Trang C
Yen My .... D

RESTAURANTS, CAFÉS &
NIGHTLIFE
Café des Amis 8
Crazy Kim's Bar 12
Cyclo Café 19
El Coyote 5
Four Seasons 3
Good Morning Vietnam 13
Guava 11
La Taverna 18
Lac Canh 20
Louisiane Brewhouse 1
Nha Trang Sailing Club 15
Ngoc Suong 21
Omar's Tandoori 14
Red Star 6
Same Same But Different ... 16
Shorty's 10
Thanh Thanh Café 4
Thanh The 2
Truc Linh .... 7, 9, 11 & 22
Why Not 17

Perfume Grass Inn 4a Biet Thu ☏058/352 4286, ⓦwww.perfume-grass.com. This reasonably priced place has lots of character. All the rooms are tastefully furnished, some with wooden floors, others with reclining chairs and bathtubs. There's also an attractive, cheap café downstairs and a relaxing rooftop terrace. Their second branch, with slightly cheaper prices, is on "Hotel Alley", next to 64 Tran Phu. ❷–❸

Phu Quy 54 Hung Vuong ☏058/352 1609, ⓔphuquyhotel@dng.vnn.vn. Welcoming, reasonably priced family-run mini-hotel. Rooms, with either a/c or fans, are small, but all are spotlessly clean; there's also a small rooftop terrace with sun-loungers. ❷–❸

Sao Mai 99 Nguyen Thien Thuat ☏058/352 6412, ⓔsaomai2ht@dng.vnn.vn. A reliable budget option, which has a $3 per night dorm, as well as en-suite doubles. A second branch at 96b Tran Phu, near the beach, is slightly more expensive. ❶–❷

Seaside 96b Tran Phu ☏058/352 8343. Rooms here have solid furniture and a cosy feel. The place is well maintained and staff are very friendly, plus it's right in front of the beach; one of the best-value options in town. ❷–❸

Yen My 22 Hoang Hoa Tham ☏058/352 5064, ⓔyenmyhotel@hotmail.com. This mini-hotel run by a friendly family is a good-value budget option, with very cheap a/c or fan rooms and free internet. ❶–❷

Moderate

52 Tran Phu 52 Tran Phu ☏058/352 4228. One of the few remaining mid-range options on the central beachfront, offering comfortable rooms with beach views for just $25, all with a/c and hot water. ❸

Green Hotel 6 Hung Vuong ☏058/352 5405, ⓦwww.greenhotelnhatrang.com. Behind the garish exterior, its rooms are comfortable with bamboo and rattan fixtures and furnishings, making it a good mid-range option. ❺–❻

Nha Trang Beach Hotel 4 Tran Quang Khai ☏058/524468, ⓦwww.nhatrangbeachhotel.com. vn. Smart mini-hotel in the budget district with a/c, hot water, TV and comfortable furnishings. ❸

Nha Trang Lodge 42 Tran Phu ☏058/352 1500, ⓦwww.nhatranglodge.com. With over 120 rooms on twelve floors, some with fantastic views of the beach, this is one of Nha Trang's flashiest and trendiest hotels. ❹–❺

Phu Quy 2 1 Tue Tinh ☏058/352 6060, ⓦwww .phuquyhotel.com.vn. A very smart mid-range option run by the owners of one of the town's best budget hotels, this 15-storey building offers some of the city's best beach views, especially from the upper-floor rooms and the tiny rooftop pool. Rooms are well-furnished and have wood floors. ❹

Vien Dong 1 Tran Hung Dao ☏058/352 3606, ⓔviendonghtl@dng.vnn.vn. Ageing but well-run operation, counting swimming pool, tennis courts and satellite TV among its amenities. Rooms in the main building are scrupulously clean, but those in the poolside annexe are less polished. ❸–❹

Violet 12 Biet Thu ☏058/352 2314, ⓦwww .violethotel.com.vn. This well-maintained mini-hotel on trendy Biet Thu has a small pool and restaurant, as well as smart rooms with new furnishings. ❸

Expensive

Ana Mandara Resort Southern end of Tran Phu ☏058/352 2222, ⓦwww.sixsenses.com. Nha Trang's most luxurious low-rise resort and the only property on this long beach with direct access. It features dreamy bungalows with all mod cons and some traditional touches, including ethnic-minority tapestries. Facilities include two pools, tennis courts, a spa and beach restaurant. ❼

Novotel 50 Tran Phu ☏058/322 1027, ⓦwww .novotel.com. Muscling in amongst the big boys on beachfront Tran Phu, this stylish hotel provides extremely comfortable rooms at competitive prices, along with a pool, spa, restaurant and bar. ❻

Six Senses Hideaway Ninh Van Bay ☏058/372 8222, ⓦwww.sixsenses.com. Choose from beach villas, rock villas, hill-top villas, over-water villas or spa-suite villas on an idyllic offshore island, but make sure you can afford the $500-plus per night price tag. ❼

Sunrise Beach Resort 12-14 Tran Phu ☏058/382 0999, ⓦwww.sunrisenhatrang .com.vn. Enjoying a superb location towards the northern end of the beach, this is Nha Trang's leading high-rise hotel, with a classical colonial design and every conceivable luxury, including sea-view jacuzzis on the balconies of top suites. ❼

Vinpearl Resort 7 Tran Phu ☏058/391 11166, ⓦwww.vinpearlresort.com. This luxurious resort is actually located on Hon Tre out in the bay, and features nearly 500 well-equipped rooms as well as the biggest pool in Southeast Asia (5000sqm). It is accessed by speedboat or cable car from the southern end of Tran Phu. ❼

Yasaka Saigon Nha Trang 18 Tran Phu ☏058/382 0090, ⓦwww.yasanhatrang.com. One of Nha Trang's most impressive high-rise hotels, in a prime location along Tran Phu. Facilities include a fitness centre, swimming pool and tennis courts. All rooms face the sea, the higher ones with fabulous views, and are well appointed and chintzy. ❻–❼

The city centre and beach

The disorienting knot of roads constituting **central Nha Trang** hugs the southern lip of the Cai River. Its beating heart is the hectic central market, semicircular **Cho Dam**, which stands on land reclaimed from the Cai; the market positively churns with life from morning to night. Most new arrivals in the city, however, make a beeline for its **municipal beach**, a grand six-kilometre scythe of soft yellow sand lapped by rolling waves, whose upper extent lies five minutes' stroll east of the market. There's a pleasant promenade running along behind the beach, with some very unusual modern sculptures and topiary set in trim lawns. The tourists who descend on the beach every day are promptly besieged by traders hawking massages, tropical fruits, t-shirts and paperbacks, though it's possible to escape their clutches by wandering further north or south along the beach or at the pool at the *Louisiane Brewhouse* (free for customers or 25,000đ). There's also a small but well-organized **water park** (daily 8.30am–5pm; 30,000đ, children 20,000đ) at the south end of Tran Phu. To avoid the midday sun, locals wait until the hour before dusk to do their bathing, at which time the surf is peppered with squealing, splashing kids.

The Alexandre Yersin Museum

A local sight well worth visiting is at the top of Tran Phu in the Pasteur Institute, where the **Alexandre Yersin Museum** (Mon–Fri 7.30–11am & 2–4.30pm; 26,000đ) profiles the life of the Swiss-French scientist who travelled to Southeast Asia in 1889 as a ship's doctor. Yersin developed a great love of the country and learned to speak Vietnamese fluently. He was responsible for the founding of Da Lat (he recognized the beneficial effects of the climate there for Europeans), and settled in Nha Trang in 1893. By the time of his death in 1943, Yersin had become a local hero, thanks not to his greatest achievement – the discovery of a plague bacillus in Hong Kong in 1894 – but rather to his educational work in sanitation and agriculture, and to his ability to predict typhoons and thus save the lives of fishermen. Significantly, his name is still given to streets, not only in Nha Trang but around the country, sharing an honour generally only granted to Vietnamese heroes. Yersin's desk is here, with his own French translations of Horace still slotted under its glass top; so too, are the barometers and telescope he used to forecast the weather, and a model boat presented to him by grateful fishermen. But it's the doctor's library, where French, English, Latin and Vietnamese tomes cover subjects from medicine to horticulture, astrology to bacteriology, that conveys most strongly Yersin's thirst for knowledge. Guided tours are given regularly, and a short video on Yersin's life is also available for viewing. The institute (which Yersin set up in 1895) is still active today, and you'll see white-coated technicians buzzing about.

Along Thai Nguyen

Thread your way southwest from the Pasteur Institute, and after a few minutes you'll hit Thai Nguyen, home to two of Nha Trang's best-known sights. Presiding over the street's eastern end, the stolid, grey-brick **Nha Trang Cathedral**, built in the 1930s, casts its shadow over the sloping cobbled track that winds round to its front doors from Nguyen Trai. Under the lofty, vaulted ceilings within the cathedral's dowdy exterior, vivid stained-glass windows depict Christ, Mary, Joseph, Joan of Arc and St Theresa. If you feel as if you're being watched as you climb up to the cathedral, it's probably the huge white Buddha image seated on a hillside above **Long Son Pagoda**, 800m west along Thai Nguyen. Stone gateposts topped by lotus buds mark the entrance to the 1930s-built pagoda. An impressive bronze Buddha stands at the head of the altar,

Scuba-diving and water sports

Nha Trang is the **dive centre of Vietnam**, as is well evidenced by the number of dive companies that operate here. It's best avoided between October and December, when the waters can get stirred up and murky, but during the dry season (Jan–May) there are dive boats kitting out and casting off every day to one of over twenty dive sites in the region. A typical day out, including a couple of dives and lunch, costs around $50 for an experienced diver, more if you need instruction. Two reliable companies are Rainbow Divers (☎058/352 4351, ⓦwww.divevietnam.com), which has a base at 90a Hung Vuong, and Sailing Club Divers (☎058/352 2788, ⓦwww.sailingclubvietnam .com), with offices in front of the *Nha Trang Sailing Club* at 72–74 Tran Phu, Both offer PADI courses, including a Discover Scuba Diving course for beginners.

If you'd rather get your kicks above water, head on down to the stretch of beach beside the *Louisiane Brewhouse*, where watersports equipment can be rented. For a mere $20 you can scare the wits out of swimmers by zapping them with a **jet-ski** spray for fifteen minutes, but keep in mind that you will be held responsible for any injuries or damages. Less environmentally disastrous are the sports of **parasailing**, **windsurfing** and **kayaking**, with prices varying according to activity.

and there are the usual capering dragons on the eaves, but it's the huge **White Buddha**, 152 steps up the hillside behind, that's the pagoda's greatest asset – and Nha Trang's most recognizable landmark. Crafted in 1963 to symbolize the Buddhist struggle against the repressive Diem regime, around its lotus-shaped pedestal are carved images of the monks and nuns who set fire to themselves in protest, among them Thich Quang Duc (see box, p.99).

Eating and drinking

Finding a decent place to **eat** presents no problem in Nha Trang, with seafood its speciality. There is no particular district of town to head for, though the budget area around Biet Thu has a wide variety of places. You don't need to leave the beach to eat during the day, as strolling vendors are on hand with their tempting snacks. There's also a night market south of the water park with many cheap food stalls.

Restaurants and cafés

Café des Amis 2d Biet Thu. Perennial favourite and heaving most nights, serving well-prepared Vietnamese and Western dishes with a good vegetarian selection; the steamed fish with ginger is particularly recommended. Most dishes are 25,000–35,000đ. 7am–10.30pm.

Cyclo Café 130 Nguyen Thien Thuat. A friendly ambience, along with a solid menu of Vietnamese and Italian food (around 40,000–50,000đ per dish), plus locally-brewed beer make this place worth checking out. 7.30am–10pm.

El Coyote 76 Hung Vuong. Tex-Mex dishes like chilli con carne and empanadas, as well as French dishes at around 80,000–90,000đ, served up in a cosy setting. 3pm–11pm

Four Seasons 40 Tran Phu. This smart beachfront restaurant serves seafood specials at around 80,000–100,000đ, plus a good range of shakes and ice creams. 7am–11pm.

Good Morning Vietnam 19b Biet Thu. Another branch of the successful nationwide chain, offering reliable pasta and pizza for around 100,000đ per dish. 10am–11pm.

La Taverna 115 Nguyen Thien Thuat. Authentic Italian atmosphere and food at this welcoming place in the budget district. Pizzas for around 110,000đ. 10am–11pm.

Louisiane Brewhouse Tran Phu Beach. This beachfront place has it all – an excellent range of Vietnamese and Western dishes, such as chicken escalope for 85,000đ, a sushi corner, a pizza corner, home-made cakes and pastries, delicious local beers, a swimming pool (free for customers), pool table and live music three nights a week. 7am–1am.

Lac Canh 44 Nguyen Binh Kiem. A table-side grill that's hugely popular among locals; some might bridle at its brusque staff, and at the eye-watering smoke off the cooked-at-table barbecues, but the food (50,000–70,000đ), compensates for these discomforts. 9am–9.30pm.

Omar's Tandoori Cafe 89B Nguyen Thien Thuat and 96a/8 Tran Phu. The place to go when you get the urge for an Indian curry. A chicken korma will set you back around 70,000đ. 7am–10pm

🏃 **Ngoc Suong** 96 Tran Phu. Smart seafood restaurant to the south of the town centre, with prices according to weight – pick your choice from a fabulous fresh display and have it prepared in a variety of ways. Low-key live music gives the place a sophisticated ambience. 10am–11pm.

Red Star 27a Hung Vuong. This place is well set up for travellers and gets plenty stopping by for its filling, good-value breakfasts, shakes or curries. They also offer cooking classes each morning. 8.30am–10.30pm.

Same Same But Different 111b Nguyen Thien Thuat. One of many places in the budget district offering a wide range of Vietnamese and Western

dishes, including good muesli, at very reasonable prices. 7am–10pm.

Shorty's 1e Biet Thu. Full English breakfast, jacket potatoes, shepherd's pie and much more comfort food, all competitively priced, at this welcoming café near the beach. 6am–11pm.

Thanh Thanh Café 10 Nguyen Thien Thuat ☎058/382 4413. Extensive menu of reasonably priced Vietnamese, Western and vegetarian dishes, but it's the wood-fire range of pizzas that is their forte; also offers city deliveries. 7am–9pm.

Thanh The 3 Phan Chu Trinh. A bright, open-fronted seafood restaurant on Phan Chu Trinh; the shrimps grilled with garlic (90,000đ) won't disappoint. 7.30am–10pm.

Truc Linh 11 and 18 Biet Thu, 80 Hung Vuong and 83 Tran Phu. Very successful operation serving up a good range of Western and Vietnamese dishes, with seafood the speciality. Prices are a little above average but the food is still good value. The branch at 18 Biet Thu is the most atmospheric. 8am–10pm.

Nightlife

Nha Trang has the advantage over Mui Ne when it comes to its buzzing **nightlife**. There are plenty of chillout and party places around the budget district and, while nightspots along the beachfront tend to be a bit pricier than ones located inland, all of them have generous **happy hours**, guaranteed to bring you back for more. Occasional crackdowns have the bars closing at midnight, but left to their own devices, most bar-owners will stay open till the wee hours.

Crazy Kim's Bar 19 Biet Thu. Two-foot-tall cocktails, happy hour that runs noon to midnight, great selection of CDs, hedonistic party atmosphere and hangover breakfasts make this place very popular with expats, tourists and brave locals, who rave till late. Proceeds from the bar go towards helping Nha Trang's street children. 9.30am–late.

Guava 17 Biet Thu. This well-designed bar, with pool table, sports on TV, funky sounds and some weird cocktails, is one of the city's most popular night haunts.11am–late.

Nha Trang Sailing Club 72–74 Tran Phu. For some years this has been a favourite spot for an eclectic group of party animals. It draws a well-heeled expat crowd and hordes of tourists to its refined beachfront bar which gets progressively less refined as the night wears on. 7am–late.

Why Not 24 Tran Quang Khai. Big place with inside and outside seating, pool table, dance floor and comfy lounge area. Serving beer and spirits, with live music some nights. 9am–late.

Listings

Airlines Vietnam Airlines, 91 Nguyen Thien Thuat (daily 7–11.30am & 1.30–5pm; ☎058/352 6768), and at Khanh Hoa Tourism, 1 Tran Hung Dao (Mon–Fri 7.30–11am & 2–4.30pm; ☎058/352 5036).
Bank Vietcombank, 17 Quang Trung, changes cash and traveller's cheques, and has an ATM. There's also a convenient branch of Agribank at 2 Hung Vuong.
Bicycles and motorbikes Just about everybody and their grandmother, including most hotels, wants to rent you a bike or motorbike in Nha Trang,

so you shouldn't have difficulty finding one; about $1 for bicycles, $4–5 for a motorbike per day; just check that it's roadworthy.
Books The best selection of new books is at the brand-new Fahasa Books at 11 Ly Thanh Ton. At Shorty's, 1e Biet Thu, you'll find a good selection of second-hand fiction and non-fiction, salvaged from the ghosts of travellers past.
Car rental Most tour operators, including Khanh Hoa Tourism at 1 Tran Hung Dao (☎058/352 8100),

can arrange car rental with driver for $40–45 per day; minibuses are also available at a slightly higher rate.

Hospital 19 Yersin, below the city stadium ☏058/382 2168.

Internet access There are hundreds of places offering internet access in Nha Trang, including 24d Nguyen Thiet Thuat, where rates are a standard 100đ per minute.

Mini–markets Dai Thuan Mini Mart, 17a Biet Thu; Maxi-Mart, 66 Quang Trung; ABC Bakery, 76a Ly Thanh Ton.

Pharmacy 27 Le Thanh Ton.

Police 5 Ly Tu Trong ☏058/382 2400.

Post office 4 Le Loi (daily 7am–9pm), has fax, IDD facilities, internet access, poste restante and DHL courier desk (closed Sun); there are also several other small post offices scattered around town.

Souvenirs Vietnam Pure Silk, 19 Le Thanh Ton, has ready-to-wear silk garments and tailor shop plus embroidery, artwork and ethnic souvenirs; Bambou, 15 Biet Thu, offers original-design T-shirts at $10 each, plus other bright and colourful souvenirs; Lac Viet, 4c Biet Thu, specializes in lacquerware ornaments and wood carvings; XQ Arts and Crafts Centre, 64 Tran Phu, displays and sells embroidered pictures, some of which are stunning works of art, from $30 upwards.

Tour operators Con Se Tre Tourist, 100/16 Tran Phu ☏058/352 7522; Hanh Café, 10 Hung Vuong ☏058/352 7467, ✉hanhcafe@dng.vnn.vn; Khanh Hoa Tourism, 1 Tran Hung Dao (☏058/352 8100, ⓦwww.nhatrangtourism.com.vn) is the official government office, so the best place to go for visa extensions; Mama Linh, 23C Biet Thu ☏058/052 2844; Sinh Café, 2a Biet Thu ☏058/352 2982, ✉info@sinhcafevn.com; TM Brothers Café, 34 Nguyen Thien Thuat ☏058/352 3556, ✉tmbrotherscafevietnam@yahoo.com.

Around Nha Trang

Several of Nha Trang's attractions are just outside the city, including the **Po Nagar Cham towers**, **Thap Ba Hot Springs** and the **National Oceanographic Institute**. A short distance north of town lie several natural areas that are worth exploring, namely the **Hon Chong Promontory**, **Monkey Island** and **Ba Ho Falls**, which can be easily visited by renting a motorbike or xe om, or joining a tour. However, the most popular activity for most visitors is to take a **boat trip to the islands** that speckle the waters around Nha Trang (see box opposite).

Hon Tre Island

The biggest island in the bay, **HON TRE** can be reached by the impressive new **cable car** (daily 9am–10pm) that runs from Phu Quy pier, next to the harbour. Over three kilometres in length, it is the world's longest cross-sea cable car: the journey takes around ten minutes and costs 100,000đ return. Once on the island, you can visit the *Vinpearl Resort* (see p.244) and the **Vinpearl Land Amusement Park** (☏058/359 0111, ⓦwww.vinpearlland.com; 250,000đ, children 175,000đ), which includes a waterpark with slides and flumes, a mini-oceanarium, 4-D movies, a shopping mall, and some rides.

The National Oceanographic Institute

Located right beside Cau Da Wharf, 6km south of Nha Trang, the **National Oceanographic Institute** (daily 6am–6pm; 15,000đ), housed in a colonial mansion and established in 1923, is a veritable Frankenstein's lab of pickling jars and glass cases yielding crustaceans, fish, seaweed and coral. In one room an eighteen-metre-long humpback whale skeleton is displayed, plus a hammerhead shark and bow-mouth guitarfish. If you've been out snorkelling you might spot some recent acquaintances in the aquarium's twenty or so tanks of primary-coloured live fishes and sea horses. There are three large open ponds in the forecourt, home to horseshoe crabs, zebra sharks and various local species of fish.

Boat trips to the islands

Several companies in Nha Trang (see "Listings" opposite) offer day-trips to a selection of islands, including a stop for **snorkelling** and a **seafood lunch** on board – all for around $6–8 per person. However, to fully enjoy the day, you'll need to fork out for several extras if you don't want to sit on the boat and wait till everyone comes back. All the companies offer similar tours, though each boat trip tends to cater to a specific crowd: if you're after a peaceful, relaxing time you won't want to be stuck with a group of party animals and loud music, as tends to be the case on Mama Linh's trips. Con Se Tre (see "Listings", opposite) runs slightly more upmarket tours at around $25 per person, which include a visit to their resort on Hon Tre. It's also worth contacting diving operators (see box, p.246) who sometimes let people join them for snorkelling at a reduced daily rate: these trips can be great fun on a sunny day, but they are no fun at all in stormy weather.

On a typical island day tour, you'll be picked up from your hotel, taken to Cau Da Wharf, 6km south of the town centre, and shuffled on to one of many boats jostling in the harbour. As the boat casts off at around 9.30am, you'll pass beneath the cable car to Hon Tre (see below), then chug between islands for about half an hour to **HON MUN** (Black Island), named after the dark cliffs that rear up from it. There's no beach to speak of on Hon Mun, but the island boasts one of the best places for snorkelling in the area, with some great coral. Boats hang around for an hour or so while people snorkel over the corals or sunbathe on the boat, and there are frequently diving groups here too. There's a 40,000đ charge to snorkel in this "protected area", though it's not clear quite how it's being protected.

After a break for lunch in the shelter of **HON MOT**, boats head for **HON TAM**, where there's a small beach (10,000đ entry), and you get the chance to stretch on the sand or splash about in the sea for an hour before heading for the final destination, the **Tri Nguyen Aquarium** (25,000đ) on **HON MIEU**. The setting here is wonderfully kitsch: visitors approach the site through giant lobsters and past cement sharks, and the strange building that houses the aquarium looks like a galleon dragged up from the depths and draped in seaweed. Inside, the tanks feature black-tipped sharks, bug-eyed groupers, hawksbill turtles and colourful sea anemones. Finally the boat heads back to the mainland and visitors are whisked back to their hotels.

Po Nagar Cham towers

One of Nha Trang's most popular sights is the **Po Nagar Cham towers** (daily 6am–6pm; small admission fee), 1.5km north of the city centre. Of the estimated ten towers, or *kalan*, constructed by the Hindu Cham people (see box, p.238 for more on the Cham civilization) on Cu Lao Hill between the seventh and twelfth centuries, only four remain, their baked red bricks weathered so badly through the centuries that restoration work on the towers has been necessary. Despite the restoration, this complex of age-old towers manages to produce an evocative atmosphere, and represents big business for the gaggles of young postcard-sellers who counter rebuffs with a plaintive "Maybe later?"

Visitors to the complex approach the towers via a curling flight of steps that is often swarming with beggars, but Cham worshippers would have entered the *mandapa*, or meditation and offerings hall, whose stone pillars are still visible on the hillside; and from there they would have mounted a set of steep steps directly up to the main tower.

The complex's largest and most impressive tower is the 25-metre-high **northern tower**, built in 817 by Harivarman I and dedicated to Yang Ino Po Nagar, tutelary Goddess Mother of the Kingdom and a manifestation of Uma,

▲ The Po Nagar Cham towers

Shiva's consort. Restored sections stand out for their lighter hue, but the lotus-petal and spearhead motifs that embellish the tower are original, as is the lintel over the outer door, on which a lithe four-armed Shiva dances, flanked by musicians, on the back of an ox. The two sandstone pillars supporting this lintel bear spidery Cham inscriptions.

Inside, a vestibule tapering to a pyramidal ceiling leads to the main chamber, where a fog of incense hangs in the air. The golden statue that originally stood in here was pilfered by the Khmer in the tenth century and replaced by the black stone statue of Uma still here today – albeit minus its head, which was plundered by the French, and now resides in a Parisian museum. The ten arms of cross-legged Uma are nowadays obscured by a gaudy yellow robe, and a doll-like face has been added. Yang Ino Po Nagar is still worshipped as the protectress of the city, and the statue is bathed during the **Merian Festival** each March.

Possessing neither the height nor the intricacy of the main *kalan*, the **central tower**, dating back to the seventh century, is dedicated to the god Cri Cambhu, and sees a steady flow of childless couples pass through to pray for fertility at its lingam. The **southern tower** is the smallest of the four, and also features a lingam inside. Beneath its boat-shaped roof, half-formed statues in relief are still visible at the **northwest tower**, and the frontal view of an elephant is just about discernible on the western facade, its serpentine trunk now blackened with age.

Thap Ba Hot Springs

A side-road heading west just to the north of the Po Nagar Cham towers takes you through distant suburbs of Nha Trang to **Thap Ba Hot Springs** (daily 7am–7.30pm; ☎058/383 4939, ⓦwww.thapbahotspring.com.vn; prices vary according to treatment chosen). There are many different options for pampering your body but if you believe, as the brochure claims, that "soaking in mineral mud is very interesting", you can ooze down into a tub of the messy stuff for half an hour (about $5) and see what wonders it does for your skin. After allowing the mud to dry on the skin, take an invigorating shower, then a swim in the mineral-water pool or stand under a mineral waterfall. Finally, finish off with a water massage from a high-pressure spray. The waters here are rich in sodium silicate chloride, which has beneficial effects on stress, arthritis and rheumatism. The place also has a VIP spa and is well known by most hotels, who can arrange transport.

Hon Chong Promontory and Beach

Crossing Tran Phu Bridge at the north end of Tran Phu leads to the **Hon Chong Promontory**, a finger of granite boulders dashed by the sea. It's quite possible to clamber down to the rocks, the largest of which is said to bear a handprint, left, if you believe the local folklore, by a clumsy giant who slipped and fell while ogling a bathing fairy. The headland above the rocks makes a refreshingly blustery venue for a fresh coconut bought at one of the stalls in the shantytown of cafés and souvenir stalls here. Looking northwest you'll spot **Nui Co Tien**, or the Heavenly Maid Mountains, so called because their three ridges resemble the head, breasts and legs of a woman.

Immediately up the coast from the promontory is **Hon Chong Beach**, scruffier and shinglier than the city beach and not so clean, but more secluded. Cheap seafood restaurants proliferate at its far end. At night, the views from here across the bay to the central beach zone are very impressive.

Monkey Island

Following the main road running north from the Cham towers and over the **Ru Ri Pass**, after 14km you'll see at Da Chung village a pair of dragons perched on a huge arch to the right of the road, which signals the jetty for departures to Hon Lao, or **Monkey Island**. Predictably enough, the island plays host to a colony of inquisitive monkeys, and a boat trip to see them is great fun – especially if you've got kids with you. The boat trip (daily 7.30am–4.45pm; 55,000đ per person return), is operated by Long Phu Tourist (T058/383 9436; W www.longphutourist.com), and takes an hour or so; boats depart every fifteen minutes or when there are six passengers, and the price includes a guide on the island. The tour includes a monkey show as well as dog and goat shows, which may not be to everybody's taste.

The same company also offers day-trips (about $10 with hotel pick-up) to nearby **Thi Island**, which has a decent beach with good swimming, and **Orchid Stream**, further east on Hon Heo Peninsula, where there are picturesque waterfalls among dramatic cliffs and forests.

Ba Ho Falls

Therapeutic properties are attributed to the waters of the three pools at **Ba Ho Falls**, the turning for which is signposted to the left about 7km further up the highway. At the lowest of the falls, the water is beautifully clear, and ideal for a refreshing dip. From there, a steep track leads through lush forest to two more pools. To get there by public transport, take a bus headed for Ninh Hoa District from Nha Trang's local station, and tell the driver your destination; a xe om from the turn-off should cost around 10,000đ.

North to Son My

Most tourists leapfrog the four-hundred-plus kilometres of coastline between Nha Trang and Hoi An on a tour bus, and it's hard to fault their decision. Though swathes of splendid coastline do exist along this stretch of the country, few have been exploited to any great extent as yet. However, this is changing fast, and visitors to places like **Doc Let**, **Whale Island** and **Bai Dai** will find good accommodation options and uncrowded beaches in front of their resort. The next significant town north of Nha Trang is **Quy Nhon**, with good accommodation options, a reasonable beach and some Cham towers that are worth visiting.

About 100km north of Quy Nhon, shortly before reaching Quang Ngai, Highway 1 passes through **Sa Huynh**, which has a long, inviting beach that is often empty. The final "attraction" of the south-central coast is near **Quang Ngai**, at the eerily quiet **Son My Village**, site of one of the American War's most horrific incidents, the My Lai massacre.

Hon Khoi Peninsula

At Ninh Hoa, about 33km north of Nha Trang, Highway 26 branches off left from Highway 1 to Buon Ma Thuot, then about 5km later, a signposted turning on the right leads 12km to splendid **Doc Let Beach**, along the Hon Khoi Peninsula. You'll be keen to linger at Doc Let: its casuarinas and white sands are perfect for a day's beach-bumming, although you do have to pay a small entrance fee for the privilege unless you are staying at one of the resorts here. If you want to stay overnight, there are a few choices. In a class of its own is the ⚘ *Ki-em Art House Resort* (☎058/367 0952; ⓦwww.ki-em.com; ❻–❼), a dreamy compound with a handful of individually decorated bungalows, a meditation room, art gallery and huge picnic tables in the garden. Run by an artist, this place is something special. It is located in the middle of the beach, next to *Paradise Resort* (☎058/367 0480, ⓔparadise_doclech@hotmail.com; ❸–❹), which has a few huge rooms and some simple bungalows, plus a shady terrace overlooking the beach. Rates at both these places include three meals a day. A reasonable budget alternative which mostly attracts Vietnamese, the *Doc Let Beach Resort* (☎058/384 9152, ⓕ058/384 9506; ❶–❷), at the south end of the beach, has pleasant huts with air-conditioning or fans, plus some cheaper fan rooms set back from the beach in a single concrete block. Just south of the *Doc Let* is the newest arrival on the scene, the *White Sand Resort* (☎058/367 0670, ⓦwww.whitesandresort.com.vn; ❻–❼), an attractive low-rise development with beautifully-furnished rooms, all with balconies. The resort also has a spa, a pool, tennis courts and free wi-fi.

If the dazzling sands and empty spaces of the Hon Khoi Peninsula get you in the mood for adventure, consider a visit to *Jungle Beach Resort* (☎091/342 9144, ⓔsyl@dng.vnn.vn; ❸), one of the most secluded places to stay on the entire Vietnamese coast. Run by a Canadian-Vietnamese couple, *Jungle Beach* has basic rooms for rent in the house, plus some smart bungalows in the garden. All meals are included in the room price, and the food is excellent. There's a glorious, deserted beach here and trails on the hillside behind are ripe for exploring. The enthusiastic owner, Sylvio, can arrange treks, and several guests have spent a week or two in the region. Finding the place is difficult – it's at the far end of the road on the northeast coast of the peninsula, past the shipyards and shrimp-farming village of Ninh Phuoc. Phone before going, and staff there will guide you or your driver in. A taxi from Nha Trang costs about $20–25.

Hon Gom Peninsula and Hon Ong (Whale Island)

Another 50km or so north along Highway 1 from the Hon Khoi Peninsula, a road branches off to the right along the **Hon Gom Peninsula**, accessing the endless beaches on both sides of this swan's neck of land. Though there is no accommodation on the peninsula as yet, if you have your own transport, it's worth taking a drive down here just to look at the wild sand dunes and islands sitting in the bay. About 15km down the peninsula, the road reaches the **Dam Mon jetty**, from where it's a five-minute hop by speedboat to **Hon Ong (Whale Island)** and the *Whale Island Resort* (☎058/384 0501, ⓦ www.whaleislandresort.com; ➏). The place has a wonderfully relaxing feel, with simple but tasteful bungalows peeking out over dense vegetation at a fabulous view of the bay. However, you have to pay extra for transfers from Nha Trang and meals, which some guests have found below par. Humpback whales and whale sharks are often seen in the area from May to August. Rainbow Divers (see box, p.246) runs dives from here, and the resort has catamarans, canoes and snorkelling equipment available for guests' use for a nominal fee.

Dai Lanh and north to Quy Nhon

Back on Highway 1, the main road also passes some impressive but empty beaches. You can get a taster 83km from Nha Trang, just beyond the Hon Gom Peninsula at the tiny fishing village of **DAI LANH**, whose appeal lies in the fact that there's absolutely nothing to do. With its patchwork of clay-tile roofs and modest fleet of blue fishing boats, the village lies at the northern end of the kilometre-long beach curving around Vung Ro Bay, a beach whose casuarinas and white sands are hemmed between the clear, turquoise waters of the South China Sea and a mantle of green mountains. The *Thuy Ta* **restaurant** at the southern end of the beach makes an ideal spot for a pit-stop between Nha Trang and Quy Nhon.

Beyond Dai Lanh, you'll have to wait until just before **Quy Nhon** to get more glimpses of idyllic beaches. Highway 1D branches off to the right from Highway 1 about 30km south of town, and passes some sheltered pristine bays as it squiggles up the coast. About 15km south of town on Highway 1D, the *Life Resort* (☎056/384 0132, ⓦ www.life-resorts.com; ➏–➐) on the attractive Bai Dai Beach has over sixty luxurious rooms and suites, and a fantastic spa: it's a good place to relax and revive as they pump you up with health drinks and yoga practice.

Quy Nhon and around

A mid-sized seaport set on a narrow stake of land harpooning the South China Sea, **QUY NHON** attracts few foreign visitors, due to its beach being less dazzling than many others along this coast, and a bit shallow for swimming. For more adventurous travellers, however, the lack of foreigners only adds to the town's intrigue, while the recently-restored Cham towers in the region and the friendly locals also add to its appeal.

Quy Nhon's origins lie in the Cham migration south, at the start of the eleventh century, under pressure from the Vietnamese to the north. They named the empire they established in the area Vijaya ("Victory"); its epicentre was the citadel of Cha Ban (see p.257), and Quy Nhon – then known as Sri Bonai – developed into its thriving commercial centre. Centuries later, the Tay Son Rebellion boiled over in this neck of the woods. During the American War the city served as a US port and supply centre, and was engorged by refugees from the vicious bombing meted out to the surrounding countryside.

Arrival and information

Flights between Ho Chi Minh City and Quy Nhon touch down at Phu Cat Airport, 35km north of town. A Vietnam Airlines minibus shuttles passengers into and out of town (25,000đ), and the company has an office at 55 Le Hong Phong (☎056/382 5313). **Buses** pull up at Quy Nhon's **long-distance bus station**, a short xe om ride west of the city centre, at the corner of Tay Son

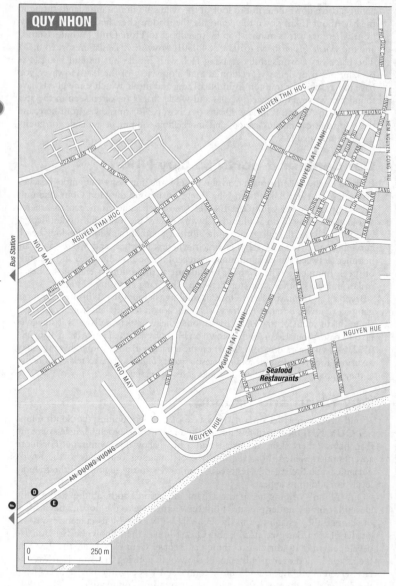

QUY NHON

Seafood Restaurants

0   250 m

and Nguyen Thai Hoc (though open-tour buses by-pass the town). Quy Nhon's branch-line **train station** is beside the Quang Trung statue at the north end of town, though service is irregular, so you'd be better off taking a taxi or xe om (around 50,000–60,000đ) to the nearby station at Dieu Tri for trains to Ho Chi Minh City or Hanoi. The best place for local travel **information** and **bicycle** ($2 a day) or **motorbike** ($10 a day) **rental** is the *Kiwi Café* (see p.256). The Vietcombank, 152 Le Loi, will **exchange** dollars and has a

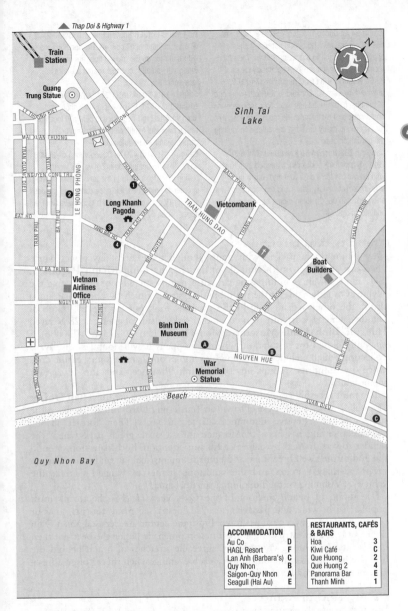

Thap Doi & Highway 1

Train Station

Quang Trung Statue

Sinh Tai Lake

Long Khanh Pagoda

Vietcombank

Boat Builders

Vietnam Airlines Office

Binh Dinh Museum

War Memorial Statue

Beach

Quy Nhon Bay

ACCOMMODATION	
Au Co	D
HAGL Resort	F
Lan Anh (Barbara's)	C
Quy Nhon	B
Saigon-Quy Nhon	A
Seagull (Hai Au)	E

RESTAURANTS, CAFÉS & BARS	
Hoa	3
Kiwi Café	C
Que Huong	2
Que Huong 2	4
Panorama Bar	E
Thanh Minh	1

24-hour ATM. Many hotels offer free **internet** or wi-fi, and there's also internet access at 2g Nguyen Hue.

Accommodation

While Quy Nhon does not have a great choice of hotels, things have improved noticeably in recent years and there are now rooms to suit most tastes and budgets.

Au Co 24 An Duong Vuong ☎056/374 7699. The best of several mini-hotels clustered together opposite the beach to the west of town. The a/c rooms have TVs and are kept spotlessly clean. ②

HAGL Resort 1 Han Mac Tu ☎056/374 7100, ⓦwww.hagl.com.vn. Located at the southwest end of the beach, this hotel has two pools, tennis courts and a couple of restaurants. Its rooms are smartly furnished and many have big balconies overlooking the garden or beach. ④

Lan Anh (Barbara's) 19 Xuan Dieu ☎056/389 2921, ⓔnzbarb@yahoo.com. Managed by a Kiwi who knows the local area well and runs a tight ship. There's a variety of a/c and fan rooms as well as a dorm (50,000đ); some rooms have balconies and sea views. ②

Quy Nhon Hotel 8 Nguyen Hue ☎056/389 2402, ⓦwww.quynhonhotel.com.vn. The spacious rooms with bathtubs on the ground floor are good value, though the smaller, cheaper rooms upstairs are less appealing. ②–③

Saigon–Quy Nhon Hotel 24 Nguyen Hue ☎056/382 0100, ⓦwww.saigonquynhonhotel .com.vn. This high-rise place is centrally located with a pool and health club. The rooms are carpeted and well-equipped. ⑤–⑥

Seagull (Hai Au) 489 An Duong Vuong ☎056/384 6377, ⓦwww.seagullhotel.com.vn. It's worth paying extra for a room in the new 11-storey wing in order to enjoy the thick-piled carpet, sturdy desk and big TV, as well as superb beach views from the upper floors. ④

The city and beaches

Quy Nhon is not packed with sights, though there are a few places worth checking out. Right in the middle of the city, the **Long Khanh Pagoda**, at 141 Tran Cao Van, is an imposing structure, its nine-tiered roof dominating the skyline. On either side of the main building stands a turret – one containing a drum, the other a giant bell. In the grounds, look out for the tall statue of Buddha, which is currently painted a rather sickly shade of green. At 28 Nguyen Hue, the **Binh Dinh Museum** (Mon–Fri 7–11am & 2–5pm; 15,000đ) is currently closed for restoration; when it re-opens it will doubtless display its collection which includes some superb examples of Cham masonry, ethnic dress worn by minority groups in Binh Dinh Province, and the usual war memorabilia.

The most accessible of Quy Nhon's Cham monuments are the **Thap Doi**, or "Double Towers", 2km west of town on Tran Hung Dao, which have been the subject of an extensive restoration in recent years. Their former shabby backstreet setting has been transformed into a small green park where the slender towers, framed by palms, command attention. Both date from around the end of the twelfth century, and embellishments such as sandstone pilasters, spearhead-shaped arches and the sandstone statues of winged Garuda, the vehicle of Vishnu, give the buildings a spiritual aura.

The strand of **beach** in front of the *Quy Nhon Hotel* is the town's most popular: fairly wide, and passably clean, it doesn't see many tourists, so your presence might draw a curious crowd. From the central area, coastal Xuan Dieu slopes away southwest, passing a smart new promenade beside the beach. It then blends into An Duong Vuong, with agreeable stretches of beach behind the hotels, where locals come out in force each evening, when there's often a fresh, salty breeze, to stroll beside the sea.

Eating and drinking

When it comes to **eating**, the two-storey 🍴 *Que Huong 2*, 125 Tang Bat Ho, has a formidable local reputation and is regularly full to bursting in the early evenings: its sister branch is at 185 Le Hong Phong. Some of the dishes are fancifully-named, such as the "fried cracky noodle and roughly-fried snake head", but everything tastes great. Alternatively, try the reliable, hole-in-the-wall restaurant named *Thanh Minh* at 151 Phan Boi Chau, where dirt-cheap, simple vegetarian fare is continuously doled out. *Nem* lovers should make for the *Hoa* at 124 Tang Bat Ho, while the *Kiwi Café* at the *Lan Anh Hotel* turns out cheap and cheerful backpacker staples. A couple of streets behind the seafront – Tran Doc and Nguyen Lac – house a few dedicated seafood restaurants, which score low on ambience but high on taste, with most dishes around 70,000–100,000đ. There are not too many places on the central seafront, but if you're looking for somewhere to savour a sundowner with a view, try the *Panorama Bar* on the top floor of the *Seagull Hotel*.

North to Quang Ngai

Ten kilometres northwest along Quy Nhon's feeder road, the throng of cafés and restaurants operating around **Phu Tai Crossroads** heralds your arrival at the junction with Highway 1. From here it's another 9km north to **Ba Di Bridge** (Cau Ba Di), where Highways 1 and 19 meet. Clearly visible from Ba Di Bridge, the restored **Banh It** Cham towers, known locally as Thap Bac, cut a dash on a hilltop over the river, and can be accessed by a road off to the right above the bridge. Their site yields tremendous views of the surrounding countryside, enhanced by the giant white statue of a seated Buddha below.

North of Ba Di, Highway 1 rushes on towards Sa Huynh. If you are travelling under your own steam you could search for the last vestiges of **Cha Ban Citadel**, the erstwhile capital of Vijaya, a couple of kilometres west of the highway around 21km north of Quy Nhon – look out for a small lane on the left signposted **Canh Tien**. This site constituted the epicentre of Champa from the early eleventh century until 1471, when Le Thanh Ton finally seized it, killing 50,000 Cham people in the process. The Tay Son brothers renamed the site Hoang De and made it their base in the mid-1770s (see p.463). After years of neglect, restoration began in 2008, but all that currently can be seen is the **Canh Tien Tower**, standing on a slight rise: its distinctive shape is visible from afar, a rectangular brick and sandstone edifice framed by sandstone pilasters.

After racing across terrain whose fertile soil supports huge coconut plantations and through **Phu Cat**, **Phu My** and **Hoai Nhon**, small towns that saw great suffering in the war, the highway nears the coast at **SA HUYNH**, a pleasing fishing backwater perched on a broad curve of palm-fringed, golden sand. Speckled with scores of blue fishing boats, sleepy Sa Huynh makes a convenient and relaxing staging post en route from Nha Trang to Hoi An, and the roaring of its excitable surf masks the noise of traffic from the road; open-tour buses often make a brief stop here. For a decent meal, pull into the *Vinh* restaurant, which serves up excellent seafood at low prices, and is just a little further north of the run-down *Sa Huynh* hotel building (currently being demolished and rebuilt) on the right.

Shrimp farms, salt flats and vast expanses of paddy characterize the countryside above Sa Huynh. Once past **Duc Pho**, an R&R base for the Viet Minh in the late 1940s, and the tobacco plantations of **Mo Duc**, you quickly hit Quang Ngai.

Quang Ngai and around

Slender **QUANG NGAI**, clinging to the south bank of the Tra Khuc River some 130km south of Da Nang, is about as pleasant as you could expect of a town skewered until recently by Vietnam's main highway. Highway 1, which once ripped through town, now skirts it to the east, leaving the town in a state of shocked silence. The area's long tradition of resistance against the French found further focus during American involvement, for which the reward was some of the most extensive bombing meted out during the war: by 1967, American journalist Jonathan Schell was able to report that seventy percent of villages in the town's surrounding area had been destroyed. A year later, the

The My Lai massacre

The massacre of civilians in the hamlets of **Son My Village**, the single most shameful chapter of America's involvement in Vietnam, began at dawn on March 16, 1968. US Intelligence suggested that the 48th Local Forces Battalion of the NVA, which had taken part in the Tet Offensive on Quang Ngai a month earlier, was holed up in Son My. Within the task force assembled to flush them out was **Charlie Company**, whose First Platoon, led by Lieutenant William Calley, was assigned to sweep through **My Lai 4** (known to locals as **Tu Cung Hamlet**). Recent arrivals in Vietnam, Charlie Company had suffered casualties and losses in the hunt for the elusive 48th, but always inflicted by snipers and booby-traps. Unable to contact the enemy face to face in any numbers, or even to distinguish civilians from Viet Cong guerrillas, they had come to feel frustrated and impotent. Son My offered the chance to settle some old scores.

At a briefing on the eve of the offensive, GIs were told that all civilians would be at market by 7am and that anyone remaining was bound to be an active Viet Cong sympathizer. Some GIs later remembered being told not to kill women and children, but most simply registered that there were to be no prisoners. Whatever the truth, a massacre ensued, whose brutal course Neil Sheehan describes with chilling under-statement in *A Bright Shining Lie*:

The American soldiers and junior officers shot old men, women, boys, girls, and babies. One soldier missed a baby lying on the ground twice with a .45 pistol as his comrades laughed at his marksmanship. He stood over the child and fired a third time. The soldiers beat women with rifle butts and raped some and sodomised others before shooting them. They shot the water buffalos, the pigs, and the chickens. They threw the dead animals into the wells to poison the water. They tossed satchel charges into the bomb shelters under the houses. A lot of the inhabitants had fled into the shelters. Those who leaped out to escape the explosives were gunned down. All of the houses were put to the torch.

Americans turned their focus upon **Son My Village**, site of the My Lai massacre (see box above). This workaday settlement is worth visiting for its moving memorial garden and museum, or the peaceful **My Khe Beach**, nearby: the best way to get there is by xe om (get your hotel owner to negotiate a fare).

Son My Village

Turn right once you're over the bridge at the top of Quang Ngai, and it's 12km east to **SON MY**, the site of an infamous massacre of civilians by American soldiers in early 1968 that's remembered at the **Son My Memorial Park** (daily 7am–5pm; 10,000đ) in the village's sub-hamlet of Tu Cung. Pacing through this peaceful and dignified place, set within a low perimeter wall, you'll be accompanied by a feeling of blanched horror, and a palpable sense of the dead all around you. Wandering the garden, visitors can see bullet holes in trees, foundations of homes burnt down, each with a tablet recording its family's losses, blown-out bomb shelters and cement statues of slain animals. The path through the centre of the garden ends at a large, Soviet-style statue of a woman cradling a dead baby over her left arm while raising her right fist in defiance. Once you've seen the garden, step into the museum to view the grisly display upstairs, though be warned that it's a disturbing place for anyone with a sensitive disposition. Here, beyond a massive marble plaque recording the names of the dead, family by family, and a montage of rusting hardware, a **photograph gallery** documents the events of March 16, 1968, from snaps of American helicopters disgorging GIs in the paddy outside the hamlet to the sordid aftermath of cold-blooded murder.

In all, the Son My body count reached 500, 347 of whom fell in Tu Cung alone. Not one shot was fired at a GI in response, and the only US casualty deliberately shot himself in the foot to avoid the carnage. The 48th Battalion never materialized. The military chain of command was able temporarily to suppress reports of the massacre, with the army newspaper, *Stars and Stripes*, and even the *New York Times* branding the mission a success. But the awful truth surfaced in November 1969, through the efforts of former GI Ronald Ridenhour and investigative journalist Seymour Hersh, and the incontrovertible evidence of the grisly colour slides of army photographer Ron Haeberle. When the massacre did finally make the cover of *Newsweek* it was under the headline "An American Tragedy" – which, as John Pilger pointed out, "deflected from the truth that the atrocities were, above all, a *Vietnamese* tragedy".

Of 25 men eventually charged with murder over the massacre, or for its subsequent suppression, only Lieutenant William Calley was found guilty, though he had served just three days of a life sentence of hard labour when Nixon intervened and commuted it to house arrest. Three years later he was paroled.

It's all too easy to dismiss Charlie Company as a freak unit operating beyond the pale. A more realistic view may be that the very nature of the US war effort, with its resort to unselective napalm and rocket attacks, and its use of body counts as barometers of success, created a climate in which Vietnamese life was cheapened to such an extent that a My Lai became almost inevitable. If indiscriminate killing from the air was justifiable, then random killing at close quarters was only taking this methodology to its logical conclusion.

Michael Bilton and Kevin Sim, whose *Four Hours in My Lai* remains the most complete account of the massacre, conclude that "My Lai's exposure late in 1969 poisoned the idea that the war was a moral enterprise." The mother of one GI put it more simply: "I gave them a good boy, and they made him a murderer."

In stark contrast, the secluded **My Khe Beach**, 3km east of My Lai, consists of seven kilometres of powder-soft sand, backed by casuarinas, and is very good for swimming. Hamlets stand along the back of the beach, while fishing boats are sometimes moored off it, and there's a handful of restaurants that only get busy at the weekend. The only **resort** here so far is the twelve-roomed *My Khe Resort* (℡055/368 6111; ❸), which has comfortable rooms with air conditioning and hot water at reasonable prices. The best part about it is the tranquil setting, which makes it a good choice for a beach getaway.

Practicalities

The junction of Quang Trung with westward-pointing Hung Vuong effectively forms central Quang Ngai. **Trains** arrive 3km west of town along Hung Vuong, while the **bus** station is a little over 500m south of the centre, and 50m east of Quang Trung on Le Thanh Ton. **Quang Ngai Tourist** is 150m north of Hung Vuong at 310 Quang Trung (℡055/381 7811; ⓦwww.quangngaitourist .com.vn), though there's rarely anyone there; the **post office** is about 100m west of the highway, at the junction of Hung Vuong and Phan Dinh Phung. **Internet access** is unusually difficult to find; try 634/01 Quang Trung, down an alley off the main road. There's an **ATM** at the *Hung Vuong Hotel*, and several others along Quang Trung.

There's nowhere outstanding **to stay** in Quang Ngai, though there are a few reasonable mid-range options and a new four-star place is currently being built to the west of the bridge heading north out of town. Once the town's best choice,

the *Central* at 784 Quang Trung (℡055/382 9999, ⓦwww.centralhotel
.com.vn; ④) is getting a bit tatty, though it does have a pool and tennis courts.
Alternatives include the *Hung Vuong* (℡055/371 0477, ⓦwww.hungvuong-hotel
.com.vn; ④) at 45 Hung Vuong, which has better-value rooms, some with carpets
and bathtubs, or the *My Tra* (℡055/384 2985, ⓔks-mytra@dng.vnn.vn; ❸–④),
just north of the bridge across the broad Tra Khuc River: some rooms here have
great views of the river, and it's away from the bustle of the town. Budget travellers
should head for the friendly *Kim Thanh* (℡055/382 3471; ❶–❷) at 19 Hung
Vuong, where the rooms are basic but clean.

As with accommodation, **places to eat** are also limited in Quang Ngai,
though the *My Tra* hotel's open-air terrace restaurant looking out across the
river makes a nice enough setting. The food is rather ordinary in all the hotels,
so you're better off heading for the *Bac Son*, next door to the *Kim Thanh* hotel,
which serves decent Vietnamese staples. The local speciality is chicken and rice,
which is very well prepared at *Nhung Com Ga* at 474 Quang Trung. At 7 Hung
Vuong, you'll find a **stall** selling *ram*, barbecued shrimp or meat folded in rice
paper and then dipped in a tasty peanut sauce.

Travel details

Trains

Dieu Tri to: Da Nang (7 daily; 5–6hr); Ho Chi Minh
City (7 daily; 12hr 30min–15hr 30min); Hué
(7 daily; 8–10hr); Nha Trang (7 daily; 4–5hr).
Muong Man to: Da Nang (6 daily; 12–17hr); Ho
Chi Minh City (9 daily; 3–5hr); Hué (6 daily;
14–18hr); Nha Trang (9 daily; 4–6hr).
Nha Trang to: Da Nang (7 daily; 9hr–12hr 30min);
Hanoi (7 daily; 24–32hr); Ho Chi Minh City
(7 daily; 7hr 10min–11hr 15min); Hué (7 daily;
12hr–16hr 10min).
Thap Cham to: Da Nang (6 daily; 12hr 25min–
13hr 30min); Ho Chi Minh City (5 daily; 6hr
40min–7hr 30min); Hué (5 daily; 16–17hr);
Nha Trang (9 daily; 1hr 30min–3hr).

Buses

Bus stations are gradually becoming more
organized, with ticket desks and scheduled departures. However, it is still almost impossible to give
the **frequency** with which buses run because of
the large number of private minibuses that ply
more popular routes, and depart only when they
have enough passengers to make the journey
worthwhile. Off the highway, to be sure of a bus it's
advisable to start your journey early – most long-
distance departures are between 5am and 9am,
and few run after midday. **Journey times** can also
vary; figures below show the normal length of time
you can expect to take by public bus.

Ba Di Bridge (Quy Nhon) to: Plei Ku (4hr).
Mui Ne to: Ho Chi Minh City (3–4hr).
Nha Trang to: Buon Me Thuot (4hr); Da Lat (3hr);
Da Nang (12hr); Hanoi (32hr); Ho Chi Minh City
(10hr); Hué (15hr).
Phan Rang to: Da Lat (3hr); Ho Chi Minh City (5hr);
Nha Trang (2hr); Phan Thiet (3hr).
Phan Thiet to: Ho Chi Minh City (4hr); Nha Trang
(5hr).
Quang Ngai to: Da Nang (4hr); Nha Trang (7hr).
Quy Nhon to: Da Nang (8hr); Nha Trang (4hr);
Quang Ngai (4hr).
Vung Tau to: Ba Ria (30min); Da Lat (6hr); Ho
Minh City (2hr); Nha Trang (7hr).

Boats

Vung Tau to: Con Son (1–2 weekly; 15hr).

Hydrofoils

Vung Tau to: Ho Chi Minh City (Mon–Fri 6 daily,
Sat & Sun 7 daily; 1hr 15min).

Flights

Con Dao to: Ho Chi Minh City (daily; 1hr).
Nha Trang to: Da Nang (daily; 1hr 20min); Hanoi
(daily; 1hr 40min); Ho Chi Minh City (daily; 1hr).
Quy Nhon to: Hanoi (daily; via Danang or Saigon;
5hr); Ho Chi Minh City (daily; 1hr 20min).

5

The central provinces

CHAPTER 5 Highlights

* **Hoi An** Sip a latte by lantern-light while waiting for your tailor-made clothes to measure up in this laid-back city. See p.266

* **My Son** Majestic Cham ruins covered in moss, grass and leaves – rise early to see them before the crowds. See p.280

* **Da Nang** Amiable city providing a jump-off point for lofty Ba Na Hill Station and the fabled Marble Mountains. See p.283

* **Hué's Imperial City** Cross the Perfume River to meander through the intricately decorated buildings that emperors once called home. See p.302

* **Phong Nha Cave** Take a boat trip into the mouth of one of Asia's most extensive cave systems. See p.330

* **Cycling from Tam Coc to Hoa Lu** A fantasy landscape of limestone crags provides the backdrop for a leisurely cycle ride through Ninh Binh's prolific rice lands. See p.336

* **Cuc Phuong National Park** Get close to some of the world's most endangered species at the excellent Primate Rescue Center. See p.339

▲ Cham towers at My Son

The central provinces

Vietnam's narrow waist comprises a string of provinces squeezed between the long, sandy coastline and the formidable barrier of the Truong Son Mountains, which mark the border between Vietnam and Laos. Ragged spurs sheer off the Truong Son range towards the South China Sea, cutting the coastal plain into isolated pockets of fertile rice land. For much of Vietnam's early history, one of these spurs, the thousand-metre-high Hoanh Son Mountains north of Dong Hoi, formed the cultural and political divide between the northern, Chinese-dominated sphere and the Indianized Champa kingdom to the south. As independent Vietnam grew in power in the eleventh century, so its armies pushed southwards to the next natural frontier, the Hai Van Pass near Hué. Here again, the Cham resisted further invasion until the fifteenth century, when their great temple complex at My Son was seized and their kingdom shattered.

Since then, other contenders have battled back and forth over this same ground, among them the Nguyen and Trinh lords, whose simmering rivalry ended in victory for the southern Nguyen and the emergence of **Hué** as the nation's capital in the nineteenth century. The Nguyen dynasty transformed Hué into a stately Imperial City, whose palaces, temples and grand mausoleums now constitute one of the highlights of a visit to Vietnam, despite the ravages they suffered during successive wars. In 1954, Vietnam was divided at the Seventeenth Parallel, only 100km north of Hué, where the Ben Hai River and the **Demilitarized Zone (DMZ)** marked the border between North and South Vietnam until reunification in 1975. Though there's little to see on the ground these days, the desolate battlefields of the DMZ are a poignant memorial to those who fought here on both sides, and to the civilians who lost their lives in the bitter conflict.

Da Nang and nearby **China Beach** are other evocative names from the American War, but the region has more to offer. The compact riverside town of **Hoi An**, with its core of traditional, wood-built merchants' houses and jaunty Chinese Assembly Halls, is a particularly captivating place. Inland from Hoi An, the Cham spiritual core, **My Son**, survives as a haunting array of overgrown ruins in a hidden valley, while the coast here presents a succession of empty, white-sand beaches that are among the finest in Vietnam.

All these highlights lie in the southernmost of the central provinces. In stark contrast, the more northerly provinces suffer from a particularly hostile climate, and were also the hardest-hit by bombing raids during the American War: from Hué most people skip straight up to Hanoi, but if you're travelling overland, there are a couple of places en route that warrant a stop. First of these is the **Phong Nha Cave**, near Dong Hoi, where boats take you into the mouth of

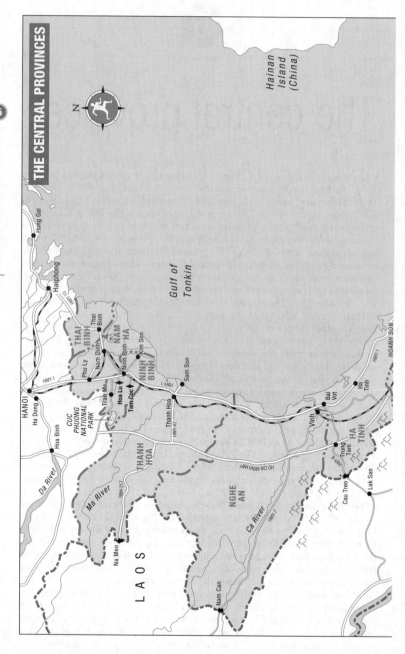

THE CENTRAL PROVINCES

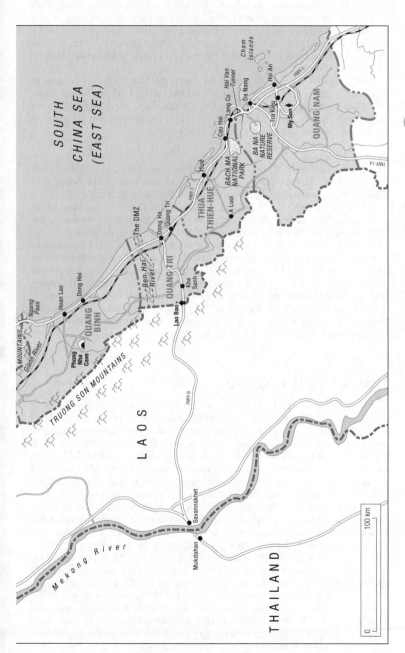

SOUTH
CHINA SEA
(EAST SEA)

*Cham
Islands*

Hoi An

HWY-1

Da Nang

Lang Co

Hai Van
Tunnel

Tra Kieu

My Son

QUANG NAM

Cau Hai

BA NA
NATURE
RESERVE

*BACH MA
NATIONAL
PARK*

Hué

HWY-1

A Luoi

THUA
THIEN-HUÉ

The DMZ

Dong Ha

Quang Tri

*Ben Hai
River*

QUANG TRI

Khe
Sanh

Hoan Lao

Dong Hoi

*Ngang
Pass*

QUANG
BINH

Gianh River

MOUNTAINS

**Phong
Nha
Cave**

Lao Bao

TRUONG SON MOUNTAINS

HWY-9

L A O S

Savannakhet

Mekong River

Mukdahan

T H A I L A N D

0   100 km

an extensive underground river system. Then right up in the north, **Ninh Binh** is the base for a number of attractions, from engaging river trips to ancient temples and reserves of primary rainforest. For those travelling by car or minibus, the usual place to break the journey between Hué and Hanoi is **Vinh**, though if you stop off at Dong Hoi for the caves you should be able to press on to Ninh Binh in a long day.

Finally, if you're heading **overland to Laos**, the four border gates open to foreigners in the central provinces are at **Lao Bao**, along Highway 9 from Dong Ha; **Cau Treo**, on Highway 8 from Vinh; **Nam Can**, northwest of Vinh on Highway 7; and **Na Meo**, on Highway 217 from Thanh Hoa. (For information on the Bo Y border gate, near Kon Tum, see p.215).

When to go

This region has a particularly complicated climate as it forms a transitional zone between the north and south of Vietnam. In general, around **Da Nang and Hué** the rainy season lasts from September to February, with most rain falling between late September and December; during this season it's not unusual for road and rail links to be cut. Hué suffers particularly badly and, even during the "dry season" from March to August, it's possible to have several days of torrential rain, giving the city an annual average of three metres. Overall, the best time to visit this southern region is in spring, from February to late May, before both temperatures and humidity reach their summer maximum (averaging around 30°C), or just at the end of the summer before the rains break. The region **north of the Hoanh Son Mountains** experiences a drier climate and a more marked rainy season, with September and October again the wettest months. Summers are hot and dry, though from August to November **typhoons** can bring periods of heavy rain and severe flooding.

Hoi An and around

The ancient core of **HOI AN** is a rich architectural fusion of Chinese, Japanese, Vietnamese and European influences dating back to the sixteenth century. In its heyday the now drowsy channel of the Thu Bon River was a jostling crowd of merchant vessels representing the world's great trading nations, and there's still a compelling sense of history in the mellow streets of this small, amiable town. Hoi An's most noteworthy monuments are the 200-year-old homes of prosperous Chinese merchants whose descendants, surrounded by astonishing collections of antiques and family memorabilia, continue to inhabit the cool, dark houses. Between their sober wooden facades, riotous confections of glazed roof tiles and writhing dragons mark the entrances to **Chinese Assembly Halls**, which form the focal point of civic and spiritual life for an ethnic Chinese community that constitutes one quarter of the population.

Granted UNESCO World Heritage status in 1999, Hoi An is now firmly on most visitors' agendas. For some it's already too much of a tourist trap with its profusion of tailors' shops and art galleries and its rapidly proliferating hotels, and the majority of visitors pause only briefly, but it takes time to tune in to the town's subtle charms. At least a day is needed to cover the central sights and sample some of Hoi An's mouthwatering speciality dishes, and by then most people are hooked. It's easy to spend longer, taking day-trips to the atmospheric Cham ruins of **My Son** or some of the other sights closer to town (see p.280), biking out into the surrounding country or opting for a leisurely sampan ride

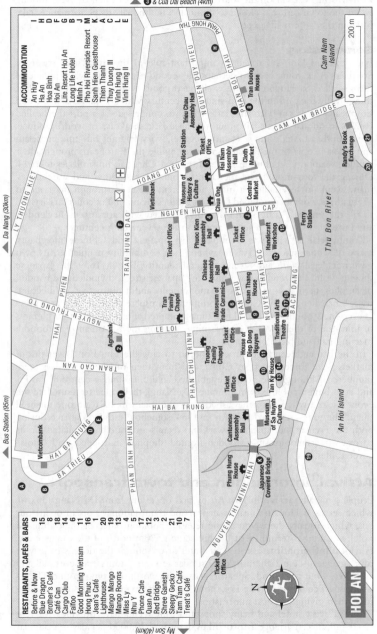

HOI AN

THE CENTRAL PROVINCES

5

267

RESTAURANTS, CAFÉS & BARS

Before & Now	9
Blue Dragon	15
Brother's Café	8
Café Can	18
Cargo Club	14
Faifoo	6
Good Morning Vietnam	16
Hong Phuc	11
Jean's Café	1
Lighthouse	20
Mango Mango	19
Mango Rooms	13
Miss Ly	4
Nhu Y	5
Phone Cafe	17
Quan An	12
Red Bridge	3
Shree Ganesh	2
Sleepy Gecko	21
Tam Tam Café	10
Treat's Café	7

ACCOMMODATION

An Huy	I
Ha An	H
Hoa Binh	D
Hoi An	F
Life Resort Hoi An	G
Long Life Hotel	B
Minh A	J
Pho Hoi Riverside Resort	M
Sanh Hien Guesthouse	K
Thien Thanh	A
Thuy Duong III	C
Vinh Hung I	L
Vinh Hung II	E

▲ Da Nang (30km)

▲ Bus Station (95m)

▲ My Son (40km)

❸ & Cua Dai Beach (4km)

on the Thu Bon River. If possible, try to time your visit to coincide with the **Full-Moon Festival**, on the fourteenth day of the lunar calendar every month, when the town centre is closed to traffic and traditional arts performances take place in the lantern-lit streets.

Some history

For centuries Hoi An played an important role in the **maritime trade** of Southeast Asia, going back to perhaps the second century BC, when people of the so-called Sa Huynh culture exchanged goods with China and India. But things really took off in the mid-sixteenth century when Chinese, Japanese and European vessels ran with the trade winds to congregate at a port then called Fai Fo. Its annual spring fair grew into an exotic showcase of world produce: from Southeast Asia came silks and brocades, ivory, fragrant oils, fine porcelain and a cornucopia of medicinal ingredients, while the Europeans brought their textiles, weaponry, sulphur, lead – and the first Christian missionaries in 1614. During the four-month fair, merchants would rent lodgings and warehouses; many went on to establish a more permanent presence through marriage to Vietnamese women, renowned for their business acumen. Tax collectors arrived to fill the imperial coffers, and the town swelled with artisans, moneylenders and bureaucrats as trade reached a peak in the seventeenth century.

Commercial activity was dominated by Japanese and Chinese merchants, many of whom settled in Fai Fo, where each community maintained its own governor, legal code and strong cultural identity. But in 1639 the Japanese shogun prohibited foreign travel and the "Japanese street" dwindled to a handful of families, then to a scattering of monuments and a distinctive architectural style. Unchallenged, the Chinese community prospered, and its numbers grew as every new political upheaval in China prompted another wave of immigrants to join one of the town's self-governing "congregations", organized around a meeting hall and place of worship.

In the late eighteenth century, silt began to clog the Thu Bon River just as markets were forced open in China, and from then on the port's days were numbered. Although the French established an administrative centre in Fai Fo, and even built a rail link from Tourane (Da Nang), they failed to resuscitate the economy, and when a storm washed away the tracks in 1916 no one repaired them. The town, renamed Hoi An in 1954, somehow escaped damage during both the French and American wars and retains a distinctly antiquated air, its narrow streets comprising wooden-fronted shophouses topped with moss-covered tiles.

Arrival, information and town transport

People generally **arrive** in Hoi An by taxi or xe om from Da Nang (30km), which serves as Hoi An's nearest airport and train station, or on an open-tour bus, which usually drops you at the relevant booking office or their affiliated hotel. Local buses terminate at the bus station 500m north of the town centre. For local **information**, ask in your hotel or try one of the dozens of private tour agencies (see p.278): most offer similar services – tours, transport, rail and air tickets – but prices and itineraries vary so it's worth shopping around. There's a tourist office of sorts on Le Loi, though the staff are more interested in selling tours than giving practical information.

Almost every hotel and many shops and tour agents have **bicycles** for rent (20,000đ), or can arrange **motorbikes** at around 70,000đ per day – a popular way to visit My Son (see p.280). While bikes are recommended for touring the outlying districts, Hoi An's central sights are all best approached **on foot**, especially since **traffic restrictions** apply in the town centre. The regulations are part of a much-needed effort to save the old town from the worst effects of fame: cars are prohibited from the core streets south of Phan Chu Trinh and west of Hoang Dieu; and all vehicles are banned in the vicinity of the market and on the Japanese Bridge, though you can push pedal bikes across.

Accommodation

The number of **hotels** in Hoi An continues to grow at an astonishing rate. The local authorities put a block on developments in the centre – too late to prevent some eyesores in the old streets – but a whole new enclave of pleasant and cheap mini-hotels has sprung up to the north of the centre along Ba Trieu; most of these have swimming pools, which provide welcome relief in warmer months. Competition means that, in general, prices have come down and standards have risen, most places will bargain and there's no longer a shortage of beds in peak season. If you do have difficulty, just head for the hotels further from the centre.

Central Hoi An

An Huy 30 Phan Boi Chau ☎0510/386 2116, ✉anhuyhotel@vnn.vn. Behind its tiny entrance, this mini-hotel is a real find, offering simple clean rooms with a/c, cable TV and full-size baths in an excellent (and very quiet) location 100m east of the market. ❸

Ha An 6 Phan Boi Chau ☎0510/386 3126, ✉tohuong@fpt.vn. Welcoming, family-run hotel, set back from the street in a quiet residential area, with a relaxing communal garden. Its 25 rooms are beautifully decorated in a mix of traditional and contemporary styles, all with en-suite bathrooms, a/c, phones and TVs. ❹

Hoa Binh 696 Hai Ba Trung ☎0510/391 6838, ✉peace_hoian@yahoo.com.vn. Large, clean rooms with satellite TV for under $10 at this popular and presentable hotel, with a swimming pool on the ground floor. ❶

Hoi An 6 Tran Hung Dao ☎0510/386 1373, ✇www.hoiantourist.com. A state-run, colonial-style hotel and former billet for US Marines, the *Hoi An* boasts 160 rooms in three low-rise blocks set among gardens. The rooms are unusually spacious and well equipped, while the hotel also boasts a restaurant, bar, money exchange, tour agent, tennis courts. and a pool that's also open to non-residents. ❹

Life Resort Hoi An 1 Pham Hong Thai ☎0510/391 4555, ✇www.life-resorts .com. This is an excellent option for those that want the luxury of a resort in central Hoi An. Just a short stroll from the market, and lying on the banks of the Thu Bon River, it blends minimalist Japanese design with maximum service and facilities including a fantastic pool, massage

rooms, two international restaurants and its own river boat. ❻

Long Life Hotel 26 Ba Trieu ☎0510/391 6696, ✇www.thanhxuanhotel.com. Also known as the *Thanh Xuan*, this welcoming mini-hotel offers quiet comfort, including a/c, cable TV, internet and full-size baths. At the back is a small courtyard that looks out into the fields. ❸

Minh A 2 Nguyen Thai Hoc ☎0510/386 1368. This little guesthouse right by Hoi An market has just six rooms in an ancient shophouse. Facilities are basic – there's no a/c and access to the shared bathroom and toilet is through the kitchen – but it's a good opportunity to stay in a traditional family home. ❷

Pho Hoi Riverside Resort 7/2 Tran Phu ☎0510/386 1633, ✇www.phohoiriverside hoian.com. Few tourists cross the bridge to peaceful Cam Nam Island, let alone stay there, but at this presentable resort you're just a short walk from central Hoi An, which you can see across the water from the outdoor bar or swimming pool. ❹

Sanh Hien Guesthouse 7 Nguyen Thi Minh Khai ☎0510/386 3631. Just three doors down from the Japanese Bridge, this 200-year-old house offers real charm, although the rooms are very basic, with fans and shared bathrooms only. ❷

Thien Thanh 16 Ba Trieu ☎0510/391 6545, ✇www.blueskyhoian.com. Comfortable and intimate mini-hotel with exceptionally attentive staff who try to make your stay as restful as possible. It has all mod cons, such as cable TV, a/c and internet access; the more expensive rooms have balconies overlooking water-spinach fields. Many guests return again and again. ❸

Thuy Duong III Ba Trieu ☎0510/391 6565, ✉thuyduongco@dng.vnn.vn. Don't be put off by the fact that Sinh open-tour buses drop you here. The rooms are comfortable, well maintained and reasonably priced, though those on the ground floor around the courtyard pool can be noisy. ❸

Vinh Hung I 143 Tran Phu ☎ 0510/386 1621, ⓔ quanghuy.ha@dng.vnn.vn. Apart from an unbeatable location and excellent service, the highlights of this lovely old Chinese shophouse are the two superbly restored rooms upstairs complete with balcony, wood panelling, antique furniture and four-poster beds as well as tiny bathrooms; they're in great demand, so book ahead. The other rooms, in a modern extension at the back, are decorated in traditional style but are dark and rather expensive for what you get. ❺

Vinh Hung II Ba Trieu ☎ 0510/386 3717, ⓔ quanghuy.ha@dng.vnn.vn. This addition to the *Vinh Hung* empire maintains similarly high standards of service and continues the traditional Chinese theme in its more expensive rooms, while the cheaper rooms are adequate if unexciting. Facilities include a small courtyard pool, restaurant, gym and internet access. ❹

Cua Dai Beach

Hai Yen 22a Cua Dai ☎ 0510/386 2445, ⓔ kshaiyen@dng.vnn.vn. Once past the saccharine-pink staircase, this quiet hotel is a good choice on the road to the beach. Decent-sized, comfortable rooms come with a bathtub, and other facilities include a restaurant, internet access, bike rental and all the usual tours and ticketing services. It also has a small tropical garden and pool. ❺

Hoi An Beach Resort Cua Dai Beach ☎ 0510/392 7011, ⓦ www.hoiantourist.com. Separated from the beach by a quiet road, this is slightly cheaper than nearby resorts. Rooms are elegant in cool, sand colours and bathrooms are generously proportioned; it's worth paying the extra for a river-view room. Other attractions include two pools, a private beach and a restaurant recommended for its well-priced local dishes. Free shuttle bus to Hoi An. ❺

Palm Garden Resort Cua Dai ☎ 0510/392 7927, ⓦ palmgardenresort.com.vn. This resort takes its name from the four hundred-odd trees dotting the complex; some at beachside have hammocks for lazing or cocktail-sipping. The rooms are spacious and well up to standard, while the seafood in the on-site restaurants is superb. ❼

Swiss–Belhotel Golden Sand Resort Cua Dai ☎ 0510/392 7555, ⓦ www.swiss-belhotel.com/hoian Aiming for a contemporary-traditional fusion, and largely getting the balance right, this resort has some of the best rooms on the strip, and by far the largest pool; little touches such as wafts of frangipani in the gardens make most stays special, though customer service is not always five-star. ❼

Victoria Hoi An Resort Cua Dai Beach ☎ 0510/392 7040, ⓦ www.victoriahotels-asia.com. Hoi An's ritziest hotel, with the top-rated bungalows opening right onto a lovely stretch of beach, while the cheapest rooms occupy two-storey villas. The *Victoria* has all the amenities you'd expect of an international-class resort, including a restaurant serving good but expensive meals, a free shuttle bus to Hoi An and a whole range of activities (for which you pay extra). ❼

The Town

The **historic core** of Hoi An consists of just three short streets running parallel to the river. Tran Phu is the oldest and is still the principal commercial street, running from Hoi An's most famous monument, the Japanese Covered Bridge, in the west, to the market in the east. One block south is Nguyen Thai Hoc, with a fine array of wooden townhouses, traditional pharmacists and an overspill of galleries, tailors and antique shops. Finally comes riverfront Bach Dang, site of the ferry station and a line of attractive, waterside café-restaurants. Just north of this central core is a scattering of sights, including two of the less visited merchants' houses, that shouldn't be overlooked.

Japanese Covered Bridge

The western extremity of Tran Phu is marked by a small arched bridge of red-painted wood, popularly known as the **Japanese Covered Bridge**, which has been adopted as Hoi An's emblem. It was known to exist in the mid-sixteenth century, and has subsequently been reconstructed several times to the same simple design. According to local folklore, the bridge was erected after Japan suffered a series of violent earthquakes which geomancers attributed to a restless

Visiting Hoi An's sights

Hoi An has a **ticket scheme** covering the majority of its most famous sights, the proceeds of which contribute to the preservation of the old centre. A ticket costing 75,000đ (valid for one day), allows access to five places: either the temple on the Japanese Covered Bridge or Chua Ong; one of the museums (the Museum of History and Culture, the Museum of Trade Ceramics or the Museum of Sa Huynh Culture); one of the participating Chinese Assembly Halls (the Phuoc Kien, Trieu Chau or Cantonese halls); one of the participating merchants' houses or family chapels (the houses of Tan Ky, Phung Hung and Quan Thang or the Tran Family Chapel); and the Hoi An Handicraft Workshop at 9 Nguyen Thai Hoc. If you want to visit more sights in the scheme, you have to fork out for another ticket.

Tickets are on sale at six **outlets**: 52 Nguyen Thi Minh Khai, 19 Ha Ba Trung, 5 Hoang Dieu, 12 Phan Chu Trinh, 37 Tran Phu and 78 Le Loi (see map, p.267). Groups of more than eight people are entitled to a free guide for the day; otherwise, you can hire one for around $15. The ticket outlets are **open** from 7am to 6pm, as are all the sights included in the scheme.

monster lying with its head in India, tail in Japan and heart in Hoi An. The only remedy was to build a bridge whose stone piles would drive a metaphorical sword through the beast's heart and fortuitously provide a handy passage across the muddy creek. Inside the bridge's narrow span are a collection of stelae and four statues, two dogs and two monkeys, which suggest that work began in the year of the monkey and ended in that of the dog. The small **temple** suspended above the water is a later addition dedicated to the Taoist god Tran Vo Bac De ("Emperor of the North"), a favourite of sailors as he controls wind, rain and other "evil influences".

The Chinese Assembly Halls

Historically, Hoi An's ethnic Chinese population organized themselves according to their place of origin (Fujian, Guangdong, Chaozhou or Hainan). Each group maintained its own assembly hall as both community centre and house of worship, while a fifth hall also provided assistance to all the local groups and to visiting Chinese merchants. The most populous group hailed from Fujian, or Phuoc Kien, and their **Phuoc Kien Assembly Hall**, at 46 Tran Phu, is a suitably imposing edifice with an ostentatious, triple-arched gateway added in the early 1970s. The hall started life as a pagoda built in the late seventeenth century when, so it's said, a Buddhist statue containing a lump of gold washed up on the riverbank. Almost a century later, the Chinese took over the decaying structure and rededicated it as a temple to Thien Hau, Goddess of the Sea and protector of sailors. She stands, fashioned in 200-year-old papier-mâché, on the principal altar flanked by her two assistants, green-faced Thien Ly Nhan and red-faced Thuan Phong Nhi, who between them can see or hear any boat in distress over a range of a thousand miles. A second sanctuary room behind and to the right of the main altar shelters a deity favoured by couples and pregnant women: the awesome Van Thien and her aides, the "twelve heavenly midwives", who decide the fundamentals of a child's life from conception onwards, including the fateful matter of gender. On the way out of the main building, take a look at the entrance porch decorated with colourful wooden friezes and delicate stone motifs.

It's worth strolling out to the **Trieu Chau Assembly Hall**, on the far eastern edge of town at 157 Nguyen Duy Hieu. Built in the late eighteenth century by Chinese from Chaozhou, or Trieu Chau, it's renowned for its remarkable display of wood carving. In the altar niche sits the gilded Ong Bon, a general in the Chinese navy believed to hold sway over the wind and waves, surrounded by a frieze teeming with bird, animal and insect life so lifelike you can almost hear it buzz. The altar table itself depicts life on land and in the depths of the ocean, while panels on either side show two decorative ladies of the Chinese court modelling the latest Japanese hair fashions. On the way to Trieu Chau hall, you'll pass **Hai Nam Assembly Hall** at 10 Tran Phu (7–11.30am & 2–5pm; not covered by ticket scheme, free), founded by the Chinese community from Hainan, or Hai Nam, and also noted for its ornately carved, gilded altar table. Its unusual history is intriguing – in 1851 a Vietnamese general plundered three merchant ships, killing 107 passengers, after which the vessels were painted black to imply they were pirate ships. A lone survivor revealed the crime to King Tu Duc, who promptly condemned the general to death and ordered that the booty be returned to the victims' families. When the hall was built later in the century, it was dedicated to the unlucky passengers.

Just east of the Japanese Bridge you can't miss the **Cantonese Assembly Hall**, its gaudy entrance arch a recent embellishment to the original late eighteenth-century hall built by immigrants from Guangdong. Though there's nothing of particular merit here, it's an appealing place, mostly because of its plant-filled courtyard, ornamented with dragon and carp carvings (see box below). Lastly, plum in the centre of town is the **Chinese Assembly Hall**, or Chua Ba (7–11.30am & 2–5pm; not covered by ticket scheme, free), built in 1740 as an umbrella organization for all Hoi An's ethnic Chinese population. Thien Hau graces the altar but the hall is nowadays used mainly as a language school where local ethnic Chinese children and adults come to learn their mother tongue. The school was closed in 1975 and only permitted to re-open in 1990.

The merchants' houses

The majority of Hoi An's original wooden buildings are found along Tran Phu and south towards the river, which is where you'll find the best-known merchant's house, at 101 Nguyen Thai Hoc. The **Tan Ky House** is a beautifully

Unravelling the architectural features of Hoi An

You can't walk far in Hoi An without confronting a **mythical beast** with a fish's body and dragon's head; though they're found all over northern Vietnam they seem to have struck a particular chord with Hoi An's architects. One of the most prominent examples tops a weather vane in the Phuoc Kien Assembly Hall, but there are plenty of more traditional representations about, carved into lantern brackets and beam ends, or forming the beams themselves. The **carp** symbolizes prosperity, success and, here, metamorphosing into a **dragon**, serves as a reminder that nothing in life comes easily. To become a dragon, and thereby attain immortality, a fish must pass through three gates – just as a scholar has to pass three exams to become a mandarin, requiring much patience and hard work.

Another typical feature of Hoi An's architecture are "**eyes**" watching over the entrance to a house or religious building. Two thick wooden nails about 20cm in diameter are driven into the lintel as protection against evil forces, following a practice that originated in the pagodas of northern Vietnam. Assembly halls offer the most highly ornamented examples: that of Phuoc Kien consists of a yin and yang with two dragons in obeisance to the sun, while the Cantonese version is a fearsome tiger. The **yin and yang** symbol became fashionable in the nineteenth century and is the most commonly used image on houses, sometimes set in a chrysanthemum flower, such as at the Tan Ky House, or as the octagonal talisman representing eight charms.

preserved example of a two-storey, late eighteenth-century shophouse, amalgamating Vietnamese, Japanese and Chinese influences in an architectural style typical of Hoi An. The present house was built by a second-generation member of the Tan Ky family, who fled China as political refugees in the late sixteenth century, and took eight years to complete. The long, narrow building has shop space at the front, a tiny central courtyard and direct access to the river at the back, from where merchandise would be hauled upstairs to storerooms safe above the floods. The house, wonderfully cluttered with the accumulated property of seven generations grown wealthy from trading silk, tea and rice, is constructed of dark hardwoods, including termite-resistant jackfruit for its main columns. The skill of local woodcarvers is evident throughout, but most stunning is the inlay work: look out for two hanging poem-boards on which mother-of-pearl brush-strokes form exquisitely delicate birds in flight. Guides, speaking French and English, are on hand to answer questions, but at times the house is completely overwhelmed with visitors – far better to come, if you can, at a quieter time (early or late in the day) to appreciate the weight of history here. Diagonally across the street, at 80 Nguyen Thai Hoc, poke your nose in at the **house of Diep Dong Nguyen**. Built at the end of the nineteenth century for a Chinese merchant, and later converted into a pharmacy, nowadays the glass medicine cases are stuffed full of dusty family heirlooms.

Just up from the covered bridge at 4 Nguyen Thi Minh Khai, **Phung Hung House** has been home to the same family for eight generations, since they moved from Hué in about 1780 to trade cinnamon and hardwoods from the central highlands, as well as silk and glass. The large two-storey house is Vietnamese in style although its eighty ironwood columns and small glass skylights denote Japanese influence, while the gallery and window shutters are in Chinese style. An upstairs living area features a shrine to the ancestors as well as a large shrine to the protector deity Thien Hau, suspended from the ceiling; prayers were said here for the safe return of family members away on trading trips. A set of seven dice in a bowl on a table in front of the altar used to be thrown to determine the auspicious time to set out on a journey, although a plastic set has replaced the bone or marble originals.

More modest is **Quan Thang House** at 77 Tran Phu. This single-storey shophouse was founded in the early eighteenth century by a captain from Fujian in China, and was home to a medicine-trading business.

On the face of it, Phan Chu Trinh, one block north of Tran Phu, is an unspectacular road but it hides two "family chapels", again houses built by wealthy Chinese merchants, but to a design reflecting their spiritual rather than predominantly commercial focus. On Phan Chu Trinh itself is the 200-year-old **Tran Family Chapel**, within a walled compound on the junction with Le Loi. Over home-made lotus-flower tea and sugared coconut you learn about the building and family traditions, going back thirteen generations (three hundred years) to when the first ancestor settled in Hanoi. The move to Hoi An came, so the story goes, when one son married a Vietnamese woman. Such was the parental disapproval that he fled south to make his fortune trading silk, pepper and ivory in Hoi An, but, miraculously, all was forgiven and the whole family turned up on the doorstep. Succeeding generations continued to shine, with one mandarin to their credit – his portrait and ceremonial sword, bearing the Imperial insignia, are displayed in the reception room. On the altar itself, oblong funerary boxes contain a name-tablet and biographical details of deceased family leaders and their wives – carved lotus blossoms indicate adherents of Buddhism. Each year the entire family – more than eighty people – gather round the altar to venerate their ancestors and discuss family affairs.

The smaller, more elaborate **Truong Family Chapel** (not covered by ticket scheme; 7.30am–noon & 2–5pm; small donation expected) is hidden down an alley beside 69 Phan Chu Trinh. The Truong ancestors, like many ethnic Chinese now in Hoi An, fled China in the early eighteenth century following the collapse of the Ming Dynasty. The ground-breaking ceremony took place in 1840 at the auspicious moment of 5am on the fifth day of the eleventh lunar month – that is, on the hour of the cat and day of the cat, in the month and year of the mouse. This family also embraces mandarin forefathers and cherishes gifts from the Hué court, but more intriguing is an inscribed panel bestowed by Emperor Bao Dai on the wife of the fifth generation who, widowed at 25 and with three children, nevertheless remained faithful to her dead husband.

Museums

Hoi An has a clutch of fairly modest historical museums, the most rewarding of which is the **Museum of Trade Ceramics** at 80 Tran Phu, housed in a traditional timber residence–cum–warehouse. It showcases the history of Hoi An's ceramics trade, which peaked in the fifteenth and sixteenth centuries, with most of the exhibits from Vietnam, China and Japan. The rear room on the ground floor houses a small display about the architecture of Hoi An.

The **Museum of Sa Huynh Culture**, occupying a two-storey French-era house at 149 Tran Phu, focuses on a distinct culture which flourished along the coast of central Vietnam between the second century BC and the second century AD; the name comes from the town 130km south of Hoi An where evidence was first discovered in 1902 (see p.257).

Towards the east end of Tran Phu, the north side of the market square is dominated by the colourful frontage of **Chua Ong**, a seventeenth-century pagoda-temple conversion dedicated to General Quan Cong. Behind the temple lies Hoi An's **Museum of History and Culture**, attractively housed in another former pagoda. Apart from the copies of ancient maps of Fai Fo, the primary appeal of this small, informative museum is its quiet courtyard and carved, wooden door panels, depicting the four sacred animals: crane, dragon, turtle and the mythical *kylin*.

The market and around

Hoi An **market** retains an appealingly traditional atmosphere, despite the number of tourists. Like most, it's best in the early morning, especially among the riverfront fresh-food stalls. Look out for jars of tiny preserved tangerines, a regional speciality, amid neat stacks of basketware, bowl-shaped lumps of unrefined cane-sugar, liniments, medicinal herbs and every variety of rice. Wandering down through the market square brings you out by the ferry docks and Bach Dang, which regularly disappears each autumn under the swollen **Thu Bon River**. The floods are bad news for Hoi An's ancient buildings, occasionally precipitating the collapse of weakened roofs and walls, and the deterioration of the fabric as pollution levels increase. For most of the year, however, you can go dry-shod along Bach Dang and watch the river scene from beneath the cheery awning of a waterside café. It's a spectacle best captured between 6 and 7am when the fishing boats are unloading their catch.

From the market, walk east along the river and you come to Phan Boi Chau, where the town takes on a distinctly European flavour – louvred shutters, balconies and stucco – in what was the beginnings of a **French quarter**. The interiors of these late nineteenth-century townhouses are characterized by vast, high-ceilinged rooms and enormous roof-spaces, markedly different from the

▲ Selling fish at the riverfront market

Chinese abodes. You can take a brief tour round **Tran Duong House**, at no. 25, the home of an enterprising man who owns a smattering of period furniture (small donation expected).

Eating and drinking

Hoi An has a fine choice of **restaurants** at which you can sample an array of local speciality dishes (see box, p.276) or opt for some fairly upmarket international cuisine. In the evenings, tables and chairs line Bach Dang, whose restaurants may look more Mediterranean than Vietnamese, but largely focus on local produce. There's also a glut of popular restaurants on Tran Phu, spreading up Nguyen Hue near the market. In addition to cut-price set meals featuring local specialties, many of Hoi An's restaurants also offer cooking classes, costing from $10 per person and best arranged a day in advance; some establishments will help you personally select your ingredients at the market. Hoi An even boasts a few **bars** nowadays, the best of which occupy restored merchants' houses along Nguyen Thai Hoc.

Before & Now 51 Le Loi. Double-storey Italian restaurant and bar inside a traditional shophouse. While the first floor serves good thick-crust pizzas, downstairs is a popular meeting point for travellers wanting a beer or one of the many inhouse cocktails.

Blue Dragon 46 Bach Dang. Offering a similar standard of food and service to many other restaurants on Bach Dang, but the *Blue Dragon* donates part of its profits to a charity that helps rural children stay in school. The fact that the tasty five-course meal is just 70,000đ is a bonus.

Brother's Café 27 Phan Boi Chau. The garden setting on the banks of the Thu Bon River is reason

enough to come to this Hoi An institution, though the food on the whole is overpriced. To experience the atmosphere without the cost, sip a coffee ($2) while the sun goes down.

Café Can 74 Bach Dang. A welcoming restaurant offering Hoi An specialities and a good-value, three-course set menu for 60,000đ. Tables tend to fill up as the sun starts to set and the service is always super friendly.

Cargo Club 107–109 Nguyen Thai Hoc ☏0510/391 0489. Despite having a good selection of local and international dishes, the real draw is the French bakery downstairs, which offers decadent pastries and an array of take-to-the-beach bread rolls.

Hoi An specialities

Hoi An has a number of tasty specialities to sample. Most famous is *cao lau*, a mouthwatering bowlful of thick rice-flour **noodles**, bean sprouts and pork-rind croutons in a light soup flavoured with mint and star anise, topped with thin slices of pork and served with grilled rice-flour crackers or sprinkled with crispy rice paper. Legend has it that the genuine article is cooked using water drawn from one particular local well. Lovers of **seafood** should try the delicately flavoured steamed manioc-flour parcels of finely diced crab or shrimp called *banh bao*, translated as "white rose", with lemon, sugar and *nuoc mam*, complemented by a crunchy onion-flake topping, adding extra flavour. A local variation of *hoanh thanh chien* (fried wonton), using shrimp and crab meat instead of pork, is also popular. To fill any remaining gaps, try Hoi An **cake**, *banh it*, triangular parcels made by steaming green-bean paste and strands of sweetened coconut in banana leaves.

The home-made ice cream also has the crowds lining up.

Faifoo 104 Tran Phu. Locals rate the *banh bao* at this well-established and attractive restaurant as the best in town, though many travellers choose the cheap five-course sampler of Hoi An specialities.

Good Morning Vietnam 102 Nguyen Thai Hoc. The popular Ho Chi Minh City-based chain has brought its winning formula – authentic pasta and pizza dishes at moderate prices (from around 90,000đ), plus a bit of ambience – north to Hoi An.

Hong Phuc 86 Bach Dang. A friendly, good-value and deservedly popular place – get here early for a table on the balcony – in a great waterside location, run by two multilingual female cousins. If you want to know the secret, you can sign up for an afternoon cookery class ($10; one-day's notice) during which you learn how to make four dishes.

Jean's Café 48 Phan Dinh Phung. Cheap prices and a jovial patron have earned this little café a place on the backpacker circuit. It serves all the old favourites – pizza, pasta, sandwiches and omelettes – as well as Vietnamese dishes.

Lighthouse Cam Nam Island ☏ 0510/393 6235. As well as a moderately-priced mix of foreign and Vietnamese dishes, Dutch owner Hans runs interesting bike-plus-cooking tours in which you zoom through the countryside, stop off at a market or two to buy ingredients, then head back home in the evening to whip up your food. Diners can get a free ride here on their boat, which can be found off Bach Dang.

Mango Rooms 111 Nguyen Thai Hoc. The menu at this chilled restaurant is constantly changing but always wonderfully creative – imagine red snapper with coriander and pineapple, or prawns in a passion fruit and chocolate sauce – and there's also an excellent wine list. Its sister restaurant – *Mango Mango* – is directly across the river from the Japanese Bridge, views of which make this it a better choice for sampling maverick owner Duc's signature cocktails.

Miss Ly 22 Nguyen Hue. *Miss Ly*'s is a pretty little place with a well-deserved reputation for serving up some of the best *cao lau* and *banh bao* in Hoi An. Try the Vietnamese set menu (45.000đ) to sample a bit of everything. They also offer a good range of vegetarian dishes, plus Vegemite on toast for homesick Aussies.

Nhu Y 2 Tran Phu. This restaurant has a strong reputation for service and value. Their speciality is grills, such as snapper on banana leaf with ginger or tuna with turmeric, or try the set dinner – a starter, choice of two main courses plus dessert for 80,000đ.

Phone Cafe 80b Bach Dang. This relaxed, homely restaurant is most notable for its cooking classes, which get you five courses worth of food for just $10, as well as a trip to the market to choose your ingredients. In the evening you can get "fresh beer" for just 4,000đ, or go for the more adventurous gin and mango shake.

Quan An 18 Hoang Van Thu. On a quiet street near the river, this simple restaurant serves mouth-watering local cuisine at very reasonable prices. The duck dishes are particularly recommended, and they also rustle up a mean fried wonton. While you're waiting, slake your thirst on a glass of chilled *bia tuoi* (local draught beer).

Red Bridge Thon 4, Cam Thanh ☏ 0510/393 3222. In just a short space of time, this restaurant has gained a reputation for serving some of Hoi An's finest modern Vietnamese cuisine. Situated 2km east of town, in incredibly scenic riverside surroundings, it will take you there on its own boat, which departs outside 74 Bach Dang (daily noon & 1.30pm and Fri–Sun 5.30pm & 7pm; 20min). It also runs half-day cooking classes which can be booked at *Hai's Scout Café* (98 Nguyen Thai Hoc).

Shree Ganesh 24 Phan Dinh Phung. You may not find many locals here, but you are sure to find lots of travellers getting their fix of hot curries (they have their own tandoor oven) and cold beers. An Indian chef oversees proceedings, and takes pride in the fact that he uses local spices and ingredients.

Sleepy Gecko Cam Nam Island. Picture-perfect sunsets are the norm at this chilled bar, which can get nice and busy in the evenings despite its isolated location on Cam Nam.

Tam Tam Café 2f/110 Nguyen Thai Hoc ☏0510/386 2212. Stylish French-run bar (serving bar meals such as sandwiches, salads, and great Aussie steaks) that's open late, with music, pool and happy-hour beers (4–9pm). Head for the comfy sofas at the back if you want to chill out, or upstairs for what many expats deem the town's best nightspot.

Treat's Café 158 Tran Phu. Upbeat bar-restaurant with good music, a shady interior courtyard, pool and cheap happy-hour deals (4–9pm). A second, less popular outlet at 31 Phan Dinh Phung enigmatically promises to be "same same but different".

Arts, handicrafts and shopping

With the influx of tourists, Hoi An is becoming a centre for the **arts**. A delightful hour-long medley of **traditional music and dance** is performed most evenings in a cramped room rather grandly known as the Traditional Arts Theatre, 75 Nguyen Thai Hoc (Mon–Sat 9pm; 45,000đ). Folk musicians also play short concerts at the Hoi An Handicraft Workshop, 9 Nguyen Thai Hoc (Mon–Sat 10.15am & 3.15pm; included in ticket scheme, see box, p.271). Once a month vehicles are banned from the town centre, coloured silk lanterns replace electric lights and shopkeepers don traditional costume to celebrate the **Full-Moon Festival** (fourteenth day of the lunar calendar). It's a tourist event, but a great occasion nonetheless: there are traditional music performances, with food stalls selling local specialities by the Japanese Bridge and on the waterfront. During the **Mid-Autumn Festival**, a much bigger affair celebrated nation-wide on the fourteenth day of the eighth lunar month, people also float lanterns on the river. In recent years – usually in spring but dates vary – Quang Nam province has also staged a week-long **cultural heritage festival** in Hoi An and My Son, including Cham dances and folk songs.

Tourism has also led to a revival in local **crafts**, though there are plenty of second-rate **souvenirs** on sale as well. Dedicated browsers can occupy several hours in the shops and galleries along Tran Phu, Nguyen Thai Hoc and Le Loi, while just over the Japanese bridge a cluster of old houses double as showrooms. Scattered here and there are **workshops** where you can see a range of local crafts, from embroidery, wood-carving and pottery to silk being made by tradi-tional methods; visits are free, though afterwards you'll be directed to the souvenir shop-cum-showroom, not that there's any obligation to buy. The most interesting are the Hoi An Handicraft Workshop at 9 Nguyen Thai Hoc, where they also give folk concerts (see above), and the House of Traditional Handi-crafts, 41 Le Loi. The Kim Bong traditional carpentry studio is also worth a look at 108 Nguyen Thai Hoc, and look out, too, for a tiny stall at 49 Le Loi where the same family has been making silk lanterns for generations.

Hoi An is now well known for its **silk** and **tailoring**, with prices generally cheaper than in Hanoi or Ho Chi Minh City. You'll find shops all over town but the original outlet was the market, where even now rows of tailors sit at sewing machines next to rainbow-coloured stacks, and for a few dollars will make up beautiful garments in a matter of hours. It's worth shopping around – ask to see some finished articles before placing an order. If you have time, it's a good idea to have one item made first to check the quality and fit. A few places with a reputation for reliability include Bi Bi Silk, 13 Phan Chu Trinh, with a good range of linen, wool and silk, and the more upmarket Yaly at 47 Nguyen Thai Hoc (✉yalyshop@dng.vnn.vn). The popular Phuong Huy makes a wide array of items such as suits and handbags and has three outlets, at 9a Nhi Trung and 25 and 26 Tran Phu. To complete the outfit you can have **shoes** made to match (where you can create your own designs such as suede running shoes with your own initials on them). Most shops can do this for you, or there are dozens of outlets towards the bridge on Hoang Dieu.

Listings

Banks and exchange You can exchange cash and traveller's cheques and get over-the-counter cash advances on credit cards at Vietcombank, 25 Hai Ba Trung, and Agribank, 2 Phan Dinh Phung and 92 Tran Phu (both locations Mon–Sat 7am–5pm). There are also several ATMs around town.

Books Randy's Book Exchange on Cam Nam Island may well be the best second-hand bookstore in Vietnam; if you can't face the walk, most guest-houses offer book exchange.

Diving Tours Cham Island Diving Centre, 98 Bach Dang (☎0510/391 0782, ⓔ laochamsailing @hotmail.com), and Hoi An's branch of the popular Rainbow Divers, 99 Le Loi (☎0510/391 1123, ⓦ www.divevietnam.com), are the best options. Both have similar prices starting at $50 for a one-day scuba dive or $20 for snorkelling. Cham Island Diving Centre also offers accommodation on the island.

Ferries From the market end of Bach Dang, small ferry boats depart for villages along the Thu Bon River every thirty minutes from 5.30am to 7.30pm.

Hospital 4 Tran Hung Dao ☎0510/386 1218.

Laundry Places along Tran Hung Dao offer laundry services at around 10,000đ per kilo.

Open–tour buses For tickets and onward reservations contact *Sinh Café*, 186 Hai Ba Trung (see opposite). Local operator Seventeen's, 17 Tran Hung Dao (see opposite), also runs minibuses to Da Nang, Hué, Nha Trang and so forth, with stops en route.

Pharmacies In addition to small pharmacies near the hospital, Bac Ai, at 68 Nguyen Thai Hoc, is well stocked.

Police 8 Hoang Dieu ☎0510/386 1204.

Post office The unusually fancy and well-organized GPO is at 4b Tran Hung Dao (daily 6am–10pm); there is also an ATM here. There's a sub-post office at 89 Phan Chu Trinh.

River trips Along Bach Dang, sampan owners will take you out on the river for about 15,000đ an hour, or you can take a boat out to the craft villages and downstream as far as the Cua Dai estuary (see below). Prices start at 100,000đ an hour for an eight-person boat, but it's worth bargaining.

Tour agencies Hotel booking desks and tour agents along Tran Hung Dao, Phan Dinh Phung and Hai Ba Trung offer outings to My Son and craft villages around Hoi An. Sinh Café, 186 Hai Ba Trung (☎0510/386 3948, ⓦ www.sinhcafevn.com), and Vinh Tours, 32 Le Loi (☎0510/391 0825, ⓔ vintour74@hotmail.com), are popular but Seventeen's, 17 Tran Hung Dao (☎0510/386 1947, ⓔ seventeenstravel@yahoo.com), has some interesting variations, including canoeing on the Thu Bon River and trips out to the Cham Islands (see p.279). All these agents can arrange onward train and plane tickets from Da Nang and handle applications for visa extensions for you for a small commission.

Around Hoi An

From Hoi An you can bike out along meandering paths to the white expanse of **Cua Dai Beach** or hop on a sampan to one of the **islands** of the Thu Bon River. River tours take you to low-lying, estuarine islands and the **craft villages** along their banks, while it's also now possible to visit the distant **Cham Islands**, renowned for their sea swallows' nests.

Cua Dai Beach

A popular bike ride takes you 4km east of Hoi An to the clean, white sands of **Cua Dai Beach**. The inevitable hawkers patrol the area, but you can minimize the hassle by walking away from the main centre, or by taking an umbrella and deck chair for the day at one of the many beachfront café-restaurants; in return you'll be expected to buy at least a drink, though many also serve excellent seafood – just be sure to check the prices before ordering. Be prepared, too, for the strict parking regulations, which require you to leave your bicycle or motorbike at the car park a few hundred metres from the beach for a handful of dong; these regulations don't

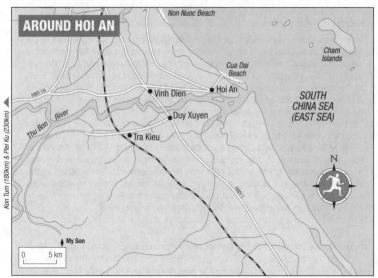

Non Nuoc Beach

Cham Islands

Cua Dai Beach

Vinh Dien • Hoi An

SOUTH CHINA SEA (EAST SEA)

Duy Xuyen

Tra Kieu

Thu Bon River

HWY-14

Kon Tum (180km) & Plei Ku (230km)

N

HWY-1

My Son

0   5 km

Quang Ngai (75km) & Nha Trang (480km) ▼

apply if you're heading to one of the resort hotels (see p.270) south along the beach road. En route by bike, you can take a detour through the beautiful, canal-riddled Cam Thanh area, which lies to the south of the main road; head east on Nguyen Duy Hieu and take a right when the road ends a couple of kilometres east of Hoi An. Alternatively, you can get to Cua Dai by taxi (25,000đ) or xe om (from 10,000đ) – just tell the driver when to pick you up.

Cam Nam Island and the craft villages

Even closer at hand, you can take a bike over either Cam Nam or An Hoi bridge and cycle round **Cam Nam Island**. Sandy tracks lead off in all directions between smallholdings and private houses, but the first lane right over Cam Nam Bridge brings you to a great viewpoint with Hoi An across the other side of the river. You can then work your way round to the south side of the island (or simply follow the metalled road from Cam Nam Bridge) and you'll reach a row of waterside restaurants serving *banh dap* (a sandwich of crispy and fresh rice-crackers served with a shellfish dipping sauce) and *hen tron* (fried clams). Even if you aren't tempted, it's a nice breezy place for a drink.

Specialist **craft villages**, inhabited by skilled artisans, developed around Hoi An during the sixteenth and seventeenth centuries. The work of one famous community of wood-carvers, from Kim Bong Village on **Cam Kim Island**, can be seen throughout Hoi An. Most carpenters have moved out of the village but a handful remain, building fishing boats or crafting furniture for export. This large island is a ten-minute ride from the Hoi An ferry station (see opposite) heading west up the river. You'll find one of the few surviving boatyards right beside the island's jetty, but it's worth taking a bike over and exploring the rest of the island. Cam Kim is also a stop on the boat trip back from My Son (see p.280).

The Cham Islands

A group of mountainous islands lying 10km offshore is clearly visible from the coast near Hoi An. Cu Lao Cham, or the **Cham Islands**, are inhabited by

Moving on from Hoi An

When it comes to onward transport, the most popular option is to hop on one of the **open-tour buses** heading north to Da Nang (from $2) and Hué (from $4) – with some services stopping briefly at the Marble Mountains, Hai Van Pass and Lang Co – or south to Nha Trang ($9–16) with stops at Sa Huynh, Song Cau and Dai Lanh. Each of the open-tour operators has an office in Hoi An where you can purchase tickets and make reservations (see p.278). While you can buy tickets almost anywhere, it's best to go to the company direct to ensure it's valid.

If you're headed to Da Nang, however, and want to spend longer at the various stops en route – the Marble Mountains, Non Nuoc Beach and the Cham Museum – a better alternative is to take a hired car ($10–15) or xe om (from 100,000đ). Afterwards you can get the driver to drop you at your hotel or at the train station or airport. Hotels and tour agencies in Hoi An will help with the arrangements. Local **buses** plying between Hoi An and Da Nang are very much a last resort: ancient vehicles, often stuffed to the gunnels, leave Hoi An bus station every half-hour or so, taking up to ninety minutes to cover the 30km (15,000đ; services stop at 5pm).

fishermen, the navy and collectors of highly prized birds' nests. Cham islanders have been harvesting sea swallows' nests since the late sixteenth century and today the government-controlled trade contributes greatly to the local economy, with prices up to $2500 per kilo for the culinary delicacy, to which extraordinary medicinal virtues are also attributed. Each spring, when thousands of the tiny, grey-and-black birds nest among the islands' caves and crevices, villagers build bamboo scaffolding or climb up ropes to prise the diminutive structures, about the size of a hen's egg, off the rock. Three thousand people live on the main island, but until 1995 even Vietnamese people weren't allowed to visit because of the naval base. Recently the island has become popular for its surrounding marine life, with 135 species of coral, 202 species of fish and 84 species of mollusks said to exist around the marine park. Boat trips take an hour each way from **Cua Dai Beach**, but there are plans for hydrofoil transport that will take just twenty minutes.

Although the development of a beach resort is rumoured, as yet there are no hotels on the islands. However Lodovico, the Italian owner of Cham Island Diving Centre (see p.278) rents out rooms in his beachside guesthouse (❸). Day-trips can be taken to the island with diving tour operators, starting at $20 for a snorkel trip.

My Son

Vietnam's most evocative Cham site, **MY SON** (daily 6.30am–4.30pm; 75,000đ), lies 40km southwest of Hoi An, in a bowl of lushly wooded hills towered over by the aptly named Cat's Tooth Mountain. My Son may be no Vietnamese Angkor Wat, but it is now on UNESCO's World Heritage list and richly deserves its place on the tourist map. The riot of vegetation that until recently enveloped the site has now largely been cleared away, but the tangible sense of faded majesty still hangs over the mouldering ruins, enhanced by the assorted lingam and Sanskrit stelae strewn around and by the isolated rural setting, whose peace is broken only by the wood-gatherers who trace the paths around the surrounding coffee and eucalyptus glades.

Excavations at My Son have revealed that Cham kings were buried here as early as the fourth century, indicating that the site was established by the rulers of the early Champa capital of **Simhapura**, sited some 30km back towards the highway, at present-day Tra Kieu. (See box on p.238 for more on the **Kingdom of Champa**.) The stone towers and sanctuaries whose remnants you see today were erected between the seventh and thirteenth centuries, with successive dynasties adding more temples to this holy place, until in its prime it comprised some seventy buildings. The area was considered the domain of gods and god-kings, and living on site would have been an attendant population of priests, dancers and servants.

French archaeologists discovered the ruins in the late nineteenth century, when the Chams' fine **masonry** skills were still evident – instead of mortar, they used a resin mixed with ground brick and mollusc shells, which left only hairline cracks between brick courses. After the Viet Cong based themselves here in the 1960s, many unique buildings were pounded to oblivion by American B52s, most notably the once magnificent A1 tower. Craters around the site and masonry pocked with shell and bullet holes testify to this tragic period in My Son's history.

Practicalities

Most people visit on a **guided tour** from Hoi An (see p.278 for agencies; approx $10 per person); a popular variation is to return part of the way by boat, stopping at a couple of craft villages along the way ($15). It's also possible to rent a motorbike or taxi ($35) or motorbike in Hoi An and travel to My Son independently; the road to the site strikes west from Highway 1 at Duy Xuyen (there are sporadic signs for My Son). If you do this, it pays to get there early (before 9am) to avoid the worst of the crowds and the heat.

While we've outlined a handful of the site's particularly noteworthy edifices below, you'll get most out of My Son simply by wandering at your leisure – but don't stray far from the towers and marked paths, as **unexploded mines** may still be in the ground. The groups of buildings labelled B, C and D most warrant

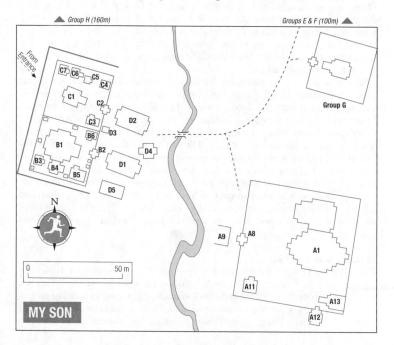

your attention: viewing these, it's possible, with a little stirring of the imagination, to visualize how a functioning temple complex would have appeared in My Son's heyday.

Group B

Archeologists regard **Group B** as the spiritual epicentre of My Son. Of the central **kalan** (sanctuary), **B1**, only the base remains, along with a lingam discovered under the foundations a few years ago; but stone epitaphs found nearby reveal that it was dedicated to the god-king Bhadresvara, a hybrid of Shiva and fourth-century King Bhadravarman, and erected in the eleventh century, under King Harivarman IV, on the site of an earlier, wooden temple. Fortunately, other elements of Group B have fared rather better, particularly **B5**, the impressive **repository room**, boasting a bowed, boat-shaped roof still in reasonably good condition. Votive offerings and other ritual paraphernalia would have been stored in B5's chimney-shaped interior, while its outer walls support ornate columns and statues of deities. The carving on the southern facade is particularly well preserved; on the west look out for a fine bas-relief depicting two elephants with their trunks entwined around a coconut tree. The carving of Vishnu sitting below the thirteen heads of the snake-god Naga that adorned the roof of **B6** was an early casualty of war, but the oval receptacle for the holy water used in purification rituals and statue-washing ceremonies is still intact inside. The two smaller temples flanking B1's south side, **B3** and **B4**, would have been dedicated to Skanda and Ganesha, the children of Shiva, while posted around the complex are the remains of seven tiny shrines honouring the gods of the elements and of the points of the compass.

Groups C and D

Originally separated from Group B by a wall, the **Group C** complex is quite distinct from it. This time the central *kalan*, **C1**, is standing and fairly well preserved, though the statue of Shiva that it was built to house long since went to Da Nang's museum, leaving only its base in place. The statues of standing gods around the walls have been allowed to stay, though, as has the carved lintel that runs across the entrance.

East of B and C, the two long, windowed *mandapa* (meditation halls) that comprise **Group D** have now both been converted into modest **galleries**. Precisely aligned with the foundations of B1 is **D1**, the **mandapa**, where the priests would meditate prior to proceeding through the (now ruined) gate **B2** to worship. It also contains a lingam, the remains of a carving of Shiva, and a statue of Nandi, Shiva's bull, while in **D2** you'll see a fine rendition of many-armed Shiva dancing, and, beside the steps up to its eastern entrance, an impressive statue of Vishnu's vehicle, Garuda. The ground between these two galleries was named the **Court of Stelae** by early archaeologists, a reference to the stone tablets, etched with Sanskrit script, that litter it. As well as these stelae, altars and statues of deities would have stood in the court, though all that remain of these are their plinths, on whose sides are sculpted images of dancing women, arms raised to carry their gods.

Groups A and G

East of Group D, signs direct you to Groups A and G. Bomb damage was particularly cruel in the vicinity of **Group A**, reducing the once spectacular *kalan*, **A1**, to a heap of toppled columns and lintels that closely resembles a collapsed hall of cards. Unusually, A1 was constructed with both an eastern and a western entrance. Within, a huge lingam base is ringed by a number of detailed, fifteen-centimetre-high figures at prayer. You'll pass **A9**, the *mandapa*, and **A8**, the gate, en route from B, C and D; **A11** would have been the repository room.

The remains of hilltop **Group G**, 60m north of Group A, are equally poorly preserved. However, you can still pick out horned gargoyles, sporting fangs and bulbous eyes, carved into the corners of the main *kalan*. The base of a lingam stands at the *kalan*'s southwestern corner, with breasts around its base.

Da Nang

Sitting on the southerly curve of a vast, well-protected bay, **DA NANG** is central Vietnam's dominant port and its third largest city. During the sixteenth and seventeenth centuries trading vessels waiting to unload at Fai Fo (Hoi An) often sheltered in nearby Da Nang Bay, until Hoi An's harbour began silting up and Da Nang developed into a major port in its own right. After 1802, when Hué

Da Nang during the war

The city of Da Nang mushroomed after the arrival of the first American combat troops on March 8, 1965. An advance guard of two battalions of Marines waded ashore at Red Beach in Da Nang Bay, providing the press with a photo opportunity that included amphibious landing craft, helicopters and young Vietnamese women handing out garlands – not quite as the generals had envisaged. The Marines had come to defend Da Nang's massive **US Air Force base**; as the troops flew in so the base sprawled. Eventually Da Nang became "a small American city", as journalist John Pilger remembers it, "with its own generators, water purification plants, hospitals, cinemas, bowling alleys, ball parks, tennis courts, jogging tracks, super-markets and bars, lots of bars". For most US troops the approach to Da Nang airfield formed their first impression of Vietnam, and it was here they came to take a break from the war at the famous **China Beach**.

At the same time the city swelled with thousands of **refugees**, mostly villagers cleared from "free-fire zones" but also people in search of work – labourers, cooks, laundry staff, pimps, prostitutes and drug pushers, all inhabiting a shantytown called Dogpatch on the base perimeter. Da Nang's population rose inexorably: 20,000 in the 1940s, 50,000 in 1955 and, some estimate, a peak of one million during the American years. North Vietnamese mortar shells periodically fell in and around the base, but the city's most violent scenes occurred when two South Vietnamese generals engaged in a little power struggle. In March 1966 Vice Air Marshal Ky, then prime minister of South Vietnam, ousted a popular Hué overlord, General Thi, following his open support of Buddhist dissidents. Demonstrations spread from Hué to Da Nang where troops loyal to Thi seized the airfield in what amounted to a **mini civil war**. After much posturing Ky crushed the revolt two months later, killing hundreds of rebel troops and many civilians. In the preceding chaos, the beleaguered rebels held forty Western journalists hostage for a brief period in Da Nang's largest pagoda, Chua Tinh Hoi, while streets around filled with Buddhist protesters.

When the North Vietnamese Army finally arrived to **liberate** Da Nang on March 29, 1975, they had less of a struggle. Communist units had already cut the road south, and panic-stricken South Vietnamese soldiers battled for space on any plane or boat leaving the city, firing on unarmed civilians. Many drowned in the struggle to reach fishing boats, while planes and tanks were abandoned to the enemy. Da Nang had been all but deserted by South Vietnamese forces, leaving the mighty base to, according to Pilger, be "taken by a dozen NLF cadres waving white handkerchiefs from the back of a truck".

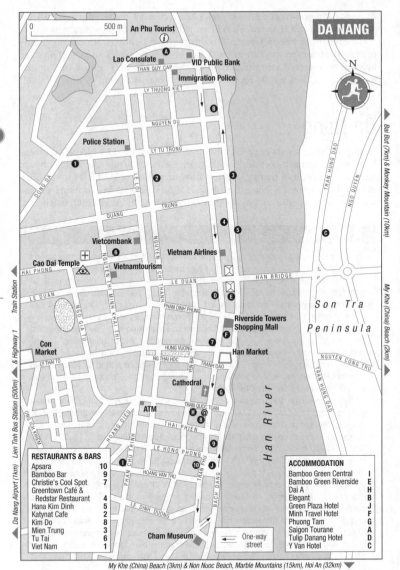

THE CENTRAL PROVINCES | Da Nang

DA NANG

0   500 m

An Phu Tourist

Lao Consulate   VID Public Bank

THAN QUY CAP

Immigration Police

LY THUONG KIET

NGUYEN DU

Police Station

LY TU TRONG

LE LOI

TRUNG

QUANG

Vietcombank

Vietnam Airlines

Cao Dai Temple

Vietnamtourism

HAI PHONG

NGUYEN CHI THANH

NGUYEN THI MINH KHAI

LE DUAN

LE DUAN

HAN BRIDGE

NGO GIA TU

PHAN DINH PHUNG

Con Market

Riverside Towers Shopping Mall

LY THAI TO

HUNG VUONG

NG THAI HOC

Han Market

TRANH DAO

YEN BAI

Cathedral

HOANG DIEU

ATM

TRAN QUOC TOAN

THAI PHIEN

PHAN CHU TRINH

LE HONG PHONG

THANG PHU

HOANG VAN THU

BACH DANG

LE DINH DUONG

Cham Museum

TRAN HUNG DAO

NGO QUYEN

Bai But (7km) & Monkey Mountain (10km)

My Khe (China) Beach (2km)

Son Tra Peninsula

NGUYEN CONG TRU

TRAN HUNG DAO

Han River

One-way street

RESTAURANTS & BARS

Apsara	10
Bamboo Bar	9
Christie's Cool Spot	7
Greentown Café & Redstar Restaurant	4
Hana Kim Dinh	5
Katynat Cafe	2
Kim Do	8
Mien Trung	3
Tu Tai	6
Viet Nam	1

ACCOMMODATION

Bamboo Green Central	I
Bamboo Green Riverside	E
Dai A	H
Elegant	B
Green Plaza Hotel	J
Minh Travel Hotel	F
Phuong Tam	G
Saigon Tourane	A
Tulip Danang Hotel	D
Y Van Hotel	C

Train Station

& Highway 1

Lien Tinh Bus Station (500m)

Da Nang Airport (1km)

My Khe (China) Beach (3km) & Non Nuoc Beach, Marble Mountains (15km), Hoi An (32km)

became capital of Vietnam, Da Nang naturally served as the principal point of arrival for foreign delegations to the royal court. However, the real spur to the city's growth came in the American War when the neighbouring air base spawned the greatest concentration of US military personnel in South Vietnam.

Walking around central Da Nang today, however, it's the earlier, French presence which is more apparent, in the leafy boulevards and colonial edifices along the riverfront promenade. Considering its size (it has a population of around 750,000), its history and the fact that this is a major transport hub offering air connections as well as road and rail links, Da Nang is an unexpectedly amiable place. Though the city harbours few specific sights of its own beyond the **Cham Museum** with its unique collection of Cham sculpture, it makes a reasonable base for exploring this stretch of coast. Some of Vietnam's best **beaches** are to be found only a few kilometres away (see p.292), while, further afield, My Son (see p.280) and Hoi An can be covered on day-trips.

Arrival, information and city transport

Da Nang's **airport** is only 3km southwest of the city. There are a couple of taxi desks inside the arrivals hall offering reasonable rates for Hoi An (from 50,000đ per person), but if you're going to the city centre, it's a little cheaper to take one of the metered taxis waiting outside (45,000đ or less). The **train station** lies 2km west of town at 122 Hai Phong. Long-distance **buses** arrive a kilometre further out at Lien Tinh bus station, 33 Dien Bien Phu, where local buses also gather on the other side of the road. **Open-tour buses** generally drop passengers at the Cham Museum, at the south end of Bach Dang.

Da Nang is big enough and its sights sufficiently spread out to make walking round town fairly time-consuming. Most hotels either **rent bikes** or can direct you to somewhere that does (around 15,000đ per day); otherwise, there's no shortage of cyclo or xe om. Self-drive **motorbikes** (around 75,000đ per day) are available from tour agencies and most hotels.

Accommodation

The majority of Da Nang's **hotels** are geared to either business travellers or tour groups. In the last few years a number of mini-hotels have opened that offer reasonable value for money, particularly on the other side of the river (Tran Hung Dao), where the views are better and surroundings quieter. Accommodation is also available at nearby China Beach or the luxurious *Furama Resort* (see p.291).

Bamboo Green Central 158 Phan Chu Trinh ☎0511/382 2996, ✉bamboogreen@dng.vnn.vn. Upmarket hotel popular with tour groups and business people. A good range of facilities, including money exchange, tour desk, restaurant and bar, plus decent – if rather bland – rooms, make this one of the best hotels in town. ❹

Bamboo Green Riverside 68 Bach Dang ☎0511/383 2591, ✉riversidets@dng.vnn.vn. The latest addition to the *Bamboo* chain makes up for smaller rooms with slightly cheaper prices and river views from most rooms, some with balconies. Facilities include internet access as well as a restaurant, bar, tour desk and ATM outside. ❹

Dai A 51 Yen Bai ☎0511/382 7532, ⓦwww .daiahotel.com. The rooms are a bit dated, but the central location and friendly welcome make this a reasonable option for those that want their own bathroom, a/c and satellite TV. Front rooms can be noisy. ❸

Elegant 22a Bach Dang ☎0511/389 2893, ✉elegant@dng.vnn.vn. Efficient business hotel on the riverfront which lives up to its name. The decor

and standard of furnishings are a cut above the competition at this price range. There's a restaurant, bar, small business centre and money-exchange facilities. ❸–❹

Green Plaza Hotel 238 Bach Dang ☎0511/322 3399, ⓦwww.greenplazahotel .vn. It's hard to miss this new twenty-floor tower on the riverside; service is excellent, and the rooms fresh and immaculate, though you'll pay extra for a river view. Non-guests are also welcome to use the *Skybar* on the top floor, which offers free high-speed internet access and wonderful views. ❻

Minh Travel Hotel 105 Tran Phu ☎0511/381 2661, ✉mtraymond@yahoo.ca. The central location and some of the lowest prices in town make this a good option for those on a strict budget. Rooms are basic but adequate with fans, or a/c for a slightly higher price. If you are willing to share a bathroom, the "student room" is only $5. ❶

Phuong Tam 174 Bach Dang ☎0511/382 4288. This riverside hotel is handy for the Cham Museum, and has well-appointed rooms with a/c and satellite TV. Those at the rear are quieter and slightly cheaper. **②**

Saigon Tourane 5 Dong Da ☎0511/382 1021, ⓦwww.saigontourane.com.vn. The most upmarket hotel in town boasts a restaurant serving international cuisine, piano-bar, health club, business centre and ATM. The rooms are very comfortable, equipped to three-star standards, albeit slightly soulless. It's also a little out of the way. **⑤**

Tulip Danang Hotel 58 Tran Phu ☎0511/384 0778, ⓔtulipdananghote@vnn.vn. This new hotel's rooms are spotless and fully equipped; as it's on a

main road rooms out back are quieter, though those on the higher floors facing the front have good views over the town and river. **④**

Y Van Hotel 21 Tran Hung Dao ☎0511/393 6156, ⓔhotelyvan@vnn.vn. Situated on the quieter side of the Han River, this new fifteen-room mini-hotel is a shining beacon among Da Nang's lacklustre mid-range accommodation options. Rooms are luxuriously furnished with all amenities including full-size baths. The rooftop bar is a great spot to watch the city at night. **③–④**

The City

The elongated oval of Da Nang occupies a small headland protruding into the southern curve of Da Nang Bay. The city faces east, fronting onto Bach Dang and the Han River, across which the narrow Son Tra Peninsula shelters it from the South China Sea. Its streets follow a rough grid plan, dissected by two main thoroughfares, Le Duan and Le Loi/Phan Chu Trinh. Hung Vuong and streets around form the commercial heart of Da Nang, running between the two central **markets**: sprawling, oppressive Cho Con in the west and orderly Cho Han by the river. Two blocks south of Han market, past the soft, salmon-mousse coloured cathedral, colonial Da Nang is represented by a few wooden and stucco houses at the eastern end of Tran Quoc Toan. From here turn right along riverfront **Bach Dang** for 750m to reach the **Cham Museum**, the city's only real tourist attraction, or left to stroll north past a collection of well-restored French-era administrative buildings, some of them now occupied by People's Committees and hotels.

The Cham Museum

Even if you're just passing through Da Nang, try to spare an hour for the small **Cham Museum** at 2 Duong 2 Thang 9 (7am–5pm; 30,000đ), particularly if you plan to visit the Cham ruins at My Son (see p.280). The museum – whose design incorporates Cham motifs – sits in a garden of frangipani trees at the south end of Bach Dang, and its display of graceful, sometimes severe, terracotta and sandstone figures gives a tantalizing glimpse of an artistically inspired culture that ruled most of southern Vietnam for a thousand years (see box, p.238). In the late nineteenth century French archeologists started collecting statues, friezes and altars from once magnificent Cham sites dotted around the hinterland of Da Nang, and opened the museum in 1916. Though this is undoubtedly the most comprehensive display of Cham art in the world, it's said many of the best statues were carried off into European private collections.

Recurring images in Cham art are lions, elephants and Hindu deities, predominantly Shiva (founder and defender of Champa) expressed either as a vigorous, full-lipped man or as a lingam, but Vishnu, Garuda, Ganesha and Nandi the bull are also portrayed. Buddhas feature strongly in the ninth-century art of Indrapura, a period when Khmer and Indonesian influences were gradually assimilated. The most distinctive icon is Uroja, a breast and nipple that represents the universal "mother" of Cham kings.

As the Viets pushed south during the eleventh century, so the Chams retreated, and their sculptures evolved a bold, cubic style. Though less refined than earlier works, the chunky mythical animals from this period retain pleasing solidity and a playful charm.

▲ Da Nang's Cham Museum

The exhibits are grouped according to their place of origin and are positioned in two main halls. In the first hall, a massive, square altar pedestal (late seventh century) from the religious centre of My Son is considered a masterpiece of early Cham craftsmanship, particularly its frieze depicting jaunty dancing-girls, and a soulful flute player. However, experts and amateurs alike usually nominate two lithe dancers with Mona Lisa smiles, their soft, round bodies seemingly clad in nothing but strings of pearls, as the zenith of Cham artistry. The piece also features two musicians on a fragment of capital produced by Tra Kieu sculptors in the late tenth century, just before the decline of the Champa kingdom.

The second hall is a new extension at the back; three times larger than the first hall, it includes a further 146 stone sculptures, dating from the seventh to the fourteenth centuries.

Cao Dai Temple

Da Nang's **Cao Dai Temple**, at 63 Hai Phong opposite the hospital, was built in 1956 and is Vietnam's second most important after Tay Ninh (see p.123). An elderly archbishop, assisted by fifteen priests, ministers to a congregation said to number 50,000 here. The temple, which sees few tourists, is a smaller, simpler version of Tay Ninh, dominated inside by the all-seeing eye of the Supreme Being and paintings of Cao Dai's principal saints, Lao-tzu, Confucius, Jesus Christ and Buddha (see box on p.126 for more on these tenets). Services were banned between 1975 and 1986 and the building locked up, but now adherents gather to worship four times a day (6am, noon, 6pm & midnight). The occasional tourists who do turn up find it has more erratic opening times than its larger sister temple outside Ho Chi Minh City; you may find the gate locked when there is no service on.

Eating and drinking

Da Nang has no shortage of places to eat, ranging from food stalls to full-blown, top-notch restaurants. Fruitful hunting grounds for local restaurants and **food**

stalls are the west end of Hai Phong and streets to the south of Hung Vuong, particularly Nguyen Chi Thanh. For a mid-morning snack, browse the little **bakeries** at the north end of Phan Chu Trinh. There are also a couple of decent **bars** where, amongst other things, you can quaff the local beers – Da Nang Export and Bière la Rue.

Apsara 222 Tran Phu. Prices are surprisingly reasonable at Danang's flashiest restaurant, with mains on the seafood-centred menu starting at 60,000đ, and soups going for half that; for an interesting change, try the *chao tom* – ground shrimp roasted on sugar cane. A band plays traditional music every night from 7–8pm.

Bamboo Bar 230 Bach Dang. Shoot some pool at this small, friendly bar; popular with expats, it can get busy of an evening (open till 1am).

Christie's Cool Spot 112 Tran Phu. This Japanese/Australian-owned bar and restaurant is where the small expat community likes to come and chat. If you suddenly have a craving for yakitori or tandoor chicken pizza, this is the place for you. You can eat at the bar or in the upstairs restaurant, where there's also a small book exchange.

Greentown Café & Redstar Restaurant 50 Bach Dang. Overlooking the river, this schizophrenic venue is popular with locals and foreigners alike. The Greentown Café is an open-air pub with pool tables and outdoor seating, while the Redstar next door offers standard Vietnamese and Western food (pizza and pasta) but is most popular for the huge cinema screen outside that plays movies and football. Upstairs there is an excellent area overlooking the river.

Hana Kim Dinh 15 Bach Dang. Da Nang's attempt at plush dining, a floating restaurant to the north of the Han Bridge, in a/c rooms or outside terraces.

It's not as expensive as it looks and the quality is good, a mix of Western and Asian foods, with fish specialities. Alternatively, settle back into one of the comfy cane chairs for a quiet coffee or early-evening drink.

Katynat Cafe 51 Nguyen Chi Thanh. The most appealing of a recent glut of youth-focused, wi-fi-friendly cafes; fruit juices and small meals are available, while women get everything half-price on Wed.

Kim Do 180 Tran Phu. This local favourite serves a broad range of Chinese cuisine, and provides comfortable, a/c dining with attentive service. The portions can be on the small side, but with a bit of care you can eat reasonably well for around 120,000đ per head.

Mien Trung 9 Bach Dang. Big, open-fronted riverside restaurant catering mostly to a local crowd. Minimal decor is offset by an extensive choice of reasonably priced Vietnamese dishes. You won't leave hungry.

Tu Tai 62 Hai Phong. Cheap and cheerful street kitchen serving a mean *com ga* (chicken rice) and other rice dishes. If they're full, try the noodles at *Mi Quang* across the street.

Viet Nam 53–55 Ly Tu Trong. It's worth the walk to this excellent, popular eatery where well-prepared and well-priced Vietnamese dishes come in small, medium or large sizes. The fresh trout is highly recommended, as are the daily specials.

Listings

Airlines Pacific Airlines, 35 Nguyen Van Linh ℡0511/358 3583; PB Air, Da Nang Airport ℡0511/365 6060, ⓦwww.pbair.com; Vietnam Airlines, 35 Tran Phu ℡0511/382 1130.

Banks and exchange Vietcombank, 140 Le Loi; Incombank, 172 Nguyen Van Linh; VID Public Bank, 2 Tran Phu. ATMs now dot the city and are located in front of some hotels, including the *Orient Hotel*, 97 Phan Chu Trinh, *Bamboo Green Riverside*, 68 Bach Dang, and the *Saigon Tourane*, 5 Dong Da. There is an Agribank branch at the airport (daily 9am–5pm) that has exchange facilities and a 24hr ATM.

Consulate The Lao consulate is located at 16 Tran Quy Cap (Mon–Fri 8–11.30am & 2–4.30pm; ℡0511/382 1208). A thirty-day tourist visa will cost $31 to $48, depending on your nationality;

you'll need two passport photos, and visas are issued on the spot.

Hospital The Family Medical Practice at 50–52 Nguyen Van Linh (℡0511/358 2699, ⓦwww .vietnammedicalpractice.com), is well respected and popular with tourists. It has foreign staff and a dental clinic and offers 24hr emergency service. Prices begin at $50 for initial consultation. Benh Vien C, 74 Hai Phong, opposite the Cao Dai Temple ℡0511/382 1480 is the local hospital and a cheaper alternative.

Immigration police 7 Than Quy Cap. The place to go if you've lost your passport or have similar difficulties.

Post office Main office at 60 Bach Dang, poste restante at no. 66; other branches at 80 Hung Vuong, 41 Tran Quoc Toan and 20 Dong Da.

Silks and tailoring Outlets line the north end of Phan Chu Trinh (try Hanh Silk Shop at no. 91), although the best quality and prices are in Hoi An. **Tour agents and open–tour buses** An Phu Tourist, 20 Dong Da ☎0511/381 8366, Ⓔanphucndn@yahoo.com; Vietnamtourism, 83 Nguyen Thi Minh Khai ☎0511/382 3660, Ⓔvitoursdad@dng.vnn.vn. An Phu Tourist's open-tour buses stop outside their office, while other operators drop off and pick up passengers outside the Cham Museum; local tour agents will be able to help with tickets and reservations.

Around Da Nang

The main places worth visiting around Da Nang are beaches, from Red Beach (Nam O) in the north where the first US Marines came ashore, down the broad, bleached-white fringe of **China Beach** (My Khe), and continuing all the way south through **Non Nuoc** to Hoi An. Of all the beaches in Vietnam, these are the most coveted by international developers, though only one resort has been completed so far along this empty, attractive coastline. A note of warning, however: there's a powerful undertow off this coast and when the northeast, winter monsoon blows up, riptides become particularly dangerous. Guards patrol the main swimming beaches during the day, where flags also indicate safe spots. Best months on the beach are April to August, with the peak season for local holidaymakers in July and August.

Heading south down the coast, past old US installations occupied these days by the People's Army, you come to a group of abrupt hills constituting the coast's other main tourist attraction, usually a stop on the trip to or from Hoi An: the **Marble Mountains**. The five limestone and marble knobbles are

---

Moving on from Da Nang

Heading on **up the coast to Hué** it's a difficult choice between road and rail over the dramatic Hai Van Pass. If you plump for the **train**, ask for seats on the right for the best views as the train hugs the cliff. Highway 1 winds much higher but keeps inland, and clouds often shroud the top. **Open-tour buses** (45,000đ) pick up passengers outside the Cham Museum or from An Phu Tourist at 20 Dong Da; services stop briefly at the Hai Van Pass and Lang Co Beach. Alternatively, hire a car and driver ($25–45) for the three-hour trip so you can enjoy the scenery at your leisure. **Local buses** for Hué leave from the main Lien Tinh bus station but go through the new road tunnel, bypassing the Hai Van Pass.

Travelling south from Da Nang, xe om compete to whisk you off to **Non Nuoc** (for the Marble Mountains and beach) for 50,000đ, and to Hoi An. A one-way ride to Hoi An (45min) should cost 100,000đ including waiting time at the Marble Mountains; the same journey by taxi or hire car will come in at around $15–20. Local buses run from outside the Han market but are way too overcrowded for a comfortable, or safe, proposition. A more popular option is one of the open-tour buses (45,000đ), with a choice of morning services via the Marble Mountains or direct afternoon services. Open-tour buses also leave daily for Nha Trang, Da Lat and other destinations en route to Ho Chi Minh City.

The most popular land crossing **into Laos** open to foreigners is Lao Bao border gate, west of Dong Ha (see box on p.325 for details, and Da Nang listings for visa information). **International bus** services run from Da Nang's Lien Tinh bus station direct to Savannakhet daily (3pm; 24hr; $24).

From Da Nang airport, Vietnam Airlines operates daily **flights** to several Vietnamese cities, including Ho Chi Minh City and Hanoi, while Jetstar also flies to Ho Chi Minh City, Hanoi and Haiphong.

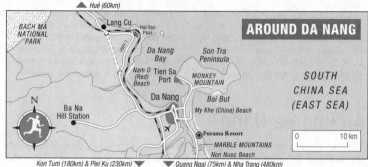

peppered with sacred caves, wrapped in legend – and liberally sprinkled with souvenir stands. For generations Non Nuoc Village at the mountains' base has resonated with the chink of stone masons chiselling away at religious statues, memorials and imitation Cham figures. Another possible excursion is to **Ba Na**, west of Da Nang, where an old French hill station has been developed as a summer retreat.

Up the coast from Da Nang, Highway 1 zigzags over the **Hai Van Pass**, affording sweeping views of the bay and north to the brilliant white sands of **Lang Co** beach. From here you can head into the mountains to explore the walking trails of **Bach Ma National Park**, where the remains of another French-era hill station are swamped by some of the most lush vegetation in the whole of Vietnam. All three places can be visited on a long day's excursion from Da Nang, or covered on the road to Hué.

East of Da Nang

Long, lumpy Son Tra Peninsula, tipped by **Monkey Mountain**, shelters Da Nang and its port from the worst winter monsoons. The peninsula's seaward side provides the city with its nearest unpolluted beach, My Khe, the original **China Beach**. Its rival to the south, the quieter **Non Nuoc Beach**, also claims the same sobriquet. If you're heading for Non Nuoc, or down the coast to Hoi An, the honeycomb cave-shrines of the **Marble Mountains**, just back from the beach, are worth a quick trot round in passing.

Monkey Mountain and China Beach

A low-lying neck of land forms the Han River's east bank and then rises 700m in the north to rolling Nui Tien Sa. The name means "descending angels", a reference to heavenly creatures who apparently would often alight on the summit for a game of chess, but most people know it as **Monkey Mountain** on account of its wildlife population. Monkeys still inhabit the promontory, which is mostly a restricted military area. Head up to the observatories, or skirt round the northern tip where you can scramble down to coves and beaches in several places. A road along the promontory's south coast provides easier access to a sandy cove called **Bai But**, about 8km from the city centre. At weekends Da Nang day-trippers fill the beach, but at other times it's a good place to escape the noise and bustle of the city. Refreshments and reasonably priced seafood are on offer at a simple bar-restaurant behind the beach. A return trip to Bai But by xe om will cost around 120,000đ including a couple of hours' waiting time.

Da Nang's nearest beach resort, My Khe, lies at the southern end of the peninsula, less than 3km southeast of the centre; better known as **China Beach**, it's where US servicemen were helicoptered in for R&R during the American War. Just behind the beach the *My Khe Hotel II*, 233 Nguyen Van Thoai (℡0511/394 1095, ⓔmkbeach@vnn.vn; ❸–❹) offers more modern facilities than its nearby sister hotel at the same price. The *Tourane Hotel*, a couple of hundred metres north, is a large renovated French colonial-style property that offers spacious yet simple rooms in villas (℡0511/393 2666, ⓔtouranehotel @dng.vnn.vn; ❸–❹). A xe om should cost 20,000đ (slightly more at night) for the ride from Da Nang.

Three kilometres further south, on the road to Hoi An and the Marble Mountains, you come to a turning for Bac My An Beach, which is home to the five-star *Furama Resort* (℡0511/384 7333, ⓦwww.furamavietnam.com; ❼). This $40-million development set in lush gardens stands out as one of Vietnam's top beach resorts. It offers luxuriously appointed rooms, international cuisine, two swimming pools plus a guarded beach and a range of recreational activities from tennis and golf to scuba-diving, ocean kayaking and windsurfing. It's soon to be joined by many more resorts, with construction lining most of the seafront towards Hoi An; *Hyatt* and *Crowne Plaza* are among the big boys moving in, as well as at least two golf courses.

The Marble Mountains

As you continue down the road to Hoi An, an unattractive stretch of storage tanks and scrubby, postwar wasteland eventually gives way to Vietnam's most southerly limestone outcrops, known as the **Marble Mountains**. Despite all the fuss, only one of the mountains' caves rates above ordinary, but it's a good place to stretch your legs and admire the views. A torch is useful for exploring the caves and, although everything is well signposted, it's still worth picking up a sketch map (small charge) at the ticket desk.

The simplest way of covering the 12km to the Marble Mountains and Non Nuoc from Da Nang is by **car**, **xe om** (50,000đ) or **bicycle**. Just past the first mountain, turn left at a T-junction down a road called Huyen Tran Cong Chua and find the main entrance on your left after a few hundred metres of marble shops. Da Nang city **buses** run infrequently out to Non Nuoc (7am–5pm), heading down Phan Chu Trinh and terminating at the Non Nuoc T-junction. Finally, if you can face the scrum, Hoi An-bound **pick-ups** will drop you off at Non Nuoc. If you're pressing on from here, Hoi An is another 20km down the coast from Non Nuoc – take a xe om (50,000đ) or squeeze onto a passing local bus.

Local **mythology** tells of the Turtle God hatching a divine egg on the shore; the shell cracked into five pieces, represented by the five small mountains. Historically, Cham people came here to worship their Hindu gods and then erected Buddhist altars in the caves, which became places of pilgrimage, drawing even the Nguyen kings to the sacred site. When Ho Chi Minh died, marble from these mountains was used for his mausoleum in Hanoi, but quarrying has since been banned. In Vietnamese the mountains are named Ngu Hanh Son, meaning the five ritual elements: Thuy Son (water mountain) and Moc Son (wood) to the east of the road; Tho Son (earth), Kim Son (gold or metal) and Hoa Son (fire) to the west.

The highest, at 107m, and most important mountain is **Thuy Son** (6am–5pm). Two staircases, built for the visit of Emperor Minh Mang, lead up its southern flank. The main, westernmost entrance, the first you reach coming from the main road, brings you to the hollow summit surrounded by jagged rocks with grottoes in every direction. In the middle, the Tam Thai Pagoda sits beside a crossroads. Turn left here, pass through a narrow defile, under a natural rock arch and you enter the antechamber to the most impressive of Thuy Son's warren of **cave pagodas**; follow the path to the left of the sandstone Quan Am statue, down steep, dark steps into the eerie half-light and swirling incense of **Huyen Khong Cave**. Locals will point out stalactites resembling wrinkled faces and so on, but the cave's best feature is its roof through which midday sunlight streams like spotlights. A wall plaque commemorates a deadly accurate women's Viet Cong guerrilla unit, which during the war destroyed nineteen planes with just 22 rockets.

Backtracking to Tam Thai Pagoda, the path heading east under a couple more rock arches climbs slightly before starting to descend towards the eastern exit, affording expansive views over Non Nuoc Beach, the Cham Islands and north to Monkey Mountain. About halfway down you pass Linh Ung Pagoda behind which lurks **Tang Chon Cave**, in this case occupied by tenth-century Cham Hindu altars and two Buddhas, one sitting and one standing.

You emerge again at the foot of the mountain in **NON NUOC** Village. Since the fifteenth century, Non Nuoc has been inhabited by stone-carvers, who coax life out of the local white, grey and rose marble. Nowadays workshops generally churn out mass-produced souvenirs using marble imported from Thanh Hoa Province, but it's fascinating to watch the masons at work – just follow your ears.

Non Nuoc Beach

Follow the paved road east from Non Nuoc Village for about 500m, round a dogleg, and you reach **Non Nuoc Beach**, promoted locally as "new China Beach". Huge, empty and consisting of clean, fine white sand, it's far enough from Da Nang to leave you unpestered. There's a cluster of cafés, restaurants and souvenir stalls beside the car park and the *Sandy Beach Resort* (℡ 0511/383 6216, Ⓦ www.sandybeachdanang.com; ❻), a four-star hotel with prices to match, is a good option for those that crave luxury. Those looking for something more modest should head back to the dogleg and turn down towards the beach on Huyen Tran Cong Chau to find a warm welcome at ⚘ *Hoa's Place* (℡ 0511/396 9216, Ⓔ hoasplace@hotmail.com; ❶), a delightfully laidback **guesthouse** offering twenty clean, good-value rooms. It has built up a cult reputation with backpackers and surfers, some guests staying for months. They also lay on very reasonably priced and convivial meals and can arrange motorbike rental or a xe om to Hoi An or Da Nang.

West of Da Nang: Ba Na Hill Station

Perched 1500m up a mountain 48km west of Da Nang, **Ba Na Hill Station** provides a welcome change from the coast. The site was first developed by the French in the 1920s, who escaped the summer heat for its cool, mountain air. After a brief heyday in the 1930s the resort was abandoned and soon fell victim to the ravages of war and the encroaching jungle. Thanks to a high annual rainfall together with temperatures at a constant 17–20°C, dense forest growth cloaks the mountain, which is home to over five hundred species of flora and 250 of fauna. In the past few years the local authorities have poured money into Ba Na, converting some of the old French villas into guesthouses and restaurants, laying forest trails and a new access road and even putting in a cable car – a great hit with the locals, who come up here at night to admire the lights of Da Nang twinkling far below. Not that the daytime **views** are to be scoffed at, taking in the Hai Van Pass, Son Tra Peninsula and Marble Mountains if you're lucky. Given the weather, you may have to content yourself with a more atmospheric scene of mountains wreathed in mist, but while it's raining on the lower slopes, the summit may be above the clouds, enjoying brilliant sunshine.

Views apart, the main attraction is exploring the **forest paths** and wandering among the ruined villas, for which half a day will suffice. You may want to avoid summer weekends when the place can be packed out. A return trip by car or xe om from Da Nang will be pricey once waiting time is factored in – bargain hard – but Da Nang tour agents (see p.289) also offer various **organized bus tours**, mostly in summer.

North of Da Nang

Thirty kilometres north of Da Nang, beyond a region of grave-pocked, sandy desolation, the first and most dramatic of three mountain spurs off the **Truong Son range** cuts across Vietnam's pinched central waist. This thousand-metre-high barrier forms a climatic frontier blocking the southward penetration of cold, damp winter airstreams which often bury the tops under thick cloud banks and earn it the title **Hai Van**, or "Pass of the Ocean Clouds". These mountains once formed a national frontier between Dai Viet and Champa, and Hai Van's continuing strategic importance is marked by a succession of forts, pillboxes and ridge-line defensive walls erected by Nguyen-dynasty Vietnamese, French, Japanese and American forces. A new road tunnel funnels traffic on Highway 1 through the mountain, leaving a more peaceful journey for those that choose to take on the pass. From the top of the pass there are superb views, weather permitting, over the sweeping curve of Da Nang Bay, with glimpses of the rail lines looping and tunnelling along the cliff.

Lang Co

Descending again into warmer air, a white-tipped spit of land comes into view round a hairpin bend, jutting into an aquamarine lagoon strung with fishing nets. Sadly, this much photographed scene is marred by the road bridge marching across it. The original bridge spanning the lagoon has the dubious distinction of being the Viet Minh bomb squads' first target in 1947 and its ruined piles are still visible. **LANG CO** village hides among coconut palms on the sandy peninsula, its presence revealed only by a white-spired church. It makes a popular lunch stop on the road between Da Nang and Hué, though a quick swim from the narrow beach will be spoilt by electricity pylons and a good deal of rubbish – head north away from the fishing village to find cleaner sand.

Lang Co has been earmarked for tourist development for years, yet it remains rather quiet, with only a few beach resorts in operation and a number of cheaper guesthouses on the other side of the highway. If you decide to **stay**, the best all-round option is *Thanh Tam* (☎054/387 4456; ❸), on the highway about 1500m north of the village; ask for a sea view. On the opposite side of the highway, *Anh Nguyen* (☎054/387 4448; ❷) has nice en-suite rooms with hot water, while nearby *Chi Na* (☎054/387 4597; ❶) is another friendly place with a handful of simple but clean rooms at slightly cheaper rates. The government-owned *Lang Co Beach Resort* (☎054/387 3555, ✉langco@dng.vnv.vn; ❹), opposite *Chi Na*, stands out a bit with its complex of green-roofed, Hué-style villas, landscaped pool and replica covered bridge. The rooms are big, light and well equipped and the beach here is kept scrupulously clean. Most of these places have restaurants, or will at least rustle up a meal, but the most popular place in town is *Sao Bien* just over the bridge when coming from the south, which busily serves an array of seafood to passing tour buses.

Lang Co lies about 40km north of Da Nang and 65km from Hué. The train station is on the lagoon's western side, or public buses will drop you off anywhere on the highway. Sinh Café open-tour buses stop at *Thanh Tam*, while An Phu Tourist uses the very run-down *Tourist Hotel* towards the southern end of the strip.

Bach Ma National Park

Well off the beaten track, **Bach Ma National Park** is being developed as an eco-tourism destination, and dedicated ornithologists and botanists may want to make the effort to get here for the chance of seeing some of the region's 330 bird species and more than 1400 species of flora. Bach Ma is also home to 83 mammal species, including the Asiatic black bear, leopard and the recently discovered saola and giant muntjac (see "Environmental issues", p.508), as well as more visible deer and macaque monkeys. The highlands were previously the location of a French summer resort, where Emperor Bao Dai also kept several luxury villas. The majority of buildings, tennis courts and rose-beds are now in ruins, but a number of villas have been restored to provide tourist accommodation. One word of warning before you set off: Bach Ma is one of the wettest places in Vietnam, with a staggering eight metres of rainfall a year at the summit. The best time to visit is from May to early September, but even then be prepared to get wet. Remember to take warm clothes since it can get chilly at the top.

Six short **nature trails** branch off the steep, tarmacked road which leads 16km from the entrance gate almost to the summit of Hai Vong Dai Mountain (1450m). The first, **Pheasant Trail** (2.5km), starts at the kilometre 8 marker (note that all distances refer to the distance from Highway 1 rather than from the park entrance) to reach a series of waterfalls and pools, where you can swim. On the way you may hear the calls of white-cheek gibbons or some of the seven types of pheasant that inhabit the park, or see the fifty-centimetre-long earthworms which the locals cook and eat as a treatment for malaria. The short but very steep **Parashorea Trail** (300m), at kilometre 14, is named after this area's towering trees, while 2km further on **Rhododendron Trail** (1.5km), leads up 689 steps to a waterfall, with views over primary forest. **Five Lakes Trail** (2km), at kilometre 17.5, ends at a series of five pools fed by a waterfall, where you can also swim. **Summit Trail** leads 800m from the end of the road to the crest of Hai Vong Dai with good views over Cau Hai lagoon and surrounding mountains. From here, instead of retracing your steps, you can walk back down the **Nature Exploration Trail** (2.5km) past ruined villas to rejoin the road at kilometre 17 beside the **Orchid House** where nearly a hundred species are carefully nurtured.

Practicalities

By far the easiest way to get to Bach Ma is with your own **transport** – 26km north of Lang Co (40km south of Hué), look for a small green sign pointing west off Highway 1 in Cau Hai Village (Phu Loc District), then drive for another 3km to the park gate – or by rented car from Hué (around $80 for three people for the return journey). Alternatively, both public and open-tour **buses** will drop you at the turning in Cau Hai, from where you can pick up a xe om for the final stretch. A xe om from Lang Co will cost a minimum of 200,000đ for the return trip. Note that, while cars are allowed inside the park, motorbikes and bicycles are not. Instead, you'll have to rent one of the park's jeeps which will take you to the summit and back again, but can't drop off or pick up passengers en route.

At the entrance to the park, stop first at the **Visitors' Centre** (7am–5pm; ☎054/387 1330, ⓦwww.bachma.vnn.vn) to buy your entrance tickets and arrange transport and accommodation (10,500đ entrance, 350,000đ for a four-seater jeep to the summit and back). If you are arriving outside these hours, phone in advance. Make sure you pick up a map of the trails, and it's also well worth investing in the excellent English-language booklet. While you're here, take a quick look round the exhibition; it's aimed at kids but is still very informative. Although it's not a requirement, it's definitely a good idea to take a **guide** ($10 for an English-speaker) when you're walking in the park, principally for your own safety – it's easy to get lost. Note that it's normal "forest etiquette" to share drinks, meals and carrying the loads. If you want to make a positive contribution to the onerous task of **reforestation**, the park has a programme whereby you can buy a sapling and help plant it in one of the denuded areas of the park.

Should you wish to stay in the park, you can opt for the **campsite** (bring your own tent), at kilometre 18, or one of a number of **guesthouses** either near the summit or beside the entrance. The five-room *Do Quyen Villa* (❶) is especially popular with its location near the summit, nestled amongst the trees. In peak season (June–Aug) it's advisable to book in advance; contact the Visitors' Centre for reservations. There's a small **restaurant** at the park entrance, where you can also buy biscuits, water and snacks, whereas meals have to be ordered in advance if you're staying at the summit. Alternatively, you can bring your own food from Cau Hai market.

Hué

Unlike Hanoi, Ho Chi Minh City and most other Vietnamese cities, **HUÉ** somehow seems to have stood aside from the current economic frenzy and, despite its calamitous history, has retained a unique cultural identity. It's a small, peaceful city, full of lakes, canals and lush vegetation, all celebrated in countless romantic outpourings by its much esteemed poetic fraternity. Since the early nineteenth century, when Hué became the capital of Vietnam, it has also been a city of scholars; there's a discernible atmosphere of refinement and easy-going tolerance in the city, though it's considered highbrow by the rest of the country,.

Hué repays exploration at a leisurely pace, and contains enough in the way of historical interest to swallow up a few days with no trouble at all. The city divides into three clearly defined urban areas, each with its own distinct character. The nineteenth-century walled **citadel**, on the north bank of the Perfume River, contains the once magnificent **Imperial City** as well as an extensive grid of attractive residential streets and prolific gardens. Across Dong Ba Canal to the east lies **Phu Cat**, the original merchants' quarter of Hué where ships once pulled in, now a crowded district of shophouses, Chinese Assembly Halls and pagodas. What used to be called the **European city**, a triangle of land caught between the Perfume River's south bank and the Phu Cam Canal, is now Hué's modern administrative centre, where you'll also find most hotels and tourist services.

Pine-covered hills, scattered with tombs and secluded pagodas, form the city's southern bounds, where the Nguyen emperors built their palatial Royal Mausoleums (see p.313). And through it all meanders the Perfume River, named somewhat fancifully from the tree resin and blossoms it carries, passing on its way the celebrated, seven-storey tower of Thien Mu Pagoda (see p.312). If you can afford the time, cycling out to Thuan An Beach (see p.320) makes an enjoyable excursion. Hué is also the main jumping-off point for day-tours of the DMZ (see p.321).

With all this to offer, Hué is inevitably one of Vietnam's pre-eminent tourist destinations. The choice and standard of accommodation are generally above average, as are its restaurants serving the city's justly famous speciality foods. Nevertheless, the majority of people pass through Hué fairly quickly, partly because high entrance fees make visiting more than a couple of the major sights beyond many budgets, and partly because of its troublesome **weather**. Hué

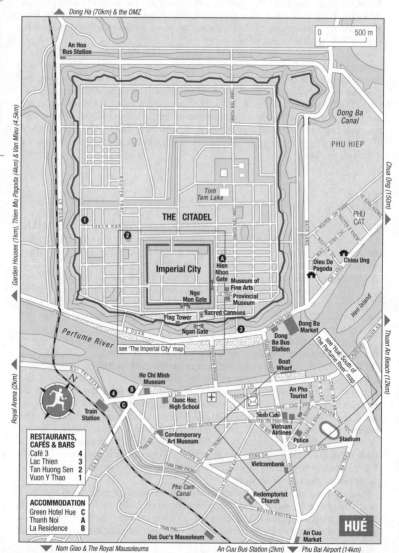

Dong Ha (70km) & the DMZ

0   500 m

An Hoa
Bus Station

Dong Ba
Canal

PHU HIEP

Tinh
Tam Lake

THE CITADEL

Garden Houses (1km), Thien Mu Pagoda (4km) & Van Mieu (4.5km)

Chua Ong (150m)

PHU
CAT

Dieu De
Pagoda

Chieu Ung

Hien
Nhon
Gate

Imperial City

Museum of
Fine Arts

Ngo
Mon Gate

Provincial
Museum

Hen Island

Flag Tower

Sacred Cannons

Ngan Gate

Dong Ba
Market

Thuan An Beach (12km)

Perfume River

see 'The Imperial City' map

Dong
Ba Bus
Station

Boat
Wharf

see Hué: South of
The Perfume River, map

Royal Arena (2km)

Ho Chi Minh
Museum

An Phu
Tourist

Quoc Hoc
High School

Sinh Café

Vietnam
Airlines

Train
Station

Contemporary
Art Museum

Police

Stadium

Vietcombank

Phu Cam
Canal

Redemptorist
Church

**RESTAURANTS,
CAFÉS & BARS**
Café 3   4
Lac Thien   3
Tan Huong Sen   2
Vuon Y Thao   1

ACCOMMODATION
Green Hotel Hue   C
Thanh Noi   A
La Residence   B

Duc Duc's Mausoleum

An Cuu
Market

HUÉ

Nam Giao & The Royal Mausoleums   An Cuu Bus Station (2km)   Phu Bai Airport (14km) suffers from the highest rainfall in the country, mostly falling over just three months from October to December when the city regularly floods for a few days, causing damage to the historic architecture, though heavy downpours are possible at any time of year.

Some history

The land on which Hué now stands belonged to the Kingdom of Champa until 1306, when territory north of Da Nang was exchanged for the hand of a Vietnamese princess under the terms of a peace treaty. The first Vietnamese to settle in the region established their administrative centre near present-day Hué at a place called Hoa Chan, and then in 1558 Lord Nguyen Hoang arrived from Hanoi as governor of the district, at the same time establishing the rule of the Nguyen lords over southern Vietnam which was to last for the next two hundred years. In the late seventeenth century the lords moved the citadel to its present location where it developed into a major town and cultural centre, **Phu Xuan**, which briefly became the capital under the Tay Son emperor Quang Trung (1788–1801). But it was the next ruler of Vietnam, Emperor Gia Long, founder of the Nguyen Dynasty, who literally put Hué on the map after 1802 when he sought to unify the country by moving the capital, lock, stock and dynastic altars, from Thang Long (Hanoi) to the renamed city of **Hué**. Gia Long owed his throne to French military support but his Imperial City was very much a Chinese concept, centred on a Forbidden City reserved for the sovereign, with separate administrative and civilian quarters.

The Nguyen emperors (see box, p.298) were Confucian, conservative rulers, generally suspicious of all Westerners yet unable to withstand the power of France. In 1884 the French were granted land northwest of Hué citadel, and they then seized the city entirely in 1885, leaving the emperors as nominal rulers. Under the Nguyen, Hué became a famous centre of the arts, scholarship and Buddhist learning, but their extravagant building projects and luxurious lifestyle demanded crippling taxes.

Hué ceased to be the capital of Vietnam when Emperor Bao Dai abdicated in 1945; two years later a huge fire destroyed many of the city's wooden temples and palaces. From the early twentieth century the city had been engulfed in social and political unrest led by an anti-colonial educated elite, which simmered away until the 1960s. Tensions finally boiled over in May 1963 when troops fired on thousands of Buddhist nationalists demonstrating against the strongly Catholic regime of President Ngo Dinh Diem (see p.472). The protests escalated into a wave of self-immolations by monks and nuns until government forces moved against the pagodas at the end of the year, rounding up the Buddhist clergy and supposed activists in the face of massive public demonstrations.

During the 1968 **Tet Offensive** Hué was torn apart again when the North Vietnamese Army (NVA) held the city for 25 days. Communist forces entered Hué in the early hours of January 31, hoisted their flag above the citadel and found themselves in control of the whole city bar two small military compounds. Armed with lists of names, they began searching out government personnel, sympathizers of the Southern regime, intellectuals, priests, Americans and foreign aid workers. Nearly three thousand bodies were later discovered in mass graves around the city – the victims were mostly civilians who had been shot, beaten to death or buried alive. But the killing hadn't finished: during the ensuing counter-assault as many as five thousand North Vietnamese and Viet Cong, 384 Southern troops and 142 American soldiers died, plus at least another thousand civilians. Hué was all but levelled in the massive fire power unleashed on NVA forces holed up in the citadel but it took a further ten days of agonizing, house-to-house combat to drive the Communists out, in what Stanley Karnow described as "the most bitter battle" of the entire war. Seven years later, on March 26, 1975, the NVA were back to liberate Hué in its pivotal position as the first major town south of the Seventeenth Parallel.

The mammoth task of **rebuilding** Hué has been going on now for more than twenty years but received a boost in 1993 when UNESCO listed the city as a World Heritage Site, which served to mobilize international funding for a whole range of projects, from renovating palaces to the revival of traditional arts and technical skills.

Arrival, information and city transport

Flights arriving at Hué's **Phu Bai Airport**, 15km southeast of the city centre, are met by a bus (35,000đ) which takes you to central hotels, and by metered taxis (around $11). The **train station** lies about 1.5km from the centre of town at the far western end of Le Loi, a boulevard running along the south bank of the Perfume River. Note that trains out of Hué get booked up, especially sleepers to Ho Chi Minh City and Hanoi, so make onward travel arrangements as early as possible (ticket office open daily 7–11.30am & 1.30–8pm).

Hué has two long-distance **bus stations**: services from the south pull into An Cuu station, 3km southeast of the centre on Highway 1. A xe om or cyclo into town should cost around 15,000đ. Buses from Hanoi and the north dump you at An Hoa station, 4km northwest on Highway 1, from where a xe om or cyclo to the centre costs around 20,000đ. Sinh Café and An Phu Tourist **open-tour buses** set down at their town-centre offices at no. 7 and no. 11 Nguyen Tri Phuong respectively. Note that some streets in Hué, including Nguyen Tri Phuong and Ben Nghe, have been allocated new numbers. The situation is confusing (since some old numbers remain), but we use the new numbers wherever possible.

The best bet for **tourist information** is either your hotel or one of the tour agents; staff at the *Mandarin Café* (see p.308) are particularly helpful. Every hotel and tour agent hands out photocopied **maps**, but for a detailed city plan try the big hotels and bookstalls on Le Loi.

Even Hué's wide avenues become crowded during rush hour (7–9am & 4–6pm), but generally the most enjoyable way of **getting around** the city's

The Nguyen Dynasty

In 1802 Prince Nguyen Anh, one of the southern Nguyen lords, defeated the Tay Son Dynasty with the help of a French bishop, Pigneau de Behaine. When Nguyen Anh assumed the throne under the title Emperor Gia Long he thus founded the **Nguyen Dynasty**, which ruled Vietnam from Hué until the abdication of Emperor Bao Dai in 1945. Eleven of the Nguyen emperors are buried in Hué (see p.313 for information on several of their mausoleums), the exceptions being Ham Nghi and Bao Dai; the latter died in Paris in 1997 after four decades in exile, while Ham Nghi was exiled to Algeria and eventually buried there.

Gia Long	1802–20	Ham Nghi	1884–85
Minh Mang	1820–41	Dong Khanh	1885–89
Thieu Tri	1841–47	Thanh Thai	1889–1907
Tu Duc	1847–83	Duy Tan	1907–16
Duc Duc	1883	Khai Dinh	1916–25
Hiep Hoa	1883	Bao Dai	1926–45
Kien Phuc	1883–84		

scattered sights – and especially of touring the Royal Mausoleums – is by **bicycle**. Most hotels and guesthouses, plus a few cafés, offer bike rental (10,000–15,000₫ per day) and **motorbikes** (60,000–75,000₫). A popular option is to take a guided **motorbike tour** of Hué and its environs (from $10) offered by a number of tour agents (see p.309); you either ride pillion or take your own bike. All the above places can usually help with **car rental** (around $35 per day). Hué has no shortage of cyclos or xe om and also boasts metered **taxi services** (see p.309).

Accommodation

The majority of accommodation in Hué is located south of the Perfume River; **top-class** establishments overlook the river, while **budget hotels** and **guest-houses** are scattered in the streets behind, particularly the backpacker enclave of Hung Vuong and Nguyen Tri Phuong, and along Pham Ngu Lao. A few hotels have opened up within the citadel, though as yet you'll find better value south of the river. Thanks to a dramatic increase in the number of private hotels, there's now an oversupply of rooms most of the year and you should be able to bargain. All the accommodation below is marked on the map on p.300, except where otherwise stated.

Binh Duong III 4/34 Nguyen Tri Phuong ☎054/383 0145, ✉binhduong1@dng .vnn.vn. The real highlight of this friendly hotel is that each room is equipped with a computer for free internet access. In addition, it has large, spotless rooms with a/c, cable TV and full-size tubs. *Binh Duong I* – slightly cheaper but not as plush – is just up the alley. ②

Binh Minh I 36 Nguyen Tri Phuong ☎054/382 5526, ⊛www.binhminhhue.com. Bright, welcoming hotel in a great location with a range of clean, homely rooms, some with balconies looking towards the mountains. A popular and good-value option. Rooms are cheaper when booked through the website. ②

Canh Tien Guesthouse 9/66 Le Loi ☎054/382 2772, ✉tvphuong1@dng.vnn.vn. Immaculately clean and with spacious rooms with cable TV, a/c and spotless bathrooms. The owner, Phuong, is the head of foreign languages at the local university, so the odds are he can understand anyone, and is always keen to share a beer. ①

Century Riverside Inn 49 Le Loi ☎054/382 3390, ⊛www.centuryriversidehue.com. International hotel on the banks of the Perfume River with swimming pool, bar, post office and souvenir shops. The comfortable but characterless rooms, some very small, are overpriced. ⑥

Dong Tam 7/66 Le Loi ☎054/382 8403. Pink and plush-looking from the outside – especially when the sun is shining on the pool out front – this secluded guesthouse features rooms that, while simple, are a real steal at $10 and up. ①

Duy Tan 12 Hung Vuong ☎054/382 5001, ✉nkduytan@dng.vnn.vn. Large, government-run

hotel with big, old-fashioned yet comfortable rooms on the main drag; not bad value if you fancy something a bit less frenetic than many of the other budget options. ④

Green Hotel Hue 2 Le Loi ☎054/382 4668, ⊛www.greenhotel-hue.com. See map, p.296. A large and architecturally adventurous hotel right next to the train station. Green is the theme in the fresh, rattan-furnished rooms, four levels of which curl around a central outdoor swimming pool. ⑥

Huong Giang 51 Le Loi ☎054/382 2122, ⊛www.huonggiangtourist.com. One of Hué's top hotels, built in 1962 and well renovated, with a pool, gardens, tennis court and other four-star facilities. It's a more homely establishment than the next-door *Century Riverside*, but can't match the *Saigon Morin* for service and room size. Larger rooms overlooking the river offer better value for money. ⑤

Imperial Hotel 8 Hung Vuong ☎054/388 2222, ⊛www.imperial-hotel.com.vn. The first five-star hotel in Hué dominates the skyline near the Perfume River; plush carpets lead the way to suitably well-appointed rooms, while the complex also includes a fitness centre, swimming pool and classy restaurant. ⑦

La Residence 5 Le Loi ☎054/383 7475, ⊛www.la-residence-hue.com. See map, p.296. Formerly the French governor's residence (hence the name), and overlooking the Perfume River, this intensively renovated hotel blends early-twentieth-century Art Deco design with excellent services. ⑥

Phu An 42 Nguyen Tri Phuong ☎054/382 1168, ✉phuanhotel@dng.vnn.vn. New, towering mini-hotel

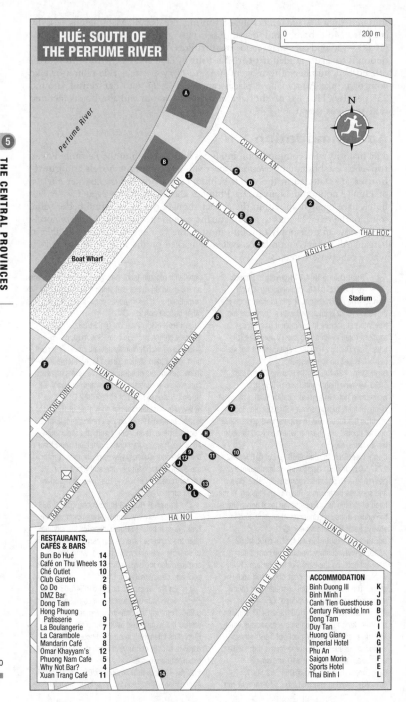

HUÉ: SOUTH OF THE PERFUME RIVER

0   200 m

Perfume River

Boat Wharf

Stadium

N

RESTAURANTS, CAFÉS & BARS

Bun Bo Hué	14
Café on Thu Wheels	13
Ché Outlet	10
Club Garden	2
Co Do	6
DMZ Bar	1
Dong Tam	C
Hong Phuong Patisserie	9
La Boulangerie	7
La Carambole	3
Mandarin Cafe	8
Omar Khayyam's	12
Phuong Nam Cafe	5
Why Not Bar?	4
Xuan Trang Café	11

ACCOMMODATION

Binh Duong III	K
Binh Minh I	J
Canh Tien Guesthouse	D
Century Riverside Inn	B
Dong Tam	C
Duy Tan	I
Huong Giang	A
Imperial Hotel	G
Phu An	H
Saigon Morin	F
Sports Hotel	E
Thai Binh I	L

that is a hub of traveller activity due to its popular communal area downstairs that doubles as a restaurant and tour service. Rooms range from cheap with fan only to large fully equipped ones with balconies. ❶
Saigon Morin 30 Le Loi ☎054/382 3526, ⓦwww.morinhotel.com.vn. Hué's most famous French-era hotel has been painted pink and renovated to four-star standards, but still retains some of its colonial charm, not least in the garden courtyard. The rooms are a good size, if a little bland, and kitted out with all the equipment you'd expect, including mini-bar, bathtub and hairdryer. There's a rooftop bar, two restaurants, a small pool ($5 to non-residents), internet access and so forth. Prices reflect the standard of service and location. ❻

Sports Hotel 15 Pham Ngu Lao ☎054/382 8096, ⓦwww.huestays.com. The most amiable budget hotel on Pham Ngu Lao sports large and newly furnished rooms, all of which have a/c and cable TV; some have excellent views over the surrounding area. ❷
Thai Binh I 10/9 Nguyen Tri Phuong ☎054/382 8058, ⓔksthaibin@hotmail.com. Spotlessly clean, friendly and popular hotel with a good range of well-equipped rooms, down a quiet alley beside *Binh Minh I*. ❷
Thanh Noi 57 Dang Dung ☎054/352 2478, ⓔthanhnoi@dng.vnn.vn. See map, p.296. One of the few hotels north of the river, near the citadel, offering a touch of character in its Imperial-style decor and nice outdoor setting with pool and garden. ❸

The citadel

Hué's days of glory kicked off in the early nineteenth century when Emperor Gia Long laid out a vast **citadel**, comprising three concentric enclosures, ranged behind the prominent flag tower. Within the citadel's outer wall lies the **Imperial City**, containing administrative offices, parks and dynastic temples, with the royal palaces of the **Forbidden Purple City** at its centre. Though wars, fires, typhoons, floods and termites have all taken their toll, it's these Imperial edifices, some now restored to their former magnificence, that constitute Hué's prime tourist attraction. Apart from one museum, there are no specific sights in the outer citadel, but it's a pleasant area to cycle round, especially the northern sector where you'll find many lakes and the prolific **gardens** for which Hué is famed.

In accordance with ancient tradition the citadel was built in an **auspicious location** chosen to preserve the all-important harmony between the emperor and his subjects, heaven and earth, man and nature. Thus the complex is oriented southeast towards the low hummock of Nui Ngu Binh ("Royal Screen Mountain"), which blocks out harmful influences, while to either side two small islands in the Perfume River represent the Blue Dragon's benevolent spirit in balance with the aggressive White Tiger. Just in case that wasn't protection enough, the whole 520 hectares are enclosed within seven-metre-high, twenty-metre-thick brick and earth walls built with the help of French engineers, and encircled by a moat and canal. Eight villages had to be relocated when construction began in 1805, and over the next thirty years tens of thousands of workmen laboured to complete more than three hundred palaces, temples, tombs and other royal buildings, some using materials brought down from the former Imperial City in Hanoi.

The flag tower and the sacred cannons

The citadel's massive, ten-kilometre-long perimeter wall has survived intact, as has its most prominent feature, the **flag tower**, or *Cot Co* (also known as *Ky Dai*, "the King's Knight"), which dominates the southern battlements. The tower is in fact three squat, brick terraces topped with a flagpole first erected in 1807, where the yellow-starred Viet Cong flag flew briefly during the 1968 Tet Offensive. Ten gates pierce the citadel wall: enter through Ngan Gate, east of the flag tower, to find a parade ground flanked by the nine **sacred cannons**, which

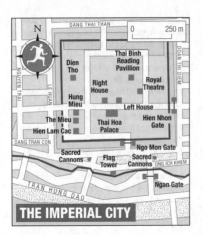

were cast in the early nineteenth century in bronze seized from the Tay Son army. The cannons represent the four seasons and five ritual elements (earth, fire, metal, wood and water); originally they stood in front of Ngo Mon Gate, symbolizing the citadel's guardian spirits.

The Imperial City

A second moat and defensive wall inside the citadel guard the **Imperial City** (7am–5pm; 55,000đ), which follows the same symmetrical layout about a north–south axis as Beijing's Forbidden City. The city, popularly known as *Dai Noi* ("the Great Enclosure"), has four gates – one in each wall – though by far the most impressive is south-facing **Ngo Mon**, the Imperial City's principal entrance. In its heyday the complex must have been truly awe-inspiring, a place of glazed yellow and green roof tiles, pavilions of rich red and gilded lacquer, and lotus-filled ponds – all surveyed by the emperor with his entourage of haughty mandarins. However, many of its buildings were badly neglected even before the battle for Hué raged through the Imperial City during Tet 1968, and by 1975 a mere twenty of the original 148 were left standing among the vegetable plots. Some are in the midst of extensive restorations, and those which have been completed, notably **Thai Hoa Palace** and the **The Mieu** complex, are stunning. Among the others, the charming **Thai Binh Reading Pavilion** and a pair of octagonal music pavilions are less formal mementoes of the dynasty. The rest of the Imperial City, especially its northern sector, is a grassed-over expanse full of birds and butterflies where you can still make out foundations and find bullet pockmarks in the plasterwork of ruined walls.

Ngo Mon Gate

In 1833 Emperor Minh Mang replaced an earlier, much less formidable gate with the present dramatic entrance way to the Imperial City, **Ngo Mon**, considered a masterpiece of Nguyen architecture. Ngo Mon (the "Noon" or "Southwest" Gate) has five entrances: the emperor alone used the central entrance paved with stone; two smaller doorways on either side were for the civil and military mandarins, who only rated brick paving, while another pair of giant openings in the wings allowed access to the royal elephants. The bulk of Ngo Mon is constructed of massive stone slabs, but perched on top is an elegant pavilion called the **Five Phoenix Watchtower** as its nine roofs are said to resemble five birds in flight when viewed from above. Note that the central roof, under which the emperor passed, is covered with yellow-glazed tiles, a feature of nearly all Hué's royal roofs. Emperors used the watchtower for two major ceremonies each year: the declaration of the lunar New Year; and the announcement of the civil service exam results, depicted here in a lacquer painting. It was also in this pavilion that the last Nguyen emperor, Bao Dai, abdicated in 1945 when he handed over to the new government his symbols of power – a solid gold seal weighing ten kilos and a sheathed sword encrusted with jade.

Thai Hoa Palace

Walking north from Ngo Mon along the city's symmetrical axis, you pass between two square lakes and a pair of *kylin*, mythical dew-drinking animals that are harbingers of peace, to reach **Thai Hoa Palace** ("the Palace of Supreme Harmony"). Not only is this the most spectacular of Hué's palaces, its interior glowing with sumptuous red and gold lacquers, but it's also the most important since this was the throne palace, where major ceremonies such as coronations or royal birthdays took place and foreign ambassadors were received. On these occasions the emperor sat on the raised dais, wearing a golden tunic and a crown decorated with nine dragons, under a spectacular gilded canopy. He faced south across the **Esplanade of Great Salutations**, a stone-paved courtyard where the mandarins stood, civil mandarins to the left and military on the right, lined up in their appointed places beside eighteen stelae denoting the nine subdivided ranks. A French traveller in the 1920s witnessed the colourful spectacle, with "perfume-bearers in royal-blue, fan-bearers in sky-blue waving enormous yellow feather fans, musicians and guardsmen and ranks of mandarins in their curious hats and gorgeous, purple-embroidered dragons, kow-towing down, down on their noses amidst clouds of incense – and all in a setting of blood-red lacquer scrawled with gold".

The palace was first constructed in 1805, though the present building dates from 1833 when the French floor tiles and glass door panels were added, and was the only major building in the Imperial City to escape bomb damage. Nevertheless, the throne room's eighty ironwood pillars, swirling with dragons and clouds, had been eaten away by termites and humidity and were on the point of collapse when rescue work began in 1991. During the restoration every column, weighing two tonnes apiece, had to be replaced manually and then painted with twelve coats of lacquer, each coat taking one month to dry. Behind the throne room a souvenir shop now sells books and tapes of Hué folk songs where once the emperor prepared for his grand entrance. It also contains two large dioramas depicting the Imperial City and flag tower in their heyday.

The Forbidden Purple City

From Thai Hoa Palace the emperor would have walked north through the Great Golden Gate into the third and last enclosure, the **Forbidden Purple City**. This area, enclosed by a low wall, was reserved for residential palaces, living quarters of the state physician and nine ranks of royal concubines, plus kitchens and pleasure pavilions. Many of these buildings were destroyed in the 1947 fire, leaving most of the Forbidden Purple City as open ground, a "mood piece", haunted by fragments of wall and overgrown terraces.

However, a handful of buildings remain, including the restored **Left House** and **Right House** facing each other across a courtyard immediately behind Thai Hoa Palace. Civil and military mandarins would spruce themselves up here before proceeding to an audience with the monarch. Of the two, the Right House (actually to your left – the names refer to the emperor's viewpoint) is the more complete with its ornate murals and gargantuan mirror in a gilded frame, a gift from the French to Emperor Dong Khanh. Walking northeast from here you pass behind the Royal Theatre, built in 1826 and now belonging to the University of Fine Arts, to find the **Thai Binh Reading Pavilion**, an appealing, two-tier structure surrounded by bonsai gardens. The pavilion was built by Thieu Tri and then restored by Khai Dinh, who added the kitsch mosaics. The only other buildings left standing near here are a pair of octagonal pavilions, where the emperor came to listen to music and commune with nature.

The Ancestral Altars

The other main cluster of sights lies a short walk away in the southwest corner of the Imperial City. Again, they are all aligned on a south–north axis, kicking off with **Hien Lam Cac** ("Pavilion of Everlasting Clarity"), a graceful, three-storey structure with some notable woodwork, followed by the **Nine Dynastic Urns**. Considered the epitome of Hué craftsmanship, the bronze urns were cast during the reign of Minh Mang and are ornamented with scenes of mountains, rivers, rain clouds and wildlife, plus one or two stray bullet marks. Each urn is dedicated to an emperor: the middle urn, which is also the largest at 2600 kilos, honours Gia Long. They stand across the courtyard from the long, low building of **The Mieu**, the Nguyens' dynastic temple erected in 1822 by Minh Mang to worship his father. Since then, altars have been added for each emperor in turn, except Duc Duc and Hiep Hoa, who reigned only briefly, and Bao Dai who died in exile in 1997; the three anti-French sovereigns – Ham Nghi, Thanh Thai and Duy Tan – had to wait until after Independence in 1954 for theirs. Take a look inside to see the line of altar tables, most sporting a portrait or photo of the monarch. Behind each is a bed equipped with a sleeping mat, pillows and other accoutrements and, finally, a shrine holding funeral tablets for the emperor and his wife or wives. Anniversaries of the emperors' deaths are still commemorated at The Mieu, attended by members of the royal family in all their finery.

Exit The Mieu by its west door, beside a 170-year-old pine tree trained in the shape of a flying dragon, and follow the path north into the next compound to find **Hung Mieu**. This temple is dedicated to the Nguyen ancestors and specifically to the parents of Gia Long, and is distinguished by its fine carving. North again, **Dien Tho**, the queen mother's residence, is worth a look. Built in a mix of Vietnamese and French architectural styles, the palace later served as Bao Dai's private residence, and the downstairs reception rooms are now set out with period furniture, echoing the photos of the palace in use in the 1930s.

▲ The Mieu in the Imperial City

The museums
Instead of leaving the Imperial City via Ngo Mon Gate, cut east to exit via the well-preserved Cua Hien Nhon ("Gate of Humanity"). From here it's a short walk to the **Museum of Fine Arts** at 3 Le Truc (7am–7pm; 22,000đ), which boasts an interesting display of former royal paraphernalia. Its most valuable exhibits are the lively paintings on glass which adorn the ironwood columns, and a series of stone gongs. But the museum's greatest asset is the building it's housed in, **Long An Palace**, built in 1845 inside the Imperial City and then moved to its present location to become the National University Library. The palace was renovated in 1995 and decorated with rich browns, highlighting the wealth of furniture decorated with mother-of-pearl inlay.

Directly across Le Truc, the **Provincial Museum** (7.30am–5pm; free) is worth visiting for its well-presented coverage of Hué during the American War. Photos, documents and original film clips cover both the Buddhist demonstrations in 1963 and the 1968 battle, including footage of the National Liberation Front flag being hoisted above the citadel.

Phu Cat

Hué's civilian and merchant quarter grew up alongside the citadel on a triangular island now divided into **Phu Cat**, Phu Hiep and Phu Hau districts. This part of town has a completely different atmosphere: it's a lively, crowded, dilapidated area centred on Chi Lang, in Phu Cat District, which still boasts some single-storey, wood and red-tiled houses as well as more ornate, colonial-era shophouses. The area was once home to the Chinese community, and five **Assembly Halls** still stand along Chi Lang. Old trees shade the Dong Ba Canal on the island's southwestern side, where Bach Dang was the site of anti-government demonstrations in the 1960s, centred around **Dieu De Pagoda**. There's nothing compelling to draw you onto the island, particularly if you've already seen the Chinese temples of Hoi An and Ho Chi Minh City, but the area provides a bustling contrast to the otherwise sedate streets of Hué.

The Chinese Assembly Halls
Chinese immigrants to Hué settled in five congregations around their separate **Assembly Halls**, of which the most interesting is **Chua Ong**, 319 Chi Lang. Founded by the Phuoc Kien (Fujian) community in the mid-1800s and rebuilt on several occasions, including after Viet Cong mortars hit a US munitions boat on the river nearby in 1968 and destroyed the pagoda plus surrounding houses. Surprisingly, there's no Buddha on the main altar but instead several doctors of medicine, along with General Quan Cong to the right and Thien Hau to the left, both protectors of sailors. The story goes that Quan Cong sat on the main altar until a devastating cholera epidemic in 1918 when he was displaced by the doctors, and the outbreak ended soon after. Of the other halls, **Chieu Ung**, at no. 223, is worth dropping in to. The gilded altar displays some skilled carpentry. This pagoda was also founded in the nineteenth century by ethnic Chinese from Hai Nam, and has been rebuilt at least twice since.

Dong Ba Market
En route to or from Phu Cat you pass **Dong Ba Market**, the epicentre of Hué commercial life, a rambling covered market at the southeast corner of the citadel. Fruit, fish and vegetable vendors overflow into the surrounding spaces, while in the downstairs hall you'll find Hué's contribution to the world of fashion, the *non bai tho*, or **poem hat**. These look just like the

normal conical hat but have a stencil, traditionally of a romantic poem, inserted between the palm fronds – and only visible when held up to the light. The market is within walking distance of the centre, but a more enjoyable way to get there is to hop on one of the sampans that shuttle back and forth from beside the Dap Da causeway.

The European city

Although the French became the de facto rulers of Vietnam after 1884, they left the emperors in the citadel and built their administrative city across the Perfume River on the south bank. The main artery of the **European city** was riverside Le Loi where the French Resident's office stood (now the *Le Residence* hotel), together with other important buildings such as **Quoc Hoc High School** and the *Frères Morin* hotel (now the *Saigon Morin*). Residential streets spread out south of the river as far as the Phu Cam Canal, and are linked to the citadel by Clemenceau Bridge, renamed Trang Tien Bridge after 1954. Apart from the high school, the only major sight is the **Ho Chi Minh Museum**, not just the obligatory gesture in this case as Ho did spend much of his childhood in Hué. The extraordinary, tiered spire of the **Redemptorist Church** dominates the southern horizon with its improbable blend of Gothic and Cubism created by a local architect in the late 1950s. The church caters to some of Hué's 20,000 Catholics and is interesting to view in passing, though the interior is less striking. Admirers of modern Vietnamese art should call in at the **Museum of Contemporary Art**, 1 Pham Boi Chau (7.30–11am & 2–5pm; free) – in fact an exhibition of the works of Diem Phung Thi, who was born in Hué in 1920. The old villa provides the perfect setting for her chunky "modules" developed from Chinese calligraphy.

The Ho Chi Minh Museum and Quoc Hoc High School

Ho Chi Minh was born near Vinh in Nghe An Province (see p.334), but spent ten years at school in Hué (1895–1901 and 1906–1909) where his father worked as a civil mandarin. The modern **Ho Chi Minh Museum** at 7 Le Loi (Tues–Sun 7.30–11am & 2–4.30pm; 10,000đ) presents these years in the context of the anti-French struggle and then takes the story on to 1960s' peace protests in Hué and reunification. The most interesting material consists of family photos and rare glimpses of early twentieth-century Hué. You can still see the house where Ho lived for a time with his father in Duong No Village on the way to Thuan An Beach (see p.320), but the primary school he attended near Dong Ba Market no longer exists.

Ho Chi Minh was the most famous student to attend **Quoc Hoc High School**, which stands almost opposite his museum on Le Loi. The school was founded in 1896 as the National College, dedicated to the education of royal princes and future administrators who learnt the history of their European "motherland" – all in French until 1945. Ho studied here for at least a year before being expelled for taking part in anti-government demonstrations. Other revolutionary names that appear on the roster are Prime Minister Pham Van Dong, General Giap and Party Secretary Le Duan, while former president of South Vietnam Ngo Dinh Diem was also a student. Even during the 1960s Quoc Hoc had a justly earned reputation for breeding dissident intellectuals, and after reunification in 1975 some staff were sent for "re-education".

Eating

It's not only Hué people who say their cuisine is the best in Vietnam, combining as it does special dishes originating from the Imperial kitchens, vegetarian meals prepared with exquisite care in the pagodas and simple but delicious "frugal meals" which are the essence of Hué home cooking; see the box below for more on Hué's **speciality foods**.

Much of the local cuisine originated from **Imperial meals**, which involved many elaborate dishes presented like works of art before the royal family. Some of the large hotels, such as the *Saigon Morin* and *Huong Giang*, now stage "royal meals" for tourists, including traditional music and the opportunity to embarrass yourself in Imperial togs. All this frivolity doesn't come cheap, though – the food is rich and plentiful, but at more than $80 for two it's really aimed at tour groups and business entertaining.

If you fancy something sweet, the *Hong Phuong* **patisserie** at 36 Nguyen Tri Phuong, next to the *Binh Minh I* hotel, is a good spot for coffee and pastries. Or you could try Hué's most famous *chè* outlet down the alley beside 29 Hung Vuong, where you can sample a refreshing **drink** made from green bean and coconut (*chè xanh dua*), fruit (*chè trai cay*) or, if you're lucky, lotus seed (*chè hat sen*).

Most of the places listed below are found **south of the Perfume River**, near the hotels and guesthouses, but a few restaurants **in the citadel** make convenient lunch stops or are worth an excursion in their own right. Several of the smaller hotels serve decent food, usually all day, and there's no shortage of cafés or cheap and cheerful local hostelries scattered throughout the city. All those listed places below are marked on the map on p.300, except where otherwise stated.

Hué specialities

One good argument for staying in Hué an extra couple of days is its many speciality foods, best sampled at local stalls and street kitchens. The most famous Hué dish is **banh khoai**, a small, crispy yellow **pancake** made of egg and rice flour, fried up with shrimp, pork and bean sprouts and eaten with a special peanut and sesame sauce (*nuoc leo*), plus a vegetable accompaniment of star fruit, green banana, lettuce and mint. Hué is also well known for its **noodles** and has its own spicy version of the rice-noodle soups, called *bun bo*, *bun ga* or *bun bo gio heo* depending on the meat used – beef, chicken or beef and pork – and flavoured with citronella, shrimp and basil.

There are even special **snacks**, usually eaten around four or five o'clock in the afternoon. Order *banh beo* and you get a whole trayful of individual dishes containing a small amount of steamed rice-flour dough topped with spices, shrimp flakes and a morsel of pork crackling; add a little sweetened *nuoc mam* sauce to each dish and tuck in with a teaspoon. *Banh nam*, or *banh lam*, is a similar idea but spread thinly in an oblong, steamed in a banana leaf and eaten with rich *nuoc mam* sauce. Manioc flour is used instead of rice for *banh loc*, making a translucent parcel of whole shrimps, sliced pork and spices steamed in a banana leaf, but this time the *nuoc mam* is pepped up with a dash of chilli. Finally, *ram it* consists of two small dollops of sticky rice-flour dough, one fried and one steamed, to dip in a spicy sauce.

One Hué dish that most people steer clear of, for fear of health repercussions, is *com hen* whose main ingredient is a small **shellfish** of the mussel family (*hen*) dredged up from around the Perfume River's Hen Island and further down the estuary. It's a popular and very tasty breakfast dish in summer, the main *hen* season, but can occasionally be found at other times of year in restaurants at the west end of Truong Dinh. *Com hen* is complicated to prepare, but its main constituents are *hen*, rice vermicelli noodles, shrimp sauce and chilli.

Bun Bo Hué 11b Ly Thuong Kiet. Join breakfasting locals for spicy *bun bo* at this big, popular and scrupulously clean outlet.

Café 3 3 Le Loi. See map, p.296. A cheap and cheerful streetside café serving the standard range of Western and Vietnamese dishes, from spring rolls to fruit shakes. They also have an interesting range of tours on offer

Café on Thu Wheels 3/34 Nguyen Tri Phuong. Jot your own Thu-related pun on the wall at this tiny café-bar, which has long been a popular backpacker pit-stop (though service standards have dropped in recent years). The high-octane Ms Thu also runs excellent motorbike tours around Hué.

Club Garden 8 Vo Thi Sau ☏054/382 6327. One of several upscale garden restaurants along this street serving classic Vietnamese cuisine, with reasonably priced set menus. Try and reserve a table outside.

Co Do 22 Ben Nghe. Small and inexpensive no-frills restaurant offering a limited menu of local dishes. Lemongrass and chilli are the predominant flavours, accompanying squid, chicken or shrimps. Some people may find the seasoning on the heavy side, but the food is all very fresh and well prepared.

Dong Tam 48/7 Le Loi. This vegetarian restaurant run by a Buddhist family is an oasis of calm. The short menu includes vegetarian *banh khoai* and good-value combination plates, as well as decent set menus starting at 20,000đ. It's best at lunchtime when the food's freshest and you can sit in the garden courtyard.

La Boulangerie Nguyen Tri Phuong. A French charity runs this café and bakery school for local orphans in the hope that they gain employment after graduation. Their shop has an array of light and delicious French pastries, perfect for breakfast or packed away for long boat rides.

La Carambole 19 Pham Ngu Lao ☏054/381 0491. Innovative and attractive French–Vietnamese owned restaurant serving good-quality international dishes, such as quiche, sandwiches, banana flambé and the like, as well as local foods. Other plus points are the range of set menus (from around $6) and the attentive service. Reservations recommended.

Lac Thien 6 Dinh Tien Hoang. See map, p.296. Probably Hué's friendliest and most interesting restaurant, located on the citadel side, *Lac Thien* is run by a deaf-mute family who communicate by sign language. The food is excellent, taking in the Hué staples, and prices remain reasonable, despite its fame. Enquire about their wooden bottle openers, and you will be given one and asked to send them photos from around the world holding it to the camera.

Mandarin Café 24 Tran Cao Van. A leading light of Hué's backpacker business, this unassuming café off the main road rustles up cheap but very tasty Vietnamese and Western fare. Owner-photographer Mr Cu and his staff are also excellent sources of information and can assist with boat trips, bike and car rental and tours.

Omar Khayyam's 34 Nguyen Tri Phuong. Deservedly popular restaurant for its authentic Indian fare, which includes a good vegetarian and *thali* selection.

Phuong Nam Cafe 38 Tran Cao Van. Simple local eatery that serves local specialities, including some of the best spring rolls in town. Tables outside on the street are often full with Hué's tiny expat community, but it is popular with locals as well.

Tan Huong Sen 96b Nguyen Trai. See map, p.296. Just west of the citadel, and set in a middle of a small lagoon (complete with walking plank), the bamboo-decorated restaurant offers good-value, fresh seafood in unique surroundings. It's a popular dating spot for locals.

Vuon Y Thao 3 Thach Han ☏054/352 3018. See map, p.296. It's worth splashing out to eat at this restaurant on the western edge of the citadel, where you feast on beautifully presented Imperial foods (150,000đ for a set meal) in the garden of a colonial villa. Traditional music can be arranged on request.

Why Not Bar? 21 Vo Thi Sau. Comfy, open-air pub that serves the usual Vietnamese fare in addition to good burgers, toasties and hotdogs. It often gets crowded at night when the music cranks up.

Xuan Trang Café 14 Hung Vuong. Above-average backpackers' place with an extensive and reasonably priced menu; its ice creams and Hué speciality dishes are recommended.

Nightlife and entertainment

Under the Nguyen emperors Hué was the cultural and artistic as well as political capital of Vietnam. A rich tradition of dance and music evolved from popular culture, from the complex rituals of the court and from religious ceremonies. Though much of this legacy has been lost over the last fifty years, considerable effort has gone into reviving Hué folk songs, *Ca Hué*, which you can now sample, drifting down the Perfume River on a balmy Hué evening.

Historically the Perfume River was a place of pleasure where prostitutes cruised in their sampans and artists entertained the gentry with poetry and music. While the former officially no longer exist, today's **folk-song performances** are based on the old traditions, eulogizing the city's beautiful scenery or the ten charms of a Hué woman – including long hair, dreamy eyes, flowing *ao dai* and a conical hat – while she waits for her lover beside the river. Tickets (60,000đ) can be arranged through hotels and tour agents, or you can catch free performances in the courtyard of the *Saigon Morin*.

If you like your nightlife a bit more upbeat, then try the *DMZ Bar* at 44 Le Loi for beers, pool and dancing or the friendly *Café on Thu Wheels* and *Why Not Bar*? (see opposite) for cheap beer and loud music. More laidback options include the *Saigon Morin's* rooftop bar.

The city authorities have also instigated a **biennial arts festival** (held in June) featuring not only folk songs, kite-flying, water-puppetry and other local traditions, but also international groups.

Listings

Airlines Vietnam Airlines, *Thuan Hoa Hotel*, 7 Nguyen Tri Phuong ☎054/382 4709.

Airport bus A privately run bus service shuttles to and from the airport (35,000đ). Organize a hotel pick-up via your reception.

Banks and exchange Vietcombank, 78 Hung Vuong, exchanges cash and traveller's cheques and has a 24hr ATM outside. More convenient is the exchange bureau outside the *Saigon Morin* hotel, which is also open longer hours (Mon–Sat 7am–10pm) with a 24hr ATM.

Hospital Hué Central Hospital, 16 Le Loi ☎054/382 2325.

Internet access If your hotel doesn't have internet access then head to the backpacker enclave of Hung Vuong and Nguyen Tri Phuong for internet cafés.

Pharmacies You'll find well-stocked pharmacies at 9 Hoang Hoa Tham (actually round the corner on Tran Cao Van) and 7 Ben Nghe.

Post office The GPO occupies a grand new building at 8 Hoang Hoa Tham, and also has internet facilities. Sub-branches are located at 38 Le Loi and in the station complex.

Taxi For a metered taxi call Mai Linh Taxi (☎054/389 8989) or Hué Taxi (☎054/381 8181).

Tours and onward transport *Mandarin Café*, 24 Tran Cao Van ☎054/382 1281, ✉mandarin@dng.vnn.vn), *Sinh Café*, 7 Nguyen Tri Phuong (☎054/384 5022, ✉sinh5hue@dng.vnn.vn), and Green Travel, 8 Hung Vuong (☎054/384 9643, ✉phigreentravel@yahoo.com), all offer reliable tours of Hué and the surrounding sights, including Perfume River boat trips, the DMZ and Bach Ma National Park. For motorbike tours, contact *Café on Thu Wheels*, 3/34 Nguyen Tri Phuong (☎054/383 2241, ✉minhthu1970@hotmail.com) or *Mandarin Café*. Most places can also help arrange hire cars and other onward transport. Open-tour bus operators with offices in Hué include *Sinh Café*, Green Travel and An Phu Tourist at 11 Nguyen Tri Phuong ☎054/383 3897. Buses to Laos leave every morning – *Sinh Café* go every other day at 6.30am, while Malinh-tourism (12 Hung Vuong ☎054/382 5252) have a daily bus leaving at 6am. Both head to Vientiane ($34) via Savannakhet ($20).

Around Hué

For the most part the Nguyen emperors lived their lives within Hué's citadel walls, but on certain occasions they emerged to participate in important rituals at symbolic locations around the city. Today these places are of interest more for their history than anything much to see on the ground, though the mouldering **Royal Arena** still hints at past spectacles. A visit to at least a couple of the **Royal Mausoleums**, however, is not to be missed – it's in these eclectic architectural confections in the hills to the south of Hué that the spirit of the Nguyen emperors lives on. Taking a boat along the **Perfume River** to get to the best mausoleums also offers the chance to stop

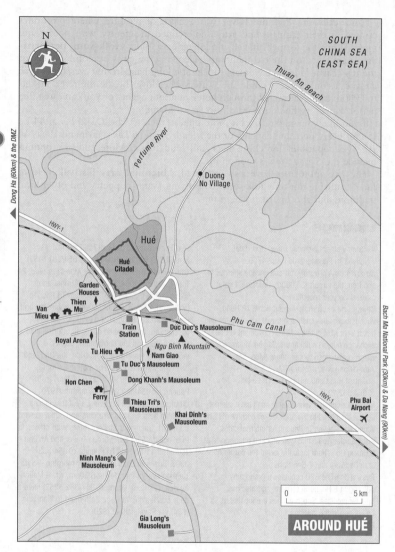

off at the **Thien Mu Pagoda** and **Hon Chen Temple** on the way (see box opposite).

Thuan An Beach is a bike ride away, if you have the time and energy, making for an attractive journey across the estuary with views of fish farms to either side, though the beach itself is nothing spectacular. Further afield, one of the most popular excursions from Hué is a whirlwind day-trip round the **DMZ** (see p.320). **Bach Ma National Park** (see p.294) is also within striking distance.

West along the Perfume River

Hug the north bank of the Perfume River west of the citadel and you'll stumble across a few interesting sights, including the pagodas of **Thien Mu** and **Van Mieu**, the traditional garden houses of **Kim Long Village**, and the Temple of **Hon Chen**. Most people arrive on a boat tour, but the first three sights can be visited on an easy bike ride from the centre of Hué (6km; 30min): follow Le Duan (Highway 1) south from the citadel as far as the train tracks and then just keep heading west along the river where the road eventually gets quieter. You'll pass through the quiet lanes of Kim Long en route to Thien Mu, with Van Mieu a further 500m west. If you've got time it's a pleasant cycle ride on from Van Mieu (see p.313) along an empty country lane beside the river.

The Garden Houses

Travelling by road to Thien Mu along the north bank of the river you pass through **Kim Long** village, a peaceful area of quiet lanes and canals where in the late nineteenth-century mandarins and other Imperial officials built their houses, surrounded by lush gardens. The seven most interesting of these "**garden houses**" have now been preserved and are open to the public. They're still lived in and, although there's no entry fee, a donation is expected (up to 15,000đ would be appropriate). Note that it's best to avoid meal times and to dress conservatively.

The houses are strung along Phu Mong lane, which heads north from the riverbank just before 86 Kim Long; the turning is a good kilometre west of the train tracks and a little hard to spot, so keep your eyes peeled. The first of the houses you come to, on the right behind an entrance arch at no. 20, was built by one of Emperor Gia Long's most senior generals. It's nevertheless a simple structure, consisting of a temple dedicated to the general and the house where his descendants now live. Continuing along Phu Mong lane, take the first turning right to find the next house, second on the left behind a wire-mesh fence, at 2 Diem Tham Quan. This house originally belonged to a minister of foreign affairs under Emperor Tu Duc and is one of the few which still retains the original connecting passage between the house and temple. In front of the temple, a water basin backed by a stone screen represents the lake and mountain

Boat trips on the Perfume River

A sizeable number of people still live in boats on the **Perfume River** and the waterways of Hué, such as the Dong Ba and Phu Cam canals, despite government efforts to settle them elsewhere. It's possible to join them, if only temporarily, by taking a boat trip, puttering about in front of the citadel on a misty Hué morning, watching the slow bustle of river life. A day's boating on the Perfume River is a good way to soak up some of the atmosphere of Hué and do a little gentle sightseeing off the roads. The standard **boat trip** takes you to **Thien Mu Pagoda**, **Hon Chen Temple** and the most rewarding mausoleums, usually those of **Tu Duc**, **Khai Dinh** and **Minh Mang**. However, if you want to visit some of the others or spend more time exploring, it's usually possible to take a bicycle on the boat and cycle back to Hué, though double-check this when you book the trip. Most tour agents (see "Listings", p.309) and hotels offer river tours starting at $2 per person, including a very meagre lunch but no guide. However, all entrance fees are extra, which can work out costly at 55,000đ per mausoleum. If you'd rather do it independently, the same agents can arrange charter boats from $30 for the day, or hone your bargaining skills at the boat wharf beside the Trang Tien Bridge.

required by geomantic principles to defend the family from evil influences. The mangosteen tree, a rarity in Hué, growing behind the screen is said to have sprouted from a seed given to the mandarin by Tu Duc.

Perhaps the most interesting of the garden houses is the last, **An Lac Vien**, 1c Phu Mong. To reach it, head east for another 500m or so along Phu Mong, take a right fork and then follow the lane round to the end. It was built in 1888 by a junior mandarin under Thanh Thai. His grandson can give you an English-language leaflet and proudly show you round the house, full of family heirlooms, and – his pride and joy – the garden. Here he grows all manner of fruits (banana, sapodilla, persimmon, plum and papaya, to name but a few) for the family altar, vegetables and a number of medicinal plants, while the canal at the bottom of the garden doubles as a fish farm.

Thien Mu Pagoda

Also known as *Linh Mu* ("Pagoda of the Celestial Lady"), **Thien Mu Pagoda** stands on the site of an ancient Cham temple. In 1601 Lord Nguyen Hoang left Hanoi to govern the southern territories. Upon arriving at the Perfume River he met an elderly woman who told him to walk east along the river carrying a smouldering incense stick and to build his city where the incense stopped burning. Later Lord Hoang erected a pagoda in gratitude to the lady, whom he believed to be a messenger from the gods, on the site where they met. The pagoda was founded in 1601, making it the oldest in Hué.

During the 1930s and 1940s Thien Mu was already renowned as a centre of Buddhist opposition to colonialism, and then in 1963 it became instantly famous when one of its monks, the Venerable Thich Quang Duc, burned himself to death in Saigon, in protest at the excesses of President Diem's regime (see box, p.99). The monk drove down from Thien Mu in his powder-blue Austin car, which is now on display just behind the main building with a copy of the famous photograph that shocked the world. Thien Mu has continued to be a focus for Buddhist protest against repression and a sore spot for the government.

▲ Thien Mu Pagoda

Despite its turbulent history, the pagoda is a peaceful place where the breezy, pine-shaded terrace affords wide views over the Perfume River. Approaching by either road or river you can't miss the octagonal, seven-tier brick **stupa**, built by Emperor Thieu Tri in the 1840s; each tier represents one of Buddha's incarnations on earth. Two **pavilions**, one on each side, shelter a huge bell, cast in 1710, weighing over 2000 kilos and said to be audible in the city, and a large stele erected in 1715 to record the history of Buddhism in Hué. Walk inland to find the main sanctuary, fronted by a gilded Maitreya Buddha.

Van Mieu

Confucianism had been the principal state religion in Vietnam since the eleventh century and the Nguyens were a particularly traditional dynasty. Early in his reign, in 1808, Gia Long dedicated a national temple to Confucius, known as **Van Mieu** or Van Thanh (the "Temple of Literature"), to replace that in Hanoi. Nothing much remains of the complex, beyond a collection of 32 stone stelae listing the names of 297 recipients of doctorates from exams held between 1822 and 1919. Two other stelae, under small shelters, record edicts from Minh Mang and Thieu Tri banning the "abuse of eunuchs and royal maternal relatives". You get a fine view of the royal landing stage and temple gate passing by on a Perfume River boat trip (see box, p.311).

Hon Chen Temple

Beyond Van Mieu boats head south to stop at the rocky promontory of **Hon Chen Temple** (20,000đ), named "Temple of the Jade Bowl" after the concave hill under which it sits. Again it's the scenery of russet temple roofs among towering trees that is memorable, though the site has been sacred since the Cham people came here to worship their divine protectress Po Nagar, whom the Vietnamese adopted as Y A Na, the Mother Goddess. Emperor Minh Mang restored Hon Chen Temple in the 1830s, but it was Dong Khanh who had a particular soft spot for the goddess after she predicted he would be emperor. He enlarged the temple in 1886, declared himself Y A Na's younger brother and is now worshipped alongside his favourite goddess in the main sanctuary, **Hue Nam**, up from the landing stage and to the right. Of several shrines and temples that populate the hillside, Hue Nam is the most interesting, particularly for its unique nine-tier altar table and a small, upper sanctuary room accessible via two steep staircases.

Festivals at Hon Chen were banned between Independence and 1986 but have now resumed, taking place twice yearly in the middle of the third and seventh lunar months. The celebrations, harking back to ancient rituals, include trance-dances performed by mediums, usually females dressed in brightly coloured costumes, who are transported by a pulsating musical accompaniment.

Hon Chen Temple is 9km from Hué and is only accessible from the river. If you don't want to take a **tour**, hire a sampan either from the **ferry** station directly opposite the temple (accessible from the riverside road), or from Minh Mang pier: it can be as cheap as 30,000đ per person for the return trip.

The Royal Mausoleums

These wise kings of Annam, who make death smile.

Charles Patris, late 1800s

Unlike previous Vietnamese dynasties, which buried their kings in the ancestral village, the Nguyen built themselves magnificent **Royal Mausoleums** in the valley of the Perfume River among low, forested hills to the south of Hué. For historical reasons only seven mausoleums were built, but each one is a unique expression of the monarch's personality, usually planned in detail during his lifetime to serve as his palace in death. It's here more than anywhere else in Hué that the Nguyen emperors excelled in achieving a harmony between the works of man and his natural surroundings and, along with the Imperial City, these are Hué's most rewarding sights.

It often took years to find a site with the right aesthetic requirements that would also satisfy the court cosmologists charged with interpreting the underlying supernatural forces. Artificial lakes, waterfalls and hills were added to improve the geomantic qualities of the location, at the same time creating picturesque, almost romantic, **garden settings** for the mausoleums, of which the finest examples are those of Tu Duc and Minh Mang.

Though details vary, all the mausoleums consist of three elements: a **temple** dedicated to the worship of the deceased emperor and his queen; a large, stone **stele** recording his biographical details and a history of his reign, usually written by his successor; and the royal **tomb** itself. The main temple houses the funerary tablets and possessions of the royal couple, many of which have been stolen, while nearby stand ancillary buildings where the emperor's concubines lived out their years. In front of each stele-house is a paved courtyard, echoing the Imperial City's Esplanade of Great Salutations, where officials and soldiers lined up to honour their emperor, but in this case the mandarins, horses and elephants are fashioned in stone; military mandarins are easily distinguished by their swords, whereas the civil variety clutch sceptres. Obelisks nearby symbolize the power of the monarch, and lastly, at the highest spot, there's the royal tomb enclosed within a wall and a heavy, securely fastened door. Traditionally the burial place was kept secret as a measure against grave-robbers and enemies of the state, and in extreme cases all those who had been involved in the burial were killed immediately afterwards.

Visiting the mausoleums

The mausoleums are intoxicating places, occasionally grandiose but more often achieving an elegant simplicity, where it's easy to lose yourself wandering in the quiet gardens. Of the seven, the contrasting mausoleums of Tu Duc, Khai Dinh and Minh Mang are the most attractive and best-preserved, as well as being easily accessible. These are also the three covered by the boat trips, so they can get crowded; don't let this put you off – but if you do want something more off the beaten track then those of Gia Long, Dong Khanh and Thieu Tri are worth calling in on. Finally, Duc Duc's temple and mausoleum are very modest but they are the closest to Hué and still tended by members of the royal family. Even if time allows, however, you probably won't want to visit all the mausoleums at a **ticket price** of 55,000đ each. If you are lucky enough to arrive on a public holiday, entry is free. The mausoleums are **open** from 7am to 5pm every day, but note that it's best to avoid weekends if possible when they're at their busiest.

To get to the mausoleums you can either rent a **bicycle** or **motorbike** for the day (see p.299), or take a **motorbike tour**, which normally includes at least one mausoleum, with one of the tour agents listed on p.309. The most popular option, however, is a Perfume River boat trip (see box, p.311). On a **boat tour**, you'll face a couple of longish walks, while with your own wheels you'll have to negotiate your own ferry crossings, but will have more time to explore, and won't be restricted to the three main mausoleums. A good compromise is to take a bike on board a tour boat and cycle back to Hué from the last stop.

The Mausoleum of Tu Duc

Emperor Tu Duc was a romantic poet trying to rule Vietnam at a time when the Western world was challenging the country's independence. Although he was the longest-reigning of the Nguyen monarchs, he was a weak ruler who preferred to hide from the world in the lyrical pleasure gardens he created. The **Mausoleum of Tu Duc** is the most harmonious of all the mausoleums, with elegant pavilions and pines reflected in serene lakes. The walled, twelve-hectare park took only three years to complete (1864–67), allowing Tu Duc a full sixteen years for boating and fishing, meditation, drinking tea made from dew collected in lotus blossoms and composing some of the four thousand poems he is said to have written,

besides several important philosophical and historical works. Somehow he also found time for fifty-course meals, plus 104 wives and a whole village of concubines living in the park, though – possibly due to a bout of smallpox – he fathered no children. Perhaps it's not surprising that Tu Duc was also a tyrant who pushed the three thousand workmen building his mausoleum so hard that they rebelled in 1866, and were savagely dealt with.

Entering by the southern gate, **Vu Khiem**, brick paths lead beside a lake covered in water lilies and lotus to a small three-tiered **boating pavilion** which looks across to larger **Xung Khiem Pavilion**, where Tu Duc drank wine and wrote poetry; *khiem*, meaning "modest", appears in the name of every building. From the lake, steps head up through **Khien Cung Gate**, the middle door painted yellow for the emperor, into a second enclosure containing the main temple, **Hoa Khiem**, which Tu Duc used as an office before his death. The royal funerary tablets here are unusual in that Tu Duc's, bearing a dragon, is smaller than the phoenix-decorated tablet of the queen. Beyond is a second temple, **Luong Khiem**, which served as the royal residence, and the elegant **royal theatre**, while behind the storerooms opposite once stood the quarters for Tu Duc's numerous concubines.

The second group of buildings, to the north, is centred on the emperor's tomb, preceded by the salutation court and stele-house. Tu Duc's stele, weighing twenty tonnes, is by far the largest; unusually, Tu Duc wrote his own self-critical eulogy, running to over four thousand characters, to elucidate all his difficulties. Behind the stele is a kidney-shaped pond, representing the crescent moon, and then a bronze door leading into a square enclosure where the unadorned tomb shelters behind a screen adorned with the characters for longevity. Emperor Kien Phuc, one of Tu Duc's adopted sons, is also buried here, just north of the lake.

Tu Duc's Mausoleum is 7km from central Hué **by road**. From the **boat** jetty, it's a walk of 2km from the river on a dirt track, or take one of the **xe om** waiting on the riverbank (10,000đ). On the way you pass incense sticks out to dry and people making – and selling – Hué's famous conical hats.

The Mausoleum of Khai Dinh

By way of a complete contrast, the **Mausoleum of Khai Dinh** is a monumental confection of European baroque, highly ornamental Sino-Vietnamese style and even elements of Cham architecture. Its most attractive feature is the setting, high up on a wooded hill, but it's worth climbing the 130-odd steps to take a look inside the sanctuary itself, still in its original state. Khai Dinh was the penultimate Nguyen emperor and his mausoleum is a radical departure from its predecessors, with neither gardens nor living quarters and only one main structure. Khai Dinh was also a vain man, a puppet of the French very much taken with French style and architecture, and though he only reigned for nine years it took eleven (1920–31) to complete his mausoleum, and it cost so much he had to levy additional taxes for the project.

The approach is via a series of grandiose, dragon-ornamented stairways leading first to the salutation courtyard, with an unusually complete honour guard of mandarins, and on to the stele-house. Climbing up a further four terraces brings you to the **principal temple**, built of reinforced concrete with slate roofing imported from France, whose extravagant halls are a startling contrast to the blackened exterior. Walls, ceiling, furniture, everything is decorated to the hilt, writhing with dragons and peppered with symbolic references and classic imagery such as the Four Seasons panels in the antechamber. Most of this lavish display, not as garish as it might sound, is worked in glass and porcelain mosaic – even the central canopy, which looks like fabric. A life-size gilded bronze statue of the emperor holding his royal sceptre sits under the canopy, while his altar table and funerary tablet are up on the mezzanine floor behind. His portrait stands on the incense table in the antechamber. Khai Dinh was a particularly flamboyant dresser and it's rumoured that he brought back a string of fairy lights from France and proceeded to wear them around the palace, twinkling, until the batteries ran out.

Khai Dinh's Mausoleum is 10km from Hué **by road**. Arriving **by boat**, it's a 1.5-kilometre walk, heading eastwards up a valley with a giant Quan Am statue on your right until you see the mausoleum on the opposite hillside.

The Mausoleum of Minh Mang

Court officials took fourteen years to find the location for the **Mausoleum of Minh Mang** – for which the mandarin responsible was awarded two promotions – and then only three years to build (1841–43), using ten thousand workmen. Minh Mang, the second Nguyen emperor, was a capable, authoritarian monarch who was selected for his serious nature and distrust of Western religious infiltration. He was also passionate about architecture – it was Minh Mang who completed Hué citadel after Gia Long's death – and designed his mausoleum along traditional Chinese lines, with all the principal buildings symmetrical about an east–west axis. But the mausoleum's stately grandeur is softened by fifteen hectares of superb landscaped gardens, almost a third of which is taken up by lakes reflecting the handsome, red-roofed pavilions.

Inside the mausoleum a processional way links the series of low mounds bearing all the main buildings. After the salutation courtyard and stele-house comes the **principal temple** (*Sung An*), where Minh Mang and his queen, who died at the age of 17, are worshipped. Despite this early loss, Minh Mang managed to father 142 children with his 33 wives and 107 concubines. Though beautifully restored, the only point of interest about the temple itself is that local Christians vandalized it in 1885 to protest against Minh Mang's virulent anti-Catholicism. Continuing west you reach **Minh Lau**, the elegant, two-storey "Pavilion of Pure Light" standing among clouds of frangipani trees, symbols of

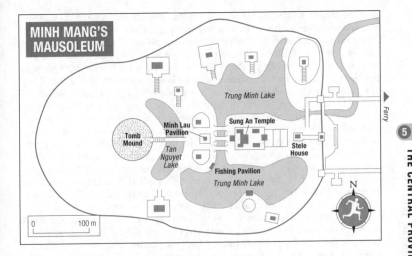

longevity; beyond, two stone gardens trace the Chinese character for long life. From here the ceremonial pathway crosses a crescent lake and ends at the circular burial mound.

With the new bridge (part of the new highway connecting to the airport) it is now easy to get here from Khai Dinh's Tomb. Simply follow the road to the highway, cross over the river and turn left after fifty metres for Minh Mang's Mausoleum. The entrance is then a couple of hundred metres' walk through a barrage of souvenir-sellers. Note that **sampans** are available to Gia Long's Mausoleum and the Hon Chen Temple (see p.313) from the other side of the river, from a small village just west of the bridge.

The Mausoleum of Gia Long

As the first Nguyen ruler, Gia Long had his pick of the sites, and he chose an immense natural park 16km from Hué on the left bank of the Perfume River. Unfortunately his **mausoleum** – begun in 1814 and completed shortly after his death in 1820 – was badly damaged during the American War and there's not a great deal to see beyond some fine carving, and a double tomb with pitched roofs housing Gia Long and his wife. However, this is the least-visited of Hué's mausoleums and is recommended for the boat trip and the peaceful stroll through sandy pine forest, though some visitors complain of attracting a convoy of persistent soft-drink sellers for the duration of the two-kilometre walk. You approach the complex from the north to find the main temple, tomb and stele-house all aligned on a horizontal axis, looking south across a lake towards Thien Tho Mountain.

The easiest way to reach Gia Long's Mausoleum is **by road** as far as the Minh Mang boat station, from where **sampans** can be hired (20min each way; 30,000đ return).

The Mausoleum of Dong Khanh

Dong Khanh was put on the throne by the French in 1885 as titular head of their new protectorate. A pliant ruler with a fondness for French wine, perfume and alarm clocks, he died suddenly at the age of 25 after only three years on the throne; having never got round to planning his final resting place he was buried near the temple he dedicated to his father. As a result this is a modest, country-side **mausoleum** with a rustic charm but is particularly well preserved.

The mausoleum consists of two parts: the main temple, and then the tomb and stele in a separate, walled enclosure on a slight rise 100m to the northwest. The complex was built mostly by Dong Khanh's son, Khai Dinh, after 1889, though has been added to since. The **main temple** holds most interest: the first thing you notice are the coloured-glass doors and windows, but the faded murals on each side wall showing scenes of daily life are far more attractive. Twenty-four glass-paintings, illustrated poems of Confucian love, hang on the temple's ironwood columns and, at either end of the first row, there are two engravings of Napoleon and the Battle of Waterloo. The three principal altars honour Dong Khanh with his two queens to either side, while his seven concubines have a separate altar in the back room. Finally, don't miss the altar to Y A Na in a small side-chamber, off to the right as you enter: Dong Khanh often consulted the goddess at Hon Chen Temple (see p.313) and dedicated an altar to her after she appeared in a dream and foretold that he would be emperor.

Dong Khanh's Mausoleum is only 500m from Tu Duc's. Follow the **road** round to the southeast or take a **short cut** over the hill by the **footpath** from between the refreshment stalls, forking left twice before you see Dong Khanh's tomb on your right and the temple straight ahead behind some trees.

The Mausoleum of Thieu Tri

Emperor Thieu Tri was the son of Minh Mang and shared his father's aversion to foreign influences – it's said he destroyed anything Western he found in the Imperial palaces – and his taste in architecture. His **mausoleum** follows the same basic pattern as Minh Mang's though without the attractive walled gardens, and is split into two sections placed side by side. As it's also smaller it took less than a year to build (1847–48), but its most distinctive feature is that it faces northwest, a traditionally inauspicious direction, and many people believed that this was the reason the country fell under the French yoke a few years later. Although the salutation courtyard, stele-house and tomb are suffering from serious neglect, the temple itself is in reasonable shape. It contains numerous poems, in mother-of-pearl or painted on glass, since Thieu Tri was a prolific poet who would pen a stanza or two at a moment's notice.

To get here from Hué follow the **road** towards Khai Dinh's Mausoleum, but after Cau Lim Bridge branch right beside a faded sign saying "Lang Thieu Tri" opposite the Social Welfare School. The mausoleum is 6km from the centre of Hué.

The Mausoleum of Duc Duc

Three emperors are buried at the **Mausoleum of Duc Duc** which, although it's the closest to Hué, is rarely visited. Duc Duc and his wife are buried in a walled compound, while emperors Thanh Thai and Duy Tan are interred in a separate row of graves behind the main temple, built in 1899. Duc Duc was forced to resign by his senior courtiers after a mere three days as emperor in 1883 and died a year later in prison, while his son, **Thanh Thai**, was also removed in 1907 after a suspected anti-French conspiracy. The French then put Thanh Thai's 8-year-old son, **Duy Tan**, on the throne, but he fled the palace nine years later amid another revolutionary plot, and was eventually exiled with his father to the French territory of Réunion in the Indian Ocean. Duy Tan died in a World War II plane crash in 1945, fighting on the side of the Allies, but Thanh Thai was allowed back to Vietnam in 1947 and died in Saigon in the 1950s. Descendants of the Imperial family, two French-speaking nephews of

Bao Dai, still live in the temple buildings and possess a historic collection of family photos including some of the funeral of Thanh Thai.

Find the mausoleum down **Duong Duy Tan** (opposite 74 Tran Phu), 100m along on the right; someone will show you around for a small donation.

South of the centre

Aside from the mausoleums there are a number of other regal sights worth seeing south of the city; all are easily accessible by bike or xe om. Just 3km from central Hué – at the end of Dien Bien Phu – is **Nam Giao**, once the site of Imperial rites, while the splendid **Tu Hieu Pagoda** is buried in the pine forests northeast of Tu Duc's Mausoleum. Directly west of the train station is the **Royal Arena**, once the site of much imperial merriment.

Nam Giao

First and foremost in the ceremonial and religious life of the nation was **Nam Giao** ("Altar of Heaven"), where the emperor reaffirmed the legitimacy of his rule in sacred rituals, held here roughly every three years from 1807 to 1945. The ceremonies were performed on a series of terraces, two square-shaped and one round, symbolizing heaven, earth and man in descending order. Before each occasion the monarch purified himself, keeping to a strict regime of vegetarian food and no concubines for several days. He then carried out the sacrifices, with the assistance of some five-thousand attendants, to ensure the stability of both the country and the dynasty. Nam Giao makes a good place for a relaxing walk, though there's not too much to get your teeth into. In the grounds – on the far right of the complex as viewed from the entrance – is a small museum featuring interesting photographs of regal days.

Tu Hieu Pagoda

Though not the most famous pagoda in Hué, **Tu Hieu** is one of the most attractive, and it does have an Imperial link since this is where royal eunuchs retired to and were worshipped after their deaths. The pagoda was founded in 1843 and still houses an active community of forty monks who extend a warm welcome to their occasional visitors. The main altar is dedicated to Sakyamuni, with the Buddhist trinity sitting up above, while a secondary shrine room behind contains altars to several famous mandarins and the eunuchs. Between the two buildings is a small courtyard festooned with orchids and a 100-year-old star-fruit vine. To find the pagoda, take the road towards Tu Duc's Mausoleum from the Nam Giao T-junction and near the top of the hill look out for two tall columns announcing "Tu Hieu". Turn right here down a dirt road and then fork left to reach the pagoda's triple-arched gate behind which lies a peaceful, crescent-moon lake. There is no charge to visit the Tu Hieu Pagoda.

The Royal Arena

On the south bank of the Perfume River stands the **Royal Arena**, or Ho Quyen, where the emperors amused themselves with fights between elephants and tigers. Not that this was entirely sport: elephants symbolized the unequalled might of the sovereign while tigers represented rebel forces, and the arena was built on the site of an old Cham fort just to underline the message of Imperial power. It was, apparently, a pretty one-sided fight which the elephant was never allowed to lose, and contemporary accounts suggest that in later years the tigers were tied to a stake and had their claws removed. Originally the contests were held on open ground in front of the citadel, but after a tiger attacked Minh Mang they were staged in the arena from 1830 until the last fight in 1904.

The Royal Arena still exists almost in its original state, though the royal pavilion has rotted away. For the best view, climb up the staircase on the north wall to where the emperor would have sat facing south over the small arena. After they died, the elephants were worshipped nearby in a small temple, **Long Chau Dien**, which stands to the west of the arena, although almost completely hidden by undergrowth and with only a couple of elephant statues to see: follow the path round the arena's south side to find the temple, overlooking a small lake.

The Royal Arena is 4km from central Hué, taking Bui Thi Xuan along the Perfume River's south bank through Phuong Duc, a famous metal-casting village. At 198 Bui Thi Xuan, turn left up a dirt track and take the left fork after 20m to see the arena's brick steps in front of you. If you want to combine the arena with the Royal Mausoleums, you can use a rough backroad from Phuong Duc village, though this takes a far steeper route than the main one via Dien Bien Phu.

Thuan An Beach

Northeast of Hué, the Perfume River ends in a vast estuary lagoon, sheltered by a long sandy spit with **Thuan An Beach** at its northern end, a quiet place where residents of Hué come to escape the summer heat. The beach itself is inferior to Hoi An's Cua Dai or Da Nang's China Beach (see p.278 & p.290 respectively), but nice enough once you get away from the litter and the pestering, sometimes aggressive, deck-chair attendants – head south down the beach for the quieter, cleaner sands. You'll also find a number of small seafood restaurants along here; check the prices before ordering.

Thuan An is 14km from Hué by road, through flat rice country and via a causeway which floods easily in the monsoon season (late Sept to early March), when the sea here also gets very rough. On the way you pass through Duong No Village, 8km outside Hué, where Ho Chi Minh once lived with his father. It's a pleasant **cycle** ride or, alternatively, you can take a local **bus** from Hué's Dong Ba bus station, beside Dong Ba Market on the river's north bank, for the thirty-minute ride, but note that the last bus back leaves around 4pm. If you have your own transport, you'll have to pay a nominal **parking fee** at the beach.

The DMZ and around

Quang Tri and Quang Binh, the two provinces either side of the **DMZ** (Demilitarized Zone; see box opposite), were the most heavily bombed and saw the highest casualties, civilian and military, American and Vietnamese, during the American War. Names made infamous in 1960s' and 1970s' America have been perpetuated in countless films and memoirs: Con Thien, the Rockpile, Hamburger Hill and Khe Sanh. For some people the DMZ will be what draws them to Vietnam, the end of a long and difficult pilgrimage; for others it will be a bleak, sometimes beautiful, place where there's nothing particular to see but where it's hard not to respond to the sense of enormous desolation.

North of the DMZ is one of the region's main attractions – the tunnels of **Vinh Moc**, where villages created deep underground during the American war have been preserved. The area's other points of interest lie south of the Ben Hai

The DMZ

Under the terms of the 1954 Geneva Accords, Vietnam was split in two along the Seventeenth Parallel, pending elections intended to reunite the country. The demarcation line ran along the Ben Hai River and was sealed by a strip of no-man's-land 5km wide on each side known as the **Demilitarized Zone**, or DMZ. All Communist troops and supporters were supposed to regroup north in the Democratic Republic of Vietnam, leaving the southern Republic of Vietnam to non-Communists and various shades of opposition. When the elections failed to take place, the river became the de facto border until 1975.

In reality both sides of the DMZ were anything but demilitarized after 1965, and anyway the border was easily circumvented – by the Ho Chi Minh Trail to the west (see box, p.327) and sea routes to the east – enabling the North Vietnamese to bypass a string of American fire bases overlooking the river. One of the more fantastical efforts to prevent Communist infiltration southwards was US Secretary of Defense Robert McNamara's proposal for an electronic fence from the Vietnamese coast to the Mekong River, made up of seismic and acoustic sensors that would detect troop movements and pinpoint targets for bombing raids. Though trials in 1967 met with some initial success, the "McNamara Line" was soon abandoned: sensors were confused by animals, especially elephants, and could be triggered deliberately by the tape-recorded sound of vehicle engines or troops on the march.

Nor could massive, conventional bombing by artillery and aircraft contain the North Vietnamese, who finally stormed the DMZ in 1972 and pushed the border 20km further south. Exceptionally bitter fighting in the territory south of the Ben Hai River (I Corps Military Region) claimed more American lives in the five years leading up to 1972 than any other battle zone in Vietnam. Figures for North Vietnamese losses during that period are not known, but it's estimated that up to thirty percent of ordnance dropped in the DMZ failed to detonate on impact and that these have, since 1975, been responsible for up to ten thousand deaths and injuries. So much fire power was unleashed over this area, including napalm and herbicides, that for years nothing would grow in the impacted, chemical-laden soil, but the region's low, rolling hills are now almost entirely reforested with a green sea of pine, eucalyptus, coffee and acacia.

River, and while it's not possible to cover everything in a day, the most interesting of the places described here are included on organized tours from Hué (see "Listings", p.309 for recommended operators). Alternatively, it's possible to use **Dong Ha** as a base or cover a more limited selection of sights on the drive north. If you have limited time then the Vinh Moc tunnels should be high on your list, along with a drive up Highway 9 to **Khe Sanh**, both for the scenery en route and the sobering battleground itself. Note that, although you can now visit the DMZ without a local guide, this is not recommended as most sites are unmarked and, more importantly, the guides (arranged in Dong Ha; see p.323) know which paths are safe – local farmers are still occasionally killed or injured by **unexploded ordnance** in this area.

Quang Tri

American troops weren't the first to suffer heavy losses in this region: during the 1950s French soldiers dubbed the stretch of Highway 1 north of Hué as *la rue sans joie*, or "street without joy", after they came under constant attack from elusive Viet Minh units operating out of heavily fortified villages along the coast. Later, in the 1972 Easter Offensive, Communist forces overran the whole area, capturing **QUANG TRI** town, some 60km from Hué, from the South

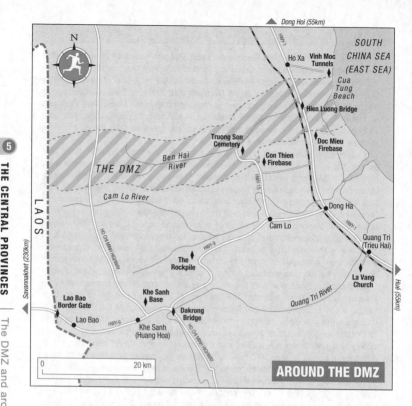

AROUND THE DMZ

Vietnamese Army (ARVN) and holding it for four months while American B-52s pounded the township and surrounding countryside, before it was retaken at huge cost to both sides as well as to hapless civilians caught up in the battle. Quang Tri was simply wiped off the map, and though a town of sorts has risen in its stead, known officially as **Trieu Hai**, you could be forgiven for missing it. Keep your eyes peeled for one of its few identifying features, the small, pockmarked shell of **Long Hung Church** to the east of the road, 55km from Hué, kept as a memorial to victims of 1972. Soon after, a track on the opposite side of the highway leads 4km southwest to the more impressive ruin of **La Vang Church**, beside which stands an extraordinary monument of *Alice in Wonderland* mushrooms supposedly representing the apparition of the Virgin Mary to persecuted Catholics on this spot in 1798.

The town itself lies off to the right of the highway down Tran Hung Dao, the last surfaced road before you reach the Quang Tri River. There's not a lot to see, but if you've got your own transport the remains of **Quang Tri Citadel** (daily 7am–5pm; 12,000đ) are worth a look. To find the citadel, continue on Tran Hung Dao for 2km, passing a market on your left, then turn right down a dirt road, Ly Thai To, which leads to the entrance. The square, walled structure, resembling a smaller version of the citadel in Hué, was originally built from earth in 1806 by the Nguyen Dynasty, fortified with bricks in 1827, and served in turn as a base for the French and the ARVN before being overrun and destroyed in 1972. Parts of the wall and moat remain, and the south gate, through which visitors enter, has been rebuilt. Inside is a war memorial, the remains of a nineteenth-century French prison consisting of fourteen tiny cells measuring 1m by 2m, and a small war **museum** with English captions (included in entrance fee). The museum houses some excellent photos of the fierce hand-to-hand fighting that took place towards the end of 1972 as ARVN troops eventually retook the city after 81 days. Stick to established paths, as unexploded ordnance may still lurk.

Back on the highway, the road and rail line share a bridge over the Quang Tri River from where it's only another 13km to the town of Dong Ha, which took over as provincial capital when Quang Tri ceased to exist.

Dong Ha

As a former US Marine Command Post and then ARVN base, **DONG HA** was also obliterated in 1972, but unlike Quang Tri it has bounced back, thanks largely to its administrative status and location at the eastern end of Highway 9 which leads through Laos to Savannakhet on the Mekong River (see box, p.325 for details of cross-border travel). The future looks rosy as well: a new deep-water port has been built to serve landlocked Laos, a number of special economic zones are under construction along the border, and Highway 9 has been upgraded as part of the massive Trans-Asian Highway project.

As the closest town to the DMZ, Dong Ha attracts a lot of tourist traffic, though few people choose to stay here, preferring the comfort and facilities of Hué. It is essentially a two-street town: Highway 1, known here as Le Duan, forms the main artery as it passes through on its route north, while Highway 9 takes off inland at a central T-junction.

Practicalities

Dong Ha's **bus station** lies one street north of the central T-junction on the left, while its **train station** is a kilometre south towards Hué and just west of the highway. The market and bridge over the Cua Viet River, a kilometre beyond the bus station, mark Dong Ha's northern extremity, where Tran Hung Dao branches left to the **post office** (spot the telltale radio mast). **Information**, car rental and **guides** can be found at Sepon Travel (☎053/3855289, ✉sepontravel@vnn.vn), situated at 189 Le Duan (across the highway from the bus station), and *Trung Tam Quan Guesthouse* next door (see below). Both sell tickets for **open-tour buses** and for DMZ tours ($11), on which you join the coach originating in Hué, and **motorbike** rental (90,000đ per day). The town's **bank** at 1 Le Quy Don – the second main road on the left as you head north on Highway 1 from the bus station – can exchange US dollars, handle advances on Visa and MasterCard and change traveller's cheques. There is also an **ATM** next door to the Sepon Travel office.

Dong Ha's **accommodation** is dominated by a string of dreary, damp, state-run guesthouses. A welcome exception is the long-running favourite *Phung Hoang II*, 146 Highway 1 (☎053/385 4567, ✉phunghoanghotel2001@yahoo .com; ❸) about 200m south of the bus station with a range of en-suite rooms. Alternatively, the *Melody Hotel*, 62 Highway 1 ☎053/355 4664; ❷) is a little gem that keeps its rooms super clean and its guests happy; the staff are also adept at helping with trips to DMZ attractions. For those on a real budget, the tiny *Trung Tam Quan Guesthouse*, 201 Highway 1 ☎053/385 2972, ✉ttquan@dng .vnn.vn; ❶) has just two fan rooms with reasonably clean shared toilets and a hot-water shower.

Dong Ha's best **restaurants** are the *Tan Chau II* at 222 Highway 1, near the *Phung Hoang II* hotel, and the *Hiep Loi*, 200m north of the intersection of

The battle of Khe Sanh

The **battle of Khe Sanh** was important not because of its immediate outcome, but because it attracted worldwide media attention and, along with the simultaneous Tet Offensive, demonstrated the futility of America's efforts to contain their enemy. In 1962 an American Special Forces team arrived in Khe Sanh Town to train local Bru minority people in counter-insurgency, and then four years later the first batch of Marines was sent in to establish a forward base near Laos, to secure Highway 9 and to harass troops on the Ho Chi Minh Trail. Skirmishes around Khe Sanh increased as intelligence reports indicated a massive build-up of North Vietnamese Army (NVA) troops in late 1967, possibly as many as forty thousand, facing six thousand Marines together with a few hundred South Vietnamese and Bru. Both the Western media and American generals were soon presenting the confrontation as a crucial test of America's credibility in South Vietnam and drawing parallels with Dien Bien Phu (see p.439). As US President Johnson famously remarked, he didn't want "any damn Dinbinfoo".

The **NVA attack** came in the early hours of January 21, 1968; rockets raining in on the base added to the terror and confusion by striking an ammunition dump, gasoline tanks and stores of tear gas. There followed a seemingly endless, nerve-grinding NVA artillery barrage, when hundreds of shells fell on the base each day, interspersed with costly US infantry assaults on the surrounding hills. In an operation code-named **"Niagara"**, General Westmoreland called in the air battalions to silence the enemy guns and break the siege by unleashing the most intense bombing raids of the war: in nine weeks nearly a hundred thousand tonnes of bombs pounded the area round the clock, averaging **one airstrike every five minutes**, backed up by napalm and defoliants. Unbelievably the NVA were so well dug in and camouflaged that they not only withstood the onslaught but continued to return fire, despite horrendous casualties, estimated at ten thousand. On the US side around five hundred troops died at Khe Sanh (although official figures record only 248 American deaths, of which 43 occurred in a single helicopter accident), before a relief column broke through in early April, seventy-odd days after the siege had begun. NVA forces gradually pulled back and by the middle of March had all but gone, having successfully diverted American resources away from southern cities prior to the Tet Offensive. Three months later the Americans also quietly withdrew, leaving a plateau that resembled a lunar landscape, contaminated for years to come with chemicals and explosives; even the trees left standing were worthless because so much shrapnel was lodged in the timber.

highways 1 and 9. Further down Highway 1 just out of town, is the friendly *Dong Que Restaurant*, which also provides travel information. Otherwise, there's no shortage of no-nonsense places serving com and pho all along Highway 1, including the highly popular restaurant at the *Trung Tam Quan Guesthouse*.

West along Highway 9

Heading west from Dong Ha on Highway 9, you begin to climb into the foothills of the Truong Son range. Where the highway veers south, a sheer-sided isolated stump 230m high dominates the valley: the **Rockpile**. For a while American troops, delivered by helicopter, used the peak for directing artillery to targets across the DMZ and into Laos, but the post was abandoned after 1968. The highway continues over a low pass and then follows a picturesque valley past the **Dakrong Bridge**, which carries a spur of the Ho Chi Minh Highway before climbing among ever-more forested mountains to emerge at **KHE SANH** (now officially rechristened **Huang Hoa**), 63km from Dong Ha.

This bleak, one-street settlement, its frontier atmosphere reinforced by the smugglers' trail across the border to Laos only 19km away (see box below for more on crossing the border), sits on the edge of a windswept plateau that was the site of a pivotal battle in the American War (see box opposite). Due to the high concentration of chemical and explosive contamination after the war, it's only recently that the soil around Khe Sanh has been able to support vegetation again, and the hills are now green with coffee plantations. A few optimistic teenagers still peddle "genuine" dog-tags, and guides point out the red gash of the airstrip, but nothing else remains: when American troops were ordered to abandon Khe Sanh, everything was blown up and bulldozed flat. The only memorial is a small **museum** (daily 7am–5pm; 20,000đ), 2km north of Khe Sanh Town, commemorating the siege – made even more poignant by the hauntingly beautiful mountains all around.

Northwest to the Truong Son Cemetery and Con Thien Firebase

Thirty-odd kilometres northwest of Dong Ha along highways 9 and 15, **Truong Son War Martyr Cemetery** is dedicated to the estimated twenty-five thousand men and women who died on the Truong Son Trail, better known in the West as the Ho Chi Minh Trail (see box, p.327). Many bodies were never recovered, but a total of 10,036 graves lie in the fourteen-hectare cemetery among whispering glades of evergreen trees. Arranged in five geographical regions, the graves are subdivided according to native province, and centred round memorial houses listing every name and grave number in the sector. Each headstone announces *liet si* ("martyr"), together with as many details as are known: name, date and place of birth, date of enrolment, rank and the date they died.

To reach the cemetery from Dong Ha, drive west on Highway 9 as far as Cam Lo Town (12km) and then turn north for 22km following signs along Highway 15. On the way, roughly 12km out of Cam Lo, you pass the site of

Lao Bao border crossing into Laos

Of the five **border crossings** open to foreigners between Vietnam and Laos, the most popular is still **Lao Bao**, 80km west of Dong Ha along Highway 9. It's an vattractive ride, through misty mountains on a reasonable road, and the crossing is hassle-free beyond having to walk a kilometre between inspection posts. Frequent local **buses** and **minibuses** run from Dong Ha to the border and back (2hr; 30,000–45,000đ), though some terminate at Lao Bao Village, in which case you'll have to pick up a **xe om** for the final 3km. On the Laotian side, buses leave for Savannakhet, from where there are connections north to Vientiane by road, river (both unpredictable during the rains) and air, or you can head straight over the Mekong River to Mukdahan in Thailand. A quicker and more comfortable alternative is to take the morning air-conditioned **tourist bus** direct from Dong Ha to Savannakhet (8hr; 190,000đ), which leaves around 8am on odd-numbered days of the month and returns on even-numbered days. Alternatively, there's an **overnight bus** all the way from Da Nang to Savannakhet (see box, p.289) as well as daily services from Hue to Vientiane via Savannakhet (see box, p.309). In theory you can obtain a fifteen-day **visa** for Laos at the border ($30; two passport photos required), but check beforehand for the latest situation. Otherwise, the safest option is to get your visa in advance at the Lao consulates in Da Nang or in Ho Chi Minh City, or at their embassy in Hanoi (see p.288, p.119 & p.386 respectively).

Con Thien Firebase. Again, there's precious little left to see, beyond a view north to what were once NVA positions, chillingly close on the opposite bank of the Ben Hai River. The largest American installation along the DMZ, Con Thien Fire Base was first established by the Special Forces (Green Berets) and then handed over to the Marines in 1966, whose big guns could reach from here far into North Vietnam. In the lead-up to the 1968 Tet Offensive, as part of the NVA's diversionary attacks, the base became the target of prolonged shelling, followed by an infantry assault during which it was briefly surrounded. The Americans replied with everything in their arsenal, including long-range strafing from gunships in the South China Sea and carpet-bombing by B-52s. The North Vietnamese were forced to withdraw temporarily, but then completely overran the base in the summer of 1972.

North of Dong Ha

The American front line comprised a string of fire bases set up on a long, low ridge of hills looking north across the DMZ and the featureless plain of the Ben Hai River. Although there's nothing much to see now, you pass the site of one of these, **Doc Mieu Firebase** to the east of Highway 1 about 14km north of Dong Ha. Before the NVA overran Doc Mieu in 1972, the base played a pivotal role in the South's defence. From here American guns shelled seaborne infiltration routes and, for a while, this was the command post for the "McNamara Line", calling in airstrikes from Da Nang to pound targets – both real and faked – along the Ho Chi Minh Trail.

Just beyond Doc Mieu, Highway 1 drops down into the DMZ, running between paddy fields to the Ben Hai River, which lies virtually on the Seventeenth Parallel. You will see two bridges, the newly built one which is open to traffic and the unused **Hien Luong Bridge** that runs parallel to it. Until it was destroyed in 1967, the original Hien Luong Bridge was painted half red and half yellow as a vivid reminder that this was a physical and ideological boundary separating the two Vietnams. The reconstructed iron-girder bridge officially re-opened in 1975 as a symbol of reunification, and for many years represented an important psychological barrier between north and south.

The Vinh Moc tunnels

In Ho Xa township, 7km north of the Ben Hai River and 28km from Dong Ha, a faded pink signpost opposite a petrol station indicates a right turn which takes you 15km to an amazing complex of tunnels where over a thousand people sheltered, sometimes for weeks on end, during the worst American bombardments. A section of the **Vinh Moc tunnels** has been restored and opened to visitors as a powerful tribute to the villagers' courage and tenacity, with a small museum at the entrance providing background information (7am–5pm; 25,000đ including English-speaking guide and flashlight). The tour

The Ho Chi Minh Trail

At the end of its "working" life, the Ho Chi Minh Trail had grown from a rough assemblage of animal tracks and **jungle paths** to become a highly effective **logistical network** stretching from near Vinh, north of the Seventeenth Parallel, to Tay Ninh Province on the edge of the Mekong Delta. Initially it took up to six months to walk the trail from north to south, most of the time travelling at night while carrying rations of rice and salt, medicines and equipment; in four years one man, Nguyen Viet Sinh, is reputed to have carried more than fifty tonnes and covered 40,000km, equivalent to walking round the world. By 1975, however, the trail – comprising at least three main arteries plus several feeder roads leading to various battlefronts and totalling over **15,000km** – was wide enough to take tanks and heavy trucks, and could be driven in just one week. It was protected by sophisticated anti-aircraft emplacements and supported by regular service stations (fuel and maintenance depots, ammunition dumps, food stores and hospitals), often located underground or in caves and all connected by field telephone. Eventually there was even an oil pipeline constructed alongside the trail to take fuel south from Vinh to a depot at Loc Ninh. All this absorbed thousands of men and women in maintenance work, as engineers, gunners and medical staff, while as many as fifty thousand Youth Volunteers repaired bridges and filled in bomb craters under cover of darkness.

The trail was conceived in early 1959 when **General Giap** ordered the newly created Logistical Group 559 to reconnoitre a safe route by which to direct men and equipment down the length of Vietnam in support of Communist groups in the south. Political cadres blazed the trail, followed in 1964 by the first deployment of ten thousand regular troops, and culminating in the trek south of 150,000 men in preparation for the **1968 Tet Offensive**. It was a logistical feat that rivalled Dien Bien Phu (see p.439) in both scale and determination: this time it was sustained over fifteen years and became a symbol to the Vietnamese of both their victory and their sacrifice. For much of its southerly route the trail ran through **Laos** and **Cambodia**, sometimes on paths forged during the war against the French, sometimes along riverbeds and always through the most difficult, mountainous terrain plagued with leeches, snakes, malaria and dysentery.

On top of all this, people on the trail had to contend with almost constant bombing. By early 1965, **aerial bombardment** had begun in earnest, using napalm and defoliants as well as conventional bombs, to be joined later by carpet-bombing B-52s. Every day in the spring of 1965 the US Air Force flew an estimated three hundred bombing raids over the trail and in eight years dropped over two million tonnes of bombs, mostly over Laos, in an effort to cut the flow. Later they experimented with seismic and acoustic sensors to eavesdrop on troop movements and pinpoint targets, but the trail was never completely severed and supplies continued to roll south in sufficient quantities to sustain the war.

takes around fifty minutes and although these tunnels are bigger (the ceiling is almost 2m high in places) than those of Cu Chi it's not recommended for the claustrophobic.

When American bombing raids north of the DMZ intensified in 1966 the inhabitants of Vinh Linh District began digging down into the red laterite soils, excavating more than fifty tunnels over the next two years. Although they were also used by North Vietnamese soldiers, the tunnels were primarily built to shelter a largely civilian population who worked the supply route from the Con Co Islands lying 28km offshore. Five tunnels belonged to Vinh Moc, a village located right on the coast where for two years 250 people dug more than 2km of tunnel, which housed all six hundred villagers over varying periods from early 1967 until 1969, when half decamped north to the relative safety of Nghe An Province. The tunnels were constructed on three levels at 10, 15 and 20–23m deep (though nowadays you can't visit the lowest level) with good ventilation, freshwater wells and, eventually, a generator and lights. The underground village was also equipped with a school, clinics and a maternity room where seventeen children were born. Each family was allocated a tiny cavern, the four-person space being barely larger than a single bed. They were only able to emerge at night and lack of fresh air and sunlight was a major problem, especially for young children who would sit in the tunnel mouths whenever possible. In 1972, the villagers of Vinh Moc were finally able to abandon their underground existence and rebuild their homes, rejoined by relatives from Nghe An a year later.

Dong Hoi to Ninh Binh

North of the DMZ, Vietnam shrinks to a mere 50km wide and is edged with sand dunes up to 80m high, marching inland at a rate of 10m per year despite efforts to stabilize them with screw-pine and cactus. The narrow coastal plain is walled in by the jagged Truong Son Mountains and drained by short, flood-prone rivers; one of these, the Son, has created an extensive underground drainage system that constitutes one of the few sights of any note in the region. **Phong Nha Cave**, where the river emerges, attracts a steady stream of visitors, mostly on excursions from Hué or the nearby town of **Dong Hoi**.

There's little to tempt the tourist on the route north from Dong Hoi, and most people push straight on through to Ninh Binh or Hanoi. The road passes through Ha Tinh and Nghe An, two of Vietnam's poorest provinces, each with areas of exceptionally dense highland forests on the Lao border, harbouring **rare species** such as the Asian elephant and tiger. Since 1992 scientists have identified two new species of mammal (previously known only to local hunters) in these hills: the elusive **saola ox** and the more numerous **giant muntjac deer**.

Those travelling by road usually overnight in **Vinh**, where there's the opportunity to visit **Ho Chi Minh's birthplace** in the nearby village of Kim Lien. For motorcyclists and others in need of accommodation en route, both **Ha Tinh** and **Thanh Hoa** furnish the basic requirements.

Dong Hoi and Phong Nha Cave

The first town of any size north of the Seventeenth Parallel is **DONG HOI** which was flattened in the American War's bombing raids. The town has risen from its ashes to become a prosperous provincial capital of over sixty thousand people, built on a grand scale with well-ordered streets, a massive theatre hall and an attractive riverfront boulevard – though bereft of any particular sights. Those tourists who do stop in Dong Hoi are usually heading for the **Phong Nha Cave**, a genuinely impressive cave system recognized by UNESCO as a World Heritage Site.

Tourism is becoming big business in Dong Hoi as Phong Nha attracts ever more visitors and developers eye up the region's beaches; there's even a tiny airport with services to Hanoi and Ho Chi Minh City. The town's southern extremity is marked by the broad expanse of the Nhat Le River and a **monument**, said to be a gateway of the eighteenth-century citadel, a couple of hundred metres further on. Continuing north you reach the landmark post office radio mast on a crossroads which constitutes the town centre: south of this junction Highway 1 is named Quang Trung, north of it is Ly Thuong Kiet; Tran Hung Dao leads west, while east takes you 50m to riverfront Quach Xuan Ky, where a bridge crosses over the Nhat Le estuary. Heading east from the monument, Me Suot leads down to a lively, riverside **market** and an area of covered stalls where in summer vendors sell ice-cold glasses of sweet-bean *chè*.

Practicalities

There's no long-distance **bus station** in Dong Hoi – just stand on the highway and flag a bus down. The **train station** is 3km out of town west along Tran Hung Dao. The provincial **tourist office**, Quang Binh Tourism at 102 Ly Thuong Kiet (☎052/382 8228, ✉qbtouristcompany@dng.vnn.vn), provides car rental and English-speaking guides, though you can easily organize transport to Phong Nha through your hotel. Vietcombank at 54 Nguyen Huu Canh handles **foreign exchange** and has a 24-hour ATM; to find it take Le Loi leading west from the monument and turn right onto Nguyen Huu Can after about 100m. There is also a 24-hour ATM at the *Sun Spa Resort* (see below).

One of the best **accommodation** options in town is the well-designed, spotless and friendly *Hoang Linh* on Mac Dinh Chi (☎052/382 1608, ℱ052/382 9960; ❷–❸) – ask for a corner room where the two large windows look out on the water. To get there from the south turn left off Highway 1 down the first street after crossing over the bridge on the south side of town, then turn left again to the riverfront. Tucked down a backstreet immediately northwest of the monument, *Tan Binh*, 4 Le Van Huu (☎052/382 2181, ℱ052/382 3132; ❷) is clean, friendly and equipped with cable TV, as is the slightly cheaper *Kim Lien* next door (☎052/382 2154; ❶–❷). For those who want a beach setting, the luxurious five-star *Sun Spa Resort*, My Canh Beach (☎052/384 2999, ⓦwww.sunsparesortvietnam.com; ❻) – just 500m from the town – is easily the best place to stay in the area; it offers everything you would expect for the price, with over three hundred staff, and a restaurant serving international cuisine at reasonable prices. For cheaper views of the beach, however, *Ke Bang*, 28 Ho Xuan Huong (☎052/384 1063, ℱ052/382 4673; ❷) is a simple but pleasant place in a relaxing location beside the mouth of the estuary about 500m north of town – ask for a sea-view room.

Dong Hoi's most popular **restaurant** – where all the tour buses stop – is the *Anh Dao* next door to *Hoang Linh* hotel, run by a Hué emigré and serving reasonably priced Vietnamese and international foods. Hué specialities, such as *banh beo* and *banh khoai*, are also available at a strip of small restaurants on Co Tam, one block north of the market; *Huyen Nga* at no. 5b is especially popular with locals. As usual, the market itself is home to a number of cheap and cheerful foodstalls. And look out for signs announcing the **local speciality** of *chao luon*, a thick eel soup sold at roadside restaurants.

Phong Nha Cave

Since time immemorial the underground river emerging at **Phong Nha Cave** has held a mystical fascination for the local population. The earliest-known devotees were ninth- and tenth-century Cham people, followed by Vietnamese who petitioned the **guardian spirits** during periods of drought, with great success by all accounts. When Europeans started exploring the caves early in the twentieth century it's said the rainmaker took everlasting umbrage. However, the explorers were undeterred and by the 1950s, tunnels 2km long had been surveyed and the number of visitors warranted a small hotel. Owing to the intervening wars, when Phong Nha provided safe warehousing – you can see evidence of an American rocket attack on the cliff above the cave entrance – nothing further happened until a British expedition was allowed to investigate in 1990. They began pushing upriver, eventually penetrating deep into the limestone massif, and what they discovered is a spelunker's delight: 8km of underground waterway, vast chambers full of magical rock formations and intriguing side-channels waiting to be explored.

For the less intrepid, tour boats take you on an attractive, thirty-minute trip meandering up the peaceful Son River. The tour begins by climbing steps up a relatively steep cliff face to **Tien Son Cave**, and a grand view of the valley. After descending, you will rejoin your boat and explore 600m of Phong Nha Cave, drifting between rippling walls of limestone, awed by the scale of Phong Nha and its immense stalactites and stalagmites, lit by multicoloured spotlights. Listen for the bats overhead, but look out for their droppings. The boats drop you at the far end to see a Cham inscription and then again to walk through a dry cave back to the entrance. Note, however, that the boats may not operate **after heavy rain** if the water level is too high.

To **get to the cave**, Dong Hoi's hotels and Quang Binh Tourism can help with car rental (from $40 for a half-day), or alternatively it's a long xe om ride from Dong Hoi. Some Hué tour agents offer Phong Nha excursions, but at five hours on the road each way it's too far for a comfortable day-trip and most overnight

---

Cau Treo and Nam Can border crossings into Laos

There are border crossings into Laos at Cau Treo and Nam Can: since both are remote with haphazard bus connections, it's essential to get up-to-date advice from the bus station or local guesthouses before attempting either crossing.

Cau Treo lies 105km southwest of Vinh on Highway 8. Early-morning **public buses** (5–9am) depart from Vinh's provincial bus station (Ben Xe Cho Vinh) as far as Trung Tam, the last settlement of any size before the border. From there you'll have to pick up a **minibus** or **xe om** for the last 25km to Cau Treo or, better still, **hitch** a ride on a truck heading all the way to Lak Sao, 20km across the border in Laos. There are also **tourist buses** to Vientiane from Hanoi, which you may be able to pick up en route: most reach Vinh just after midnight.

It is also possible to catch a bus from Vinh to the **Nam Can** border crossing, 240km northwest of Vinh up Highway 7, which is mainly used by people heading to and from Louang Phabang. Daily buses leave Vinh early in the morning, costing 40,000đ, and take six to seven hours. On the Laotian side, the nearest main town with accommodation is Phonsavan, roughly 100km from the border.

In theory, you can obtain a fifteen-day Lao **visa** at the border at Cau Treo and Nam Can ($30; two passport photos required), but check with the embassy before for current information. Otherwise you can obtain Lao visas at either the Lao consulate in Ho Chi Minh City or Da Nang, or at their Hanoi embassy (see p.119, p.288 & p.386, respectively).

in Dong Hoi anyway. Once you've got transport sorted out, finding the cave isn't difficult: take Highway 1 north for 15km to Hoan Lao where a signpost indicates a left to Phong Nha, heading west until you reach Son Trach Village 30km later (1hr); for the last bit you join the new Ho Chi Minh Highway. The whole village is devoted to servicing boat-trippers: there's a Visitors' Centre where you can buy **tickets** (6.30am–4.30pm; 50,000đ entrance to the caves plus 150,000đ per boat), and the excellent-value **guesthouse** *Thanh Dat* 200m before the Visitors' Centre (☎052/367 5328; ❶–❷), offering air-conditioned, en-suite rooms. A line of **restaurants** with similar menus and standards is situated directly next to the Visitors' Centre compound; *Quan Hoa Phung* has the best view of the river.

Vinh and around

VINH is a sprawling grey city with a sad past, sitting astride Highway 1 – which throws up dust and a steady trickle of tourists breaking their journey between Hué and Hanoi or heading to or from Laos. Soviet-style apartment blocks and socialist town planning on a grand scale may hold a certain historical interest, but there's nothing attractive about the town and for most people its saving grace is a selection of reasonable-standard hotels. Nevertheless, the province of Nghe An savours its proud history, having spawned a wealth of revolutionary figures, many of them enshrined in street names: Le Hong Phong, Nguyen Thi Minh Khai, Phan Boi Chau and, top of the list, Ho Chi Minh. **Ho's birthplace** and childhood home are found in **Kim Lien** Village, 14km from Vinh, a place of pilgrimage for Vietnamese, though rather sterile for most foreign visitors. **Cua Lo** beach resort lies 19km north of the city, comprising a straggle of overpriced hotels beside a long, unspoilt beach with good white sand but too much rubbish to make you want to linger.

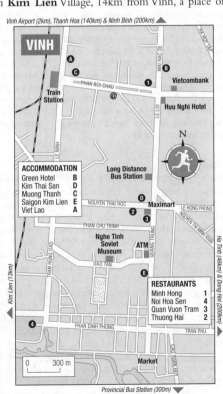

Arrival and information

Vinh's main axis is Highway 1, called Quang Trung and then Le Loi in the centre. Heading up Quang Trung, after about 500m you'll find the *Saigon Kim Lien Hotel*, good for **information**, followed by the long-distance **bus station** (Ben Xe Vinh) a kilometre further on; public buses from Trung Tam (and the border with Laos; see box opposite) terminate at the provincial bus station (Ben Xe Cho Vinh) at the south end of Quang Trung behind Vinh market. **Open-tour**

VINH

Vinh Airport (2km), Thanh Hoa (140km) & Ninh Binh (200km)

Vietcombank

Train Station

Huu Nghi Hotel

ACCOMMODATION
Green Hotel	B
Kim Thai San	D
Muong Thanh	C
Saigon Kim Lien	E
Viet Lao	A

Long Distance Bus Station

Maximart

Nghe Tinh Soviet Museum

ATM

Kim Lien (13km)

Ha Tinh (46km) & Dong Hoi (200km)

RESTAURANTS
Minh Hong	1
Noi Hoa Sen	4
Quan Vuon Tram	3
Thuong Hai	2

0   300 m

Market

Provincial Bus Station (300m)

buses can set down passengers in Vinh en route, but confirm onward travel with the relevant company beforehand. Two kilometres north of the market the nine-storey *Huu Nghi Hotel* dominates a major crossroads: turn left here to find an **internet** café at 32 Phan Boi Chao and the **train station**, at the end of the street (ticket office hours 6.30am–11pm); right brings you to the **Vietcombank** at 9 Nguyen Si Sach, with a 24-hour ATM. There's another 24-hour ATM at 33 Quang Trung. Vinh **airport**, with flights to Ho Chi Minh City only, lies a short taxi ride (30,000–45,000đ) north of the city. The main **post office** is nearly a kilometre east of the *Saigon Kim Lien* beside the unmissable radio tower, but there are more convenient sub-branches outside the train station and at 73 Le Loi. Car and motorbike rental are available through most hotels, and you can pick up xe om anywhere in town.

For details of **heading to Laos** via Cau Treo (105km southwest of Vinh) or Nam Can (240km northwest of Vinh) see the box on p.330.

Accommodation

Because it's such a transport hub, Vinh has a large number of **hotels**, which means places are willing to bargain. Many hotels, however, sit right on the highway, so wherever possible go for a room at the back.

Green Hotel 2 Mai Hac De ☎038/384 4788, ℉038/384 8873. If you're after a few creature comforts near the train station, this place has old-fashioned but decent-size rooms. Other plus points are the small pool and friendly welcome. ❸

Kim Thai San 107 Nguyen Thai Hoc ☎038/384 4409, ℉038/327 5156. Very friendly mini-hotel, situated just off the busy streets. The rooms are spacious, clean and all en suite. Each floor has a communal balcony. ❶

Muong Thanh 1 Phan Boi Chau ☎038/353 5666. Service is friendly and the rooms well-priced at this large hotel, near the station. There's a swimming pool on the second floor. ❸

Saigon Kim Lien 25 Quang Trung ☎038/383 8899, ⓦ www.saigon-tourist.com/saigon-kimlien. Vinh's top hotel opened in 1990 to commemorate the hundredth anniversary of Ho Chi Minh's birth. Prices are surprisingly affordable for comfortable and well-proportioned rooms. Facilities include a recommended restaurant, bar, pool, business centre and money exchange. ❹

Viet Lao 2 Le Ninh ☎038/353 8847. Just north of the train station, this is a reasonable budget option if you're breaking a long journey; the rooms are institutional but all have satellite TV and en-suite bathrooms. ❶

The City

Vinh has fared particularly badly in the twentieth century. As an industrial port-city dominating major land routes, whose population was known for rebellious tendencies, the town became a natural target during both French and American wars. In the 1950s French bombs destroyed large swathes of Vinh, after which the Viet Minh burnt down what remained rather than let it fall into enemy hands; the rebuilt town was flattened once again during the American air raids. Reconstruction proceeded slowly after 1975, mostly financed by East Germany; the decrepit hulks of barrack-like apartment blocks, totally unsuited to the Vietnamese climate, still dominate the city centre. Things are beginning to improve, however, as trade with Laos brings more money into the region: Vinh's streets are being repaved and pavements laid; smart new villas and hotels are being built; and there's even a multi-storey supermarket stocked with all manner of goodies. Vinh's only sight, the **Nghe Tinh Soviet Museum** (daily: April–Sept 6.30–11am & 2–5.30pm; Oct–March 7–11.30am & 1–5.30pm; free) celebrates a mass uprising against French rule in the 1930s (see Contexts, p.466), relating the causes, development and aftermath of the uprising, but is really only for the specialist.

Kim Lien: Ho Chi Minh's birthplace

Ho Chi Minh was born in 1890 in Hoang Tru Village, **KIM LIEN** commune, 14km west of Vinh. The two simple houses made of bamboo wattle and palm-leaf thatch are 1959 reconstructions, now surrounded by fields of sweet potatoes. Ho's birthplace is said to be the hut by itself on the left as you approach, while behind stands the brick-built family altar. At the age of 6 Ho moved 2km west, to what is now called Lang Sen (Lotus Village), to live with his father in very similar surroundings. The two Sen houses are also replicas, built in 1955, with nothing much to see inside, but the complex is peaceful and alive with dancing butterflies. A **museum** nearby (daily: April–Sept 7–11.30am & 1.30–5pm; Oct–March 7.30am–noon & 1.30–5pm; free) illustrates Ho's world travels with memorabilia and photos.

To reach Kim Lien by **car or motorbike**, take Phan Dinh Phung in front of Vinh market and follow signs along the new highway until you reach the turning for Lang Sen and Kim Lien. The signed route takes you first to Ho's birthplace and then loops round to find the museum beside a car park and Ho's father's house a little further back, down a path beside a small lotus pond. A **xe om** to both sites from Vinh should set you back around 100,000đ, including waiting time.

Eating

There's not much choice for **places to eat**. The smartest option is the restaurant at the *Saigon Kim Lien* hotel which serves well-priced Asian and European dishes. On a fine day, *Noi Hoa Sen*, in the middle of a lake at the west end of Phan Dinh Phung, makes a pleasant and inexpensive place to eat, while *Quan Vuon Tram* at 49b Le Loi is a popular choice for the evening. This beer garden serves jugs of *bia hoi* accompanied by chicken curry, spicy beef, pork skewers and the like – ask for their one and only English-language menu. Otherwise, there's a whole host of street kitchens on Le Loi, with a group outside the bus station and another towards the *Huu Nghi Hotel* and spreading down Phan Boi Chau: *Minh Hong* at 3 Phan Boi Chau and *Thuong Hai* at 144a Nguyen Thai Hoc are popular with the locals and serve standard Vietnamese fare.

Ninh Binh and around

The provincial capital **NINH BINH** is another dusty town straddling Highway 1, no more attractive than those to the south but slightly smaller and with sugar-loaf hillocks encroaching on the western horizon. While the town itself has little to detain you, the surrounding hills shelter **Tam Coc**, where sampans slither through the limestone tunnels of "Ha Long Bay on land", and one of Vietnam's ancient capitals, **Hoa Lu**, represented by two darkly atmospheric dynastic temples. Both places can be tackled in one day by car or

The life of Ho Chi Minh

So inextricably is the life of **Ho Chi Minh** intertwined with Vietnam's emergence from colonial rule that his biography is largely an account of the country's struggle for independence in the twentieth century. As Ho adopted dozens of pseudonyms and never kept diaries, uncertainty clouds his public life and almost nothing is known about the private man beneath the cultivated persona of a celibate and aesthete, totally dedicated to his family – a concept that embraced all the Vietnamese people.

Ho's **origins** were humble enough – he was born in 1890 Nguyen Sinh Cung, the youngest child of a minor mandarin who was dismissed from the Imperial court in Hué for anti-colonialist sympathies. For a while Ho attended Hué's Quoc Hoc High School until he was expelled for taking part in a student protest and left Vietnam in 1911 on a steamship bound for France. Then began several years of wandering the world, including spells in the dockyards of Brooklyn and as pastry chef under Escoffier in London's *Carlton Hotel*, before returning to France in the aftermath of World War I, to earn his living retouching photographs. In Paris, Ho became an increasingly active **nationalist**, going by the name Nguyen Ai Quoc ("Nguyen the Patriot"), and caused quite a stir during the Versailles Peace Conference when he published a petition demanding democratic constitutional government for Indochina. For a while Ho joined the French Socialists, but when they split in 1920 he defected to become one of the founder members of the French Communist Party, inspired by Lenin's total opposition to imperialism.

Ho's energetic role in French Communism was rewarded when he was called to Moscow in 1923 to begin a career in **international revolution**, and a year later he found himself posted to southern China as a Comintern agent. Within a few months he had set up Vietnam's first Marxist-Leninist organization, the Revolutionary Youth League, which attracted a band of impassioned young Vietnamese eager to hear about the new ideology. But in 1927, Chiang Kai-shek, leader of the Chinese nationalists, turned against the Communists and Ho was forced to flee. For a while he lived in Thailand, disguised as a Buddhist monk, before turning up in Hong Kong in 1930 where he was instrumental in founding the **Vietnamese Communist Party**. By now

motorbike, or by bicycle via the back lanes. To the east, the stone mass of **Phat Diem Cathedral** wallows in the rice fields, an extraordinary amalgam of Western and Oriental architecture that still shepherds an active Catholic community. Further afield, **Cuc Phuong** is one of Vietnam's more accessible national parks and contains some magnificent, centuries-old trees. More boat trips are in store at **Kenh Ga**, to visit a limestone cave, and at **Van Long** nature reserve, both on the Cuc Phuong road. These last sights are more distant: the cathedral requires a half-day outing, while Cuc Phuong and either Kenh Ga or Van Long can be combined in a long day-trip. Hanoi is only 90km (2hr) away and the Hoa Lu/Tam Coc–Bich Dong circuit makes a popular and inexpensive day tour out of the capital. However, with more time, it's far better to take advantage of Ninh Binh's hotels and services to explore the area at a more leisurely pace.

Ninh Binh itself claims just one sight of its own: a kilometre to the north a picturesque little pagoda nestles at the base of **Non Nuoc Mountain**. This knobbly outcrop – no more than 60m high – is noted for an eminently missable collection of ancient poetic inscriptions and views east over a power station to the graphically named "Sleeping Lady Mountain".

Practicalities

Ninh Binh's pint-sized **train station** and the refreshingly well-organized **bus station** both lie on the east side of town, a short walk across the Van River from the French authorities had placed a death sentence on Ho's head, for insurrection, and while in Hong Kong he was arrested on trumped-up charges, released and then re-arrested before finally escaping with the help of prison hospital staff, who managed to persuade everyone, including the French police, that Ho had died of tuberculosis.

Ho disappeared again for a few years while the fuss died down, before reappearing on China's southern border in the late 1930s. From here he re-entered Vietnam for the first time in thirty years, in early 1941, wearing Chinese-style tunic, rubber-tyre sandals and carrying just a small rattan trunk plus his precious typewriter. He was aged 51, had dysentery, malaria and tuberculosis, and was about to embark on the most momentous task of his life. In the mountains of northern Vietnam, Ho, now finally known as Ho Chi Minh (meaning "He Who Enlightens"), was joined by Vo Nguyen Giap, Pham Van Dong and other young militants. Together they laid the groundwork for the anticipated national uprising, establishing a united patriotic front, the League for the Independence of Vietnam – better known by its abbreviated name, the **Viet Minh** – and training the guerrilla units that would eventually evolve into the Vietnamese People's Army. But events conspired against Ho: in 1942 he was arrested as a Franco-Japanese spy when he crossed back into China to raise support for the nationalist cause, and he languished for more than a year in various prisons, writing a collection of poetry later published as the "Prison Diary".

Meanwhile, however, events were hotting up, and when the Japanese occupation of Vietnam ended in August 1945, the Viet Minh were ready to seize control. Ho Chi Minh, by this time seriously ill, led them to a brief period in power following the August Revolution, and then ultimately to Independence in 1954. For the next fifteen years, as **President of the Democratic Republic of Vietnam**, Uncle Ho took his country along a sometimes rocky socialist path, continually seeking reunification through negotiation and then war. But he didn't live to see a united Vietnam: early in 1969 his heart began to fail and on September 2, Vietnam's National Day, he died. Since then, myth and fact have converged in a cult placing Ho Chi Minh at the top of Vietnam's pantheon of heroes, true to Confucian tradition – though against Ho's express wishes.

the post office. **Open–tour buses** drop you at their affiliated hotels and guest-houses, all of which can help with **information**, tours and transport; staff at the *Thuy Anh*, *Thanh Thuy* and *Xuan Hoa* hotels are particularly knowledgeable about the area, with tours of the main sights starting at around $10. The going rate for motorbike rental is around 75,000đ and 20,000đ or less for a bicycle per day. You can **exchange** cash (dollars and euros only) and traveller's cheques at the Incombank located on the main strip, Tran Hung Dao, where there's also an ATM.

Accommodation

The standard and range of **hotels** in Ninh Binh continues to improve, and the increased competition means it's usually possible to bargain. Don't be put off by places along the main roads, some of which have double and even triple glazing.

New Guesthouse 3 Hoang Hoa Tham ☏030/387 2137. Six basic rooms with fans and hot water, right beside the train station. They can also help with train ticket bookings. ❶

Queen 21 Hoang Hoa Tham ☏030/387 1874, ℮luongvn2001@yahoo.com. A few doors along from the train station on a pleasant tree-lined street, this small, friendly hotel is basic but clean, with a large sister hotel opposite. ❶

Thanh Binh 31 Luong Van Tuy ☏030/387 2439 ℮thanh_binh_hotel@yahoo.com. Clean, well-equipped rooms off the highway make this a good alternative to the nearby *Thuy Anh* and *Thanh Thuy* if those are full. The meals here are also recommended. ❷

Thanh Thuy 128 Le Hong Phong ☏030/387 1811, ℮tuc@hn.vnn.vn. From the front it may not look like much, but walk through the passage, past the excellent courtyard beer garden and you will see why so many people stay here. The new section of the hotel is situated at the back, away from the street, and offers twenty clean, fully equipped rooms. Those in the old section with fans are the cheapest. There's a small but decent restaurant offering a limited range of tasty, fresh food. ❶–❷

Thuy Anh 55a Truong Han Sieu ☏030/387 1602, ⓦwww.thuyanhhotel.com. Ninh Binh's smartest hotel offers efficient service and a range of immaculately kept rooms, from a couple with fan and shared bathroom up to huge rooms furnished and equipped to a high standard. The food in the downstairs restaurant is very good, and there's also a bar on the sixth floor with views over Ninh Binh. The full range of tours and transport, including good-quality bicycles and motorbikes for rent, completes the picture. ❸

Xuan Hoa 1 & 2 31d Pho Minh Khai ☏030/388 0970, ⓦwww.xuanhoahotel .com. Owner Xuan's two hotels are situated almost side-by-side just off the main drag, 20m apart in quiet surroundings overlooking a lake. The rooms are spotless, modern and well equipped, and some have views of Tam Coc. They also offer excellent home cooking and tour services. ❶–❷

Eating

Ninh Binh has a fairly limited choice of **eating** places, though all the hotels provide excellent food at surprisingly reasonable prices. Best for both value and quality is *Xuan Hoa*, where Hoa (wife of owner Xuan) creates some excellent dishes. The *Thuy Anh* also provides good food (their sweet 'n' sour chicken is excellent) in friendly surroundings, as does the *Thanh Thuy*, while the banana pancakes at *Queen* deserve a special mention. There are also a couple of good-value independent restaurants to head for: the *Hoang Hai*, just down from the *Thuy Anh* at 36 Truong Han Sieu, serves an excellent fish steamboat (*lau ca*), and you'll also find good fare at the popular *Com 112* at 112 Le Hong Phong. Otherwise, check out the roadside braziers around the market and the **cafés** in streets west of Tran Hung Dao, where the little courtyard behind *Café Be*, 142 Cu Chinh Lan, is a decent place for a coffee or beer. The rooftop **bar** of the *Thuy Anh* hotel provides a scenic spot to unwind at the end of a heavy day's sightseeing.

Tam Coc and Bich Dong

The film *Indochine* put the **Tam Coc "three caves" region**, 7km southwest of Ninh Binh, firmly on the tourist map, and the government is now pouring money into developing it: the access road has been upgraded, there's a new Visitors' Centre and concrete lines the canal banks – but fortunately only as far as the first bridge. They're even trying to clamp down on the over-zealous – occasionally aggressive – peddling of embroideries and soft drinks by the sampan-rowers. Despite all this, it's hard not to be won over by the mystical, watery beauty of the area, which is a miniature landlocked version of Ha Long Bay. The two-hour sampan-ride is a definite highlight, meandering among dumpling-shaped, karst hills in a flooded landscape where river and rice paddy merge serenely into one; keep an eye open for mountain goats high on the cliffs, and bright, darting kingfishers. Journey's end is **Tam Coc**, three long, dark tunnel-caves (Hang Ca, Hang Giua and Hang Cuoi) eroded through the limestone hills with barely sufficient clearance for the sampan after heavy rains. On the way back, you can ask to stop at **Thai Vi Temple**, a short walk from the river. Dating from the thirteenth century and dedicated to the founder of the Tran Dynasty, it's a peaceful, atmospheric spot.

If you have time after the boat trip, follow the road leading southwest from the boat dock (see below) for about 2km to visit the cave-pagoda of **Bich Dong**, or "Jade Grotto". Stone-cut steps, entangled by the thick roots of banyan trees, lead up a cliff face peppered with shrines to the cave entrance, believed to have been discovered by two monks in the early fifteenth century. On the rock face above,

▲ Boat trip through Tam Coc

two giant characters declare "Bich Dong". The story goes that they were engraved in the eighteenth century by the father of Nguyen Du (author of the classic *Tale of Kieu*), who was entrusted with construction of the complex. The cave walls are now scrawled with graffiti but the three Buddhas sit unperturbed on their lotus thrones beside a head-shaped rock which bestows longevity if touched. Walk through the cave to emerge higher up the cliff, from where steps continue to the third and final temple and viewpoint over the waterlogged scene.

Practicalities

Day-trips from Hanoi start at $15 per person in a minibus and also include lunch and a side-trip to Hoa Lu. From Ninh Binh, the easiest and most enjoyable way to reach Tam Coc is to rent a **bicycle** or **motorbike**; the turning, signed (with a large photo sign) to "Bich Dong", is 4km south on Highway 1, before the cement factory. Hiring a **xe om** for the excursion will cost about 75,000đ including waiting time. From Tam Coc, there's a partly unpaved back road, which takes you on a delightful ten-kilometre cycle ride through rice fields and limestone karst scenery to Hoa Lu (see p.338 for details).

To avoid the worst of the crowds at Tam Coc, it's best to set off either very early in the morning or in the late afternoon (boats run between 7am and 5pm). **Tickets** (30,000đ) are on sale at the Visitors' Centre – on the right 100m before the boat dock, located in Van Lam Village; it's another 60,000đ for a two-person boat. **Restaurants** and **cafés** catering to tour groups line the approach to Van Lam, and some of the smaller places aren't too bad. There's also a clutch of cheap noodle and rice stalls beside the entrance to Bich Dong.

Hoa Lu

Twelve kilometres northwest of Ninh Binh, **Hoa Lu**, site of the tenth-century capital of an early, independent Vietnamese kingdom called Dai Co Viet, makes another rewarding excursion. The fortified royal palaces of the Dinh and Le kings are now reduced to archeological remains, but their dynastic temples, seventeenth-century copies of eleventh-century originals, still rest quietly in a narrow valley surrounded by wooded, limestone hills. Though the temple

337
—

buildings and attractive walled courtyards are unspectacular, the inner sanctuaries are compelling – mysterious, dark caverns where statues of the kings, wrapped in veils of pungent incense, are worshipped by the light of candles.

First stop at the site should be the more imposing **Den Dinh Tien Hoang**, on the left as you approach from the car park and ticket office, dedicated to King Dinh Tien Hoang (also known as Dinh Bo Linh), who seized power in 968 AD and moved the capital south from Co Loa in the Red River Delta to this secure valley far from the threat of Chinese intervention. Dinh Tien Hoang's gilded effigy can be seen in the temple's second sanctuary room, flanked by his three sons. Dinh Tien Hoang was born near Hoa Lu. He was the illegitimate son of a provincial governor and was known as a reforming monarch who ruled with a firm hand; he is reputed to have placed a bronze urn and caged tiger in front of his palace and decreed that "those who violate the laws will be boiled and gnawed". However, in 979 an assassin, variously rumoured to be a mad monk or a palace hitman, killed the king and his two eldest sons as they lay in a drunken sleep.

In the anarchy that followed, Le Hoan, commander of Dinh Tien Hoang's army and supposed lover of his queen (whom Le Hoan later married), wrested power and declared himself King Le Dai Hanh in 980. The second temple, **Den Le Dai Hanh**, is dedicated to the earlier of the two Le dynasties which itself spiralled into chaos 25 years later while the king's three sons squabbled over the succession. Le Dai Hanh is enshrined in the temple's rear sanctuary with his eldest son and Queen Duong Van Nga. On the way out, signs direct you to an adjacent archeological dig where some tenth-century foundations have been unearthed, along with tiles and pottery shards.

After visiting the two temples, energetic types could climb the steps of neighbouring "Saddle Mountain" (*Nui Ma Yen*) for a panoramic view of Hoa Lu and its surroundings. The new **Bai Dinh Pagoda** is currently under construction nearby and already features the largest Buddha in Vietnam, consisting of a hundred tonnes of sculptured bronze. Due to be completed in 2010, it is already on some tour group itineraries, in part because of the excellent views of the surrounding countryside.

Practicalities

Hoa Lu is just as popular as Tam Coc and the temples can be swamped, particularly mid-morning and early afternoon when tour groups arrive from Hanoi. The hawkers can also be just as enthusiastic, though fortunately they aren't allowed to pursue you into the temples. **Admission** to both temples is 10,000đ. Day-trips from Hanoi to Tam Coc stop at Hoa Lu and cost from $15 per person on a minibus. From Ninh Binh, the quickest way to Hoa Lu is to rent a motorbike for the day or take a xe om (90,000đ for the round trip), but if time allows this is definitely one to do by **bicycle** in combination with Tam Coc (see p.336); allow at least one hour for the journey. The best route from Ninh Binh is to head up Tran Hung Dao, and turn left after number 58 – from here, it's pretty much straight all the way. En route you'll pass *Thach Ban Quan*, a friendly cafe just 3km from Hoa Lu that can rustle up a small meal for hungry cyclists; you can also stay the night for a couple of dollars, quite a temptation given the surrounding amphitheatre of mountains.

Phat Diem

Strike southeast from Ninh Binh and there's no mistaking that you've stumbled on a Christian enclave, where church spires sprout out of the flat paddy land on all sides; it's said that 95 percent of the district's population attend church on a regular basis. These coastal communities of northern Vietnam were among the first to be targeted by Portuguese missionaries in the sixteenth century. This area owes its particular zeal to the Jesuit Alexandre de Rhodes who preached here in 1627. The greatest monument to all this religious fervour is the century-old stone cathedral, **Phat Diem**, situated 30km from Ninh Binh in **Kim Son Village**. Note that opening times vary, so check in Ninh Binh before setting off.

The first surprise is the cathedral's monumental **bell pavilion**, whose curved roofs and triple gateway could easily be the entrance to a Vietnamese temple save for a few telltale crosses and a host of angels. The structure is built entirely of dressed stone, as is the equally impressive cathedral facade sheltering in its wake; both edifices rest on hundreds of bamboo poles embedded in the marshy ground. Behind, the tiled double roof of the **nave** extends for 74m, supported by 52 immense ironwood pillars and sheltering a cool, dark and peaceful sanctuary. The **altar** table is chiselled from a single block of marble, decorated with elegant sprays of bamboo, while the altarpiece above glows with red and gold lacquers in an otherwise sober interior. Twelve priests conduct daily services here for a diocese that musters 140,000 Catholics.

The cathedral was conceived and designed by Father Tran Luc (also known as Father Sau), whose tomb lies behind the bell tower, and was more than ten years in the preparation, as stone and wood were transported from the provinces of Thanh Hoa and Nghe An, though it apparently took a mere three months to build in 1891. During the French War, the Catholic Church formed a powerful political group in Vietnam, virtually independent of the French administration but also opposed to the Communists. The then bishop of Phat Diem, Monseigneur Le Huu Tu, was outspokenly anti-French and an avowed nationalist, but, as his diocese lay on the edge of government-held territory, the French supplied him with sufficient arms to maintain a militia of two thousand men in return for containing Viet Minh infiltration. However, in December 1951 the Viet Minh launched a major assault on the village and took it – with suspicious ease for French tastes, who felt the Catholics were withholding information on enemy activities in the area, if not actually assisting them. When paratroops came in to regain control, the Viet Minh withdrew, taking with them a valuable supply of weapons. The author Graham Greene was in Phat Diem at the time, on an assignment for *Life Magazine*, and watched the battle from the bell tower of the cathedral – later using the scene in *The Quiet American*.

Practicalities

Day-trips from Hanoi start at $8 per person on a minibus. Frequent public **buses** depart from Ninh Binh bus station for the hour's journey **to Kim Son**, though note that the last bus back leaves around 3.30pm. Otherwise, it's near enough to reach by rented **motorbike**, or the return trip by **xe om** will cost around 100,000đ. If you're riding here yourself, take the road heading straight east from Ninh Binh's Lim Bridge and, when you get to Kim Son Village, 100m after passing an elegant covered bridge, take a right turn to the cathedral; follow the compound wall anticlockwise to reach the entrance, where you can buy a small but informative booklet explaining the cathedral's colourful history. The bell is rung daily at noon, and visitors are allowed to accompany the bell-ringer up the stairs (block your ears though).

Cuc Phuong National Park

In 1962 Vietnam's first national park was established around a narrow valley between forested limestone hills on the borders of Ninh Binh, Thanh Hoa and Hoa Binh provinces, containing over two hundred square kilometres of tropical evergreen rainforest. **Cuc Phuong** is well set up for tourism and sees a steady stream of visitors, attracted principally by the excellent primate rescue centre, but also by the easy access to impressively ancient trees. With more time, you can walk into the park interior, overnight in a Muong village and experience the multi-layered forest. The most enjoyable time for walking in these hills is October to January, when mosquitoes and leeches take a break and temperatures are relatively cool – but this is also peak season. Flowers are at their best during February and March, while April to May are the months when lepidopterists can enjoy the "butterfly festival" as thousands of butter-flies colour the forest.

Even now the park has not been fully surveyed but is estimated to contain approximately three hundred **bird species** and ninety **mammal species**, some of which were first discovered in Cuc Phuong, such as red-bellied squirrels and a fish that lives in underground rivers. Several species of bat and monkey, including the critically endangered Delacour's langur, inhabit the park, while bears and leopards roam its upper reaches. Hunting has taken its toll, though, and you're really only likely to see butterflies, birds and perhaps a civet cat or a tree squirrel, rather than the more exotic fauna. What you can't miss, though, is the luxuriant **vegetation** including 1000-year-old trees (living fossils up to 70m high), tree ferns and kilometre-long corkscrewing lianas, as well as a treasure-trove of medicinal plants.

Some of the luckier victims of illegal hunting are now to be seen in the **Endangered Primate Rescue Center** (daily 9–11am & 1.30–4pm; ⓦwww .primatecenter.org) located near the park gate. Opened in 1993, the centre not only cares for rescued animals, but also tries to rehabilitate them by releasing them into an adjacent semi-wild area. In addition, they run crucial research, conservation and breeding programmes. At any one time there may be between sixty and a hundred animals here, including Delacour's langur, with its distinc-tive black body and white "shorts", the Cat Ba, or Golden-headed langur, and the Grey-shanked douc langur, as well as various lorises and gibbons. It's a unique opportunity to see these incredibly rare species at close quarters.

Of several **walks** in the park, one of the most popular starts at Car Park A, 18km from the park gate. For seven steamy kilometres (roughly 2hr) a well-trodden path winds through typical rainforest to reach the magnificent **cho xanh tree**, a 45-metre-high, 1000-year-old specimen of *Terminalia myriocarpa* – its dignity only slightly marred by a viewing platform. Dropping back down to the flat, take a left turn at the unmarked T-junction to bring you back to the road higher up at Car Park B. This second car park is also the start of the "Adventurous Trail", an eighteen-kilometre hike through the park to Muong villages, noted for their gigantic wooden waterwheels, for which you'll need a guide ($20 minimum) plus a night's accommodation at the top ($5, excluding food).

Much is made of Cuc Phuong's **prehistoric caves**, the most accessible of which is Dong Nguoi Xua, only 300m from the road, 7km from the park gate. Joss sticks burn in the cave mouth near three tombs estimated to be over 7000 years old but there's nothing to see that justifies the steepish climb; if you decide to go, bring a torch for the upper reaches, and watch out for some decidedly dangerous steel staircases.

Practicalities

Cuc Phuong **park gate**, just beyond which you'll find the Primate Center and then the **Visitors' Centre** (daily 7–11am & 1.30–4pm; ⓣ030/384 8006, ⓔdulichcucphuong@hn.vnn.vn), lies 45km north and west of Ninh Binh; head north on Highway 1 for 10km to find the sign indicating "Cuc Phuong" to the left.

From the gate it's a further 18km to the heart of the forest. There are no public buses so you'll either have to rent a **car** or **motorbike** in Ninh Binh, or haul out there with a **xe om** (around $30 for the round trip). Visiting the park is also feasible as a day-trip out of Hanoi – an option offered by several tour agencies (see p.349).

Entry **tickets** are on sale at the Visitors' Centre (20,000đ, plus a further 10,000đ for an obligatory guide to the Primate Center) where you can also arrange **accommodation** (❶–❸), ranging from unexpectedly comfortable, if somewhat expensive, bungalows and bamboo chalets to a basic hostel, located either at the headquarters or in the interior. Day-trips from Hanoi start at $15 per person in a minibus and include lunch and guide. Or if you are already there it is easy to organize **guided treks**, including overnighting in a Muong village, through the Visitors' Centre or through hotels in Ninh Binh, such as *Thuy Anh* and *Thanh Thuy* (see pp.335–336). Be aware that Cuc Phuong is some way above the plains and winter nights can get chilly.

Van Long and Kenh Ga

TRAN ME, a town 23km from Ninh Binh on the road to Cuc Phuong, is the departure point for a couple of very different but worthwhile boat trips. It's possible to do them both in a day, or either one can be combined with a visit to Cuc Phuong or Hoa Lu.

The more beguiling of the two takes you round the shallow, reed-filled lagoons of **Van Long Nature Reserve**, signed to the right about 2km to the east of Tran Me. The road ends beside the ticket office (just past a new hotel complex), where you pay 35,000đ per person for a ninety-minute trip, being poled across the wetlands and among the limestone outcrops in a low-slung bamboo sampan. Take your binoculars: the crags are home to a small, isolated population of Delacour's langur, and the reed beds provide refuge for migratory waterfowl. At present there's a good chance you'll have the place to yourself, with only the eerie cries of monkeys and birds to break the silence, but this is unlikely to last. Hawkers are banned from using boats, but already they gather round the ticket office whenever a tour bus appears and there is even talk about opening restaurants along the dyke.

The second boat trip departs from a canal bank about 4km away on the south side of Tran Me; take the lane immediately after the post office with its landmark radio tower. In this case a skinny motor launch takes you on a 45-minute ride (40,000đ per person) through scenery which is certainly attractive but doesn't quite stand up beside that of Tam Coc or Van Long. However, the main purpose is to visit **Kenh Ga**, a village accessible only by water. The village boasts houses and even an ornate church, but many families live on boats and the whole place seems to be engaged in watery pursuits: boatyards turn out concrete-hulled barges to take gravel and quarried stone downstream; there are fish farms and great flocks of ducks, and sampans bustle about, often propelled by people rowing with their feet. Kenh Ga (Chicken Canal) supposedly gets its name from a hot spring where chickens were soaked in the near-boiling water to make them easier to pluck. The water is also said to be good for digestion, skin ailments and general recuperation and the site was developed for bathing, but the facilities are very run-down now. Better to press on to the final destination, **Van Trinh grotto**, a little-visited cave system where the guide will point out gnarled rocky outcrops which conjure up images of turtles, dragons, elephants and wizened faces. The local tourist authority has now installed lighting and concrete pathways, but you'll still need stout shoes, especially during the dry season when boats can't pull up outside the cave and you may have to walk the final kilometre.

Practicalities

Van Long and Kenh Ga can be reached independently by **car** or **motorbike**; count on at least 120,000đ for a **xe om** for the return trip from Ninh Binh. Hotels in Ninh Binh and a few Hanoi tour agencies also offer **organized tours** combining both places, with prices starting at around $15 per person for a one-day excursion.

There are cheap food stalls in Tran Me, but the most convenient place to eat is the small **restaurant** next to the Kenh Ga ticket office. There is no menu but a good choice is the local fish and a dish of their excellent spring rolls. If you order before you set off on the boat trip, the meal will be ready on your return.

Travel details

Trains

Da Nang to: Hanoi (6 daily; 15–20hr); Ho Chi Minh City (6 daily; 16–21hr); Hué (6 daily; 2hr 30min–3hr); Nha Trang (6 daily; 9–12hr).

Dong Ha to: Dong Hoi (5 daily; 1hr 20min–2hr 10min); Hanoi (4 daily; 12–15hr); Hué (5 daily; 1hr 20min).

Dong Hoi to: Dong Ha (4 daily; 1hr 40min–2hr 35min); Hanoi (5 daily; 10–12hr); Hué (5 daily; 2hr 35min–4hr); Ninh Binh (3 daily; 9–11hr); Vinh (6 daily; 3hr 30min–5hr).

Hué to: Da Nang (6 daily; 2hr 20min–3hr); Dong Ha (5 daily; 1hr–1hr 20min); Dong Hoi (6 daily; 2hr 40min–3hr 30min); Hanoi (6 daily; 13–16hr); Ho Chi Minh City (6 daily; 19–24hr); Nha Trang (6 daily; 11hr 20min–15hr); Ninh Binh (3 daily; 14hr).

Ninh Binh to: Dong Hoi (4 daily; 10hr); Hanoi (3 daily; 2hr 30min); Hué (4 daily; 13–14hr); Vinh (4 daily; 4hr).

Thanh Hoa to: Hanoi (5 daily; 3hr 30min); Ninh Binh (3 daily; 1hr 20min); Vinh (5 daily; 2hr 30min).

Vinh to: Dong Ha (5 daily; 5hr–7hr 30min); Dong Hoi (6 daily; 4–5hr); Hanoi (6 daily; 6hr–6hr 30min); Hué (6 daily; 6–9hr); Ninh Binh (3 daily; 4hr).

Buses

Bus stations are gradually becoming more organized, with ticket desks and scheduled departures. However, it is still almost impossible to give the frequency with which buses run because of the large number of private minibuses that ply more popular routes, and depart only when they have enough passengers to make the journey worthwhile. Highway 1 sees a near-constant stream of buses passing through to various destinations, and it's possible to flag something down at virtually any time of the day. Off the highway, to be sure of a bus it's advisable to start your journey early – most long-distance departures are between 5am and 9am, and few run after midday. Journey times can also vary; figures below show the normal length of time you can expect to take by public bus.

Da Nang to: Dong Ha (5hr); Hoi An (1hr 30min–2hr); Hué (3–4hr); Quang Ngai (5hr); Quiy Nhon (11hr); Savannakhet (24hr).

Dong Ha to: Dong Hoi (2hr); Hué (2hr 30min); Lao Bao (2hr); Savannakhet (8hr).

Dong Hoi to: Dong Ha (2hr); Hué (4–5hr); Vinh (4hr).

Hoi An to: Da Nang (1hr 30min–2hr); Quang Ngai (4hr).

Hué to: Da Nang (3–4hr); Dong Ha (2hr 30min); Dong Hoi (5hr).

Ninh Binh to: Haiphong (3hr); Hanoi (2hr); Kim Son (Phat Diem) (1hr); Son La (8hr); Thanh Hoa (1hr 30min); Vinh (5hr).

Thanh Hoa to: Hanoi (3hr); Ninh Binh (1hr 30min); Vinh (4hr).

Vinh to: Dong Ha (6–7hr); Dong Hoi (4hr); Hué (8–10hr); Ninh Binh (5hr); Thanh Hoa (4hr); Trung Tam (2hr); Vientiane (12–14hr).

Flights

Da Nang to: Buon Ma Thuot (4 weekly; 1hr 10min); Hanoi (4 daily; 1hr 10min); Ho Chi Minh City (5 daily; 1hr 10min); Nha Trang (1 daily; 1hr 5min); Plei Ku (daily; 50min); Quy Nhon (4 weekly; 1hr).

Hué to: Hanoi (3 daily; 1hr 10min); Ho Chi Minh City (3 daily; 1hr 20min).

Vinh to: Ho Chi Minh City (daily; 1hr 45min).

6

Hanoi and around

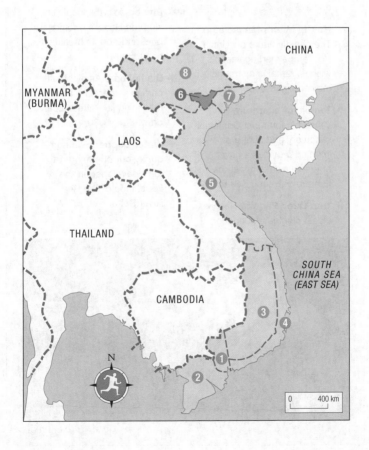

CHAPTER 6

Highlights

* **The Old Quarter** Wander through the intoxicating tangle of streets that make up Hanoi's commercial heart. See p.360

* **The Opera House** Check out this stately signature-piece of French colonial architecture, which was modelled on the one in Paris. See p.363

* **Ho Chi Minh's Mausoleum** The ghostly figure of "Uncle Ho", embalmed against his wishes, remains a strangely moving sight. See p.366

* **Temple of Literature** Vietnam's foremost Confucian sanctuary and centre of learning provides a haven of green lawns amidst the hubbub of Hanoi. See p.369

* **Tran Quoc Pagoda** Hanoi's oldest religious foundation attracts a constant stream of petitioners and sightseers. See p.372

* **Museum of Ethnology** Discover the staggering variety and creativity of Vietnam's ethnic minorities. See p.373

* **Pho bo** Join the locals and slurp on Hanoi's traditional beef-and-noodle breakfast soup. See p.374

* **Bia hoi bars** As night falls parties gather for a few refreshing jars of the local brew. See p.380

* **Water-puppets** Vietnam's quirky but charming art form developed in the floodlands of the Red River Delta. See p.381

▲ The Old Quarter, Hanoi

6

Hanoi and around

B
y turns exotic, squalid, gauche and hip, the high-octane Vietnamese capital of **Hanoi** provides a full-scale assault on the senses. Its crumbly, lemon-hued colonial architecture is a feast for the eyes: swarms of buzzing motorbikes invade the ear, while the delicate scents and tastes of delicious street food can be found all across a city that – unlike so many of its regional contemporaries – is managing to modernize with a degree of grace. Despite its political and historical importance, as well as the incessant noise drummed up by a population of over six million, Hanoi exudes a more intimate, urbane appeal than Ho Chi Minh City.

At its centre lies a tree-fringed lake and shaded avenues of classy French villas dressed up in jaded stucco, but the rest of Hanoi is bursting at the seams and nowhere is this more evident than in the teeming traffic and the vibrant, intoxicating tangle of streets known as the **Old Quarter**, the city's commercial heart since the fifteenth century. Delving back even further, a handful of Hanoi's more than six hundred temples and pagodas hail from the original, eleventh-century city, most notably the **Temple of Literature**, which encompasses both Vietnam's foremost Confucian sanctuary and its first university. Many visitors, however, are drawn to Hanoi by more recent events, seeking explanations among the exhibits of the **Military History Museum** and in **Ho Chi Minh's Mausoleum** for the extraordinary Vietnamese tenacity displayed during the wars of the twentieth century.

Modern Hanoi has an increasingly confident, "can do" air about it and a buzz that is even beginning to rival Ho Chi Minh City. There's more money about nowadays and the wealthier Hanoians are prepared to flaunt it in the ever-more sophisticated restaurants, cafés and designer boutiques that have exploded all over the city. Hanoi now boasts glitzy, multistorey shopping malls and wine warehouses; beauty parlours are the latest fad and some seriously expensive cars cruise the streets. Almost everyone else zips around on motorbikes rather than the deeply untrendy bicycle. The authorities are trying – with mixed success – to temper the anarchy with laws to curb traffic and regulate unsympathetic building projects in the Old Quarter, coupled with an ambitious twenty-year development plan that aims to ease congestion by creating satellite towns. Nevertheless, the city centre has not completely lost its old-world charm nor its distinctive character.

Hanoi, somewhat unjustly, remains less popular than Ho Chi Minh City as a jumping-off point for touring Vietnam, with many making the journey from south to north. Nevertheless, it provides a convenient base for **excursions** to Ha Long Bay, and to Sa Pa and the northern mountains, where you'll be able to get away from the tourist hordes and sample life in rural Vietnam (see

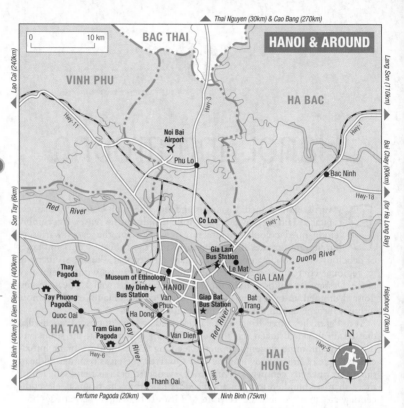

Chapters Seven and Eight respectively). There are also a few attractions much closer at hand, predominantly religious foundations such as the **Perfume Pagoda**, with its spectacular setting among limestone hills, and the spiral-shaped citadel of **Co Loa**, just north of today's capital. The Red River Delta's fertile alluvial soil supports one of the highest rural population densities in Southeast Asia, living in bamboo-screened villages dotted among the paddy fields. Some of these communities have been plying the same trade for genera-tions, such as ceramics, carpentry or snake-breeding. While the more successful **craft villages** are becoming commercialized, it's possible, with a bit of effort, to get well off the beaten track to where Confucianism still holds sway.

The **best time to visit** Hanoi is during the three months from October to December, when you'll find warm, sunny days and levels of humidity below the norm of eighty percent, though it can be chilly at night. From January to March, cold winds from China combine with high humidity to give a fine mist which often hangs in the air for days. March and April usually bring better weather, before the extreme summer heat arrives in late April, accompanied by monsoon storms which peak in August and can last until early October, causing serious flooding throughout the delta.

Some history

When Tang Chinese armies invaded Vietnam in the seventh century, they chose a small **Red River fort** as capital of their new protectorate, named, optimistically,

Annam, the "Pacified South". Three centuries later the rebellious Vietnamese ousted the Chinese from their "Great Nest", *Dai La*, in 939 AD. After that, the citadel lay abandoned until 1010 when **King Ly Thai To**, usually credited as Hanoi's founding father, recognized the site's potential and established his own court beside the Red River. It seems the omens were on his side for, according to legend, when the king stepped from his royal barge onto the riverbank a golden dragon flew up towards the heavens. From then on **Thang Long**, "City of the Soaring Dragon", was destined to be the nation's capital, with only minor interruptions, for the next eight hundred years.

Ly Thai To and his successors set about creating a city fit for "ten thousand generations of kings", choosing auspicious locations for their temples and palaces according to the laws of geomancy. They built protective dykes, established a town of artisans and merchants alongside the **Imperial City**'s eastern wall, and set up the nation's first university, in the process laying the foundations of modern Hanoi. From 1407, the country was again under Chinese occupation, but this time only briefly before the great hero **Le Loi** retook the capital in 1428. The Le Dynasty kings drained lakes and marshes to accommodate their new palaces as well as a growing civilian population, and towards the end of the fifteenth century Thang Long was enjoying a **golden era** under the great reformer, King Le Thanh Thong. Shortly after his death in 1497, however, the country dissolved into anarchy, while the city slowly declined until finally Emperor Gia Long moved the royal court to Hué in 1802.

By the 1830s Thang Long had been relegated to a provincial capital, known merely as *Ha Noi*, or "City within the River's Bend", and in 1882 its reduced defences offered little resistance to **attacking French forces**, led by Captain Rivière. Initially capital of the French Protectorate of Tonkin, a name derived from *Dong Kinh*, meaning "Eastern Capital", after 1887 Hanoi became the centre of government for the entire Union of Indochina. Royal palaces and ancient monuments made way for grand residences, administrative offices, tree-lined boulevards and all the trappings of a **colonial city**, more European than Asian. However, the Vietnamese community lived a largely separate, often impoverished existence, creating a seedbed of insurrection.

During the 1945 August Revolution, thousands of local nationalist sympathizers spilled onto the streets of Hanoi and later took part in its defence against returning French troops, though they had to wait until 1954 for their city finally to become the **capital of an independent Vietnam**. Hanoi sustained more serious damage during the air raids of the American War,

The Christmas Bombing

In December 1972 President Nixon ordered intensive bombing raids on Hanoi and Haiphong, targeting transport arteries, power stations, factories and military installations, in the hope of influencing the Paris peace negotiations. This controversial "**Christmas Bombing**" inflicted considerable damage on residential districts, causing an estimated 1300 deaths in Hanoi. The area southwest of the train station was the worst hit. More than two hundred people died in and around Kham Thien Street on December 26, but the most infamous strike was that on Bach Mai hospital in which, miraculously, only eighteen people were killed though seven bombs fell on the cardiology unit alone. Vietnamese forces did manage to wreak some revenge, destroying between fifteen and twenty B-52s. At the time the North Vietnamese feared Hanoi would be wiped off the map and even laid out plans for a new capital; in the event, central Hanoi survived relatively unscathed.

particularly the infamous Christmas Bombing campaign of 1972 (see box, p.347). The subsequent political isolation together with lack of resources preserved what was essentially the city of the 1950s, somewhat faded, a bit battered and very overcrowded. These characteristics are still in evidence today, even as Hanoi is reinventing itself as a dynamic international capital. New market freedoms combined with an influx of tourists since the early 1990s have led to a huge growth in privately run hotels and restaurants, several of international standard, and in boutiques, craft shops and tour agencies. As ancient – and antiquated – buildings give way to glittering high-rises, and as traffic congestion increases, the big question is how much of this historic and charming city will survive the onslaught of modernization.

Arrival and information

Hanoi's smart international **Noi Bai Airport** (☎04/3886 6527), 35km north of the city, is equipped with several **exchange** bureaux and **ATMs**, as well as a **tourist information** desk (8am–midnight). By far the cheapest option for getting into town are the #7 and #17 **city buses** (2hr; 5000đ), which depart from outside the arrivals hall every fifteen to twenty minutes from 5.30am to 10.30pm; #7 takes you to Kim Ma bus station, to the west of centre, and #17 to Long Bien station on the northern edge of the Old Quarter. Note that you may be charged extra for bulky luggage. Quicker are the shuttle buses run by **Noi Bai Minibus** and **Airport Minibus** (45min–1hr), which also leave from outside the terminal and drop you near the Vietnam Airlines office just south of Hoan Kiem Lake; these should cost $2, though you may have to haggle. **Taxis** cost a fixed-rate $15 for the 45-minute ride into town; always insist on being taken to your chosen hotel, as some drivers will try to direct you elsewhere in order to gain a commission. This is a serious problem with some budget and mid-range hotels in the Old Quarter; the safest option is to get your hotel to send a taxi to meet you.

Hanoi's **train station** is roughly a kilometre west of centre, on Le Duan. Arriving from Ho Chi Minh City and all points south or from China, you exit the main station onto Le Duan. However, trains from the east and north (Haiphong, Lang Son and Lao Cai) pull into platforms at the rear of the main station, bringing you out among market stalls on a narrow street called Tran Quy Cap.

Hanoi's three main long-distance **bus stations** are all located several kilometres from the centre, and you'll need to catch a city bus (see p.353 for details of routes) or hop on a xe om. Buses **from the south** generally terminate at Giap Bat station, 6km south of town on Giai Phong, while those **from the northeast** (Lang Son, Cao Bang, Ha Long and Haiphong) usually arrive at Gia Lam station, 4km away on the east bank of the Red River. However, some Ha Long and Haiphong services, including the through bus from Cat Ba operated by Hoang Long company, drop you at the more central Luong Yen bus station on the eastern edge of the French Quarter. Services **from the northwest** (Son La, Mai Chau and Lao Cai) arrive at either Giap Bat or the new My Dinh station, about 10km west of centre. Note that some buses **from Mai Chau and Hoa Binh** terminate in Ha Dong, a suburb of Hanoi also roughly 10km west on Highway 6; jump on one of the waiting city buses for the forty-minute ride into town. **Open-tour buses** stop at various points around the Old Quarter.

For details of **moving on** from Hanoi, see p.388.

Tour agents

Over the years, Hanoi's tourist-service industry has become increasingly sophisticated and now comprises a dizzying array of dedicated **tour agents**. The situation is further complicated by the tendency for newcomers to adopt the same name as a successful rival, or something that sounds similar; there are dozens of outfits claiming to be affiliated to Ho Chi Minh City *Sinh Café*, for example. To be on the safe side, it's best to go to one of the longer-established and more reliable agents such as those listed below.

Buffalo Tours 94 Ma May ☏04/3828 0702, ⓦwww.buffalotours.com. Long-established experts in organizing tailor-made private tours throughout Indochina, with a particular focus on adventure and special interest holidays; prices are a little high but the service is extremely professional.

Ethnic Travel 35 Hang Giay ☏04/3926 1951, ⓦwww.ethnictravel.com.vn. Popular operation with a genuine passion for low-impact, environmentally-conscious travel; a maximum group size of six also makes for a more personal adventure.

Exotissimo 26 Tran Nhat Duat ☏04/3828 2150, ⓦwww.exotissimo.com. One-stop travel shop offering all travel-related services from visas and ticketing to tours aimed at the middle market and above. It's a highly professional operation, with a strong focus on adventure tours and responsible tourism.

Explore Indochina 2 Tran Thanh Tong ☏0913 524658, ⓦwww.exploreindochina .com. Reliable tours on "old-school Soviet motorbikes", with a few interesting alternatives to the usual northern mountain routes; tours vary in length from three days to two weeks.

Explorer Tours 85 Hang Bo ☏04/323 0713, ⓦwww.explorer.com.vn. Specializes in private group-tours of Ha Long Bay, but also offers Hanoi day-trips and tours of the northern mountains.

Handspan Adventure Travel *Tamarind Café*, 80 Ma May ☏04/3926 2828, ⓦwww .handspan.com. Environmentally conscious adventure-tour specialist. Options range from sea-kayaking in Ha Long Bay to exploring the north on foot or by mountain bike, staying in minority villages. The tours are well organized, with good equipment and back-up, and are restricted to small groups.

Hanoi Toserco 8 To Hien Thanh ☏04/3978 0004, ⓦwww.tosercohanoi.com. The Hanoi home to *Sinh Café's* open-tour buses offers cheap tours aimed squarely at the backpacker market, from day-trips in and around Hanoi to full-blown Sa Pa and Ha Long Bay excursions.

Kangaroo Café 18 Bao Khanh ☏04/3828 9931, ⓦwww.kangaroocafe.com. This Australian-run café is recommended for its innovative, well-organized small-group and adventure tours. Helpful staff and a simple restaurant serving wholesome local, Western and vegetarian food round out the picture.

Love Planet Tours & Books 25 Hang Bac ☏04/3828 4864, ⓦwww.loveplanettravel .com. A reliable operator with many years' experience of meeting travellers' needs, Love Planet provides a great all-round service, including tours (covering a range of budgets), tickets and good advice. They also boast Vietnam's biggest collection of secondhand books.

Queen Travel 65 Hang Bac ☏04/3826 0860, ⓦwww.queencafe.com.vn. Aims at the middle market and above with tailor-made and small-group tours.

Sunshine Travel 49 Luong Ngoc Quyen ☏04/3926 2641, ⓦwww .vietnamsunshinetravel.com. A reliable low-to-middle market agency offering tours throughout Vietnam. It also has a good reputation for its visa services (ⓦwww .visavietnam.com).

Vietnam Indochina 71 Bo De ☏04/3872 2319, ⓦwww.vietnamholidays.biz. A small but enthusiastic and efficient company offering customized tours countrywide.

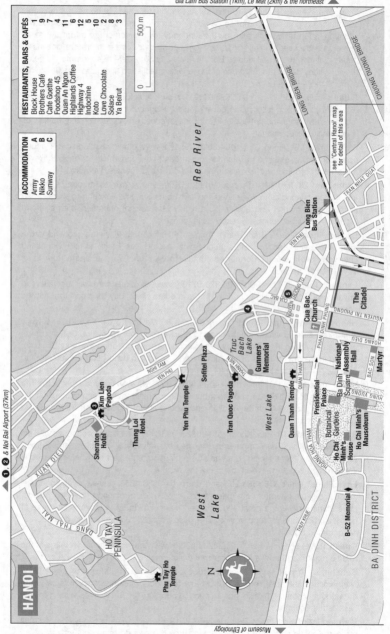

HANOI

ACCOMMODATION

Army	A
Nikko	B
Sunway	C

RESTAURANTS, BARS & CAFÉS

Block House	1
Brothers Café	9
Cafe Goethe	7
Foodshop 45	4
Quan An Ngon	11
Highlands Coffee	6
Highway 4	12
Indochine	5
Koto	10
Love Chocolate	2
Solace	8
Ya Beirut	3

0 — 500 m

Gia Lam Bus Station (1km), Le Mat (2km) & the northeast

& Noi Bai Airport (37km)

Museum of Ethnology

Red River

LONG BIEN BRIDGE

CHUONG DUONG BRIDGE

see 'Central Hanoi' map
for detail of this area

Long Bien
Bus Station

TRAN NHAT QUAN

YEN PHU

GIA BAC

Cua Bac
Church

The
Citadel

NGUYEN TRI PHUONG

HOANG DIEU

BAC SON

Martyr

PHAN DINH PHUNG

National
Assembly
Hall

Ba Dinh
Square

Ho Chi Minh's
Mausoleum

HUNG VUONG

Presidential
Palace

Botanical
Gardens

Ho Chi
Minh's
House

B-52 Memorial

THUY KHUE

HOANG HOA THAM

QUAN THANH

Quan Thanh Temple

West Lake

Tran Quoc Pagoda

*Truc
Bach
Lake*

Gunners'
Memorial

THANH NIEN

Sofitel Plaza

NGHI TAM

YEN PHU

Yen Phu Temple

Kim Lien
Pagoda

Thang Loi
Hotel

Sheraton
Hotel

XUAN DIEU

DANG THAI MAI

HO TAY
PENINSULA

*West
Lake*

Phu Tay Ho
Temple

N

BA DINH DISTRICT

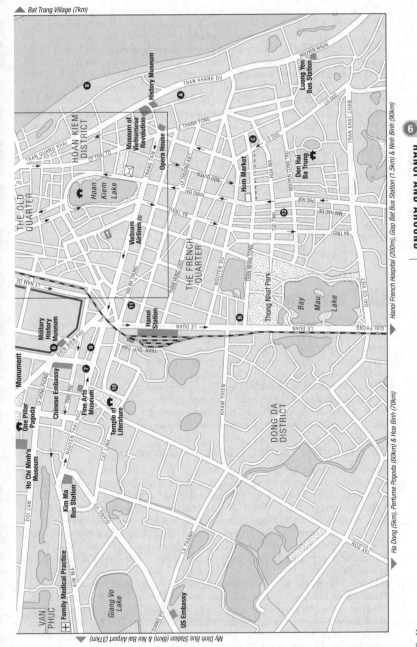

Bat Trang Village (7km)

HOAN KIEM DISTRICT

THE OLD QUARTER

TRAN QUANG KHAI

LY THAI TO

Hoan Kiem Lake

History Museum

Museum of Vietnamese Revolution

Opera House

LE THANH TONG

TRANG TIEN

NGUYEN KHOAI

Luong Yen Bus Station

LO DUC

TRAN KHAT CHAN

TRAN KHANH DU

Ⓐ

Ⓒ

Hom Market

Den Hai Ba Trung

HOA MA

NGUYEN CONG TRU

LO DUC

HANG BAI

LE THUONG KIET

NGO QUYEN

HANG BAI

BA TRIEU

Vietnam Airlines

THE FRENCH QUARTER

NGUYEN DU

TRAN NHAN TONG

TUE TINH

MAI HAC DE

PHO HUE

BA TRIEU

Ⓘ

TRAN HUNG DAO

TRAN QUOC TOAN

Ⓚ

Ⓑ

Thong Nhat Park

Bay Mau Lake

DAI CO VIET

GIAI PHONG

Hanoi French Hospital (200m); Giap Bat Bus Station (1.5km) & Ninh Binh (90km)

Hanoi Station

LE DUAN

TRAN QUY CAP

LY NAM DE

Military History Museum

Ⓕ

Monument

One Pillar Pagoda

DIEN BIEN PHU

Chinese Embassy

TRAN PHU

LE HONG PHONG

Ho Chi Minh's Museum

DOI CAN

NGUYEN THAI HOC

Ⓖ

Ⓙ

Fine Arts Museum

Ⓗ

Temple of Literature

CAT LINH

KHAM THIEN

DONG DA DISTRICT

Kim Ma Bus Station

KIM MA

GIANG VO

LA THANH

TAY SON

Family Medical Practice

VAN PHUC

Giang Vo Lake

GIANG VO

US Embassy

My Dinh Bus Station (8km) & Noi Bai Airport (37km)

Ha Dong (5km), Perfume Pagoda (60km) & Hoa Binh (70km)

6

HANOI AND AROUND

351

Information

The big state-run tour agencies, such as Vietnamtourism at 30a Ly Thuong Kiet (☎04/3826 4089, ⓦ www.vn-tourism.com), are more interested in signing you up for a tour than dishing out **information**. A far better option is to try one of the well-established and reliable private **tour agencies** (see box, p.349), which can provide information on visas, tours, transport and so forth. Most also arrange day **city tours**, starting at $10 a person for a full-day tour up to $100 for a luxury option, including meals. For a more in-depth introduction to the city, Hidden Hanoi (☎0912 254045 or 04/3852 6295, ⓦ www.hiddenhanoi .com.vn) offers a range of small-group walking tours, including the Old Quarter, French Quarter and a Temple Tour (90min–2hr; $15–20 per person; reservations required). Alternatively, you can buy leaflets outlining self-guided architectural tours of the Old Quarter, French Quarter and Old Citadel from the museum at 87 Ma May (see p.361).

Maps of the city are available from a wide variety of outlets, including bookshops and stalls on Trang Tien: those with a street index and inset of the Old Quarter are the most useful. Several publications carry **listings** information, but by far the most useful and easiest to track down is *Vietnam Pathfinder*, a free monthly mini-magazine: also handy is *Time Out*, produced weekly with the *Vietnam Investment Review*. Tourist-oriented cafés, restaurants, bars and so forth usually provide copies of these magazines for customers to read.

City transport

Despite the chaotic traffic, getting around **on foot** remains the best way to do justice to Hanoi's central district, taking an occasional **motorbike** ride to scoot between more distant places. Alternatively, take a leisurely tour by **cyclo**. **Cycling** is not recommended, since traffic discipline is an unfamiliar concept in Hanoi: teenagers on their Hondas ride without fear, and everyone drives without signalling or even looking. If you prefer something solid between you and the maelstrom, there are numerous **taxi** companies operating in Hanoi and tariffs aren't exorbitant. Finally, the much improved **city buses** are mainly useful for getting out to the long-distance bus stations.

Motorbike taxis, taxis and cyclo

Motorbike taxis (xe om), which hover at every intersection, provide the main form of cheap, inner-city transport. An average journey within the city centre should cost around 10,000đ and a trip out to Ho's Mausoleum or West Lake in the region of 15,000đ. Always establish terms before setting off. It's wise to write down the figures, making it clear whether you're negotiating in dollars or dong, and for a one-way or return journey; having the exact change ready at the end of the journey can also save argument. Drivers are obliged to carry spare helmets for passengers, but it still can be a fairly hair-raising ride.

Metered **taxis** wait outside the more upmarket hotels and at the north end of Hoan Kiem Lake, or you can call one up (see "Listings", p.387). With a short ride across the city centre averaging 20,000đ, and 40,000đ to the suburbs, taxis are definitely worth considering for hopping around the city. Note that prices are metered in dong, though it looks like dollars – for example, 20.00 on the meter means 20,000đ, not $20.

Cyclo have been replaced by xe om as the most popular form of public transport, and they now mainly cater to tour groups taking a leisurely amble round the Old Quarter. If you fancy doing the same, the simplest option is to get your hotel to arrange it for you. Otherwise, be prepared to bargain hard, aiming at around $2–3 per hour. Cyclo are banned from certain roads in central Hanoi, so don't be surprised if you seem to be taking a circuitous route or are dropped off round the corner from your destination.

Motorbike and car rental

Self-drive **motorbikes** are only for the brave in the inner city but are definitely worth considering for exploring sights further afield. Again, most rental outlets are located in the Old Quarter (see "Listings", p.386). Rental costs $4–5 per day for the standard 110cc Honda Wave, usually with the helmet thrown in. Again, always use the designated parking areas (*gui xe may*); the rate for motorbikes should be 5000đ or under.

Virtually every tour agency will gladly arrange **car rental**, and though the traffic congestion makes this a cumbersome method of sightseeing in the central districts, for day-trips out of Hanoi it offers greater flexibility than tours. Prices start at around $40 per day for an air-conditioned car with driver; as few drivers speak English, you may also want to hire a guide for another $15–30 a day.

City buses

Most travellers only use Hanoi's **city buses** to get to or from Noi Bai Airport (see p.348). Other **useful routes** connect the far-flung long-distance bus stations: #3 runs between Gia Lam and Giap Bat with stops on Hang Tre (or Tran Quang Khai, heading south), Tran Hung Dao and outside the train station. From the centre of town count on roughly thirty minutes to either Gia Lam or Giap Bat. Route #34 plies between Gia Lam and My Dinh (40min) via Hai Ba Trung and the Opera.

Buses on most routes run approximately every fifteen to twenty minutes between 5am and 9pm, and are fairly empty except during rush hour (7–9am and after 4pm) when some routes can be hideously overcrowded. The **fares** are heavily subsidized, with a flat rate of 3000đ within the city centre and 5000đ to the airport and the outer suburbs; pay the ticket collector on board.

Accommodation

Hanoi's **hotel** scene has changed dramatically over recent years to the extent that there's now an oversupply at all levels. Big international hotels continue to open, but are now being given a run for their money by a handful of classy boutique hotels. As a result, prices at the top end continue to fall and there are some excellent bargains to be had – ask about special discounts and promotional rates. Rates have also been dropping – and standards rising – at the budget level, spurred by an explosion of backpacker-oriented places all vying for the tourist dollar. Finding a room shouldn't cause any problems, even during the Tet New Year holiday, when the rest of the city all but shuts down. Be aware that several hotels adopt the same name, for example there are multiple *Prince* and *Camellia* hotels, so you'll need the exact address if arriving by xe om or taxi. Insist on being taken to the hotel you've specified: some drivers will try to persuade you it has closed, moved or changed name, and take you somewhere which pays

6

HANOI AND AROUND | Accommodation

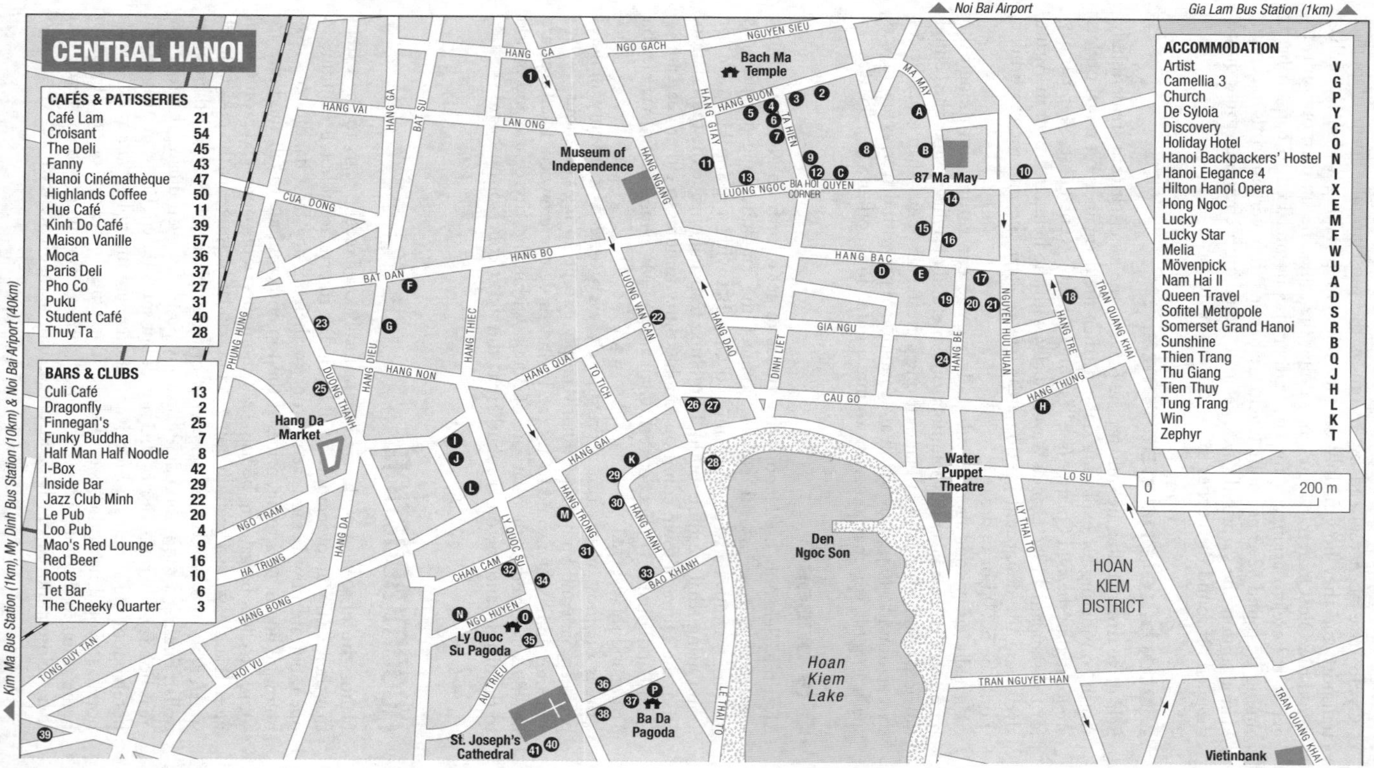

CENTRAL HANOI
CAFÉS & PATISSERIES
Café Lam 21
Croisant 54
The Deli 45
Fanny 43
Hanoi Cinémathèque 47
Highlands Coffee 50
Hue Café 11
Kinh Do Café 39
Maison Vanille 57
Moca 36
Paris Deli 37
Pho Co 27
Puku 31
Student Café 40
Thuy Ta 28
BARS & CLUBS
Culi Café 13
Dragonfly 2
Finnegan's 25
Funky Buddha 7
Half Man Half Noodle 8
I-Box 42
Inside Bar 29
Jazz Club Minh 22
Le Pub 20
Loo Pub 4
Mao's Red Lounge 9
Red Beer 16
Roots 10
Tet Bar 6
The Cheeky Quarter 3
ACCOMMODATION
Artist V
Camellia 3 G
Church P
De Syloia Y
Discovery C
Holiday Hotel O
Hanoi Backpackers' Hostel N
Hanoi Elegance 4 I
Hilton Hanoi Opera X
Hong Ngoc E
Lucky M
Lucky Star F
Melia W
Mövenpick U
Nam Hai II A
Queen Travel D
Sofitel Metropole S
Somerset Grand Hanoi R
Sunshine B
Thien Trang Q
Thu Giang J
Tien Thuy H
Tung Trang L
Win K
Zephyr T
0 200 m
Noi Bai Airport
Gia Lam Bus Station (1km)
Kim Ma Bus Station (1km), My Dinh Bus Station (10km) & Noi Bai Airport (40km)
Bach Ma Temple
Museum of Independence
87 Ma May
Bia Hoi Quyen Corner
Water Puppet Theatre
Den Ngoc Son
Hoan Kiem Lake
HOAN KIEM DISTRICT
Hang Da Market
Ly Quoc Su Pagoda
Ba Da Pagoda
St. Joseph's Cathedral
Vietinbank
HANG CA
NGO GACH
NGUYEN SIEU
MA MAY
HANG VAI
HANG GA
BAT SU
LAN ONG
HANG BUOM
TA HIEN
HANG GIAY
LUONG NGOC QUYEN
HANG NGANG
CUA DONG
HANG BO
HANG BAC
BAT DAN
PHUNG HUNG
LUONG VAN CAN
HANG DAO
GIA NGU
DINH LIET
HANG BE
NGUYEN HUU HUAN
HANG TRE
TRAN QUANG KHAI
HANG THIEC
HANG DIEU
HANG NON
HANG QUAT
TO TICH
CAU GO
HANG THUNG
DUONG THANH
HANG GAI
HANG TRONG
HANG HANH
LO SU
LY THAI TO
NGO TRAM
HANG DA
LY QUOC SU
HA TRUNG
CHAN CAM
BAO KHANH
HANG BONG
NGO HUYEN
TONG DUY TAN
HOI VU
AU TRIEU
LE THAI TO
TRAN NGUYEN HAN

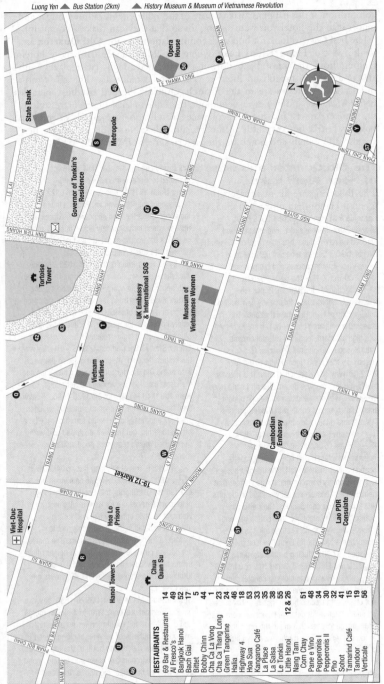

HANOI AND AROUND

6

RESTAURANTS

69 Bar & Restaurant	14
Al Fresco's	49
Bangkok Hanoi	52
Bach Giai	17
Bittet	5
Bobby Chinn	44
Cha Ca La Vong	1
Cha Ca Thang Long	23
Green Tangerine	24
Halia	46
Highway 4	18
Hoa Sua	53
Kangaroo Café	33
La Place	35
La Salsa	38
Le Tonkin	55
Little Hanoi	12 & 26
Nang Tam	51
Com Chay	48
Pane e Vino	34
Pepperonis I	30
Pepperonis II	32
Pho	41
Sohot	15
Tamarind Café	19
Tandoor	56
Verticale	56

355

commission. If this happens, make a note of the vehicle registration number and report it to the hotel you were aiming for so that they can make a complaint.

The best place to look for budget accommodation is in the **Old Quarter**, and to the west of **Hoan Kiem Lake**, where you'll find dozens of private hotels ranging from the most basic dormitories to increasingly ritzy places with air-conditioning, broadband internet access and satellite TV. The city's most sought-after addresses are in the **French Quarter**, headed by the venerable *Sofitel Metropole* and its newer neighbour, the *Hilton Hanoi Opera*. Here, among the quieter streets and more open spaces, you'll also find a rash of modern business hotels, but very little in the bargain stakes. North of the centre, there are also a few high-end hotels on the eastern shores of West Lake.

The Old Quarter and west of Hoan Kiem Lake

The following are all marked on the Central Hanoi map on pp.354–355.

Camellia 3 31 Hang Dieu ☏04/3828 5704, ⓦwww.camellia-hotels.com. Friendly staff and spruced-up rooms make this little hotel on the west side of the Old Quarter a decent option. Rates include free internet access and buffet breakfast. ❷

🏃 **Church 9** Nha Tho ☏04/3928 8118, ⓔchurchhotel@vnn.vn. Prices are surprisingly affordable at this classy new boutique hotel on one of Hanoi's trendiest streets. The standard rooms aren't large, but all are furnished to a high standard, featuring tasteful creams, natural wood and original artworks. ❺

Discovery 22 Luong Ngoc Quyen ☏04/3926 2462, ⓦwww.discoveryhotel9.com. This friendly, family-run hotel tucked up an alley off Luong Ngoc Quyen is a welcome addition to Hanoi's budget scene. Its six rooms come with fridges, phones, TVs, a/c and minuscule en-suite bathrooms. ❷

🏃 **Hanoi Backpackers' Hostel 48** Ngo Huyen ☏04/3828 5372, ⓦwww .hanoibackpackershostel.com. With a superb location, super-friendly staff, free internet access and quiet, comfy dorm rooms, it's no wonder that Vietnam's first hostel is usually packed to the gills with fun-seeking backpackers. Staff also run regular barbeque nights on the rooftop bar, and organize hugely popular – some might say debauched – tours of Ha Long Bay (see p.403). Bunk beds $7.50 including breakfast; rooms ❷

🏃 **Hanoi Elegance 4**, 3 Yen Thai ☏04/3938 0963, ⓦwww.hanoielegancehotel.com. Newest and most reasonably priced of this swish new chain, with three other branches in Hanoi (see website for details). It gets the basics spot on, and is full of nice touches that make the price-tag reasonable when it would otherwise be a little high for the room size. ❹

Holiday Hotel 9 Ngo Huyen ☏04/3938 0565. On a relatively quiet sidestreet just north of the cathedral,

this small hotel has amiable staff, and large, well-furnished rooms at reasonable prices. ❸

Hong Ngoc 39 Hang Bac ☏04/3926 0322, ⓔhongngochotel@hn.vnn.vn. Prices a little above the norm reflect the high standard of fixtures and fittings, which include safety boxes in every room, generous bathrooms and furniture that's a touch different. It's also spotlessly clean. ❸

Lucky 12 Hang Trong ☏04/3825 1029, ⓦwww .luckyhotel.com.vn. Some of the furniture could do with upgrading, but overall this is the best of the bunch along Hang Trong for comfortable accommodation at a range of prices; all the rooms have safety boxes, fridges, phones, a/c and satellite TV, plus balconies at higher rates. ❹

Lucky Star 11 Bat Dan ☏04/3923 1781, ⓦwww .luckystarhotel.com. Welcoming hotel on the west side of the Old Quarter, with cheerful floor tiles and the latest satellite TVs, amongst other things. ❸

Nam Hai II 40 Ma May ☏04/3926 1688, ⓦwww .namhai2hotel.com. The wood panelling, wooden collages and heavy dark-wood furniture may be a bit overbearing, but the well-equipped and well-maintained rooms represent good value for money. ❸

🏃 **Queen Travel 65** Hang Bac ☏04/3826 0860, ⓦwww.queencafe.com.vn. In the heart of the Old Quarter, this homely hotel (only nine rooms) stands out for its eye-catching Vietnamese-style entrance hall and for the attention to detail in the guestrooms, not to mention a friendly, family atmosphere. The rooms are decked out in restful creams and beiges offset by the dark wooden floorboards and bamboo furniture, and are equipped with DVD players and free wi-fi. ❹

Sunshine 42 Ma May ☏04/3926 1559, ⓦwww .hanoisunshinehotel.com. With just eleven rooms and a well-justified reputation for helpful staff and good standards of service, booking ahead is a must at this welcoming hotel at the top end of Ma May. Guestrooms are clean and spacious and come with all the usual mod cons. Tour and travel services and free internet access round out the picture. ❸

Thien Trang 24 Nha Chung ☏ 04/3826 9823, ✉ thientranghotel24@hotmail.com. Prices remain surprisingly affordable at this small and friendly hotel located in the trendy cathedral area. The rooms are nothing fancy, but clean and well kept: those at the cheaper end have no windows, while the top-floor room boasts a private roof terrace and great views over the town. ❷–❸

Thu Giang 5a Tam Thuong alley ☏ 04/3828 5734, ✉ thugiangn@hotmail.com. A family-run hotel with tiny, no-frills rooms from $6: $10 buys you more space, a/c and TV. Not much in the way of facilities but an interesting location and the hosts make you very welcome. ❶

Tien Thuy 9 Hang Thung ☏ 04/3934 3608, ⓦ www.sunshinehotel.com.vn. Well-managed hotel close to Hoan Kiem Lake offering twenty fully equipped if slightly aging rooms at reasonable rates; bathrooms are unusually generous and all fitted with bathtubs. Buffet breakfast included in price. ❸

Tung Trang 13 Tam Thuong alley ☏ 04/3828 6267, ✉ tungtranghotel@yahoo.com. A step above the rest along this alley, the *Tung Trang* offers more spacious rooms, all with TVs, a/c and en-suite bathrooms. It's worth paying a couple of dollars extra for a bigger room with a window. ❷

Win 34 Hang Hanh ☏ 04/3828 7371, ✉ winhotel @yahoo.com. Perennially popular, friendly hotel on the ultra-cool Hang Hanh café strip. While the ten rooms are kitted out with all the usual amenities (a/c, satellite TV, fridges, phones and so forth) and well maintained, they're looking a little worn considering the price tag. ❷

The French Quarter

The following are all marked on the Central Hanoi map on pp.354–355, unless otherwise stated.

Army 33c Pham Ngu Lao ☏ 04/3825 2896, ✉ armyhotel@fpt.vn. See map, p.351. This mid-range hotel set among trees on a quiet backstreet next to the Ministry of Defence offers reasonable value for such a central location. Spacious if somewhat old-fashioned rooms occupy low-rise blocks around a large, salt-water swimming pool. ❻

Artist 22a Hai Ba Trung ☏ 04/3825 3044, ✉ artist_hotel@yahoo.com. One of the few cheap options in the French Quarter, this old hotel is recommended for its lovely location around a tree-filled courtyard at the end of a long alley: the rooms, however, aren't super clean. ❸

De Syloia 17a Tran Hung Dao ☏ 04/3824 5346, ⓦ www.desyloia.com. A stylish, boutique business hotel with just 33 impeccably furnished rooms, some a touch on the small side, behind its mock-colonial facade. Service is good and it also boasts a decent restaurant. ❼

🏃 **Hilton Hanoi Opera** 1 Le Thanh Tong ☏ 04/3933 0500, ⓦ www.hilton.com. Arguably Hanoi's top city-centre address for all-round value, this five-star hotel is carefully designed to blend in with the neighbouring Opera House. Facilities include 269 cheerful and well-proportioned rooms with excellent bathrooms and some local touches in the ceramics, contemporary paintings and chunky furniture. In-house services include three restaurants, a business centre, and a fitness centre with outdoor swimming pool and spa services. ❼

Melia 44b Ly Thuong Kiet ☏ 04/3934 3343, ⓦ www.solmelia.com. While this high-rise hotel is pitched at the executive traveller, it's worth checking out the online deals. Luxurious rooms have an appealingly funky design, but bathrooms at the cheaper end are small considering the price tag. There's an elevated open-air swimming pool, as well as a gym and a choice of restaurants. ❼

Mövenpick 83a Ly Thuong Kiet ☏ 04/3822 2800, ⓦ www.moevenpick-hotels.com. Standard-setting business hotel housed in a colonial-style building near the train station. Rooms are tastefully decorated and equipped with flatscreen TVs, but the hotel's most distinctive feature is a female-only floor, which has slightly different rooms and direct access to the excellent fitness centre. ❼

Nikko 84 Tran Nhan Tong ☏ 04/3822 3535, ⓦ www.hotelnikkohanoi.com.vn. See map, p.351. A luxurious hotel on the French Quarter's southern fringes, where well-appointed rooms feature comprehensive five-star facilities. Its Japanese ownership is apparent in its distinct, minimalist feel, and it is home to the excellent *Benkay* restaurant. Other facilities include a business centre, health club and outdoor swimming pool. ❻

🏃 **Sofitel Metropole** 15 Ngo Quyen ☏ 04/3826 6919, ⓦ www.accorhotels .com/asia. Opened in 1901 since when It has hosted numerous Illustrious guests, the *Metropole* remains one of the most sought-after hotels in Hanoi despite increasingly fierce competition. Though rooms in the modern Opera Wing exude international-class luxury, they lack the old-world charm of the original building, with its wooden floorboards and louvred shutters. In-house services include a business centre, a small open-air swimming pool, fitness centre and a choice of bars and restaurants, notably *Spices Garden*, serving upmarket Vietnamese fare. ❼

Somerset Grand Hanoi 49 Hai Ba Trung ☏ 04/3934 2342, ⓦ www.somersetgrandhanoi.com.

These serviced apartments, with up to three bedrooms and fully equipped kitchens, can be rented by the night and make a more homely alternative to an upmarket hotel. They also represent surprisingly good value, including access to facilities such as an open-air pool, a gym and a crèche. Make sure you book well in advance. ⑥

Sunway 19 Pham Dinh Ho ☎ 04/3971 3888, ⓦ www .sunway-hotel.com. See map, p.351. An award-winning, four-star boutique hotel where consistently high standards of service and comfortable rooms make up for a slightly inconvenient location. There's an in-house restaurant and live music nightly in the lobby bar, not to mention the obligatory fitness centre. ⑥

Zephyr 4-6 Ba Trieu ☎ 04/3934 1256, ⓦ www.zephyrhotel.com.vn. This three-star place offers value for money with its forty taste-fully decorated and fully equipped rooms in a prime location just a stone's throw from Hoan Kiem Lake. ⑥

The City

Hanoi city centre comprises a compact area known as **Hoan Kiem District**, which is neatly bordered by the Red River embankment in the east and by the rail line to the north and west, while its southern extent is marked by the roads Nguyen Du, Le Van Huu and Han Thuyen. The district takes its name from its present-day hub and most obvious point of reference, **Hoan Kiem Lake**, which lies between the cramped and endlessly diverting **Old Quarter** in the north, and the tree-lined boulevards of the **French Quarter**, arranged in a rough grid system, to the south. West of this central district, across the rail tracks, some of Hanoi's most impressive monuments occupy the wide open spaces of the former **Imperial City**, grouped around Ho Chi Minh's Mausoleum on Ba Dinh Square and extending south to the ancient walled gardens of the Temple of Literature. A vast body of water confusingly called **West Lake** sits north of the city, harbouring a number of interesting temples and pagodas, but the attractive villages that once surrounded it have now largely given way to upmarket residential areas and a smattering of luxury hotels.

Hoan Kiem District

The commercial core of Hanoi is **Hoan Kiem District**, home to the city's banks, airlines and the GPO, plus most of the hotels, restaurants, shopping streets and markets. But there's a lot more to the area, not least the lake itself and nearby **temples**, which date back to the earliest days of the city. Though you'll want to spend time on these individual sights, it's the abundant streetlife and architectural wealth that give the area its special allure.

Hoan Kiem Lake

Early morning sees **Hoan Kiem Lake** at its best, stirring to life as walkers, joggers and *tai chi* enthusiasts limber up in the half-light. Space is at a premium in this crowded city, and the lake's strip of park meets multiple needs, at its busiest when lunch-hour hawkers are out in force, and easing down slowly to evenings of old men playing chess and couples seeking twilight privacy on benches half-hidden among the willows. The lake itself is small – you can walk round it in thirty minutes – and not particularly spectacular, but to Hanoians this is the soul of their city.

A squat, three-tiered pavilion known as the **Tortoise Tower** ornaments a tiny island in the middle of Ho Hoan Kiem, "Lake of the Restored Sword". The names refer to a legend of the great Vietnamese hero, Le Loi, who led a successful uprising against the Chinese in the fifteenth century. Tradition has it that Le Loi netted a gleaming sword while out fishing in a sampan and when

▲ Den Ngoc Son Temple at Hoan Kiem Lake

he returned as King Le Thai To, after ten years of battle, he wanted to thank the spirit of the lake. As he prepared the sacrifice there was a timely peal of thunder and the miraculous sword flew out of its scabbard, into the mouth of a golden turtle (Vietnamese use the same word for turtle and tortoise) sent by the gods to reclaim the weapon. At least one hardy giant turtle still lives in the lake, but the one you're most likely to see is a heavily varnished specimen captured in 1968. It's preserved and on view on a second island accessible via the striking **The Huc Bridge**, an arch of red-lacquered wood poetically labelled the "place where morning sunlight rests". Beside the bridge stands a nine-metre-high obelisk, the **Writing Brush Tower**, on which three outsized Chinese characters proclaim "a pen to write on the blue sky".

Crossing over to the island you find the secluded **Den Ngoc Son**, "Temple of the Jade Mound" (daily 8.30am–6pm; 3000đ), sheltering among ancient trees. This small temple was founded in the fourteenth century and is dedicated to an eclectic group: national hero General Tran Hung Dao, who defeated the Mongols in 1288, sits on the principal altar; Van Xuong, God of Literature; physician La To; and a martial arts practitioner, Quan Vu. The temple buildings date from the 1800s and are typical of the Nguyen Dynasty; in the antechamber, look out for the dragon heads, carved with bulbous noses and teeth bared in manic grins.

Around the lake

A good way to get your bearings in Hanoi is to make a quick circuit of Hoan Kiem Lake, a pleasant walk at any time of year and stunning when the flame trees flower in June and July. In the 1960s these paths, like many others in the city, were studded with hundreds of individual air-raid shelters – concrete-lined holes big enough for one person, topped with a manhole cover. Heading south from the Writing Brush Tower, you can't miss the stony-faced, grey marble **Hanoi People's Committee** building, about halfway down the lake. Just to its south stands an equally imperious statue of Hanoi's founding father, King Ly Thai To, erected in 2004 in anticipation of celebrations to mark the city's millennium in 2010. At dusk, the expanse of polished stone paving around it provides an incongruous venue for Hanoi's small but keen band of break-dancers. The next block south is occupied by the **General Post Office**, opposite which stands a small brick tower, all that remains of an enormous pagoda complex, Chua Bao An, after French town planners cleared the site in 1892.

Rounding the lake's southern tip and heading up its west shore, you might want to take a detour to **St Joseph's Cathedral** (daily 5am–noon & 2–7pm) at the far end of attractive Nha Tho ("Big Church") Street, lined with trendy restaurants, cafés and boutiques. Look out on the way for the arched entrance to **Ba Da Pagoda**, which houses an impressive array of Buddhas. Hanoi's neo-Gothic cathedral was constructed in the early 1880s, partly financed by two lotteries, and though the exterior is badly weathered its high-vaulted interior is still imposing. Among the first things you notice inside are the ornate altar screen and the stained-glass windows, most of which are French originals. Over the black marble tomb of a former cardinal of Vietnam stands one of several statues commemorating martyred Vietnamese saints, in this case André Dung Lac who was executed in 1839 on the orders of the fervently anti-Christian emperor Minh Mang. The cathedral's main door is open during services (the celebration of Mass was allowed to resume on Christmas Eve 1990 after a long hiatus); at other times walk round to the small door in the southwest corner.

Walking north from the cathedral along Ly Quoc Su brings you to **Ly Quoc Su Pagoda**, at no. 52, a small pagoda with a genuinely interesting collection of statues. Ly Quoc Su (sometimes also known as Minh Khong) was a Buddhist teacher, healer and royal adviser who cured the hallucinating King Ly Than Tong of believing he was a tiger. Quoc Su's image resides alongside that of the white-bearded Tu Dao Hanh (see "Thay Pagoda", p.389) on the principal altar of this twelfth-century temple – when it later became a pagoda they simply added a few Buddhas behind. In front of the altar, two groups of statues face each other across the prayer floor: four secular, female figures sit opposite three perfectly inscrutable mandarins of the nineteenth century, clothed in rich red lacquer. From Ly Quoc Su retrace your steps to Hoan Kiem Lake and continue northwards to where *Thuy Ta* café (see p.379) offers respite from the traffic and a fine place to relax.

The Old Quarter

Walk north from Hoan Kiem Lake, across Cau Go, and suddenly you're in the tumultuous streets of the **Old Quarter**, a congested square kilometre which was closed behind massive ramparts and heavy wooden gates until well into the nineteenth century. Apart from one gate, at the east end of Hang Chieu, the walls have been dismantled, and there are few individual sights in the quarter; the best approach is simply to dive into the back lanes and explore.

Everything spills out onto pavements which double as workshops for stone-carvers, furniture-makers and tinsmiths, and as display space for merchandise ranging from pungent therapeutic herbs and fluttering prayer flags to ranks of Remy Martin and shiny-wrapped chocolates. With so much to attract your attention at ground level it's easy to miss the **architecture**, which reveals fascinating glimpses of the quarter's history, starting with the fifteenth-century merchants' houses otherwise found only in Hoi An (see p.272). Hanoi's aptly named **tube-houses** evolved from market stalls into narrow single-storey shops, windows no higher than a passing royal palanquin, under gently curving, red-tiled roofs. Some are just two metres wide, the result of taxes levied on street frontages and of subdivision for inheritance, while behind stretches a succession of storerooms and living quarters up to 60m in length, interspersed with open courtyards to give them light and air; to get a better idea of the layout, pop into the beautifully restored example at **87 Ma May** (daily 9am–noon & 1–5pm 5000đ). Nowadays, the majority of facades bear distinctly European touches – faded wooden shutters, sagging balconies and rain-streaked moulding – dating from the early 1900s when the streets were widened for pavements. Certain occupants were too wealthy or influential to be shifted and you can find their houses still standing out of line along Hang Bac, Ma May and Hang Buom, three of the Old Quarter's most interesting and attractive streets. Ma May also retains its own **dinh**, or communal house (at no. 64), which traditionally served as both meeting hall and shrine to the neighbourhood's particular patron spirit, in this case a fourteenth-century mandarin and ambassador to the Chinese court.

Bach Ma Temple and the Guiding Light Mosque
Walking north along Ma May and onto **Hang Buom**, you pass a wealth of interesting detail typical of the quarter's patchwork architecture: simple one-storey shophouses, some still sporting traditional red-tiled roofs; elaborate plaster-work and Art Deco styling from colonial days; and Soviet chic of the 1960s and 1970s – each superimposed on the basic tube-house design. Hang

What's in a name

The Old Quarter's **street names** date back five centuries to when the area was divided among 36 artisans' guilds, each gathered around a temple or a *dinh* (communal house) dedicated to the guild's patron spirit. Even today many streets specialize to some degree, and a few are still dedicated to the original craft or its modern equivalent. The most colourful examples are Hang Quat, full of bright-red banners and lacquerware for funerals and festivals, and Hang Ma, where paper products have been made for at least five hundred years. Nowadays gaudy tinsel dances in the breeze above brightly coloured votive objects, which include model TVs, dollars and cars to be offered to the ancestors. A selection of the more interesting streets with an element of specialization is listed below. *Hang* means merchandise.

Street name	Meaning	Modern speciality
Ha Trong	Drum skin	Bag menders, upholsterers
Hang Bo	Bamboo baskets	Haberdashers
Hang Buom	Sails	Imported foods and alcohol, confectionery
Hang Chieu	Sedge mats	Mats, ropes, bamboo blinds
Hang Dau	Oil	Shoes
Hang Dieu	Pipes	Cushions, mattresses
Hang Duong	Sugar	Clothes, general goods
Hang Gai	Hemp goods	Silks, tailors, souvenirs
Hang Hom	Wooden chests	Glue, paint, varnish
Hang Ma	Paper votive objects	Paper goods
Hang Quat	Ceremonial fans	Religious accessories
Hang Thiec	Tin goods	Tin goods, mirrors
Hang Vai	Fabrics	Bamboo ladders
Lan Ong	Eighteenth-century scholar-physician	Traditional medicines, towels

Buom is also home to the quarter's oldest and most revered place of worship, **Bach Ma Temple** (daily 7.30–11.30am & 1.30–6pm). The temple was founded in the ninth century and later dedicated to the White Horse (*Bach Ma*), the guardian spirit of Thang Long who posed as an ethereal site foreman and helped King Ly Thai To overcome a few problems with his citadel's collapsing walls. The present structure dates largely from the eighteenth century and its most unusual features are a pair of charismatic, pot-bellied guardians in front of the altar who flaunt an impressive array of lacquered gold teeth. In front stands an antique palanquin, used each year to celebrate the temple's foundation on the twelfth day of the second lunar month.

As you explore the quarter you'll come across a great many other sacred sites – temples, pagodas, *dinh* and venerable banyan trees – hidden among the houses. One of the more surprising is the **Guiding Light Mosque** at no. 12 Hang Luoc, which was built in the 1890s by an Indian Islamic community of traders and civil servants, and now serves Muslims from Hanoi's diplomatic community as the only mosque in northern Vietnam.

Dong Xuan and Long Bien Bridge

East of the mosque, the city's largest covered market, **Dong Xuan**, occupies a whole block behind its original, 1889 facade. Its three storeys are dedicated to clothes and household goods, while fresh foodstuffs spill out into a bustling street market stacked with multicoloured mounds of vegetables. Head one block east again and you find two ramps taking bicycles and pedestrians up onto **Long Bien Bridge**, a road and rail bridge completed in 1902 and originally named after the then governor-general of Indochina, Paul Doumer. Until Chuong Duong Bridge was built in the 1980s, Long Bien was the Red River's only bridge and therefore of immense strategic significance. During the American War this was one of Vietnam's most heavily defended spots, which American bombs never managed to knock out completely. If you have time, take a bicycle ride across the 1700-metre span of iron lattice-work, but spare a thought for the maintenance staff: in the 1960s, perhaps the last time it was done, it took a hundred workers five years to repaint the bridge.

The Museum of Independence, To Tich and Hang Quat

Cutting back southwards, it was at 48 Hang Ngang that Ho Chi Minh drafted the Declaration of Independence for the Democratic Republic of Vietnam in 1945. The house where he lived for those heady months is now the **Museum of Independence** (Mon–Fri 8–11.30am & 2–4.30pm; free). A desultory exhibition downstairs shows yet more photos of Uncle Ho with beaming children, but it's worth taking a look at the two first-floor rooms where he slept, wrote and debated, seemingly surrounded by oversized Western period furniture.

From here it's only a couple of minutes' walk down to Hoan Kiem Lake, passing through the traditional street market selling fresh meat, fish and vegetables under an improvised canopy of low-slung sacks that clogs the lanes just behind Cau Go. This southern edge of the Old Quarter, particularly Hang Gai, is where you'll find the biggest concentration of silk and embroidery shops, but before leaving the old streets completely take a quick detour up **To Tich**, a short lane of wood-turners, souvenir shops and juice bars whisking up colourful fresh-fruit combinations, to walk among **Hang Quat**'s bright-red prayer flags.

The French Quarter

After the hectic streets of the Old Quarter, the grand boulevards and wide pavements of Hanoi's **French Quarter** to the south and east of Hoan Kiem Lake are a welcome relief. Again it's the architecture here that's the highlight, with a few specific attractions spread over a couple of kilometres. The first French concession was granted in 1874, an insalubrious plot of land on the banks of the Red River, southeast of where the Opera House stands today. Once in full possession of Hanoi, after 1882, the French began to create a city appropriate to their new protectorate, starting with the area between the old concession and the train station, 2km to the west. Gradually elegant villas filled plots along the grid of tree-lined avenues, then spread south in the 1930s and 1940s towards what is now Thong Nhat (Reunification) Park, a peaceful but rather featureless expanse of green marking the French Quarter's southern boundary.

The Opera House

In the process of building their capital the French destroyed many ancient Vietnamese monuments, including one of Hanoi's oldest pagodas, Bao Thien, which was demolished to make way for the cathedral. They were replaced, however, with some fine, Parisian-style buildings such as the stately **Opera House** (now officially known as the Municipal Theatre), near the eastern end of Trang Tien. Based on the neo-Baroque Paris Opéra, complete with Ionic columns and grey slate tiles imported from France, the theatre was erected on reclaimed land and finally opened in 1911 after ten years in the building. It was regarded as the jewel in the crown of French Hanoi, the colonial town's physical and cultural focus, until 1945 when the Viet Minh proclaimed the August Revolution from its balcony. After Independence, audiences were treated to a diet of Socialist Realism and revolutionary theatre, but now the building has been restored to its former glory after a massive face-lift. Crystal chandeliers, Parisian mirrors and sweeping staircases of polished marble have all been beautifully preserved, although, unfortunately, there's no access to the public unless you go to a performance (see p.380 for box office details). Otherwise, feast your eyes on the exterior – particularly stunning under evening floodlights or, better still, the soft glow of a full moon.

The History Museum

One block east of the Opera House is Hanoi's excellent History Museum, on Trang Tien (Tues–Sun 8–11.30am & 1.30–4.30pm; 15,000đ). Buried among trees and facing the river, the museum isn't immediately obvious, but its architecture is unmissable – a fanciful blend of Vietnamese palace and French villa which came to be called "Neo-Vietnamese" style. The museum was founded in the 1930s by the Ecole Française d'Extrême Orient, but after 1954 changed focus to reflect Vietnam's evolution from Paleolithic times to Independence. Exhibits, including many plaster reproductions, are arranged in chronological order on two floors: everything downstairs is pre-1400, while the second floor takes the story up to August 1945.

The ground floor

On the **ground floor**, the museum's prize exhibits are those from the **Dong Son culture**, a sophisticated Bronze Age civilization that flourished in the Red River Delta from 1200 to 200 BC. The display includes a rich variety of implements, from arrowheads to cooking utensils, and a lamp in the form of a graceful figurine, but the finest examples of Dong Son creativity are several huge, ceremonial bronze drums, used to bury the dead, invoke the monsoon or celebrate fertility rites. The remarkably well-preserved **Ngoc Lu Drum** is the highlight, where advanced casting techniques are evident in the delicate figures of deer, birds and boats ornamenting the surface – you can see the detail more clearly in the rubbing in the display case behind. Other notable exhibits on this floor include recent finds from excavations in Hanoi's citadel, a willowy Amitabha Buddha of the eleventh century, pale-green celadon ware from the same era and a group of wooden stakes from the glorious thirteenth-century battle of the Bach Dang River (see p.406).

The second floor

Displays on the museum's **second floor** illustrate the great leap in artistic skill that took place in the fifteenth century following a period of Chinese rule. Pride of place goes to a three-metre-tall stele inscribed with the life story of Le Loi, who spearheaded the resistance against the Chinese and founded the dynasty. More interesting are the extensive collection of ceramics and exhibits relating to the nineteenth-century Nguyen Dynasty and the period of French rule. A series of ink-washes depicting Hué's imperial court in the 1890s are particularly eye-catching, as are the embroidered silks and inlaid ivory furniture once used by the emperors cloistered in the citadel.

The Museum of Vietnamese Revolution

The **Museum of Vietnamese Revolution**, 216 Tran Quang Khai (Tues–Sun 8–11.45am & 1.30–4.15pm; 10,000đ), is housed in a classic colonial building that started life as a customs house. The museum catalogues the "Vietnamese people's patriotic and revolutionary struggle", from the first anti-French movements of the late nineteenth century to post-1975 reconstruction. Much of the tale is told through documents, including the first clandestine newspapers and revolutionary tracts penned by Ho Chi Minh, and illustrated with portraits of Vietnam's most famous revolutionaries. Among them are many photos you won't see elsewhere. There's good coverage of Dien Bien Phu and the War of Independence, and a small but well-presented exhibition on the American War, a subject that is treated in greater depth at the Military History Museum (see p.368).

Residence of the Governor of Tonkin and the Metropole

Back at the Opera House, walking two blocks north on Ly Thai To brings you to the junction with Ngo Quyen, dominated by two very different buildings. The imposing Art Deco structure with a circular portico, once the French Bank of Indochina, now houses the **State Bank** in its lofty halls. Diagonally opposite stands one of Hanoi's most attractive colonial edifices, the immaculately restored **Residence of the Governor of Tonkin**, constructed in 1918; it's now known as the State Guest House and used for visiting VIPs. Unfortunately you can't get inside, but as you peer in take a closer look at the elegant, wrought-iron railings, pitted with bullet-mark souvenirs of the 1945 Revolution. More recently the building's terraces appeared in the film *Indochine* (see p.535).

In comparison, the bright, white Neoclassical facade of the **Metropole** – nowadays *Sofitel Metropole* hotel – just south at 15 Ngo Quyen, verges on the austere. The then *Grand Metropole Palace* opened in 1901, and soon became one of Southeast Asia's great hotels. Even during the French War, Bernard Fall, a journalist killed by a landmine near Hué in 1967, described the hotel as the "last really fashionable place left in Hanoi", where the barman "could produce a reasonable facsimile of almost any civilized drink except water". After Independence it re-emerged as the *Thong Nhat* or *Reunification Hotel*, but otherwise stayed much the same, including en-suite rats and lethal wiring, until 1990 when Sofitel transformed it into Hanoi's first international-class hotel. The *Metropole's* illustrious visitors' book includes Charlie Chaplin and Paulette Goddard on honeymoon in 1936 and Graham Greene, who first came here in 1952. Twenty years later Jane Fonda stayed for two weeks while making her famous broadcast to American troops.

Trang Tien

Trang Tien, the main artery of the French Quarter, is still a busy shopping street where you'll find bookshops and art galleries, as well as the Trang Tien Plaza with its flash boutiques and somewhat incongruous supermarket. South of Trang Tien you enter French Hanoi's principal residential quarter, consisting of a grid of shaded boulevards whose distinguished villas are much sought after for restoration as embassies or offices or as desirable, expatriate residences. These houses, which like those of the Old Quarter survived largely due to lack of money for redevelopment, run the gamut of early twentieth-century European architecture from elegant Neoclassical through to 1930s Modernism and Art Deco, with an occasional Oriental flourish.

To take a swing through the area, drop down Hang Bai onto Ly Thuong Kiet and start heading west. Just round the corner, the **Museum of Vietnamese Women**, 36 Ly Thuong Kiet (Tues–Sun 8am–4pm; 20,000đ), puts a different perspective on national history. Once again, it's the twentieth century that provides the most absorbing material, while the top-floor display of ethnic minority costumes is worth a quick look. Two blocks further west, you arrive at **Cho 19–12** (19 Dec Market), a short covered street of stalls selling mainly fresh fruit, vegetables and meat, including the twisted carcasses of roast dog. Beyond, the Hanoi Towers complex looms over the sanitized remnants of French-built **Hoa Lo Prison** at 1 Hoa Lo (Tues–Sun 8.30–11.30am & 1.30–4.30pm; 5000đ), nicknamed the "Hanoi Hilton" by American prisoners of war in wry comment on its harsh conditions and often brutal treatment. The jail became famous in the 1960s when the PoWs, mostly pilots and crew members, were shown worldwide in televised broadcasts. There's a heavy dose of propaganda, too, in the two rooms dedicated to the PoWs, peddling the message that they were well treated, clothed and fed. Fortunately, the museum mostly concentrates on the pre-1954 colonial period when the French incarcerated many nationalist leaders at Hoa Lo, including no fewer than five future general secretaries of the Vietnamese Communist Party. Some of the cells – which were still in use up to 1994 – have been preserved, along with rusty shackles and instruments of torture. Other rooms display photos and information on the more famous political prisoners, though only the captions are in English.

At the next junction west, turn left down Quan Su to find the arched entrance of **Chua Quan Su**, the Ambassadors' Pagoda, founded in the fifteenth century as part of a guesthouse for ambassadors from neighbouring Buddhist countries, though the current building dates only from 1942. Nowadays Quan Su is one of Hanoi's most active pagodas: on the first and fifteenth days of the lunar month, worshippers and mendicants throng its forecourt, while inside an iron lamp, ornamented with sinuous dragons, hangs over the crowded prayer-floor and ranks of crimson-lacquered Buddhas glow through a pungent haze of burning incense. The compound, shaded by ancient trees, is headquarters of the officially recognized Central Buddhist

Congregation of Vietnam and is a centre of Buddhist learning, hence the well-stocked library and classrooms at the rear. Shops roundabout specialize in Buddhist paraphernalia.

Ho Chi Minh's Mausoleum and around

Hanoi's most important cultural and historical monuments are found in the district immediately west of the Old Quarter, where the Ly kings established their Imperial City in the eleventh century. The venerable **Temple of Literature** and the picturesque **One Pillar Pagoda** both date from this time, but nothing else remains of the Ly kings' vermilion palaces, whose last vestiges were cleared in the late nineteenth century to accommodate an expanding French administration. Most impressive of the district's colonial buildings is the dignified Residence of the Governor-General of Indochina, now known as the **Presidential Palace**. After 1954 some of the surrounding gardens gave way in their turn to Ba Dinh parade ground, the National Assembly Hall and two great centres of pilgrimage: **Ho Chi Minh's Mausoleum** and **Museum**. The nearby Botanical Gardens, however, survived to provide a welcome haven from modern Hanoi's hustle and bustle. East of Ba Dinh Square the **citadel** encloses a restricted military area. Its most famous feature is the **Cot Co Flag Tower** which dominates the extreme southwest corner, next to one of Hanoi's most rewarding museums, the **Military History Museum**. Although there's a lot to see in this area, it's possible to cover everything described below in a single day, with an early start at the mausoleum and surrounding sites, leaving the **Fine Arts Museum** along with the Military History Museum and Temple of Literature until later in the day.

Ba Dinh Square and Ho Chi Minh's Mausoleum

The wide, open spaces of **Ba Dinh Square**, 2km west of Hoan Kiem Lake, are the nation's ceremonial epicentre. It was here that Ho Chi Minh read out the Declaration of Independence to half a million people on September 2, 1945, and here that Independence is commemorated each National Day with military parades. The National Assembly Hall, venue for Party congresses, stands on the square's east side, while the west is dominated by the severe grey bulk of **Ho Chi Minh's Mausoleum** (April–Oct Tues–Thurs 7.30–10.30am, Sat & Sun 7.30–11am; Nov–March Tues–Thurs 8–11am, Sat & Sun 8–11.30am; free). In the tradition of great Communist leaders, when Ho Chi Minh died in 1969 his body was embalmed, though not put on public view until after 1975. The mausoleum is probably Hanoi's most popular sight, attracting hordes of visitors at weekends and on national holidays; from school parties to ageing confederates, all come to pay their respects to "Uncle Ho".

Visitors to the mausoleum must leave bags and cameras at one of the reception centres, the most convenient being that at 8 Hung Vuong, from where you'll be escorted by soldiers in immaculate uniforms. Respectful behaviour is requested, which means **appropriate dress** (no shorts or sleeveless vests) and removing hats and keeping silence within the sanctum. Note that each autumn the mausoleum usually closes for a few weeks while Ho undergoes maintenance.

Inside the building's marble entrance hall Ho Chi Minh's most quoted maxim greets you: "nothing is more important than independence and freedom." Then it's up the stairs and into a cold, dark room where this charismatic hero lies under glass, a small, pale figure glowing in the dim light, his thin hands resting on black covers. Despite the rather macabre overtones, it's hard not to be affected by the solemn atmosphere, though in actual fact Ho's last wish was to be cremated and his ashes divided between the north, centre and south of the country, with each site marked only by a simple shelter. The grandiose building where he now lies seems sadly at odds with this unassuming, egalitarian man.

The Presidential Palace and Ho Chi Minh's house

Follow the crowd on leaving Ho's mausoleum and you enter the grounds of the **Presidential Palace** via the side gate. The palace was built in 1901 as the humble abode of the governor-general of Indochina – all sweeping stairways, louvred shutters and ornate wrought-iron gates of the Belle Époque – and these days is used to receive visiting heads of state. It's closed to the public but you can admire the outside as you walk through the palace gardens to **Ho Chi Minh's house** (daily: April–Oct 7.30–11am & 1.30–4pm; Nov–March 8–11am & 2–4pm; 5000đ). After Independence in 1954 President Ho Chi Minh built a modest dwelling for himself behind the palace, modelling it on an ethnic minority stilthouse, a simple structure with open sides and split-bamboo screens. Ho and his Politburo used to gather in the ground-level meeting area, while his study and bedroom upstairs are said to be as he left them, sparsely furnished, unostentatious and very highly polished. Ho lived here for the last eleven years of his life, even during the American War, tending his garden and fishpond; tradition has it that he died in the small hut next door.

The One Pillar Pagoda

Close by Ho's stilthouse, the **One Pillar Pagoda** rivals the Tortoise Tower as a symbol of Hanoi. It is the most unusual of the hundreds of pagodas sponsored by devoutly Buddhist Ly Dynasty kings in the eleventh century, and represents a flowering of Vietnamese art. The tiny wooden sanctuary, dedicated to Quan Am whose statue nestles inside, is only three square metres in size and is supported on a single column rising from the middle of an artificial lake, the whole structure designed to resemble a lotus blossom, the Buddhist symbol of enlightenment. In fact this is by no means the original building – the concrete pillar is a real giveaway – and the last reconstruction took place after departing French troops blew up the pagoda in 1954.

The pagoda's **origins** are uncertain but a popular legend recounts that it was founded in 1049 by King Ly Thai Tong, an ardent Buddhist with no male offspring. The goddess Quan Am appeared before the king in a dream, sitting on her lotus throne and holding out to him an infant boy. Soon after, the king married a village girl who bore him a son and heir, and he erected a pagoda shaped like a lotus blossom in thanks. The fact that King Ly Thai Tong already had a son born in 1022, six years before he came to the throne, gives greater credence to a less romantic version. According to this story, King Ly Thai Tong dreamt that Quan Am invited him to join her on the lotus throne. The king's advisers, deeming this an ill omen, advised him to found a pagoda where they could pray for their sovereign's longevity.

Whatever the truth, most people find the pagoda an anticlimax – partly because of its size and the concrete restoration work, and partly because of the overpowering presence of Ho Chi Minh's Museum. Behind the pagoda grows a **bo tree**, said to be an offshoot of the one under which the Buddha gained enlightenment, which was presented to Ho Chi Minh on a visit to India in 1958. Finally, take a peek in the adjacent **Dien Huu Pagoda** (daily 6–11am & 2–6pm): inside is a delightfully intimate courtyard full of potted plants and bonsai trees.

Ho Chi Minh's Museum

The angular, white building just 200m west of the One Pillar Pagoda is **Ho Chi Minh's Museum** (daily 8–11am & 2–4pm; Mon & Fri closed 2–4pm; 15,000đ), built with Soviet aid and inaugurated on May 19, 1990, the hundredth anniversary of Ho's birth. The museum celebrates Ho Chi Minh's life and the pivotal role he played in the nation's history; not surprisingly, this is also a favourite for school outings. Exhibits around the hall's outer wall focus on Ho's life and the "Vietnamese Revolution" in the context of social-ism's international development, including documents, photographs and a smattering of personal possessions, among them a suspiciously new-looking disguise Ho supposedly adopted when escaping from Hong Kong (see box on p.334 for more on Ho's life story). Running parallel on the inner ring are a series of heavily metaphoric "spatial images", six tableaux portraying signifi-cant places and events, from Ho's birthplace in Nghe An to Pac Bo cave and ending with a symbolic rendering of Vietnam's reunification. Go in for the surreal nature of the whole experience, but don't expect to come away having learnt much more about the man.

The Military History Museum and the Cot Co Flag Tower

From Ho Chi Minh's Museum, head back east past Ba Dinh Square to Dien Bien Phu, a road lined with gnarled trees and former colonial offices - inter-spersed with gingerbread villas. Around 500m from the square, Lenin's statue still stands opposite a white arcaded building housing the **Military History Museum** at 28 Dien Bien Phu (Tues–Thurs, Sat & Sun 8–11.30am & 1–4.30pm; 20,000đ). While ostensibly tracing the story of the People's Army from its foundation in 1944, in reality the museum chronicles national history from the 1930s to the present day, a period dominated by the French and American wars, though it's noticeably quiet on China and Cambodia.

The museum forecourt is full of weaponry: pride of place goes to a Russian MiG 21 fighter, alongside artillery from the battle of Dien Bien Phu (see box, p.439) and a tank from the American War, while the second courtyard is dominated by the mangled wreckage of assorted American planes piled against a tree. The exhibition proper starts on the arcaded building's second floor and runs chronologically from the 1930 Nghe Tinh Uprising, through the August Revolution to the "People's War" against the French, culminating in the decisive **battle of Dien Bien Phu**. If there's sufficient demand, they'll show an English-language video to accompany the battle's diorama; despite the heavy propaganda overlay, the archive footage is fascinating, including Viet Minh hauling artillery up mountain slopes and clouds of French parachutists. Naturally, General Giap and Ho Chi Minh make star appearances – after the ubiquitous still images, it's a shock to see Ho animated. The American War, covered in a separate hall at the rear, receives similar treatment with film of the relentless drive south to "liberate" Saigon in 1975.

Within the museum compound stands the thirty-metre **Cot Co Flag Tower**, one of the few remnants of Emperor Gia Long's early nineteenth-century citadel, where the national flag now billows in place of the emperor's yellow banner. In 1812, Vietnamese architects added several towers to the otherwise European-designed citadel, and when the French flattened the ramparts in the 1890s they kept Cot Co as a handy lookout post and signal-ling tower. From the terrace you look out over today's citadel, harbouring the army headquarters and relics of the fifteenth-century Imperial City, which are slowly being restored for the city's millennial celebrations in 2010.

The public are occasionally allowed in to see progress, but for the moment only the citadel's north gate, on Phan Dinh Phung opposite Chau Bac Church, is permanently on view, its brickwork heavily scarred in a French bombardment in 1882.

Vietnam Fine Arts Museum

From the Military History Museum follow Hoang Dieu Avenue south, past the wonderfully flamboyant Chinese embassy, and turn right on Cau Ba Quat to find a three-storey colonial block with chocolate-brown shutters. The **Vietnam Fine Arts Museum** at 66 Nguyen Thai Hoc (Tues, Thurs, Fri & Sun 8am–5pm; Wed & Sat 8.30am–9pm; 20,000đ) not only boasts the country's most comprehensive collection of fine art, but it is also unusually well presented, with plenty of information in English. Arranged chronologically, the museum illustrates the main themes of Vietnam's artistic development, kicking off with a collection of Dong Son drums (see p.364) and graceful Cham dancers. Though once again many are reproductions, there are some fine pieces, notably among the seventeenth- and eighteenth-century Buddhist art which spawned such masterpieces as Tay Phuong's superbly lifelike statues (see p.390). Other highlights include extensive collections of folk art and ethnic minority art, and an interesting exhibition of twentieth-century artists charting the evolution from a solidly European style through Socialist Realism to the emergence of a distinct Vietnamese school of art.

The Temple of Literature

Across busy Nguyen Thai Hoc Avenue is Hanoi's most revered temple complex, the **Temple of Literature**, or **Van Mieu**, both Vietnam's principal Confucian sanctuary and its historical centre of learning (daily: April–Sept 7.30am–5.30pm; Oct–March 8am–5pm; 5000đ). The temple is also one of the few remnants of the Ly kings' original city and retains a strong sense of harmony despite reconstruction and embellishment over the nine hundred years since its dedication in 1070.

▲ Traditional musicians at the Temple of Literature

Entry is through the two-tiered Van Mieu Gate on Quoc Tu Giam. The temple's ground plan, modelled on that of Confucius's birthplace in Qufu, China, consists of a succession of five walled courtyards. The first two are havens of trim lawns and noble trees separated by a simple pavilion; entry to the third is via the imposing Khue Van Cac, a double-roofed gateway built in 1805, its wooden upper storey ornamented with four radiating suns. Central to the third courtyard is the Well of Heavenly Clarity – a rectangular pond – to either side of which stand the temple's most valuable relics, 82 stone **stelae** mounted on tortoises. Each stele records the results of a state examination held at the National Academy between 1442 and 1779, though the practice only started in 1484, and gives brief biographical details of successful candidates. It's estimated that up to thirty stelae have gone missing or disintegrated over the years, but the two oldest, dating from 1442 and 1448, occupy centre spot on opposite sides of the pond.

Passing through the Gate of Great Success brings you to the fourth courtyard and the main temple buildings. Two pavilions on either side once contained altars dedicated to the 72 disciples of Confucius, but now house administrative offices and souvenir shops. At Tet (Vietnamese New Year) this courtyard is the scene of calligraphy competitions and "human chess games", with people instead of wooden pieces on the square paving stones.

The temple's **ceremonial hall**, a long, low building whose sweeping tiled roof is crowned by two lithe dragons bracketing a full moon, stands on the courtyard's north side. Here the king and his mandarins would make sacrifices before the altar of Confucius, accompanied by booming drums and bronze bells echoing among the magnificent ironwood pillars. Directly behind the ceremonial hall lies the **temple sanctuary**, at one time prohibited even to the king, where Confucius sits with his four principal disciples, resplendent in vivid reds and golds.

Becoming a mandarin

Examinations for admission to the **Imperial bureaucracy** were introduced by the Ly kings in the eleventh century as part of a range of reforms that served to underpin the nation's stability for several centuries. Vietnam's exams were based on the Chinese system, though included Buddhist and Taoist texts along with the Confucian classics. It took until the fifteenth century, however, for academic success, rather than noble birth or patronage, to become the primary means of entry to the civil service. By this time the system was open to **all males**, excluding "traitors, rebels, immoral people and actors", but in practice very few candidates outside the scholar-gentry class progressed beyond the lowest rung.

First came **regional exams**, *thi huong*, after which successful students (who could be any age from 16 to 61) would head for Hanoi, equipped with their sleeping mat, ink-stone and writing brush, to take part in the second-level *thi hoi*. These **national exams** might last up to six weeks and were as much an evaluation of poetic style and knowledge of the classic texts as they were of administrative ability; it was even felt necessary to ban the sale of strong liquor to candidates in the 1870s. Those who passed all stages were granted a doctorate, *tien si*, and were eligible for the third and final test, the *thi dinh*, or **palace exam**, set by the king himself. Some years as few as three *tien si* would be awarded whereas the total number of candidates could be as high as six thousand, and during nearly three hundred exams held between 1076 and 1779, only 2313 *tien si* were recorded. Afterwards the king would give his new mandarins a cap, gown, parasol and a horse on which to return to their home village in triumphal procession.

The fifth and final courtyard housed the **National Academy**, regarded as Vietnam's first university, which was founded in 1076 to educate princes and high officials in Confucian doctrine. Later the academy held triennial examinations to select the country's senior mandarins (see box opposite), a practice that continued almost uninterrupted until 1802 when Emperor Gia Long moved the nation's capital to Hué. In 1947 French bombs destroyed the academy buildings but they have now been painstakingly reconstructed, including an elegant two-storey pavilion housing a small museum and an altar dedicated to a noted director of the university in the fourteenth century, Chu Van An. Upstairs, three more statues honour King Ly Thanh Tong, the founder of Van Mieu; Ly Than Tong, who added the university; and Le Thanh Tong, instigator of the stelae. The exhibits are mostly post-eighteenth century, including 1920s photos of the temple, and students' textbooks, ink-stones and other accoutrements, such as a wine gourd for the fashion-conscious nineteenth-century scholar. Recitals of traditional music are held in the side-pavilion according to demand.

West Lake

Back in the mists of time, a gifted monk returned from China, bearing quantities of bronze as a reward for curing the emperor's illness. The monk gave most of the metal to the state but from a small lump he fashioned a bell, whose ring was so pure it resonated throughout the land and beyond the mountains. The sound reached the ears of a golden buffalo calf inside the Chinese Imperial treasury; the creature followed the bell, mistaking it for the call of its mother. Then the bell fell silent and the calf spun round and round, not knowing which way to go. Eventually, it trampled a vast hollow which filled with water and became **West Lake**, *Ho Tay*. Some say that the golden buffalo is still there, at the bottom of the lake, but can only be retrieved by a man assisted by his ten natural sons.

More prosaically, West Lake is a shallow lagoon left behind as the Red River shifted course eastward to leave a narrow strip of land, reinforced over the centuries with massive embankments, separating the lake and river. The lake was traditionally an area for royal recreation or spiritual pursuits, where monarchs erected summer palaces and sponsored religious foundations, among them Hanoi's most ancient pagoda, **Tran Quoc**. In the seventeenth century, villagers built a causeway across the lake's southeast corner, creating a small fishing lake now called **Truc Bach** and ringed with little cafés.

In the last decade or so, West Lake has once again become Hanoi's most fashionable address, complete with exclusive residential developments, lakeside clubs, spas and a clutch of luxury hotels. For now, however, a lakeside walk still makes a pleasant excursion with one or two sights to aim for, while Hanoi's newest cultural asset, the **Museum of Ethnology**, southwest of the lake, is best tackled by car or bus. Alternatively, the attractions grouped along the causeway, described below, are only about 500m north of the Presidential Palace and can easily be combined with a visit to the monuments around Ba Dinh Square.

The causeway and Truc Bach Lake

The name **Truc Bach** derives from an eighteenth-century summer palace built by the ruling Trinh lords which later became a place of detention for disagreeable concubines and other "errant women", who were put to work weaving fine white silk, *truc bach*. The palace no longer exists but eleventh-century **Quan Thanh Temple** (daily 8am–4.30pm; 2000đ) still stands on the lake's southeast bank, erected by King Ly Thai To and dedicated to the Guardian of the North, Tran Vo, who protects the city from malevolent spirits. Quan Thanh has been rebuilt several times, most recently in 1893, along the way losing nearly all its original features, but it's well worth wandering into the shady courtyard to see the **statue** of Tran Vo, cast in black bronze in 1677 and seated on the main altar. The statue, nearly 4m high and weighing 4 tonnes, portrays the Taoist god accompanied by his two animal emblems, a serpent and turtle; it was the creation of a craftsman called Trum Trong whose own statue, fashioned in stone and sporting a grey headscarf, sits off to one side. The shrine room also boasts a valuable collection of seventeenth- and eighteenth-century poems and parallel sentences (boards inscribed with wise maxims and hung in pairs on adjacent columns), most with intricate, mother-of-pearl inlay work.

The gate of Quan Thanh is just a few paces south of the **causeway**, Thanh Nien, an avenue of flame trees that is a popular picnic spot in summer when a cooling breeze comes off the water and hawkers set up shop along the grass verges. Where the road bears gently right, keep your eyes peeled for a small memorial in the pavement on the Truc Bach side, which is dedicated to teams of **anti-aircraft gunners** stationed here during the American War. In particular the memorial commemorates the downing of Navy Lieutenant Commander John McCain, who parachuted into Truc Bach Lake in October 1967 and survived more than five years in the "Hanoi Hilton". He went on to run for US president in 2008, only to be beaten by Barack Obama.

Continuing along the causeway you come to Hanoi's oldest religious foundation, **Tran Quoc Pagoda**, occupying a tiny island off Thanh Nien in West Lake (daily 7–11.30am & 1.30–6pm; free). The pagoda's exact origins are uncertain but it's usually attributed to the sixth-century early Ly Dynasty during a brief interlude in ten centuries of Chinese domination. In the early seventeenth century, when Buddhism was enjoying a revival, the pagoda was moved from beside the Red River to its present, less vulnerable location. Entry is along a narrow, brick causeway lying just above the water, past a collection of imposing brick stupas, the latest of which – towering over its more modest neighbours – was erected in 2003 on the death of the then master of the pagoda. The sanctuary's restrained interior and general configuration are typical of northern Vietnamese pagodas though there's nothing inside of particular importance. Note that visitors are requested not to wear shorts.

Around West Lake

The east side of West Lake is now largely built up, but it does have a sprinkling of mildly interesting sights. On Yen Phu Avenue, halfway up the Red River embankment from the causeway, an arch on the left – inscribed "Lang Yen Phu" – marks the entrance to a narrow lane, down which **Yen Phu Temple** merits a quick detour for its massive entrance hall and a jolly group of statuettes making offerings before the altar. Continuing north, past ostentatious villas – fantasy houses combining a touch of Spanish hacienda with a slice of French château – you get an idea of the pace of development in this district, which for a while outstripped any attempt at planning or design controls. The most notorious example was illegal construction work just east of here, which caused cracks up to 200m long in the city's 1000-year-old flood defences. After a much publicized enquiry, in which a few heads rolled, some offending structures were torn down. Ever since, there have been persistent rumours that all buildings between the embankment and the river will have to go.

About a kilometre from the causeway, the red-tiled roofs of **Kim Lien Pagoda** huddle in the shadow of the *Sheraton Hotel*. The pagoda's best attributes are its elaborate carvings and unplastered brick walls dating from an eighteenth-century rebuild. Even if pagodas aren't your thing, you could always come out here to indulge yourself at the nearby Zen Spa (see "Listings", p.387). The surrounding district, **Nghi Tam**, was traditionally a flower-producing area and you'll still find one or two pockets of chrysanthemum, peach or kumquat – depending on the time of year – between the encroaching buildings. If you're an early riser, it's worth venturing this way at sunrise when Hanoi's flower-sellers gather on a dusty patch of ground to select their choice of blooms at the wholesale **flower market** (see "Shopping and markets", p.382).

Turning left onto Xuan Dieu, and then left again on Dang Thai Mai, takes you along the **Ho Tay Peninsula** through upmarket housing estates to a row of popular lakeside restaurants and **Phu Tay Ho**. This temple is dedicated to Thanh Mau, the Mother Goddess, who in the seventeenth century appeared as a beautiful girl to a famous scholar out boating on the lake. She refused to reveal her name, just smiled enigmatically, recited some poetry and disappeared. But when the scholar worked out her identity from the poem, local villagers erected a temple where they still occasionally worship the goddess in trances – as at Hon Chen Temple in Hué (see p.313). Phu Tay Ho attracts few tourists and the petitioners here are mostly women and young people asking for favours by burning their fake dollars under the banyan trees; according to Chinese belief, the bats depicted on the facades are symbolic of five wishes – for longevity, security, success, happiness and health.

Museum of Ethnology

Although the **Museum of Ethnology** (Tues–Sun 8.30am–5.30pm; 20,000đ) is a bit of a trek, out in the suburbs of Hanoi on Nguyen Van Huyen, it more than repays the effort, particularly if you'll be visiting any of the minority areas. Spread across two floors, the displays are well presented and there's a fair amount of information in English on all the major ethnic groups. Musical instruments, games, traditional dress and other domestic items which fill the showcases are brought to life through musical recordings, photos and plenty of life-size models, as well as captivating videos of festivals and shamanistic rites. This wealth of creativity amply illustrates some of the difficulties ethnologists are up against – the museum also acts as a research institute charged with producing ethnologies for Vietnam's 54 main groups plus their confusion of sub-groups (for more on the ethnic minorities, see Contexts, p.492). The grounds contain a growing collection of minority houses relocated from all over Vietnam, dominated by a beautiful example of a Bahnar communal house. To find the museum, follow Thuy Khue Avenue along the southern edge of West Lake and then keep heading west to find the museum 6km out of town, signposted left off Hoang Quoc Viet. City bus #14 stops on the main road 500m from the museum, or a taxi from the Old Quarter should cost around 60,000đ.

On the way back into central Hanoi, you might want to make a brief detour to Ngoc Ha Village, where the mangled undercarriage of an American **B-52 bomber** lies half-submerged in a small lake. The plane was one of 23 shot down in December 1972 and now serves as a memorial to those who died during intensive raids known as the "Christmas Bombing" (see box, p.347). The lake lies just off Hoang Hoa Tham Avenue towards its eastern end, where a small sign points 100m down a narrow lane between nos. 55 and 57.

Eating

The choice of eating options in Hanoi now rivals Ho Chi Minh City in terms of quality, range and sophistication. You'll find everything from humble **food stalls** and **street kitchens**, the best dishing out top-quality food for next to nothing, to an increasing number of stylish international **restaurants**, mostly found around Hoan Kiem Lake and in the French Quarter: check English-language listings magazines such as *Pathfinder* or the excellent *New Hanoian* website (Ⓦ www.newhanoian.com) for the latest newcomers. There's no shortage, either, of **cafés**, whether one-room coffee houses serving thick, strong cups of the local brew, or fancy Western-style places serving cappuccinos and café lattes. Check out, too, some of the first-class **patisseries** and the handful of **ice-cream parlours**, catering to all tastes, from green-tea flavour to young rice or rum 'n' raisin.

If you are self-catering, there are two well-stocked and easily accessible **supermarkets**, *Citimart*, on the ground floor of Hanoi Towers, and *Intimex*, over the road from Hoan Kiem Lake's western edge. You may also want to find out more about the local cuisine by taking **cooking classes** (though they are cheaper in Hoi An; see p.275). The best course in the capital is at Hidden Hanoi, 137 Nghi Tam, near the *Sheraton Hotel* (Ⓦ www.hiddenhanoi.com.vn), which runs classes (Mon–Sat 11am–2pm) for $40 per person, including lunch: *Highway 4* (see opposite; from $26) and *Hoa Sua* (see p.377; from $22) both run similar courses, too.

Street food

For sheer value for money and atmosphere your best option is to eat either at the rock-bottom, stove-and-stools **food stalls** or at the slightly more upmarket **street kitchens**, most of which specialize in just one or two types of food. You'll find food stalls and street kitchens scattered across the city, often with no recognizable name and little to choose between individual establishments, but there are a few that stand out from the crowd: we've listed below some of the best places to sample typical Hanoi street dishes.

14 Hang Ga The place to try *banh cuon*, a Hanoi snack consisting of almost transparent rice-flour pancakes usually stuffed with minced pork and black mushrooms and sprinkled with fried shallots.

52 Ly Quoc Su Come here for *banh goi*, fried pastries filled with vermicelli, minced pork and mushrooms, and eaten with a thin sweet sauce, parsley and chilli.

67 Hang Dieu The speciality dish is *bun bo nam bo*, generous bowlfuls of lean beef and noodles, topped with a mound of roasted nuts, garlic and basil.

1 Hang Manh and **1 Pho Hue** Both serve *bun cha*, a Hanoian favourite consisting of barbequed pork chunks in fish sauce, served up with a plate of cold rice noodles.

34 Cau Go and **48b Phan Boi Chau** These two places specialize in *bun rieu cua*, crab noodle soup laced with tomatoes, spring onions and fried shallots, and usually eaten for breakfast.

104 Hang Bac and **45 Ly Quoc Su** Both serve delicious *nem chua nuong*, grilled spring rolls, usually served up with cucumber and/or green mango.

Pho Hoan Kiem and **31 Le Van Huu** Both good places to try *nom*, finely shredded papaya topped with dried beef, chilli and peanuts, and sometimes slices of barbecued quail.

Pho Gia Truyen 49 Bat Dan and **10 Ly Quoc Su** Hanoians come here for breakfast to eat the city's most famous dish, *pho bo*, a beef noodle soup with chopped spring onion.

Restaurants

One step up from the street kitchens (see opposite), at the inexpensive end of the scale, are the excellent-value local **restaurants**. Moving up a notch you'll find a growing number of moderately priced Western-style establishments which serve a range of cuisine, from classic Vietnamese dishes to increasingly sophisticated Western fare, via sandwiches, pizzas and burgers for the homesick. Top-notch restaurants offering Vietnamese or international cuisine in atmospheric surroundings are on the increase, too, as Hanoi challenges Ho Chi Minh City's culinary supremacy.

When it comes to number and variety of budget and mid-price eating places, the **Old Quarter** and the streets to the west of Hoan Kiem Lake take some beating, while Hanoi's glitziest dining rooms tend to be located in the **French Quarter**. Here several moderately priced restaurants are charmingly housed in renovated colonial villas; there's also a smattering of less formal, local eating places and cafés to suit more modest budgets. Further out of the centre there are a few places scattered in the outer districts that come in useful for a respite from sightseeing around Ho Chi Minh's Mausoleum and West Lake.

Restaurants tend to be small: in the listings below, we've given phone numbers for those where it's advisable to make **reservations**. Note also that even though this is the capital city, you still need to **eat early**: whatever the advertised closing time might be, local places stop serving before 8pm and peak time is 6–7pm, while Western-style restaurants and hotels tend to allow an extra hour or two.

The Old Quarter and west of Hoan Kiem Lake

The following are all marked on Central Hanoi map on pp.354–355.

69 Bar & Restaurant 69 Ma May. Exposed beams and brickwork give a rustic feel to this traditional house now converted to a lively bar-cum-restaurant. Some of the more innovative dishes include caramelised pork claypot with coconut cream, while the brave can sample home-made rice wine such as Fire Arrow and Violet Ticky. 9am–11pm.

Bach Giai 23 Hang Mam. One of a growing number of Old Quarter restaurants making the most of their tube-house decor. This unpretentious and inexpensive place offers traditional foods, from breakfast pho and rice soups to full meals. The spring rolls and beef with pepper come highly recommended. 7am–10pm.

Bittet 51 Hang Buom. Hidden down a long, dark passage at the back of a tube-house (see p.360), this small and bustling restaurant serves platters of *bittet* – a Vietnamese corruption of French *biftek* – with lashings of garlic and chips for 30,000đ. Or you can opt for roast chicken, roast pigeon, crab or prawn. 5–9pm.

Cha Ca La Vong 14 Cha Ca ☎04/3825 3929. Although it's definitely seen better days, this place – founded in 1871 – is a local institution. It serves just one dish: *cha ca*, fried fish with fresh dill cooked at your table on a brazier, then eaten with cold rice noodles, chilli and peanuts. At 70,000đ, it's moderately expensive for what you get. 11am–2pm & 4.30–10pm.

Cha Ca Thang Long 31 Duong Thanh. Patronized by locals, this is a newer and less touristy version of *Cha Ca La Vong* (see above). Again, there's only one dish – do-it-yourself fried fish with lashings of fresh dill – for 80,000đ a head, but portions are generous. 10am–3pm & 5–10pm.

Green Tangerine 48 Hang Be ☎04/3825 1286. The setting is a 1920s Art Deco villa and its lovely, plant-filled courtyard. The food is Vietnamese–French fusion: rich and unusual flavour combinations such as smoked duck breast with goat's cheese and red tuna carpaccio with frozen yoghurt and lime. The two-course set lunch (147,000đ) is excellent value. Otherwise, this is definitely one for a splurge – a meal for two will set you back $40 or more. 11am–11pm; reservations essential.

Highway 4 5 Hang Tre ☎04/3926 0639. Midway between a restaurant and a bar, *Highway 4* offers moderately priced mainly north Vietnamese dishes – steamboat and earthen-pot dishes, as well as more innovative fare such as their famous catfish spring rolls – to accompany traditional rice wine liquors. These come in more than thirty varieties, the medicinal benefits of which are explained in the English-language menu. There is a range of seating over three floors, culminating in a great roof terrace (reservations recommended). 10am–1am; food served to 11pm.

Kangaroo Café 18 Bao Khanh. Popular Australian-run tour agent-cum-café (see p.349) serving fresh, wholesome food – including a good selection of vegetarian fare – using organic produce as far as possible. The all-day breakfasts and bangers-and-mash are recommended. 7.30am–10pm.

La Place 4 Au Trieu. Sweet little place with views of the cathedral square from its picture windows. The dishes are small but well prepared, and on the upper floor they provide crayons and paper tablecloths so you can doodle away the sometimes considerable wait for your meal. The coconut chicken curry is a popular choice (60,000đ), though the spring rolls are even better. 8am–10.30pm.

La Salsa 25 Nha Tho. Decently-priced tapas (from 20,000đ), gazpacho and the like in a knockout location opposite the cathedral; the two-course set lunches are good value at 95,000đ, while of an evening, the ground-floor bar is also a popular drinking hole for local expats. 10am–11pm.

Little Hanoi 9 & 14 Ta Hien ☏04/3926 0168. Cosy, friendly and great-value restaurant on a bustling sidestreet, serving lip-smacking Vietnamese home cooking among bamboo knick-knacks. Try the fried tuna with lemon butter or the house special, spicy fried chicken with five tastes, including lashings of garlic and ginger. Even though they have two outlets, you might need to book ahead. 10am–11pm.

Little Hanoi 21 Hang Gai. Not to be confused with the above, this intimate café-restaurant on a busy junction just off Hoan Kiem Lake is perennially popular for its good-value salads, soups, filled baguettes (to eat in or take away) and other light meals, plus an extensive range of bar drinks. 7.30am–11pm.

Pepperonis I & Pepperonis II 29 Ly Quoc Su & 31 Bao Khanh. With two outlets in the cathedral area, this cheap-and-cheerful pizza chain has found a winning formula in its all-you-can-eat buffets: pasta and salad lunch buffet (Mon–Fri 11am–1pm; 48,000đ) and evening pizza buffet (Mon, Wed & Fri 6–9.30pm; 78,000đ); get there early to grab a table. 8am–midnight.

Sohot 2 Au Trieu. This place has it all – a wide selection of excellent food, swish decor, views of the cathedral, and prices around half what they should be. As such it has become hugely popular with affluent Hanoian youths; come for an insight into where the city is heading. 9am–11pm.

Tamarind Café 80 Ma May. A little pricey but worth it for the well-presented contemporary vegetarian food (organic where possible), fresh fruit juices and herbal teas, with a laidback vibe and decor to match: plump sofas, Japanese calligraphy prints and arty Asian-style seating platforms at the rear. It's also home to Handspan's booking desk (see p.349). 6am–11pm.

Tandoor 24 Hang Be. A perennially popular Indian restaurant with simple decor but cracking curries: fish tikka, mutton vindaloo and an extensive range of mouthwatering vegetarian dishes. The thali set meals offer excellent value at 55,000đ to 75,000đ. 11am–2.30pm & 6–10.30pm.

The French Quarter

The following are all marked on the Central Hanoi map on pp.354–355, unless otherwise stated.

Al Fresco's 23 Hai Ba Trung ☏04/3826 7782. The sister restaurant to Pepperonis (see opposite) is a relaxed place with a pleasant balcony on the first floor. Café, bar and grill in one, the menu includes good-quality Aussie and international fare, including ribs, salads, steaks and a choice of thin- or thick-crust pizzas from 92,000đ upwards, all served in hefty portions. 10am–10.30pm.

Bangkok Hanoi 52a Ly Thuong Kiet. Give your taste buds a work out with a fiery thom yam soup followed by a green, yellow or red Thai curry, washed down with a Singha beer. Despite the fancy exterior, it's not too pricey – main dishes start at around 40,000đ. 10am–10pm.

Bobby Chinn 1 Ba Trieu ☏04/3934 8577. Hanoi's standard-setting dining experience features Asian-Californian fusion food, mood music, contemporary Vietnamese art and an oh-so-laidback chill-out zone screened by silk-gauze partitions – indulge yourself with an Egyptian water-pipe (shisha). The limited lunchtime menu offers salads, sandwiches and pasta dishes from around $8, while in the evening a starter and main course will set you back around $30. The menu is seasonal but usually contains signature dishes such as filet mignon, blackened barramundi and, as a side dish, grapes wrapped in goat's cheese with a pistachio crust. 11am–11pm.

Halia 83b Ly Thuong Kiet. A Singaporean restaurant serving European food in the business-heavy Pacific Place complex – "cosmopolitan" may be le mot juste. Lobster linguini and sauteed mushrooms with duck egg jump out from a slightly overpriced menu, though the set lunches ($18; 11.30am–2.30pm) are good value. 11am–11pm.

Highway 4 54 Mai Hac De ☏04/976 2647. The sister outlet to Highway 4 (see p.375) is very much a restaurant – bigger, less rustic and more spacious – but otherwise follows the same successful formula: varied seating areas, a well-priced menu of classic Vietnamese flavours and, of course, the lip-smacking liquors and herbal teas.

Vietnamese street food

From hawkers with cauldrons of soup hanging from shoulder poles, to push carts, market stalls and makeshift "street kitchens", Vietnam's street food is unsurpassed. Often better quality than what's found in restaurants, it's much cheaper and a lot more fun. Though the choice is enormous, most vendors are highly specialized, serving one type of food or even just a single dish, but they cook it to perfection. All you need is a bit of judicious selection – look for places with a fast turnover, where the ingredients are obviously fresh – and a smattering of basic vocabulary.

A wealth of flavours

Throughout Vietnam street vendors sell rice-flower crackers, corn cobs (steamed, fried or grilled), fish balls, whole dried squid barbecued over coals, a myriad of freshly cooked fritters, glutinous rice and Chinese-style dumplings filled with tasty morsels and intriguing parcels steamed in banana leaves.

Thanks to Vietnam's varied topography and climate, its cooks have an unusually broad range of ingredients to call on, from temperate fruits and vegetables grown in the cool uplands to the tropical bounty of the Mekong Delta, so you'll find a great deal of regional variation in the food on offer: typical **northern** dishes include hotpots, rice gruels and sweet and sour soups, while **southern** flavours include curries and spicy dipping sauces, often married with a touch of sugar and coconut milk to balance the heat. Throughout Vietnam you'll find a strong **vegetarian** tradition, a legacy of Buddhism, while the French introduced dairy products, wheat-flour bread and pastries – baguette-sellers are a common sight in Vietnam's markets.

Street vendor ▲

Pho bo ▼

Northern foods

The quintessential street food is **pho bo**, a beef noodle soup, originating in Hanoi but now found throughout Vietnam. It's primarily a breakfast dish, and on cold northern mornings you can't miss the great, steaming cauldrons. Perch on one of the low stools and, after helping yourself to crunchy bean sprouts and salad greens heaped on the table, add a sprinkling of red chillies and a squeeze of lime to taste and tuck into a hearty bowlful of broth garnished with slivers of beef.

Another not-to-be-missed northern delicacy is **bun cha**: small pieces of pork are barbecued on an open brazier, giving off an unmistakable aromatic smoke, then served on a bed of cold rice noodles with a bowl of herbs and salad greens and a sour-sweet dipping sauce. *Bun cha* is often accompanied by a plate of **nem** (spring rolls), deep-fried and filled with minced pork, rice vermicelli, finely chopped mushrooms and herbs. Or ring the changes with deep-fried crabmeat rolls, **nem cua be**.

Look out, too, for **banh cuon** – steamed, almost transparent, rice-flour pancakes folded over a dollop of minced pork and black mushrooms, garnished with deep-fried shallots and served with a light, sweetish dipping sauce.

Central and southern foods

While Hué is best known for its Imperial cuisine, it also has its own distinct street food. The traditional breakfast dish is **bun bo**, a flavoursome, slightly spicy take on the ubiquitous beef and rice-noodle soup, with citronella, shrimp and basil providing some extra zest. And make sure to try **banh khoai** – a cross between an omelette and a pancake; these crispy little egg and rice-flour crêpes combine shrimp, pork and bean sprouts. They're served with a peanut and sesame sauce, herbs and various greens, plus star fruit and green banana.

Hoi An's most famous dish is **cao lau**, a soup of rice-flour noodles, bean sprouts and pork crackling laced with mint and star anise. A close second, though, are the beautifully named **banh bao** ("white rose") – delicate parcels of minced crab or shrimp in manioc-flour wrappings,

▲ Nem

▼ Banh khoai

▼ Banh xeo

Foodstalls at the market ▲

Street food ▼

sprinkled with crispy onion flakes and a light, slightly sweet lemon dressing.

Heading south, **banh xeo** – sizzling pancake – is similar to Hué's *banh khoai*; wrap a small portion of pancake in rice paper with some herbs and salad leaves, then dunk it in a tangy sauce. A popular southern version of *nem* (spring rolls) sees barbecued pork strips, green banana and star fruit rolled in semi-transparent rice paper wrappers, and eaten with a rich peanut sauce.

Streetwise

Eating street food might seem a bit intimidating at first, but don't be put off. Since most vendors and many street kitchens serve only one dish, and since everything is cooked in front of you, you can get a long way by simply pointing at what you want. If a whole range of prepared dishes and raw ingredients are on display, the place serves **com binh dan**, or people's meals. Again, select the dishes you want by pointing, but ask how much it costs before you tuck in (you pay at the end). Next find a spare seat and the food will be brought to you when it's ready.

On each table there'll be chopsticks, metal spoons, small squares of paper (which serve as tiny napkins) and tooth-picks. Select a pair of chopsticks, and a spoon if you're having soup, and wipe them thoroughly with some napkins – it won't necessarily make them any cleaner but you'll look like an expert. You'll also find condiments such as salt and pepper, limes and chilli flakes or chilli sauce and bottles of **nuoc mam**, Vietnam's famously pungent fish sauce, and often a bowl of salad greens, too, from which you help yourself.

There may be a waste bin under the table for the bones, shells, toothpicks, napkins and other debris, but if not, just chuck it all on the floor. It's fine to slurp your noodles and to hold your rice bowl up to your mouth and shovel away.

Phone ahead if you want a seat on the roof terrace. 10am–1am; food served until 11pm.

🏃 **Hoa Sua** 28a Ha Hoi ☎04/3942 4448. Well-presented Vietnamese and European food with a heavy French influence served on the plant-filled patio or in the a/c colonial villa buried in the backstreets – it's not well signed, but don't give up. *Hoa Sua* is part of a non-profit-making vocational training school giving disadvantaged children a start in the restaurant trade. Try a Vietnamese combo platter (35,000–48,000d), or one of the daily specials, but save room for a wicked dessert. Live music Sat (7–10pm). Mon–Fri 11am–10pm, Sat & Sun 7.30am–10pm.

Indochine 16 Nam Ngu ☎04/3942 4097. See map, p.350. Food of consistently high quality at reasonable prices keeps this well-established restaurant up there with its younger rivals. Beautifully presented, original Vietnamese specialities, from seafood spring rolls to steamboat or the famous prawn on sugar cane, is served either in the colonial villa or its patio-courtyard. Evenings are popular with tour groups, so reservations are recommended. Traditional Vietnamese music Tues & Thurs (7.30–9.30pm). 11am–2pm & 5.30–10pm.

🏃 **Koto** 59 Van Mieu ☎04/3747 0337. See map, p.351. Deservedly popular restaurant staffed by erstwhile street kids under a charity programme to train them in hospitality skills. Start the day with muesli and fresh fruits or a full buffet breakfast, then stop by later for a gourmet sandwich or a barbecued duck salad, but make sure you leave room for dessert. All proceeds are ploughed back into the charity, and you can also visit the training school by prior arrangement. 7am–10pm.

Le Tonkin 14 Ngo Van So ☎04/3943 3457. The garden lends more atmosphere to this sister restaurant of *Indochine* (see above), but otherwise it follows the same formula: elegant but not exorbitant dining which makes a great introduction to Vietnamese cuisine. Traditional music on Mon & Fri (7.30–9.30pm). 11am–2pm & 5.30–10pm.

Nang Tam Com Chay 79a Tran Hung Dao. Small, vegetarian restaurant down a quiet alley off Tran Hung Dao and named after Vietnamese Cinderella character. *Goi bo*, a main-course salad of banana flower, star fruit and pineapple, is recommended, or try one of the well-priced set menus all under 35,000d a head. The food's all tasty and MSG-free, though purists might not like the way some dishes emulate meat. 11am–2pm & 5–10pm.

Pane e Vino 3 Nguyen Khac Can. Popular with the local Italian community for its authentic cuisine and relaxed atmosphere. The menu ranges from *pecorino* salad and minestrone soup through *osso bucco*, roast lamb and veal *saltimbocca* to zabaglione and the obligatory tiramisu – not to mention the gourmet pasta and pizza dishes; count on around $15–20 per head for three courses, $3–7 for a pizza. There's a daily set lunch ($7.50) and a popular Fri night buffet with traditional music (7pm; $7). 8am–11pm.

🏃 **Quan An Ngon** 18 Phan Boi Chau. See map, p.351. A southern import, this open-air food court is a good place to sample upmarket street food in pleasant surroundings. Choose from the menu or see what takes your fancy at stalls cooking up Hanoi and Hué specialities around the garden seating area – there are more tables in the colonial villa behind. Avoid peak hours if you want to sit outside. 6.30am–10pm.

🏃 **Verticale** 19 Ngo Van So. Spice is the word at this converted colonial house – the laboratory-like ground floor is pungent with French chef Didier's cooking. Possibly the most carefully constructed dishes in the country, such as ocean *escabeche* and swordfish with avocado, and a good location – the open top level is perfect for an evening wine. Set meals from $30. 11am–2pm, 6pm–10pm; terrace bar open til midnight.

West and north of the centre

The following are all marked on the Hanoi map on pp.350–351.

Brothers Café 26 Nguyen Thai Hoc. Through a traditional entranceway on this busy main road, you'll find a peaceful courtyard restaurant with tables set out under the trees. They only serve buffets, which are well priced at $10 for lunch and $14 in the evening. 11.30am–2pm & 6.30–10pm.

Cafe Goethe 56 Nguyen Thai Hoc. Portions can be small for a restaurant with German pretensions, though prices are reasonable (from 70,000d for mains) and the outdoor courtyard is a pleasant place to eat. Part of the Goethe Institute, and handy for those touring the Temple of Literature and Fine Arts Museum. 8am–10pm.

Foodshop 45 59 Truc Bach. It's worth going out of your way to eat at this welcoming Indian restaurant in an interesting residential district overlooking Truc Bach Lake. The Indian-trained chef magics up a knockout range of curries and accompaniments, such as toothsome tandoor dishes and a cracking Kadhai chicken with big chunks of meat. Excellent value for money. 10am–10.30pm.

Ya Beirut 4/28 Xuan Dieu. Hidden down an alley opposite the *Sheraton* is Vietnam's first Lebanese restaurant; prices are reasonable from 100,000d for filling mains. The menu has English explanations for those that don't know their *hummus* from their *sambousik*. 4–10pm, Fri, Sat & Sun til 11pm.

Hanoi's unusual eats

In addition to the traditional favourite street food such as *bun cha* and pho, it's not uncommon to find dishes featuring goat, dog, rat, snake and porcupine. Ethically some readers may find this disturbing but the eating of animals is deeply entrenched in Vietnamese culture, and an invitation to share in the feast is to be considered an honour.

If you want to sample **dog meat** (*thit cho*), a northern speciality eaten mostly in winter and never during days one to ten of the lunar calendar month, then head out of Hanoi along the Red River dyke to **Nghi Tam Avenue**. There are dozens of stilt-house restaurants to choose from, though *Tran Muc* is consistently regarded as the best; alternatively, just head for the busiest. The dog meat comes boiled (*luoc*) or grilled (*cha nuong*) and served with green banana and tofu (*rua man*), and is washed down with rice wine.

Le Mat snake village – 4km over Chuong Duong Bridge in the Gia Lam District – is home to a slew of **snake-meat** restaurants, some of which play to the crowd with elaborate theatrics, including killing the snake in front of you. It's then served up in every possible form, from soup and crispy-fried skin accompanied by rice wine liquors laced with blood and bile. The guest of honour gets to eat the still pumping heart – beware, it's alleged to have amphetamine properties. Though not the cheapest of Le Mat's restaurants, *Quoc Trieu* (℡04/3827 2988; 10am–10pm) has a reliable reputation and leaves out the gory bits.

Cafés and patisseries

Hanoi's French legacy is particularly apparent in the city's adoption of **café** culture. The city boasts hundreds of local **cafés**, offering minimum comfort but great coffee – usually small, strong shots of the local brew – although the epicentre of Hanoi's café-bar scene is Bao Khanh/Hang Hanh, a bustling street near Hoan Kiem Lake, where young Vietnamese hang out. In addition, there is an ever-increasing number of sophisticated Western-style cafés, most of which also serve food, and a crop of outlets selling fine pastries, yoghurts and ice cream. Prices vary enormously: a standard *ca phé* (shot of filtered Vietnamese coffee; add *sua* for sweetened condensed milk) starts at 6,000đ at the less salubrious street-side shacks, rises to 15,000đ at places with indoor seating and aircon, then hits 30,000đ or more at upmarket establishments. Western-style lattes, cappucinos and the like start at around 35,000đ.

For a more traditional sugar-fix, try **chè**, halfway between a drink and a dessert; there's a clutch of outlets on the ground floor of Hom market, and a little place at 24 Ta Hien. For a few thousand dong you'll get a mug of thick, sweet soup, packed with beans, jelly, coconut and all kinds of seasonal fruits; in winter they also serve it hot, which brings out the sweetness more. **Juice bars** are also becoming increasingly popular: there are several along To Tich, on the Old Quarter's southern edge, which whisk up the fruit while you wait. For **ice cream**, *Fanny* at 48 Le Thai To serves up a bewildering array of flavours.

Cafés

The following are all marked on the Central Hanoi map on pp.354–355, unless otherwise specified.

Block House 61 To Ngoc Van. See map, p.350. Near the northern end of West Lake you'll find this curious military bunker whose dimly-lit innards have been plastered with newspaper pages; most people, however, sip their drinks on a roof affording unbeatable views of the lake.

Café Lam 60 Nguyen Huu Huan. This shabby but atmospheric one-room café made its name as a place for artists and young intellectuals to hang out. A few paid their bills with paintings, some of which still adorn the walls, and there's a bohemian vibe.

Hanoi Cinémathèque 22a Hai Ba Trung. Duck down the alley of the *Artist* hotel to find this delightful courtyard café-bar belonging to a cinema club (see p.386).

Highlands Coffee A Vietnamese Starbucks clone with an ever-increasing number of outlets; the best location is outside the Hanoi Opera House, closely followed by the one outside the Military History Museum (see map, p.351).

Hue Café 26 Hang Giay. This tiny store sells strong coffee from the Central Highlands; though quality is high and every cup is freshly ground, prices are very low. Also available is "weasel coffee", made from beans passed through said mammal's digestive system and far more delicious than it sounds; 250-gram bags make quite the souvenir for unsuspecting friends.

Kinh Do Café 252 Hang Bong. "Café 252" became famous after Cathérine Deneuve complimented the patron on his yoghurts, which still merit praise, as do the home-baked pastries. The decor's changed little over the years, though they now offer a wider range of foods, including well-prepared Vietnamese dishes, making it popular with locals, tourists and Francophile movie buffs.

Love Chocolate 26 To Ngoc Van. See map, p.350. Located some distance from the centre near the northern side of West Lake, but it's well worth the hike to this faux English living room; think mint paint, pot plants and flowery curtains, with batches of delicious home-made cookies rustled up daily.

Moca 14–16 Nha Tho. Located in the hip cathedral area, *Moca's* huge picture windows are ideal for people-watching over a mug of the creamiest, frothiest café latte in town. In winter hunker by the open fire.

Paris Deli 13 Nha Tho & 6 Phan Chu Trinh. Excellent coffee, tea and cakes at this French-style bakery and café with outlets in prime spots near the cathedral and the Opera House. They also serve reasonably priced sandwiches, savoury snacks and main meals.

Pho Co 11 Hang Gai. Hunting down the entrance to this fascinating place is hard enough: go through the art gallery, then beneath the birdcages and into a hushed courtyard, where you place your order. Head up the stairs, past the family altar, up a spiral staircase and one more flight of regular steps, and you'll finally reach a roof terrace high above Hoan Kiem Lake, where you can sample coffee with added egg white, if you dare.

Puku 60 Hang Trong. One of the main hangout venues for Hanoi expats, and deservedly so: good food and coffee – try the Kiwi breakfast at 70,000d – comfy sofas on the lower level, breezy views from the upper, and wi-fi access all around. Head down the hard-to-find alleyway and up the stairs on the left.

Student Café 2b Au Trieu. An amazingly cheap place considering its location directly in front of the cathedral: strong coffee and decent fruit shakes are available for 6,000d, and tiny meat toasties for even less. You get a small plastic chair to sit on – like being back in kindergarten – and another for your food or drink.

Thuy Ta 1 Le Thai To. A breezy lakeside café that's great for breakfast, afternoon tea or an evening beer. It also serves pastries, ice creams and a variety of light meals.

Patisseries and bakeries

Le Croissant 21 Ha Hoi. The bakery of the *Hoa Sua* (see p.377) turns out excellent breads, cakes, pastries and savoury snacks.

The Deli 59a Ly Thai To. On the ground floor of the *Press Club*, producing a mouthwatering array of home-made breads, quiches, cold cuts, cakes and suchlike to eat in or take away. It also has an extensive wine selection.

Maison Vanille 49 Phan Chu Trinh. Real Parisian-style bakery-cum-deli with all sorts of goodies from walnut bread and fruit tarts to cheese, paté and cold cuts. They also serve salads and other light meals in the upstairs café-restaurant.

Drinking, nightlife and entertainment

For a capital city, Hanoi is pretty sleepy: most **bars** outside the big hotels sweep up around midnight and **nightclubs** don't stay open much later. The authorities blow hot and cold over enforcing a midnight **curfew** on bars and clubs, but one or two places always seem to keep pouring until the last customer leaves: check the English-language listings magazines (see p.352) for the current situation. Each November, the Minsk Club puts on a popular **music festival**, featuring a wide range of acts from home and abroad; check ⓦwww .minskclubvietnam.com for details.

On the traditional side, even if you're not particularly into Western **classical music**, it's well worth catching a concert or ballet at the Opera House on Trang Tien, where occasional performances take place in truly sumptuous surroundings of plush red fabrics, mirrors and chandeliers; tickets (from 150,000đ) are available from the Opera House (daily 8am–5pm) or can be booked by phone or online (☎04/3565 1806 or 0912 021516, ⓦwww.ticketvn.com).

As for **traditional entertainment**, a performance of the water-puppets, Vietnam's charming contribution to the world of marionettes, should be high on everyone's itinerary. It's also worth catching some music, opera or dance at the *Ly Club* (see opposite). Otherwise, apart from the odd group playing traditional music at some of Hanoi's main tourist sights, there's little on offer in the cultural sphere that's easily accessible just yet. Very occasionally, events are listed in the English-language press, but are more likely to be announced on street banners or outside the venues themselves, so you'll have to ask around to see if there's anything interesting happening.

Bars, pubs and clubs

Hanoi's bar and club scene can't be described as wild, but the choice of **nightspots** is improving. You're no longer restricted to characterless hotel bars or psuedo-pubs, as the number of dedicated drinking holes, some of them packing a bit of designer flair, gradually increases, particularly on Ta Hien, a street packed with funky bars. Nevertheless, the busiest venues are without doubt the **bia hoi** outlets selling pitchers of the local brew. The most popular spot for foreigners to experience the bia hoi is at the cluster of outlets on the junction of Ta Hien and Luong Ngoc Quyen, known as "Bia Hoi Corner"; on busy nights customers sit across the junction, moving their plastic chairs in and out like a tide as the police come and go. Also worth trying is *Bia Tuoi Hoang Dat*, at 124a Hai Ba Trung, an upmarket bia hoi on four floors. Note that the Vietnamese tend to drink early, and by midnight few bars remain open. The following establishments are all marked on the Central Hanoi map on pp.354–355 unless otherwise specified.

Culi Café 40 Luong Ngoc Quyen. An Aussie-owned café-bar-restaurant in the Old Quarter. Choose between bar stools and music/sports videos in the downstairs bar or the chilled lounge above. Prices are cheap and the food's not bad.

Dragonfly 15 Hang Buom. Part stylish bar, part lively club, part comfy lounge, this venue has something for everyone; one of the better places to be locked in when the police are out on prohibition patrol.

Finnegan's 16a Duong Thanh. Quite why so many backpackers spend their Hanoi evenings in an Irish bar is open to question, though it's true that good Guinness goes down well anywhere. This is certainly the place to meet fellow travellers.

Funky Buddha 2 Ta Hien. A focus on fixtures, fittings and lighting has made this one of Hanoi's best-looking bars, and the drink prices remain reasonable too.

Half Man Half Noodle 62 Dao Duy Tu. Friendly little bar hidden away in the Old Quarter and a haunt of Hanoi's English-language teachers, though don't expect much action before 11pm.

I–Box 32 Le Thai To. Indulgent sofas, mock leopard-skin lampshades and vampish red velour set the tone in this café-bar. It's great for a quiet drink during the day, and in the evenings they often crank up the atmosphere with live music. Happy hour 5–8pm.

Inside Bar 28 Hang Hanh. One of Hanoi's more bizarre bars, this tiny drinking hole tucked down a corridor is not for claustrophobics. It's friendly, though, and cheap and generally stays open into the wee hours.

Jazz Club Minh 31 Luong Van Can ☎04/3828 7890. Live jazz every night led by the charismatic – and highly accomplished – Quyen Van Minh, Hanoi's answer to Ronnie Scott. Performances start at 8.30pm.

Le Pub 25 Hang Be. A good range of drinks at reasonable prices – including genuinely *cold* beers – plus above-average food, decent music and friendly bar staff ensures a real pub atmosphere at this English-run outlet in an Old Quarter tube-house. There are different drink promotions most days.

Loo Pub 1 Ta Hien. With toilet-shaped seating and deliberately suspicious-looking brown sand on the floor, this bar is one of the most distinctive – and noisy – in Hanoi. Worth a peep, if only for novelty value.

Mao's Red Lounge 7 Ta Hien. Cheap prices and strong cocktails make this two-level bar one of the most popular places on Hanoi's nighttime strip; at weekends, it can achieve a rowdiness quite at odds with its loungey setting and mood music.

Red Beer 97 Ma May. Microbrewery serving lip-smacking Belgian Red Beer and German pilsner lager, plus a limited range of soft drinks. Some of the food has a certain beery touch, too, such as steamed cuttle fish with Red Beer.

Roots 2 Luong Ngoc Quyen. The reggae and Latin music pumping out of the sound system make this a weekend favourite for those who want to dance; a slightly out-of-the-way location makes this one of the best bets for late-night drinking.

Solace Off Chuong Duong Do. One of those places you never really intend to end up at, but do anyway. A nightclub on a docked Red River boat, this was once one of the most popular places around; though things have gone downhill, it can still be good fun.

Tet Bar 2a Ta Hien. Hot, smoky and packed. The service is pleasingly prompt – even when you're desperate for a toasted sandwich at 2am – and you get a fair whack of grog for your dong.

The Cheeky Quarter 1 Ta Hien. Good music, great food and table football are on the cards here, though given the size and layout things can feel decidedly dead on an off-night.

Traditional Vietnamese entertainment

While in Hanoi most people devote an hour to the **water–puppets** (*mua roi nuoc*) – literally, puppets that dance on the water – a uniquely Vietnamese art form that originated in the Red River Delta (see p.513 for more background). Traditional performances consist of short scenes depicting rural life or historic events accompanied by mood-setting musical narration. By far the most popular, and most polished, of Hanoi's troupes is the Thang Long Water Puppet Troupe, which presents an updated repertoire and uses modern stage effects to create an engaging spectacle. They give several performances daily at the small, air-conditioned Kim Dong Theatre, 57 Dinh Tien Hoang (front rows 60,000đ, behind 40,000đ; ☏04/3824 9494 ⓦwww.thanglongwaterpuppet.org). Though these shows are largely put on for tourists, you can't help but admire the artistry and be charmed by the puppets' antics.

If that's whetted your appetite, you might like to try one of the weekly **cultural performances** held in a beautiful traditional theatre at the *Ly Club*, 51 Ly Thai To (☏04/3936 3069; Thurs 7pm; $6). Each week the club showcases a sampler of different musical and theatrical styles, including Cheo, Chau Van and Quan Ho (see Contexts, p.512, for more on these art forms).

Apart from the **folk music** groups playing at the Temple of Literature (see p.369) and one or two other tourist venues, at present these are the only easily accessible venues regularly showcasing Vietnamese traditional culture in Hanoi. However, the situation is evolving rapidly, so keep an eye on the English-language press, or ask around. It's also worth dropping by the theatres to see what's on. In the city centre, try the Hong Ha Theatre, 51 Duong Thanh (☏04/3825 2803), which hosts a varied programme of Hat Tuong, Cheo and Cai Luong, and the Labour Theatre (Rap Cong Nhan), 42 Trang Tien (☏04/3824 5707), offering traditional and contemporary music, dance and theatre.

Shopping and markets

When it comes to shopping for crafts, silk, accessories and souvenirs, Hanoi now offers the best overall choice, quality and value for money in the country. **Specialities** of the region are embroideries, wood- and stone- carvings, inlay work and lacquer, and the best areas to browse are the south of the Old Quarter and the streets around St Joseph's Cathedral. Though smarter establishments increasingly have fixed prices, at many shops you'll be expected to **bargain** (see Basics, p.65, for some tips), and the same goes, naturally, for market stalls. Hanoi has over fifty **markets**, selling predominantly foodstuffs (see below); for a greater variety of wares, **Cho Dong Xuan** and **Cho Hom** sell almost everything. There's also a weekly **night market** (Fri–Sun 6.30–11pm) in the Old Quarter when Hang Dao is closed to traffic. Stalls sell mainly clothes, toys and gimmicks aimed at locals, but it's worth a wander for the atmosphere if nothing else.

Food and flower markets

Hanoi's most numerous – and pungent – markets are those concentrating on **foodstuffs**. You'll rarely be too far from one, but among the most interesting is **Cho 19–12**, a traditional fresh-food market packed into two short alleys between Hai Ba Trung and Ly Thuong Kiet. Also worth exploring are Hanoi's largest covered market **Cho Dong Xuan**, located on Dong Xuan, with numerous sections to explore; and **Cho Hom** on Pho Hue.

One of Hanoi's more unusual and colourful markets, though you'll have to be up early to catch it, is the **flower market** held each dawn beside Nghi Tam Avenue at its most northerly junction with Yen Phu; action starts around 4am (5am in winter), and lasts around two hours. This is primarily a wholesale market catering to the city's army of itinerant flower-sellers, so prices are that bit cheaper than in town and you'll find people peddling wicker baskets, ferns and ribbons besides bundles of fresh-cut blooms.

Fabrics, handicrafts and souvenirs

Compared with Thailand, Vietnamese **silk** is slightly inferior quality but prices are lower and the tailoring is still good value. Though Hoi An is really Vietnam's tailoring capital, Hanoi has so many silk shops concentrated on Hang Gai, at the southern edge of the Old Quarter, that it's now referred to as "Silk Street";

▲ Hanoi street hawker

competition is fierce, but take care since you'll find a fair amount of tat among the more reputable outlets (see below). Classy designer boutiques offering excellent quality at premium prices are also now concentrating around the cathedral. Most bigger places have multilingual staff, accept credit cards and offer less expensive souvenirs as well, such as ties, purses, mobile-phone holders – very natty – and sensuous, silk sleeping bags.

Embroideries and drawn threadwork also make eminently packable souvenirs. Standard designs range from traditional Vietnamese to Santa Claus and robins, but you can also take along your own artwork for something different. Many of the big-name silk and accessories shops also sell embroidered items.

One of the more interesting shops is Craft Link (see below), run by a not-for-profit organization working with ethnic minorities and other small-scale producers of traditional **crafts**. They also organize a charity bazaar each November at the Museum of Ethnology, which is a great occasion attended by many of the craftspeople involved, including representatives from the minority villages.

Most ordinary souvenir shops also stock **ethnic minority crafts**, particularly the Hmong and Dao bags, coats and jewellery that are so popular in Sa Pa. Though it's virtually impossible to tell, in fact the majority of these are now made by factories in and around Hanoi, partly to meet the huge demand and partly to get a slice of the action. Of course, everyone will insist their goods are genuine, and they are very well made, but it's something to be aware of.

Another pretty portable souvenir is **lacquerware**. Chopsticks, boxes, bowls, vases – the variety of items coated in lacquer is endless. Natural lacquer gives a muted finish, usually in black or rusty reds. However, lacquerware in a rainbow array of colours – made from imported synthetic rather than natural lacquer – is now very popular in Old Quarter souvenir shops.

Other popular mementoes are embroidered and printed **T-shirts**: although the selection is limited, you'll find no shortage of places to buy them, notably on Hang Gai and Trang Tien. **Silk lanterns**, **water-puppets** and **silver items** – both plated and solid silver – make manageable souvenirs, as do hand-painted **greetings cards**, usually scenes of rural life or famous beauty spots on paper or silk; the best are unbelievably delicate and sell for next to nothing. It's illegal to export **antiques** from Vietnam, but you'll find plenty of "antique" jewellery or watches on sale, and beautifully crafted copies of ancient religious statues.

For more unusual mementoes, have a look at the traditional Vietnamese **musical instruments** on sale at a clutch of little workshops on Hang Manh and round the corner on Hang Non. Several small shops on Hang Bong supply Communist Party **banners and badges** as well as Vietnamese flags. **Propaganda posters** are another popular souvenir from the Communist days. You'll find a selection, both originals and copies, at 17 Nha Chung.

Clothes and accessories Kana, 41 Hang Trong, stocks traditional Vietnamese designs and some Western variations, while it's all French chic at Song, 27 Nha Tho (🌐www.valeriegregorimckenzie.com), and ethnic embroideries at Sapanesque, 45a Ly Quoc Su. Indigo, 65 Ma May, is a fair-trade outlet selling a limited range of clothes and bags in cotton, silk and linen. Aussie-owned Things of Substance, 5 Nha Tho, designs for Western sizes. At the other end of the spectrum, Ipa-Nima, 59g Hai Ba Trung, and its offshoot Tina Sparkle, 17 Nha Tho (🌐www.ipa-nima.com), make outrageous bags – and Ipa-Nima's decadent decor is worth a look. Beautiful handmade silk clothes are available at Co, 18 Nha To, and Marie-Linh, 74 Hang Trong (🌐www.marie-linh.com), while most of the silk shops and some of the embroidery shops listed below also sell ready-made clothes and accessories. For jewellery, Phuc Tin, 49 Hai Ba Trung & 22 Hang Gai (🌐www.phuctin.com), sells traditional and contemporary designs by a master silversmith and made in the family's workshop.

Embroidery Vietnam Quilts, 16 Hang Tre (ⓦwww .vietnam-quilts.org), is a not-for-profit organization raising funds for a variety of causes through the sale of quilts; all are made by women in rural provinces. For the very finest, albeit expensive, embroidered bedlinen, tablecloths, cushion covers and so forth, head for Chi Vang, 17 Trang Tien, or May, 7 Nha Tho. Chef Collection, 21d Ha Hoi, sells household items and souvenirs embroidered by disabled students under *Hoa Sua*'s vocational training programme (see p.377).

Handicrafts Craft Link, 39 & 43 Van Mieu, is a not-for-profit organization working with small-scale producers of traditional crafts, particularly among the ethnic minorities, helping develop increasingly high-quality designs. Another shop worth seeking out is Tribal Pan Flutes, 38 Hang Bac, a real Aladdin's cave of minority crafts.

Interiors For elegant if pricey home accessories and gifts try L'Image, 34 Nha Chung; Mosaïque, 22 Nha Tho; Dome, 71 Hang Trong (ⓦwww.dome .com.vn); and Hanoi Moments, 101 Hang Gai. La Casa, 12 Nha Tho (ⓦwww.lacasavietnam.com), sells unusual and upmarket household items from an Italian designer, while Nguyen Frères, 3 Phan Chu Trinh & 9 Dinh Tien Hoang, specializes in high-end antique and reproduction furniture, and also sells more portable souvenirs.

Lacquerware You'll find lacquer everywhere, but for something special Minh Tam, 2 Hang Bong, uses top-quality lacquer for his unusual designs, often incorporating eggshell to give a crazed finish, and gold leaf on black lacquer for a more dramatic effect.

Musical instruments Browse the shops on Hang Manh, where Thai Khue Music Shop, at 1a, and Ta Tham, at 16a, sell a range of unusual instruments from packable pipes and flutes to lithophones and bronze gongs from the central highlands.

Shoes To complete your outfit, Pinocchio, 71 Hang Trong & 52 Hang Bong, is the place to go for the most gorgeous handmade shoes with lacquered wooden soles and silk or leather uppers. Alternatively, most silk shops sell or will run you up a pair of dainty embroidered slippers.

Silk and tailoring Hanoi's most famous silk shops, Khai Silk, 121 Nguyen Thai Hoc (with branches at 96 Hang Gai and in the *Sofitel Metropole* hotel), and Kenly Silk, 108 Hang Gai (ⓦwww.kenlysilk.com), sell expensive but high-quality Vietnamese silks (raw, taffeta, satin even knitted) as well as other fabrics. They also sell ready-made clothes and have a reputation for reliable tailoring. Other places to try for both fabrics and tailoring include: Cocoon, 20 Nha Chung; F-Silk, 82 Hang Gai, 4 Le Thai To & 49 Hai Ba Trung; Hadong Silk, 102 Hang Gai; and Hanoi Silk, in the *Sheraton* and *Sofitel* Plaza (ⓦwww .hanoisilkvn.com). Finally, Emerald Silk, 9 Bao Khanh, is chock-a-block with a rainbow array of silk items at very reasonable prices.

Galleries

As Vietnamese art continues to attract international recognition, so ever more **art galleries** appear on the streets of Hanoi. Many of these are no more than souvenir shops selling paintings of variable quality but usually at affordable prices, while many of the big galleries, such as Apricot Gallery, 40b Hang Bong (ⓦwww.apricot-artvietnam.com), and Viet Fine Arts Gallery, 96 Hang Trong (ⓦwww.vietfinearts.com), are essentially commercial concerns. However, there are a number of galleries showcasing more experimental work and promoting promising newcomers; ⓦwww.hanoigrapevine.com is one of the best sources of up-to-date information. Now and again the Alliance Francaise (see opposite) and the Geothe Institute (see p.386) also put on interesting exhibitions. At the other end of the spectrum, you can watch artists running up bootleg "masterpieces" in broad daylight at a number of shops at the north end of Hang Trong. In recent years, a few photographers have also set up shops which double as exhibition space.

Art Vietnam Gallery 7 Nguyen Khac Ngu ⓦwww .vietnamesefineart.com. Stunning exhibition space on three floors featuring varied works from leading contemporary artists. Gallery owner Suzanne Lecht also organizes cultural events and arranges studio tours on request.

Centre for Exhibition & Art Exchange 2f/43 Trang Tien ⓦwww.ceae-artgallery.com. This government-run gallery combines a small rental space, which changes every month or so and may be showing something of interest, with a regular, commercial gallery at the rear.

Dien Dam Gallery 4b Dinh Liet. Shop-cum-gallery of award-winning photographer Lai Dien Dam.

Duc's House on Stilts Dock 82, Duong Buoi, Ba Dinh District ☎04/3762 5452. Nguyen Manh Duc is one of Vietnam's most innovative installation and performance artists. His studio, a Muong stilthouse relocated from Hoa Binh, has become a focus for cutting-edge arts.

Fine Art Exhibition House 16 Ngo Quyen. It's worth popping into this rental space to see what's on offer.

Gallery Mai Hien 99 Nguyen Thai Hoc ⊕04/3846 9614. Famous lacquer artist Bui Mai Hien exhibits in her second-floor gallery, at the back of the courtyard. By appointment only.

Green Palm Gallery 110 Hang Gai ⓦwww .greenpalmgallery.com. Big, well-established gallery showcasing the big names alongside lesser-known artists.

Hanoi Studio 13 Trang Tien. Commercial gallery hosting three or four interesting and well-displayed exhibitions a year promoting young local artists.

Life Photo Gallery 39 Trang Tien. Showcases the work of Do Anh Tuan, one of Vietnam's leading photographers.

Mai Gallery 113 Hang Bong ⓦwww .maigallery-vietnam.com. Commercial contemporary art gallery which also fosters new talent.

Ryllega Gallery 1a Trang Tien ⊕04/3933 2878. A few times a year this tiny gallery is the venue for experimental video and performance art.

Salon Natasha 30 Hang Bong. Pioneering private gallery, set up in 1990, where Russian-born Natasha and her artist husband Vu Dan Tan live, work and act as an informal meeting place for Hanoi's more experimental artists.

Studio Dao Anh Khanh To 19, Gia Thuong, Ngoc Thuy Village, Long Bien ⊕04/3827 1216, ⓦwww.daoanhkhanh.com. Dao Anh Khanh's Muong stilthouse in landscaped gardens makes a wonderful exhibition space and is also a centre for performance and installation art. By appointment only.

Suffusive Art Gallery 2b Bao Khanh ⓦwww .suffusiveart.com. One-room gallery hosting exhibitions by young artists.

Trinh Tuan–Cong Kim Hoa Studio 2f/17 Ly Quoc Su ⊕04/3824 5975. Vietnam's leading lacquer artists live and work in this small studio-gallery. By appointment only.

Thanh Long Gallery 41 Hang Gai. Exhibits leading contemporary artists and hosts the occasional avant-garde exhibition.

Young Gallery 28 Dao Duy Tu. Small new gallery promoting a broad range of young artists, including video and installation arts, in its monthly exhibitions.

Listings

Airlines Aeroflot, 4 Trang Thi ⊕04/3825 6742; Air Asia, 30 Le Thai To ⊕04/3726 2262; Air France, 1 Ba Trieu ⊕04/3825 3484; Asiana Airlines, 360 Kim Ma ⊕04/3771 4094; British Airways, 25 Ly Thuong Kiet ⊕04/3934 7239; Cathay Pacific, 49 Hai Ba Trung ⊕04/3826 7298; China Airlines, 18 Tran Hung Dao ⊕04/3824 2688; China Southern Airlines, 27 Ly Thai To ⊕04/3826 9233; Japan Air Lines, 1 Ba Trieu ⊕04/3826 6693; Lao Airlines, 41 Quang Trung ⊕04/3942 5362; Malaysia Airlines, 49 Hai Ba Trung ⊕04/3826 8820; Pacific Airlines, 36 Dien Bien Phu ⊕04/3733 2162; Qantas Airways, 4 Pham Ngu Lao ⊕04/3933 3026; SAS, 49 Hai Ba Trung ⊕04/3934 2626; Singapore Airlines, 17 Ngo Quyen ⊕04/3826 8888; Thai Airways, 44b Ly Thuong Kiet ⊕04/3826 6893; Vietnam Airlines, 1 Quang Trung ⊕04/3825 6666.

Airport For flight information, call ⊕04/3886 6527 or 04/3832 0320, or check ⓦwww .hanoiairportonline.com.

Alliance Française L'Espace, 24 Trang Tien (Mon–Fri 8am–8.30pm; ⊕04/3936 2164, ⓦwww.ambafrance-vn.org). Extensive programme of films (subtitled in English), concerts and

exhibitions, plus a members-only media centre (200,000đ per annum).

Banks and exchange Most travellers use 24hr ATMs which are widespread throughout the city; those operated by Vietcombank and HSBC accept the most overseas cards. The Vietcombank head office, 198 Tran Quang Khai (foreign exchange services Mon–Fri 8–11.30am & 1–3.30pm; all other services Mon–Fri 7.30–11.30am & 1–5pm), handles all services including cash withdrawals on credit cards and telegraphic transfers. It has branches at 108 Cau Go, 120 Hang Trong and 2 Hang Bai, amongst other locations.

Books and bookshops By far the best resources are Bookworm, 4b Yen The (closed Mon), with a great selection of new and second-hand English-language books for sale or exchange; Love Planet Travel, 25 Hang Bac; and Book Exchange at 35 Hang Giay. All these places also buy used books. You'll find a few guidebooks and glossy hardbacks in souvenir shops at top-class hotels and at the *Press Club* at 59a Ly Thai To, while stalls on Trang Tien sell pirated English-language publications, including guides, phrasebooks and novels. There are also several state-run bookshops on Trang Tien.

Car rental Cars with drivers can be arranged through tour and travel agencies (see box, p.349).

Cinema The two main venues showing regular English-language films are the multi-screen National Cinema Centre, 87 Lang Ha, and Megaplex, at the top of Vincom Towers. If you're in Hanoi a while, it's well worth joining the members-only Hanoi Cinémathèque, 22a Hai Ba Trung (ⓣ04/3936 2648; 200,000đ per year), for its range of international non-mainstream movies. The Alliance Française (see p.385) and the Goethe Institute (see below) both show films in their native language.

Dentists The Family Medical Practice Dental Clinic in the Van Phuc Diplomatic Compound, 298 Đ Kim Ma (Mon–Fri 8.30am–4.30pm; ⓣ04/3823 0281, ⓦwww.vietnammedicalpractice.com), has a 24hr emergency service (ⓣ0903 446126). The Hanoi French Hospital and International SOS (see below) also provide dental care.

Embassies and consulates Australia, 8 Dao Tan, Van Phuc ⓣ04/3831 7755, ⓦwww.vietnam.embassy.gov.au; Cambodia, 71 Tran Hung Dao ⓣ04/3825 3788, ⓔarch@fpt.vn; Canada, 31 Hung Vuong ⓣ04/3734 5000, ⓔhanoi@international.gc.ca; China, 46 Hoang Dieu ⓣ04/3845 3736, ⓔchinaemb_vn@mfa.gov.cn; Lao PDR, 40 Quang Trung ⓣ04/3822 9084; Malaysia, 43–45 Dien Bien Phu ⓣ04/3734 3836, ⓔmwhanoi@hn.vnn.vn; Myanmar, A3 Van Phuc Compound, Kim Ma ⓣ04/3845 3369, ⓔmyan.emb@fpt.vn; New Zealand, 63 Ly Thai To ⓣ04/3824 1481, ⓔnzembhan@fpt.vn; Singapore, 41–43 Tran Phu ⓣ04/3823 3966, ⓦwww.mfa.gov.sg/hanoi; Thailand, 63–65 Hoang Dieu ⓣ04/3823 5092; UK, 31 Hai Ba Trung ⓣ04/3936 0500, ⓦwww.britishembassy.gov.uk/vietnam; US, 7 Lang Ha ⓣ04/3772 1500, ⓦhanoi.usembassy.gov. For information on visas to China and Laos, see p.388.

Emergencies Dial ⓣ113 to call the police, ⓣ114 in case of fire and ⓣ115 for an ambulance; better still, get a Vietnamese-speaker to call on your behalf.

Goethe Institute 56–58 Nguyen Thai Hoc (ⓣ04/3734 2251, ⓦwww.goethe.de/hanoi). Puts on an interesting programme of films, concerts and exhibitions.

Hospitals and clinics The Hanoi French Hospital, 1 Phuong Mai, offers international-class facilities including an outpatients clinic (Mon–Fri 8.30am–noon & 2–5pm, Sat 8.30am–noon; ⓣ04/3577 1100, ⓦwww.hfh.com.vn; $50 consultation), dental and optical care, surgery and a 24hr emergency service (ⓣ04/3574 1111). Alternatively, the Family

Medical Practice, Van Phuc Compound, 298 I Kim Ma, is well known for its reasonable pricing (Mon–Fri 8.30am–5.30pm, Sat 8.30am–12.30pm; ⓣ04/3843 0748, ⓦwww.vietnammedicalpractice.com; $50 consultation). It has an outpatients clinic and a 24hr emergency service. International SOS, at 31 Hai Ba Trung, provides routine care (Mon–Fri 8am–7pm, Sat 8am–2pm; ⓣ04/3934 0666, ⓦwww.internationalsos.com) in addition to its 24hr emergency service (ⓣ04/3934 0555). Of the local hospitals, best bet is the outpatients clinic of the Viet Duc Hospital at 8 Phu Doan (Mon–Sat 8am–4.30pm; ⓣ04/3828 9852). Outside these hours, head to their emergency department in the main hospital building at 14 Phu Doan (ⓣ04/3825 3531); $20 for the initial consultation.

Language courses The Vietnamese Language Centre of Hanoi Foreign Language College, 1 Pham Ngu Lao (ⓣ04/3826 2468), offers individual instruction from $7 per hour. The centre also arranges student exchanges and student visas. Alternatively, Hidden Hanoi (ⓣ0912 254045 or 04/3852 6295, ⓦwww.hiddenhanoi.com.vn) runs a range of language classes, from the survival "Holiday Vietnamese" (90min; $15 per person) to one-week intensive courses and individual tuition.

Laundry Most hotels have a laundry service, while top hotels also offer dry cleaning. Alternatively, try one of the low-priced laundries (*giat la*) in the Old Quarter, such as at 9 Luong Ngoc Quyen, 20 & 59 Hang Be, 39 Ma May or along Ta Hien; the standard rate is 12,000–15,000đ per kilo for a one-day service.

Maps Hanoi city maps are available at outlets along Trang Tien, newsstands and souvenir shops around Hoan Kiem Lake. For more detailed regional and national maps, the Map & Photo Shop, 5 Hang Be, stocks by far the best selection.

Motorbike rental Outlets in the Old Quarter – especially along Ta Hien and Hang Bac – offer motorbike rental from $7 a day. Cuong's Adventure Biking, 1 Luong Ngoc Quyen, buys, sells, rents & repairs bikes, while Nguyen Nghia (26, 31 & 42 Hang Bac & 37 Ta Hien) is recommended for reliable machines and reasonable rates. The Minsk Club (ⓦwww.minskclubvietnam.com) is an invaluable source of information and occasionally arranges one-off motorbiking excursions and other events.

Newspapers and magazines A decent selection of foreign-language papers and magazines is on sale at Thang Long Bookshop (see p.385) and other outlets on Trang Tien. Alternatively, try the big hotels and the *Press Club*, 59a Ly Thai To.

Pharmacies The Hanoi French Hospital, Family Medical Practice and International SOS (see

"Hospitals and clinics" above) all have pharmacies. Of the local retail outlets, those at 2 Hang Bai and 3 Trang Thi stock a wide selection of imported medicines. Traditional medicines can be bought on Lan Ong.

Post offices The GPO occupies a whole block at 75 Dinh Tien Hoang (daily 6.30am–9pm). The main entrance leads to general mail and telephone services, while international postal services, including parcel dispatch (Mon–Fri 7.30–11.30am & 1–4.30pm), are located in the southernmost hall, with poste restante next door. Useful sub-post offices are at 66 Trang Tien, 66 Luong Van Can, 20 Bat Dan, and on the ground floor of Hanoi Towers at 49 Hai Ba Trung.

Spas and salons For pure pampering at unbeatable prices, indulge yourself at Zen Spa, Yen Phu (☎04/3719 9889, ⓦ www.zenspa.com.vn), near West Lake in the grounds of the *Thang Loi* hotel. The treatments, which include facials, flower baths and foot and body massages, are derived from traditional minority therapies and take place in a replica stilthouse, complete with wooden tubs, bamboo showers and mood music. Prices start at $18 for a 20min flower bath, up to $100 for a 3hr session. In the city centre, the luxury Qi Shiseido Salon and Spa, 27 Ly Thuong Kiet (☎04/3824 4703, ⓦ www.qispa.com.vn), also has a good reputation. Otherwise, there are plenty of smaller, cheaper salons in the Old Quarter and around the cathedral, where you'll pay from around $7 for a foot massage and $12 for a body massage.

Sports and activities All the five-star hotels have swimming pools and fitness centres which are sometimes open to non-residents for a daily fee; (expect to pay around $5): the *Army Hotel*'s large, open-air saltwater pool is popular in summer. Hanoi has a couple of golf driving ranges: the Hanoi Club, 76 Yen Phu (☎04/3823 8115, ⓦ www.hanoi-club .com), where you drive floating balls out over West Lake; and the Lang Ha Driving Range, 16a Lang Ha (☎04/3835 0909), in the southwestern suburbs. The Kings' Island Golf Course, 36km west of Hanoi at Dong Mo in Ha Tay Province (☎034/368 6555, ⓦ www.kingsislandgolf.com), has two eighteen-hole courses open to non-members, though members get priority at weekends. Information regarding runs organized by Hanoi Hash House Harriers is available on their website (ⓦ www .hhhh.wso.net).

Taxis Reasonably reliable, metered taxis wait outside the big hotels, or ask your hotel to call one for you. Hanoi Taxi (☎04/3853 5353), CP Taxi (☎04/3826 2626), Mai Linh Taxi (☎04/3822 2666) and Van Xuan Taxi (☎04/3822 2888) all have a decent reputation.

Tour agents See box, p.349.

Around Hanoi

There are no compelling sights in the Hanoi area, although the cave-shrine of the **Perfume Pagoda** is one of the country's most sacred locations. It's without doubt the most popular day-trip from Hanoi, though some people may find that the low-key nature of the grotto itself coupled with the long climb and barrage of hawkers en route ultimately make for a bit of a let-down. Of more appeal are the dozens of historic buildings, of which the most strongly atmospheric are the **Thay Pagoda** and **Tay Phuong Pagoda**, buried deep in the delta, both of which are fine examples of traditional Vietnamese architecture. You could spend months exploring the delta's villages – in particular the **craft villages**, which remain more traditional than most you'll find in Vietnam, concentrating on one craft, such as embroidery, conical hats or noodle-making, to the exclusion of all else. These villages are difficult to get to on your own, but **Bat Trang** pottery village is an interesting example within easy striking distance of Hanoi; for the rest you'll really need to take a guide. Finally, the ancient citadel of **Co Loa**, just north of the Red River, merits a stop in passing, mostly on account of its historical significance since there's little to recall its former grandeur.

The Perfume Pagoda

Sixty kilometres southwest of Hanoi the Red River Delta ends abruptly where steep-sided limestone hills rise from the paddy fields. The most

For addresses and telephone numbers of airlines and embassies in Hanoi, see "Listings" on p.385 & p.386 respectively.

Planes

Two **city buses** (every 15–20min between 5am and 9pm; 2hr; 5000đ) run out to the **airport**: the #7 departs from Kim Ma bus station, to the west of town; and the #17 from Long Bien bus station on the northern edge of the Old Quarter. Quicker and more convenient are **minibuses** (45min–1hr; $2), which leave every hour on the half-hour from opposite the Vietnam Airlines office on Quang Trung. A **taxi** costs from $15 (45min).

Trains

Tickets are available in the main station building, at 120 Le Duan (daily 7.30am–12.30pm & 1–10.50pm). It's best to make onward travel arrangements well in advance, especially for sleeper berths to Hué and Ho Chi Minh City. China-bound trains leave from the main station, but all other services **to the north and east** depart from a back station on Tran Quy Cap. Again, it's wise to book tickets on the night train to Lao Cai (for Sa Pa) at least a couple of days in advance. If the station has sold out of tickets for Lao Cai or Hué, try the tour agents as they get their tickets from intermediaries who buy them in bulk. Current timetables and prices can be found on the Vietnam Railways website (ⓦwww.vr.com.vn/English).

Buses

Hanoi has three main long-distance bus stations: **Giap Bat**, 6km south of town on Giai Phong; **Gia Lam** station, 4km northeast on the other side of the Red River; and **My Dinh**, about 10km west on Pham Van Dong. Usually buses to the south leave from Giap Bat, those to the northwest leave from Giap Bat and My Dinh and those to the northeast from Gia Lam. Services to Haiphong depart from Giap Bat and Gia Lam and from the more conveniently located **Luong Yen** station, on the eastern edge of the French Quarter. Luong Yen is also the departure point for the direct Cat Ba service operated by the Hoang Long company. The ubiquitous **open-tour buses** leave from various locations every night to make the trek down to **Hué** and **Hoi An**, but it's a long, uncomfortable and noisy journey: many wish they'd shelled out on a train or plane ticket instead.

Travel to China and Laos

The **China** border is currently open to foreigners at Lao Cai, Dong Dang near Lang Son, and Mong Cai (see p.426, p.456 & p.417 respectively). Direct **train services** between Hanoi and Beijing (42hr) leave Hanoi on Tuesdays and Fridays at 6.30pm; note that only soft-sleeper tickets are available and that in Vietnam you can board the train only in Hanoi. You'll need your passport with a valid Chinese visa when you buy the ticket.

There are currently six land crossings into **Laos** (see p.29 for information), and visas are in theory available at all of them except Na Meo – check locally for the latest situation – though to be on the safe side, it's advisable to get them in advance at the Lao consulate in Hanoi (see p.386). Several companies offer direct overnight bus services from Hanoi to Vientiane (18–24hr). For those flying into Laos, fifteen-day visas are also available on arrival at **Vientiane airport**.

Organized tours

Tour agencies in Hanoi (see p.349) can put together **individual programmes** including vehicle rental, guide and accommodation, or whatever combination you want. Most also run a selection of **day-trips**, of which the most popular are to Ha Long Bay and the Ninh Binh area, as well as the sights around the capital itself.

easterly of these forested spurs shelters north Vietnam's most famous pilgrimage site, the **Perfume Pagoda**, Chua Huong, hidden in the folds of Ha Tay Province's Mountain of the Perfumed Traces, and said to be named after spring blossoms that scent the air. The easiest and most popular way to visit the pagoda is on an **organized tour** out of Hanoi (from $25, including the boat ride, lunch and entry fee), or with a hired **car** and driver. Alternatively, it's a two- to three-hour **motorbike** ride: follow Highway 6 through Ha Dong, from where a sign points you left down the QL21B heading due south through Thanh Oai and Van Dinh, to find My Duc Village and the Ben Yen (Yen River boat station). A four-person **boat** costs 55,000đ, including the entrance ticket.

The Perfume Pagoda, one of more than thirty peppering these hills, occupies a spectacular **grotto** over 50m high. The start of the journey is a tranquil hour's ride by row-boat up a silent, flooded valley among karst hills where fishermen and farmers work their inundated fields. From where the boat drops you, a stone-flagged path shaded by gnarled frangipani trees brings you to the seventeenth-century Chua Thien Chu ("Pagoda Leading to Heaven"), in front of which stands a magnificent, triple-roofed bell pavilion. Quan Am, Goddess of Mercy, takes pride of place on the pagoda's main altar; the original bronze effigy was stolen by Tay Son rebels in the 1770s and some say they melted it down for cannonballs (note that respectful attire – shorts and skirts below the knee and no sleeveless tops – is required for entry to Chua Thien Chu). To the right of the pagoda as you face it a **path** leads steeply uphill for two kilometres (1hr) to the Perfume Pagoda, also dedicated to Quan Am. It is a hot and not particularly interesting walk up the mountain or a quick but expensive ride on the cable car (50,000đ single). The grotto reveals itself as a gaping cavern on the side of a deep depression filled with vines and trees reaching for light beneath the inscription "supreme cave under the southern sky". A flight of 120 steps descends into the dragon's-mouth-like entrance where gilded Buddhas emerge from dark recesses wreathed in clouds of incense – a torch comes in handy at this point.

Note that the hike is hard going and can be highly treacherous on the descent during wet weather; you'll need good walking shoes and remember to drink plenty of water, especially in the hot summer months. It's a good idea to bring your own, or be prepared to pay above the odds at drinks stalls along the route.

Thay Pagoda (the Master's Pagoda)

Thay Pagoda (Chua Thay; 25,000đ), or the **Master's Pagoda** – also known as Thien Phuc Tu ("Pagoda of the Heavenly Blessing") – was founded in the reign of King Ly Nhan Tong (1072–1127) and is an unusually large complex fronting onto a picturesque lake in the lee of a limestone crag. The pagoda lies 30km from Hanoi in Sai Son Village, between Ha Dong and Son Tay. As this isn't a popular tour destination, you'll probably need to hire a **car** and driver for the excursion, or rent a **motorbike**. The easiest route is via Highway 6, taking a right turn in front of Ha Dong post office (*buu dien*) onto the TL72/TL80 to Quoc Oai, where the pagoda is signed 4km off to the right. Note that this is a popular weekend jaunt out of Hanoi, at its busiest on Sundays.

The Master was the ascetic monk and healer **Tu Dao Hanh** (sometimes also known as Minh Khong) who "burned his finger to bring about rain and cured diseases with holy water", in addition to countless other miracles. He was head monk of the pagoda and an accomplished water-puppeteer – hence the lake's dainty theatre-pavilion – and, according to legend, was reincarnated first as a

Buddha and then as the future King Ly Than Tong in answer to King Ly Nhan Tong's prayers for an heir. To complicate matters further, Ly Than Tong's life was then saved by the monk Tu Dao Hanh. Anyway, the Thay Pagoda is dedicated to the cult of Tu Dao Hanh in his three incarnations as monk (the Master), Buddha and king.

Despite many restorations over the centuries, the pagoda's dark, subdued interior retains a powerful atmosphere. Nearly a hundred **statues** fill the prayer halls: the oldest dates back to the pagoda's foundation, but the most eye-catching are two seventeenth-century giant **guardians** made of clay and papier-mâché, which weigh a thousand kilos apiece and are said to be the biggest in Vietnam. Beyond, the highest altar holds a Buddha trinity, dating from the 1500s, and a thirteenth-century wooden statue of the Master as a bodhisattva, dressed in yellow garb and perched on a lotus throne. On a separate altar to the left he appears again as King Ly Than Tong, also in yellow, accompanied by two dark-skinned, kneeling figures which are said to be Cambodian slaves, while to the right sits a mysterious, lavishly decorated wooden chamber. The monk's mortal remains and a statue with articulated legs repose in this final, securely locked sanctuary – though a photo on the altar shows the statue's beady eyes staring out of a gaunt, unhappy face – to be revealed only once a year: at 1pm on the fifth day of the third lunar month the village's oldest male bathes Tu Dao Hanh with fragrant water and helps him to his feet. Traditionally, this event was for the monks' eyes only, but nowadays anyone can see, as long as they're prepared to put up with the scrum. The celebrations, attended by thousands, continue for three days and include daily processions as well as a famous **water-puppet festival** held on the lake (fifth to seventh days of the third lunar month).

In front of the pagoda are two attractive covered bridges with arched roofs built in 1602 and dedicated to the sun and moon: one leads to an islet where spirits of the earth, water and sky are worshipped in a diminutive Taoist temple; the second takes you to a well-worn flight of steps up the limestone hill. When Tu Dao Hanh was near death he followed the same route up to Thanh Hoa cave (Dong Thanh Hoa), now a sacred place hidden behind a screen of aerial banyan roots which lies between a mini-pagoda and a temple dedicated to the monk's parents. Though the sanctuaries themselves are well tended, there's nothing special to see beyond expansive views of a typical delta landscape over the pagoda roofs.

Tay Phuong Pagoda and Tram Gian Pagoda

Only 6km west of the Thay Pagoda, the much smaller "Pagoda of the West", **Tay Phuong Pagoda** (20,000đ), perches atop a fifty-metre-high limestone hillock supposedly shaped like a buffalo. Among the first pagodas built in Vietnam, Tay Phuong's overriding attraction is its invaluable collection of over seventy jackfruit-wood **statues**, some of which are on view at Hanoi's Fine Arts Museum (see p.369). The highlights are eighteen arhats, disturbingly lifelike representations of Buddhist ascetics as imagined by eighteenth-century sculptors, grouped around the main altar; again, a torch would help pick out the finer details. As Tay Phuong is also an important Confucian sanctuary, disciples of the sage are included on the altar, each carrying a gift to their master, some precious object, a book or a symbol of longevity, alongside the expected Buddha effigies. Tay Phuong's most notable **architectural features** are its heavy double roofs, whose graceful curves are decorated with phoenixes

▲ Statue inside the Thay Phuong Pagoda

and dragons, its unplastered brick walls and an inviting approach via 237 time-worn, red-brick steps. Hawkers from the nearby village peddle the local speciality sweetmeat, *banh che lam*, made of sticky rice pounded together with green bean and sugar.

With time to spare, you could combine a day's outing to the Thay and Tay Phuong pagodas with a quick detour to the **Tram Gian Pagoda**, roughly 7km southeast of Quoc Oai Village along a country lane and 3km north of Highway 6; if you're coming from Hanoi, the pagoda's signed to the right of the highway at the kilometre 21 marker. Again, the large, peaceful temple sitting on a wooded hill is best known for its rich array of statues. Though not as fine as those of Tay Phuong, they number over 150, including more arhats in the side corridors, alongside some toe-curling depictions of the underworld, and an impressive group on the main altar. Among them sits the unmistakable, pot-bellied laughing Maitreya, the carefree Buddha, in stark contrast to the black emaciated figure behind him. According to legend, this is the mumified and lacquered body of Duc Thanh Boi (St Boi), who was born nearby in the thirteenth century. He is credited with numerous miracles, including the ability to fly, and with saving the country from a catastrophic drought by summoning rain, though he had to wait for sainthood until a century after his death when devotees disinterred his body to find it in a perfect state of preservation.

The craft villages

For centuries villages around Vietnam's major towns have specialized in single-commodity production, initially to supply the local market, and sometimes going on to win national fame for the skill of their artisans. A few communities continue to prosper, of which the best known near Hanoi are Bat Trang pottery village and Van Phuc for silk. These are well-run, commercial operations where family units turn out fine, hand-crafted products, and they are used to foreigners coming to watch them at work. Most other villages are far less touristy, and the more isolated may treat visitors with suspicion. Nevertheless, it's worth taking a guide for the day to gain a rare glimpse into a gruelling way of life that continues to follow the ancient rhythms, using craft techniques handed down the generations virtually unchanged.

Hanoi tour agents offer organized **day-trips** to a selection of craft villages for around $15 to $25 per person. Note that some villages levy a small entry fee.

Bat Trang

BAT TRANG, across the Red River in Hanoi's Gia Lam District, is an easy jaunt by road over Chuong Duong Bridge, then immediately right along the levy; note that pedal cyclists have to use Long Bien Bridge, a short distance further north. After 10km heading generally south, following signs to Xuan Quan, a right turn indicates the village entrance. A half-day **xe om excursion** is expensive when waiting time is included; better are the #47 **buses** (3000đ) from Long Bien bus station, which depart every 15 minutes or so.

Bat Trang has been producing **bricks** and **earthenware** since the fifteenth century, and the oldest part of the village beside the river has a medieval aura, with its narrow, high-walled alleys spattered with handmade coal-pats (used as fuel in the kilns) drying in the sun; to reach this area, continue straight ahead at the end of the main street (Duong Giang Cao) and keep going generally west. Through tiny doorways, you catch glimpses of courtyards stacked with moulds and hand-painted pots, while all around rise the squat brick chimneys of the traditional coal-fired kilns. Around two thousand families live in Bat Trang, producing time-honoured blue-and-white **ceramics** alongside more contemporary designs as well as mass-produced floor tiles and balustrades to feed Hanoi's building boom. The village has expanded rapidly in recent years, thanks largely to a healthy export market, and now boasts some 2500 kilns. Most are now gas-fired, but air pollution and respiratory infections remain a problem. Showrooms along the main drag offer a bewildering choice. Prices are not necessarily any cheaper than in Hanoi itself, though the range is superior and it's easier to bargain. In some of the bigger workshops (such as Hoa Lan Ceramics, 81 Duong Giang Cao) you can paint your own design and have the piece delivered to your hotel once it's fired.

Van Phuc and Chuong

The silk village of **VAN PHUC**, 11km west of Hanoi on Highway 6, is often included as a quick stop on trips to the Perfume Pagoda or can be combined with visits to the Thay and Tay Phuong pagodas (see p.389 & p.390) – the village is about a kilometre north of Ha Dong post office on the Quoac Hai road. Once you're through the entrance arch, the clatter of electric looms from the thirty-odd workshops fills the air. You're welcome to wander into any of them, and will be given a brief explanation, but there's nothing much to detain you unless you're shopping for silk. Material is a shade cheaper than in Hanoi, while finished items such as scarves and clothes can be as little as half the price.

Further west, conical hats are the staple product of **CHUONG** village (also known as Phuong Trung) which lies just off Highway 21b a couple of kilometres south of Thanh Oai on the road to the Perfume Pagoda (see p.387). It's best to visit on market days (held six times each lunar month), when hats are piled high in golden pyramids. At other times it's possible to see artisans deftly assembling the dried leaves on a bamboo frame. Traditionally the designs varied according to the different needs: thick and robust for working in the fields, more delicate for outings to the temple and other special occasions, and flat, ornamented hats for fashion-conscious aristocrats. Nowadays the vast majority of families produce the basic conical hat for everyday wear, though two still specialize in the more elaborate designs demanded by theatre and dance troupes.

Co Loa citadel

The earliest independent Vietnamese states grew up in the Red River flood plain, atop low hills or crouched behind sturdy embankments. First to emerge from the mists of legend was Van Lang, presided over by the Hung kings from a knob of high ground marked today by a few dynastic temples north of Viet Tri (Vinh Phu Province). Then the action moved closer to Hanoi when King An Duong ruled Au Lac (258–207 BC) from an immense citadel at **CO LOA** (Old Snail City), 16km due north of the present capital. These days the once massive earthworks are barely visible and it's really only worth stopping off here in passing, to take a look at a couple of quiet temples with an interesting history.

King An Duong built his citadel inside three concentric ramparts, spiralling like a snail shell, separated by moats large enough for ships to navigate; the outer wall was 8km long, 6 to 8m wide and at least 4m high, topped off with bamboo fencing. After the Chinese invaded in the late second century BC, Co Loa was abandoned until 939 AD, when Ngo Quyen established the next period of independent rule from the same heavily symbolic site. Archaeologists have found rich pickings at Co Loa, including thousands of iron arrowheads, displayed here and in Hanoi's History Museum (see p.363), which lend credence to at least one of the Au Lac legends. The story goes that the sacred Golden Turtle gave King An Duong a magic crossbow made from a claw that fired thousands of arrows at a time. A deceitful Chinese prince married An Duong's daughter, Princess My Chau, persuaded her to show him the crossbow and then stole the claw before mounting an invasion. King An Duong and his daughter were forced to flee, whereupon My Chau understood her act of betrayal and nobly told her father to kill her. When the king beheaded his daughter and threw her body in a well, she turned into lustrous, pink pearls.

Co Loa's **temple complex** (daily 6am–6pm; 3000đ) is signposted to the right of busy Highway 3, down a tree-lined road running beside what looks just like any other delta embankment though it's said to be a remnant of the fortifications. First thing you come to after a couple of kilometres is an archer's statue standing in a small pond; continue straight on here (west) to find the principal temple, **Den An Duong Vuong**, facing a refurbished lake, with a graceful stele-house to one side. Inside the recently rebuilt temple, a sixteenth-century black-bronze statue of the king resides on the main altar, resplendent in his double crown, while a subsidiary altar is dedicated to Kim Quy, the Golden Turtle. More interesting, however, is the second group of buildings, 100m north of the archer, where a large, walled courtyard contains a beautifully simple open-sided hall, furnished with huge, ironwood pillars, and containing some of the archeological finds. Next door is the princess's small temple, **Den My Chau**. Sadly, it's all new concrete, but inside she is still honoured in the surprising form of a dumpy, armchair-shaped stone clothed in embroidered finery and covered in jewels but lacking a head.

Travel details

Trains

Hanoi to: Da Nang (6 daily; 14–20hr); Dong Dang (2 daily; 6hr); Dong Ha (4 daily; 12–16hr); Dong Hoi (6 daily; 9–13hr); Haiphong (2 daily; 2–3hr); Ho Chi Minh City (6 daily; 30–40hr); Hué (6 daily; 11–16hr); Lao Cai (4 daily; 7–9hr); Ninh Binh (3 daily; 2hr 20min); Thanh Hoa (6 daily; 3–5hr); Vinh (8 daily; 5–9hr).

Buses

Bus stations are gradually becoming more organized, with ticket desks and scheduled departures. However, it is still almost impossible to give the **frequency** with which buses run because of the large number of private minibuses that ply more popular routes, and depart only when they have enough passengers to make the journey worthwhile. Off the highway, to be sure of a bus it's advisable to start your journey early – most long-distance departures are between 5am and 9am, and few run after midday. **Journey times** can also vary; figures below show the normal length of time you can expect to take by public bus.

Hanoi to: Bai Chay (Ha Long City; 4hr); Cao Bang (8hr); Haiphong (2hr 30min); Hoa Binh (1hr 30min); Hué (12hr); Lang Son (3hr); Mai Chau (3hr); Ninh Binh (2hr); Son La (6–7hr); Thai Nguyen (3hr); Thanh Hoa (3hr).

Flights

Hanoi to: Buon Ma Thuot (4 weekly; 1hr 40min); Da Lat (12 daily; 1hr 40min); Da Nang (4 daily; 1hr 15min); Dien Bien Phu (1–2 daily; 1hr); Dong Hoi (3 weekly; 1hr 30min); Ho Chi Minh City (14 daily; 2hr); Hué (3 daily; 1hr 10min); Nha Trang (1–2 daily; 1hr 40min).

7

Ha Long Bay and the northern seaboard

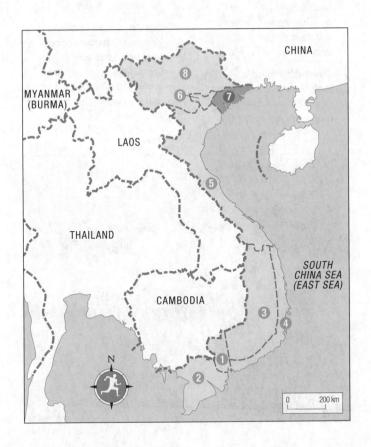

CHAPTER 7

Highlights

* **Haiphong's colonial architecture** Fine examples include the municipal theatre, for which materials were shipped from France. See p.401

* **Cruising Ha Long Bay** Passing through the maze of limestone pinnacles punctuating the turquoise waters is an unmissable experience. See p.403

* **Overnighting on a junk** Spend at least one night onboard, taking a moonlight dip in the Bay's phosphorescent waters and waking far from the hustle and bustle of the cities. See p.405

* **Rock-climbing** Get your fill of juggy overhangs on Cat Ba, one of the region's freshest new rock-climbing destinations. See p.406

* **Cat Ba** With its cluttered harbour, lush interior and easy access to some of Ha Long Bay's most beguiling scenery, this is the best place to base yourself in the region. See p.406

▲ Cat Ba harbour

7

Ha Long Bay and the northern seaboard

The mystical scenery of **Ha Long Bay** is what draws people to the northeast coast of Vietnam. Thousands of bizarrely-shaped limestone islands jut out of the emerald sea; navigating the silent, secretive channels, past bobbing clusters of fishing boats, and stopping to scramble through caves or swim beneath overhanging cliffs are some of the highlights of a trip to Vietnam. Tourism now rivals fishing as the prime activity, but the bustling harbour retains a certain authenticity and the tourist hordes are easily swallowed up in the bay's generous proportions, with many overnighting aboard a traditional wooden junk; their tea-coloured sails are just for show since almost all vessels are motor-driven, but there's a timeless, romantic air to floating amongst pristine moonlit peaks. By far the largest island in the bay, the wonderful **Cat Ba** makes an appealing base for exploring the area with some fine scenery as well as being home to **Cat Ba National Park**, a forest and maritime reserve requiring the usual mix of luck and dedication to see anything larger than a mosquito.

The two main jumping-off points for the bay and its islands are Haiphong and Ha Long City: though most travellers pass straight through, both are well set up for tourism. **Haiphong** is the more appealing, despite being north Vietnam's second-largest city and a major port: broach the industrial outskirts and you'll find a surprisingly agreeable centre with some nineteenth-century architecture. Further up the coast, **Ha Long City** is split by a strait into two mismatched halves - the largely unappealing sprawl of high-end hotels and seaside kitsch known as **Bai Chay**, and the neighbouring **Hong Gai**, an earthy, industrious town largely dedicated to fishing.

It's a further 150km up the coast to the Chinese border with the booming markets of **Mong Cai** and the long, sweeping beach at **Tra Co**: hydrofoil services along the coast make travel up to Mong Cai uncharacteristically smooth.

Haiphong

Traffic heading out of Hanoi to the northeast coast funnels over the rust-coloured waters of the Red River on Highway 1 and then branches east on Highway 5 across the northern delta's most prolific rice fields. Road's end is

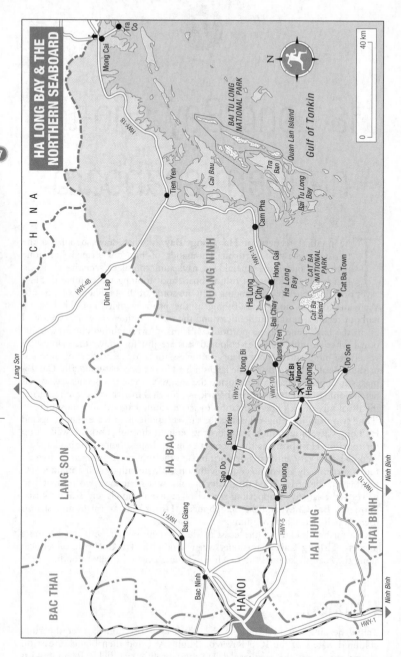

HA LONG BAY & THE NORTHERN SEABOARD

CHINA

LANG SON

BAC THAI

HA BAC

QUANG NINH

HAI HUNG

THAI BINH

Gulf of Tonkin

BAI TU LONG NATIONAL PARK

CAT BA NATIONAL PARK

Ha Long Bay

Bai Tu Long Bay

Cat Ba Island

Quan Lan Island

Tra Ban

Cai Bau

Tra Co

Mong Cai

HWY-18

Tien Yen

Dinh Lap

HWY-4B

Cam Pha

Hong Gai

Ha Long City

Bai Chay

Quang Yen

Uong Bi

HWY-18

HWY-10

Cat Bi Airport

Haiphong

Do Son

Cat Ba Town

Dong Trieu

Sao Do

Hai Duong

HWY-5

HWY-10

HWY-1

Bac Giang

Bac Ninh

HANOI

HWY-1

▲ Lang Son

▲ Ninh Binh

► Ninh Binh

N

0   40 km

HAIPHONG, a city of two million souls, where a vast, smoke-belching cement factory dominates the outskirts: it comes as a pleasant surprise, however, to find in the centre of this moderately quiet, orderly city an older district with low-key sites and subtle charms, shaded by ranks of flame trees. Broad avenues of well-tended colonial villas add to the impression of quiet prosperity and the city has a cosmopolitan flavour, evident in a profusion of suited businessmen talking deals in hotel lobbies.

Some history

Haiphong lies 100km from Hanoi on the Cua Cam River, one of the main channels of the Red River Estuary. Originally a small **fishing village** and military outpost, its development into a **major port** in the seventeenth century stems more from its proximity to the capital city than from favourable local conditions. In fact it was an astonishingly poor choice for a harbour, 20km from the open sea with shallow, shifting channels, no fresh water and little solid land. The first quay was only built in 1817 and it was not until 1874, when Haiphong was ceded to the French, that a town began to develop. With remarkable determination, the first settlers drained the mosquito-ridden marshes, sinking foundations sometimes as deep as 30m into huge earth platforms that passed for building plots. Doubts about the harbour lingered, but then, in 1883, the nine-thousand-strong **French Expeditionary Force**, sent to secure Tonkin, established a supply base in Haiphong and its future as the north's principal port was secured.

In November 1946 Haiphong reappeared in the history books when rising tensions between French troops and soldiers of the newly declared Democratic Republic of Vietnam erupted in a dispute about customs control. Shots were exchanged over a Chinese junk suspected of smuggling, and the French replied with a **naval bombardment** of Haiphong's Vietnamese quarter, killing many civilians (estimates range from one to six thousand), and only regained control of the streets after several days of rioting. But the two nations were now set for war – a war that ended, appropriately, with the citizens of Haiphong watching the last colonial troops embark in 1955 after the collapse of French Indochina.

Merely a decade later the city was again under siege, this time by American planes targeting a major supply route for Soviet "aid". In May 1972 President Nixon ordered the **mining of Haiphong harbour**, but less than a year later America was clearing up the mines under the terms of the Paris ceasefire agreement. By late 1973 the harbour was deemed safe once more, in time for the exodus of desperate **boat people** at the end of the decade as hundreds of refugees escaped in overladen fishing boats (see box, p.477).

Arrival, information and city transport

Haiphong **train station** is located on the southeast side of town, within easy walking distance of the centre. **Buses** from Ninh Binh and the south usually pitch up at Niem Nghia bus station, out in the southwest suburbs on Tran Nguyen Han, about 3km and 20,000đ by xe om from the centre. Most Hanoi services drop you closer in at Tam Bac bus station, beside Sat Market at the west end of Tam Bac Lake. Buses from Bai Chay and the northeast come into Lac Long bus station near the mouth of the Tam Bac River. The **Ben Binh ferry station**, 500m north of the city centre, is the terminus for ferries and **hydrofoils** from Cat Ba, while Haiphong's **Cat Bi Airport** (flights to Ho Chi Minh City only) is 7km southeast of the city. A taxi from the airport is around 60,000đ. There is no tourist office, but staff at the *Harbour View* speak English and can help with **information**.

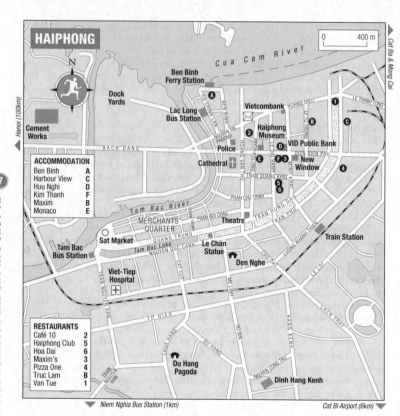

HAIPHONG

0   400 m

Hanoi (100km)

Cat Ba & Mong Cai

Cua Cam River

Ben Binh
Ferry Station

Dock
Yards

Lac Long
Bus Station

Vietcombank

HOANG DIEU

LE THANH TONG

Cement
Works

BACH DANG

Haiphong
Museum

VID Public Bank

DIEN BIEN PHU

Police

New
Window

Cathedral

TRAN QUANG KHAI

ACCOMMODATION

Ben Binh	A
Harbour View	C
Huu Nghi	D
Kim Thanh	F
Maxim	B
Monaco	E

PHAN CHU TRINH

Tam Bac River

MERCHANTS
QUARTER

PHAN BOI CHAU

Theatre

TRAN HUNG DAO

TRAN PHU

Train Station

Sat Market

Tam Bac
Bus Station

Tam Bac Lake

NGUYEN DUC CANH

Le Chan
Statue

Den Nghe

LUONG KHANH THIEN

LE LOI

Viet-Tiep
Hospital

CAT CUT

ME LINH

HO SEN

LACH TRAY

HANG KENH

RESTAURANTS

Café 10	2
Haiphong Club	5
Hoa Dai	6
Maxim's	3
Pizza One	4
Truc Lam	B
Van Tue	1

TO HIEU

CHUA HANG

DU HANG

Du Hang
Pagoda

NGUYEN CONG TRU

Dinh Hang Kenh

Niem Nghia Bus Station (1km)

Cat Bi Airport (6km)

Xe om and **cyclo** are readily available and a good way of getting around the central district, although it's quite possible to tackle most of it on foot. There's no official bike or motorbike rental, but you might be able to arrange something through your hotel. For longer distances a **taxi** or **car rental** is the only answer.

Accommodation

Haiphong has a fair number of hotels, but – with a few noteworthy exceptions – prices tend to be high and the quality not great. Budget accommodation of an acceptable standard is in particularly short supply and generally fills up early. Most hotels cluster on and around Dien Bien Phu, the city's main artery, with others dotted around town.

Ben Binh 6 Ben Binh ☎031/384 2260, ℱ031/384 2524. Handy for the ferry station and set in pleasant gardens, though the old-fashioned rooms are expensive for what you get. ❸

Harbour View 4 Tran Phu ☎031/382 7827, ⓦwww.harbourviewvietnam.com. This mock-colonial, international-class hotel is as plush as Haiphong gets. It boasts two restaurants, a piano bar and a pocket-sized pool,

not to mention very stylish rooms and impeccable service. ❻

Huu Nghi 60 Dien Bien Phu ☎031/382 3244, ℮huunghihotel@hn.vnn.vn. The central strip's glitziest hotel is housed in an unsympathetic eleven-storey block, one of the tallest buildings in town. Some rooms are looking a bit worn, but facilities include a small pool, tennis court and fitness centre. ❺

Kim Thanh 67 Dien Bien Phu ☎031/374 7216, ⓔvntourism.hp@bdvn.vnmail.vnd.net. A reasonable budget choice on the central strip. Don't expect much in the way of frills, but the rooms are clean and well maintained and the staff friendly. ❷

Maxim 3k Ly Tu Trong ☎031/374 6540, ⓔmaximhotelvn@yahoo.com. You'd be wise to book ahead at this attractive new hotel offering excellent value for money with its well-equipped rooms, with satellite TV, a/c, phones and fridges.

It's worth paying a couple of dollars extra for a room with a window – and great views from the top floors. There's free internet access and the hotel is also home to one of Haiphong's best restaurants, the *Truc Lam* (see p.402). ❷

Monaco 103 Dien Bien Phu ☎031/374 6468, ⓔmonacohotel@vnn.vn. With its museum-like reception hall and arty guestrooms, some with kitchenettes, this small three-star hotel provides the best value rooms in town. ❸

The city centre

Despite its recent history, old Haiphong is surprisingly well preserved. The crescent-shaped nineteenth-century core, which holds most places of interest, lies between the curve of the Tam Bac River and the loop of the train tracks. To the north of the main artery, Dien Bien Phu, you'll find an area of broad, sleepy avenues and Haiphong's most attractive **colonial architecture**. On Dien Bien Phu itself is a mix of hotels, banks and shops and the classic wine-red facade of the **Haiphong Museum** (Tues & Thurs 8–10.30am, Wed & Sun 7.30–9.30pm; 2000đ) at no. 66. Even during its advertised opening hours the museum is often closed, but you're not missing much – it houses a motley collection of stuffed animals and a few moderately interesting photos of Haiphong under French rule. Instead, head southwest towards the square tower of Haiphong **cathedral**, built in the late nineteenth century and recently renovated after years of neglect, and continue down bustling Hoang Van Thu to the buttermilk-yellow **theatre**. Constructed of materials shipped from France in the early 1900s, it faces onto a wide, open square – a site remembered locally for the deaths of forty revolutionaries during the street battles of November 1946 "after a valiant fight against French invaders".

In earlier times the Bonnal Canal ran past this square, linking the Tam Bac and Cua Cam rivers. For most of its length it's now gardens, cutting a green swathe through the city, but the canal's western section survives as Tam Bac Lake. The wide, shady boulevards bordering the lake and gardens make for a pleasant stroll, and the massive bronze statue of the city's heroine, Le Chan (see below), made in the bold style of Soviet Social Realism, adds to the area's appeal. North of the lake you'll find Haiphong's **merchants' quarter**, a lively area of street markets, chandlers and ironmongers between Tran Trinh and Cho Sat. **Sat Market**'s nineteenth-century halls have been replaced by an ugly, six-storey block, but there's still plenty of streetlife around. Also of interest in the central district is **Den Nghe**, on the corner of Me Linh and Le Chan, an unusually cramped temple noted for its sculptures. The finest carvings are on the massive stone table in the first courtyard, but make sure you also look above the perfumed haze of incense for some detailed friezes. General Le Chan, who led the Trung Sisters' Rebellion (see p.460), is worshipped at the main altar; on the eighth day of each second lunar month she receives a birthday treat – platefuls of her favourite food, crab with rice noodles.

Across the train tracks

There are a couple of sights of passing interest across the train tracks from Haiphong centre, both about 2km to the south. The more rewarding is **Du Hang Pagoda**, on Chua Hanh. In its present form, the pagoda dates from the late seventeenth century and is accessed through an imposing triple-roofed bell tower. Interestingly, the architecture reveals a distinct Khmer influence in the form of vase-shaped pinnacles ornamenting the roof and pillars of the inner courtyard – according to Buddhist legend these contain propitious *cam lo*, or sweet dew. Beside it lies a small, walled garden of burial stupas.

It's worth going on to **Dinh Hang Kenh**, a kilometre east on Nguyen Cong Tru, if you haven't yet seen a *dinh*, or communal house. This one is a low, graceful building with a sweeping expanse of tiled roof facing across a spacious courtyard to an ornamental lake. Despite the surrounding apartment blocks, it's still an impressive sight. Thirty-two monumental ironwood columns hold up the roof and populate the long, dark hall which is also noted for its carvings of 308 dragons sculpted in thirty writhing nests – now clothed in the dust of ages.

Eating, drinking and entertainment

Haiphong is well endowed with a fair range of **places to eat** and **drink**. Apart from the big hotels, nowhere is particularly upmarket, but you'll find restaurants serving good-value seafood and some increasingly fancy bia hoi outlets, including Haiphong's very own microbrewery. In the evenings, the cafés and small restaurants around the theatre and along the boulevards lining the canal gardens – Tran Phu and Tran Hung Dao – make a great place to watch the world go by. Alternatively, join the throng promenading up and down, pausing at ice-cream parlours or beneath the flickering lights of popcorn vendors. If you're looking for more action, there's a clutch of live-music venues, though even these shut up shop at midnight.

Café 10 10 Dinh Tien Hoang. Inexpensive little local eatery whose decor is a cut above the competition. It serves a mix of Vietnamese and Western dishes, from noodle soups and omelettes at breakfast to sandwiches, spring rolls and beef curry for lunch or dinner.

Haiphong Club 17 Tran Quang Khai. The most appealing of Haiphong's restaurant-cum-live-music venues thanks to comfy chairs and a bit of (fake) greenery. It serves drinks, snacks and main meals all day at moderate prices, though it costs slightly more after 4.30pm. The noise level cranks up at 9pm when local bands – of variable talent – take to the stage. 8am–midnight.

Hoa Dai 39 Le Dai Hanh. Ignore the similar-sounding place across the road and join the locals here for ultra-fresh seafood. There are no prices on the menu, so check before ordering, but you'll eat well for between 50,000đ and 100,000đ per person.

Maxim's 51 Dien Bien Phu. This restaurant-bar follows the same basic pattern as the *Haiphong Club*: all-day dining and live music after 8.30pm,

though here it's only the drinks that cost more after 6.30pm. 7.30am–midnight.

Pizza One 11a Tran Phu. Cheap-and-cheerful little restaurant serving a range of mostly Western dishes. Zero ambience, but the pizzas aren't bad.

Truc Lam 3k Ly Tu Trong. This restaurant hidden on the second floor of the *Maxim* hotel (see p.401) packs more style than most in Haiphong. The food is very tasty, too, with treats such as German sausages with garlic and herb mashed potatoes, lamb chops and a succulent beef bourguignon – they're not always on the menu, so just ask. You'll eat well for around 100,000đ a head. 10am–10pm.

Van Tue 1a Hoang Dieu. Gleaming vats, wooden tables and waiters bustling about with jugs of pilsner and great platters of food lend a real beer-hall buzz to the basement of this popular restaurant and microbrewery – the two upper floors are more refined but less fun. There's a bewildering menu of Vietnamese and European dishes, with prices starting at around 35,000đ. 9.30am–11pm.

Listings

Airlines Vietnam Airlines, 166 Hoang Van Thu, near the theatre ☎031/381 0890.

Banks and exchange There are 24hr ATMs dotted about town, including one outside

Vietcombank, one outside the *Harbour View*, and another in the foyer of the *Huu Nghi*.

Hospital Ben Vien Viet–Tiep (Vietnam–Czech Friendship Hospital), 1 Nha Thuong ☎031/385 4185.

Post office The GPO is at the junction of Nguyen Tri Phuong and Hoang Van Thu.

Taxi For metered taxis call Haiphong Taxi ☎031/384 1999; Mai Linh Taxi ☎031/383 3666; or VN Taxi ☎031/383 8383.

Ha Long Bay

From Guilin in China to Thailand's Phang Nga Bay, the limestone towers that typify the scenery of **Ha Long Bay** are by no means unique, but nowhere else are they found on such an impressive scale: an estimated 1969 islands pepper the 1553 square kilometres of Ha Long Bay itself, with a further two thousand more punctuating the coast towards China. Local legend tells of a celestial dragon and her children, sent by the Jade Emperor to stop an invasion, which spat out great quantities of pearls to form islands and razor-sharp mountain chains in the path of the enemy fleet. After the victory the dragons, enchanted by their creation, decided to stay on, giving rise to the name *Ha Long* ("dragon descending"), and to the inevitable claimed sightings of sea monsters.

In 1469 King Le Thanh Tong paid a visit to Ha Long Bay and was so inspired by the scenery that he wrote a poem, likening the islands to pieces on a chess-board; ever since, visitors have struggled to capture the mystery of this fantasy world. Nineteenth-century Europeans compared the islands to Tuscan cathedrals, while a local tourist brochure opts for meditative "grey-haired fairies", and the bay is frequently referred to as the eighth natural wonder of the world. With so much hyperbole, some find Ha Long disappointing, especially since this stretch of coast is also one of Vietnam's more industrialized regions with a major shipping lane cutting right across the bay to Ha Long City's Cai Lan port, earmarked to become the north's major deepwater port. The huge influx of tourism has, of course, added to the problem, not least the litter and pollution from fume-spluttering boats. The winter weather is another factor to bear in mind; it's coldest in February and March, but from November on there can be chilly days of drizzly weather when the splendour and romance of the bay are harder to appreciate.

Getting there and around

The vast majority of visitors come on **organized tours** from Hanoi, travelling by road to Ha Long City, on the bay's northern shore, where they spend a day or two cruising the bay on replica wooden junks (see box on p.405 for details). While an organized tour is without doubt the easiest option, it's perfectly possible – though not necessarily any cheaper – to do it under your own steam. Cat Ba is just a boat-ride away from the jumping-off points of Ha Long City and Haiphong, both of which can easily be reached by public transport from Hanoi.

Moving on from Haiphong

Moving on, there are two **trains** a day from Haiphong to Hanoi, and at least one **flight** to Ho Chi Minh City. Hanoi-bound **buses** leave every ten to fifteen minutes from Tam Bac bus station, but if you're coming off a ferry it's easier to get a **minibus** from the Lac Long bus station, which is within walking distance of Ben Binh ferry pier. For details of **hydrofoils** and **ferries** to Cat Ba Island, see p.409.

▲ Boat in Ha Long Bay

The caves

Ha Long Bay is split in two by a wide channel running north–south: the larger, western portion contains the most dramatic scenery and best caves, while to the east lies an attractive area of smaller islands, known as Bai Tu Long, or "Children of the Dragon", though with few specific sights (see p.416). Of the dozen or so caves open to visitors, only about half feature regularly on tour itineraries.

The bay's most famous cave is also the closest to Bai Chay, so is a favourite for day-trippers: **Hang Dau Go** ("Grotto of the Wooden Stakes") is where General Tran Hung Dao amassed hundreds of stakes deep inside the cave's third and largest chamber before the Bach Dang River battle of 1288 (see box, p.406). On the same island, a steep climb to **Hang Thien Cung** ("Grotto of the Heavenly Palace") is rewarded by a rectangular chamber 250m long and 20m high with a textbook display of sparkling stalactites and stalagmites – supposedly petrified characters of the Taoist Heavenly Court.

Further south, past hidden bays, needle-sharp ridges and cliffs of ribbed limestone, lies an area particularly rich in caves. The most visited, which features on almost all one- and two-day itineraries, is **Hang Sung Sot** (also known as the Surprise Cave). Inside its three echoing chambers spotlights pick out the more interesting rock formations, including a "Happy Buddha" and rather surprising pink phallus. At the top you come out onto a belvedere with good views over the flotilla of junks below and sampans hawking souvenirs and soft drinks. Also in this area is **Ho Dong Tien** ("Grotto of the Fairy Lake") and **Dong Me Cung** ("Grotto of the Labyrinth") where, in 1993, ancient fossilized human remains were found.

Dau Be Island, on the southeastern edge of Ha Long Bay, encloses **Ho Ba Ham** ("Three Tunnel Lake"), a shallow lagoon wrapped round with limestone

Organized tours of Ha Long Bay

Every Hanoi tour agent offers **Ha Long Bay excursions**. If you're pushed for time, you can even come here on a day-trip, but really to do the bay justice you need to devote at least two days, preferably **overnighting on board**. There's an enormous range of tours on offer at prices that vary according to the group size, the facilities on the boat, whether you sleep on board and so forth. On the whole, however, the most popular option is a three-day, two-night excursion, spending one night on board and the second on Cat Ba Island. The **price** of such tours starts at around $40–50 per person for the basic package, rising to somewhere around $150 on the more luxurious boats. Other **options** include camping on outlying islands, rock-climbing, adventure kayaking and visiting more remote parts of the bay such as Quan Lan Island.

One of the most important factors to bear in mind when **booking a tour** is the maximum number of people on board: unless you opt for one of the big, luxury boats with plenty of space, it's really worth going with a small group of ten to sixteen people. Check if the cabins are en suite and whether they have air-conditioning. Equally, in winter, the bay can get quite cold so make sure you have warm clothes, and that you get a refund if the trip is cancelled due to bad weather: this is your right under Vietnamese law.

Competition is so fierce among travel agencies that at any given time several companies will offer good tours at low prices, though which company is the cheapest varies from month to month – shop around, and ask fellow travellers for recommendations. The following are all reputable operators offering distinctive tours.

Buffalo Tours ℡04/3828 0702, ⓦwww.buffalotours.com. Impeccable tours on one of the best junks around – the *Jewel of the Bay*. The seafood is rarely anything short of delectable, the wine list none too shabby, and kayaking is included in the cost of the trip. Starts at $185 per person.

Emeraude ℡04/3934 0888, ⓦwww.emeraude-cruises.com. By far the most luxurious vessel cruising the bay, the *Emeraude* is a replica of a nineteenth-century paddle-steamer. Five-star facilities include a restaurant, two bars, beauty salon and massage rooms and spacious sundecks where you can indulge in sunrise *tai chi* classes.

Handspan ℡04/3926 0581, ⓦwww.handspan.com. Reliable operator with excellent vessels and a range of tours; perhaps of most interest is the trip around the less-visited Bai Tu Long Bay ($165 per person), which eschews the usual caves for excursions to fish farms and local schools.

Kangaroo Café ℡04/3828 9931, ⓦwww.kangaroocafe.com. This Aussie-owned outfit pride themselves on the small size of their groups (no more than sixteen); fewer passengers means that more attention is paid to the onboard meals, which are nothing short of superb. Two nights on board for $155.

Slo Pony Adventures ℡031/368 8450, ⓦwww.slopony.com. American-run team that have single-handedly established Cat Ba as a rising star in the rock-climbing world: they also organize the hugely popular "Rock Long Rock Hard" Ha Long tours booked through Hanoi Backpackers (a two-night tour $150, including climbing; see p.356). Other agencies also offer Cat Ba rock-climbing trips at slightly cheaper prices, but minus the qualified guide – there are far safer ways to save a couple of dollars.

walls and connected to the sea by three low-ceilinged tunnels that are only navigable by sampan at low tide. This cave is sometimes included in day-trips out of Bai Chay but is most easily visited from Cat Ba.

The battles of Bach Dang River

The **Vietnamese navy** fought its two most glorious and decisive battles in the Bach Dang Estuary, east of Haiphong. The first, in 938 AD, marked the end of a thousand years of Chinese occupation when General **Ngo Quyen** led his rebels to victory, defeating a vastly superior force by means of a brilliant ruse. Waiting until high tide, General Ngo lured the **Chinese fleet** upriver over hundreds of iron-tipped stakes embedded in the estuary mud, then counter-attacked as the tide turned and drove the enemy boats back downstream to founder on the now-exposed stakes.

History repeated itself some three centuries later during the struggle to repel **Kublai Khan**'s Mongol armies. This time it was the great **Tran Hung Dao** who led the Vietnamese in a series of battles culminating in the Bach Dang River in 1288. The ingenious strategy worked just as well second time round when over four hundred vessels were lost or captured, finally seeing off the ambitious Khan.

Cat Ba Island

Dragon-back mountain ranges mass on the horizon 20km out of Haiphong as you approach **Cat Ba Island**. The island, the largest member of an archipelago sitting on the west of Ha Long Bay, boasts only one settlement of any size – Cat Ba Town, a fishing village now redefining itself as a tourist centre. The rest of the island is largely unspoilt and mostly inaccessible, with just a handful of paved roads across a landscape of enclosed valleys and shaggily forested limestone peaks, occasionally descending to lush coastal plains. In 1986 almost half the island and adjacent waters were declared a **national park** in an effort to protect its diverse ecosystems, which range from offshore coral reefs and coastal mangrove swamps to tropical evergreen forest. Its value was further recognized in 2004, when the Cat Ba Archipelago was approved as an UNESCO Biosphere Reserve. One of the most rewarding ways to explore the area is by boat from Cat Ba Town, passing through the labyrinth of **Lan Ha Bay**, a miniature version of neighbouring Ha Long Bay but one which receives fewer visitors. There are **floating villages** and **oyster farms** in the area, which can be included in tour itineraries. Other options are **kayaking**, **rock-climbing** and visits to isolated **beaches** where the water is noticeably cleaner than elsewhere in the bay. Be warned, though: Cat Ba is by no means undiscovered and during the local summer holidays (June to mid-Aug) hotels and beaches in the area can be swamped.

Archeological evidence shows that humans inhabited Cat Ba's many limestone caves at least six thousand years ago. Centuries later these same caves provided the perfect wartime hideaway – the military presence on Cat Ba has always been strong, for obvious strategic reasons. When trouble with China flared up in 1979, hundreds of ethnic Chinese islanders felt compelled to flee and the exodus continued into the next decade as "boat people" sailed off in search of a better life, depleting the island's population to fewer than fifteen thousand. Now that prosperity has come in the form of tourism, the population is growing rapidly.

Getting there

The most popular way of getting to Cat Ba is on a tour **from Hanoi** – many companies offer three-day tours of Ha Long Bay with one night on board and the second on Cat Ba (see box, p.405). If you'd rather travel independently, the quickest and most convenient option is a combined bus and high-speed ferry

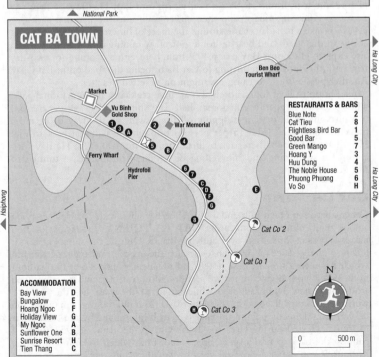

CAT BA ISLAND

Halong City ▲   Ha Long City ▲

Haiphong ◄

Titop Island

Gia Luan Harbour

Hang Sung Sôt
Ho Dong Tien

Dong Me Cung

C a t   B a   I s l a n d

CAT BA NATIONAL PARK

Ang Coi

Park Headquarters

▲ *Yen Ngua*

Viet Hai

Viet Hai Harbour

● Quan Cave

Dau Be Island

Lan Ha Bay

Cat Ba   Ben Beo

See "Cat Ba Town" map

Monkey Island

Cat Ong Island

N

0   4 km

CAT BA TOWN

▲ National Park

Ha Long City ►

Haiphong ◄

Ben Beo Tourist Wharf

Market

Vu Binh Gold Shop

❶ ❸ Ⓐ   ❷   ◆ War Memorial

Ferry Wharf

Ⓢ   Ⓑ   ❹

Hydrofoil Pier

❻ ❼
Ⓒ
Ⓓ
Ⓕ
Ⓖ

Ⓔ

❽

🌴 Cat Co 2

🌴 Cat Co 1

Ha Long City ►

Ⓗ 🌴 Cat Co 3

N

0   500 m

RESTAURANTS & BARS

Blue Note	2
Cat Tieu	8
Flightless Bird Bar	1
Good Bar	5
Green Mango	7
Hoang Y	3
Huu Dung	4
The Noble House	5
Phuong Phuong	6
Vo So	H

ACCOMMODATION

Bay View	D
Bungalow	E
Hoang Ngoc	F
Holiday View	G
My Ngoc	A
Sunflower One	B
Sunrise Resort	H
Tien Thang	C

service from Hanoi run by Hoang Long Tourist Company (4–7 daily; 4hr; 120,000đ; see p.388). Alternatively, hop on one of the **hydrofoils** that depart from Haiphong's Ben Binh ferry pier (1–4 daily; 1hr–1hr 30min; 130,000đ). Ordinary **ferries** also sail from Haiphong (2hr 30min; 80,000đ), calling in at Cat Hai on route; weather permitting, it's more comfortable to travel on the roof of these overladen antique vessels. Ferries and hydrofoils from Haiphong take you down the Cua Cam River through a procession of wallowing coal barges, picking their way through a maze of sandbanks and shifting channels. They then cross the **Bach Dang Estuary**, one of the most famous battle sites in Vietnamese history (see box, p.406), before turning south across open sea to the west coast of Cat Ba Island. It's this second half of the voyage that offers the most spectacular scenery as you sail in the shadow of increasingly dramatic cliffs towards Cat Ba Town, tucked into a fold on the island's southern tip.

From Ha Long City, the easiest option is to get the tourist boat leaving around noon from Bai Chay tourist wharf; the most direct boats take around four hours (see box on p.414 for details). Alternatively, there's a daily hydrofoil from Hong Gai to Cat Ba at 3.45pm (25min; 120,000đ); the ticket price including a 40-minute minibus ride from the pier to Cat Ba Town.

Organized tours

Most hotels in Cat Ba Town arrange **boat tours**, with little to choose between them on price ($12–20 per person per day), though the quality varies considerably; *My Ngoc* runs reliable tours, but it pays to ask fellow travellers for up-to-date advice on the best choices. One of the most picturesque trips from Cat Ba is to sail north into **Lan Ha Bay**, perhaps pay a visit to a floating village, and then either walk into the national park (see p.411) or take a half-day cruise around the maze of limestone islands, stopping at one of the coral-sand beaches for a spot of swimming or kayaking. You can also explore **Ha Long Bay** (see p.403) from here, either as a one- or two-day trip, with the option of returning to Cat Ba or being dropped off in Bai Chay. Another possibility is to camp overnight on deserted beaches.

In addition to boat tours, hotels also arrange **trekking** in the national park. There are two standard excursions: a half-day "short trek" ($7–9 per person) to Yen Ngua peak, perhaps stopping off for a swim on the way back, and a full-day "long trek" ($12–15 per person) through the national park to Viet Hai village for lunch, then back by boat through fjord-like Lan Ha Bay with a stop for swimming and snorkelling or kayaking through cave tunnels to find secret lagoons.

Cat Ba Town

Caught between green hills and a horseshoe bay alive with coracles scurrying among multicoloured fishing boats, **CAT BA TOWN**'s west-facing location makes it perfect for sunsets over outlying islands. Outside the summer peak, it retains a pretty laidback ambience despite the recent onslaught of tourism which has seen a slew of new hotels and restaurants open along the harbour front. The town is divided into two sections: most tourist facilities are grouped around the new hydrofoil pier, while 800m to the west lies the original, workaday fishing village with a bustling market and its accompanying food and bia hoi stalls. Directly behind the pier is a small hill topped by the town's war memorial, erected during Ho Chi Minh's visit to the island in 1953; follow a path up the back to find a quiet, breezy spot from which to contemplate the harbour. If you prefer a close-up view of life afloat, hire one of the **coracles**, essentially water-taxis, that hover around the harbour steps; with hard bargaining an hour shouldn't cost more than 20,000đ.

To the east of town, on the far side of the peninsula, are three small, sandy **beaches**, romantically named Cat Co 1, Cat Co 2 and Cat Co 3. The two most southerly – Cat Co 1 and 3 – are more popular and home to resort developments: they are linked by a **cliffside path** that's a joy to walk at any time, day or night. Cat Co 2 is quieter and cleaner, with snacks and drinks available, but little shade; you may be able to walk there from Cat Co 1 on a cliff-hugging boardwalk, though this has been under repair for some time.

Arrival and information

There are several **arrival points** around the island, some almost an hour by bus from Cat Ba Town. Minibuses meet almost all arrivals, and in most cases a ride to Cat Ba Town is included in the price of your ferry or hydrofoil ticket or tour.

Cat Ba's **information office** is on the main drag, though its owner is also the boss of a hotel and travel agency, so the advice given is far from impartial; instead, the People's Committee website (Ⓦ www.catba.com.vn) provides the basics and most local hotels will help you out. Hotels also offer **tours** of Cat Ba island and the bay (see "Organized tours", p.405), but for exploring the island independently, your best bet is to rent a **motorbike** with or without a driver: xe om cruise around town and most hotels offer motorbike rental from $6 per day. You can also rent **mountain bikes** for $3 a day, but unless you're pretty fit, you may find the steep hills hard going in the heat.

At the time of writing, the bank in Cat Ba Town does not handle foreign exchange, and there are no ATMs on the island. Your best option for **changing money** and **traveller's cheques**, therefore, is the Vu Binh gold shop (7am–10pm) on the main road by the market – look for the giant credit card logos painted outside. It can exchange major currencies or traveller's cheques, and give credit card advances. Hotels and restaurants will also change cash and traveller's cheques, but at poor rates. The **post office** (7am–noon & 12.30–10pm) is beside *The Noble House* on the harbour front, near the hydrofoil pier.

Accommodation

Thanks to a building boom, **accommodation** on Cat Ba represents good value on the whole. The exception is during the peak summer holiday period of June through August, when the place is absolutely packed and prices can more than double. Most are budget hotels, generally clean and comfortable and equipped with satellite TV and air-conditioning, but there's also an increasing number of more upmarket places. While hotels away from the harbour tend to be slightly cheaper, it's well worth opting for somewhere on the front with rooms overlooking the bay.

Bay View ☎031/368 8241. English-owned hotel that prides itself on providing good, clean rooms at rock-bottom prices. The food is excellent, and non-residents can make use of their cheap and reliable laundry facilities. ❶

Bungalow ☎031/350 8408. Cat Ba Town lacks the remote feel of most of the island, but there's a real sense of mountain-sheltered isolation at this cluster of rustic bungalows on Cat Co 2 beach. Rooms contain nothing but mattresses and mosquito nets (communal showers only), but the setting is superb. ❷

Hoang Ngoc ☎031/368 8788. This new family-run guesthouse has that Cat Ba rarity – an elevator. The rooms are fresh and pleasant, and there's a communal balcony on every floor; the eighth-floor rooftop also turns into a small bar at night. ❷

Holiday View ☎031/388 7200, Ⓔholidayview hotel@vnn.vn. You can't miss this fourteen-storey monstrosity sticking up to the east of the pier. It does, however, boast three-star comforts, including a restaurant and terrace café, and its rooms are tastefully decorated, if a tad bland. ⑤

My Ngoc ☎031/388 8199. This big hotel to the west of the hydrofoil pier offers cheap rates for its seafront location. Ask for a room in the newer block – no balconies, but they're bigger and better equipped. It also arranges reasonable tours. ❶

Sunflower One ☎031/388 8429, ⊛www .sunfloweronehotel.com.vn. Spacious and smartly furnished rooms make this a good choice if you're after a bit of comfort. Though not on the harbour, the upper floors get sea views. To find it,

walk east from the pier and turn left by the *Vien Dong* hotel. ❸

Sunrise Resort ☎031/388 7360, ⓔcatba-sunriseresort@vnn.vn. If you want to feel the sand between your toes, head for this low-rise resort hotel on Cat Co 3 beach. The burgundy-trimmed rooms all have sea-view balconies; best value are the deluxe rooms, whose "Extra King Size" beds are colossal. Hotel facilities include a restaurant, bar, pool and sauna. ⑥

Tien Thang ☎031/388 8568. A spruce hotel to the east of the pier; its rooms are not huge, but come with TVs, a/c and phones as standard; some also have balconies. ❷

Eating

The number of **restaurants** on Cat Ba is gradually expanding, with some offering tasty food – especially seafood – at reasonable prices. For a real challenge, order one of the huge crabs on display in some restaurants, and crack your way through to its succulent meat. As usual, you'll find food stalls in and around the market, and there's a sprinkling of places serving breakfast pho soups up the road from the post office. The **floating restaurants** in Cat Ba harbour and off Ben Beo tourist wharf seem a nice idea but there are so many reports of people getting ripped off they're best avoided. Coracles ferry you out to them for free (or, rather, included in the bill) if you want to try your luck; the problem is, once you're out there you're a bit stuck.

Cat Tieu A floating restaurant without the possibility of extortion, since it's connected to the Cat Co 3 road by gangplank – a rickety adventure in itself. The menu is extensive but you may need a few goes before landing on something that they actually have; recommended are the huge clam and shoot soups (25,000đ).

Green Mango Cat Ba's classiest restaurant offers a chilled atmosphere to match fusion dishes such as black barramundi with braised banana, and pan-roast salmon with wasabi mashed potato. Prices are a little steep – at least 130,000đ for a full meal – but since some of the cheaper dishes could be better prepared it's worth splashing out on something special.

Hoang Y Friendly local joint with a well-deserved reputation for serving ultra-fresh seafood at reasonable prices; shrimp with lemon and garlic hits the spot, or try whole steamed fish with lashings of ginger. Copycat restaurants with similar names have opened, so make sure you pick the original: it's at #197 on the harbour road.

Huu Dung Also known as the *Coca Cola*, this little stilthouse restaurant is an old favourite for its warm welcome and broad menu of soups, rice and noodle dishes and seafood. It's up the road past the *Sunflower One* hotel.

The Noble House Though quality is on the wane, this is still the place to head for hearty Western breakfasts, pizzas, pasta and other comfort foods, or you can opt for local dishes, including fresh seafood. Work it off afterwards playing pool or table football in the upstairs bar.

Phuong Phuong Cheap prices, decent food and more than usually friendly staff make this a popular option on the harbour front. It serves a broad range of standard Vietnamese and seafood dishes.

Vo So Located in the *Sunrise Resort*, with surprisingly reasonable prices given the opulent surroundings. Salads, soups and pasta dishes are offered as well as the Vietnamese regulars, and some of the desserts are simply irresistible.

Drinking and nightlife

In the evenings, locals and visitors stroll along the harbour front, stopping to enjoy a beer or juice at the drink stalls. Most fun-seekers gravitate to the *Good Bar* above the *Noble House*, which gets pretty wild whenever there's a crowd. For a cosier atmosphere, try the Kiwi-run *Flightless Bird Bar* (known to locals as the "Penguin Bar", there being no word for Kiwi in Vietnamese), further down towards the market. Another good option is the locally-owned *Blue Note*, which lives up to its name with blues music, low lighting and a laidback vibe.

Cat Ba National Park

One of Cat Ba's main draws is its rugged unspoilt scenery. A recommended outing is to rent a motorbike or a car for the day and explore the island's few paved roads and its isolated beaches. The main cross-island road climbs sharply out of Cat Ba Town, giving views over distant islands and glimpses of secluded coves, and then follows a series of high valleys. After 8km look out on the right for the distinctive **Quan Y Cave** (15,000đ), a gaping mouth embellished with concrete, not far from the road. During the American War the cave became an army hospital big enough to treat 150 patients at a time.

Eight kilometres further on you reach the gates of **Cat Ba National Park** (15,000đ), established in 1986. Its most famous inhabitant is a sub-species of the critically endangered **golden-headed langur**, a monkey found only on Cat Ba and now probably numbering fewer than sixty individuals. Considerably more visible will be the rich diversity of plant species, including some 350 of medicinal value, as well as birds, snakes and plenty of mosquitoes. Alongside repellent, remember to take lots of water, good boots and a hat if you plan to do any **walks** in the park. A compass wouldn't come amiss either, as people have got seriously lost.

There are two main **trails** through the park. The "short trek" (2–3hr from the gates of the park) takes you to a viewpoint at the top of Yen Ngua peak. The path is easy enough to follow, but it's a steep climb, scrambling over tree roots and rocks in places, and extremely slippery in wet weather. Not everyone agrees that the views merit the effort. If you've got the time and energy, the "long trek" (4–5hr) is a more rewarding experience, especially if you finish up with a boat ride back to Cat Ba Town. It involves a strenuous eighteen-kilometre hike via

▲ Cat Ba Harbour

Frog Lake (Ao Ech), over a steep ridge for a classic view over countless karst towers, then dropping down to Viet Hai village where you can buy basic foodstuffs. From there it's about an hour's walk through lush scenery to the jetty. The easiest way to tackle this walk is on an organized tour arranged by agents in Cat Ba (see p.408). If you want to do it yourself, you'll need to take a guide from the national park headquarters and arrange for a boat to meet you at the end. A xe om from Cat Ba to the park headquarters should cost under 50,000đ one way.

Ha Long City

In 1994 Hong Gai and Bai Chay, two towns on the north shore of Ha Long Bay, were amalgamated to create a new provincial capital called **HA LONG CITY**. For the moment, locals still use the old names – as do ferry services, buses and so on – as a useful way to distinguish between the two towns, each with its own distinct character, lying either side of the narrow Cua Luc channel and linked by a bridge. The epicentre of tourist activity is **Bai Chay**, a rather unattractive beach resort which offers an enormous choice of accommodation and is also the main departure point for boat tours. For those in search of more local colour, or who are put off by Bai Chay's overwhelming devotion to tourism, **Hong Gai** provides only basic tourist facilities but has a more bustling, workaday atmosphere.

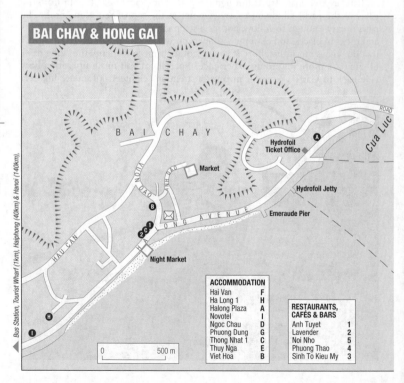

BAI CHAY & HONG GAI

B A I   C H A Y

Hydrofoil Ticket Office

Market

Hydrofoil Jetty

Emeraude Pier

ONG AVENUE

Night Market

Cua Luc

ROAD

HAU CAN

Bus Station, Tourist Wharf (1km), Haiphong (40km) & Hanoi (140km)

ACCOMMODATION	
Hai Van	F
Ha Long 1	H
Halong Plaza	A
Novotel	I
Ngoc Chau	D
Phuong Dung	G
Thong Nhat 1	C
Thuy Nga	E
Viet Hoa	B

RESTAURANTS, CAFÉS & BARS	
Anh Tuyet	1
Lavender	2
Noi Nho	5
Phuong Thao	4
Sinh To Kieu My	3

0   500 m

Bai Chay

Neon signs and flashing fairy lights blaze out at night along the **Bai Chay** waterfront, advertising north Vietnam's most developed resort, with shoulder-to-shoulder hotels and a picturesque backdrop of wooded hills. While Bai Chay is swamped in summer with local holidaymakers and tourists from China, out of season it's a pretty sleepy place and decidedly less sleazy. Apart from strolling the seafront boulevard and taking a quick look at its very indifferent beach, Bai Chay has nothing to distract you from the main business of touring Ha Long Bay. If you're staying here, you can take a turn through the **night market**, a somewhat desultory array of overpriced souvenirs, on the seafront at the junction of Ha Long Avenue and Vuon Dao, the budget-hotel strip. More interesting is the **Royal Amusement Park** (6–10.30pm; 100,000đ), further west along the front. Of various entertainments on offer, best are the water-puppet performances and the "cultural shows" offering a jazzed-up sampler of "traditional" song and dance. The park also boasts a surprisingly well-presented museum of Vietnamese art and history.

Arrival and information

Most foreign visitors to Bai Chay stay only as long as it takes to board their Ha Long Bay junk, which leave from the tourist wharf two kilometres west of town (see box, p.414). Frequent **bus** services **from Hanoi and Haiphong** to Bai Chay pull in at a bus station west of the centre (30,000đ by xe om). Although buses **from Mong Cai** drop you in Hong Gai (see p.415), Mong Cai hydrofoils

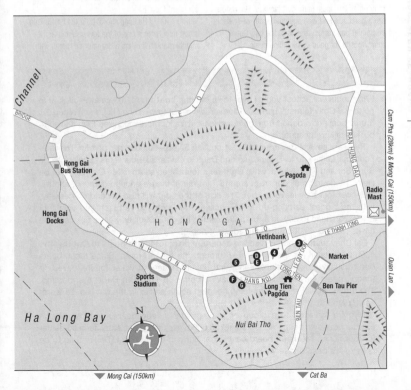

dock at a pier near the *Halong Plaza*. There are two departures daily to Mong Cai, at 8am and 1pm (3hr; $15); buy tickets from the Pearl Cape (Mui Ngoc) office (℡033/384 7888) just across the road from the pier – remember to take your passport.

For **changing money**, Vietcombank, opposite the Royal Amusement Park at the west end of Ha Long Avenue, handles all major currencies and traveller's cheques as well as credit card advances. There's also a 24-hour ATM here, and a more convenient one beside the entrance to the *Heritage Halong* hotel. The **post office** is at the bottom of Vuon Dao, with an internet café next door.

Accommodation

Despite a continuing increase in the number of hotels in Bai Chay, there are still temporary **room shortages**, particularly during the Vietnamese summer season (June to early Sept) and holiday weekends. The budget hotels are located along Vuon Dao, while Ha Long Avenue is home to the bigger, swankier establishments.

Ha Long 1 Ha Long Ave ℡033/384 6320, ℻033/384 6318. This converted French villa built in 1936 has seen better days, but still has more atmosphere than most Bai Chay hotels. Rooms are furnished to a reasonable standard; the best are on the third floor, with big balconies overlooking the bay. ❹
Halong Plaza 8 Ha Long Ave ℡033/384 5810, ⓦwww.halongplaza.com. A smart four-star hotel offering all the usual upmarket facilites. The rooms are a good size and well equipped, with wi-fi; some command panoramic sweeps of the bay. Check their website for good-value online deals. ❻

Novotel Ha Long Ave ℡033/384 8108, ⓦwww.novotelhalongbay.com. One of the most immaculately designed hotels in Vietnam – plush carpets lead to subtly lit and delicately scented rooms where you can see the outside world from every shower cubicle. The infinity pool outside is another nice touch, and the onsite restaurant serves excellent food. ❻
Thong Nhat 1 Ha Long Ave ℡033/384 6145. This smart new hotel is one of the few catering to the middle market. It offers a dozen or so rooms with

Boat tours and charters

While touts will accost you all over town offering **boat tours**, the safest option is to go to Bai Chay tourist wharf two kilometres west of town along Ha Long Avenue. All tourist boats now depart from here and while it's a lot more organized than it used to be, it's still pretty confusing.

There are several **day-trips** on offer, costing 50,000–60,000đ per person. The four-hour tour takes you to Thien Cung and Dau Go caves; six-hour tours usually include Sung Sot and Titop Island; while eight-hour tours head south to Me Cung and Ho Ba Ham. These tours all depart at around 7am, but if there's enough demand, another four-hour tour may leave at 1pm. The size of the boat will also depend on demand, with the biggest carrying up to 45 passengers. Once you've purchased your tour ticket, you need to buy an **entry ticket** for the bay (30,000đ), as well as tickets to the caves (10,000–40,000đ) from an adjacent booth.

Bai Chay tourist wharf is also the departure point for tourist boats **to Cat Ba** (4hr; 100,000đ), taking a leisurely amble through the bay en route. Since these boats don't usually stop for sightseeing, you shouldn't need a ticket for the caves. In theory, boats leave around noon, having come up from Cat Ba in the morning. There may, however, be something heading south earlier in the day, so it's worth asking around.

If you're travelling in a group or want greater independence, you can always **charter** your own boat. Prices start at 700,000đ, excluding cave entry, for a 25-seater for four hours. Meals on board cost extra, but can be excellent. Drinks tend to be pricey – it's best to take your own.

balconies and a good standard of equipment, if slightly overpriced. ❷
Viet Hoa 35 Vuon Dao ☎033/384 6035. One of the better budget hotels on Vuon Dao, this is a clean and welcoming place offering cheerful fan or a/c rooms. They're a decent size and all come with TVs and fridges as standard. ❷

Restaurants

Fresh **seafood** is the natural speciality of Ha Long Bay, with excellent lobster, crab and freshly caught fish on offer. Despite the onslaught of passing traffic and souvenir-vendors at the throbbing epicentre of Ha Long's tourist mecca, the most popular place to eat in Bai Chay remains the strip of **restaurants** on Ha Long Avenue between the post office and the *Heritage* hotel. There's nothing much to choose between them, but the *Lavender* is worth trying for an unusually varied menu and good-value meals. Alternatively, head for one of the cheaper, local eating houses round the corner on Vuon Dao – the *Anh Tuyet* is clean and friendly. For basic com pho outlets, head up Vuon Dao towards the market; there's a good choice of food stalls in the market itself.

Hong Gai

In contrast to Bai Chay, **HONG GAI** has a compelling, raw vitality plus an attractive harbour to the east, crowded with scurrying coracles. It's worth spending an hour or so wandering the harbourside paths where a picturesque village lies strung out under the limestone knuckle of **Nui Bai Tho**. This mountain is named after a collection of poems (*bai tho*) carved into the rock, that detail Ha Long Bay's beauty, kicking off with King Le Thanh Tong's in 1468. Nowadays most are hidden behind houses clinging to the cliff edge, but keep an eye open as you follow Ben Tau lane from Long Tien, winding through the fishing village, and you might spot one or two of the weathered inscriptions; no one seems quite sure which are the royal verses.

Also worth a look is the small but colourful **Long Tien Pagoda** on Long Tien. There are frequently ceremonies taking place in its small courtyard, offering fascinating glimpses into local rituals.

Arrival and information

Buses to and from Mong Cai operate out of Hong Gai bus station on the west side of town; from here, it's around 30,000đ into town by xe om. **Ferries** to and from Cat Ba and Quan Lan use Ben Tau pier, on the east side of Nui Bai Tho. Incombank, 120 Le Thanh Tong, provides **foreign exchange** services, including credit card advances, but only accepts dollars and euros in cash and traveller's cheques. There's also a handy Vietcombank ATM inside the **post office** (daily 6.30am–10pm) on Le Thanh Ton.

Accommodation and eating

Hotels in Hong Gai may be basic, but standards are improving and the atmosphere of the town has a certain charm. There are a number of acceptable options along Le Thanh Tong, of which the best are grouped around a square near the junction with Long Tien. Here, the *Ngoc Chau*, 15b Cay Thap (☎033/362 0499; ❷), and *Thuy Nga*, 11 Cay Thap (☎033/362 2675; ❷), are newish places with a range of good-value rooms. West along Hang Noi, you'll find another clutch of slightly older budget hotels, of which the *Phuong Dung* at no. 78 (☎033/382 8952; ❶) and the *Hai Van* at no. 76 (☎033/382 6279, ⓕ033/382 7092; ❶) are clean and welcoming.

The best **eating** in Hong Gai is at the *com binh danh* outlets on the opposite side of the square from the *Ngoc Chau* hotel. Though there's little to choose between them, *Phuong Thao*, on the corner at 16 Doan Thi Nien, has a good reputation. You'll also find food stalls round the market, where ingredients come fresh from fishing boats in the harbour next door. For something smarter, try the surprisingly swish second-floor restaurant at *Noi Nho*, 269 Le Thanh Tong, which offers everything from sandwiches to snails, but is best for seafood. Finally, the little juice bar *Sinh To Kieu My*, at 2 Le Quy Don, whisks up some mean fresh-fruit shakes.

Bai Tu Long

East of Ha Long Bay, stretching up towards the Chinese border, lies an attractive area of islands, known as **Bai Tu Long** or "Children of the Dragon". Some of the larger islands feature important forest reserves and are home to a number of rare species, such as the pale-capped pigeon, while dugong (sea cows) inhabit the surrounding waters. In 2001, **Bai Tu Long National Park** was created to protect the 15,700 hectares of marine and island habitat.

Though there are few specific sights in the area, and consequently little tourist development, tour boats from Bai Chay and Cat Ba occasionally venture out this way, and the odd intrepid tourist heads as far as **Quan Lan Island**, a long skinny island on the outer fringes of the bay. Although there has been much talk of developing the larger islands in Bai Tu Long as eco-tourism destinations, so far only Quan Lan has seen any development and even this is fairly minimal. The island's main attractions are the empty, sandy and relatively clean beaches fringing its east coast. A cycle ride on its only road makes a pleasant jaunt through rice paddies and over the dunes to the north tip. Otherwise, there's not much to do apart from enjoying simply being off the tourist trail.

Daily boats to Quan Lan leave from Hong Gai's Ben Tau pier at 1.30pm (4hr 30min; 130,000đ); xe om and xe may (three-wheeler motorbike taxis) wait at Quan Lan pier, on the island's southern tip, to take people three kilometres north to the main village (15,000đ). Here you'll find a **post office** – spot the radio mast – and, opposite it, the friendly *Ngan Ha Hotel* (☎033/387 7296; ❶), offering simple but good-value **accommodation**, as well as meals and bike rental. The other places to stay are spread out along the beach on the island's southeast coast. The smartest is the *ATI Resort* (☎033/387 7471, ℱ033/387 7257; ❸), signed off to the right 1500m from the ferry pier, with comfortable but overpriced wooden cabins – boasting fans and hot water – scattered among the dunes. You can also rent bikes here, and there's a **restaurant**, though you're better off eating at the com pho places in the village. Very basic wooden cabins, albeit with bathrooms and electricity, are available at *Quan Hai* (☎0913 388632, ℮quanhai_baitulong@yahoo.com; ❶) at the southern end of the beach; phone in advance and someone will come to meet you. Basic meals are available. Note that both places on the beach have electricity in the evenings only.

North to the Chinese border

Few travellers head on up the coast to **Mong Cai**, unless they're looking for an adventurous route into China (see box on p.456 for general information on crossing into China) or a back road to **Lang Son** (see p.454). Mong Cai is simply a thriving frontier town, booming on the back of cross-border trade, but the journey there offers great views. This is particularly so if you travel by **hydrofoil**, passing through the eastern extent of Ha Long Bay. The hydrofoil comes to rest in a protected bay near the northeast border, where at low tide you have to transfer to a smaller boat (in rough weather this can be precarious). On coming ashore, foreigners must present their passports to the immigration police (same procedure on leaving). The final fifteen-kilometre bus ride into town passes duck farms and buffaloes ruminating in paddies, before reaching the broad boulevards of Mong Cai, lined with karaoke and massage signs.

Travelling by **road** offers an altogether different experience. The first stretch with views over Ha Long Bay is promising enough, though the road is choked with trucks from the huge open-cast coal mines of **Cam Pha**, where the whole landscape is shrouded in grey dust. You wouldn't want to linger, but the scene possesses a certain post-apocalyptic power. About 20km beyond Cam Pha the scenery gradually revives, as the highway winds through a spur of hills, with signs of shifting agriculture practised by local Thai people, while down below mangroves invade marshy, saltwater lagoons. Then suddenly you're out onto densely populated coastal plains, a fertile landscape painted every conceivable shade of green, where the only town of any size since Cam Pha, **Tien Yen**, marks the turning to Lang Son, a slow 100km away to the west on a rough road. North of Tien Yen, it's all flat rice-growing country until an incongruous clump of high-rise hotels and apartment blocks announces Mong Cai.

Mong Cai and around

Since the border re-opened for trade in 1992, **Mong Cai** has been booming, as witnessed by the massive hexagonal **central market** (8am–noon), north of the main roundabout and dominating the town centre, and the vast Chinese-built casino and hotel development under construction across the river. Vietnamese tourists flock here to snap up cheap Chinese clothes; the Chinese for gambling, girls and to visit the nearby seaside resort of Tra Co. Few Westerners pass through, which means hardly anyone speaks English (Chinese is the second language of choice), but the town's compact centre, radiating from a large roundabout, is easy to negotiate and the raw, frontier feel has a certain attraction.

Once you've explored Mong Cai's markets, the main excursion takes you 7km southeast to **Tra Co**, a windswept beach resort frequented by Vietnamese and Chinese tourists in summer. Though there's the usual ribbon of rubbish and the water is unlikely to tempt you in, the seventeen-kilometre-long strand is good for peaceful walks past the curious boats of bamboo and styrofoam lying like beached whales on the grey, hard-packed sand. A one-way **taxi** ride out here costs around 100,000đ, while a **xe om** will set you back 20,000đ.

Practicalities

South of the central roundabout lies the **post office** and a clutch of **internet cafés**. The town's long-distance bus station – for buses to and from Hong Gai - is about 400m west across the river. The **Chinese border** is just a kilometre away to the north; walk straight up Tran Phu to the junction and turn left to reach the **border gate** (daily 7am–5pm). The **hydrofoil offices**, from where buses leave to start the journey to Bai Chay or Haiphong, are both near the central roundabout: Pearl Cape (or Mui Ngoc), 1 Tran Phu (T033/388 3988), which operates services to Bai Chay, has its office on the roundabout, while Greenlines, for Haiphong, is a short walk to the east at

44 Hung Vuong (☎033/388 1214). The most useful **bank** is Vietcombank at 2 Van Don, north of the market, with a 24-hour ATM. There's also another ATM at the post office.

With the growth in tourist traffic across the border, there's now more choice of **accommodation** in Mong Cai. For best all-round value, you can't beat the bright, well-scrubbed rooms at the *Truong Minh*, 36 Trieu Duong (☎033/388 3368, ℱ033/388 6048; ❶), mid-way between the border and the central market. Further east along the same street, the *Thanh Tam*, 71 Trieu Duong (☎033/388 1373; ❶), is another good option, or try the *Le Thanh*, 55 Chu Van An (☎033/377 0181; ❶), on a backstreet south of the central market. Finally, close to the border gate, the *Hoang Hiep*, 12 Hoang Quoc Viet (☎033/388 7999, ℱ033/377 8666; ❷), offers a touch more style, although rooms are a little pricey for what you get, and at weekends it may be full with Vietnamese tour groups.

Eating is more of a hit-and-miss affair, as few places have menus and almost no one speaks English. The streets near the central market turn into open-air restaurants in the evening, each stall thronged with customers. One friendly place is the *Minh Thuy*, 70 Trieu Duong, the best of several *com binh dan* joints near the *Thanh Tam* hotel. If you want to get in off the street, head for the *Lang Tu* restaurant, east along Hung Vuong from the central roundabout. It serves inexpensive meals including do-it-yourself barbecues and good seafood.

Travel details

Trains

Haiphong to: Hanoi (2 daily; 2hr–2hr 20min).

Buses

Bus stations are gradually becoming more organized, with ticket desks and scheduled departures. However, it is still almost impossible to give the frequency with which buses run because of the large number of private minibuses that ply more popular routes, and depart only when they have enough passengers to make the journey worthwhile. Journey times can also vary; figures below show the normal length of time you can expect to take by public bus.

Bai Chay to: Haiphong (3hr); Hanoi (4hr).
Haiphong to: Bai Chay (3hr); Hanoi (2hr 30min); Ninh Binh (4–5hr).
Hong Gai to: Mong Cai (3hr 30min).
Mong Cai to: Hong Gai (3hr 30min).

Ferries

Cat Ba to: Haiphong (2 daily; 2–3hr); Hong Gai (1 daily; 2hr).
Haiphong to: Cat Ba (2 daily; 2–3hr).
Hong Gai to: Cat Ba (1 daily; 2hr 30min).

Hydrofoils

Bai Chay to: Mong Cai (2 daily; 3hr).
Cat Ba to: Haiphong (1–4 daily; 45min); Hong Gai (1–4 daily; 30min).
Haiphong to: Cat Ba (1–4 daily; 45min); Mong Cai (1 daily; 4hr–4hr 30min).
Mong Cai to: Bai Chay (2 daily; 3hr); Haiphong (1 daily; 4hr–4hr 30min).

Flights

Haiphong to: Ho Chi Minh City (1 daily; 2hr).

8

The far north

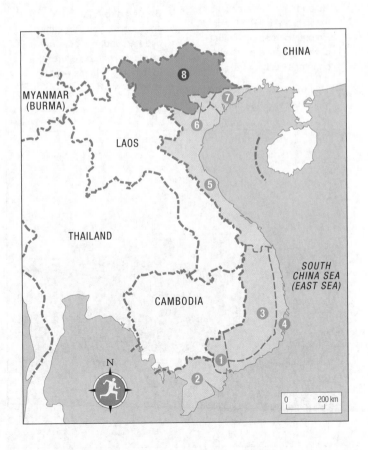

CHAPTER 8

Highlights

✱ **Trekking around Sa Pa**
A hugely popular activity, offering great views of the landscape as well as the chance to spend time with the colourfully dressed montagnards. See p.431

✱ **Weekend markets** Bac Ha and Can Cau weekend markets are full of Flower Hmong, perhaps the most dazzling dressers in the country. See p.434 & p.435

✱ **Thai minority villages** Around Mai Chau visitors can stay in Thai stilthouses and see shows of traditional dancing. See p.443

✱ **Ha Giang** Gateway to the country's northernmost and wildest province, where the scenery is simply stunning. See p.447

✱ **Ba Be Lake** A laidback spot, where you can either glide around in a boat on its glassy waters, or trek to minority villages near its shore See p.452

▲ The landscape around Sa Pa is great for trekking

8

The far north

As Vietnam fans out above Hanoi towards the Chinese and Laos borders, it attains its maximum width of 600km, the majority of it a mountainous buffer zone wrapped around the Red River Delta. Much of the region is wild and inaccessible, yet it contains some of Vietnam's most awe-inspiring scenery, sparsely populated by a fascinating mosaic of ethnic minorities. Most impressive on both counts is the northwest region where the country's highest mountain range and its tallest peak, Fan Si Pan, rise abruptly from the Red River Valley. Within the shadow of Fan Si Pan lies **Sa Pa**, an easily accessible former French hill station, famous for its minority peoples and for its superb scenery with opportunities for trekking out to isolated hamlets. Nearby, **Bac Ha** has one of the most colourful of all minority groups in the form of the Flower Hmong, whose markets are great fun. The attractions of these two towns and the historic battlefield of **Dien Bien Phu**, site of the Viet Minh's decisive victory over French forces in 1954, draw most tourists to the northwest region, while those with enough time are well rewarded if they follow the scenic route back to Hanoi, passing through **Son La**, **Moc Chau** and **Mai Chau**.

The little-travelled provinces east of the Red River Valley also deserve attention, especially the stunning scenery and mountain people in the border area of **Ha Giang** and **Cao Bang provinces**. The northeast region also features **Ba Be National Park**, where Vietnam's largest natural lake hides among forested limestone crags and impenetrable jungle. Not surprisingly, infrastructure throughout the northern mountains is poor: facilities tend to be thin on the ground, and some roads are in terrible condition. However, this area is becoming increasingly popular with tourists as Hanoi's tour agents organize new tours and independent travellers venture into uncharted terrain by jeep or motorbike.

Some recent history

Remote uplands, dense vegetation and rugged terrain suited to guerrilla activities, plus a safe haven across the border, made this region the perfect place from which to orchestrate Vietnam's independence movement. For a short while in 1941, **Ho Chi Minh** hid in the Pac Bo Cave on the Chinese frontier, later moving south to Tuyen Quang Province, from where the Viet Minh launched their August Revolution in 1945. These northern provinces were the first to be **liberated** from French rule, but over in the northwest some minority groups, notably from among the Thai, Hmong and Muong, supported the colonial authorities and it took the Viet Minh until 1952 to gain control of the area. Two years later, they staged their great victory over the French at Dien Bien Phu, close to the Laos border.

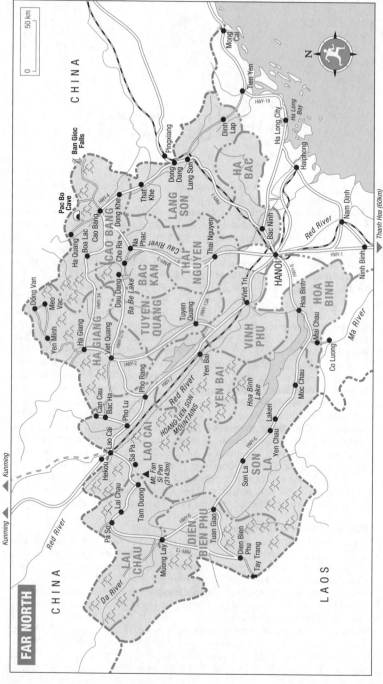

FAR NORTH

During the late 1970s **Sino-Vietnamese** relations became increasingly sour for various reasons, not least Vietnam's invasion of Cambodia. Things came to a head on February 17, 1979 when the Chinese sent 200,000 troops into northern Vietnam, destroying most of the border towns: seventeen days later, however, the invasion force was on its way home, some 20,000 short. Though much of the infrastructural and political damage from the war has been repaired, unmarked minefields along 1000km of frontier pose a more intractable problem: most areas – including all which regularly receive tourists – have been cleared and declared safe, but in the more remote areas it's sensible to stick to well-worn paths.

Getting around

The mountains of northern Vietnam remain relatively unexplored, largely because of the limited road network and the difficulties of getting around by public transport. Even major highways are little more than single-track, though roads are continuing to improve. It is possible to do a complete loop of the **northwest** with no backtracking, linking Sa Pa, Lai Chau, Dien Bien Phu, Son La and Mai Chau. By cutting across from Sa Pa or Bac Ha to Ha Giang, the northwest route can be combined with a tour of the **northeast** that takes in Ha Giang, Ba Be Lake, Cao Bang and Lang Son.

Travelling through the northern provinces using local **buses** is possible, though uncomfortable: **renting a vehicle** gives you more freedom to stop at villages or jaunt off along side tracks. Either a four-wheel-drive jeep or Landcruiser, or a motorbike, is recommended; the cost of hiring a jeep and driver (for three to four passengers) in Hanoi averages around $60 per day, while scooters and motorbikes go for between $5 and $8 per day. When **planning your route**, base your itinerary on an average speed of about 40km per hour. Whether you travel by public transport or with your own vehicle, you need to allow around six days' actual **travelling time** to cover the northwestern region; by cutting out side-trips to Dien Bien Phu and Mai Chau you can reduce this to a minimum of four days on the road. Touring the entire northeast requires at least six days including a tour of Ha Giang Province, but more if you want to spend time on Ba Be Lake, or visit Pac Bo Cave or Ban Gioc Waterfall near Cao Bang. Bear in mind that travelling these roads is unpredictable, becoming downright hazardous during the rains (see p.13), and it's advisable to allow some **flexibility** in your programme. If you've got only limited time, Sa Pa, Mai Chau and Ba Be National Park make rewarding two- or three-day **excursions out of Hanoi**, either by public transport or hired vehicle. The other alternative is to join an organized tour with one of Hanoi's tour agencies.

The major towns in the north have **ATMs**, but in smaller towns you'll have to make sure you bring enough dong and dollars with you: the odd bank may also change traveller's cheques.

When to go

The **best time** to visit the northern mountains is from September to November or from March to May, when the weather is fairly settled with dry sunny days and clear cold nights. **Winters** can be decidedly chilly, especially in the northeast where night frosts are not uncommon from December to February, but the compensation is daybreak mists and breathtaking sunrise views high above valleys filled with early-morning lakes of cloud. The **rainy season** lasts from May to September, peaking in July and August, when heavy downpours wash out bridges, turn unsealed roads into quagmires and throw in

The northern minorities

Around six million minority people (nearly two-thirds of Vietnam's total) live in the northern uplands, mostly in isolated villages. The largest ethnic groups are Thai and Muong in the northwest, Tay and Nung in the northeast, and Hmong and Dao dispersed throughout the region. Historically, all these peoples migrated from southern China at various times throughout history: those who arrived first, notably the Tay and Thai, settled in the fertile valleys where they now lead a relatively prosperous existence, whereas late arrivals, such as the Hmong and Dao, were left to eke out a living on the inhospitable higher slopes (for more on these diverse groups, see Contexts, p.492). Despite government efforts to integrate them into the Vietnamese community, most continue to follow a way of life little changed over the centuries. For an insight into the minorities' traditional cultures and highly varied styles of dress, visit Hanoi's informative **Museum of Ethnology** or the **Museum of Ethnology** in Thai Nguyen (see p.373) before setting off into the mountains.

Visiting minority villages

The remoteness of Vietnam's minority villages provides much of their appeal, though many are easily accessible from hub towns such as Sa Pa, Bac Ha, Son La, Mai Chau, Ba Be and Cao Bang. A popular, hassle-free way to visit is to join one of the **organized trips** offered by Hanoi tour agencies (see p.349). The usual destinations are Sa Pa and Bac Ha, coinciding with the Sunday market, or Mai Chau, with the standard package including guided visits to at least two different minorities plus, in the case of Mai Chau, a night in a stilthouse. The four-day Sa Pa tour costs from $90 per person depending on transport and accommodation arrangements, while two days with one night in Mai Chau costs around $30. In Sa Pa and Bac Ha, most **guesthouses** offer trekking and home-stay trips with their own guides, though note that not all the guides can speak English.

Village etiquette

Behaviour that we take for granted may cause offence to some ethnic minority people; remember you're a guest. Apart from being sensitive to the situation and

the occasional landslide for good measure. Peak season for foreign tourists is from September to November, while the rainy summer months of July and August are when Hanoians head up to the mountains to escape the stifling heat of the delta.

The northwest

Vietnam's most mountainous provinces lie immediately west of the Red River Valley, dominated by the country's highest range, Hoang Lien Son. Right on the border where the Red River enters Vietnam sits **Lao Cai** Town, a major crossing point into China and gateway to the former hill station of **Sa Pa** and nearby **Bac Ha**, both now firmly on the tourist map for their colourful minority groups and weekly markets. From Sa Pa a road loops west across the keeping an open mind, the following simple rules should be observed when visiting the ethnic minority areas.

- **Dress modestly**, in long trousers or skirt and T-shirt or shirt.
- Be sensitive to people's wishes when taking **photographs**, particularly of older people who are suspicious of the camera; always ask permission first.
- Only go **inside a house** when invited and remove your shoes before entering.
- Small **gifts**, such as fresh fruit from the local market, are always welcome. However, there is a view that even this can foster begging, and that you should only ever give in return for some service or as a sign of appreciation for hospitality. A compromise is to **buy craft work** produced by the villagers – most communities should have some embroidery, textiles or basketry for sale.
- As a mark of respect, learn the local **terms of address**, either in dialect or at least in Vietnamese, such as *chao ong, chao ba* (see p.541).
- Try to **minimize your impact** on the often fragile local environment; take litter back to the towns and be sensitive to the use of wood and other scarce resources.
- Growing and using **opium** is illegal in Vietnam and is punished with a fine or prison sentence; do not encourage its production by buying or smoking opium.

Trekking practicalities

It's important to wear the right **clothing** when walking in these mountains: strong boots with ankle support are the best footwear, though you can get away with training shoes in the dry season. Choose thin, loose clothing – long trousers offer some protection from thorns and leeches; wear a hat and sunblock; take plenty of water; and carry a basic medical kit. If you plan on spending the night in a village you'll need warm clothing as temperatures can drop to around freezing, and you might want to take a sleeping bag, mosquito net and food, though these are usually provided on organized tours. Finally, dogs can be a problem when entering villages, so it's a good idea to carry a strong stick when trekking, and always be watchful for the poisonous snakes that are common in this area.

immense flank of **Fan Si Pan**, the country's tallest peak, to join the Song Da (Black River) Valley running south, through the old French garrison towns of **Muong Lay** (formerly Lai Chau, see box on p.437 for more on changing names) and **Son La**, via a series of dramatic passes to the industrial town of Hoa Binh on the edge of the northern delta. The only sight as such is the historic battlefield of **Dien Bien Phu**, close to the Lao border, but it's the scenery that makes the diversion worthwhile. Throughout the region, sweeping views and mountain grandeur contrast with ribbons of intensively cultivated valleys, and here more than anywhere else in Vietnam the **ethnic minorities** have retained their traditional dress, architecture and languages. After Sa Pa, the most popular tourist destination in these mountains is **Mai Chau**, an attractive area inhabited by the White Thai minority, within easy reach of Hanoi.

Lao Cai

Follow the Red River Valley northwest from Hanoi, and after 300km pushing ever deeper into the mountains, you eventually reach the border town of **LAO CAI**, the railhead for Sa Pa and a popular route into China for travellers heading to Kunming. It exudes none of the trading frenzy of other border towns and even its **market**, the only point of interest apart from the border itself, is a small, local affair peddling medicinal leaves, roots and bark from the surrounding forests as well as cheap Chinese imports. Vietnamese traders head over the border to Hekou market, a mass of ramshackle huts clearly visible across the river; coming the other way, but in smaller numbers, are groups of Chinese day-trippers.

Practicalities

Most people arriving from Hanoi will pitch up at Lao Cai **train station**, located next to a **post office** on the east bank of the Red River, nearly 3km due south of the Chinese border. The **bus station** is 400m along Phan Dinh Phung, which runs directly opposite the train station; note that almost nobody arrives by bus from Hanoi, as the road is in a wretched state.

If you want to head into town, follow the road north from the station towards the border and after 2km you reach Coc Leu Bridge, spanning the river to link up with the bulk of Lao Cai Town over on the opposite bank. Immediately across the bridge, the town's market is on the left. To get to Lao Cai's one and only **ATM**, continue up the hill from the bridge for 150m and turn left at the first set of traffic lights. To reach the border, continue north past the bridge for another kilometre. Getting about Lao Cai is most easily done by **motorbike**; hordes of xe om shuttle between the train station and frontier or across to the bus station.

For those travelling **on to Sa Pa**, a slew of tourist buses (40,000đ) meet the Hanoi train in the early morning for the ninety-minute journey to Sa Pa Town. Local buses (25.000đ) also run from here and the nearby bus station, though times are highly irregular. Xe om (from 80,000đ) are always on the prowl, though this is not the best way to tackle the switchback climb if you're a sensitive traveller. Note that there have been several thefts on the **night train** between Hanoi and Lao Cai and reports of pickpocketing on Hanoi's station platform. It's also worth noting that you can take a motorbike onto the train with you for around $10: if you can, get help from a Vietnamese speaker to fill in the necessary from.

Accommodation and eating

There's little reason to linger in Lao Cai itself and if you are simply passing through after getting the night train, you can freshen up with a shower ($2 including towel and soap) at the *Hotel Terminus* (☎020/383 5470), opposite the station. If you need **to stay** overnight, try the *Thien Hai* (☎020/383 6666,

---

Onward travel to China

The border crossing into China is via the Hekou Bridge **border gate** (daily 7am–10pm), on the east bank of the Red River. Queues are longest in the early morning, when local traders get their day pass over to Hekou. There are no Chinese trains to Kunming, as the line has been out of service for many years due to flooding and landslides. However, it is possible to make your own way to Lao Cai, cross the border on foot, then carry on in China by bus (taking twelve hours for the 520km journey to Kunming); you'll need to have arranged your Chinese visa beforehand.

Travellers entering China occasionally have their guidebooks to the country confiscated (hiding it might help), while those **entering Vietnam** at Lao Cai may be asked for a "fee" of a couple of dollars for paperwork, processing or the like.

@www.thienhaihotel.com; ❹), immediately on your left as you exit the train station. The best option on Phan Dinh Phung, the road heading away from the station, is the huge *Viet Hoa Guesthouse* (☎020/383 0082; ❷), though it looks far grander from the outside than it is inside.

The ground-floor **restaurant** at the *Hotel Terminus* serves up cheap and tasty dishes in a convenient location, while the **food stalls** opposite the train station are also good. The tenth-floor cafe of the *Thien Hai* is the place to hang out over a coffee, while waiting for the train.

Sa Pa and around

Forty kilometres southwest of Lao Cai and the tourist capital of Vietnam's mountainous north, **SA PA** is perched dramatically on the western edge of a high plateau, facing the hazy blue peak of **Fan Si Pan**. Its refreshing climate and vaguely alpine landscape struck a nostalgic chord with European visitors, who travelled up from Lao Cai by sedan chair in the early twentieth century, and by 1930 a flourishing hill station had developed, complete with tennis court, church and over two hundred villas. Nowadays only a handful of the old buildings remain, the rest lost to time and the 1979 Chinese invasion, as well as those involved in the current hotel development spree. Although height restrictions are finally being enforced on new buildings, the damage has already been done and Sa Pa's days as an idyllic haven in the hills have been concreted over. However, what the modern town lacks in character is more than compensated for by its magnificent scenery, and it makes an ideal base for tours of the area's varied collection of **minority villages**.

The region is home to many **ethnic groups**, principally Hmong, Dao and Giay. (For more on minority peoples see Contexts, p.492.) The group most frequently seen in Sa Pa is the Black Hmong, who are not intimidated by the presence of foreigners in their midst. In fact, young Hmong girls can often be seen walking hand in hand with Westerners they have befriended prior to making their sales pitch. By contrast, the Red Dao, another common group here, are very shy and not at all happy to be photographed, despite their eye-catching dress.

Sa Pa's invigorating air is a real tonic after the dusty plains, but cold nights make warm clothes essential throughout the year: the sun sets early behind Fan Si Pan, and temperatures fall rapidly after dark. During the coldest months (Dec–Feb), night temperatures often drop below freezing and most winters bring some snow, so it's worth finding a hotel room with heating. Often a thick fog straight out of a Sherlock Holmes novel can creep over the whole town, lending a spooky feel to the market. You'll find the best **weather** from September to November and March to May, though even during these months cold, damp cloud can descend, blotting out the views for several days.

Arrival, information and transport

Though many people visit Sa Pa on an organized **tour** from Hanoi, the town is well set up for independent travel. The most popular route is by **train** to Lao Cai, and then the connecting **tourist bus** (40,000đ) up to Sa Pa; while the night train saves on both time and accommodation, a daylight journey gives great views along the Red River Valley. The tourist buses drop off on Cau May, Sa Pa's main street.

Heading back to Lao Cai, local buses (also 40,000đ) leave from various points, including Cau May and the church. Guesthouse owners can also often arrange

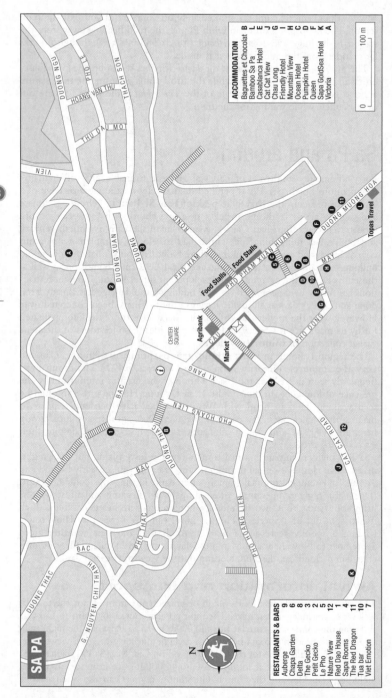

SA PA

ACCOMMODATION

Baguettes et Chocolat	B
Bamboo Sa Pa	L
Casablanca Hotel	E
Cat Cat View	G
Chau Long	J
Friendly Hotel	I
Mountain View	C
Ocean Hotel	D
Pumpkin Hotel	F
Queen	K
Sapa GoldSea Hotel	A
Victoria	A

0 — 100 m

RESTAURANTS & BARS

Auberge	9
Chapa Garden	6
Delta	8
The Gecko	3
Petit Gecko	2
Le Pho	5
Nature View	12
Red Dao House	4
Sapa Rooms	1
The Red Dragon	11
Tua bar	10
Viet Emotion	7

N

a pick-up, organize jeeps for small groups back to Lao Cai and book train tickets; note that hard sleeper and soft seat tickets on the night train are often in short supply at Lao Cai, so to be sure of a place book in advance in Sa Pa. Several private operators now attach luxury carriages onto the Hanoi–Sa Pa night trains, including the **Victoria Express**, reserved for guests at the *Victoria Sapa Hotel* (see p.430), and the **Pumpkin Train** (Ⓦ www.et-pumpkin.com), and the **Fanxipan Express**, which can both be booked through Hanoi travel agents (see p.349).

Though there's a dedicated **tourist information** office (daily 7.30–11.30am & 1.30–5pm) at the top of Cao May, Sa Pa's guesthouses remain the best source of advice on visiting minority villages; guides are available for around $15–20 per day. Trips offered by Topas Travel at 24 Muong Hoa (Ⓣ 020/387 1331, Ⓦ www.topas-adventure-vietnam.com) and Handspan Adventure Travel in Hanoi (Ⓣ 04/3926 2828, Ⓦ www.handspan.com) are safe and popular, though fierce competition means that you'll find far lower prices if you shop around. The tourist office sells detailed walking maps of the area, though most agencies hand out their own versions for free.

Accommodation

Despite the glut of guesthouses and hotels in Sa Pa, rooms can still be in **short supply** in the summer months, pushing up prices by as much as fifty percent. Prices also go up at **weekends** from September to November, when the streets are busy with foreigners, but there are usually enough beds to go round. Since weekend hotel prices are higher and the town crawling with tourists, it's worth considering a midweek visit. Needless to say, rooms with views command higher prices. Foreigners can also now stay in many of Sa Pa's surrounding **minority villages**; guesthouses and travel agencies can help with arrangements.

Baguettes et Chocolat Thac Bac Ⓣ 020/387 1766, Ⓔ hoasuaschoolsp@hn.vnn.vn. Run by the Hoa Sua School for disadvantaged youth, this is a quiet and comfy place that looks over the town. It has only two twins and two doubles, but the delightful decor and friendly service make it popular. The price includes breakfast in the fantastic ground-floor café. ❷

Bamboo Sa Pa Muong Hoa Ⓣ 020/387 1075, Ⓔ bamboosapa@hn.vnn.vn. Some of the smartest rooms in town, with excellent views, bathtubs and fake fireplaces. Minority shows in the large restaurant at weekends. ❹

Casablanca Hotel Dong Loi Ⓣ 020/387 2667, Ⓔ guesthousecasablancasapahotel @gmail.com. By far the best value of Sa Pa's growing army of boutique hotels, with gorgeously decorated rooms – all with satellite TV – and a friendly, on-the-ball owner. ❸

Cat Cat View Cat Cat Rd Ⓣ 020/387 1946, Ⓦ www.catcathotel.com. One of the town's longest-standing mini-hotels, *Cat Cat* has a building on each side of the road and a huge variety of rooms, some with fantastic panoramic views across to Mount Fan Si Pan. Popular with

budget travellers who socialize on the communal balconies. ❶–❹

Chau Long 24 Dong Loi Ⓣ 020/387 1245, Ⓦ www.chaulonghotel.com.vn. Small but smart rooms, all with bathtubs, in this attractive building. Opposite, the pricier four-star wing has excellent facilities and better views. ❹–❺

Friendly Hotel 11 Muong Hoa Ⓣ 020/387 3689. The best budget choice in town has amiable service, fantastic views from some upper-floor rooms, and bedding that puts many of the big boys to shame. Breakfast, however, is poor value for money – head elsewhere. ❶

Mountain View 52 Cau May Ⓣ 020/387 1334. A popular choice, with bright, clean, comfy rooms, and good vistas. Its outdoor restaurant (see p.431) is a great place to watch the sun go down. Slightly cheaper, but slightly shabbier, is the *Royal*, a sister hotel across the road. ❶–❸

Ocean Hotel 18 Pham Xuan Huan Ⓣ 020/387 1573. Though the service is sub-par and little English is spoken, corner rooms at the *Ocean* (also known as the *Dai Duong*) have one meaty advantage – there's almost as much window as there is wall, making for great views. ❷

Pumpkin Hotel 42 Cau May ☎020/387 2350, ℮pumpkinsapa@gmail.com. The owners at this cheapie have aimed for a fresh look with their peach-and-lemon paint scheme, and views are good from the communal balconies; just watch out for the trinket-selling Hmong girls that often take up residence on the front steps. ❷

Queen Muong Hoa ☎020/387 1301, ℮sapaqueenhotel@yahoo,com. Getting on in years, but this budget choice in the centre is well kept and friendly, and has some of the cheapest rooms in town. Most of them have decent views, but can be noisy. ❶

Sapa GoldSea Hotel 58 Fanxipan ☎020/387 2180, ⓦwww.sapagoldsea-hotel.com.vn. There's a sense of remoteness at this hotel, despite its location just a short walk down the road from Cat Cat. The rooms are split between two buildings: views from some are splendid though others are crowded by foliage – ask to see them first. ❸

Topas Eco–lodge ☎020/387 1331, ⓦwww.topas-eco-lodge.com. Situated a 45min drive from Sa Pa, the *Topas Eco-lodge* is made up of 25 luxurious but eco-friendly alpine lodge-style cottages, set on a clifftop with spectacular views looking down over a glorious valley and the ethnic minority village of Ban Ho. Their office in Sa Pa offers transport to the lodge and a number of tours. ❺

Victoria Hoang Dieu ☎020/387 1522, ⓦwww.victoriahotels-asia.com. The *Victoria*'s 77 rooms bring a touch of luxury to Sa Pa and find a regular clientele among expat residents of Hanoi looking for an accessible weekend break. Pool, tennis courts, sauna and jacuzzi on site, as well as an excellent restaurant and a rabbit farm for the kids. Guests can travel here on the Victoria Express, a luxury carriage on the 9.55pm Hanoi–Lao Cai train daily bar Sat. ❼

The Town

Sa Pa itself is ethnically Vietnamese, but its shops and market serve the minority villages for miles around. What initially attracted visitors was the **weekend market**, which runs from Friday to Sunday. These days it's housed in a concrete eyesore, a far cry from the original Saturday "love market" where the local ethnic minorities would come to court their sweethearts. The love market has now moved on elsewhere, a result of too many intrusive camera flashes and voyeuristic tourists, though plenty of minority people still turn up to peddle ethnic-style bags and shirts to trekkers. More authentic market fairs can be found on the other side of the Red River at **Can Cau** (Sat) and **Bac Ha** (Sun; see p.434). The weekends are still bright and lively in Sa Pa, though, with the women coming dressed in their finery – the most eye-catching are the Red Dao, who wear scarlet headdresses festooned with woollen tassels and silver trinkets. Black Hmong are the most numerous group – over a third of the district's population – and the most commercially minded, peddling their embroidered indigo-blue waistcoats, bags, hats and heavy, silver jewellery at all hours.

Eating and drinking

Sa Pa has the widest range of food in the north outside Hanoi; one benefit of the building boom is that there is plenty of choice, many serving a mixture of local cuisine and foreign dishes. To go where the locals are, try the series of street stalls along Pham Xuan Huan, parallel to Cau May, that serve pho and rice; some stay open late into the night, when the focus shifts to barbequed meat and rice wine. For nightlife, the *Red Dragon* (see below) serves beer and cocktails, or you can shoot some pool at the *Tua Bar* on Dong Loi.

Auberge Muong Hoa. Popular restaurant with a great terrace area that serves cheap and decent Vietnamese fare or local interpretations of Western dishes. A good place to mingle with other travellers.

Baguettes et Chocolat Thac Bac. Part of a chain that trains disadvantaged children in hospitality; it offers excellent pastries and, as the name suggests, filling baguettes and chocolate sweets, in a comfortable colonial setting. It also sells custom-made hampers to take on your trekking journey.

Chapa Garden Pham Xuan Huan. This secluded, Norwegian-run restaurant with delectable cuisine (mains from 120,000d), fine wine and a crackling fireplace has something of an Alpine atmosphere. The friendly staff are all Black Hmong, and there's always a local choice among the Western items on the menu.

Delta Cau May. With a prime location and a good wine list, the *Delta* is better known for its pizzas than its pasta, but is still a popular place for late-night diners.

The Gecko Ham Rong. Well-designed, French-run venue; the dishes are pricey but their originality – clay pot with caramelised fish, for example – makes them a welcome relief from Sa Pa's usual Viet-Western fare. Opposite, its sister restaurant, the tiny *Petit Gecko*, is slightly cheaper and styled like a Black Hmong house, but serves similar fare.

Le Pho Pham Xuan Huan. Slurp down Sa Pa's best pho in a pleasant, orange-trimmed setting; 32,000đ may seem a steep price for this simple dish, but cardamom and aniseed are among the more adventurous ingredients thrown into the mix.

Mountain View Cau May. One of the most scenic spots in Sa Pa, the outdoor area is the perfect place to sample traditional north Vietnamese fare and look out over the valley. The huge Lao Cai beers they sell also make it a jovial choice for when the sun has set.

Nature View Fan Si Pan. You could pay for the views alone and still feel that you'd got value for money; throw in a selection of reasonably-priced Vietnamese and Western dishes and it's a good deal. Pizzas, however, are better at *Viet Phap Y* across the road.

Red Dao House Thac Bac. Too twee for some but there's a certain kitsch appeal to this large and slightly pricey restaurant; the menu has plenty of authentic Sa Pa cuisine, and as the name suggests, staff are all Red Dao.

Sapa Rooms Fan Si Pan. You could spend the whole day here, grazing on home-made muffins and carrot juice for breakfast, awesome fries for lunch, and fish fried with coriander and chilli for dinner. Prices are very reasonable, and many customers return again and again.

Tavan *Victoria* hotel. The service and quality is what you'd expect from the *Victoria*. Specializing in French cuisine with locally grown produce, the meals are delicious but with a price to match. Also offers an excellent breakfast buffet that is perfect fuel for early morning treks.

The Red Dragon Muong Hoa. A slice of England in Sa Pa. Run by English expat John and his wife, the effort that goes into the food (think home-made sausages and shepherds' pie) make this a great option. They also have a good range of beers in the bar upstairs, where travellers swap stories till the midnight closing time.

Viet Emotion Cau May. Spanish tapas and a healthy range of cocktails are on the menu at this two-floor gem; try the *bu nuong ngu vi*, pork grilled with cardamom, or start the day with a filling set breakfast.

Listings

Banks and money There are several ATMs dotted around Sa Pa, and the Agribank (Mon–Fri 7.30–11am & 1.30–5pm) on Cau May can exchange cash and traveller's cheques.

Internet Most guesthouses have internet access.

Motorbikes & jeeps Xe om can be arranged through your guesthouse; self-drive is available (from $5 per day) but you need to be an experienced biker to tackle the stony, mountain tracks; make sure you test the bike for faults before leaving town. It's also possible to hire your own jeep and driver (around $30 per day) via guesthouses, depending on availability, but if you want to tackle the whole northwestern circuit you'll find cheaper long-term prices in Hanoi.

Post office Ham Rong (Mon–Fri 8–11.30am & 1–4pm). Service is poor and mail delivery times are exceptionally long. Hanoi is a better option.

Around Sa Pa

There are several Hmong villages within easy walking distance of town, though if you are heading to the more remote villages, it's strongly advisable to go accompanied by a local guide. All hotels and tour agents in Sa Pa can organize treks to all the villages below, with prices starting at around $15 per day: for around an extra $10 a day, you can include home-stay accommodation in a village. When booking a guide locally (see p.429 for a couple of reliable outfits), make sure you get one from Sa Pa and not from Hanoi, as only a local will speak the dialects necessary to communicate within the villages. Always wear strong shoes, carry water, waterproofs and a basic medical kit.

Cat Cat and Sin Chai

Since it's just 3km from Sa Pa, most people walk independently to the Black Hmong village of **CAT CAT** – follow the track west from the market square, and continue past the steeple-shaped forestry department building. The village hides among fruit trees and bamboo, where chickens and pot-bellied pigs scavenge through trailing pumpkin vines, though the sheer number of visitors makes the experience feel less authentic than it really is. Look out for tubs of indigo dye, used to colour the hemp cloth typical of Hmong dress, and for interlocking bamboo pipes that supply the village with both water and power for de-husking rice. Cat Cat waterfall is just below the village, the site of an old hydroelectric station and now a pleasant place to rest before tackling the homeward journey. For a longer walk, instead of cutting down to Cat Cat Village, continue on the main track turning right at the last bend before a river to follow a footpath up the valley towards Fan Si Pan. After 4km you'll reach **SIN CHAI** Village, a much larger Hmong settlement (nearly a hundred houses) spread out along the path.

South down the Muong Hoa Valley

You have to venture further afield to reach villages of minorities other than Hmong. One of the most enjoyable treks is to follow the main track down the Muong Hoa Valley for 9km to a wooden suspension bridge and **TA VAN** Village, on the opposite side of the river. Ta Van actually consists of two villages: immediately across the bridge is a Giay community, while further uphill to the left is a Dao village. From here, it's possible to walk back towards Sa Pa on the west side of the river, as far as another Hmong village, **LAO CHAI**, before rejoining the main track. If you don't want to walk all the way back up to Sa Pa, you can pick up a motorbike taxi at one of the huts you'll find every two to three kilometres along the track. Alternatively, you can take a xe om from Sa Pa for the round trip, but negotiate an acceptable price first.

Following the main road another 3km south from the turn-off to Ta Van, a track leads to the Dao settlement of **GIANG TA CHAI**. The path branches off to the right, just after a stream crosses the road and before a small shop. After crossing a suspension bridge, take the left fork, directly across a stream, after which it's a kilometre to the village. Giang Ta Chai can also be reached by footpath from Ta Van, but you'll need a guide; some tours include all three of the above villages, with Ta Van the usual home-stay base.

From the last turn-off the road deteriorates rapidly for another 6km until it finally dwindles to a footpath just after **SU PAN**, an unprepossessing collection of huts which is home to a number of different minorities (mainly Red Dao). From here, heading 4km straight down into the valley, and bearing right at each fork, brings you to the Tay village of **BAN HO**, which straddles the river at a suspension bridge; the settlement comes into view at the bottom of the valley soon after you leave Su Pan. Ban Ho is the staging point for two-, three- and four-day treks in the next valley, best tackled in the company of a guide.

North of Sa Pa

An excursion to **TA PHIN** Village takes you northeast of Sa Pa, along the main Lao Cai road for 6km and then left on a dirt track for the same distance again, past the blackened shell of an old French seminary. Finally, a scenic footpath across the paddy leads to a community of Red Dao scattered among a group of low hills; on the way look out for a beautifully engineered rice-husker beside a small stream. The village is known for its handicrafts, though it's now rather commercial and the locals can sometimes be quite aggressive when it comes to selling their beer. The easiest way to find Ta Phin is to take a xe om from Sa Pa (around 80,000đ each way) and get dropped off at the start of the footpath; as the leg between Sa Pa and the start of this path isn't so attractive, you might also want to keep it for the return journey.

New villages are being explored all the time as more tourists arrive seeking out ever more remote spots. **BANG KHOANG** is a Dao settlement with over a hundred families located 16km north of Sa Pa; look for a right turn after about 10km along the Lai Chau road and follow the road to the village. From here, the road continues to the Hmong settlement **TA GIANG PHINH**, home to 150 families. Both of these villages are best explored by jeep or motorbike in a day-trip from Sa Pa.

Mount Fan Si Pan

Vietnam's highest mountain, **Fan Si Pan** (3143m) lies less than 5km as the crow flies from Sa Pa, but it's an arduous three- to five-day round trip on foot. The usual route starts by descending 300m to cross the Muong Hoa River, and then climbs almost 2000m on overgrown paths through pine forest and bamboo thickets, before emerging on the southern ridge. The reward is a panorama encompassing the mountain ranges of northwest Vietnam, south to Son La Province and north to the peaks of Yunnan in China. Although it's a hard climb, the most difficult aspect of Fan Si Pan is its climate: even in the most favourable months of November and December it's difficult to predict a stretch of settled clear weather and many people are forced back by cloud, rain and cold. A **guide** is essential to trace indistinct paths, hack through bamboo and locate water sources; Hmong guides are said to know the mountain best. Sa Pa hotels and tour agents can arrange guides and porters as required.

Bac Ha and around

The small town of Bac Ha, nestling in a high valley 40km northeast of Highway 7, makes a popular day-excursion from Sa Pa. There's little to see in the town itself except on Sunday, when villagers of the Tay, Dao, Nung, Giay

▲ Flower Hmong ethnic people, Bac Ha

and above all Flower Hmong ethnic minorities trek in for the lively **market**. At 1200m above sea level compared to Sa Pa's 1600m, Bac Ha is less spectacularly beautiful, although it's still scenic, with cone-shaped mountains bobbing up out of the mist, and it's also much less touristy, giving out a workaday sense of a bustling agricultural community rather than an alpine resort. If you're travelling independently it's worth spending a whole weekend in Bac Ha, in which case you'd also be able to take in the rustic and colourful market at **Can Cau** on Saturday. Bac Ha also makes a good base for trips out to the surrounding Flower Hmong villages of **Ban Pho** and **Coc Ly**.

Arrival and information

Coming **from Hanoi**, get off the bus or train at Pho Lu, from where there are several buses a day to Bac Ha from the bus station (90min; 17,000đ), which lies on the highway just across from the railway station. Coming **from Lao Cai**, there are four daily buses to Bac Ha (2hr; 28,000đ), though times are irregular. If you missed the last bus, which theoretically leaves at 3pm, hop on a bus to Pho Lu and change there. If you're coming **from Sa Pa** on a Sunday, your best bet is to take a tour from one of Sa Pa's guesthouses for around $15, which includes spending the morning at the market, a trek in the afternoon and a ride back to Sa Pa, with the option of being dropped off at Lao Cai station. Alternatively, rent a motorbike from your guesthouse in Sa Pa to make the spectacular three-hour journey through the mountains. Bac Ha has no **exchange** facilities, so make sure you bring an adequate supply of dong and dollars. **Internet** access is available at the *Cong Fu* (see below).

Accommodation

The range of accommodation available in Bac Ha is limited, with few people spending more than one night in town: all the places listed below are within a minute's walk of – and visible from – the main four-way junction in the town centre. The two most expensive places in town are also the most popular: just west of the junction, the *Sao Mai* (℡020/388 0288, Ⓔsaomai@hn.vnn.vn; ❸), has big, comfortable rooms with satellite TV and a restaurant, and offers many tours of the local area; on the road heading to Can Cau, the *Cong Fu* (℡020/388 0254, Ⓦwww.congfuhotel.com; ❸), has adequate rooms, some of which directly overlook the market. At the junction itself are several reasonably priced places with little to choose between them – the *Tuan Anh* (℡020/388 0377; ❷) is a good option, though be warned that your sleep may be interrupted in this area: extremely loud public information broadcasts often thunder from nearby loudspeakers at around 5am.

The Town

Bac Ha provides a stark contrast to Sa Pa, with little in the way of tourist facilities beyond a few pho and bia hoi stalls. The Sunday **market**, the town's one big attraction, gradually fills up from 8 to 10am, and from then till lunchtime it's a jostling mass of colour, mostly provided by the stunningly dressed Flower Hmong women looking for additional adornments to their costume. The scene is filled out with a sizeable livestock market, meat and vegetable sellers, wine sellers and vendors of farming implements. The town returns to a dusty shadow of its former self by 5pm when the ethnic tribes return to their outlying villages. As Sa Pa becomes saturated with tourists seeking out a more authentic experience, so Bac Ha has attempted to emulate

Sa Pa's success by developing its own trekking business focused around the nearby rural markets. For the moment, however, it lacks sufficient infrastructure – which, in many ways, is the key to its charm.

At the northern end of town on the left along the main road, lies the remarkable folly of **Vua Meo**, or Cat King House. Two storeys of pure wedding cake surround a courtyard built in 1924 by the French as a palace for a Hmong leader, Vuong Chiz Sinh, whom they had installed as the local "king" (Meo, or "Cat" in Vietnamese, is a disparaging term formerly applied to the Hmong). The building is now the office of the local People's Committee, but visitors are free to wander through the courtyard.

Restaurants

Bac Ha's **restaurants** are bursting with tourists on Sundays and practically deserted at all other times, but don't expect the same quality that you'd find in Sa Pa. The tour buses tend to head for the *Ngan Nga*, on the north side of the main drag, thanks to its cheap, no-nonsense menu. Most of the hotels serve food – the *Sao Mai* features Western as well as Vietnamese dishes but is only open at weekends, while the *Tran Sin* serves basic meals in decent portions. There are two restaurants in town called *Cong Fu*, one in the *Cong Fu* hotel and another on the market road: both serve excellent food, though the latter is cheaper.

The villages around Bac Ha

It's only a short stroll to the picturesque Flower Hmong hamlet of **BAN PHO**, 3km from town. To get there head west out of town past the *Sao Mai Hotel*, turning left at the first major road, which continues up the hill for a couple of kilometres after the village, and affords good views of the valley. Around halfway along this vaguely clockwise loop, you can climb down on some rather dodgy trails to the idyllic Nung village of **NA THA**, from where there is a clearer path directly back to Bac Ha.

The village of **CAN CAU**, 18km north of Bac Ha, hosts a market each Saturday, which is every bit as colourful as that in Bac Ha, albeit smaller, and is located in a fairy-tale setting among rolling hills. It consists of a disparate mix of livestock on sale – including horses, ponies, buffalo and cattle – with traders trekking in from as far afield as China in search of bargains, plus many vendors selling bright panels of cloth, which attract the Flower Hmong women, already resplendent in their bright outfits. As with Bac Ha, the busy hours are around 10am to lunchtime, and there are some beautiful items of clothing on sale that make great souvenirs. Relatively few visitors get there so the fair retains much of its authenticity, a situation that is likely to change now that there is a reasonably good road. Other than the market there's nothing at all to see in Can Cau, but the ride, across a high, empty range with panoramic views on either side, is glorious. To get there, simply follow the main road north out of town the whole way. You can go there on a tour ($15 per person in a group of four), but it's not really necessary if you can ride a motorbike, as the market is right by the main road. The trusty xe om is another option. Further north of Can Cau, the largely Hmong town of **SIMA CAI** has its own ethnically diverse Sunday market, attended by Flower Hmong, Nung and Black Dao: it's best visited on a guided tour.

East of Bac Ha, the village of **THAI GIANG PHO**, home to Hmong, Tay and Fula people, is a six-hour round trip by motorbike or jeep from town, for which you'll need a guide, but be prepared for some rough overland driving.

The *Sao Mai* and *Cong Fu* hotels organize trips to all the above villages, as well as to the Tuesday flower market at **COC LY**, where the Flower Hmong women

From Bac Ha, it's possible to go directly to **Ha Giang** (see p.447) and continue exploring the little-known northeast, though for this you will need your own transport. Head back down out of the hills towards Lao Cai, but after crossing the bridge over the Chay River, turn left on Highway 70 and follow it about 40km to Pho Rang. This is a good place for a break as there are reasonable food stalls just beyond the bridge on the left and a lively market off to the right a little further down the main street. Turn left just before the bridge and follow Highway 279 to Viet Quang, then left again on Highway 2, which takes you into Ha Giang. The trip takes about six hours, depending on road conditions. Another option, though only possible in good weather and with good wheels, is to head directly east to **Viet Quang** via Xin Man and Huong Su Phi: the road is awful but the views are nothing short of spectacular.

stand side by side selling carefully selected flowers to neighbouring minority groups. The latter trip includes transport by jeep and a boat trip down the Blue River Valley and costs $18 per person. There are also possibilities of two- and three-day trips costing $15 per person per day, including overnight stays in the minority villages.

West to Dien Bien Phu

West of Sa Pa the road climbs over the **Hoang Lien Son range**: the going is rough all the way to the 2100m-high **Tram Tom Pass** ("Heaven's Gate"), which marks the boundary with Lai Chau province, but once over the top you'll have a smooth and incredibly scenic glide down. The road hugs the wall of an immense valley into the most sparsely populated region of Vietnam's far north: look out for tumbling waterfalls in the upper reaches, while on lower ground there's a colourful mosaic of **ethnic groups**. The most interesting of these are the Lu, who number less than 5,000 across Lai Chau, Laos, northern Thailand and the Chinese province of Yunnan. It's possible to stay at a Lu village, though you'll need a permit: this can be organized by travel agencies in Sa Pa (see p.429), or at the security bureau in Tam Duong (look for a lemon-coloured building in the centre of town). The Lu women often wear distinctive triangular hair clasps, and Lu society runs on extremely traditional lines, so if you do visit, stick to your most unobtrusive behaviour.

Lai Chau

About two hours' drive from Sa Pa, the town of **LAI CHAU** (not to be confused with the former Lai Chau now called Muong Lay), is getting uglier by the minute despite being surrounded by immaculate mountain scenery. Its main interest to travellers is as a base to visit the Monday **market** of great ethnic variety at **Pa So** Village (formerly Phong Tho), 30km further west. Lai Chau has only a handful of hotels, and they're all somewhat overpriced, except the *Muong Thanh* (☎023/379 0888; ❸), visible to the right as you're about to drop into town: it's surrounded by tea fields and affords fantastic views from the upper floors. Lai Chau's single main street is unappealing but holds the rest of the hotels, including the *Anh Huan* (☎023/387 8456; ❶), which is cheap and close to the market. Easily the best accommodation option around Pa So village is the impressive *Lan Anh II* (☎023/385 2682; ❿www.lananhhotel.com ❷) situated 3km beyond the village on the riverbank. It has comfortable rooms and a good restaurant.

From Lai Chau the route veers south, following the gently attractive **Nam Na Valley**: the higher slopes are farmed by groups of Black Hmong and Dao, though the valley floor is predominantly peopled with Thai villages of impressively solid stilthouses. Some of the White Thai communities in this region are surprisingly modern and orderly, as they are recent creations housing those whose original villages were affected by damming.

Muong Lay

Road and river track a wooded gorge before emerging at the confluence with the Da River near the town of **Muong Lay**, some 200km (5–6hr) from Sa Pa. The landscape to the north and south of town is some of the most rugged in the northwest, and thus prone to occasional landslides that can delay progress for long periods. After crossing the Da River the road skirts east of the town, past a T-junction where Muong Lay's one street branches right to the market and an attractive hotel, while the **bus station** is further along on the main highway. Some years ago Muong Lay lost its status as provincial capital to Dien Bien Phu, since when it's been in slow decline – some sections may even disappear altogether if plans for a second Da River dam go ahead. Today, however, it's a small, sleepy town with no real centre, just tentacles of buildings stranded above the flood plain. One eerie sight is the shell of the former Cultural Hall that was gutted by a flash flood and now looks like some futuristic sculpture of concrete and weeds. For most travellers this is a one-night stop between Sa Pa and Dien Bien Phu; after a quick walk round the small market, where you can snack on freshly cooked rice cakes, and a wander through the Black Thai village on the hillside west of town, there's little else to do – other than enjoy not being on the road.

Muong Lay boasts a surprisingly characterful **hotel**, the *Lan Anh* (☎023/385 2370, ⓦwww.lananhhotel.com; ❷), set in a leafy compound down a sidestreet to the right beyond the market. It has over forty rooms housed in a few attractive wooden buildings, all fitted with four-poster beds: while the cheaper rooms can be cramped, the mid-range ones are roomier and a better option. The hotel can also arrange local **tours** of up to six days, though most popular is a half-day trip that takes in a Hmong village, a Black Thai village, and a half-hour boat ride. The town's other accommodation option is the *Song Da* (☎023/385 2527; ❶) on the main highway 100m past the T-junction heading south, but this would only appeal to those on a very strict budget. For **food**, the best place in town – in fact, the best place in the northwest, outside of Sa Pa – is the restaurant at the *Lan Anh*, which serves excellent northern cuisine at reasonable prices.

Trading places

Only in Vietnam can things become so confusing. A few years ago, the government decided to change the names of certain towns in the northwest region, which is not that uncommon. However, when places began adopting the old names of nearby towns that already had changed their names, travelling became much harder than it needed to be. While some signs have been slow to change, we use the **new names**.

In Lai Chau Province, Binh Lu has changed to Tam Doung, and Tam Doung to Lai Chau. In Dien Bien Province, Lai Chau Town has changed to Muong Lay Town, and Moung Lay to Muong Tra.

Dien Bien Phu

South of Muong Lay the road splits: Highway 6 takes off southeast to Tuan Giao and is the shortest route to Son La; Highway 12 ploughs on south for more than 100km (about 3–4hr), making slow progress at first but then zipping through the second 50km, to the heart-shaped valley of **DIEN BIEN PHU**, scene of General Giap's triumph in a battle that signalled the end of French Indochina (see box opposite). Though the town's trickle of tourists tend to be French history buffs, it's starting to become more popular as a base for trips to local minority villages: the valley's population is predominantly Thai (53 percent), while the Viet are concentrated in the urban area. With the recent opening of the border to foreigners, it's also being used as an alternative gateway to Laos.

Arrival and information

Daily flights from Hanoi arrive at the **airfield**, 1.5km north out of town, with the Vietnam Airlines office next door: it's a ten-minute walk into town from here, though a xe om only costs 10,000đ. Most people visit here, however, on the more interesting but gruelling road journey, arriving at the **bus station**, at the T-junction a couple of hundred metres from the town centre on the western edge of town. This is also where you catch the numerous minibuses for Son La and beyond (first one leaves at 6am). Head right from the busy roundabout and market if coming from the bus station to find an **Agribank** (Mon–Fri 7.30–11am & 1.30–5pm), which can change US dollars, and the **post office**.

The town and battle sites

The town's **museum** (daily 7.30–11am & 1.30–5pm; 5000đ) is set back slightly from the road on the right-hand side as you head south out of town. The displays of weaponry include American-made guns of World War II vintage captured from French troops. Alongside them languish Viet Minh guns, also American-made but newer: these were booty from the Korean War which came via China into Vietnam, to be dragged up the battlefield's encircling hills. Familiar photos of the war-torn valley become more interesting in context, as does the scale model where a guide describes the unfolding catastrophe – the message is perfectly clear, even in Vietnamese.

Directly opposite the museum is the **Viet Minh Cemetery**, where some of the fallen heroes are buried under grey marble headstones marked only with a red and gold star. In 1993 an imposing imperial gateway and white-marble wall of names was added in time for the fortieth anniversary of the battle. The outside of this wall features bas-reliefs in concrete of battle scenes.

A small hill overlooking the cemetery, known as **Hill A1** to the Vietnamese and as Eliane 2 to French defenders, was the scene of particularly bitter fighting before it was eventually overrun towards the end of the battle. You can inspect a reconstructed bunker on the summit and various memorials, including the grave of a Viet Minh hero who gave his life while disabling the French tank standing next to him, and you also get a panorama over the now peaceful, agricultural valley.

There's little to see at the last battle site, a reconstruction of **de Castries' bunker** (daily 7.30–11am & 1.30–5pm; 5000đ), located on a dusty country road across the river a couple of kilometres from central Dien Bien Phu; it's best to get here by bike (can be rented from most guesthouses for 20,000đ a day), crossing the river on the fantastically rickety Muong Thanh bridge (closed to anything with more than two wheels) before turning left. Captured tanks, anti-aircraft guns and other weaponry rust away in the surrounding fields. Carry on past the bunker and you'll come to a concrete enclosure with a memorial to "Those who died here for France".

The Battle of Dien Bien Phu

In November 1953 General Navarre, Commander-in-Chief in Indochina, ordered the French Expeditionary Force's parachute battalions to establish a base in Dien Bien Phu. Taunted by Viet Minh incursions into Laos, with which France had a mutual defence treaty, Navarre asserted that this would block enemy lines through the mountains, force the Viet Minh into open battle and end the war in Indochina within eighteen months – which it did, but not quite as Navarre intended. His deputy in Dien Bien Phu was **Colonel de Castries**, an aristocratic cavalry officer and dashing hero of World War II, supposedly irresistible to women, although Graham Greene, visiting the base in January 1954, described him as having the "nervy histrionic features of an old-time actor".

Using bulldozers dropped in beneath seven parachutes apiece, the French cleared two airstrips and then set up nine heavily fortified positions on low hills in the valley floor, reputedly named after de Castries' mistresses – Gabrielle, Eliane, Béatrice and so on. Less than a quarter of the garrison in Dien Bien Phu were mainland French: the rest were either from France's African colonies or the Foreign Legion (a mix of European nationalities), plus local Vietnamese troops including three battalions drawn from the Thai minority. There were also nineteen women in the thick of things (a stranded French nurse, plus eighteen Vietnamese and Algerian women from the Expeditionary Force's mobile brothel).

Meanwhile, **General Giap**, Commander of the People's Army, quietly moved his own forces into the steep hills around the valley, mobilizing an estimated 300,000 porters, road gangs and auxiliary soldiers in support of up to 50,000 battle troops. Not only did they carry in all food and equipment, often on foot or bicycle over vast distances, but they then hauled even the heaviest guns up the slopes, hacking paths through the dense steamy forest as they went. Ho Chi Minh described the scene to journalist Wilfred Burchett by turning his helmet upside down: "Down here is the valley of Dien Bien Phu. There are the French. They can't get out. It may take a long time, but they can't get out." In early 1954 Giap was ready to edge his troops even closer, using a network of tunnels dug under cover of darkness. By this time the international stakes had been raised: the war in Indochina would be discussed at the Geneva Conference in May, so now both sides needed a major victory to take to the negotiating table.

French commanders continued to believe their position was impregnable until the first shells rained down on March 10. Within five days Béatrice and Gabrielle had fallen, both airstrips were out of action and the siege had begun in earnest; the French artillery commander, declaring himself "completely dishonoured", lay down and took the pin out of a grenade. All French supplies and reinforcements now had to be parachuted in, frequently dropping behind enemy lines, and when de Castries was promoted to general even his stars were delivered by parachute; at the end of the battle, 83,000 parachutes were strewn across the valley floor. The **final assault** began on May 1, by which time the rains had arrived, hindering air support, filling the trenches and spreading disease. Waves of Viet Minh fought for every inch of ground, until their flag flew above de Castries' command bunker on the afternoon of May 7. The following morning, the day talks started in Geneva, the last position **surrendered** and the valley at last fell silent after 59 days. A ceasefire was signed in Geneva on July 21, and ten months later the last French troops left Indochina.

The Vietnamese paid a high price for their victory, with an estimated 20,000 dead and many thousands more wounded. On the French side, out of a total force of 16,500, some 10,000 were captured and marched hundreds of kilometres to camps in Vietnam's northeastern mountains; less than half survived the rigours of the journey, diseases and horrendous prison conditions.

More than fifty years on, the Battle of Dien Bien Phu remains one of the most significant military conflicts of the twentieth century, with its importance in Vietnam's struggle for independence commemorated in nearly every town by a street named in honour of that famous victory.

Accommodation

Muong Thanh ☎ 0230/381 0043,
✉ ksmuongthanh@yahoo.com. This long-running
favourite has seventy rooms of varying size and
facilities, a great restaurant and a small swimming
pool. It's located on Him Lam; turn left at the
town's main roundabout if coming from the bus
station and continue for another 800m. ❷
Him Lam Hotel ☎ 0230/381 1999, ☏ 0230/381
1369. Dien Bien Phu's newest and most extravagant accommodation lies a few kilometres out of
town on Him Lam, in a peaceful setting on a
riverbank. The rooms are good and the location
superb, but note that the small collection of

trapped bears and monkeys on site are used for
the extraction of bile and other fluids – a great
hotel, but not the most ethical choice. ❸
Dien Bien Phu–Hanoi ☎ 0230/382 5103,
✉ dienbienphu-hnhotel@vnn.vn. This place has
simple but acceptable rooms – the VIP choices
are good value – as well as helpful, English-
speaking staff and a tour service. Turn right at the
roundabout towards the museum. ❷
Viet Hoang on the Thanh Binh road ☎ 0230/373
5046. The best of a poor bunch near the bus
station, it has decent rooms, some of which have
balconies. ❶

Eating and drinking

Quality **restaurants** are in short supply, with the *Muong Thanh* hotel offering
the town's best food: locals tend to patronize the com pho stalls around the
roundabout and along the main roads – it's worth wandering around and
choosing the one with the biggest crowd. Look out for the region's speciality
dish, which is the Thai minority's black rice (*com gao cam*).

Highway 6

East of Dien Bien Phu the road climbs into steep mountains and passes
through constantly changing panoramas before dropping into **TUAN
GIAO**, where Highway 6 takes off north to Muong Lay or south to Son La.
Tuan Giao is a convenient lunch stop on a day of tough travel, and the
obvious place to eat is *Hoang Quat*, 100m before the T-junction, where it
comes as a surprise to see tablecloths and an English menu; the owner can
also help travellers find accommodation if necessary. You'll need to be
fortified to face the steep climb that follows to the Pha Din ("Heaven and
Earth") Pass, one of the highest in the north. If you're lucky there are great
views from the top, but more often than not it's enveloped in clouds. After a
long descent, the road eventually passes through the small town of **THUAN
CHAU**, where there's a lively market of predominantly Black Thai people
each morning until 9 or 10am. The last stretch passes through a valley
bordered by massive karst pillars before reaching a softer landscape of paddy
and banana plantations, where water wheels feed sculpted terraces, to the
industrious town of **SON LA**.

Onward travel to Laos

Dien Bien Phu is only 35km by road from the **border with Laos**, which is now open
to foreigners: it's possible to get a visa at the border (prices dependent on
nationality), though to be sure, this is best done in advance in Hanoi (see p.386).
Buses to **Muang Khoa**, a further 70km over the border in Laos (92,000đ) leave Dien
Bien Phu at 5.30am on Monday, Wednesday, Friday and Sunday; at other times you
can get a xe om to the border (100,000đ), though it's a 3km checkpoint-to-checkpoint
walk and you may find it hard to get onward transport.

Son La and around

Son La's welcoming, low-key charm is enhanced by its valley-edge setting, and it merits more than the usual overnight stop. If time allows, there's enough of interest to occupy several days, taking in the old French prison and some nearby caves, as well as making forays to nearby **minority villages** on foot or by motorbike.

Arrival information and accommodation

Son La's **bus station** is located 5km east of town, so it's necessary to take a xe om into the centre (15,000đ). The best place for **information** is the helpful *Trade Union Hotel* (see below), where you can also hire transport and English-speaking guides, or arrange to see Thai dancing and sample rice wine. The major part of Son La lies off the highway, strag-

▲ Tham Tat Tong Water Cave (2km)

ACCOMMODATION
Bien Phong	E
Hoa Ban 2	A
Sunrise	D
Thanh Mai	B
Trade Union Hotel	C

RESTAURANTS
| Hai Phi | 1 |
| Huong Tra | 2 |

Que Lam Ngu Che Cave

Covered Market

Nam La River

TO HIEU

French Prison (Museum)

Petrolimex Fuel Station

Food Stalls

Agribank

HIGHWAY 6

SON LA

0   250 m

Minority Villages Walk & Ban Mong Village (23km)

Dien Bien Phu (170km)

Bus Station (5km)

Airport (20km)

▼ Ban Mong Village (6km)

gling for little more than a kilometre along the west bank of the Nam La River. There's just one main street, To Hieu, where you'll find all the important municipal buildings, including the Agribank, at no. 9, which will **exchange** dollars, and a **post office**. **Motorbikes** are available for rent for $7 a day.

When it comes to **accommodation**, the *Trade Union Hotel* (☎022/385 2804, ✉congdoanhotelsla@yahoo.com; ❸) is a welcome exception to the generally gloomy and uninviting government-run places found in many Vietnamese towns. Its range of almost a hundred rooms is the best in town, and it organizes a variety of local trips. The nearby *Sunrise* (☎022/385 8799, ✉buixuandai @yahoo.com; ❸) is new, more intimate and offers good clean rooms and friendly English-speaking staff. The *Thanh Mai* (☎022/385 2984, ❷) is a spotless, newly-built guesthouse, situated above an **internet** café, and a good budget option. On the other side of the river, the *Bien Phong* (☎022/385 2373; ❷) has spacious rooms and is popular with local business groups. To the north of town, the *Hoa Ban 2* (☎022/385 2395; ❶–❷) is basic and only a good option if you want to be close to the caves.

The Town

At the far end of To Hieu, in front of the *Hoa Ban 2 Hotel*, a parallel road heads back south on the opposite side of the river, past the covered **market** – selling local minority handicrafts, including handmade cloth and lively embroideries – to rejoin Highway 6. Between these two roads, patches of paddy and vegetable plots are slowly being consumed by new buildings, and two bridges have been built to ease the constant bustle of traffic.

Son La's principal tourist sight is the **French prison**, Bao Tang Son La (daily 7.30–11am & 1.30–5pm; 5000đ), which occupies a wooded promontory above To Hieu and offers good views over town. The two turn-offs from the highway are both marked with chunky stylized signs suggesting incarceration; walk uphill to find the prison gates and an arched entrance, still announcing

"Pénitencier", leading into the main compound. This region was a hotbed of anti-French resistance, and a list of political prisoners interred here reads like a roll call of famous revolutionaries – among them Le Duan and Truong Chinh, veteran Party members who both went on to become general secretary. Local hero To Hieu was also imprisoned for seditionary crimes but he died from malaria while in captivity in 1944. Most of the buildings lie in ruins, destroyed by a French bombing raid in 1952, but a few have been reconstructed, including the two-storey kitchen block (*bep*), beneath which are seven punishment cells. Political prisoners were often incarcerated in brutal conditions: the two larger cells (then windowless) held up to five people shackled by the ankles. Behind the kitchens, don't miss the well-presented collection of prison memorabilia. Enter the second arched gate and upstairs in the building on your right you'll find an informative display about the dozen or so minorities who inhabit the area, including costumes, handicrafts, jewellery and photos.

Eating and drinking

For **food**, the *Trade Union Hotel* and the *Sunrise* have very good restaurants, but the former is open to residents only (closes 10.30pm). The *Hai Phi* is also a good option, especially if you like goat dishes, and is a popular venue for large gatherings. If you didn't find black rice (*com gao cam*) in Dien Bien Phu, then try it here in one of the com pho stalls near the big junction at the south end of town. Son La's nightlife is non-existent, but the *Huong Tra*, situated over a pond on the east side of town, is at least a mildly scenic spot to have a beer.

Around Son La

There are several **caves** around town that are worth a look, the most convenient being **Que Lam Ngu Che Cave** (daily 7.30–11am & 1.30–5.30pm; free), which is situated just north of the *Hoa Ban 2 Hotel* and has a small shrine inside surrounded by strange formations in the rock. A 500-year-old poem written by King Le Thai Tong carved into the stone remains visible today on the outside of the cave. You can go there alone – just look for the sign 150m north of the hotel, or a guide from the *Trade Union Hotel* will take you for a small fee. **Tham Tat Tong Water Cave** is located a couple of kilometres further north out of town, and at the time of writing was closed to visitors, but any excuse to walk in the countryside around Son La brings rich rewards, such as meetings with friendly villagers, lush panoramas of karst hills and paddy fields alive with butterflies. Follow the road north from the *Hoa Ban 2 Hotel* for nearly 2km and turn left just before a concrete bridge onto a footpath tracing the river upstream over an ancient stone bridge – according to local legend, built by a Black Thai queen a thousand years ago. Continue up the road another 150m until just before the road bends to the right, then turn left down a small path for 50m, to reach a barbed-wire enclosure where the river emerges from the hillside. There's also a second, dry cave directly overhead – a short scramble up beside the wire – in which, when open, you can walk the first 50m of a system said to be 7km long. Women at the gate will give you a torch to use for 10,000đ. Just beyond the turning for Tham Tat Tong Cave is one of Son La's nearest, though still rarely visited, **minority villages**. Instead of turning left at the concrete bridge continue on the road towards a cliff-face punched with a round cavern, reputed to contain gold, about 70m up. Turn left before the cliff and you pitch up in **BAN CO**, a Black Thai community of about fifty stilthouses constructed of bamboo, and fenced round with hedges of poinsettia and hibiscus. The dress of the Black Thai women is particularly striking – especially the brightly embroidered headscarves that they drape over their long hair piled up in huge buns.

Their tight-fitting blouses with rows of silver buttons, often in the shape of butterflies, are also distinctive. In colder weather, many wear a green, sleeveless sweater over the blouse, or a modern jacket in pink, blue, green or maroon.

If you've got more time, a popular jaunt takes you out to **BAN MONG**, another Thai village six scenic kilometres along a luxuriant valley south of Son La. The houses of this village are solid, wooden structures surrounded by gardens of fruit trees rather than vegetables. A scummy pond at the village edge is in fact a hot spring that provides water for the bathhouse and laundry at a constant 30°C. To get to Ban Mong, take the turning off Highway 6 opposite the prison, or take a xe om from Son La for the return trip (20,000đ return).

It's also possible to take in Ban Mong as part of a longer trek which heads northwest out of Son La before wheeling south through the villages of several minorities, eventually linking up with the hot spring. It's about six hours' walking in all, so you'll need a whole day, and take food and plenty of water, as there are no shops until you get to Ban Mong. As the route's fairly complicated it's best to drop by the *Trade Union Hotel*, where you can take their one-day tour covering all the attractions mentioned above. Certain minority villages stage events for tour groups, such as traditional Thai dancing or supping the local home brew, a sweet wine made of glutinous rice; it's drunk from a communal earthenware container using bamboo straws, and hence named *ruou can*, or stem alcohol.

Onto Mai Chau

From Son La Highway 6 climbs east, passing **YEN CHAU** – a town famed for its fruit – and some very pretty Black Thai villages on the right after about 80km, particularly **LA KEN**, which can be visited by crossing swaying suspension bridges over the river. From here the road climbs onto a thousand-metre-high plateau where the cool climate favours tea and coffee cultivation, mulberry to feed the voracious worms of Vietnam's silk industry and herds of dairy cattle, initially imported from Holland, to quench Hanoi's thirst for milk, yoghurt and ice cream. Just less than 120km out of Son La, the sprawling market town of **MOC CHAU** provides a convenient place for a break. For the next 4km heading towards Hanoi, the road is dotted with stalls selling local **milk products** such as three kinds of flavoured milk, and blocks of condensed milk (which they advertise as chocolate when cocoa is added), as well as green tea. The rigid lines of tea bushes that border the road round Moc Chau create curious patterns, and though there are few side roads, this is a region in which some might want to linger. Most, however, head on down Highway 6, through valleys where the Hmong live in distinctive houses built on the ground under long, low roofs, and surrounded by fruit orchards, to **MAI CHAU**, which lies up a side valley south of Highway 6.

Mai Chau and around

The **minority villages** of the Mai Chau Valley, inhabited mainly by White Thai, are close enough to Hanoi (135km) to make this a popular destination, particularly at weekends when it's often swamped with large groups of students. The valley itself, however, is still largely unspoilt, a peaceful scene of pancake-flat rice fields trimmed with jagged mountains.

Arrival and transport

Most people visit Mai Chau on an organized **tour** out of Hanoi, which usually includes overnighting in a minority village, or as part of a longer trip into the northwest mountains by jeep or motorbike.

Mai Chau is not the easiest place to get to by **public transport** but it is possible. **From Son La** take any bus heading east to Hoa Binh or Hanoi and ask the driver to let you off at the Mai Chau junction, around 65km after Moc Chau; at the junction pick up one of the waiting xe om for the final 6km up the valley. **From Hanoi**, there are a few daily buses (1.15pm; 35,000đ) from My Dinh bus station to Mai Chau. **Leaving Mai Chau**, a local bus departs at 5am, 6am and 6.30am bound for Hanoi, arriving four hours later; alternatively, take a xe om to the junction with Highway 6 and flag down a bus going in your direction. You could also take a long xe om ride to the border at, though this will cost at least $20.

Mai Chau Village

Mai Chau is the valley's main settlement, though it's still just a village – a friendly, quiet place which has a bustling morning **market** when minority people trek in to haggle over buffalo meat, star fruit, sacks of tea or groundnuts. Unlike in Sa Pa, the minorities here have largely forsaken their traditional dress, but there's plenty of colour on the road outside the market where bright hanks of yarn, freshly dyed in primary hues, hang up to dry.

Tour groups tend to stay in the villages of Ban Lac and Pom Coong to the west of Mai Chau and go on organized walks around the valley. If you are one of the rare independent travellers here, a tempting choice is to turn left (east) at the "Guesthouse" sign in the middle of Mai Chau, walk a kilometre across paddy fields to the village of **Ben Van**, which is hemmed in by mountains and has great charm and friendly inhabitants, and stay at a stilted guesthouse. The *Number 1 Ban Van Guesthouse* (☎0218/386 7182; ❶), the first guesthouse on the right, has a nice setting next to the rice fields. By far the most salubrious accommodation in Mai Chau itself is at the *Mai Chau Lodge* (☎0218/386 8959, ⓦwww.maichaulodge.com; ❻), which sits somewhat incongruously amid bucolic scenery: though a little overpriced, its rooms are tastefully decorated with wooden fixtures, and the staff are extremely helpful. Alternatively, Mai Chau has a couple of cheaper, but rather lacklustre accommodation options. On the south side the *Mai Chau Guesthouse* (☎0218/386 7262; ❶), with fourteen

▲ Ploughing in Mai Chau

very basic rooms is fine if you're not fussy, although the karaoke behind it is extremely loud at night. The *Ngoc Bach Guesthouse* (☎0218/386 7340; ❶) is more modern but has similar basic rooms and less helpful staff.

Other than the excellent **restaurant** at the *Mai Chau Lodge* (lunch $12, dinner $15), the best food in town is dished up at the *Toan Thang*, 200m before the *Mai Chau Guesthouse*, which serves freshly caught fish but has no English menu. *Cafe Hoan*, next to the *Mai Chau Guesthouse*, offers a scenic spot looking over the fields, to have a coffee. There are also many **food stalls** clustered around the market back in town, some serving lip-smacking kebabs. In the mornings you'll find hawkers here selling piping-hot banana fritters and coffee.

The Mai Chau Valley

Just south of the *Mai Chau Guesthouse*, a road to the right (west) leads across a few paddy fields to **BAN LAC**, home to a prosperous community of White Thai, though these days their wealth is derived more from tourist dollars than from farming. This is where most people stay on a two-day tour from Hanoi – it's a settlement of some seventy houses (about four hundred people) where you can buy handwoven textiles, watch performances of traditional dancing and sleep overnight. Nowadays just about every house in the village doubles as a guesthouse, and many have sit-down toilets fitted below the houses. Some house owners have even changed their roofs from tile back to the original thatch, perhaps to fulfil visitors' expectations. If you turn up without a tour group, just ask around and someone will put you up for about $5 per person for the night, plus $1–2 for a meal depending largely on how much you eat. While too touristy for some, Ban Lac does offer the chance to stay in a genuine stilthouse – an edifying experience, particularly at dawn if your sleeping quarters happen to be above the henhouse. During the day the lanes between houses are draped with scarves, bags and dresses, with villagers urging passersby to stop for a quick look. Though it seems a bit commercial, the vendors are not as pushy as their Black Hmong counterparts in Sa Pa, and if it does get tiring then a few minutes' walk in any direction from the centre leads out to paddies and a view of the ring of purple mountains which make for some of north Vietnam's most classic scenery. In the evenings, the traditional dance performances staged for tour groups after dinner are also interesting, with coy, long-haired girls acting out agricultural chores in a graceful manner. After the show, the audience is invited to join them in a dance, as well as a sup of local wine from a big bowl through a bamboo straw.

Many houses in Ban Lac rent out **bicycles**, which are an ideal way to explore the valley (20,000d per day). One interesting route is to cycle 12km south on Highway 15 to **CO LUONG**, passing timeless rural scenes and reflections of mountains in the flooded paddy fields. At Co Luong, the Ma River joins the road, and huge limestone walls and dense bamboo growth adorn the riverbank. An active market on Saturday mornings is worth the trip, to see the array of handicrafts and fish.

Hoa Binh

There's one final pass to go over before Highway 6 leaves the northwest mountains. It's a steady climb along precipitous hillsides up to a col at 1200m, and then an ear-popping descent through sugar-cane plantations to **HOA BINH**, on the edge of the Red River plain. The town's proximity to Hanoi, 76km on a fast road, plus its hotels and easy access to a variety of minority villages mean that Hoa Binh soaks up a lot of tourist traffic. Unless you need the bus connections, it's preferable to stop over in Mai Chau or push on all the way to Hanoi.

During the French War Hoa Binh was the scene of a disastrous French raid into Viet Minh-held territory, which reads like a dress rehearsal for the epic rout of Dien Bien Phu. In November 1951, French paratroop battalions seized Hoa Binh in a daring attempt to hamper enemy supply routes. They met with little resistance and dug in, only to find themselves marooned as Giap's forces cut both road and river access. In February the following year the French fought their way out towards Hanoi in a battle that came to be known as the "hell of Hoa Binh".

The main highway thunders straight through the centre of modern Hoa Binh but a hint of quieter days lingers in its shaded main boulevard, Cu Chin Lan. Less than 2km above the city to the northwest, the 620-metre-wide **Hoa Binh Dam** chokes the Da River to create a lake over 200km long, stretching all the way to Son La. The reservoir is earmarked for tourist development, but its main purpose is to feed Vietnam's largest hydroelectric plant which came on stream in 1994 and has gone some way to solving Vietnam's chronic power shortage. Hoa Binh Tourism (ⓦwww.hoabinhtourism.com) at the *Hoa Binh Hotel 1* offers guided tours of the complex, but otherwise you get a worm's-eye view of the dam from the pontoon bridge that links Hoa Binh's main street with industrial suburbs across the Da River. Muong, Thai, Hmong and Dao **minorities** all live in the vicinity, but you'll need to arrange a guide and transport if you want to visit them. Again, Hoa Binh Tourism can help but they're geared primarily to tour groups. Their most popular outing is a day's boat trip on the Da River, visiting Muong and Dao villages ($50 per boat for fifteen people), and they can also arrange a night's accommodation in a showpiece Muong village ($10 per person plus food).

A very scenic way to travel from Hoa Binh to Mai Chau is by **boat** down the Ma River. A boat holding ten people takes two hours and offers a glimpse of life on the riverbank ($50 per boat). Note: it docks in Co Luong, 12km south of Mai Chau (35,000đ by motorbike). Bookings can be made through Hoa Binh Tourism.

Practicalities

Hoa Binh's main **bus station** lies on its eastern edge, where you'll find the usual gaggle of xe om waiting to take you the kilometre into town (10,000đ). Buses for Hanoi leave regularly, but note that some terminate at Ha Dong, where you have to pick up a Hanoi city bus. Keep an eye on your bags as thefts have been reported on this route.

The most popular **places to stay** for foreigners are the *Hoa Binh 1* and *2* (ⓣ0218/385 2051 & 385 2537, ⓕ0218/385 4372; ❸–❹), located opposite each other on a hillside 2km west of the town centre along Highway 6. Both have about thirty wood-panelled rooms in long stilthouses, and restaurants. The *Hoa Binh 2* also features folk dancing and music displays and sampling of Thai rice wine from the communal pot. Alternatively, the *Thu Huong* (ⓣ0218/385 3950; ❷), 100m before *Hao Binh 2*, is a basic but clean choice, where the front rooms have good views over the countryside. More luxurious is the Vietnamese-owned *V Resort* (ⓣ0218/387 1954, ⓦwww.vresort .com.vn; ❹–❺), situated 20km from Hoa Binh, with a variety of attractions such as a mini putt course, a zoo and natural mineral spas. A xe om will take you there from Hoa Binh, or if travelling from Mai Chau, get off at the Pho Cun junction 10km before Hoa Binh and head right a further 10km to Bai

Chao. As well as the restaurants at the *Hoa Binh* hotels, there's also a group of local **restaurants**, cafés and ice-cream parlours at the west end of Cu Chin Lan, about 50m before the T-junction.

The northeast

The provinces of northeast Vietnam, looping eastwards from Ha Giang to Lang Son, lack the grandeur of their counterparts west of the Red River Valley, with the notable exception of the area round Dong Van and Meo Vac. In general the peaks here are lower and the views smaller-scale and of an altogether softer quality; there are also less minority folk wearing traditional dress. Getting to see everything is not as straightforward as in the northwest either, and you may have to choose between an exploration of the border zone in **Ha Giang Province** or a stay at **Ba Be Lake** along with a visit to attractions near **Cao Bang**. However, with enough time, it's possible to visit all these places without returning to Hanoi.

Highlights of the northeast are its **rural landscapes**, from traditional scenes of green-engulfed villages to dramatic limestone country, typified by pockets of cultivation squeezed among rugged outcrops whose lower slopes are wrinkled with terraces. However, population densities are still low, leaving huge forest reserves and high areas of wild, open land inhabited by **ethnic minorities** practising swidden farming (see p.492). While many have adopted a Vietnamese way of life, in remoter parts the minorities remain culturally distinct – particularly evident when local markets, their dates traditionally set by the lunar calendar, are in full swing.

Ha Giang and around

HA GIANG is the capital of the north's most remote and least-visited province, where Vietnam's border juts into China and almost reaches the Tropic of Cancer. Until the early 1990s, this region was the scene of fierce fighting between Vietnam and China, and it is still considered a "sensitive area", though its inhabitants nowadays are peaceful and welcoming. The town itself has a few attractions, but the main reason for coming is to head on to **MEO VAC** and **DONG VAN**, both set in valleys surrounded by forbidding peaks and connected by a hair-raising road with spectacular views. The round trip from Ha Giang is about 300km and takes two full days of driving along narrow, bumpy roads, which may become impassable during the rainy season. This border area is home to several **minority groups**, including the White Hmong and the Lo Lo, the latter having only a few thousand members; most towns along the route have a **Sunday market** attended by villagers from the surrounding valleys, where you're likely to be the only foreigner.

One of the reasons for this lack of visitors is that foreigners currently must obtain a **permit** ($10) from the police or a tour agent to travel anywhere outside Ha Giang town. As the permit costs the same price for any length of time, you should apply for as many days as possible, as you won't be able to extend it and, given the beauty of the area, you may well want to. Previously foreigners were required to hire a guide, too, though this is currently no longer the case: however, as the situation is likely to change further, it's essential to make enquiries before heading to the area.

The Town

Ha Giang is a sizeable town, and though its buildings are of no great architectural merit, its setting is very impressive, with the tall Mo Neo and Cam mountains crowding it in. The ochre waters of the Lo River carve southward through the centre of town, and traffic is thick on the bridges that connect the west and east districts. The town's **market** is located in a purpose-built hall just northeast of the northern bridge, and is a frenzy of activity in the early morning when members of **minority groups** can often be seen. If you plan to go to Dong Van, however, you're likely to see more authentic markets along the way. The Ha Giang **museum** (daily 8–11am & 2–4pm, with late opening Wed, Sat & Sun 7–9pm; free), is just west of the northern bridge. It's well worth a visit to get a preview of the outfits of the many different minority groups who inhabit the region, as well as to see artefacts such as bronze drums and ancient axe-heads that have been unearthed by digs in the region. Archeological evidence shows that there has been a settlement here for tens of thousands of years, and the region seemingly flourished during the Bronze Age judging by the number of beautifully designed drums that have been found.

Practicalities

Ha Giang lies 318km from Hanoi; buses leave from the My Dinh Bus Station (near My Dinh Stadium, 20km southwest of Hanoi) and Gia Lam Bus Station and take six hours to reach Ha Giang via Highway 2, passing through **Viet Tri** on the banks of the Lo River, and **Viet Quang** (also known as Bac Quang) just 60km before Ha Giang. With a rented vehicle, it's also possible to approach from **Bac Ha** (see p.433) by heading south on Highway 70 to **Pho Rang**, then taking Highway 279, which winds its way eastward to Viet Quang, and finally north to Ha Giang. Either way the journey takes the best part of a day.

The town of Ha Giang straddles the Lo River, with two bridges connecting the older part on the east bank and the newer part on the west bank. The **bus station** is on Nguyen Trai which runs along the west side of the Lo River; the main **post office** and several hotels, guesthouses and restaurants are also along this street. On the east side are more hotels and restaurants, as well as many shops. The town's main **tour agent** (Ha Giang Tourist Company) is located on Tran Hung Dao, near the **bank** just west of the northern bridge, while the **immigration police** are next door. You need to visit them or a tour agent to arrange a **permit** for onward travel towards the border.

Accommodation and eating

There are plenty of **places to stay** in town, and though staff speak very little English this shouldn't be a problem. Arriving from the south along Nguyen Trai, one of the first places you come to is the *Ha Duong* (☎0219/386 2555; ❶), which has spacious but bland rooms. A little further in towards town is the *Sao Mai* (☎0219/386 3019; ❶–❷), which, despite its outside appearance, has good rooms with bathtubs. Further up the road, the newer *Hoang Hoa* (☎0219/386 3797, ✉hoanghoahotel@yahoo.com; ❶) and the cosy *Duc Giang* (☎0219/387 5648; ❶–❷) are both fine. Closer to town, the *Huy Hoan* (☎0219/387 5648; ❷) tries to sell itself as the best hotel in town, but the rooms are cramped and the service indifferent, while the quieter *Hoang Anh* on Ba Trieu (☎0219/386 3559; ❶–❷) is off the main highway and popular with tour groups.

There are several **restaurants** along Tran Hung Dao, one of the most popular being *Pham Ba Cuong*, which offers tasty Chinese cuisine and has a small English menu. Staff will also take you into the kitchen where you can pick and choose what you want. Certainly the most novel place is the *Trang Chien* floating restaurant, which is often full at night, and specializes in tasty steamboats. You can find the usual soup and rice places around the market on the east side of town.

Meo Vac and Dong Van

Highway 4C heads north out of town, at first following the Lo River Valley, then heading east to follow the Mien River. After about 20km the road begins to climb into the hills before crossing Quan Ba Pass ("Heaven's Gate"), where roadside steps lead up to a fine view – when the weather is clear – over **Quan Ba**, 45km from Ha Giang, and the patchwork fields and dramatic hills around it. There's a **market** in Quan Ba on Sundays where, apart from the White Hmong, who are the biggest group in this region, you might see Red Dao, Tay, Giay, Co Lao, Pu Peo and Lo Lo people.

After Quan Ba, the road follows a pretty stream for some distance, with steep mountain flanks rising on both sides. After climbing over treeless, terraced hills which serve to increase the feeling of remoteness, it then descends into **Yen Minh**, some 97km from Ha Giang. This makes a good lunch stop, especially since there is a very reasonable restaurant, the *Phuc Cai*, which has good tofu and potato dishes. It is located directly opposite the *Minh Hai* (☎0219/385 2109; ❶), where it's possible to base yourself, though the newer *Hai Son* (☎0219/3852091; ❶) 20m down the road is slightly better; however, Meo Vac and Dong Van have more comfortable options.

Just 4km east of Yen Minh, the road splits. The northern fork goes to Dong Van and the southern one to Meo Vac, and this is where the fun really begins. You can follow either road as they join up to form a loop; described below is the route via Meo Vac, which has slightly more accommodation options than Dong Van. There's virtually no traffic on the road, which passes through rugged limestone landscapes, the scenery gradually getting wilder and more dramatic, and little evidence of settlements at the roadside. For much of the way, the terrain is pocked with blackened knuckles of rock that must make for difficult farming, though small fields of corn are planted here and there, and cone-shaped bundles of corn stalks, used for fodder and fuel, are scattered among the rock-strewn landscape. The locals, for the most part White Hmong, stoop low under heavy burdens of wood, and it's all too evident that life here is tough.

In **MEO VAC**, the *Nho Que* (☎0219/387 1322; ❶) is easily the best place in town, although the eight rooms do resemble a 1950s motel. Its best feature is the large rooftop where you can get a nice view of the surrounding mountains. If this is full, the *People's Committee Guest House* (☎0219/387 1176; ❶) is marginally better than sleeping on the street. There's little to see in town apart from a small statue of Uncle Ho and the town's new market that overflows on Sundays, but it's the setting, with a ring of barren mountains forming a bowl around it, which is impressive. Several food stalls can be found around the market, and there are a few basic soup and rice restaurants dotted around.

The next stage of the journey, covering just 22km on the way to Dong Van, is the most spectacular part of the whole trip. The road climbs up the side of a massive canyon to the Ma Phi Leng Pass at around 1500m, and the views down to the Nho Que River, a ribbon of turquoise far below, are simply dizzying. **DONG VAN** is in a similar setting to Meo Vac, and has the usual market, and a guesthouse *Hoang Ngoc* (☎0219/385 6020; ❶), which is friendly and clean. From Dong Van, the road heads back west to the junction outside Yen Minh, and for the first section to **Sai Phin**, the scenery is superb – a constant string of cone-shaped peaks standing above fields in the valley below. After 15km from Dong Van, look out on the left for the sturdy building of the People's Committee at Sai Phin. If you ask here, someone will walk you down to the village to look at the **Vuong Palace**, a large, two-storey residence with three courtyards which was built by the French for the local Hmong king. The thick walls show intricate craftsmanship, and have slits set into them that were used to defend the place with rifles in bygone days. In the shade of pine trees beside the gateway to the palace are several impressive tombs of members of the Vuong family.

West of Sai Phin, the constantly changing views continue until finally the road descends from the hills into Yen Minh, and from here you must follow the same route back to Ha Giang.

Cao Bang and around

Cao Bang lies approximately halfway along the route from Ha Giang to Lang Son, and has enough appeal to merit a stopover. The journey from Ha Giang along Highway 34, via Bao Lac, takes the better part of a day, passing through small villages and excellent scenery. Few travellers venture this far north, but those who do usually make the pilgrimage out to **Pac Bo Cave**, where Ho Chi Minh lived on his return to Vietnam in 1941, and to **Ban Gioc Falls**, Vietnam's highest waterfall, right on the border with China. The province is home to several ethnic minorities, notably the Dao, Nung and Tay who still maintain their traditional way of life in the more remote uplands.

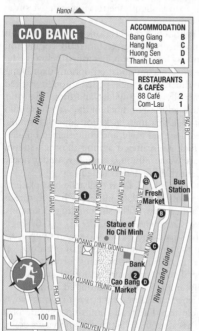

Cao Bang

Cao Bang is a likeable place: its centre may be dusty and noisy, but its riverside setting, with dense clumps of bamboo backed by sugar-loaf mountains helps to blur the edges. The town is built on the southwestern bank of the **Bang Giang River**, on a spur of land formed by the confluence with the Hien River. Highway 3 drops steeply down from the hills and enters town from the west, crossing a bridge onto a tree-lined avenue of self-important edifices, including the People's Committee, theatre, bank and post office, before turning right along the river. The narrow, shady park on top of the low hill in the centre of town is worth a wander, and the **statue of Uncle Ho** is a reminder of the fact that this region was vital to the thrust for independence that he led. Held daily, the enormous **markets** form the town's focal points. If possible, try to visit the fresh produce market around sunrise when minority women trek into town and bamboo rafts laden with produce dock beside the bridge. Once you've exhausted the market, the only thing to do is head for the hills north of town.

Practicalities

Cao Bang's **bus station** is on Pac Bo, on the east side of the river, near the Bang Giang Bridge. The **post office**, on a hill in the centre of town, is recognizable from its radio mast, while there are a couple of **ATMs** around town – the easiest to find is outside the *Bang Giang* **hotel** (℡026/385 3431, Ebanggiang_dl @yahoo.com; ❷), right next to the bridge. It's the largest hotel in town, with restaurants and shops on site, though the uninspiring rooms are rather overpriced. Far better value is the ⚑*Huong Sen* (℡026/385 4654; ❷) with river views from most rooms, cable TV, friendly staff and an excellent restaurant in the lobby: the rooms vary in style and size, so ask to see at least a couple. Alternatively, the *Huang Thom* (℡026/385 6128; ❷) has comfy rooms, cable TV and breakfast included in the price; it can also organize trips and permits to Ban Gioc Falls and Pac Bo Cave. For a budget option, the *Nga Hang* (℡026/385 6256; ❶) is about as cheap as you'll get: it's a no-nonsense riverside guesthouse a short walk from the bridge, with rooms that are just about clean.

For **eating**, the best option is *Com-Lau*, just north of Uncle Ho, which has an English menu and serves excellent Vietnamese fare, especially the seafood spring rolls and sweet and sour beef. The *Bang Giang* has a tiny English menu and serves reasonable food but in a very depressing dining room, while the *Huong Sen* has no English menu, but since most of the meals are on display it's easy to point. First stop on cold mornings should be for a **breakfast soup** ladled from the huge steaming cauldrons in the market, while the wallside snack-shacks south of the market on Kim Dong have a rustic late-night appeal. For a cup of coffee and a bit of people-watching, try *88 Café* on Kim Dong, just west of the *Huong Sen*.

Pac Bo Cave

Such a lot is made of **Pac Bo Cave** that it comes as a surprise to learn that Ho Chi Minh lived in it for only seven weeks, during February and March 1941. If you're not a fan of Ho memorabilia then neither the cave nor the small museum justifies the fifty-kilometre excursion (2hr each way) from Cao Bang, though the first part of the journey, passing minority villages moored in rice-paddy seas against craggy blue horizons, is a memorable ride.

Pac Bo is situated right on the border with China. When Ho Chi Minh walked over from Guangxi Province in January 1941, he took his first steps on Vietnamese soil for thirty years. At first he lived in a Nung village but soon left for the nearby cave where he set about co-ordinating the independence movement, and translating the history of the Soviet Communist Party into Vietnamese. The French soon discovered his hideaway and Ho had to move again, this time to a jungle hut not far away where the Viet Minh was founded in May 1941. Later that same year he left for China, to drum up support for his nascent army, and when he next returned to Pac Bo it was after Independence, as a tourist, in 1961. The **cave** today is a strange mixture of shrine and picnic spot, while exhibits in the small **museum** (daily 7.30–11.30am & 1.30–4.30pm; free) include Ho's Hermes Baby typewriter, bamboo suitcase and Mauser pistol.

Some tours **from Hanoi** include a visit to the cave on their itineraries, though it's possible to go it alone. To get to Pac Bo **from Cao Bang**, head northwest across the Bang Giang River on the Ha Quang road until you see a signpost directing you off to the right. From this junction it's another 4km to the entrance (currently no charge). Getting to the cave **by public transport** is not easy, as few buses ply the route between Cao Bang and Ha Quang; if you do take a bus, ask to be dropped off at the turning for Pac Bo, two hours from Cao Bang, where you can pick up a xe om for the last leg.

Over the Ma Phuc Pass

If revolutionary relics aren't your thing, take the road northeast towards Tra Linh and Quang Uyen and lose yourself among sugar-loaf scenery beyond the **Ma Phuc Pass**. The road from Cao Bang shoots straight up the valleyside and after a disappointing start you're suddenly looking down on a tortured landscape of scarred limestone peaks and streamless valleys typical of karst scenery. The region is inhabited by Nung people who cultivate the valley floors and terraced lower slopes, living in distinctive wooden houses that are built partly on ground level and partly raised on stilts. Even if you don't have time to explore further, views from the top of the pass – a mere 20km out of Cao Bang – more than repay the effort. Just before the top, the road splits: pick either direction for some great scenery but the right fork takes you to the only specific sight in the area, the **Ban Gioc Falls**, whose location exactly on the frontier with China made them a bone of contention during the border war. Several tour groups include the falls on their itinerary, but if you come here alone, hotels in Cao Bang such as the *Huang Thom* can arrange a permit for $10. Over 90km and two hours' driving each way, Ban Gioc is really a full day's outing; note that the falls are less than spectacular in the dry season.

Ba Be National Park

Vietnam's largest natural lake, Ho Ba Be, forms the core of the delightful **Ba Be National Park**, a feast of limestone and tropical forest. The lake is 7km long, up to 30m deep and up to a kilometre wide. A few islands decorate the surface and the whole lot is enclosed by steep, densely wooded slopes, with some tall and ancient trees breaking out here and there into white limestone cliffs. The main attractions here are **boat trips** to visit caves, waterfalls and minority villages, with the added bonus of seeing at least a few of the 220 animal, 417 plant and 49 fish species recorded here. Bears, tigers and one of Vietnam's rarest and most endangered primates, the Tonkin snub-nosed langur (*Rhinopithecus avunculus*), live in a few isolated communities on the fringes of the park, but nearer the lake there's a good chance of spotting the more common macaque monkeys and garrulous, colourful flocks of parrots. Few people are around to disturb the wildlife and outside the months of July and August, when Hanoians take their holidays, you'll usually find only a handful of tourists. What puts some people off Ba Be is difficulty of access by public transport, but if you join a tour from Hanoi or hire your own transport it becomes easier to justify, especially when combined with a visit to a minority market. Even then, though, a two-night stay is sufficient for most people.

Getting there

The simplest way of getting to Ba Be National Park is to join a tour or arrange your own transport. **Hanoi tour agencies** (see p.349) can help with vehicle hire or line up a full programme, either as a three-day excursion or as part of the Cao Bang–Lang Son circuit (4–5 days): total travelling time from Hanoi to Ba Be is around five to six hours.

From Cao Bang, Highway 3 climbs up to a high pass (800m), which marks the watershed between the Red River Valley to the south and China's Pearl River in the north. Over the col lie the **Ngan Son Mountains**, which are the domain of several ethnic minorities, among them the Nung, Dao and San Chay (whose women typically carry a broad, curved knife tucked in the back of their belts). There are few villages in sight on these wild uplands, just the occasional split-bamboo hut selling wild honey (*mat ong*) beside the road. In fact, apart from **Ngan Son**, lost in a vast, treeless valley, there's no settlement of any size between Cao Bang and journey's end, 80km later in **Na Phac**, a small market town 200km from Hanoi. If you're here on market day – held at five-day intervals, starting on the first day of the lunar month – you'll be treated to an arresting display of minority dress. From the Na Phac turning on Highway 3 a road threads west across country to Ba Be (47km) via **CHO RA**, another small town that comes to life on market days (every Sun). If you've got your own vehicle, you can take an interesting alternative route on a back road through stunning rural landscapes: just north of Phu Thong on Highway 3 (near the 174km marker), turn left and after 30km you'll come out beside Cho Ra's *Ba Be 1* hotel (see p.454).

Public transport to Ba Be is also possible – buses leave from Gia Lam bus station in Hanoi and pull up in Cho Ra, from where a xe om to Ba Be Lake will cost around 30,000đ. If coming from Ha Giang with your own transport, enquire about the condition of Highway 279, which cuts across from Viet Quang; if this road is not passable, you will need to go back down Highway 2 to Tuyen Quang, then head east on Highway 37 to Thai Nguyen, and follow Highway 3 north from there.

Information and itineries

On arrival, first stop for independent travellers should be the park headquarters (entrance fee 11,000đ), which is located a couple of kilometres from the boat jetty on the east side of the lake. Here you can get **information** about two- to five-day tours (from $25 per person), the most popular of which are **boat trips** to the caves and waterfalls. Most trips are in spacious, covered motorboats, but it's also possible to row (or be rowed) around parts of the lake in a narrow dug-out canoe – a more appropriate way to move about in such a tranquil environment; daily rental for both motorboats and canoes is from $35 a day.

The Ba Be itinerary usually begins with a boat trip along the Nang River to **Hang Puong**, where the waters have tunnelled a three-hundred-metre-long, bat-filled cave through a mountain. From here they go on to the **Dau Dang Waterfall**, a stretch of beautiful but treacherous rapids. Take care if you walk on the slippery rocks around the falls as there has been at least one tourist fatality here. Next up is a visit to a **Tay** village on the lakeside, and on longer trips an overnight stay in a stilthouse. A road around the south end of the lake has made **Pac Ngoi** less of an isolated Tay community than it used to be, but several other villages in the area, such as **Buoc Luom**, **Ban Vang** and **Bo Lu**, can accommodate visitors too. Few Tay wear traditional dress these days, and you're most likely to see it at a **minority show** at the *National Park Guest House* (see below).

Accommodation and eating

The most convenient and comfortable **place to stay** is the *National Park Guest House* or *Vuon Quoc Gia Ba Be* (☎0281/389 4136, ℱ0281/389 4126; ❸), located next to park headquarters, which offers fifty pricey rooms, a restaurant and occasional minority shows. In the summer months (June–Aug) it is often booked out by party cadres, who find it a good location for meetings, so it's best to reserve ahead. For added privacy you can stay in cottages located 100m away, opposite the guesthouse, which are newer though slightly more expensive. Alternatively, you can spend a night in a stilthouse in **Pac Ngoi**, a lakeside Tay village 7km from the park headquarters; home-stays here or in other nearby villages can be arranged through the national park (ⓦwww.babenationalpark.org). Cho Ra is 17km away, and has guesthouses if you're stuck: the *Ba Be* 1 (ⓣ0281/387 6115; ❷–❸) has large, clean rooms and expansive views from the back.

The speciality in many local **restaurants** is fish from the lake, and the best place to try it is at the *National Park Guest House*, where they serve whatever's fresh on the day. The guesthouses in Cho Ra also serve food, though the kitchens close early, and there are a few com pho stalls around the only road junction in town. Snacks and drinks are available at the boat jetty by Ba Be Lake.

Southeast to Lang Son

At Cao Bang you join **Highway 4**, an ambitious road that was originally part of a French military network linking the isolated garrisons right across northern Vietnam's empty mountain country. This road is more subject than many others in the north to falling into disrepair, and the 140km journey to Lang Son takes about four hours, depending on conditions. Beyond **Dong Khe**, a nondescript town roughly 40km out of Cao Bang, the virtually traffic-free road climbs through a gorge of sheer limestone cliffs before cresting the dramatic **Dong Khe Pass**. In 1950 this pass was the scene of a daring ambush in which the Viet Minh gained their first major victory over the French Expeditionary Force. In the ensuing panic, forts all along the border were abandoned, an estimated six thousand French troops were killed or captured, and the Viet Minh netted 950 machine guns, eight thousand rifles and a few hundred trucks.

That Khe lies exactly halfway between Cao Bang and Lang Son, and beyond here the road winds through **Na Sam**, an attractive town snuggled beneath a dramatic setting of outcrops. The villages in this area are inhabited by Nung and Tay; their bamboo rafts and huge wooden waterwheels, which form part of sophisticated irrigation works, grace the river that weaves along beside the road. Unfortunately this rural idyll comes to an abrupt end, as the speedy Highway 1 from Dong Dang brings you hurtling into Lang Son.

Lang Son

For most people, **LANG SON** is just a meal stop or overnight rest on the journey through the northeast or en route to China, only 18km away to the north. With a fast highway now linking Lang Son to Hanoi, reasons to linger are even fewer, though the surrounding countryside does have an endearing quality in the form of endless karst outcrops studding the plain. Having acquired the status of a city, Lang Son has a self-important feel, and its booming economy is evident in new construction sites all over town. The few sights worth seeing include the Ky Lua Market, the Den Ky Cung Temple, the Tam Thanh and Nhi Thanh caves and huge colonial houses in the old town south of the river. At present no nearby tourist attractions are promoted, though the area round Mau Son Mountain, just east of town, is good hiking country. For the intrepid, Lang Son is the start of a little-travelled back road (Highway 4B) cutting across 100km of empty country to Tien Yen on the east coast, offering a route to (or from) Ha Long Bay.

Arrival and information

Most of Lang Son's facilities are found on the north bank of the river. There is no official tourist office, but hotel staff at the *Van Xuan* are helpful. The **post office** is located on Le Loi, a little further east. Next door to the post office, at 51 Le Loi, the Incombank changes US dollars and has an **ATM**. Most hotels also **exchange** dollars and yuan. There are also a couple of **internet cafés** along Le Loi towards the train station. Ngo Quyen branches off to the right from Le Loi, where about 100m along you'll find the **bus station**, though most long-distance buses will drop you on Le Loi or Tran Dang Ninh, the town's main north–south artery.

Accommodation

Market forces have spawned new **hotels** and Lang Son is fairly well provisioned with inexpensive accommodation, although at weekends rooms still fill up with holidaymakers, mostly male, trekking over from China.

Hoang Nguyen 84 Tran Dang Ninh ☏025/387 4575. A mainstay for years thanks to its family-run atmosphere; it's just south of the market, near the junction of Tran Dang Ninh and Le Loi. **❶**

Hoang Son Hai 57 Duong Tam Thanh ☏025/387 0199, ✉nguyentienhung@yahoo.com. The grandest-looking hotel in town, though the rooms are overpriced for what you get. Head along Le Loi from the train station, and keep going straight after it hits Tran Dang Dinh. **❷**

Van Xuan 147 Tran Dang Ninh ☏025/371 0440, ✉thanh_loan_hotel@hn.vnn.vn. The city's best choice by far – just north of the market,

overlooking Phai Loan Lake – has attentive staff and a modern feel; the back rooms have good lake views. If it's full, the *Hoa Binh* just down the road at No.127 is almost as good and a similar price. **❷**

Yen Yen Mau Son Mountain, 30km east of Lang Son (☏025/387 4575). At the top of the mountain, just over 1000m high, this delightful guesthouse has excellent views over the valley, a decent restaurant and rooms with fireplaces. The surrounding hillsides are dotted with Dao villages set among orchards of peaches and pears: to get here, head east of town along Highway 4B and after about 14km turn along the road to Mau Son Mountain. **❶**

The Town

The Ky Cung River splits Long Son in two, leaving the main bulk on the north side of the Ky Lua Bridge and the provincial offices to the south. Highway 1 is called Tran Dang Ninh as it passes through town, and it's along here that you'll find the town's main attraction, bustling **Ky Lua Market**. Just east of the highway, this is well worth investigating, especially in the early morning when Tay, Nung and Dao women come to trade. From the market, walk a kilometre downhill to the river and take a quick look at the small temple, **Den Ky Cung** (daily 6am–6.30pm; free), tucked under the bridge on the north bank. Founded over 500 years ago, this temple is dedicated to Quan Tuan Tranh, an army officer of the border guard who is reputed to have slain hundreds of Chinese in battle before he himself fell. There's nothing much to see inside apart from a photo of Uncle Ho visiting Lang Son in 1960. Following the road that branches off the highway at Den Ky Cung for about 500m will bring you round a bend in the river to the new, three-storey edifice of **Dong Kinh Market**, a temple to Chinese kitsch, where illuminated Buddhas sit in front of posters of Huangguoshu Falls, China's highest waterfall. The broad boulevards south of the bridge are also worth exploring. The atmosphere is less frenetic than in the centre, and there are some interesting colonial buildings in the tree-lined backstreets. If the weather is good and you have time to spare, take a walk along Da Tuong in the southwest of town, which passes remnants of an ancient wall and heads on into a nearby labyrinth of karst hills. Also worth exploring are the nearby caves (daily 6am–6pm; 5000đ each). To get to them go 100m past the *Hoang Son Hai* (see above) where you will come to a junction. Turn left and continue for 200m to see the **Nhi Thanh Cave**, which follows the Ngoc Tuyen River underground and is worth a look. For the **Tam Thanh Cave**, which

Across the border to China

The majority of people taking this route into China travel **by train**, using one of the two weekly services direct from Hanoi to Beijing (see p.388 for details). Note also that you can only board this train in Hanoi (and not at Dong Dang), though on the Chinese side it's possible to disembark up the line; pleasant Nanning is the first major city.

Alternatively, you can use the **road crossing** known as the **Huu Nghi** (Friendship) **border gate**, which lies 18km north of Lang Son and 4km from Dong Dang at the end of Highway 1. If you're travelling by **local bus**, your best bet is to overnight in Lang Son (see above) and then take a motorbike to the border gate. Otherwise, frequent **minibuses** shuttle between Lang Son's Le Loi Street and Dong Dang (look for those marked "Tam Thanh" at the front), but you'll then have to hop on a motorbike for the last leg.

The tiny Huu Nghi border gate is open between 7am and 6pm; there's a walk of less than a kilometre between the two checkpoints. On the Chinese side, infrequent minibuses head to Pingxiang (15km) for the nearest accommodation: it's also the nearest money exchange, so you'll need to have got some yuan in Lang Son for the minibus fare. Note that China is **one hour ahead** of Vietnam.

However you cross the border, you must have a Chinese **visa**, available from the embassy in Hanoi (see p.386).

features series of nice rockpools and multi-coloured lighting displays, continue straight on at the junction for 200m. Past the ticket office, 150m further down the road, is a staircase that leads high above to the top of a rocky hill and to a cheesy garden equipped with fake bulls and deer, but has great views over the town.

Eating

There are few fancy places to eat in Lang Son, though the ☀ *New Century*, a large **restaurant** on Phai Loan Lake opposite the Ky Lua Market has an English menu and is extremely popular with the locals and Chinese visitors. Soup and rice stalls dot the area around the markets.

Travel details

Trains

Dong Dang to: Hanoi (1 daily; 6hr 10min).
Lang Son to: Hanoi (1 daily; 5hr 40min).
Lao Cai to: Hanoi (5 daily; 8–10hr).

Buses

Bus stations are gradually becoming more organized, with ticket desks and scheduled departures. However, it is still almost impossible to give the frequency with which buses run because of the large number of private minibuses that ply more popular routes, and depart only when they have enough passengers to make the journey worthwhile. Journey times can also vary; figures below show the normal length of time you can expect to take by public bus.

Bac Ha to: Lao Cai (2hr).
Cao Bang to: Hanoi (7hr); Lang Son (4hr).
Dien Bien Phu to: Muong Lay (4hr); Son La (5hr); Sa Pa (10hr); Hanoi (12hr).
Cao Bang to: Hanoi (7hr); Lang Son (4hr).
Ha Giang to: Hanoi (6hr).
Lang Son to: Cao Bang (4hr); Hanoi (3hr).
Lao Cai to: Sa Pa (1hr 15min).
Mai Chau to: Hoa Binh (2hr).
Muong Lay to: Dien Bien Phu (4hr); Sa Pa (7hr).
Sa Pa to: Dien Bien Phu (10hr); Lao Cai (1hr 15min) Muong Lay (7hr).
Son La to: Dien Bien Phu (5hr); Hanoi (6–7hr); Hoa Binh (7hr), via the Mai Chau junction (5hr).

Flights

Dien Bien Phu to: Hanoi (2 daily; 1hr).

Contexts

Contexts

History

Vietnam as a unified state within its present geographical boundaries has only existed since the early nineteenth century. The national history, however, stretches back thousands of years to a legendary kingdom in the Red River Delta. From there the Viet people pushed relentlessly down the peninsula of Indochina on the "March to the South", Nam Tien. The other compelling force, and a constant theme throughout its history, is Vietnam's ultimately successful resistance to all foreign aggressors.

The beginnings

The earliest evidence of human activity in Vietnam can be traced back to a Paleolithic culture that existed some five hundred thousand years ago. These hunter-gatherers slowly developed agricultural techniques, but the most important step came about 4000 years ago when farmers began to cultivate irrigated rice in the Red River Delta. The communal effort required to build and maintain the system of dykes and canals spawned a stable, highly organized society, held to be the original Vietnamese nation. This embryonic kingdom, **Van Lang**, emerged sometime around 2000 BC and was ruled over by the semi-mythological Hung kings from their capital near today's Viet Tri, northwest of Hanoi. Archeological finds indicate that by the first millennium BC these people, the Lac Viet, had evolved into a sophisticated Bronze Age culture whose influence spread as far as Indonesia. Undoubtedly their greatest creations were the ritualistic **bronze drums**, discovered in the 1920s near Dong Son, and revered by the Vietnamese as the first hard evidence of an indigenous, independent culture.

In the mid-third century BC a Chinese warlord conquered Van Lang to create a new kingdom, **Au Lac**, with its capital at Co Loa, near present-day Hanoi. For the first time the lowland Lac Viet and the hill peoples were united. After only fifty years, around 207 BC, Au Lac was itself invaded by a Chinese potentate and became part of **Nam Viet** (Southern Viet), an independent kingdom occupying much of southern China. For a while the Lac Viet were able to maintain their local traditions and an indigenous aristocracy. Then, in 111 BC the Han emperors annexed the whole Red River Delta and so began a thousand years of Chinese domination.

Chinese rule

A millennium under Chinese rule had a profound effect on all aspects of Vietnamese life, notably the social and political spheres. With the introduction of **Confucianism** came the growth of a rigid, feudalistic hierarchy dominated by a mandarin class. This innately conservative elite ensured the long-term stability of an administrative system which continued to dominate Vietnamese society until well into the nineteenth century. The Chinese also introduced technological advances, such as writing, silk production and large-scale hydraulic works, while Mahayana Buddhism first entered Vietnam from China during the second century AD.

At the same time, however, the Viet people were forging their national identity in the continuous struggle to break free from their powerful northern neighbour; on at least three occasions the Vietnamese ousted their masters. The first and most celebrated of these short-lived independent kingdoms was established by the **Trung sisters** (Hai Ba Trung) in 40 AD. After the Chinese murdered Trung Trac's husband, she and her sister rallied the local lords and peasant farmers in the first popular insurrection against foreign domination. The Chinese fled, leaving Trung Trac ruler of the territory from Hué to southern China until the Han emperor dispatched twenty thousand troops and a fleet of 2000 junks to quell the rebellion three years later. The sisters threw themselves into a river to escape capture, and the Chinese quickly set about removing the local lords. Though subsequent uprisings also failed, the sisters had demonstrated the fallibility of the Chinese and earned their place in Vietnam's pantheon of heroes.

Over the following centuries Vietnam was drawn closer into the political and cultural realm of China. The seventh and eighth centuries were particularly bleak as the powerful Tang Dynasty tightened its grip on the province it called **Annam**, or the "Pacified South". As soon as the dynasty collapsed in the early

Funan and Champa

While China has always exerted a strong influence over north Vietnam, in the south it was initially the Indian civilization that dominated, though as a cultural influence rather than as a ruling power. From the first century AD Indian traders sailing east towards China established **Hindu enclaves** along the southern coast of Indochina. The largest and most important of these city-states was **Funan**, based on a port city called Oc Eo, near present-day Rach Gia in the Mekong Delta (see p.164). By the early third century, Funan had developed into a powerful trading nation with links extending as far as Persia and even Rome. But technological developments in the fifth century enabled larger ships to sail round Indochina without calling at any port, and Funan gradually declined.

At around the same time, another Indianized kingdom was developing along the narrow coastal plains of central Vietnam. Little is known about the origins of **Champa**, but Chinese records indicate the creation of a "barbarian" state in the area towards the end of the second century. Champa's subsequent history is a complicated tale of shifting allegiances between its Chinese, Khmer and, later, Vietnamese neighbours (see box, p.238). For most of its existence, however, Champa was a Hindu kingdom, based on wet-rice farming and maritime trade, ruled over by divine kings who worshipped first Shiva and later embraced Buddhism. Until the late tenth century, Champa extended from the Hoanh Son Mountains, north of Dong Hoi, down to the Mekong Delta. Their power base was largely the territory around today's Da Nang, and their spiritual heartland the temple complex of My Son. Cham kings sponsored a vast array of sacred buildings, and the red-brick ruins of their towers and temples can be seen all along the coast of south-central Vietnam. While they never attained the magnificence of Angkor, their greatest legacy was a striking architectural style characterized by a wealth of exuberant sculpture.

In general, the Chinese tolerated the relatively weak kingdom on their borders, though they exacted tribute and plundered Champa on several occasions. After the mid-tenth century, however, Vietnamese independence changed the situation dramatically as the Viets, in search of new land, turned their attention southwards. By the end of the eleventh century Champa had lost its territory north of Hué, and four centuries later the whole kingdom became a vassal state under Viet hegemony. For a while Cham princes continued as nominal rulers until the state was finally absorbed into Vietnam in the nineteenth century.

tenth century a series of major rebellions broke out, culminating in the battle of the **Bach Dang River** in 938 AD (see box, p.406). Ngo Quyen declared himself ruler of **Nam Viet** and set up court at the historic citadel of Co Loa, heralding what was to be nearly ten centuries of Vietnamese independence.

Independent Vietnam

The period immediately following independence from Chinese rule in 939 AD was marked by factional infighting. Ngo Quyen died after only five years on the throne and Nam Viet dissolved in anarchy while twelve warlords disputed the succession. In 968 one of the rivals, Dinh Bo Linh, finally united the country and secured its future by paying tribute to the Chinese emperor, a system which continued until the nineteenth century. Dinh Bo Linh took the additional precaution of moving his capital south to the well-defended valley of Hoa Lu, where it remained during the two short-lived Dinh and Early Le dynasties.

These early monarchs laid the framework for a centralized state. They reformed the administration and the army, and instigated a programme of road building. But it was the following **Ly Dynasty**, founded by **Ly Thai To** in 1009, that consolidated the independence of **Dai Viet** (Great Viet) and guaranteed the nation's stability for the next four hundred years. One of the first actions of the new dynasty was to move the capital back into the northern rice-lands, founding the city of Thang Long, the precursor of modern Hanoi.

Ly Thai To's successor, **Ly Thai Tong** (1028–54), carried out a major reorganization of the national army, turning it into a professional fighting force, able to secure the northern borders and expand southwards. So confident was this new power that in 1076 the army of Dai Viet, under the revered General Ly Thuong Kiet, launched a pre-emptive strike against the Sung Chinese and then held off their counter-attack.

Having ousted the declining Ly clan in 1225, the following **Tran Dynasty** won spectacular military victories against the **Mongol invasions** of 1257, 1284 and 1288. On the first two occasions, Mongol forces briefly occupied the capital before having to withdraw, while the last battle is remembered for a rerun of Ngo Quyen's ploy in the Bach Dang River. This time it was General Tran Hung Dao, a prince in the royal family, who led Viet forces against the far superior armies of Kublai Khan. While the Mongol navy foundered in the Bach Dang River, its army was also being trounced and the remnants driven back into China; soon after, the khan died, and with him the Mongol threat.

In the confusion that marked the end of the Tran Dynasty, an ambitious court minister, Ho Qui Ly, usurped the throne in 1400. Though the **Ho Dynasty** lasted only seven years, its two progressive monarchs launched a number of important reforms. They tackled the problem of land shortages by restricting the size of holdings and then rented out the excess to landless peasants; the tax system was revised and paper money replaced coinage; ports were opened to foreign trade; and public health care introduced. Even the education system was broadened to include practical subjects along with the classic Confucian texts.

Just as the Ho were getting into their stride, so the new Ming Dynasty in China were beginning to look south again across the border. Under the pretext of restoring the Tran, Ming armies invaded in 1407 and imposed direct rule a few years later. This time, however, the **Chinese occupation** faced a much tougher problem as the Viet people were now a relatively cohesive force. The

Ngo	939–65 AD	Ho	1400–07
Dinh	968–80	(Ming Chinese	1407–28)
Early Le	980–1009	Later Le	1428–1788
Ly	1009–1225	Tay Son	1788–1802
Tran	1225–1400	Nguyen	1802–1945

Chinese tried to undermine Viet culture by outlawing local customs and destroying Vietnamese literature, works of art and historical texts. Slowly, Vietnamese resistance gravitated towards the mountains of Thanh Hoa, south of Hanoi, where a local landlord and mandarin, **Le Loi**, was preparing for a war of national liberation. For ten years Le Loi's well-disciplined guerrilla force harassed the enemy until he was finally able to defeat the Chinese army in open battle in 1427.

Le Loi, as King Le Thai To, founded the third of the great ruling families, the **Later Le Dynasty**, and set in train the reconstruction of Dai Viet, though he died after only five years on the throne. Initially the Le Dynasty reaped the economic rewards of its expanding empire, but eventually their new provinces spawned wealthy semi-autonomous rulers strong enough to challenge the throne. As the Le declined in the sixteenth century, two such powerful clans, the **Nguyen and Trinh**, at first supported the dynasty against rival contenders. Towards the end of the century, however, they became the effective rulers of Vietnam, splitting the country in two. The Trinh lords held sway in Hanoi and the north, while the Nguyen set up court at Hué; the Le, meanwhile, remained monarchs in name only.

The arrival of the West

The first Western visitors to the Vietnamese peninsula were probably **traders** from ancient Rome who sailed into the ports of Champa in the second century AD. Marco Polo sailed up the coast in the thirteenth century on his way to China, but more significant was the arrival of a Portuguese merchant, Antonio Da Faria, at the port of Fai Fo (Hoi An) in 1535. The Portuguese established their own trading post at Fai Fo, then one of Southeast Asia's greatest ports, crammed with vessels from China and Japan, and were soon followed by other European maritime powers. At this time Vietnam was breaking up into regional factions and the Europeans were quick to exploit growing tensions between the Nguyen and Trinh lords, providing weapons in exchange for trading concessions. However, when the civil war ended in 1674 the merchants lost their advantage. Gradually the English, Dutch and French closed down their trading posts until only the Portuguese remained in Fai Fo.

With the traders came **missionaries**. Portuguese Dominicans had been the first to arrive in the early sixteenth century, but it wasn't until 1615, when Jesuits set up a small mission in Fai Fo, that the Catholic Church gained an established presence in Vietnam. The mission's initial success in the Nguyen territory encouraged the Jesuits to look north. The man they chose for the job was a 28-year-old Frenchman, **Alexandre de Rhodes**, a gifted linguist who, only six months after arriving in Fai Fo, in 1627, was preaching in Vietnamese.

His talents soon won over the Trinh lords in Hanoi, where de Rhodes gave six sermons a day and converted nearly seven thousand Vietnamese in just two years. During this time he was also working on a simple **romanized script** for the Vietnamese language, which otherwise used a formidable system based on Chinese characters. De Rhodes merely wanted to make evangelizing easier, but his phonetic system eventually came to be adopted as Vietnam's national language, *quoc ngu*.

The missionaries found a ready audience, especially among peasant farmers and others near the bottom of the established Confucian hierarchy. It didn't take long before the ruling elite felt threatened by subversive Christian ideas; missionary work was banned after the 1630s and many priests were expelled, or even executed. But enforcement was erratic, and by the end of the seventeenth century the Catholic Church claimed several hundred thousand converts. Then, towards the end of the eighteenth century, the Catholic missions also provided an opening for French merchants wishing to challenge Britain's presence in the Far East. When a large-scale rebellion broke out in Vietnam in the early 1770s, these entrepreneurs saw their chance to establish a firmer footing on the Indochinese peninsula.

The Tay Son rebellion

As the eighteenth century progressed, insurrections flared up throughout the countryside. Most were easily stamped out, but in 1771 three brothers raised their standard in Tay Son village, west of Quy Nhon, and ended up ruling the whole country. The **Tay Son rebellion** gained broad support among dispossessed peasants, ethnic minorities, small merchants and townspeople attracted by the brothers' message of equal rights, justice and liberty. As rebellion spread through the south, the Tay Son army rallied even more converts when they seized land from the wealthy and redistributed it to the poor. By the middle of 1786 the rebels had overthrown both the Trinh and Nguyen lords, again leaving the Le Dynasty intact. When the Le monarch called on the Chinese in 1788 to help remove the Tay Son usurpers, the Chinese happily obliged by occupying Hanoi. At this the middle brother (Nguyen Hué) declared himself **Emperor Quang Trung** and quick-marched his army 600km from Hué to defeat the Chinese at Dong Da, on the outskirts of Hanoi. With Hué as his capital, Quang Trung set about implementing his promised reforms, but when he died prematurely in 1792, aged 39, his 10-year-old son was unable to hold onto power.

One of the few Nguyen lords to have survived the Tay Son rebellion in the south was Prince Nguyen Anh. The prince made several unsuccessful attempts to regain the throne in the mid-1780s. After one such failure he fled to Phu Quoc Island where he met a French bishop, Pigneau de Béhaine. With an eye on future religious and commercial concessions, the bishop offered to make approaches to the French on behalf of the Nguyen. A treaty was eventually signed in 1787, promising military aid in exchange for territorial and trading concessions, though France failed to deliver the assistance due to a financial crisis preceding the French Revolution. The bishop went ahead anyway, raising a motley force of four thousand armed mercenaries and a handful of ships. The expedition was launched in 1789 and Nguyen Anh entered Hanoi in 1802 to claim the throne as **Emperor Gia Long**. Bishop de Béhaine didn't live to see the victory or to enforce the treaty: he died in 1799 and received a stately funeral.

The Nguyen Dynasty

For the first time, **Vietnam**, as the country was now called, fell under a single authority from the northern border all the way down to the point of Ca Mau. In the hope of promoting unity, Gia Long established his capital in the centre, at Hué, where he built a magnificent citadel in imitation of the Chinese emperor's Forbidden City. The choice of architecture was appropriate: Gia Long and the **Nguyen Dynasty** he founded were resolutely Confucian. The new emperor immediately abolished the Tay Son reforms, reimposing the old feudal order; land confiscated from the rebels was redistributed to loyal mandarins, the bureaucracy was reinstated, and the majority of peasants found themselves worse off than before. Gradually the country was closed to the outside world and to modernizing influences that might have helped it withstand the onslaught of French military intervention in the mid-nineteenth century. On the other hand, Gia Long and his successors did much to improve the infrastructure of Vietnam, developing a road network, extending the irrigation systems and rationalizing the provincial administration. Under the Nguyen, the arts, particularly literature and court music, also flourished.

By refusing to grant any trading concessions, Gia Long disappointed the French adventurers who had helped him to the throne. He did, however, permit a certain amount of religious freedom, though his successors were far more suspicious of the missionaries' intentions. After 1825 several edicts were issued forbidding missionary work, accompanied by sporadic, occasionally brutal, persecutions of Christians, both Vietnamese converts and foreign priests. Ultimately, this provided the French with the excuse they needed to annex the country.

French conquest and rule

French governments grew increasingly imperialistic as the nineteenth century wore on. In the Far East, as Britain threatened to dominate trade with China, France began to see Vietnam as a potential route into the resource-rich provinces of Yunnan and southern China. Not that France had any formal policy to colonize Indochina; rather it came about in a piecemeal fashion, driven as often as not by private adventurers or the unilateral actions of French officials. In 1847, two French naval vessels began the process when they bombarded Da Nang on the pretext of rescuing a French priest. Reports of Catholic persecutions were deliberately exaggerated until Napoleon III was finally persuaded to launch an armada of fourteen ships and 2500 men in 1858. After capturing Da Nang in September, the force moved south to take Saigon, against considerable opposition, and the whole Mekong Delta over the next three years. Faced with serious unrest in the north, Emperor Tu Duc signed a treaty in 1862 granting France the three eastern provinces of the delta plus trading rights in selected ports, and allowing missionaries the freedom to proselytize. Five years later, French forces annexed the remaining southern provinces to create the colony of **Cochinchina**.

France became embroiled in domestic troubles and the French government was divided on whether to continue the enterprise, but their administrators in Cochinchina had their eyes on the north. The first attempt to take Hanoi and open up the Red River into China failed in 1873; a larger force was dispatched in 1882 and within a few months, France was in control of Hanoi and the lower reaches of the Red River Delta. Spurred on by this success, the French parliament financed the first contingents of the **French Expeditionary Force** just as the Nguyen were floundering in a succession crisis following the death of Tu Duc. In August 1883, when the French fleet sailed into the mouth of the Perfume River, near Hué, the new emperor was compelled to meet their demands. **Annam** (central Vietnam) and **Tonkin** (the north) became protectorates of France, to be combined with Cochinchina, Cambodia and, later, Laos to form the **Union of Indochina** after 1887.

Despite much talk of the "civilizing mission" of imperial rule, the French were more interested in the economic potential of their new possession. Governor-general Paul Doumer launched a massive programme of **infrastructural development**, constructing railways, bridges and roads and draining vast areas of the Mekong Delta swamp, all funded by raising punitive taxes, with state monopolies on opium, alcohol and salt accounting for seventy percent of government revenues. During the Great Depression of the 1930s markets collapsed; peasants were forced off the land to work as indentured labour in the new rubber, tea and coffee estates or in the mines, often under brutal conditions. Heavy taxes exacerbated **rural poverty** and any commercial or industrial enterprises were kept firmly in French hands, or were controlled by the small minority of Vietnamese and Chinese who actually benefited under the new regime.

On the positive side, mass vaccination and health programmes did bring the frequent epidemics of cholera, smallpox and plague under control. **Education** was a thornier issue: overall, education levels deteriorated during French rule, particularly among unskilled labourers, but a small elite from the emerging urban middle class received a broader, French-based education and a few went to universities in Europe. Not that it got them very far: Vietnamese were barred from all but the most menial jobs in the colonial administration. It was this frustrated and alienated group, imbued with the ideas of Western liberals and Chinese reformers, who began to challenge French rule.

The anti–colonial struggle

For a population brought up on legends of heroic victories over superior forces, the ease with which France had occupied Vietnam was a deep psychological blow. The earliest resistance movements focused on the restoration of the monarchy, such as the "Save the King" (*Can Vuong*) movement of the 1890s, but any emperor showing signs of patriotism was swiftly removed by the French administration. Up until the mid-1920s, Vietnam's fragmented anti-colonial movements were easily controlled by the *Sûreté*, the formidable French secret police. On the whole, the nationalists' aims were political rather than social or economic, and most failed to appeal to the majority of Vietnamese. Gradually, however, the nationalists saw that a more radical approach was called for, and an influential leader named **Phan Boi Chau** finally called for the violent overthrow of the colonial regime.

Meanwhile, over the border in southern China, the **Revolutionary Youth League** was founded in 1925. Not only was this Vietnam's first Marxist-Leninist organization, but its founding father was **Ho Chi Minh**. Born in 1890, the son of a patriotic minor official, Ho was already in trouble with the French authorities in his teens. He left Vietnam in 1911, then turned up in Paris after World War I under one of his many pseudonyms, Nguyen Ai Quoc ("Nguyen the Patriot"). In France, Ho became increasingly active among other exiled dissidents exploring ways to bring an end to colonial rule. At this time one of the few political groups actively supporting anti-colonial movements were the Communists; in 1920 Ho became a founding member of the French Communist Party and by 1923 he was in Moscow, training as a Communist agent. His task was to unite the nascent Vietnamese anti-colonial movements under one organization, the Revolutionary Youth League. Among his many talents, Ho Chi Minh was an intelligent strategist and a great motivator; though he was now committed to Marxist-Leninist ideology, he understood the need to appeal to all nationalists, playing down the controversial goal of social revolution. (See box on p.334 for more on Ho Chi Minh.)

Although many other subsequently famous revolutionaries worked with Ho, it was largely his fierce dedication, single-mindedness and tremendous charisma that held the nationalist movement together and finally propelled the country to independence. The first real test of Ho's leadership came in 1929 when, in his absence, the League split into three separate Communist parties. In Hong Kong a year later, Ho persuaded the rival groups to unite into one **Indochinese Communist Party** whose main goal was an independent Vietnam governed by workers, peasants and soldiers. In preparation for the revolution, cadres were sent into rural areas and among urban workers to set up party cells. The timing couldn't have been better: unemployment and poverty were on the increase as the Great Depression took hold, while France became less willing to commit resources to its colonies.

Throughout the 1930s Vietnam was plagued with strikes and labour unrest, of which the most important was the **Nghe Tinh uprising** in the summer of 1930. French planes bombed a crowd of twenty thousand demonstrators marching on Vinh; within days, villagers had seized control of much of the surrounding countryside, some setting up revolutionary councils to evict wealthy landlords and redistribute land to the peasants. The uprising demonstrated the power of socialist organization, but proved disastrous in the short term – thousands of peasants were killed or imprisoned, the leaders were executed and the Communist Party structure was badly mauled. Most of the ringleaders ended up in the notorious penal colony of Poulo Condore (Con Dao Island; see p.221), which came to be known as the "University of the Revolution". It's estimated that the French held some ten thousand activists in prison by the late 1930s.

World War II

The German occupation of France in 1940 suddenly changed the whole political landscape. Not only did it demonstrate to the Vietnamese the vulnerability of their colonial masters, but it also overturned the established order in Vietnam and ultimately provided Ho Chi Minh with the opportunity he had been waiting for. The immediate repercussion was the **Japanese occupation** of Indochina after Vichy France signed a treaty allowing Japan to station troops in the colony, while leaving the French administration in place. By mid-1941 the region's coalmines, rice fields and military installations were all under Japanese control. Some Vietnamese nationalist groups welcomed this turn of events as the Japanese made encouraging noises about autonomy and "Asia for the Asians". Others, mostly Communist groups, declared their opposition to all foreign intervention and continued to operate from secret bases in the mountainous region that flanks the border between China and Vietnam.

By this time, Ho Chi Minh had reappeared in southern China, from where he walked over the border into Vietnam, carrying his rattan trunk and trusty Hermes typewriter. The date was February 1941; Ho had been in exile for thirty years. In **Pac Bo Cave**, near Cao Bang, Ho met up with other resistance leaders, including Vo Nguyen Giap, to start the next phase in the fight for national liberation; the League for the Independence of Vietnam (*Viet Nam Doc Lap Dong Minh*), better known as the **Viet Minh**, was founded in May 1941.

Over the next few years Viet Minh recruits received military training in southern China; the first regular armed units formed the nucleus of the **Vietnamese Liberation Army** in 1945. Gradually the Viet Minh established liberated zones in the northern mountains to provide bases for future guerrilla operations. With Japanese defeat looking ever more likely, Ho Chi Minh set off once again into China to seek military and financial support from the Chinese and from the Allied forces operating out of Kunming. Ho also made contact with the American Office of Strategic Services (forerunner of the CIA), which promised him limited arms, much to the anger of the Free French who were already planning their return to Indochina. In return for **American aid** the Viet Minh provided information about Japanese forces and rescued Allied pilots shot down over Vietnam. Later, in 1945, an American team arrived in Ho's Cao Bang base where they found him suffering from malaria, dysentery and dengue fever; it's said they saved his life.

Meanwhile, suspecting a belated French counter-attack, Japanese forces seized full control of the country in March 1945. They declared a nominally independent state under the leadership of Bao Dai, the last Nguyen emperor, and imprisoned most of the French army. The Viet Minh quickly moved onto the offensive, helped to some extent by a massive famine that ravaged northern Vietnam that summer. Then, in early August, US forces dropped the first atom bomb on Hiroshima, precipitating the **Japanese surrender** on August 14.

The August Revolution

The Japanese surrender left a power vacuum which Ho Chi Minh was quick to exploit. On August 15, Ho called for a national uprising, which later came to be known as the **August Revolution**. Within four days Hanoi was seething with pro-Viet Minh demonstrations, and in two weeks most of Vietnam came under their control. Emperor Bao Dai handed over his imperial sword to Ho's provisional government at the end of August and on September 2, 1945 Ho Chi Minh proclaimed the establishment of the **Democratic Republic of Vietnam**, cheered by a massive crowd in Hanoi's Ba Dinh Square. For the first time in eighty years Vietnam was an independent country. Famously, Ho's Declaration of Independence quoted from the American Declaration: "All men are created equal. They are endowed by their Creator with certain inalienable rights, among these are life, liberty and the pursuit of happiness." But this, and subsequent appeals for American help against the looming threat of recolonization, fell on deaf ears as America became increasingly concerned at Communist expansion.

The **Potsdam Agreement**, which marked the end of World War II, failed to recognize the new Republic of Vietnam. Instead, Japanese troops south of the

▲ Ho Chi Minh proclaimed the establishment of the Democratic Republic of Vietnam in 1945

Sixteenth Parallel were to surrender to British authority, while those in the north would defer to the Chinese Kuomintang. Nevertheless, by the time these forces arrived, the Viet Minh were already in control, having relieved the Japanese of most of their weapons. In the **south**, rival nationalist groups were battling it out in Saigon, where French troops had also joined in the fray. The situation was so chaotic that the British commander proclaimed martial law and, amazingly, even deployed Japanese soldiers to help restore calm. Against orders, he also rearmed the six thousand liberated French troops and Saigon was soon back in French hands. A few days later, General Leclerc arrived with the first units of the French Expeditionary Force, charged with reimposing colonial rule in Indochina.

Things were going more smoothly in the north, though the two hundred thousand Chinese soldiers stationed there acted increasingly like an army of occupation. The Viet Minh could muster a mere five thousand ill-equipped troops in reply; forced to choose between the two in order to survive, Ho Chi Minh finally rated French rule the lesser of the two evils, reputedly commenting, "I prefer to smell French shit for five years, rather than Chinese shit for the rest of my life." In March 1946, Ho's government signed a treaty allowing a limited French force to replace Kuomintang soldiers in the north. In return, France recognized the Democratic Republic as a "free state" within the proposed French Union; the terms were left deliberately vague. The treaty also provided for a referendum to determine whether Cochinchina would join the new state or remain separate.

While further negotiations dragged on during the summer of 1946, both sides were busily rearming as it became apparent that the French were not going to abide by the treaty. By late April the Expeditionary Force had already exceeded agreed levels, and there was no sign of the promised referendum; in September 1946 the talks effectively broke down. Skirmishes between Vietnamese and French troops in the northern delta boiled over in a dispute over customs control in Haiphong; to quell the rioting, the French navy bombed the town on November 23, killing thousands of civilians. This was followed by the announcement that French troops would assume responsibility for law and order in the north. By way of reply, Viet Minh units attacked French installations in Hanoi on December 19, and then, while resistance forces held the capital for a few days, Ho Chi Minh and the regular army slipped away into the northern mountains.

The French War

For the first years of the **war against the French** (also known as the First Indochina War, or Franco-Viet Minh War) the Viet Minh kept largely to their mountain bases in northern and central Vietnam. While the Viet Minh were building up and training an army, the Expeditionary Force was consolidating its control over the Red River Delta and establishing a string of highly vulnerable outposts around guerrilla-held territory. In October 1947 the French attempted an ambitious all-out attack against enemy headquarters, but it soon became obvious that this was an unconventional "war without fronts" where Viet Minh troops could simply melt away into the jungle when threatened. In addition, the French suffered from hit-and-run attacks deep within the delta, unprotected by a local population who either actively supported or at least tolerated the Viet Minh. Although the French persuaded Bao Dai to return as head of the Associated State of Vietnam in March 1949, most Vietnamese regarded him as a mere puppet and his government won little support.

The war entered a new phase after the Communist victory in China in 1949. With military aid flowing across the border, Bao Dai's shaky government was seen as the last bastion of the free world; America was drawn in and funded the French military to the tune of at least $3 billion by 1954. The Viet Minh, under the command of General Giap, recorded their first major victory, forcing the French to abandon their outposts along the Chinese border and gaining unhindered access to sanctuary in China. Early in 1951, equipped with Chinese weapons and confident of success, the Viet Minh launched an assault on Hanoi itself, but in this first pitched battle of the war, suffered a massive defeat, losing over six thousand troops in a battle that saw napalm deployed for the first time in Vietnam. But Giap (known as "the snow-covered volcano" for his ice-cold exterior concealing a fiery temper) had learnt his lesson, and for the next two years the French sought in vain to repeat their success.

By now France was tiring of the war and in 1953 made contact with Ho Chi Minh to find some way of resolving the conflict. The Americans were growing increasingly impatient with French progress, and at one stage threatened to deploy tactical nuclear weapons against the Viet Minh; the Russians and Chinese were also applying pressure to end the fighting. Eventually, the two sides agreed to discussions at the Geneva Conference, due to take place in May the next year to discuss Korean peace. Meanwhile in Vietnam, a crucial battle was unfolding in an isolated valley on the Lao border, near the town of **Dien Bien Phu**. Early in 1954 French battalions established a massive camp here, deliberately trying to tempt the enemy into the open. Instead the Viet Minh surrounded the valley, cut off reinforcements and slowly closed in (see p.439 for the full story). After 59 days of bitter fighting the French were forced to surrender on May 7, 1954, the eve of the Geneva Conference. The eight years of war proved costly to both sides: total losses on the French side stood at 93,000, while an estimated two hundred thousand Viet Minh soldiers had been killed.

The Geneva Conference

On May 8, a day after the French capitulation at Dien Bien Phu, the nine delegations attending the **Geneva Conference** trained their focus upon Indochina. Armed with the knowledge that they now controlled around 65 percent of the country, the Viet Minh delegation arrived in buoyant mood. But the lasting peace they sought wasn't forthcoming: hampered by distrust, the conference succeeded only in reaching a stopgap solution, a necessarily ambiguous compromise which, however, allowed the French to withdraw with some honour and recognized Vietnamese sovereignty at least in part. Keen to have a weak and fractured nation on their southern border, the Chinese delegation spurred the Viet Minh into agreeing to a division of the country; reliant upon Chinese arms, the Viet Minh were forced to comply.

Under the terms of July 1954's **Geneva Accords** Vietnam was divided at the Seventeenth Parallel, along the Ben Hai River, pending nationwide free elections to be held by July 1956; a demilitarized buffer zone was established on either side of this military front. France and the Viet Minh, who were still fighting in the central highlands even as delegates machinated, agreed to an immediate ceasefire, and consented to a withdrawal of all troops to their respective territories – Communists to the north, non-Communists plus supporters of the French to the south. China, the USSR, Britain, France and the Viet Minh agreed on the accords, but crucially neither the United States nor Bao Dai's government endorsed them, fearing that they heralded a reunited, Communist-ruled Vietnam.

In the long term, the Geneva Accords served to cause a deep polarization within the country and to widen the conflict into an ideological battle between the superpowers, fought out on Vietnamese soil. The immediate consequence, however, was a massive exodus from the north during the stipulated 300-day period of "**free movement**". Almost a million (mostly Catholic) refugees headed south, their flight aided by the US Navy, and to some extent engineered by the CIA, whose distribution of scaremongering, anti-Communist leaflets was designed to create a base of support for the puppet government it was concocting in Saigon. Approaching a hundred thousand **anti-French guerrillas** and sympathizers moved in the opposite direction to regroup, though, as a precautionary measure, between five and ten thousand Viet Minh cadres remained in the south, awaiting orders from Hanoi. These dormant operatives, known to the CIA as "**stay-behinds**" and to the Communists as "winter cadres", were joined by spies who infiltrated the Catholic move south. In line with the terms of the ceasefire, Ho Chi Minh's army marched into Hanoi on October 9, 1954, even as the last French forces were still trooping out.

The Geneva Accords were still being thrashed out as Emperor Bao Dai named himself president and **Ngo Dinh Diem** ("Zee-em") prime minister of South Vietnam, on July 7. A Catholic, and vehemently anti-Communist, Diem knew that Ho Chi Minh would win the lion's share of votes in the proposed elections, and therefore steadfastly refused to countenance them. His mandate "strengthened" by an October 1955 **referendum** (the prime minister's garnering of 98.2 percent of votes cast was more indicative of the blatancy of his vote-rigging than of any popular support), Diem promptly ousted Bao Dai from the chain of command, and declared himself president of the Republic of Vietnam.

Diem's heavy-handed approach to Viet Minh dissidents still in the South was hopelessly misguided: although the subsequent **witch-hunt** decimated Viet

Minh numbers, the brutal and indiscriminate nature of the operation caused widespread discontent – all dissenters were targeted, Viet Minh, Communist or otherwise. As the supposed "free world democracy" of the South mutated into a police state, over fifty thousand citizens died in Diem's pogrom.

Back in Hanoi...

In Hanoi, meanwhile, Ho Chi Minh's government was finding it had problems of its own as, aided by droves of Chinese advisers, it set about constructing a socialist society. Years of warring with France had profoundly damaged the country's infrastructure, and now it found itself deprived of the South's plentiful rice stocks. Worse still, the **land reforms** of the mid-1950s, vaunted as a Robin Hood-style redistribution of land, saw thousands of innocents "tried" as landlords by ad hoc **People's Agricultural Reform Tribunals**, tortured and then executed or set to work in labour camps. "Reactionaries" were also denounced and punished, often for such imperialist "crimes" as possessing works of the great French poets and novelists. The **Rectification of Errors Campaign** of 1956 at least released many victims of the reforms from imprisonment, but as Ho Chi Minh himself said, "one cannot wake the dead".

With Hanoi so preoccupied with getting its own house in order, Viet Minh guerrillas south of the Seventeenth Parallel were for several years left to fend for themselves. For the most part, they sat tight in the face of Diem's reprisals, although guerrilla strikes became increasingly common towards the end of the 1950s, often taking the form of assassinations of government officials. Only in 1959 did the erosion of their ranks prompt Hanoi to shift up a gear and endorse a more overtly military stance. Conscription was introduced in April 1960, cadres and hardware began to creep down the **Ho Chi Minh Trail** (see p.327), and at the end of the year Hanoi orchestrated the creation of the **National Liberation Front** (NLF), which drew together all opposition forces in the South. Diem dubbed its guerrilla fighters **Viet Cong**, or VC (Vietnamese Communists) – a name which stuck, though in reality the NLF represented a united front of Catholic, Buddhist, Communist and non-Communist nationalists.

America enters the fray

American dollars had been supporting the French war effort in Indochina since 1950. In early 1955 the White House began to bankroll Diem's government and the training of his army, the **ARVN** (Army of the Republic of Vietnam). Behind these policies lay the fear of the chain reaction that could follow in Southeast Asia, were South Vietnam to be overrun by Communism – the so-called **Domino Effect** – and, more cynically, what this would mean for US access to raw materials, trade routes and markets. Though President John F. Kennedy baulked at the prospect of large-scale American intervention, by the summer of 1962 there were twelve thousand American advisers in South Vietnam.

Despite all these injections of money, Diem's incompetent and unpopular government was losing ground to the Viet Cong in the battle for the hearts and minds of the population. Particularly damaging to the government was its

Strategic Hamlets Programme. Formulated in 1962 and based on British methods used during the Malayan Emergency, the programme forcibly relocated entire villages into fortified stockades, with the aim of keeping the Viet Cong at bay. Ill-conceived, insensitive and open to exploitation by corrupt officials, the programme had the opposite effect, driving many disgruntled villagers into the arms of the resistance. In fact, the majority of strategic hamlets were empty within two years, as villagers drifted back to their ancestral lands.

Militarily, things were little better. If America needed proof that Diem's government was struggling to subdue the guerrillas, it came in January 1963, at the **Battle of Ap Bac**, where incompetent ARVN troops suffered heavy losses against a greatly outnumbered Viet Cong force. Four months later, Buddhists celebrating Buddha's birthday were fired upon by ARVN soldiers in Hué, sparking off riots and demonstrations against religious repression, and provoking **Thich Quang Duc**'s infamous self-immolation in Saigon (see box, p.99). Fearing that the Communists would gain further by Diem's unpopularity, America tacitly sanctioned the November 1 **coup** that ousted Diem, who escaped with his brother to Cho Lon, only to be shot the following day.

The capital staggered from coup to coup, but corruption, nepotism and dependence upon American support remained constant. In the countryside, meanwhile, the Viet Cong were forging a solid base of popular support. Observing Southern instability, Hanoi in early 1964 proceeded to send battalions of **NVA** (North Vietnamese Army) infantrymen down the Ho Chi Minh Trail, with ten thousand Northern troops hitting the trail in the first year. For America, unwilling to see the Communists granted a say in the running of the South, yet unable to envisage Saigon's generals fending them off, the only option seemed to be to "**Americanize**" the conflict.

In August 1964, a chance came to do just that, when the American destroyer the USS *Maddox* allegedly suffered an unprovoked attack from North Vietnamese craft; two days afterwards, the *Maddox* and another ship, the *C Turner Joy*, reported a second attack. Years later it emerged that the *Maddox* had been taking part in a covert mission to monitor coastal installations, and that the second incident almost certainly never happened. Nevertheless, reprisals followed in the form of 64 **bombing** sorties against Northern coastal bases. And back in Washington, senators voted through the **Tonkin Gulf Resolution**, empowering Johnson to deploy regular American troops in Vietnam, "to prevent further aggression".

Operation Rolling Thunder

An NVA attack upon the highland town of Plei Ku in February 1965 curtailed several months of US procrastination about how best to prosecute the war in Vietnam, and elicited **Operation Flaming Dart**, a concerted bombing raid on NVA camps above the Seventeenth Parallel. **Operation Rolling Thunder**, a sustained carpet-bombing campaign, kicked in a month later; by the time of its suspension three and a half years later its 350,000 sorties had seen twice the tonnage of bombs dropped (around eight hundred daily) as had fallen on all World War II's theatres of war. Despite such impressive statistics, Rolling Thunder failed either to break the North's sources and lines of supply, or to coerce Hanoi into a suspension of activities in the South. Bombing served only to strengthen the resilience of the North, whose population was mobilized to rebuild bridges, roads and railways as quickly as they were damaged. Moreover, NVA troops continued to infiltrate the South in increasing numbers.

As far back as 1954, the American politician William F. Knowland had warned that "using United States ground forces in the Indochina jungle would be like trying to cover an elephant with a handkerchief – you just can't do it". His words fell on deaf ears. The first regular **American troops** from the 3rd US Marine Division landed at Da Nang in March 1965; by the end of the year, two hundred thousand GIs were in Vietnam, and approaching half a million by the winter of 1967. In addition, there were large numbers of Australians and South Koreans, plus smaller units of New Zealanders, Thais and Filipinos.

The war these troops fought was a dirty, dispiriting and frustrating one: for the most part, it was a guerrilla conflict against an invisible enemy able to disappear into the nearest village, leaving them unable to trust even civilians. Missions to flush active Viet Cong soldiers out of villages, which were initiated towards the end of 1965, became known as **Search and Destroy** operations; the most infamous of these resulted in the **My Lai massacre** (see p.258). Other jargon was coined, too, and added to the lexicon of conflict: in the highlands, **fire bases** were established, from where howitzers could rain fire upon NVA troop movements; elsewhere, **free fire zones** – areas cleared of villagers to enable bombing of their supposed guerrilla occupants – were declared; and **scorched earth**, the policy of denuding and razing vast swathes of land in order to rob the Viet Cong of cover, was introduced. And all the while, generals in the field were quick to establish that most symbolic arbiter in this insane war, the **body count**, according to which missions succeeded or failed.

In the **North**, outrage at the merciless bombing campaign meted out by a remote foreign aggressor engendered a sense of anti-colonial purpose; in the **South**, there was only disorientation. To some, the immensity of the US presence seemed to preclude the possibility of a protracted conflict, and was therefore welcome; to others, it felt so much like an invasion, especially when GIs began to uproot them and destroy their land, that they supported or joined the NLF. The Viet Cong themselves were no angels, though, often imposing a reign of terror, augmented by summary executions of alleged traitors. What's more, successive Saigon governments were corrupt and unpopular, but the alternative was the Northern Communists so gruesomely depicted by American propaganda.

To survive, villagers quickly learned to react, and to say the right thing to the right person. Trying to appease the two sets of soldiers they encountered in the space of a day was like treading a tightrope for villagers, creating a climate of hatred and distrust that turned neighbours into informants. Since children were conscripted by whichever side reached them first, brothers and sisters often found themselves fighting on opposing sides.

The Tet Offensive

On January 21, 1968, around forty thousand NVA troops laid siege to a remote American military base at **Khe Sanh**, near the Lao border northwest of Hué. Wary that the confrontation might become an American Dien Bien Phu – an analogy that in reality held no water, given the US's superior air power – America responded, to borrow the military jargon of the day, "with extreme prejudice", notching up a Communist body count of over ten thousand in a carpet-bombing campaign graphically labelled "Niagara". However, such losses were seen as a necessary evil by the Communists, for whom Khe Sanh was primarily a decoy to steer US troops and attention away from the **Tet Offensive** that exploded a week later. In the early hours of January 31, a combined force of seventy thousand Communists (most of them Viet Cong) violated a New Year truce to launch offensives on over a hundred urban centres across the South. The campaign failed to achieve its objective of imposing Viet Cong representation in the Southern government; only in Hué did Viet Cong forces manage to hold out for more than a few days.

But success did register across the Pacific, where the offensive caused a sea change in popular perceptions of the war. Thus far, Washington's propaganda machine had largely convinced the public that the war in Vietnam was under control; events in 1968 flew in the face of this charade. Around two thousand American GIs had died during the Tet Offensive, but symbolically more damaging was the audacious assault mounted, on the first day of the offensive, by a crack Viet Cong commando team on the compound of the **US Embassy in Saigon**. The Communists had pierced the underbelly of the American presence in Vietnam: by the time the compound had been secured over six hours later, five Americans had died – and with them the popular conviction that the war was being won.

This shift in attitude was soon reflected in President Johnson's **vetoing** of requests for a massive troop expansion. On March 31, he announced a virtual cessation of bombing; a month later, the first bout of diplomatic sparring that was to grind on for five years was held in Paris; and, before the year was out, a full end to bombing had been declared.

Nixon's presidency

Richard Nixon's ill-starred term of office commenced in January 1969, on the back of a campaign in which he promised to "end the war and win the peace". His quest for a solution that would facilitate an American pull-out without tarnishing its image led Nixon to pursue the strategy of "**Vietnamization**", a gradual US withdrawal coupled with a stiffening of ARVN forces and hardware. Though the number of US troops in Vietnam reached an all-time peak of 540,000 early on in 1969, sixty thousand of these were home for Christmas, and by the end of 1970 only 280,000 remained. Over the same time period, ARVN numbers almost doubled, from 640,000 to well over a million.

However, the NVA had for several years been stockpiling both men and supplies in **Cambodia**, and in March 1969 US covert bombing of these targets commenced. Code-named **Operation Menu**, it lasted for fourteen months, yet elicited no outcry from Hanoi since they had no right to be in neutral Cambodia in the first place. The following spring, an American-backed coup replaced Prince Sihanouk of Cambodia with Lon Nol and thus eased access for US troops, and a **task force** of twenty thousand soldiers advanced on Communist installations there. The American public was outraged: dismayed that Nixon, far from closing down the war, was in fact widening the conflict, they rallied at mass anti-war demonstrations.

After **Ho Chi Minh's death** on September 2, 1969, the stop-start **peace talks** in Paris dragged along with Le Duc Tho representing the North, and Nixon's national security adviser Henry Kissinger at the American helm. Two stumbling blocks hindered any advancement: the North's insistence on a coalition government in the South with no place for then-president, Thieu, and the US insistence that all NVA troops should move north after a ceasefire. Tit-for-tat military offensives launched early in 1972 saw both sides attempting to strengthen their hand at the bargaining table: Hanoi launched its **Easter Offensive** on the upper provinces of the South; while Nixon countered by resuming the **bombing of the North**. Towards the year's end, negotiations recommenced, this time with Hanoi in a mood to compromise – not least because Nixon let rumours spread of his **Madman Theory**, which involved the use of nuclear weaponry – but the draft agreement produced in October (Nixon was keen to see a resolution before the US elections in Nov) was delayed by President Thieu in Saigon. By the time it was finalized in January 1973 Nixon had flexed his military muscles one last time, sanctioning the eleven-day **Christmas Bombing** of Hanoi and Haiphong (see p.347), in which twenty thousand tonnes of ordnance was dropped and 1600 civilians perished.

Under the terms of the **Paris Accords**, signed on January 27 by the United States, the North, the South and the Viet Cong, a ceasefire was established, all remaining American troops were repatriated by April, and Hanoi and Saigon released their PoWs. The Paris talks failed to yield a long-term political settlement, instead providing for the creation of a **Council of National Conciliation**, comprising Saigon's government and the Communists, to sort matters out at some future date. The agreements allowed the NVA and ARVN troops to retain whatever positions they held. For this fudged deal, Kissinger and Le Duc Tho were awarded the Nobel Prize for peace, though only Kissinger accepted.

The fall of the South

The Paris Accords accomplished little beyond smoothing the US withdrawal from Vietnam: with the NVA allowed to remain in the South, it was only a matter of time before **renewed aggression** erupted. Thieu's ARVN, now numbering a million troops and in robust shape thanks to its new US-financed equipment, soon set about retaking territory lost to the North during the Easter Offensive. The Communists, on the other hand, were still reeling from losses accrued during that campaign. By 1974, things were beginning to sour for the South. An economy already weakened by heavy **inflation** was further drained by the **unemployment** caused by America's withdrawal; corruption in the military was rife, and unpaid wages led to a burgeoning desertion rate. By the end of the year, the South was ripe for the taking.

Received wisdom in Hanoi was that a slow build-up of arms in the South, in preparation for a conventional push in 1976, would be the wisest course of action. Then, over the Christmas period of 1974, an **NVA drive** led by General Tran overran the area north of Saigon now called Song Be Province. Duly encouraged, Hanoi went into action, and towns in the South fell like ninepins under the irresistible momentum of the **Ho Chi Minh Campaign**. Within two months, Communist troops had occupied Buon Ma Thuot, taking a mere 24 hours to finish a job they'd anticipated would require a week. Hué and Da Nang duly followed, and by April 21 Xuan Loc, the last real line of defence before Saigon, had also fallen. ARVN defiance disintegrated in the face of the North's unerring progress: a famous image from these last days shows a highway scattered with the discarded boots of fleeing Southern soldiers. President Thieu fled by helicopter to Taiwan, and leadership of Saigon's government was assumed by **General Duong Van Minh** ("Big Minh"). Minh held the post for just two days before NVA tanks crashed through the gates of the Presidential Palace and Saigon fell to the North on April 30. Only hours before, the last Americans and other Westerners in the city had been **airlifted out** in the frantic helicopter operation known as "Frequent Wind" (see p.100).

The **toll** of the American War in human terms is staggering. Of the 3.3 million Americans who served in Vietnam between 1965 and 1973, some 58,000 died, and more than 150,000 received wounds that required hospitalization. The ARVN lost 250,000 troops, while perhaps two million civilians were killed in the South. Hanoi declared that over two million North Vietnamese civilians and one million troops died during the war. Many more on both sides are still listed as "missing in action" (MIA). Since 1975, an estimated 35,000 people – a third of them children – have been killed by left-over ordnance, while contamination from Agent Orange and other chemicals continues to cause health problems (see p.504). In the US, some half a million veterans suffer from post-traumatic stress disorder, while veteran suicides have now exceeded the total number of US fatalities during the conflict.

Reunified Vietnam

By July 1976, Vietnam was once again a **unified nation** for the first time since the French colonization in the 1850s. At first the new leaders trod softly, softly in order to impress the international community, but Southerners eyed the future with profound apprehension. Their fears were well founded, as Hanoi was in no mood to grant Saigon autonomy: the Council of National Reconciliation, provided for by the Paris Accords, was never established, and the NLF's **Provisional Revolutionary Government** worked beneath the shadow of the Military Management Committee, and therefore Hanoi, until the **Socialist Republic of Vietnam** was officially born, in July 1976. The impression of a conquering army was exacerbated when Northern cadres – the *can bo* – swarmed south to take up all official posts.

Monumental **problems** faced the nascent republic. For many years, the two halves of Vietnam had lived according to wildly variant political and economic systems. The North had no industry, its agriculture was based on co-operative farms, and much of its land had been bombed on a massive scale. In stark contrast, American involvement in the South had underwritten what John Pilger describes as "an 'economy' based upon the services of maids, pimps, whores, beggars and black-marketeers", buttressed by American cash that dried up when the last helicopter left the embassy in Saigon.

The changes that swept the country weren't limited to economics. Bitterness on Hanoi's part towards its former enemies was inevitable, yet instead of making moves towards national conciliation – and despite the fact that many families had connections in both camps – recriminations drove further wedges between the peoples of North and South. Anyone with remote connections to America was interned in a **re-education camp**, along with Buddhist monks, priests, intellectuals and anyone else the government wanted to be rid of. Hundreds of thousands of Southerners were sent, without trial, to these camps, where some remained for over a decade. The quagmire Vietnam found itself in after reunification prompted many of its citizens to flee the country in unseaworthy vessels, an exodus of humanity known as the **boat people** (see box opposite).

Three weeks before the fall of Saigon in 1975, **Pol Pot**'s genocidal regime had seized power in Cambodia: within a year his troops were making **cross-border**

The "boat people"

In 1979 the attention of the world was caught by images of rickety fishing boats packed with Vietnamese **refugees** seeking sanctuary in Hong Kong and other Southeast Asian harbours. An untold number – some say a third – fell victim to typhoons, starvation and disease or pirates, who often sank the boats after raping the women and seizing the refugees' meagre possessions. Others somehow fetched up on the coast of Australia or were picked up by passing freighters. The prime destination, however, was Hong Kong, where 68,000 asylum-seekers arrived in 1979 alone. The exodus was at its peak in 1979, but it had been going on, largely unnoticed, since reunification four years earlier, and continued up to the early 1990s. Over this period an estimated 840,000 boat people arrived safely in "ports of first asylum", of whom more than 750,000 were eventually resettled overseas.

The first refugees were mostly **Southerners**, people who felt themselves too closely associated with the old regime or their American allies, and feared Communist reprisals. Some were former nationalists and a few were even ex-Viet Cong, disillusioned with the new government's extremism. Then, in early 1978, nationalization of private commerce was instituted in the South, hitting hard at the **Chinese** community, which controlled much Southern business and the all-important rice trade. As anti-Chinese sentiment took hold, thousands made their escape in fishing boats followed in the late 1970s by more **Vietnamese**, driven by a series of bad harvests, severe hardship and the prospect of prolonged military service in Cambodia.

By 1979 the situation had become so critical that the international community was forced to act, offering asylum to the more than two hundred thousand refugees crowding temporary camps around Southeast Asia. Under the auspices of the UN, the **Orderly Departure Programme** (ODP) also enabled legal emigration of political refugees to the West, resettling over half a million in more than forty Western countries.

In 1987, the South China Sea was once again full of Vietnamese people in overcrowded boats. This **second wave** were mostly Northerners fleeing desperate poverty rather than fear of persecution, with Hong Kong again bearing the brunt of new arrivals. Governments were less sympathetic this time round and, in an attempt to halt the flow, from early 1989 boat people were denied automatic refugee status. Instead, a screening process was introduced to identify "genuine" refugees; the rest, designated "economic migrants", were encouraged to return under the **Voluntary Repatriation Scheme**, which offered concrete assistance with resettlement.

Then, in early 1996, all parties finally agreed that the only "viable solution" was to send the remaining forty thousand failed asylum-seekers still in Southeast Asian camps back home. In theory deportations were to take place "without threat or use of force", though clashes with security forces became more violent as the programme gained momentum. The situation was worst in Hong Kong, where there was pressure to clear the camps before the handover to China in 1997. The rate of repatriation – both voluntary and, increasingly, forced – was stepped up throughout the region and by mid-1997 nearly all the boat people had been either resettled or returned to Vietnam.

The UN High Commission for Refugees (UNHCR), which monitored returnees in Vietnam up until 2000, said there was little evidence of persecution or discrimination. Others, however, claimed that the monitoring was inadequate and ineffective, and cited examples of returnees being imprisoned. At the same time, various international bodies, such as the European Union, helped returnees reintegrate into the community through job creation schemes, vocational training programmes and low-interest loans. In 1998, a scheme known as ROVR got under way, resettling mostly Southerners who were able to prove some sort of relationship with the Americans during the war.

As the Vietnamese economy improved and as relations between America and Vietnam started to thaw around the turn of the millennium, so the ODP and ROVR programmes were gradually wound up. Their completion marked the end – at least as far as officialdom was concerned – of the whole sorry saga of the boat people.

forays into regions of Vietnam that had once fallen under Khmer sway, around the Mekong Delta and north of Ho Chi Minh City (as Saigon had been renamed). One such venture led to the massacre at **Ba Chuc** (see p.170), in which almost two thousand people died. Reprisals were slow in coming, but by 1978 Vietnam could stand back no longer; on Christmas Day of that year 120,000 **Vietnamese troops invaded Cambodia** and ousted Pol Pot. Whatever the motives for the invasion, and even though it brought an end to Pol Pot's reign of terror, Vietnam was further ostracized by the international community. In February 1979, Beijing's response came in the form of a punitive **Chinese invasion** of Vietnam's northeastern provinces; Chinese losses were heavy, and after sixteen days they retreated. Meanwhile, Pol Pot had withdrawn across the Thai border, from where his army was able to continue attacking the Vietnamese army of occupation. The Vietnamese remained in Cambodia until September 1989, by which time an estimated fifty thousand troops had died, the majority of them Southern conscripts.

Doi Moi

A severe famine in 1985 and the 775 percent inflation that crippled the country in 1986 were just two of the many symptoms of the **economic malaise** threatening to tear Vietnam apart during the late 1970s and early 1980s. An experimental hybrid of planned and market economies tried out in 1979 came to nothing, and by the early 1980s the only thing keeping Vietnam afloat was Soviet aid. Treaties made it illegal for Americans to do business with the Vietnamese, who, largely due to American pressure, were unable to look to the IMF or World Bank for development loans.

The party's conservative old guard resisted change for as long as it could, but the death of General Secretary Le Duan in 1986 finally cleared the way for more reformist politicians to attempt to reverse the country's fortunes: **Nguyen Van Linh** took over as general secretary, and a raft of market-based economic reforms, known as **doi moi** or "renovation", followed. This encompassed limited moves towards decentralizaton and privatization; collectivized agriculture was abandoned in favour of individual land-holdings and attempts were made to attract foreign capital by liberalizing foreign investment regulations. Political reforms came a poor second, although the congress did instigate purges on corrupt officialdom and gave the press freer rein to criticize. With the **collapse of Communism** across Europe in 1989, though, the press was again silenced, and in a keynote speech Nguyen Van Linh rejected the concept of a multi-party state; all economic reforms, however, remained in place, and the government set in motion efforts to end Vietnam's isolation.

International rehabilitation, which had already begun with the withdrawal of troops from Cambodia in 1989, gathered momentum in the 1990s, as efforts to aid the US search teams looking for remains of the two thousand-plus American soldiers still unaccounted for (MIAs, or Missing in Action) were stepped up. In 1993, a year after the reformist **Vo Van Kiet** became prime minister, the Americans duly lifted their veto on aid, and Western cash began to flow. By the year's end, inflation was down to five percent. The rapprochement with the US continued into 1994, as the US trade embargo was lifted by President Clinton, and in February 1995 the two countries opened liaison offices in each other's capitals. Vietnam was admitted into **ASEAN** (the Association of

Southeast Asian Nations) in July 1995, and the same month saw full **diplomatic relations restored** with the US.

During the next two years foreign investment continued to flood in, pushing economic growth rates close to ten percent per annum. Revenues from oil, manufacturing and tourism took off and everyone was forecasting Vietnam as the next **Asian tiger**. For all the optimism, however, cracks were beginning to appear: the economic upturn was benefiting city-dwellers (particularly in Ho Chi Minh City) far more than the rural population; top bureaucrats were openly criticized in **corruption** scandals; and an alarmed government launched a campaign against "**social evils**" – videos, advertising, pornography and other Western imports which were seen to be undermining traditional society.

By 1997 the honeymoon period was definitely over. Economic growth flagged as foreign companies scaled back, or pulled out altogether, frustrated by an overblown bureaucracy, miles of red tape and regulations in a constant state of flux. As the economic crisis in Southeast Asia took hold, Vietnam's mostly inefficient, state-run industries became increasingly uncompetitive, and smuggling grew at an alarming rate. In May 1997, widespread corruption, growing agricultural unemployment and the ever-widening gulf between urban and rural Vietnam sparked off **demonstrations** by thousands of dissatisfied farmers in Thai Binh Province, part of the traditionally Communist north.

The twenty–first century

National **elections** in July 1997 brought a long-awaited change of government, ushering in a band of younger, more worldly-wise ministers under Prime Minister **Phan Van Khai**, who was re-elected in 2002. In 2006 his chosen successor **Nguyen Tan Dung** took over, continuing Khai's economic reforms – no simple task given the inherent constraints of a "state capitalism" system – and the battle against corruption, resulting in a number of high-profile **anti-corruption trials**. Meanwhile, the progress of **international reconciliation** and **trade liberalization** included the ratification in 2001 of a bilateral trade agreement between Vietnam and America, and membership of the World Trade Organization (WTO) in late 2006.

Progress on **human rights**, meanwhile, has been erratic to say the least. Indeed, one of the government's biggest challenges is how to reconcile the inherent contradictions between economic liberalization and central political control, while also satisfying the growing aspirations of Vietnamese people. Combine this with the need to speed up the restructuring and privatization – or "equitization" as the Vietnamese prefer to call it – of debt-ridden state enterprises without letting unemployment and economic and social inequality spiral out of control, and it's perhaps not surprising that reform has been painfully slow: a healthy increase in GDP per head disguises the fact that Vietnam remains near the bottom of global league tables for economic and press freedom. Despite this, things are moving slowly in the right direction: according to World Bank figures, the number of households living in poverty has dropped from seventy percent in the 1980s to under thirty percent today. Likewise, child mortality has fallen and the average life expectancy is now around 71 years, compared to 65 in 1990.

Religion and beliefs

The moral and religious life of most Vietnamese people is governed by a complex mixture of Confucian, Buddhist and Taoist philosophical teachings interwoven with ancestor worship and ancient, animistic practices. Incompatibilities are reconciled on a practical level into a single, functioning belief system whereby a family may maintain an ancestral altar in their home, consult the village guardian spirit, propitiate the God of the Hearth and take offerings to the Buddhist pagoda.

The primary influence on Vietnam's religious life has been Chinese. But in southern Vietnam, which historically fell within the Indian sphere, small communities of Khmer and Cham still adhere to Hinduism, Islam and Theravada Buddhism brought direct from India. From the fifteenth century on, **Christianity** has also been a feature, represented largely by Roman Catholicism but with a small Protestant following in the south. Vietnam also claims a couple of home-grown religious **sects**, both products of political and social turmoil in the early twentieth century: Cao Dai and Hoa Hao.

The **political dimension** has never been far removed from religious affairs in Vietnam, as the world was made vividly aware by Buddhist opposition to the oppressive regime of President Diem in the 1960s. After 1975, the Marxist–Leninist government of reunified Vietnam declared the state atheist, while theoretically allowing people the right to practise their religion under the constitution. In reality, churches and pagodas were closed down, religious leaders sent for re-education, and followers discriminated against if not actively persecuted.

Since 1986 the situation has eased, with the right to **religious freedom** being reaffirmed in the 1992 constitution. A number of high-profile prisoners held on religious grounds have been released, while party leaders have publicly demonstrated the new freedoms by visiting pagodas and churches. As a result an increasing number of Vietnamese are once again openly practising their faith. Indeed, as Vietnam faces the onslaught of new ideas and the "social evils" spawned by the breakdown of its moral codes, people are looking to religion both for personal guidance and as a stabilizing force in society. Despite such moves toward greater freedom of worship, however, the government continues to exercise close control on religious groups through such practices as monitoring appointments, training institutions and publications. It is regularly accused of failing to make real progress on **human rights** issues and came in for particularly severe criticism for its crackdown on ethnic minority Christians following widespread unrest in the central highlands in 2001 and 2004. Later in 2004 the US designated Vietnam a "Country of Particular Concern" because of its violations of religious freedom. The Vietnamese government subsequently released a number of prisoners and passed legislation outlawing forced recantations, amongst other measures. Human rights organizations, however, say it is being interpreted and enforced unevenly.

Ancestor worship

One of the oldest cults practised in Vietnam is that of ancestor worship, based on the fundamental principles of filial piety and of obligation to the past, present and future generations. No matter what their religion, virtually every

Vietnamese household, even hardline Communist, will maintain an **ancestral altar** in the belief that the dead continue to live in another realm. Ancestors can intercede on behalf of their descendants and bring the family good fortune, but in return the living must pay respect, perform prescribed ceremonies and provide for their ancestors' wellbeing. At funerals and subsequent anniversaries, quantities of paper money and other **votive offerings** (these days including television sets and cars) are burnt, and choice morsels of food are regularly placed on the altar. Traditionally this is financed by the income from a designated plot of land, and it is the responsibility of the oldest, usually male, member of the family to organize the rituals, tend the altar and keep the ancestors abreast of all important family events; failure in any of these duties carries the risk of inciting peeved ancestors to make mischief.

The ancestral altar occupies a central position in the home. On it are placed several wooden tablets, one for each ancestor going back five generations. One hundred days after the funeral, the deceased's spirit returns to reside in the tablet. People without children to honour them by burning incense at the altar are condemned to wander the world in search of a home. Some childless people make provision by paying a temple or pagoda to observe the rituals, while the spirits of others may eventually take up residence in one of the small shrine houses (*cuong*) you see in fields and at roadsides. Important times for remembering the dead are **Tet**, the lunar new year, and **Thanh Minh** ("Festival of Pure Light"), which falls on the fifth day of the third lunar month.

Spirit worship

Residual animism plus a whole host of spirits borrowed from other religions have given Vietnam a complicated mystical world. The universe is divided into **three realms**: the sky, earth and man, under the overall guardianship of Ong Troi, Lord of Heaven, assisted by spirits of the earth, mountains and water. Within the hierarchy are four **sacred animals** who appear everywhere in Vietnamese architecture: the dragon, representing the king, power and intelligence; the phoenix, embodying the queen, beauty and peace; the turtle, symbol of longevity and protector of the kingdom; and the mythical *kylin*, usually translated as unicorn, which represents wisdom.

In addition each village or urban quarter will venerate a **guardian spirit** in either a temple (*den*) or communal house (*dinh*). The deity may be legendary, for example the benevolent horse-spirit Bach Ma of Thang Long (modern Hanoi), and will often come from the Taoist pantheon. Or the guardian may be a historical figure such as a local or national hero, or a man of great virtue. In either case people will propitiate these tutelary spirits – represented on the altar by a gilded throne – with offerings, and will consult them in times of need. The *dinh* also serves as meeting house and school for the community.

Buddhism

The Buddha was born **Siddhartha Gautama** to a wealthy family sometime during the sixth century BC in present-day Nepal. At an early age he renounced his life of luxury to seek the ultimate deliverance from worldly

▲ Buddhist monks

suffering and strive to reach **nirvana**, an indefinable, blissful state. After several years Siddhartha attained enlightenment while sitting under a bodhi tree, and then devoted the rest of his life to teaching the **Middle Way** that leads to nirvana. The Buddha preached that existence is a cycle of perpetual reincarnation in which actions in one life determine one's position in the next, but that it is possible to break free by following certain precepts, central to which are non-violence and compassion. The Buddha's doctrine was based on the **Four Noble Truths**: existence is suffering; suffering is caused by desire; suffering ends with the extinction of desire; the way to end suffering is to follow the eightfold path of right understanding, thought, speech, action, livelihood, effort, mindfulness and concentration.

The history of Buddhism in Vietnam

It's estimated that up to two-thirds of the Vietnamese population consider themselves Buddhist. The vast majority are followers of the Mahayana school which was introduced to northern Vietnam via China in the second century AD. Within this, most Vietnamese Buddhists claim allegiance to the Pure Land sect (*Tinh Do*), which venerates A Di Da or Amitabha Buddha above all others, while the meditational Zen sect (*Thien*) has a moderate following, predominantly in northern Vietnam.

In fact Buddhism first arrived in southern Vietnam nearly one hundred years earlier as **Theravada**, or the "Lesser Vehicle", following Indian trade routes through Burma and Thailand. Theravada is an ascetical form of the faith based on the individual pursuit of perfection and enlightenment, which failed to find favour beyond the Khmer communities of the Mekong, where it still claims about one million followers. One of the salient features of **Mahayana** Buddhism, in contrast, is the belief that intermediaries, **bodhisattvas**, have chosen to forgo nirvana to work for the salvation of all humanity, and it was this that enabled Mahayana to adapt to a Vietnamese context by incorporating local gods and spirits into its array of bodhisattvas. The best-known bodhisattva is

The Vietnamese word *chua*, translated as "pagoda", is an exclusively Buddhist term, whereas a temple (*den*) may be Taoist, Confucian or house a guardian spirit. **Pagoda architecture** reached a pinnacle during the Ly and Tran dynasties, but thanks to Chinese invasions and local, anti-Buddhist movements few examples remain. A majority of those still in existence are eighteenth- or nineteenth-century constructions, though many retain features of earlier designs. Generally, pagoda **layout** is either an inverse T or three parallel lines of single-storeyed pavilions. The first hall is reserved for public worship, while those beyond, on slightly raised platforms, contain the prayer table and principal altar. Other typical elements are a **bell tower**, either integral to the building or standing apart, and a **walled courtyard** containing ponds, stone stelae and, particularly in Mahayana pagodas, the white figure of Quan Am symbolizing charity and compassion.

The most interesting feature inside the pagoda is often the **statuary**. Rows of Buddhas sit or stand on the main altar, where the Buddhist trinity occupies the highest level: A Di Da or Amitabha, the Historical Buddha; Thich Ca Mau Ni or Sakyamuni, born Siddhartha Gautama, the Present Buddha; and Di Lac, or Maitreya, the Future Buddha. Lower ranks comprise the same characters in a variety of forms accompanied by bodhisattvas: look out for pot-bellied Maitreya as the laughing carefree Buddha who grants wishes; the omnipotent Avalokitesvara of a "thousand" arms and eyes; and the Nine Dragon Buddha (Tuong Cuu Long). This latter is a small statue, found more often in northern Vietnam, of Sakyamuni encircled by dragons, standing with one hand pointing to the sky and the other to the earth. According to legend, nine dragons descended from the sky to bathe the newborn Buddha, after which he took seven steps forward and proclaimed, "on earth and in the sky, I alone am the highest."

Two unmistakable figures residing in all pagodas are the giant **guardians of Buddhist law**: white-faced "Mister Charitable" (Ong Thien), holding a pearl, and red-faced "Mister Wicked" (Ong Ac). Ong Thien sees everything, both the good and the bad, while Ong Ac dispenses justice. From an artistic point of view, some of the most fascinating statues are the lifelike representations of *arhats*, ascetic Buddhist saints; the best examples are found in northern pagodas, where each figure is portrayed in a disturbingly realistic style. Finally, Mahayana pagodas will undoubtedly welcome in a few **Taoist spirits**, the favourites being Thien Hau, the Protectress of Sailors, and Thanh Mau, the Mother Goddess. Somewhere in the pagoda halls will be an altar dedicated to deceased monks or nuns, while larger pagodas usually maintain a garden for their burial stupas. Traditionally Buddhists would bury their dead, but increasingly they practise cremation.

The **best times to visit** a pagoda are the first and fifteenth days of the lunar month (new moon and full moon), when they are at their busiest. Note that it's customary to remove your shoes when stepping on the floor mats and sometimes when entering the main sanctuary – watch what the locals do, or ask, to be on the safe side.

Avalokitesvara, usually worshipped in Vietnam as **Quan Am**, the Goddess of Mercy. Mahayana Buddhism spread through northern Vietnam until it became the **official state religion** after the country regained its independence from China in the tenth century. The Ly kings (1009–1225), in particular, were devout Buddhists who sponsored hundreds of pagodas, prompting a flowering of the arts, and established a hierarchy of scholar-monks as advisers to the court. Great landowning monasteries came into being and Buddhist doctrine was incorporated into the civil service examinations along with Confucian and Taoist texts as part of the "triple world-view", *Tam Giao*. At the same time it became apparent that Buddhism was unable to provide the unifying ideology

Vietnamese deities

Buddhist deities

A Di Da or **Amitabha** The Historical Buddha, the most revered member of the Buddhist pantheon in Vietnamese pagodas.

Avalokitesvara A bodhisattva often represented with many arms and eyes, being all-powerful, or as Quan Am (see below).

Di Lac or **Maitreya** The Future Buddha, usually depicted as chubby, with a bare chest and a huge grin, sitting on a lotus throne.

Ong Ac or **Trung Ac** One of the two guardians of the Buddhist religion, popularly known as Mister Wicked, who judges all people. He has a fierce red face and a reputation for severity – of which badly behaved children are frequently reminded.

Ong Thien or **Khuyen Thien** The second guardian of Buddhism is Mister Charitable, a white-faced kindly soul who encourages good behaviour.

Quan Am The Goddess of Mercy, adopted from the Chinese goddess, Kuan Yin. Quan Am is a popular incarnation of Avalokitesvara. She is usually represented as a graceful white statue, with her hand raised in blessing.

Thich Ca Mau Ni or **Sakyamuni** The Present Buddha, born Siddhartha Gautama, who founded Buddhism.

Other characters

Ngoc Hoang The Jade Emperor, ruler of the Taoist pantheon who presides over heaven.

Ong Tau God of the Hearth, who keeps watch over every family and reports on the household to the Jade Emperor every New Year.

Quan Cong A Chinese general of the Han Dynasty revered for his loyalty, honesty and exemplary behaviour. Usually flanked by his two assistants.

Thanh Mau The Mother Goddess.

Thien Hau Protectress of Sailors.

Tran Vo Properly known as Tran Vo Bac De, Taoist Emperor of the North, who governs storms and generally harmful events.

---

required by a highly centralized state constantly fighting for its survival. Consequently, by the mid-fourteenth century Buddhism had lost its political and economic influence, and, when the Later Le Dynasty came to power in 1428, Confucianism finally eclipsed it as the dominant national philosophy.

But by then Buddhism was too deeply rooted, particularly in the folk religion of the countryside, to lose its influence completely. It enjoyed further brief periods of **royal patronage**, notably during the seventeenth and eighteenth centuries when new pagodas were built and old ones repaired. To many people it still offered a spiritual element lacking in Confucian doctrine, and during the colonial era Vietnamese intellectuals turned to Buddhism in search of a national identity. Since then the Buddhist community has been a focus of **dissent**, not least in the 1960s when images of self-immolating Buddhist monks focused world attention on the excesses of South Vietnam's Catholic President Diem. At the time, protesting Buddhists were accused of being pro-Communist, although their standpoint was essentially neutral. In the event they experienced even greater repression after reunification when pagodas were closed, and monks and nuns were sent to re-education camps.

The situation has eased considerably in recent years, and pagodas affiliated to the officially recognized Vietnam Buddhist Sangha (VBS) have been able to resume their social and educational programmes to a certain extent. Many pagodas, now bustling with life again, have been renovated after years of neglect. Nevertheless, the government continues to exert control over the VBS, and Buddhist leaders have persisted in their denunciations of the regime, campaigning for **human rights** and causing the government acute embarrassment as it seeks international approval. In particular, the authorities refuse to recognize the Unified Buddhist Church of Vietnam (UBCV), the main pre-1975 Buddhist organization. According to international human rights organizations, its leaders are regularly placed under "house arrest" with no official charges against them.

Confucianism

The teachings of Confucius provide a guiding set of moral and ethical principles, an **ideology** for the state's rulers and subjects onto which ritualistic practices have been grafted.

Confucius is the Latinized name of K'ung-Fu-Tzu (Khong Tu in Vietnamese), who was born into a minor aristocratic family in China in 551 BC. At this time China was in turmoil as the Zhou Dynasty dissolved into rival feudal states battling for supremacy. Confucius worked for many years as a court official, where he observed the nature of power and the function of government at close quarters. At the age of 50, he packed it all in and for the next twenty years wandered the country spreading his ideas on social and political reform in an effort to persuade states and individuals to live peacefully together for their mutual benefit. His central tenet was the importance of **correct behaviour** and **loyal service**, reinforced by ceremonial rites whereby the ruler maintains authority through good example rather than force. Important qualities to strive for are selflessness, respectfulness, sincerity and non-violence; the ideal person should be neither heroic nor extrovert, but instead follow a "golden mean". Confucius remained silent on spiritual matters, though he placed great emphasis on observing ancient rituals such as making offerings to heaven and to ancestors.

Confucian **teachings** were handed down in the *Analects*, but he is also credited with editing the Six Classics, among them the *Book of Changes* (*I Ching*) and the *Book of Ritual* (*Li Chi*). Later these became the basic texts for civil service examinations, ensuring that all state officials had a deeply ingrained respect for tradition and social order. Though Confucianism ultimately led to national inflexibility and the undermining of personal initiative, its positive legacy has been an emphasis on the value of education and a belief that individual merit is of greater consequence than high birth.

After the death of Confucius in 478 BC the doctrine was developed further by his **disciples**, the most famous of whom was Mencius (Meng-tzu). By the first century AD, Confucianism, which slowly absorbed elements of Taoism, had evolved into a cult and also become the state ideology whereby kings ruled under the Mandate of Heaven. Social stability was maintained through a fixed hierarchy of interdependent relationships encapsulated in the notion of filial piety. Thus children must obey their parents without question, wives their husbands, students their teacher, and subjects their ruler. For their part, the recipient, particularly the king, must earn this obedience; if the rules are broken, the harmony of society and nature is disturbed and authority loses its legitimacy. Therefore, by implication, revolution was justified when the king lost his divine right to rule.

The history of Confucianism in Vietnam

Confucian thinking has pervaded Vietnamese society ever since Chinese administrators introduced the concepts during the second century BC. Reinforced by a thousand years of Chinese rule, Confucianism (*Nho Giao*) came to play an essential role in Vietnam's political, social and educational systems. The philosophy was largely one of an intellectual elite, but Confucian teaching eventually filtered down to the village level where it had a profound influence on the Vietnamese family organization.

The ceremonial **cult of Confucius** was formalized in 1070 when King Ly Thanh Tong founded the Temple of Literature in Hanoi. But it wasn't until the foundation of the Later Le Dynasty in 1428 that Confucian doctrine gained supremacy over Buddhism in the Vietnamese court. The Le kings viewed Confucian ideology, with its emphasis on social order, duty and respect, as an effective means of consolidating their new regime. In 1442, they overhauled the education system and based it on a curriculum of Confucian texts. They also began recruiting top-level mandarins through doctoral examinations, which eventually gave rise to a scholar-gentry class at the expense of the old landed aristocracy. Confucian influence reached its peak during the reign of King Le Thanh Tong (1460–97), which heralded a golden age of bureaucratic reform when public service on behalf of both community and state became a noble ideal. At the same time, however, a strongly centralized administration, presided over by a divine ruler and a mandarin elite, eventually bred corruption, despotism and an increasingly rigid society. The arrival of Western ideas and French rule in the late nineteenth century finally undermined the political dominance of Confucianism, though it managed to survive as the court ideology until well into the twentieth century. The cult of Confucius continues in a few temples (*Van Mieu*) dedicated to the sage, and he also appears on other altars as an honoured ancestor, an exemplary figure remembered for services to the nation.

Many **Confucian ideals** have been completely assimilated into Vietnamese society. After Independence, the Communist Party struggled against inherent conservatism and the supremacy of the family as a political unit; indeed, leaders can still be heard railing against the entrenched "feudal" nature of rural Vietnam. But the party was also able to tap into those elements of the Confucian tradition that suited their new classless, socialist society: conformity, duty and the denial of personal interest for the common good. Today, however, Confucian ideals are being seriously undermined by the invasion of materialism and individual ambition.

Taoism

Taoism is based on the **Tao-te-Ching**, the "Book of the Way", traditionally attributed to **Lao-tzu** (meaning "Old Master"), who is thought to have lived in China in the sixth century BC. The Tao, the Way, emphasizes effortless action, intuition and spontaneity; the Tao is invisible and impartial; it cannot be taught, nor can it be expressed in words. It is the one reality from which everything is born, universal and eternal. However, by virtuous, compassionate and non-violent behaviour, it is possible to achieve ultimate stillness, through a mystical and personal quest. Taoism thus preached non-intervention, passivity and the futility of academic scholarship; it was viewed by Confucians as suspiciously subversive.

Central to the Tao is the **duality** inherent in nature; the whole universe is in temporary balance, a tension of complementary opposites defined as **yin** and **yang**, the male and female principles. Yang is male, the sun, active and orthodox; yin is female, the earth, flexible, passive and instinctive. Harmony is the balance between the two, and experiencing that harmony is the Tao. Accordingly all natural things can be categorized by their property of yin or yang, and human activity should strive not to disrupt that balance. In its pure form Taoism has no gods, only emanations of the Tao, but in the first century AD it corrupted into an organized religion venerating a deified Lao-tzu. The new cult had popular appeal since it offered the goal of immortality through yogic meditation and good deeds. Eventually the practice of Taoism developed highly complex **rituals**, incorporating magic, mysticism, superstition and the use of geomancy (see box below) to ensure harmony between man and nature, while astrology might be used to determine auspicious dates for weddings, funerals, starting a journey or even launching a new business. Ancient spirit worship, the cult of ancestors and the veneration of legendary or historic figures all fused happily with the Taoist idea of a universal essence.

The vast, eclectic pantheon of Taoist **gods and immortals** is presided over by Ngoc Hoang, the Jade Emperor. He is assisted by three ministers: Nam Tao, the southern star who records all births; Bac Dau, the north star who registers deaths; and Ong Tao, God of the Hearth who reports all happenings in the family household to Ngoc Hoang at the end of the year. Then there is a collection of immortals, genies and guardian deities, including legendary and historic figures. In Vietnam among the best-known are Tran Vo, God of the North, Bach Ho, the White Tiger of the West, and Tran Hung Dao, who protects the newborn and cures the sick. Confucius is also honoured as a Taoist saint. A distinctive aspect of Taoism is its use of **mediums** to communicate with the gods; the divine message is often in the form of a poem, transmitted by a writing brush onto sand or a bed of rice.

Chinese immigrants brought Taoism (*Dao Giao*) to Vietnam during the long period of Chinese rule (111 BC–939 AD). Between the eleventh and fourteenth centuries the philosophy enjoyed equal status with Buddhism and Confucianism as one of Vietnam's three "religions", but Taoism gradually declined until it eventually became a strand of folk religion. A few Taoist temples (*quan*) exist in Vietnam but on the whole its deities have been absorbed into other cults. The Jade Emperor, for example, frequently finds himself part of the Buddhist pantheon in Vietnamese pagodas.

Geomancy

The **practice of geomancy** is a pseudo-scientific study, much like astrology or reading horoscopes, which was introduced to Vietnam from China. The underlying idea is that every location has harmful or beneficial properties governed by its physical attributes, planetary influences and the flow of magnetic energy through the earth. Geomancy is used mainly in **siting buildings**, particularly tombs, palaces, temples and the like, but also ordinary dwellings.

Geomancers analyse the general **topography** of the site, looking at the location of surrounding hills, as well as rivers, streams and other bodies of water, to find the most auspicious situation and orientation. They may suggest improving the area by adding small hills or lakes and, if a family suffers bad fortune, a geomancer may be called in to divine the cause of the imbalance and restore the natural harmony.

Christianity

Vietnam's **Catholic community** is the second largest in Southeast Asia after the Philippines. Exact figures are hard to come by but estimates vary between six and eight million (seven to ten percent of the population), of which perhaps two-thirds live in the south. The south is also home to the majority of the one million or so adherents to the **Protestant** faith, known as *Tin Lanh*, or the Good News, which was introduced by Canadian and American missionaries in the early twentieth century. Perhaps two-thirds of Protestants belong to ethnic-minority groups in the central highlands and northwest mountains. There's evidence that the number of adherents has been growing rapidly, despite government restrictions on proselytizing.

The first Christian **missionaries** to reach Vietnam were Portuguese and Spanish Dominicans who landed briefly on the north coast in the sixteenth century. They were followed in 1615 by French and Portuguese Jesuits, dispatched by the pope to establish the first permanent missions. Among the early arrivals was the Frenchman Alexandre de Rhodes, a Jesuit who impressed the northern Trinh lords and won, by his reckoning, nearly seven thousand converts. The inevitable **backlash** against Christianity, which opposed ancestor worship and espoused subversive ideas such as equality, was not long in coming. In 1630 the Trinh lords expelled all Christians, including de Rhodes, who returned to France where he helped create the Society of Foreign Missions (*Société des Missions Etrangères*). This society soon became the most active proselytizing body in Indochina; by the end of the eighteenth century it had claimed thousands of converts, particularly in the coastal provinces.

Official attitudes towards Christianity fluctuated over the centuries, though the Vietnamese kings were generally suspicious of the Church's increasingly political role. The most violent **persecutions** occurred during the reign of Minh Mang (1820–41), an ardent Confucian, and reached a peak after 1832. Churches were destroyed, the faces of converts were branded with the words *ta dao*, meaning "false religion", and many of those refusing to renounce their faith were killed; 117 martyrs, both European and Asian, were later canonized. Such repression, much exaggerated at the time, provided the French with a pretext for greater involvement in Indochina, culminating in full colonial rule at the end of the nineteenth century.

Not surprisingly, Catholicism **prospered** under the French regime. Missions re-opened and hundreds of churches, schools and hospitals were built. Vietnamese Catholics formed an educated elite among a population that counted some two million faithful by the 1950s. When partition came in 1954 many Catholics chose to move south, partly because of their opposition to Communism and partly because the new leader of South Vietnam, President Ngo Dinh Diem, was a Catholic. Of the estimated 900,000 Vietnamese who left the North in 1954, it's said that around two-thirds were Catholic; many of these became refugees a second time in the 1970s.

Diem actively discriminated in favour of the Catholic community, which he viewed as a bulwark against Communism. As a result he alienated large sections of the population, most importantly Buddhists whose protests eventually contributed to his downfall. Meanwhile in North Vietnam the authorities trod fairly carefully with those Catholics who had chosen to stay, allowing them freedom to practise their religion, but the Church was severely restricted and there were some reports of persecution.

After reunification, churches were permitted to function but still came under strict **surveillance**, with all appointments controlled by the government, and members of the Church hierarchy frequently received heavy jail sentences for opposition to the regime. Since 1986 the party has been working to reduce the tension by re-opening seminaries, allowing the Church to resume religious educational work and releasing some clergy from prison. Catholics throughout Vietnam now regularly attend Mass, and, when the previous Cardinal of Hanoi died in 1990, thousands attended the funeral in the largest postwar demonstration of Catholic faith. Since the government still insists on vetting all appointments, it took more than seven years to find a new cardinal acceptable to both Vietnam and the Vatican. However, relations between the two continue to improve. All the bishoprics are now filled and there's even talk of re-establishing diplomatic relations in the not too distant future. A senior Vatican emissary visited Hanoi in 2005, though it will undoubtedly be several years before the much hoped-for papal visit occurs.

The situation is not quite so rosy as regards Vietnam's **Protestant** communities. While the government now officially recognizes the Southern Evangelical Church of Vietnam (SECV) and the smaller Evangelical Church of Vietnam (ECVN), based in the north, it remains deeply suspicious of another evangelical branch known as "Dega Protestantism" practised mainly by the ethnic minorities of the **central highlands**. It's not so much the belief system itself that the authorities are concerned about, but the movement's potential as a political force and, specifically, its alleged association with demands from certain minority groups for greater autonomy. There have been (sometimes violent) clashes between ethnic minorities in the central highlands and the authorities in recent years (see p.493). While the protests were generally sparked by disputes over land and continued poverty, some demonstrators also cited **religious persecution** amongst their grievances. As a result, the government imposed significant restrictions on all Protestant churches in the region. There are signs that the situation is easing, particularly as regards SECV-affiliated churches, though the government continues to keep a close eye on all Christian activity in the central highlands.

Cao Dai

Social upheaval coupled with an injection of Western thinking in the early twentieth century gave birth to Vietnam's two indigenous religious sects, **Cao Dai** and Hoa Hao. Of the two, Cao Dai claims more adherents, with an estimated following of around two million in south Vietnam, plus a few thousand among overseas Vietnamese in America, Canada and Britain. The sect's headquarters, the **Holy See**, resides in a flamboyant cathedral at Tay Ninh (see p.123), where they also maintain a school, agricultural co-operative and hospital. Vietnam's most northerly Cao Dai congregation worships in Hué.

The religion of Cao Dai (meaning "high place") was revealed by the "Supreme Being" to a middle-aged civil servant working in Phu Quoc, called **Ngo Van Chieu**, during several trances over a period of years from 1919 to 1925. What Chieu preached to his followers was essentially a distillation of Vietnam's religious heritage: elements of Confucian, Taoist and Buddhist thought, intermixed with ancestor worship, Christianity and Islam. According to Cao Dai beliefs, all religions are different manifestations of one **meta-religion**, Cao Dai; in the past, this took on whatever form most suited the prevailing human need, but during the twentieth century could finally be presented in its unity. Thus the **Supreme Being**, who revealed himself in 1925, has had two earlier manifestations, always in human guise: the first in the sixth century BC, appearing as various figures from Buddhism, Taoism and Christianity among many other saints and sages; the second as Sakyamuni, Confucius, Jesus Christ, Mohammed and Lao-tzu. In the third manifestation the Supreme Being has revealed himself through his divine light, symbolized as an all-seeing Eye on a sky-blue, star-spangled globe.

Cao Dai **doctrine** preaches respect for all its constituent religions and holds that individual desires should be subordinate to the common interest. Adherents seek to escape from the cycle of reincarnation by following the five prohibitions: no violence, theft or lying – nor indulgence in alcohol or sexual activity; priests are expected to be completely vegetarian though others need only eschew meat on certain days of the lunar month. The Cao Dai **hierarchy** is modelled on that of the Catholic Church, and divides into nine ranks, of which the pope is the highest. Officials are grouped into three branches, identifiable by the colour of their ceremonial robes: the Confucian branch dresses in red, Buddhist in saffron and Taoist in blue. Otherwise practitioners wear white as a symbol of purity, and because it contains every colour.

The **rituals** of Cao Dai are a complex mixture of Buddhist and Taoist rites, including meditation and seances. Prayers take place four times a day in the temples (6am, noon, 6pm and midnight) though ordinary members are only required to attend on four days per month and otherwise can pray at home. Note that shoes should always be removed when entering a Cao Dai temple or mansion. At the start of the thirty-minute-long ceremony, worshippers file into the temple in three columns, women on the left, men in the middle and on the right; they then kneel and bow three times – to the Supreme Being, to the earth and to mankind. Cao Dai's most important **ceremony**, a sort of feast day for the Supreme Being, takes place on the ninth day of the first lunar month; other special observances are the day of Taoism (fifteenth day of the second month), Buddha's birthday (fifteenth of the fourth lunar month), the day of Confucius (twenty-eighth of the eighth lunar month) and Christmas Day.

The religion of Cao Dai is further enlivened with a panoply of **saints**, encompassing the great and the good of many countries and cultures: Victor Hugo, Joan of Arc, William Shakespeare, Napoleon Bonaparte, Lenin, Winston Churchill, Louis Pasteur and Sun Yat Sen, alongside home-grown heroes such as Tran Hung Dao and Le Loi. These characters fulfil a variety of roles from prophet to bodhisattva and even spirit medium, through which followers communicate with the Supreme Being. Contact can occur by means of a ouija board, messages left in sealed envelopes or through human mediums – who enter a trance and write using a planchette (a pencil secured to a wooden board on castors, on which the medium rests his hand, sometimes known as a *corbeille à bec*). Apparently, adherents of Cao Dai once appointed an official to take down the further works of Victor Hugo by dictation from his spirit.

The ideology, which had widespread appeal, attracted **converts** in their hundreds of thousands in the Mekong Delta, but only gained official recognition from the French colonial authorities in 1926. Over the next decade the Holy See developed into a **semi-autonomous state** wielding considerable political power and backed by a paramilitary wing which mustered around fifty thousand men in the mid-1950s. Although originally nationalist, Cao Dai followers clashed with Communist troops in a local power struggle, and the sect ended up opposing both the North Vietnamese and President Diem's pro-Catholic regime. Diem moved quickly to dismantle the army when he came to power and exiled its leaders; then after 1975 the Communists purged the religious body, closing down Cao Dai temples and schools, and sending priests for re-education. However, Cao Dai survived as a religion and has gained some **new adherents** since 1990 when its temples and mansions, approximately four hundred in all, were allowed to re-open, albeit under strict control.

Hoa Hao

The second of Vietnam's local sects, **Hoa Hao**, meaning "peace and kindness", emerged in the late 1930s near Chau Doc in the Mekong Delta (see p.166). The movement was founded by a young mystic, **Huynh Phu So**, who disliked mechanical ritual and preached a very pure, simple form of Buddhism that required no clergy or other intermediaries, and could be practised at home by means of meditation, fasting and prayer. Gambling, alcohol and opium were prohibited, while filial piety was once more invoked to promote social order.

As a young man Huynh Phu So was cured of a mysterious illness by the monks of Tra Son Pagoda near his home town of Chau Doc. He continued to live at the pagoda, studying under the monk Xom, but returned to his home village after Xom died. During a storm in 1939, So entered a trance from which he emerged to develop his own Buddhist way. The sect quickly gained followers and, like Cao Dai, was soon caught up in **nationalist politics**. To the French, So was a mad but dangerous subversive; they committed him to a psychiatric hospital (where he promptly converted his doctor to Hoa Hao), and then placed him under house arrest. During World War II Hoa Hao followers were armed by the Japanese and later continued to fight against the French while also opposing the Communists. At the end of the war Hoa Hao members formed an anti-Marxist political party, prompting the Viet Minh to assassinate So in 1947.

However, the movement continued to grow, its **private army** equalling the Cao Dai's in size, until Diem came to power and effectively crushed the sect's political and military arm. The sect then splintered, with some members turning to the National Liberation Front, while most sided with the Americans. As a result, when the Communists took over in 1975 many Hoa Hao leaders were arrested and its priesthood was disbanded. Nevertheless some claim that there are now over 1.5 million Hoa Hao practising in the Mekong Delta. The government recognized the principal Hoa Hao sect in 1999, although its more radical offshoots, which are accused of anti-government activities, remain outlawed.

Vietnam's ethnic minorities

The population of Vietnam currently numbers some 86 million people, of whom around 85 percent are ethnic **Vietnamese** (known as Viet or Kinh), while approximately 800,000 are **Chinese** in origin (Hoa) – see box, p.502. The remaining eleven million people comprise 52 **ethnic minority** groups divided into dozens of subgroups, some with a mere hundred or so members, giving Vietnam the richest and most complex ethnic make-up in the whole of Southeast Asia. The vast majority of Vietnam's minorities live in the hilly regions of the **north** and **central highlands** – all areas that saw heavy fighting in recent wars – and several groups straddle today's international boundaries.

Little is known about the origins of many of these people, some of whom already inhabited the area before the ancestors of the **Viet** arrived from southern China around four to five thousand years ago. At some point the Viet emerged as a distinct group from among the various indigenous peoples living around the Red River Delta and then gradually absorbed smaller communities until they became the dominant culture. Other groups continued to interact with the Viet people, but either chose to maintain their independence in the highlands or were forced up into the hills, off the ever-more-crowded coastal plains.

Vietnamese legend accounts for this fundamental split between **lowlanders** and **highlanders** as follows: the Dragon King of the south married Au Co, a beautiful northern princess, and at first they lived in the mountains where she gave birth to a hundred strong, handsome boys. After a while, however, the Dragon King missed his watery, lowland home and decamped with half his sons, leaving fifty behind in the mountains – the ancestors of the ethnic minorities.

Vietnam's ethnic groups are normally differentiated according to three main **linguistic families** – Austronesian, Austro-Asian and Sino-Tibetan – which are further subdivided into smaller groups, such as the Viet–Muong and Tay–Thai language groups. Austronesians, related to Indonesians and Pacific Islanders, were probably the earliest inhabitants of the area but are now restricted to the central highlands. Peoples of the two other linguistic families originated in southern China and at different times migrated south-wards to settle throughout the Vietnamese uplands.

Despite their different origins, languages, dialects and hugely varied traditional dress, there are a number of similarities among the highland groups that distinguish them from Viet people. Most immediately obvious is the **stilthouse**, which protects against snakes, vermin and larger beasts as well as floods, while also providing safe stabling for domestic animals. The communal imbibing of **rice wine** is popular with most highland groups, as are certain **rituals** such as protecting a child from evil spirits by not naming it until after a certain age. Most highlanders traditionally practise **swidden farming**, clearing patches of forest land, farming the burnt-over fields for a few years and then leaving it fallow for a specified period while it recovers its fertility. Where the soils are particularly poor, a semi-nomadic lifestyle is adopted, shifting the village location at intervals as necessary.

Recent history

Traditionally, Viet kings demanded tribute from the often fiercely independent ethnic minorities but otherwise left them to govern their own affairs. This relationship changed with the arrival of Catholic missionaries, who won many converts to Christianity among the peoples of the central highlands – called **montagnards** by the French. Under colonial rule the minorities gained a certain degree of local autonomy in the late nineteenth century, but at the same time the French expropriated their land, exacted forced labour and imposed heavy taxes. As elsewhere in Vietnam, such behaviour sparked off rebellions, notably among the Hmong in the early twentieth century.

The northern mountains

The French were quick to capitalize on ancient antipathies between the highland and lowland peoples. In the northwest mountains, for example, they set up a semi-autonomous Thai federation, complete with armed militias and border guards. When war broke out in 1946, groups of Thai, Hmong and Muong in the northwest sided with the French and against the Vietnamese, even to the extent of providing battalions to fight alongside French troops. But the situation was not clear-cut: some Thai actively supported the Viet Minh, while Ho Chi Minh found a safe base for his guerrilla armies among the Tay and Nung people of the northeast. Recognizing the need to secure the minorities' allegiance, after North Vietnam won independence in 1954 Ho Chi Minh created two **autonomous regions**, allowing limited self-government within a "unified multi-national state".

The central highlands

The minorities of the **central highlands** had also been split between supporting the French and Viet Minh after 1946. In the interests of preserving their independence, the ethnic peoples were often simply anti-Vietnamese, of whatever political persuasion. After partition in 1954, anti-Vietnamese sentiment was exacerbated when President Diem started moving Viet settlers into the region, totally ignoring local land rights. Diem wanted to tie the minorities more closely into the South Vietnamese state; the immediate result, however, was that the Bahnar, Jarai and E De joined forces in an organized opposition movement and called a general strike in 1958.

Over the next few years this well-armed coalition developed into the United Front for the Liberation of Oppressed Races, popularly known by its French acronym, **FULRO**. They demanded greater autonomy for the minorities, including elected representation at the National Assembly, more local self-government, school instruction in their own language and access to higher education. While FULRO met with some initial success, the movement was weakened after a number split off to join the Viet Cong. An estimated ten thousand or more remained, fighting first of all against the South Vietnamese and the Americans, and then against the North Vietnamese Army until 1975. After this, FULRO rebels and other anti-Communist minority groups, mainly E De, operated out of bases in Cambodia. The few who survived Pol Pot's killing fields later fled to Thailand and were eventually resettled in America.

During the **American War**, those minorities living around the Seventeenth Parallel soon found themselves on the front line. The worst fighting occurred during the late 1960s and early 1970s, when North Vietnamese troops were based in these remote uplands and American forces sought to rout them. Massive bombing raids were augmented by the use of defoliants and herbicides which, as well as denuding protective forest cover, destroyed crops and animals; this chemical warfare also killed an unknown number of people and caused severe long-term illnesses. In addition, villages were often subject to night raids by Viet Cong and North Vietnamese soldiers keen to "encourage" local support and replenish their food supplies.

It's estimated that over two hundred thousand minority people in the central highlands, both civilian and military, were killed as a result of the American War, out of a population of around one million. By 1975, 85 percent of villages in the highlands had been either destroyed or abandoned, while nothing was left standing in the region closest to the Demilitarized Zone. At the end of the war thousands of minority people were living in temporary camps, along with Viet refugees, unable to practise their traditional way of life.

Post–reunification

After reunification things didn't really get much better. Promises of greater autonomy came to nothing; even the little self-government the minorities had been granted was removed. Those groups who had opposed the North Vietnamese were kept under close observation and their leaders sent for re-education. The new government pursued a policy of **forced assimilation** of the minorities into the Vietnamese culture and glossed over their previous anti-Viet activities: all education was conducted in the Vietnamese language, traditional customs were discouraged or outlawed, and minority people were moved from their dispersed villages into permanent settlements. At the same time the government created **New Economic Zones** in the central highlands and along the Chinese border, often commandeering the best land to resettle thousands of people from the overcrowded lowlands. According to official records, 250,000 settlers were moved into the New Economic Zones each year during the 1980s. The policy resulted in food shortages among minorities unable to support themselves on the marginal lands, and the widespread degradation of over-farmed upland soils.

Doi moi brought a shift in policy in the early 1990s, marked by the establishment of a central office responsible for the ethnic minorities. Minority languages are now officially recognized and can be taught in schools, scholarships enable minority people to attend institutes of higher education, television programmes are broadcast in a number of minority languages, and there is now greater representation of minorities at all levels of government – indeed, the current secretary general of the Communist Party, Nong Duc Manh, a member of the Tay ethnic group, is the first non-Viet to hold such an elevated position. Cash crops such as timber and fruit are being introduced as an alternative to illegal hunting, logging and opium cultivation. Other income-generating schemes are also being promoted and healthcare programmes upgraded.

All this has been accompanied by moves to preserve Vietnam's **cultural diversity**, driven in part by the realization that ethnic differences have greater appeal to tourists. However, in many areas the minorities' traditional lifestyles are fast being eroded and extreme **poverty** is widespread; while minorities constitute around fourteen percent of Vietnam's population, they account for one-third of those living under the poverty line. This, along with grievances over ancestral land rights and religious freedoms, was one of the issues that sparked widespread **demonstrations** by minority people in the central highlands in 2001 and 2004. While the prime minister ordered more favourable land distribution and promised greater socio-economic development for the region, human rights organizations have criticized the authorities for their harsh treatment of demonstrators, some of whom have received jail sentences of up to twelve years. There are also continued reports of persecution of minorities who belong to unauthorised Christian groups.

Minorities in the northern highlands

The mountains of northern Vietnam are home to a large number of ethnic groups, all of them originating from southern China. The dominant minorities are the Tay and Thai, both feudal societies who once held sway over their weaker neighbours. These powerful, well-established groups farm the fertile, valley-bottom land, while Hmong and Dao people, who only arrived in Vietnam at the end of the eighteenth century, occupy the least hospitable land at the highest altitudes. These isolated groups have been better able to lead an independent life and to preserve their traditional customs, though most exist at near-subsistence levels. Local **markets**, usually held at weekly intervals, fulfil an important role in social and economic life in the highlands; the best known are at Sa Pa and Bac Ha, though there are others throughout the area (see Chapter 8 for details). Most groups maintain a tradition of **call-and-response singing**, which is performed at ceremonies and festivals.

Tay

The **Tay** are Vietnam's largest minority group living in the highlands, with an estimated population of 1.5 million, concentrated in the northeast, from the Red River Valley east to the coastal plain, where they settled over 2000 years ago. Through centuries of close contact with lowlanders, Tay society has been strongly influenced by Viet culture, sharing many common rituals and Confucian practices.

Many Tay have now adopted Viet architecture and dress, but it's still possible to find villages of thatched stilthouses, characterized by a railed balcony around the building. Nowadays it's largely the women who still wear the Tay's traditional long, belted dress of indigo-dyed cloth, with a similarly plain, knotted headscarf peaked at the front and set off with lots of silver jewellery. Tay farmers are famous for their animal husbandry, and they also specialize in fish-farming and growing high-value crops, such as anise, tobacco, soya and cinnamon.

The Tay have developed advanced irrigation systems for wet-rice cultivation, including the huge waterwheels found beside rivers in the northeast. They have had a written language – based on Chinese ideograms – since the fifteenth century, fostering a strong literary tradition; call-and-response singing is also popular, as are theatrical performances, kite-flying and a whole variety of other games. Some Tay groups in the more remote regions occasionally erect a funeral house, decorated with fluttering slips of white paper, over a new grave.

Thai

The **Thai** minority numbers around 1.3 million, and is the dominant group in the northwest mountains from the Red River south to Nghe An, though most live in Lai Chau and Son La provinces. They are distantly related to the Thai of

Thailand and to groups in southern China, their ancestral homeland. However, Thai people have been living in Vietnam for at least 2000 years and show similarities with both Viet and Tay cultures. Traditional Thai society was strongly hierarchical, ruled over by feudal lords who controlled vast land-holdings worked by the villagers. Their written language, which is based on Sanskrit, has furnished a literary legacy dating back five centuries, including epic poems, histories and a wealth of folklore. The Thai are also famous for their unique dance repertoire and finely woven brocades decorated with flowers, birds and dragons, which are on sale in local markets. From their early teens women learn how to weave and embroider, eventually preparing a set of blankets for their dowry. Thai houses are often still constructed on stilts, with wood or bamboo frames, though the architecture varies between regions.

There are two main subgroups: **Black Thai** (around Dien Bien Phu, Tuan Giao and Son La) and **White Thai** (Mai Chau, Muang Lay), whose names are often attributed to the traditional colour of the women's shirts, though this is open to dispute. Both groups wear long, narrow skirts and fitted shirts, topped with an intricately embroidered headdress.

Muong

The lower hills from the Red River Valley south through Yen Bai and Son La down to Thanh Hoa are the domain of the **Muong** ethnic minority, with the majority now living in Hoa Binh Province. Muong people, totalling roughly one million, are believed to share common ancestors with the Viet. It's thought that the two groups split around 2000 years ago, after which the Muong developed relatively independently in the highlands. Society is traditionally dominated by aristocratic families, who distribute communal land to the villagers in return for labour and tax contributions; the symbols of their authority are drums and bronze gongs.

Muong stilthouses are similar to those built by the Thai, and the main staple is rice, though fishing, hunting and gathering are all still fairly important. Muong people have a varied cultural tradition, including call-and-response singing and epic tales, and they are famed for their embroidery, typically creating bold geometric designs in black and white. Older Muong women continue to wear the traditional long black skirt and close-fitting shirt; a broad, heavily embroidered belt is the main accessory, and many women also wear a simple white headscarf.

Nung

Nung people are closely related to the Tay, sharing the same language and often living in the same villages. Their population is estimated at 850,000, mostly in Cao Bang and Lang Son provinces, where they have a long tradition of cultivating wet rice using waterwheels for irrigation. Nung farmers terrace the lower slopes to provide extra land, and are noted for the wide variety of crops they grow, including maize, groundnuts and a whole host of vegetables. In fact, the Nung are reckoned to be the best horticulturalists in Vietnam, while their blacksmiths are almost as renowned. Unusually, the traditional Nung house has clay walls and a tiled roof, and is built either flat on the ground or with only one section raised on stilts.

Most Nung are Buddhist, worshipping Quan Am, though they also honour the spirits and their ancestors. They are particularly adept at call-and-response singing, relishing the improvised double entendre. Not surprisingly, Nung traditional dress is similar to that of the Tay, though hemmed with coloured bands. Women often sport a neck scarf with brightly coloured fringes and a shoulder bag embroidered with the sun, stars and flowers, or woven in black and white interspersed with delicately coloured threads.

Hmong

Since the end of the eighteenth century, groups of Miao people have been fleeing southern China, heading for Laos, Burma, Thailand and Vietnam. Miao meant "barbarian", whereas their adopted name, **Hmong**, means "free people". In Vietnam the Hmong population now stands at just under eight hundred thousand, living in the high areas of all the northern provinces down to Nghe An. Poor farming land, geographical isolation and their traditional seclusion from other people have left the Hmong one of the most impoverished groups in Vietnam; standards of health and education are low, while infant mortality is exceptionally high. Hmong farmers grow maize, rice and vegetables on burnt-over land, irrigated fields and terraced hillsides. Traditionally they also grow poppies, though this is now discouraged by the government. Hmong people raise cattle, buffaloes and horses, and have recently started growing fruit trees, such as peach, plum and apple. They are also skilled hunters and gather forest products, including honey, medicinal herbs, roots and bark, either for their own consumption or to trade at weekly markets. Hmong houses are built flat on the ground, rather than raised on stilts.

Until recently there was no written Hmong language, but a strong oral tradition of folk songs, riddles and proverbs. Perhaps the Hmong are best known, however, for their handicrafts, particularly weaving hemp and cotton cloth which is then coloured with indigo dyes. Many Hmong women, and some men, still wear traditional indigo apparel and chunky silver jewellery. The main subgroups are **White**, **Red**, **Green**, **Black** and **Flower Hmong**; though the origin of the names is unknown, there are marked differences in dialect and social customs as well as dress and hairstyle, especially among the women.

Dao

The **Dao** (pronounced "Zao") ethnic minority is incredibly diverse in all aspects of life: social and religious practices, architecture, agriculture and dress. For several centuries, small, localized groups have settled in the northern border region after crossing over from China. Dao people now number approximately six hundred thousand in Vietnam, with related groups in Laos, Thailand and China.

Long ago the Dao adopted the Chinese writing system and have a substantial literary tradition. One popular legend records the origin of the twelve Dao clans: Ban Ho, a powerful dog of five colours, killed an enemy general and was granted the hand of a princess in marriage, who gave birth to twelve children. Ban Ho is worshipped by the Dao and the five colours of Dao embroidery represent their ancestor. The Dao boast a particularly striking traditional dress, the most eye-catching element of which is a bulky red turban. Dao people live at all altitudes, their house style and agricultural techniques varying accordingly. While groups living at lower levels are relatively prosperous, growing rice and raising livestock, those in the high, rocky mountains live in considerable poverty.

Giay

The **Giay** (pronounced "Zay") are a relatively small minority group, with a population of around fifty thousand, living at high altitudes in Lao Cai, Lai Chau and Ha Giang provinces. Traditional Giay society is feudal, with a strict demarcation between the local aristocracy and the peasant classes. All villagers work the communal lands, living in closely knit villages of stilthouses. A few Giay women still wear the traditional style of dress, distinguished by the highly coloured, circular panel sewn around the collar and a shirt-fastening on the right shoulder; the shirt itself is often of bright green, pink or blue. On formal occasions, women may also wear a chequered turban.

Minorities in the central highlands

Nearly all minority groups living in the central highlands are indigenous peoples; most are matrilineal societies with a strong emphasis on community life and with some particularly complex burial rites. Catholic **missionaries** enjoyed considerable success in the central highlands, establishing a mission at Kon Tum in the mid-nineteenth century; then early in the twentieth century Protestantism was also introduced to the region. Most converts came from among the E De and Bahnar, though other groups have also incorporated Christian practices into their traditional belief systems and the number of converts has been increasing in recent years. Likewise, **Vietnamese influence** has been stronger here than in northern Vietnam, while the **American War** caused severe disruption. Nevertheless, their cultures have been sufficiently strong to resist complete assimilation. For how much longer is a matter of debate, as thousands of lowland Viets, plus significant numbers of northern minorities, are moving into the region, clearing huge swathes of land for coffee plantations on the back of a booming export market.

Jarai (Gia–rai)

The largest minority group in the central highlands is the **Jarai**, with a population of roughly three hundred thousand. It's thought that Jarai people left the coastal plains around 2000 years ago, settling on the fertile plateau around Plei Ku. Some ethnologists hold that Cham people are in fact a branch of the Jarai, and they certainly share common linguistic traits and a matrilineal social order. Young Jarai women initiate the marriage proposal and afterwards the couple live in the wife's family home, with children taking their mother's name. Houses are traditionally built on stilts, facing north. The focus of village life is the communal house, or *rong*, where the council of elders and their elected chief meet.

Animist beliefs are still strong, and the Jarai world is peopled with spirits, the most famous of which are the kings of Water, Fire and Wind, represented by shamans who are involved in rain-making ceremonies and other rituals. Funeral rites are particularly complex and expensive: each family maintains a funeral house which they ornament with evocative sculptures of people, birds and objects from everyday life. The Jarai also have an extensive musical repertoire, the principal instruments being gongs and the unique *k'long put*, made of bamboo tubes into which the players force air by clapping their hands. During the American War the majority of Jarai villagers moved out of their war-torn homeland, many being resettled in Plei Ku; only in recent years are some slowly returning.

E De (Rhadé)

Further south, towards Buon Ma Thuot, around 270,000 people of the **E De** minority live in stilthouses grouped together in a village, or *buon*. These longhouses, which can be up to 100m in length, are boat-shaped with hardwood frames, bamboo floors and walls, and topped with a high thatched roof. As many as a hundred family members may live in a single house, under the authority of the oldest or most respected woman, who owns all family property, including the house and domestic animals; wealth is indicated by the number of ceremonial gongs. Other much prized heirlooms are the large earthenware jars used for making the rice wine drunk at festivals. Like the Jarai, E De people worship the kings of Fire and Water among a whole host of animist spirits, and also erect a funeral house on their graves. Both the original longhouse and its grave-site replica are often decorated with fine carvings.

The E De homeland lies in a region of red soils on the rolling western plateaux. In the nineteenth and twentieth centuries French settlers introduced coffee and rubber estates to the area, often seizing land from the local people they called Rhadé. Traditional swidden farming has gradually been disappearing, a process accelerated by the American War and the forced relocation of E De into permanent settlements.

Bahnar (Ba–na)

Bahnar people trace their ancestry back many centuries to communities co-existing on the coastal plains with the Cham and Jarai. Now the Bahnar minority, numbering some 170,000, mostly live in the highlands east of Plei Ku and Kon Tum. The most distinctive aspect of a Bahnar village is its *rong*, or communal house, the roof of which may be up to 20m high. This is the centre of village cultural and ceremonial life, and also the home of adolescent boys, who are taught Bahnar history, the skills of hunting and other manly matters. Village houses grouped around the *rong* are typically stilthouses with a thatched or tiled roof, and are often decorated with geometric motifs.

The Bahnar people are skilled horticulturalists, growing maize, sweet potato or millet, together with indigo, hemp or tobacco as cash crops. Bahnar groups also erect funeral houses decorated with elaborate carvings, although they are less imposing than those of the Jarai. Sometime after the burial, wooden statues, gongs, wine jars and other items of family property are placed in the funeral house.

Sedang (Xo–dang)

According to their oral histories, **Sedang** people once lived further north but are now concentrated in the area between Kon Tum and Quang Ngai and comprise a community of nearly 130,000. The Sedang were traditionally a warlike people whose villages were surrounded with defensive hedges, barbed with spears and stakes, and with only one entrance. Inter-village wars were frequent, and the Sedang also carried out raids on the peaceable Bahnar, mainly to seize prisoners rather than territory. In the past, Sedang religious ritual involved human sacrifices to propitiate the spirits – a practice that was later modified into a profitable business, selling slaves to traders from Laos and Thailand.

In the 1880s, an eccentric French military adventurer called Marie-David de Mayréna, established a kingdom in Sedang territory by making treaties with the

The Sedang played their part in one of colonial Vietnam's oddest interludes and one which finds echoes in Joseph Conrad's novella, *Heart of Darkness*, in which a mysterious voyager named Kurtz proclaims himself king, deep in the Belgian Congo – a story later borrowed by Francis Ford Coppola for his film *Apocalypse Now* (see p.533).

The career of French rogue **Marie-David de Mayréna** was a chequered one to say the least. After a stint with the French army in Cochinchina in the mid-1860s, he made his way back to Paris, only to return to the East after having failed as a banker. Back in Vietnam by the 1880s, he established himself as a planter around Ba Ria, until 1888 when the governor sent him to explore the highlands. Of the hundred or so porters and soldiers who accompanied him, only one, a Frenchman named Alphonse Mercurol, remained by the time he reached Kon Tum. Through the contacts of the French missionaries based there, Mayréna was able to arrange meetings with local tribal chiefs; soon the leaders fell under the spell of his "blue eyes" and "bold, confident stare", and he conspired to proclaim himself **King Marie I of Sedang**, while Mercurol adopted the title "Marquis of Hanoi". For three months, Mayréna ruled from a straw hut flying the national flag (a white cross on a blue background, with a red star in the centre), legislating, creating an army and even declaring war on the neighbouring Jarai people.

But Mayréna was more interested in money than sovereignty, and within months he had decamped, setting off in the hope of getting some mileage from his "title". In his book, *Dragon Ascending*, Henry Kamm quotes an erstwhile manager of Saigon's *Continental*, where Mayréna boarded on credit with assorted courtiers: "Alas, when, several days later, Mayréna moved out of the hotel, nothing was left to Laval [the then hotel manager] as payment for his services, except for a decoration, that of the National Order of the Kingdom of the Sedangs, which the king gave him before departure." Returning to Europe, Mayréna took to selling fictitious titles and mining concessions to raise cash but, inevitably, cracks began to appear in his story, and he fled back to Southeast Asia in 1890 where he died in penury on Malaya's Tioman Island, supposedly of a snake bite.

local chiefs (see box above). A few decades later, the French authorities conscripted Sedang labour to build Highway 14 from Kon Tum to Da Nang; conditions were so harsh that many died, provoking a rebellion in the 1930s. Soon after, the Viet Minh won many recruits among the Sedang in their war against the French. In the American War some Sedang groups fought for the Viet Cong while others were formed into militia units by the American Special Services. But when fighting intensified after 1965, Sedang villagers were forced to flee, and many now live in almost destitute conditions, having lost their ancestral lands.

Each Sedang extended family occupies a longhouse, built on stilts and usually facing east; central to village life is the communal house where young men and boys sleep, and where all the major ceremonies take place. Because villages historically had relatively little contact with each other, there are marked variations between the social customs of the subgroups, and so far seventeen Sedang dialects have been identified. Agricultural techniques are more consistent, mainly swidden farming supplemented by horticulture and hunting. Some Sedang farmers employ a "water harp", a combined bird-scarer, musical instrument and appeaser of the spirits. The harp consists of bamboo tubes linked together and placed in a flowing stream to produce an irregular, haunting sound.

Koho (Co–ho) and Lat

The Di Linh plateau at the very southern end of the central highlands is the home of the **Koho** minority. The community of some 130,000 is subdivided into six highly varied subgroups, including the **Lat** people of Da Lat.

The typical Koho house is built on stilts with a thatched roof and bamboo walls and flooring. Despite the fact that many Koho were converted to Christianity in the early twentieth century, spirit worship is widely practised and each family adopts a guardian spirit from the natural world. Catholic missionaries developed a phonetic script for the Koho language but the oral tradition remains strong. Unlike many minorities in this region, the Koho incorporate dance into their religious rites, and it is an important element of them; a variety of musical instruments, such as gongs, bamboo flutes and buffalo horns, are also involved. Subgroups of the Koho minority are famed for their pottery and ironwork, whereas Lat farmers have a reputation for constructing sophisticated irrigation systems.

Mnong

The **Mnong** ethnic minority is probably best known for its skill in hunting elephants and domesticating them for use in war, for transport and for their ivory. Mnong people are also the creators of the lithophone, a kind of stone xylophone thought to be among the world's most ancient musical instruments; an example is on show at the Ethnographic Museum in Buon Ma Thuot (see p.206). The Mnong have lived in the southern central highlands for centuries, and now around ninety thousand people are concentrated in the region between Buon Ma Thuot and Da Lat. Mnong houses are usually built flat on the ground and, though the society is generally matrilineal, village affairs are organized by a male chief. Mnong craftsmen are skilled at basketry and printing textiles, while they also make the copper, tin and silver jewellery worn by both sexes. In traditional burial rituals a buffalo-shaped coffin is placed under a funeral house which is peopled with wooden statues and painted with black, red or white designs.

Bru and Ta–oi

Two related minority groups had the extreme misfortune to live on the Seventeenth Parallel, near the border with Laos: the **Bru** (or Bru Van-Kieu), these days numbering around 56,000, and the **Ta-oi**, with a population of only 35,000. Bru people were caught up in the battle of Khe Sanh (see p.324) – both as refugees and as part of an American militia force – while the Ta-oi, among others, helped keep open the Ho Chi Minh Trail for the North Vietnamese Army. During the worst years of fighting, refugees fled south to E De country or crossed over into Laos, and many never returned. Those who did move back found Viet people settled on their best land – the Khe Sanh plateau was declared a New Economic Zone – and were forced into marginal areas.

Of the two groups, Bru people have always had greater contact with the outside world since the ancient Lao Bao trade route passes through their territory to Laos. Bru houses can usually be distinguished by their rounded shape, likened to a tortoise shell, and are occasionally decorated with carved birds or buffalo horns at each end. Both groups are patrilineal, practise swidden farming and worship a huge range of spirits, though ancestor worship is also central to their belief systems.

Minorities in the southern lowlands

As the Viet people pushed down the coastal plain and into the Mekong Delta they displaced two main ethnic groups, the Cham and Khmer. Up until the tenth century powerful **Cham** kings had ruled over most of southern Vietnam (see p.238); nowadays, there are approximately 130,000 Cham people, mostly living on the coast between Phan Rang and Phan Thiet, or on the Cambodian border around Chau Doc, with a small number in Ho Chi Minh City. The coastal communities are still largely Hindu worshippers of Shiva and follow the matrilineal practices of their Cham ancestors; they earn a living from farming, silk-weaving and crafting jewellery of gold or silver. Groups along the Cambodian border are Islamic and, in general, patrilineal. They engage in river-fishing, weaving and cross-border trade, with little agricultural activity. On the

Hoa and Viet Kieu

Ethnic Chinese people, known in Vietnamese as **Hoa**, form one of Vietnam's largest minority groups, estimated at around eight hundred thousand. Throughout the country's history, Chinese people, mostly from China's southern provinces, have been emigrating to Vietnam, as administrators and merchants or as refugees from persecution. In the mid-seventeenth century the collapse of the Ming Dynasty sent a human deluge southwards, and there were other large-scale migrations in the nineteenth century and then the 1940s. Until the early nineteenth century all Hoa, even those of mixed blood, were considered by the Viets to be Chinese. After that date, however, they were admitted to public office and gradually became integrated into Vietnamese society, so that now most have Vietnamese nationality. Neverthe-less, the Hoa remain slightly apart, living in close communities according to their ancestral province in China and preserving elements of their own culture, notably their language and traditional lion dances. The Hoa have tended to settle in urban areas, typically becoming successful merchants, artisans and business people, and playing an important role in the economy. Ninety percent of Hoa now live in southern Vietnam, predominantly in Cho Lon, with small groups scattered through the Mekong Delta and the central highlands.

Viet people have tended to distrust the Hoa, mainly because of their dominant commercial position and their close links with China. After 1975 the Hoa were badly hit when socialist policies were enforced, in what amounted to an anti-Chinese persecution. Tensions rose even further when China invaded Vietnam in 1979 and thousands of Hoa left the country to escape reprisals, forming a large majority of the "boat people" (see box, p.477). It's estimated that up to one third of the Hoa popula-tion eventually left Vietnam. Many settled in America, Australia and France, where they joined earlier refugees to become what the Vietnamese call **Viet Kieu**, or overseas Vietnamese, of whom there are perhaps as many as two million worldwide. In recent years the government has gradually made it easier for Viet Kieu not only to return to Vietnam but also to send money back to family members, providing an important source of extra income for individuals and becoming increasingly valuable in the wider economy, especially in the south. Not surprisingly, however, the attitudes of those who stuck it out in Vietnam towards Viet Kieu are ambivalent, and the government itself is unsure about how to handle relations with the Viet Kieu; in general their money and expertise are welcomed but not necessarily their politics, nor their Western ways.

▲ The Khmer people are indigenous to the Mekong Delta

whole, Cham people have adopted the Vietnamese way of life and dress, though their traditional arts, principally dance and music, have experienced a revival in recent years.

Ethnic **Khmer** are the indigenous people of the Mekong Delta, including Cambodia. Nowadays only about one million remain in the eastern delta under Vietnamese rule, and some of these only arrived in the late 1970s as refugees from Pol Pot's brutal regime in Cambodia. Khmer farmers are noted for their skill at irrigation and wet-rice cultivation; it's said that they farm nearly 150 varieties of rice, each suited to specific local conditions. Traditionally, the Khmer live in villages of stilthouses erected on raised mounds above the flood waters, but these days are more likely to build flat on the earth, along canals and roadways. The pagoda, however, is still a distinctive feature of Khmer villages, its brightly patterned roofs decorated with images of the sacred ancestral dragon, the *neak*. Although ancient beliefs persist, since the late thirteenth century the Khmer have been devout followers of Theravada Buddhism, as practised in Cambodia, Laos and Thailand. They produce fine silk and basketry and wear distinctive red-and-white scarves.

Environmental issues

Vietnam is endowed with a wide variety of fauna and flora, including an unusually high number of bird species and a rich diversity of primates. Current estimates suggest 16,000 plant species and 21,000 animals, including some 850 birds, though remote areas are still being explored. Over recent years, particularly in the forest reserves bordering Laos, the identification of several species of plants, butterflies, snakes, birds and even mammals that were previously unknown to scientists has caused a sensation in the scientific community.

Such diversity is largely attributable to Vietnam's range of habitats, from the subalpine mountains of the north to the Mekong Delta's mangrove swamps, in a country that is 75 percent mountainous, has over 3400km of coastline and extends over sixteen degrees of latitude. However, the list of endangered and critically endangered species is also long – over 120 types of animals and plants – as their domains are threatened by population pressure, widespread logging and pollution, particularly of the coastal zone. One of the biggest environmental challenges facing Vietnam is to preserve its rapidly diminishing forest areas by establishing methods of sustainable use.

Happily, the government does at least seem to recognize the value of Vietnam's biodiversity and the need to act quickly. It has now put in place a number of **laws** dealing with environmental issues, the most important being the Environmental Protection Law, revised in 2005, which sets out national policy covering the prevention and control of pollution, the protection, conservation and sustainable use of natural resources, and improving environmental quality. 2005 also saw the promulgation of a new Law on Tourism, which for the first time contains provisions on sustainable tourism from an environmental and social perspective, aiming to encourage greater community participation and spreading the benefits more widely. The law also includes tougher regulations on tourism-related pollution, though ensuring these laws are effectively implemented is a more thorny problem.

Ecological warfare

The word "**ecocide**" was coined during the American War, in reference to the quantity of herbicides dropped from the air to deprive the Viet Cong of their safe areas, deep under the triple-canopy forest, and their food crops. The most notorious defoliant used was **Agent Orange**, along with agents Blue and White, all named after the colour of the respective storage containers. Their active ingredient was **dioxin**, a slowly dissolving poison that has a half-life of eight to ten years in the environment – but remains much longer in human tissue. It's estimated that over eighty million litres of chemical defoliants were sprayed from American planes criss-crossing the forests and mangrove swamps of South Vietnam and the Demilitarized Zone between 1961 and 1971. Figures vary, but somewhere between twenty and forty percent of the South's land area was sprayed at least once and in some cases more frequently, destroying up to a quarter of the forest cover.

The environmental impact was perhaps greatest on the **mangrove forests**, which are particularly susceptible to defoliants. Spraying destroyed about a half of all Vietnam's mangrove swamps and forests, and since they don't regenerate naturally, they have to be replanted by hand, a slow operation with a low success rate. The herbicides also had a severe impact on **soldiers**, both Vietnamese and American, and **villagers** who were caught in the spraying or absorbed dioxins from the food chain and from drinking water. Children and the elderly were the worst affected: some died immediately from the poisons, while others suffered respiratory diseases, skin rashes and other ailments. Soon it became apparent that the dioxins were also causing abnormally high levels of miscarriage, birth defects, neurological disease and cancers. Surveys suggest that over three million Vietnamese may be affected, many of whom now receive a tiny monthly allowance from the government.

For years, doctors in Ho Chi Minh City's Tu Do Hospital, supported by international experts, have been trying to convince the American government of the link between the use of defoliants and these medical conditions, in the hope of claiming **compensation** for the victims. In 2004, a group of Vietnamese took their case to a New York court, claiming compensation from 37 American chemical companies on behalf of all victims. The case was dismissed in March 2005 on the grounds that the use of defoliants was not prohibited under international law at the time.

For their part, American war veterans who were exposed to dioxins, many of whom have children with serious birth defects, have also been seeking reparations. In 1984, a group of ex-servicemen won a landmark out-of-court settlement from the manufacturers; though the government refused to accept culpability, they were later forced to reimburse the chemical company following legal proceedings.

Apart from using herbicides, American and South Vietnamese troops cut down swathes of forest land with specially adapted bulldozers, called **Rome Ploughs**. These vehicles were capable of slicing through a three-metre-thick tree trunk, and were used to clear roadsides and riverbanks against ambushes, or to remove vestiges of undergrowth and trees left after the spraying. Finally, there were the **bombs** themselves: an estimated thirteen million tonnes of explosives were dropped during the course of the war, leaving a staggering 25 million bomb craters, the vast majority in the South. In addition to their general destructive power, explosions compact the soil to the point where nothing will grow, and napalm bombs sparked off forest fires. The worst single incident occurred in 1968 when U Minh forest, at the southern tip of Vietnam, burned for seven weeks; 85 percent of its trees were destroyed.

Since the war, Vietnamese environmentalists led by Professor Vo Quy, founder of the Center for Natural Resources and Environmental Studies at Hanoi University, have instigated **reforestation programmes**, slowly coaxing life back into even the worst-affected regions. This has involved pioneering work in regenerating tropical forest, planting native species under a protective umbrella of acacia and eucalyptus.

A symbolically significant success of local environmentalists has been the **return of the Sarus crane** to the Mekong Delta (see p.141), near the Cambodian border. The crane, a stately bird with an elaborate courtship dance, abandoned its nesting grounds when the Americans drained the wetlands and dropped herbicides and then napalm in their attempts to rout Viet Cong soldiers from the marshes. After the war thousands of landless farmers were settled in the area, but the acid soils proved difficult to farm so the provincial governor re-established a portion of the wetlands, thus restoring the cranes' natural habitat. The first Sarus cranes reappeared in 1986, after which Tam Nong Bird Sanctuary, now the Tram Chim National Park (see p.141), was set up to protect the crane and other returning species. Though the population remains highly vulnerable, as many as four hundred Sarus cranes now spend the dry season in the delta's wetlands.

Postwar deforestation

It's estimated that more than two million hectares of Vietnam's forest reserves were destroyed during the American War as a result of defoliation, napalm fires and bombing. Since 1975, however, at least three million hectares has been lost to commercial **logging**, agricultural **clearance**, forest **fires**, firewood collection – and **population pressure**. Originally, perhaps 75 percent of Vietnam's land area would have been covered by forest. By 1945 it had dwindled to 43 percent and was down to just 24 percent (roughly eight million hectares) in 1980. It's now edging back up to 36 percent, thanks to one of the world's most ambitious reforestation programmes, launched in 1998, to replant five million

Conservation and the national parks

Vietnam recognized the need for conservation relatively early, establishing its first national park (Cuc Phuong) in 1962 and adopting a **National Conservation Strategy** in 1985. The more accessible or interesting of Vietnam's 28 **national parks** are listed below, but unless you're prepared to spend a lot of time there, it's unlikely that you'll see many animals. Birds, insects and butterflies, however, are more readily visible and often the dense tropical vegetation or mountain scenery are in themselves worth the journey. To learn more about Vietnam's protected areas, and how to access them, get hold of Fauna and Flora International's excellent *Ecotourism Map of Vietnam*, available in local bookshops and through select tour operators; all proceeds go to support Vietnamese primate conservation. For further information about biodiversity in Vietnam, search the World Conservation Monitoring Centre's comprehensive website, ⓦ www.unep-wcmc.org.

Ba Be (see p.452). A park of 8000 hectares, containing Vietnam's largest natural lake, over 350 butterfly species and a few extremely rare Tonkin snub-nosed langur. The park has limited tourist facilities, but boat trips, jungle walks and overnight stays in a minority village are possible.

Bach Ma (see p.294). This park of 22,000 hectares sits on the climatological divide between the tropical forests of the south and the northern subtropical zone, and contains Vietnam's lushest tropical rainforests. It is also home to a wide variety of bird species, including several rare pheasants, and over 1400 recorded flora species. Bach Ma is well set up for tourism, with a network of marked trails, campsites and guesthouses.

Cat Ba (see p.411). The park covers only 15,200 hectares, but 5400 of these are important marine reserves, including areas of coral reef. The limestone island supports a broad range of habitats, a wealth of medicinal plants, and a critically endangered population of Golden-headed langurs. The park is accessible to tourists either on foot or by boat from Cat Ba Town.

Cat Tien (see p.190). This 74,000-hectare park is most famous for its tiny population of Java rhino, the only ones known in mainland Asia. Otherwise the park's wetlands are a haven for water birds, including the critically endangered White-winged duck and White-shouldered ibis, as well as the equally rare Siamese crocodile. Although it's relatively close to Ho Chi Minh City, Cat Tien is not easy to reach by public transport and tourist facilities are fairly limited.

hectares. Although an impressive 130,000 hectares are planted each year, this only just exceeds the area being lost to clearance, and the new growth is largely acacia and eucalyptus rather than native species. The area under "high-quality" native forest continues to shrink.

The **worst-affected areas** are Vietnam's northern mountains, the central province of Nghe An and around Plei Ku in the central highlands. In these areas soil erosion is a major problem, and countrywide floods are getting worse as a result of deforestation along the watersheds. Many rare hardwoods are fast disappearing and the fragile ecosystems are no longer able to support a wildlife population forced into ever-smaller pockets of undisturbed jungle. Much of the blame for this rapid reduction in the forest cover is often laid on the **ethnic minorities** who traditionally clear land for farming and rely on the forests for building timber and firewood. However, lowland Vietnamese settling in the mountains have also put pressure on scant resources.

Both lowland Vietnamese and minority people have cleared huge swathes of the central highlands for **coffee plantations**, while the carefully replanted coastal mangrove forest is threatened by uncontrolled development of intensive

Cuc Phuong (see p.339). Vietnam's first national park, Cuc Phuong was established in 1962 in an area of limestone hills relatively close to Hanoi. The park covers 22,000 hectares and contains a number of unique, ancient trees and provides excellent birdwatching, as well as an opportunity to see some of the world's rarest monkeys in its Endangered Primate Rescue Center. Cuc Phuong is one of the most accessible parks, where it's possible to hike and stay overnight.

Phong Nha-Ke Bang (see p.330). Established in 2002, this 86,000-hectare park along the mountain chain bordering Laos is best known for its extensive underground river system. The park itself is home to more than sixty endangered animal species, including several types of langur. At present access is limited to visiting Phong Nha Cave.

Tram Chim (see p.141). One of Vietnam's most important wetlands ecosystems, comprising 7500 hectares in the Mekong Delta and providing haven to thousands of overwintering water birds. Its most famous visitors are the critically endangered Sarus crane.

Yok Don (see p.208). Lying on the border with Cambodia, Yok Don constitutes 115,000 hectares carved out of Vietnam's most extensive forests. The area is also one of the most biologically diverse in the whole of Indochina, supporting rare Indochinese tigers and Asian elephants. Visitors can overnight in minority villages and camp; elephant-back rides are also on offer.

To support **environmental programmes** already taking place in Vietnam, contact the following organizations.

BirdLife International Wellbrook Court, Girton Rd, Cambridge CB3 0NA, UK (℡01223/277318, Ⓦwww.birdlife.org); trip reports are welcomed by their Hanoi office (Ⓦwww.birdlifeindochina.org) via email (Ⓔbirdlife@birdlife.netnam.vn).

Fauna and Flora International 4th Floor, Jupiter House, Station Rd., Cambridge CB1 2JD, UK (℡01223/571000, Ⓦwww.fauna-flora.org).

International Crane Foundation E-11376 Shady Lane Rd, PO Box 447, Baraboo, Wisconsin, 53913-0447 US (℡608/356-9462, Ⓦwww.savingcranes.org).

WWF International Ave du Mont-Blanc 27, 1196 Gland, Switzerland (℡22/364 9111, Ⓦwww.panda.org).

prawn farming. Another significant threat to the forests is the highly lucrative **timber trade**, both legal and illegal. By **replanting**, it's hoped to create sustainable forests for commercial logging and to protect the remaining areas of primary forests, but **enforcement** is hampered by lack of resources. The authorities have devolved the management and protection of the forest reserves to local communities, with some success. Meanwhile, the government is gradually establishing more protection areas, also providing for productive forest, and aims to restore forest reserves over 44 percent of Vietnam's land area by the year 2010.

Wildlife

Forest clearance, warfare, pollution and economic necessity have all contributed to the loss of natural habitat and reduced Vietnam's broad species base. In 1994, when Vietnam signed the **Convention on International Trade in Endangered Species** (CITES), which bans the traffic in animals or plants facing extinction, the species list identified 365 animal species in need of urgent protection. Among these, the Java rhino, the world's rarest large mammal, is reduced to a mere five to eight animals, while no fewer than five of the world's most endangered primate species, including the golden-headed (or Cat Ba) langur and the Tonkin snub-nosed langur, survive in small isolated communities in the northern forests. Other severely endangered species include the Indochina tiger and Asian elephant. Vietnam is also home to around 850 species of **birds**, with the highest number of endemic species in mainland Southeast Asia. Again, many of these are under threat of extinction, including the Vietnamese pheasant, small numbers of which were recently recorded in Ha Tinh and Quang Binh provinces.

Hunting continues to be a vital source of local income, as a walk round Vietnamese markets soon reveals. Wild animals and birds are sought after for their meat or to satisfy the demand for **medicinal products** and live specimens, an often illegal (but extremely lucrative) business. Since the border with China was re-opened in the early 1990s, smuggling of rare species has increased, among them the Asiatic black bear, whose gall bladder is prized as a cure for fevers and liver problems; relentless hunting has decimated the population to small numbers in the north. Similarly, Vietnam's population of wild Asian elephants is now reduced to fewer than one hundred individuals, down from two thousand in the 1970s. Not only has their habitat along the Cambodian border declined, but after 1975 poachers began hunting elephants for their tusks. Conservationists hope to maintain two or three viable populations in Dak Lak Province, where domesticated elephants are still used for transport and forestry work.

Nevertheless, quite large areas of the Vietnamese interior remain amazingly untouched, especially the Truong Son Mountains north of the Hai Van Pass, the southern central highlands and lowland forests of the Mekong Delta. These isolated areas are rich in **biodiversity** and have yielded spectacular discoveries in recent years, with much still to be explored. In 1992, Dr John MacKinnon and a team of Vietnamese biologists working in the Vu Quang Nature Reserve, an area of steamy, impenetrable jungle on the Lao border, identified a species of ox new to science, now known as the saola. Two years later the giant muntjac, a previously unknown species of deer, and a new carp were found in the same region, followed in 1997 by a smaller type of muntjac deer and the grey-shanked douc langur, and in 1999 by a striped rabbit thought to be related to the now extinct Sumatran striped rabbit. Three new bird species were also discovered in the late 1990s in the mountains of Kon Tum province: two types of laughing thrush and the black-crowned barwing.

An all-out effort is being made to protect this "biological gold mine" and other similar areas both within Vietnam and over the border in Laos. After the saola was discovered, the reserve was put strictly off limits and the total **protected area** enlarged to almost 160,000 hectares, with buffer zones and corridors linking the reserve to conservation areas in Laos. The task is fraught with difficulties, such as achieving cross-border co-operation and establishing effective policing of the reserve – especially against poaching and illegal logging – with inadequate personnel and financial resources. At the same time, the authorities have been working to find alternative sources of income and food for people living in or near the reserve, and carrying out educational work on the importance of conservation and its relevance to their daily lives.

In a related scheme, special protection areas have also been established around Yok Don and Ba Be national parks as part of a project to establish models of stable biodiversity conservation. The government has also been adding to the number of national parks and nature reserves over recent years. Among the more recent are Bai Tu Long National Park (see p.416), to the east of Ha Long Bay, and Pu Luong Nature Reserve, to the southwest of Hanoi. As a further boost to conservation efforts, in 2000 UNESCO recognized an area of mangrove forest at Can Gio in the Mekong Delta and Cat Tien National Park as Vietnam's first "Man and Biosphere" reserves.

Sustainable tourism

There's a growing awareness among tourists and travel companies of the negative impact tourism can have on the environment and local culture – the very things most people come to see. All too often the terms **eco-tourism** and **sustainable tourism** are reduced to mere marketing gimmicks, but behind them lies a serious desire, albeit ambitious, to find a new model of small-scale tourism that contributes to the long-term development of the local community without destroying its traditional social and economic structures or the often fragile environment.

Mass tourism didn't really get going in Vietnam until the mid-1990s. From just ten thousand in 1993, the number of foreign visitors (including business trips) topped four million in 2008, while the number of domestic holiday-makers currently stands at around fifteen million, and is growing even faster. Not surprisingly, the Vietnamese government is eager to promote tourism as a **key revenue-earner** and is gradually easing visa regulations, among other things, in the hope of attracting more foreign visitors. This sudden influx of sightseers, coupled with a lack of effective planning or control, is putting pressure on some of the country's most famous beauty spots.

In response, the government has gradually introduced a number of laws and initiatives placing greater emphasis on the conservation of the nation's natural – and cultural – heritage. Local authorities in **Hoi An** have banned cars from the centre and put a block on further hotel construction in addition to introducing restrictive pricing to control the flow of tourists. Some of this revenue is being ploughed back into improving the townscape – for example, renovating the old houses, hiding television aerials and burying cables. In **Ha Long Bay**, the problems of notoriously haphazard hotel development are exacerbated by **pollution** from tourist boats, fish farms and nearby coalfields, and by the presence of a major port. Concern over the future of this World Heritage Site, however, means that the issues are at least being discussed, and various measures, such as more effective management of the caves, have been put in place. One or two more remote islands are also being developed as eco-tourism destinations.

Perhaps the key areas, however, are the **uplands** of north and central Vietnam. These are increasingly popular destinations, both for their outstanding natural beauty and their communities of **ethnic minority people**. In the honey-pot market town of **Sa Pa**, for example, the number of hotels and guesthouses has mushroomed over the last decade – from none before 1991 to 150 in 2009 – and the famous weekend market attracts more tourists than minority people. Some of these people, disturbed by the unwanted attention and intrusive cameras, now shy away from Sa Pa completely, in favour of more inaccessible markets. Naturally, the tourists have also started to look elsewhere, seeking out ever more remote villages. Most of the "minority crafts" on sale are actually shipped up from Hanoi and, though they are the major attraction, the minority people themselves receive very little economic benefit from tourism; most goes to Kinh Vietnamese or foreign travel companies. There are even signs of an emerging sex industry in Sa Pa and the beginnings of both child prostitution and drug-related crime.

Sa Pa's superb setting and trekking opportunities will continue to make it a popular destination, and it's likely that the surrounding area will be developed further. The challenge is how to achieve this in a way that contributes to the **long-term development** of the local community while also preserving cultural and biological diversity. Among other initiatives, the Netherlands Development Organization (SNV; Ⓦwww.snv.org.vn), an NGO active in developing **community-based tourism** in Vietnam, is working with local authorities to draw up tourism development plans and to raise awareness of sustainable development issues. It recently established a tourism information centre in Sa Pa and is involved in providing training for local guides and hotel and restaurant owners. In Sa Pa and Son La, SNV has also helped devise trekking routes and supported local communities in managing visitor numbers, ensuring revenue is equitably distributed and establishing a code of conduct expected of tourists and tour agents. Near Hué, SNV is working with minority people to develop music and dance performances and to build a community guesthouse to attract tourists to the village.

The international conservation body Flora and Fauna International (FFI; Ⓦwww.fauna-flora.org) is also active in Vietnam, helping develop **community-based eco-tourism**. In Pu Luong Nature Reserve, for example, FFI helped install toilets and washing facilities and supplied bedding and mosquito nets in minority villages wishing to set up home-stays. At the same time, it also provided training in home-stay management and service provision and helped promote the reserve as an eco-tourism destination.

On a **personal level**, individual action is equally important. Though domestic tourism has the greatest impact through sheer weight of numbers, international travellers can play a positive role by setting examples of **responsible behaviour**. Various NGOs and groups involved in the travel industry (see p.507) have developed **guidelines** for tourists and travel companies. Some of the most important points are: to avoid buying souvenirs made from endangered species or which damage the environment – notably tortoiseshell, ivory and coral in Vietnam; as far as possible, to eat in local restaurants, buy local produce, employ local guides and stay in home-stays or locally owned hotels – not only is it usually a lot more fun, but also your money is more likely to benefit smaller communities; to be sensitive to the local culture, including appropriate standards of dress, as well as adopting a responsible attitude towards drugs, alcohol and prostitution. Finally, when booking tours, ask how much – if anything – the tour company contributes to conservation and community development at its chosen destinations. Tour agents in Vietnam with a reputation for their conscientious approach include Handspan, Exotissimo, Buffalo Tours, Footprint and Haivenu (see Basics p.33). Intrepid (see Basics, p.31) also has a long track-record of engaging in sustainable tourism.

Music and theatre

T he binding element in all Vietnam's traditional performing arts is **music**, and particularly singing (*hat*), which is a natural extension to an already musical language. The origins of Vietnamese music can be traced back as far as the bronze drums and flutes of Dong Son (see p.364), and further again to the lithophone (stone xylophone) called the *dan da*, the world's oldest known instrument. The Chinese influence is evident in operatic theatre and stringed instruments, while India bestowed rhythms, modal improvisations and several types of drum. Much later, especially during the nineteenth century, elements of European **theatre** and music were co-opted, while during the twentieth century most Vietnamese musicians received a classical, Western training based on the works of Eastern bloc composers such as Prokofiev and Tchaikovsky.

From this multicultural melting pot Vietnamese artists have generated a variety of musical and theatrical forms over the centuries, though, surprisingly, dance is less developed than in neighbouring Thailand, Cambodia and Laos. One of the most famous home-grown performance arts is water-puppetry, Vietnam's unique contribution to the world of marionettes, where puppeteers work their magic on a stage of water. The folk tradition is particularly rich, with its improvised courtship songs and the strident, sacred music of trance dances, to which the more than fifty ethnic minorities add their own repertoire of songs and instruments.

Traditionally, the professions of artists or performers were hereditary, but the wars and political upheavals of the twentieth century have contributed to the loss of much of this largely oral tradition. While certain art forms continue to attract new talent, the younger generation is, on the whole, more interested in higher-paid professions and Vietnamese pop. As revolutionary ("red") music has waned since 1986, so pre-1975 music from the South, previously outlawed as "decadent and reactionary", is back with a vengeance, mixed with a sprinkling of artists from other Asian countries and the West.

The traditional strand

Vietnam's traditional theatre, with its strong Chinese influence, is more akin to opera than pure spoken drama. A musical accompaniment and well-known repertoire of songs form an integral part of the performance, where the plots and characters are equally familiar to the audience. Nowadays, however, the two oldest forms, **Cheo** and **Tuong**, are struggling to survive, while even the more contemporary **Cai Luong** is losing out to television and video. However, other traditional arts have seen something of a revival, most notably **water-puppetry** and folk-song performances. The stimulus for this came largely from tourism, but renewed interest in the trance music of **Chau Van** and the complexities of **Tai Tu** chamber music has been very much home-grown.

Theatre

Vietnam's oldest surviving stage art, **Hat Cheo**, or "Popular Opera", has its roots in the Red River Delta where it's believed to have existed since at least the eleventh century. Performances consist of popular legends and everyday events, often with a biting satirical edge, accompanied by a selection of tunes drawn as appropriate from a common fund. Though the movements have become highly stylized over the centuries, Cheo's free form allows the actors considerable room for interpretation; the audience demonstrates its approval, or otherwise, by beating a drum.

Cheo has the reputation of being anti-establishment, with its buffoon character who comments freely on the action, the audience and current events. So incensed were the kings of the fifteenth-century Later Le Dynasty that Cheo was banned from the court, while artists and their descendants were excluded from public office. Nevertheless, Cheo survived and received official recognition in 1964 with the establishment of the Vietnam Cheo Theatre, charged with reviving the ancient art form. It is now promoted as the country's national theatre, although its local popularity continues to decline despite a body of new work dealing with contemporary issues which aims to introduce Cheo to a wider audience.

Hat Tuong (also known as *Hat Boi* or *Hat Bo*), probably introduced from China around the thirteenth century, evolved from classical Chinese opera, and was originally for royal entertainment before being adopted by travelling troupes. Its story lines are mostly historic events and epic tales dealing with such Confucian principles as filial piety and relations between the monarch and his subjects. Tuong, like Cheo, is governed by rigorous rules in which the characters are rendered instantly recognizable by their make-up and costume. Setting and atmosphere are conjured not by props and scenery but through nuances of gesture and musical conventions with which the audience is completely familiar – and which they won't hesitate to criticize if badly executed. Of the clutch of Tuong troupes still in existence, Hanoi's Vietnam Tuong Theatre is one of the most active.

While performances of Tuong are comparatively rare events these days, if you see a large building with peanut- and candy-sellers outside, the chances are that there's a performance of **Hat Cai Luong**, or "Reformed Theatre", going on inside. Cai Luong originated in southern Vietnam in the early twentieth century, showing a French theatrical influence in its spoken parts, with short scenes and relatively elaborate sets. The action is a tangle of historical drama (such as *The Tale of Kieu*) and racy themes from the street (murder, drug deals, incest, theft and revenge). Its music is a similar hodgepodge: eighteenth-century chamber music played on amplified traditional instruments for the set pieces; electric guitar, keyboards and drums during the scene changes. Cai Luong's constant borrowing from contemporary culture – from language and plots to the incorporation of hit songs – has enabled it to keep pace with Vietnam's social changes. Around thirty professional Cai Luong troupes are currently performing, of which the best known are the National Cai Luong Theatre in Hanoi and Ho Chi Minh City's Tran Huu Trang Cai Luong Theatre.

The origin of **water-puppetry** (*mua roi nuoc*) is obscure, beyond that it developed in the flooded rice paddies of the Red River Delta and usually took place in spring when there was less farm work to be done. The earliest record is a stele in Ha Nam Province dated 1121 AD, suggesting that by this date water-puppetry was already a regular feature at the royal court.

The art of water-puppetry was traditionally a jealously guarded secret handed down from father to son; women were not permitted to learn the techniques in case they revealed them to their husbands' families. This contributed to its decline until the art seemed in danger of dying out altogether. Happily, a French organization, the *Maison des Cultures du Monde*, intervened and, since 1984, with newly carved puppets, a revamped programme and more elaborate staging,

Vietnam's water-puppet troupes have played various international capitals to great acclaim – and can be seen daily in Hanoi (see p.381), Ho Chi Minh City (see p.101) and Haiphong (see p.402). Where before gongs and drums alone were used for scene-setting and building atmosphere, today's national troupes often maintain a larger ensemble, similar to Hat Cheo, including zithers and flutes. The songs are also borrowed from the Cheo repertoire, particularly declamatory styles and popular folk tunes, and the show often includes a short recital of traditional music before the puppets emerge to create their own unique illusion.

Music, dance and song

One of Vietnam's oldest song traditions is that of **Quan Ho**, or "call-and-response singing", a form which thrives in the Red River Delta, particularly Ha Bac Province, and has parallels among the north's ethnic minorities. These unaccompanied songs are usually heard in spring, performed by young men and women bandying improvised lyrics back and forth. Quan Ho traditionally played a part in the courtship ritual and performers are applauded for their skill in complimenting or teasing their partner, earning delighted approval as the exchange becomes increasingly bawdy.

Found in north and central Vietnam, **Hat Chau Van** is a form of ancient, sacred ritual music used to invoke the spirits during trance possession ceremonies. Statues of a pantheon of goddesses are placed in shrines to the Mother Goddess, Thanh Mau, found in both Buddhist pagodas and village temples. Throughout the performance of hypnotically rhythmic music (the performers may be one or many, male or female) a medium enters a trance state and is possessed by a chosen deity. Because of the anti-religious stance of the Vietnamese government until 1986, the style was practised in secret, though some pieces were adapted for inclusion in state-sponsored Cheo theatre. Chau Van is currently being revived by older practitioners in its original religious setting, promoted by a class of nouveaux riches keen for the goddesses to intercede and protect their business interests.

Although the song tradition known as **Ca Tru**, or *Hat A Dao*, dates back centuries, it became all the rage in the fifteenth century when the Vietnamese regained their independence from China. According to legend, a beautiful young songstress, A Dao, charmed the enemy with her songs of the verdant countryside and the way of life in the villages. Fascinated by her voice, the soldiers were encouraged to drink until they became incapacitated and could be pushed into the river and drowned. The lyrics of Ca Tru are often taken from famous poems and are traditionally sung by a woman. The singer also plays a bamboo percussion instrument, and is accompanied by a three-string lute (*dan day*) and drum. She has to master a whole range of singing styles, each differentiated by its particular rhythm, such as *Hat noi* (similar to speech) and *Gui thu* (a more formal style, akin to a written letter). This difficult genre has undergone something of a revival in Hanoi in recent years, while in Hué excerpts from the closely related **Ca Hué** song tradition are performed for tourists on sampans on the Perfume River (see p.309).

The traditional music accompanying Cai Luong theatre originated in eighteenth-century Hué. Played as pure chamber music, without the voice, it is known as **Nhac Tai Tu**, or "skilled chamber music of amateurs". This is one of the most delightful and tricksy of all Vietnamese genres. The players have a great degree of improvisational latitude over a fundamental melodic skeleton; they must think and respond quickly, as in a game, and the resulting independently funky rhythms can be wild. Although modern conservatory training fails to prepare students for this most satisfying of all styles, there is now a resurgence of interest among young players in learning the demands of Tai Tu.

It was also in Hué under the Nguyen emperors that the specialized body of **royal music and dance** reached its peak of sophistication. These solemn ceremonial dances again owed their origins to the Chinese courtly tradition and were categorized into a highly complex system according to the occasion on which they would be performed: ritual dances to be held in temples or pagodas, during feasts or at various civil and military functions, and dances to mark particular anniversaries were just some of the distinctions. As the Imperial court fell under European sway in the twentieth century, so the taste – and opportunity – for such music waned, until the late 1980s when it was revived by the provincial authorities with assistance from UNESCO. Hué's former Royal Theatre has now been renovated and is the venue for occasional performances of courtly music and dance by students of Hué University of Fine Arts. In 2003 UNESCO recognized Nha Nhac ("refined music") as a Masterpiece of Oral and Intangible Heritage.

Traditional instruments

A visiting US general once stepped off a plane with the intention of smoothing relations by attempting a little Vietnamese. This being a tonal language, instead of "I am honoured to be here", listeners heard "the sunburnt duck lies sleeping". The voice and its inherent melodic information are behind all Vietnamese music, and most instruments are, to some extent, made to do what voices do: delicate pitch bends, ornaments and subtle slides. According to classical Confucian theory, instruments fall into eight **categories of sound**: silk, stone, skin, clay, metal, air, wood and bamboo. Although few people play by the rules these days, classical theory also relates five occasions when it is forbidden to perform: at sunset, during a storm, when the preparations have not been made seriously, with improper costumes and when the audience is not paying attention.

▲ Traditional musicians playing at Cao Dai Cathedral

Many instruments whose strings are now made of steel, gut or nylon originally had **silk** strings; silk is now out of fashion, more for acoustic than ecological reasons. The most famous of these, and unique to Vietnam, is the monochord **dan bau** (or *dan doc huyen*), an ingenious invention perfectly suited to its job of mimicking vocal inflections. It is made from one string (originally silk obtained by yanking apart the live worm), stretched over a long amplified sounding box, fixed at one end. The other end is attached to a buffalo-horn "whammy bar" stalk which can be flexed to stretch or relax the string's tension. Meanwhile the string is plucked with a plectrum at its harmonic nodes to produce overtones that swoop and glide and quiver over a range of three octaves. Other "silk-stringed" instruments include the *dan nguyet* (moon-shaped lute), the *dan tranh* (sixteen-string zither), *dan nhi* (two-string fiddle with the bow running between the strings), *dan day* (a three-stringed lute with a long fingerboard used in Ca Tru and also unique to Vietnam), and *dan luc huyen cam* (a regular guitar with a fingerboard scalloped to allow for wider pitch bends).

The *dan da* **stone** lithophone is the world's oldest instrument, consisting of six or more rocks struck with heavy wooden mallets. Several sets have been found originating from the one slate quarry in the central highlands where the stones sing like nowhere else. The oldest *dan da* is now in Paris, but an identical set exists in Ho Chi Minh City, where it still produces pure ringing tones.

Various kinds of **drums** (*trong*) are used, played with acrobatic use of the sticks in the air and on the sides. Some originated in China, while others were introduced from India via the Cham people, such as the double-headed "rice drum" (*trong com*), which was developed from the Indian *mridangam*; the name derives from thin patches of cooked rice paste stuck on each membrane.

Representing **clay**, four thimble-size teacups are held in the fingers and often played as percussion instruments for Hué chamber music. Representing **metal**, the *sinh tien*, **coin clappers**, are another invention unique to Vietnam, combining in one unit a rasping scraper, wooden clapper and a sistrum rattle made from old coins. Bronze **gongs** are occasionally found in minority music, but Vietnam is the only country in Southeast Asia where tuned gamelan-type gong-chimes are not used.

Air, **wood** and **bamboo** furnish a whole range of wind instruments, such as the many side- and end-blown flutes used for folk songs and to accompany poetry recitals; or the *ken*, a double-reed oboe common across Asia and played, appropriately, in funeral processions and other outdoor ceremonies. Five thin bones often dangle from the *ken* player's mouthpiece to suggest the delicate fingers of a young woman, while disguising the hideous grin necessary to play the instrument. The *song lang* is a slit drum, played by the foot, used to count the measures in Tai Tu skilled chamber music, while the *k'long put*, consisting of racks of bamboo pipes, is the only percussion instrument you don't actually touch but clap in front of. Another instrument from the same folk tradition is the *t'rung*, a type of xylophone made of ladders of tuned bamboo.

New folk

Turn on the TV during the Tet Lunar New Year festivities and you can't miss the public face of Vietnamese traditional music: ethnic-costumed dancers, musicians and singers smilingly portraying the happy life of the worker. Fancy arrangements of well-known tunes from all over the country, including some token minorities' music, are spiced up with fancy hats and bamboo pianos. This choreographed entertainment known as **Modernized Folk Music** (*Nhac Dan Tôc Cai Bien*) has only been "traditional" since 1956, when the Hanoi Conservatory of Music was founded and the teaching of folk music was deliberately "improved".

For the first time, music was learned from written Western notation (leading to the neglect of improvisational skills while opening the way for huge orchestras), and conductors were employed. Tunings of the traditional eight modes were tempered to accommodate Western-style harmonies, while bizarre new instruments were invented to play bass and to fill out chords in the enlarged bands. Schools, with the mandate of preserving traditional music through "inheritance development", took over from the families and professional apprenticeships which had formerly been passed on via the oral tradition.

Not surprisingly, a new creature was born out of all this. Trained conservatoire graduates have spread throughout the country and been promoted through competitions and state-sponsored ensembles on TV, radio and even in the lobbies of classier hotels. The new corpus of music and song arrangements has become an emblem of national pride and scientific improvement. Folk songs, melodies from the ethnic minorities, Mozart and Chinese tunes are all ripe fodder for the arranger's pen. Much to the chagrin of the few remaining traditional musicians outside this system, this is now the predominant folk-based music generally heard in public. A visitor to the central highlands asked the local tribal musicians how they felt about their music being "improved". At first they replied what an honour it was for their music to be considered by city people, but after the official interview they privately confessed their horror.

Music for new folk is entertaining and accessible, albeit risking tawdriness; at its best, though, it can be an astonishing display of a lively new art form. One family of six brothers (and one sister-in-law), led by Duc Loi, formed a percussion group in Ho Chi Minh City under the name **Phu Dong**, whose members spent time in the highlands learning the instruments of several minorities. Since 1981 they have played together and developed an infectious musical personality. Circular breathing and lightning-speed virtuosity are just some of the dazzling features of a performance, and their collection of instruments is like a zoo of mutant bamboo. Most striking, though, is their use of the lithophone (*dan da*), a replica of the original, 6000-year-old stone marimba. The effect of awakening this ancient voice, whatever changes in performance practice there may have been over the last six millennia, is shattering.

Vietnamese pop

There is no shortage of pop-star wannabes in Vietnam and the fine line between karaoke hacks on CD and major commercial pop releases can be tough to pinpoint. The vast majority of pop music would be filed under **light pop-rock**, but it is also referred to as "misery pop" or "yellow music". Most composers in the country have tried their hand at writing a pop hit but only about three are acknowledged masters: Van Cao (who also wrote the national anthem), Pham Duy (now in his eighties and back in Vietnam, having spent many years writing pointed political songs from the safe distance of California) and Trinh Cong Son (whose life of wine, women and song ended in 2001). Joan Baez was not far off when she dubbed him "the Vietnamese Bob Dylan": the tunes are catchy and the lyrics right-on. His first songs were written while in hiding from the military draft, and in 1969, when his album *Lullaby* sold over two million copies in Japan,

Son's works were banned by the South Vietnamese government, which considered the lyrics too demoralizing. Even the new government sent him to work as a peasant in the fields, but after 1979 he lived in Ho Chi Minh City, painting, writing apolitical-but-catchy love songs and celebrating Vietnam's natural wonders, with over six hundred songs to his credit.

There are two main centres for Vietnamese pop-music production: **Ho Chi Minh City** and Southern California. Those in the country have the advantage of being close to the source of folk inspiration (arrangements of traditional Ca Tru and Chau Van songs are currently in vogue), and the young generation has taken singing lessons at the Conservatory (leading to a vast technical improvement of late). Singers of note include: Tran Thu Ha, My Linh, Phuong Thanh, Bang Kieu, Hong Nhung Lam Truong, Thanh Lam and Quang Dung. Albums are bootlegged under different titles so just keep an eye out for these names and you'll be fine.

Meanwhile in Orange County, **California**, the scene is busy but somewhat stagnant. The stars of yesterday and today are: Khanh Ha, Don Ho, Lam Nhat Tien, Nhu Quynh, Y Lan, Khanh Ly and Tuan Ngoc. Look out, too, for Jimmi Nguyen, Trizzie Phuong Trinh and Thanh Ha, all of whom perform regularly in Vietnam. Some of these are the performing children of former superstars, so in many cases the entertainment genes have been passed on despite relocation and social upheaval.

The ubiquitous **pop-rock band** comprises a singer, bass guitar and one or two electronic keyboards, hailed throughout the country as the greatest labour-saving device, despite their cheesy sound. Indeed, in rural areas where there is no electricity, these portable keyboards run happily on batteries, and all the rhythm buttons that are so rarely used elsewhere – rumba, tango, bossa nova and surf-rock – are here employed liberally. The slap-echo on the singer's microphone is intentional; without it, they say, it sounds "unprofessional". Each evening, when the traffic noise dies down, you can hear the mournful laments of neighbouring karaoke bars mingling together, the ghostly echoes of lonely pop singers reverberating from another dimension.

Discography

There are more recordings of traditional music available outside the country than in. But if you find yourself in Hanoi, stop by the Vietnamese Institute of Musicology at 32 Nguyen Thai Hoc (🕸 www.vn-style.com/vim) and check out their extensive database of field recordings.

Traditional

Samplers

Hò! Roady Music from Vietnam Trikont, Germany. Crass, crazy, funky street music taken from pop cassettes and recorded in situ with mopeds and car horns in the soundscape. It opens in cracking style with a plucked *dan bau* doing "Riders in the Sky" with what sounds like fireworks as well. There's a wild funeral brass band and all sorts of surprises. Highly recommended.

Music from Vietnam Vol 1 Caprice, Sweden. An introduction (in conservatoire style) featuring songs, instrumental tracks and theatrical forms. Featured instruments include the *dan bau, dan nguyet* and *k'long put*. Music includes Quan Ho folk songs, Cai Luong and Hat Cheo theatre, Hat Chau Van possession ritual and Nhac Dan Toc Cai Bien new folk.

Stilling Time: Traditional Musics of Vietnam Innova, US. A sampler

of field recordings from all over Vietnam, including songs and gong music of the ethnic minorities. An introduction to the many surprises in store for the musical traveller. Recorded and compiled by Philip Blackburn.

Theatre

The Art of Kim Sinh King, Japan. Blind singer/guitarist Kim Sinh has something of a cult following and knows how to wrench the emotions from those old Cai Luong opera songs. His venerable musical personality is more affecting than many of the commercial Cai Luong releases available, and one struggles not to make comparisons to the blues. This recording has influenced a whole generation of California guitarists.

Vietnam: Traditions of the South Audivis/UNESCO, France. Southern ritual music from the

eclectic Cao Dai, Buddhist and indigenous spirit-possession religions, as well as a good helping of Cai Luong theatre music (the traditional, not the cheesy Western-style band!). The liner notes and recording quality are on the dry side but the music is very lively.

Vietnamese Folk Theatre: Hat Cheo King, Japan. Cheo theatre, expertly played by the Quy Bon family and recorded in Hanoi. Features a Chau Van possession ritual and the famous story of the cross-dressing Thi Mau going to a temple.

Song and classical music

Anthology of World Music: The Music of Viet Nam Rounder, US. This is the Vietnamese equivalent of the Rosetta Stone, the earliest published recordings of some of the standards of the repertoire, performed by the masters of their day. Music and Theatre of the Court, Ritual Music and Entertainment Music, and the Music of South Vietnam. The presentation may seem a little dusty by modern flashy conservatoire standards but it's still revelatory.

Ca Tru: The Music of North Viet Nam Inedit, France. Performed by the Hanoi Ca Tru Thai Ha Ensemble. A tenacious vestige of Vietnam's 500-year tradition of women's "songs for bamboo tokens", Ca Tru (or Hat A Dao) is a private entertainment forced underground until recently. Solo voice (with "bouncing seeds"

vibrato), lute and chopsticks titillate male visitors for hours on end.

Music from Vietnam Vol 2: The City of Hué Caprice, Sweden. Ceremonial music with *shawms*, drums and a big gong, a military ensemble and a great court orchestra, as well as more intimate chamber groups of singers with *dan bau, dan nguyet, dan nhi* and *dan tranh*. Three local instrumental and vocal groups give the enticing flavour of this city, and the disc features the sprightly aged Nguyen Manh Cam, former drummer to the emperor. Good notes.

Vietnam: Buddhist Music from Hué Inedit, France. An atmospheric recording, full of ceremonial presence. It begins with sonorous drums and bells before two oboes enter for music marking the ascent to the "Esplanade of Heaven". The complete ceremony of Khai Kinh, "Opening the Sacred Texts", is recorded in one of Hué's best pagodas, the Kim Thien. Not easy listening, but the music is nevertheless impressive. Good notes.

Ethnic minority music

Gongs: Vietnam, Laos Playasound, France. Before there were skipping records or Steve Reich patterns there were these delicious mellifluously clangorous loops filling the jungle nights.

Music from Vietnam Vol 3: Ethnic Minorities Caprice, Sweden. The mosaic of cultures residing in the central and northern mountains has some astonishing musical traditions. This excellent and accessible selection kicks off with a piece from the E De: a beautiful "free-reed" cow-horn solo followed up by clattering poly-rhythmic gong patterns. There's also music from the Nung, Muong and Hmong. Wonderful pipes, flutes, mouth organs and songs. Good notes.

New folk

Echoes of Ancestral Voices: Traditional Music of Vietnam Move, Australia. Music performed by husband and wife duo Dang Kim Hien and Le Tuan Hung. No fireworks, just a fragile, uncompromising intensity.

Moonlight in Vietnam Henry Street/Rounder, US. New music expertly played on Vietnam's most extraordinary musical instruments, including the *dan bau*, *k'long put* and a stick-fiddle with a resonating disc

Vietnam: Poésies et Chants Ocora, France. Master musician Tran Van Khe and friends chant poetry (*ngam tho*) and ravish the *dan tranh* and *dan nguyet* (in the Nhac Tai Tu skilled chamber music repertory). Specialized and intimate performances with excellent notes and translations.

Musiques des Montagnards Chant du Monde, France. Two CDs of extraordinary archival and recent recordings (1958–1997) from the central and northern highlands. Fourteen ethnic groups are covered and excellently described in the copious 119 page booklet.

Northern Vietnam: Music and Songs of the Minorities Buda Musique/Musique du Monde, France. A selection of recordings from the Giay, Nung, Tay, Dao, Thai and Hmong ethnic groups. A love song, courting melodies, wedding music, funeral music and the extraordinary Hmong *khen*.

held in the player's mouth. The players are a Vancouver-based ensemble led by *dan bau* virtuoso Ho Khac Chi.

The Music of Vietnam Vols 1.1 & 1.2 Celestial Harmonies, US. Accessible, virtuoso and expertly recorded, these discs document an array of Vietnam's best conservatoire-- mediated styles. Through a compelling series of pieces, this is an entertaining overview of the full range of Vietnamese instruments. Full documentation.

Pop

Don Ho *Ru Em/Lullaby* Thuy Nga, US. Heart-throb lullabies from one of California's hottest singers.

Khanh Ha *Doi Da Vang/Vacant Rock-strewn Hill* Khanh Ha Productions, US. Bilingual singing legend compared (favourably) to Barbra Streisand and Celine Dion.

My Linh *Toc Ngan/Short Hair* My Linh Productions, Vietnam. Hot arrangements of pieces all written for her sultry, crackly voice.

Nguyen Thanh Van *Ho Khoan Le Thuy/River Song* Van Nguyen Productions, US. Passion, pathos and folk references from this San Francisco-based artist.

Pham Duy *Voyage Through the Motherland* Co Loa, US. The first Vietnamese CD-ROM, featuring patriotic songs, karaoke options, video and fine photos. A real "coffee table" disc.

Y Lan *Muon Hoi Tai Sao/I Want to Ask Why* Y Lan Productions, US. From a well-known artistic family, she became a café owner before becoming a regular at the *Ritz* and *Paris By Night* circuit.

With contributions by Philip Blackburn (from *The Rough Guide to World Music*)

Books

O f the vast canon of books written on the subject of Vietnam, the overwhelming majority concern themselves, inevitably, with the American War. Indigenous attempts to come to terms with the conflicts that have caused Vietnam such pain are only now beginning to filter through the country's overcautious censorship. Some of the few novels that have reached the West in recent years are also reviewed below.

For a decent copy of a book on Vietnam, your best bet is to scour bookshops before you set off from home – only Hanoi and Ho Chi Minh City have ranges of literature of any breadth, and then often only in photocopied offprint form. The exceptions to this are books produced by local publishers, notably The Gioi Publishers, which you'll have difficulty finding outside Vietnam.

Travel writing

Maria Coffey *Three Moons in Vietnam*. Delightfully jolly jaunt around Vietnam by boat, bus and bicycle. Coffey conspires to meet more locals in one day than most travellers do in a month, making this a valuable snapshot of modern Vietnam.

Sue Downie *Down Highway One*. In 1988 Sue Downie was one of the first Westerners since the American War to travel the length of Highway 1. Returning in the early 1990s, she witnesses the changes – not all good – transforming the country and people's daily lives.

Graham Greene *Ways of Escape*. Greene's global travels in the 1950s took him to Vietnam for four consecutive winters; the coverage of Vietnam in this slim autobiographical volume is intriguing, but tantalizingly short, its memories of dice-playing with French agents over vermouths and opium-smoking in Cho Lon are evidently templates for scenes in *The Quiet American*.

Christopher Hunt *Sparring with Charlie*. Hunt can be a maddening travelling companion, but this account of his jaunt down the Ho

Chi Minh Trail on a Russian-made motorbike is undeniably a page-turner.

Norman Lewis *A Dragon Apparent*. When in 1950 Lewis made the journey that would inspire his seminal Indochina travelogue, the Vietnam he saw was still a land of longhouses and Imperial hunts, though poised for renewed conflict; the erudite prose of this doyen of travel writers reveals a Vietnam now long gone.

W. Somerset Maugham *The Gentleman in the Parlour*. The fruit of Maugham's grand tour from Rangoon to Haiphong to recharge his creative batteries, *The Gentleman in the Parlour*, finds him less than enamoured of Vietnam, his last stop. Nevertheless, his accounts of the Hué court teetering on the brink of extinction, and of a run-in with an old acquaintance in a Haiphong café, are vintage Maugham.

Karin Muller *Hitchhiking Vietnam*. A feisty American, Karin Muller went searching for the "real Vietnam", a Vietnam untouched by commercialism and Western culture. On the way she gets deported, is arrested on numerous occasions and meets some motley characters, but eventually finds what she's looking for among the minorities of the northwest mountains. Beautifully told, with great compassion and a never-failing sense of humour.

Andrew X. Pham *Catfish and Mandala*. After twenty years in America, Pham takes a gruelling bike ride through Vietnam to rediscover the country, his family and – in the process – himself. A compelling insight into the frustrations and fascinations of Vietnam.

Gontran de Poncins *From a Chinese City*. Believing that "the ancient customs of a national culture endure longer in remote colonies than in the motherland", de Poncins opted for a sojourn in Cho Lon as a means to a better understanding of the foibles of the Chinese; the resulting document of life in 1955 Cho Lon is a lively period piece, backed up by fluid illustrations.

Pam Scott *Hanoi Stories* and *Life in Hanoi*. Hanoi and its inhabitants – both local and expat, from its celebrities to its cyclo drivers – viewed through the lens of an Australian who came on business and stayed ten years.

James Sullivan *Over the Moat*. Cultures collide as Sullivan courts a Hué shop-girl he met while cycling

through Vietnam in 1992. Part love-story, part travelogue.

Paul Theroux *The Great Railway Bazaar*. His elaborate circumnavigation of Europe and Asia by train took Theroux, in 1973, to a South Vietnam still bewildered by the recent American withdrawal. In bleak sound-bite accounts of rides from Saigon to Bien Hoa and Hué to Da Nang, he describes the war's awful legacy of poverty, suffering and infrastructural breakdown, but marvels at the country's unbowed, and unexpected, beauty.

Gabrielle M. Vassal *On and Off Duty in Annam*. An enchanting wander through turn-of-the-century southern Vietnam, penned by the intrepid wife of a French army doctor. A stint in Saigon is followed by a boat trip to Nha Trang (where she was carried ashore "on the backs of natives through the breakers") and a gutsy foray into the central highlands; amazing prints of the Vietnamese and *montagnards* she encountered further enhance the account.

Justin Wintle *Romancing Vietnam*. Wintle's genial but lightweight yomp upcountry was one of the first of its kind, post-*doi moi*, and remains a pleasing aperitif to travels in Vietnam.

Vietnamese abroad

Donald Anderson (ed.) *Aftermath: An Anthology of Post-Vietnam Fiction*. As the war's tendrils crept across the Pacific to America, they touched not only the people who fought, but also those who stayed at home. In their depictions of Americans, Amerasians and Asians regathering the strands of their lives, these short stories run the gamut of emotions provoked by war.

Robert Olen Butler *A Good Scent from a Strange Mountain*. Pulitzer Prize-winning collection of short stories that ponder the struggles of Vietnamese in America to maintain the cultural ley lines linking them with their mother country, and the gulf between them and their Americanized offspring. War veteran Olen Butler's assured prose ensures the voices of his Vietnamese characters find perfect pitch.

🏃 **Le Ly Hayslip** *Child of War, Woman of Peace.* In this follow-up to *When Heaven and Earth Changed Places* (see p.527), Hayslip's narrative shifts to America, where the cultural disorientation of a new arrival is examined.

Vietnamese literature

John Balaban and Nguyen Qui Duc (eds.) *Vietnam: A Traveller's Literary Companion.* The editors of this entertaining volume of short stories, written by Vietnamese writers based both at home and abroad, chose to avoid tales of war and politics during their selection process, though both themes inevitably make their presence felt.

🏃 **Bao Ninh** *The Sorrow of War.* This is a ground-breaking novel, largely due to its portrayal of Communist soldiers suffering the same traumas, fear and lost innocence as their American counterparts.

Steven Bradbury *Poems from the Prison Diary of Ho Chi Minh Tinfish.* This beautifully rendered selection of the poems Ho penned while behind bars in 1942, in which he looks to birdsong and moonlight to ease the loneliness of prison life, provide a touching glimpse of the man behind the myth.

Alastair Dingwall (ed.) *Traveller's Literary Companion to South-East Asia.* Among the bite-sized essays inside this gem of a book is an enlightening thirty-page segment on Vietnam, into which are crammed biopics, a recommended reading list, historical, linguistic and literary backgrounds. Excerpts range from classical literature to the writings of foreign journalists in the 1960s.

🏃 **Duong Thu Huong** *Novel Without a Name.* A tale of young Vietnamese men seeking glory but finding only loneliness, disillusionment and death, as war abridges youth and curtails loves. A depiction of dwindling idealism, and a radical questioning of the political motives behind the war. Other highly acclaimed works by the same author include *Paradise of the Blind* and *Memories of a Pure Spring.*

🏃 **Duong Van Mai Elliot** *The Sacred Willow.* Mai Elliot brings Vietnamese history to life in this compelling account of her family through four generations.

Wayne Karlin, Le Minh Khue and Truong Vu (eds.) *The Other Side of Heaven.* A unique anthology of postwar fiction by Vietnamese and American authors. Though written by former enemies from all sides of the conflict, these stories echo back and forth the unifying themes of sorrow, pain and survival.

Le Minh Khue *The Stars, The Earth, The River.* Fourteen short stories by one of Vietnam's leading contemporary writers, an ex-sapper who gently details the seesaw of "tragedy and hope" which defines her war-torn generation.

Nguyen Du *The Tale of Kieu.* Vietnamese literature reached its zenith with this tale of the ill-starred love between Kieu and Kim.

🏃 **Nguyen Huy Thiep** *The General Retires and Other Stories.* Perhaps Vietnam's pre-eminent writer, Nguyen Huy Thiep articulates the lives of ordinary Vietnamese in these short stories – instead of following the prevailing trend of re-imagining the lives of past heroes.

Novels set in Vietnam

Marguerite Duras *The Lover*. Young French girl meets wealthy Chinese man on a Mekong Delta ferry; the ensuing affair initiates her into adulthood, with all its joys and responsibilities. The novel's depiction of a dysfunctional, hard-up French family in Vietnam provides an interesting slant on colonial life, showing it wasn't all vermouths and tennis.

Graham Greene *The Quiet American*. Greene's prescient and cautionary tale of the dangers of innocence in uncertain times, which anticipated America's boorish manhandling of Vietnam's political situation by several years, is still the best single account of wartime Vietnam. Its regular name-drops of familiar locales – Tay Ninh, the *Continental*, Dong Khoi – make it doubly enjoyable.

Anthony Grey *Saigon*. Vietnamese history given a blockbuster makeover: a rip-roaring narrative, whose Vietnamese, French and American protagonists conspire to be present at all defining moments in recent Vietnamese history, from French plantation riots to the fall of Saigon.

Nguyen Kien *Tapestries*. This rich and beautifully woven novel is based on the extraordinary real-life story of the author's grandfather, who eventually became an embroiderer in the royal court of Hué. The context is a country on the cusp of change as French influence gains the upper hand.

Tim O'Brien *Going After Cacciato*. A highly acclaimed, lyrical tale of an American soldier who simply walks out of the war and sets off for Paris, pursued by his company on a fantastical mission that takes them across Asia. The savage reality of war stands out vividly against a dream-world of peace and freedom.

History

William J. Duiker *The Communist Road to Power in Vietnam*. One of America's leading analysts of the political context in Vietnam takes a long close look at why Communist Vietnam won its wars – as opposed to why France and America lost.

William J. Duiker *Ho Chi Minh: A Life*. Duiker turns his spotlight on the patriot and revolutionary who led Vietnam to independence. It's a thoroughly researched and exhaustive tome, particularly good on Ho's political evolution, though fails to get under the skin of this enigmatic man.

Bernard Fall *Hell in a Very Small Place*. The classic account of the siege of Dien Bien Phu, capturing the claustrophobia and the fear, written by a French-born American journalist.

Bernard Fall *Street Without Joy*. Another masterpiece by Fall, charting the French debacle in Indochina, which became required reading for American generals and GIs – though it didn't prevent them committing exactly the same mistakes just a few years later.

David Halberstam *Ho*. Diminutive, sympathetic and highly readable biography of Vietnam's foremost icon, though no attempt is made to apportion blame for the disastrous land reforms of the 1950s.

Stanley Karnow *Vietnam: A History*. Weighty, august tome that elucidates the entire span of Vietnamese history.

Michael Maclear *Vietnam: The Ten Thousand Day War*. A solid introductory account of the French and American wars, from Ho's alliance with Archimedes Patti, to the fall of Saigon.

Nguyen Khac Vien *Vietnam: A Long History*. Published by Hanoi's The Gioi Publishers, and therefore heavily weighted in favour of the Communists, but easier to get hold of in Vietnam than most histories.

Keith Weller Taylor *The Birth of Vietnam* University of California Press. As a GI, Taylor was struck by the "intelligence and resolve" of his enemy. This meticulous account of the dawn of Vietnamese history, trawling the past from the nation's first recorded history up to the tenth century, is the result of his attempt to uncover their roots.

Martin Windrow *The Last Valley: Dien Bien Phu and the French Defeat in Vietnam*. This meticulously researched and detailed account of the battle of Dien Bien Phu gives a brutally realistic picture of what it was like for the French soldiers (many actually Vietnamese, Thai and North African) trapped in what came to be known as the "toilet bowl". Windrow's sympathy and admiration for the soldiers – on both sides – comes across loud and clear.

The American War

Mark Baker *Nam*. Unflinching firsthand accounts of the GI's descent from boot camp into the morass of death, paranoia, exhaustion and tedium. Gut-wrenchingly frank at times, the book depicts war as a rite of passage, and moral deterioration as a prerequisite to survival.

Tad Bartimus (ed.) *War Torn: Stories of War from the Women Reporters Who Covered Vietnam*. Nine pioneering women journalists who covered the American War tell their tales, from the struggle to get there in the first place and be recognized in what was then an almost exclusively male profession to their reactions to the war itself and coming to terms with the aftermath.

Michael Bilton and Kevin Sim *Four Hours in My Lai*. Brutally candid and immaculately researched reconstruction of the events surrounding the My Lai massacre of 1968; as harrowing a portrayal of the depths plumbed in war as you'll ever read.

Philip Caputo *A Rumour of War*. One of the classics of the American War, Caputo's straightforward narrative is a powerful account of the numbing daily routine of the ordinary US soldier's life, the strange exhilaration of combat and the brutalization that accompanies war.

Denise Chong *The Girl in the Picture*. Kim Phuc was the little girl running naked away from her napalm-bombed village in what is arguably the most famous – and most harrowing – photo taken during the American War. Not only did she survive the burns, just, but her resilience and capacity for forgiveness are quite remarkable. Denise Chong tells Kim's story simply, letting the horrific events speak for themselves.

Michael Clodfelter *Mad Minutes and Vietnam Months*. Combat reminiscences from a man who found war's false promise of "courage, sacrifice, glory and adventure" displaced by monotony and, occasionally, atrocity.

W.D. Ehrhart *Going Back: An Ex-Marine Returns to Vietnam.* A veteran of the battle for Hué, Ehrhart returned to Vietnam in 1985. *Going Back*, a record of that trip, mixes diary, memory and Ehrhart's own poetry to very readable effect.

Horst Faas and Tim Page (eds.) *Requiem.* Turning through this compendium of shots by photographers who subsequently lost their lives in Vietnam, Laos or Cambodia will haunt you for weeks. Never was a book more aptly named.

James Fenton *All the Wrong Places.* In Vietnam at the moment of Saigon's liberation, Fenton somehow managed to hitch a lift on the tank that rammed through the palace gates; his easy prose and poet's eye for detail make his account an engrossing one.

Frances Fitzgerald *Fire in the Lake.* Pulitzer Prize-winning analysis of the historical, political and cultural context of the war, this time told from the Vietnamese perspective.

Albert French *Patches of Fire.* Examining his experiences of the infantryman's life in Vietnam and his attempts to exorcise his war-conjured demons back in the States, French's autobiography is at once moving and engrossing.

Le Ly Hayslip *When Heaven and Earth Changed Places.* For giving a human face to the slopes, dinks and gooks of American writing on Vietnam, this heart-rending tale of villagers trying to survive in a climate of hatred and distrust is perhaps more valuable than any history book.

Michael Herr *Dispatches.* Infuriatingly narcissistic at times, Herr's spaced-out narrative still conveys the mud, blood and guts of the American war effort in Vietnam. Herr's distinctive tone is also evident

in the classic war movie, *Apocalypse Now* (see p.533), for which he wrote the screenplay.

John Laurence *The Cat from Hué.* Highly acclaimed for his coverage of the Vietnam conflict for CBS News from 1965 to 1970, Laurence has written not only an evocative memoir but also a moving testimony to the courage of the American troops who, like him, came of age in the battlefields of Vietnam.

Tom Mangold and John Penycate *The Tunnels of Cu Chi.* The most thorough, and the most captivating, account yet written of the guerrilla resistance mounted in the tunnels around Cu Chi.

Robert Mason *Chickenhawk.* Few people can be better qualified than Mason to deliver an account of the American War: a helicopter pilot with over a thousand missions under his belt, his blood-and-guts, bird's-eye account of the war is harrowing but compelling.

Harold G. Moore and Joseph Galloway *We Were Soldiers Once… and Young.* This blow-by-blow account of the ferocious battle of the Ia Drang valley, among the earliest encounters of the American War, makes compelling reading as the authors recapture the chaos and fear alongside moments of incredible courage and the sheer determination to survive.

Tim O'Brien *The Things They Carried* and *If I Die in a Combat Zone.* Through a mix of autobiography and fiction O'Brien lays to rest the ghosts of the past in a brutally honest reappraisal of the war, his own actions and the events he witnessed (see also O'Brien's novel *Going After Cacciato*, reviewed on p.525).

John Pilger *Heroes.* Journalist Pilger's systematic dismantling of the myth that America's role was in any way a justifiable "crusade" makes his Vietnam reportage required reading.

William Prochnau *Once Upon a Distant War.* Now that all the journos ever to set foot in Vietnam have published memoirs, Prochnau presents a new twist – the intriguing story of the people (amongst them Neil Sheehan, David Halberstam and Peter Arnett) who wrote the stories of Vietnam.

Neil Sheehan *A Bright Shining Lie.* This monumental and fluently rendered account of the war, hung around the life of the soldier John Paul Vann, won the Pulitzer Prize for Sheehan; one of the true classics of Vietnam-inspired literature.

Dang Thuy Tram *Diaries of a War Physician.* The story behind these diaries written by a young North Vietnamese doctor killed in action is as poignant as the entries themselves. Their release caused a storm in Vietnam in 2005. So far only an online English-language version is available at ⓦwww.vietnam.ttu.edu.

Justin Wintle *The Vietnam War.* Written in reaction to the shelves of long-winded texts available on the subject, Wintle's succinct overview manages to condense this mad war into fewer than two hundred pages.

Tobias Wolff *In Pharaoh's Army.* A former adviser based in My Tho, Wolff's honest, gentle autobiographical tale takes a wry look at life away from the "front line".

Postwar Vietnam

Bui Tin *Following Ho Chi Minh.* An erstwhile colonel in the North Vietnamese Army, Bui Tin effectively defected to the West in 1990, since when he has been an outspoken critic of Vietnam's state apparatus. These memoirs don't flinch from addressing the underside – corruption, prejudice, naivety and insensitivity – of the party.

Adam Fforde and Stefan de Vylder *From Plan to Market.* Highbrow, laudably researched book plotting the route Vietnam has taken from Stalinist central planning to market economy. Fforde and de Vylder hold the fabric of *doi moi* up to the light for examination in the mid-1990s.

David Lamb *Vietnam, Now: A Reporter Returns.* War journalist David Lamb returned to Vietnam for a four-year stint in 1997. While the war is a constant presence, this is primarily a commentary on contemporary Vietnam and its

prospects for the future. Lamb is ultimately optimistic, though his criticisms of the government – notably its failure to reconcile the still-deep divisions between north and south – were sufficient to get the book banned.

Tim Page *Derailed in Uncle Ho's Victory Garden.* The war photographer with a legendary ability to defy death, returns to Vietnam in the 1980s. Buried among the flashbacks and meandering discourse, Page's eye for detail and his delight in the bizarre give a flavour of postwar Vietnam.

Neil Sheehan *Two Cities: Hanoi and Saigon.* Sheehan returned to Vietnam in 1989 to witness firsthand the legacy of the war. Down south, the memories really begin to flow as encounters and travels trigger wartime flashbacks, interspersed with commentary on re-education camps and other deprivations of the dark, pre-*doi moi* years.

🏃 **Robert Templer** *Shadows and Wind*. This hard-hitting book casts a critical eye over Vietnam's decades of reform, from corruption and censorship to the emergence of a consumer-oriented youth culture. Though written in the late 1980s, the informative and balanced analysis still holds true today.

Culture and society

James Goodman *Uniquely Vietnamese*. Asia-based author Goodman has produced an informative catalogue of Vietnamese ingenuity, ranging from conical hats to Cheo theatre, from local festivals to water-puppets and the haunting, one-stringed *dan bau*.

Gerald Cannon Hickey *Shattered World*. Detailed but readable account of ethnic minorities living in Vietnam's central highlands by one of the region's leading ethnologists. A fascinating analysis of the minorities' tragic struggle to survive both war and peace.

Henry Kamm *Dragon Ascending*. Pulitzer Prize-winning correspondent Kamm lets the Vietnamese – art dealers, ex-colonels, academics, doctors, authors – speak for themselves. This they do eloquently, resulting in a convincing portrait of contemporary Vietnam.

Norma J. Livo and Dia Cha *Folk Stories of the Hmong*. The Hmong's fading oral tradition is captured in this unique collection, gleaned from US immigrants, while its scene-setting introduction offers a valuable overview of Hmong culture, accompanied by illustrations of traditional costume and embroidered "storycloths".

William S. Logan *Hanoi: Biography of a City*. A heritage adviser, Logan peels back the layers of history revealed in Hanoi's architecture and streetscapes to provide an academic but engaging account of the city. In doing so, he also examines the challenges facing Hanoi at the start of the new millennium as it strives to preserve its unique heritage while also meeting the needs of its citizens.

Robert S. McKelvey *The Dust of Life*. Moving oral histories by Vietnamese Amerasians abandoned by their American fathers and discriminated against by the Vietnamese.

Mai Pham *Pleasures of the Vietnamese Table*. Saigon-born chef and restaurateur rediscovers her Vietnamese culinary roots and puts together one of the best Vietnamese cookbooks.

Nguyen Van Huy and Laurel Kendall (eds.) *Vietnam: Journeys of Mind, Body and Spirit*. A broad range of contemporary commentators present an evocative snapshot of Vietnamese society and culture at the start of the new millennium.

🏃 **Christina Noble** *Bridge Across My Sorrows*. Life-affirming autobiography by a Dublin woman spurred by a dream to channel her considerable strengths into helping Ho Chi Minh City's *bui doi*, or street children. In her sequel, *Mama Tina*, Noble continues the story of her work in Vietnam, and describes her more recent campaign for children's rights in Mongolia.

Vietnam's Culture: Frequently Asked Questions. Booklets on various cultural themes available in local bookshops. Subjects covered include Cheo theatre, martial arts, traditional medicine and Hanoi's Old Quarter.

Vietnam on film

Gilbert Adair *Hollywood's Vietnam: From the Green Berets to Full Metal Jacket*. Adair's excitable prose guides you past the fire-fights, f-words and R&R hijinks, to a real appreciation of how Hollywood reflected shifting American attitudes to the war.

Jeremy Devine *Vietnam at 24 Frames a Second*. The most wide-ranging analysis of Vietnam movies, covering more than four hundred films.

Linda Dittmar and Gene Michaud (eds.) *From Hanoi to Hollywood*. Collected essays on the way the American War encroached on Hollywood.

Vietnam in the movies

The embroilment of France and the US in Vietnam and its conflicts has spawned hundreds of movies, ranging from fond soft-focused colonial reminiscences to blood-and-guts depictions of the horrors of war. As a means of brushing up on your Indochinese history, their value is questionable: for the most part, they're hardly objective. Yet, through the reflections they cast of the climates in which they were created, these films amplify the West's efforts to come to terms with what went on there, and for this reason they demand attention.

Early depictions

Hollywood was setting movies in Indochina long before the first American troops splashed ashore at Da Nang. As early as 1932, Jean Harlow played a sassy Saigon prostitute to smouldering Clark Gable's rubber-plantation manager, in the steamy pot-boiler, **Red Dust**. At this early stage, however, Vietnam was no more than an exotic backdrop.

Even by the mid-1950s, as the modest beginnings of American involvement elicited from Hollywood its first real moves to acquaint itself with Vietnam, the country was often treated less as a nation with its own discernible identity and unique set of political issues, and more as a generic Asian theatre of war, in which the righteous **battle against Communism** could be played out. In its portrayal of noble and libertarian French forces, aided by American military specialists, confronting the evil of Communism, **China Gate** (1957) is an early example of this trend. Dedicated to the French *colons* who "advanced this backward society to its place as the rice bowl of Asia", its laboured plot, concerning an attempt to destroy a Viet Minh arms cache, is of much less interest than its heavy-handed politics.

Vietnam provided Hollywood with a golden opportunity to project its militaristic fantasies, and a chance to tap into the prejudices brought to the surface by more than a decade of anti-Japanese World War II movies – prejudices that painted American involvement as a reprise of past battles with the inscrutable **Asian hordes**. Rather more depth of thought went into the making of **The Quiet American** (1958), in which Michael Redgrave played the British journalist and cynic, Fowler, while Audie Murphy (America's most decorated soldier in World War II) played Pyle, the eponymous "hero" of Graham Greene's novel. To Greene's chagrin, Pyle was depicted not as a representative of the American government, but of a private aid organization – something which the author felt blunted his anti-American message; nevertheless, the movie retained its source's sense of the futility of attempting to make sense of Vietnam's political quagmire.

Gung ho!

The military mandarins who led America into war failed to get the message, though: with American troops duly deployed in a far-flung corner of the globe by 1965, it was only a matter of time before **John Wayne** produced a patriotic movie to match. This came in the form of the monumentally bad

The Green Berets (1968), in which a paunchy Wayne starred as "Big" Bill Kirby, a loveable colonel leading an adoring team of American soldiers into the central highlands. That Wayne, while on a promotional trip out to Vietnam, handed out cigarette cases inscribed with his signature and the message "Fuck Communism", speaks volumes about the film's subtlety. Kicking off with a stirring marching song ("Fighting soldiers from the sky, Fearless men who jump and die..."), the movie depicts American soldiers in spotless uniforms and perma-grins fighting against no less a threat than total "Communist domination of the world", yet still abiding, as the critic Gilbert Adair has it, "by Queensberry rules". In stark contrast to the squeaky-clean GIs are the barbaric Viet Cong, depicted as child-abusing rapists who whoop and holler like madmen as they overrun a US camp, all to the strains of suitably eerie Oriental music.

Sweeping Vietnam under the carpet

The war in Vietnam was a much dirtier affair than *The Green Berets* made it seem, its politics far less cut and dried. As the struggle turned into tragedy and popular support for it soured, movie moguls sensed that the war had become **taboo**. "Vietnam is awkward," said the journalist Michael Herr, "...and if people don't even want to hear about it, you know they're not going to pay money to sit there in the dark and have it brought up." It was to be a full decade before another major combat movie was released. Instead, film-makers trained their gaze upon returning Vietnam veterans' doomed attempts to ease back into society. The resulting pictures were low in compassion: America's national pride had been collectively compromised by the failure to bring home a victory, and sympathy and forgiveness were at a premium.

A raft of **exploitation movies** was churned out, boasting names such as *Born Losers* (1967), *Angels from Hell* (1968) and *The Ravager* (1970), in which the mental scars of Vietnam provided topical window-dressing to improbable tales of martial arts, motorbikes and mayhem. At best, vets were treated as dysfunctional vigilantes acting beyond the pale of society – most famously in **Taxi Driver** (1976), which has Robert De Niro's disturbed insomniac returnee, Travis Bickle, embarking on a one-man moral crusade to purge the streets of a hellish New York. At worst, they were wacko misfits posing a threat to small-town America. With veterans being portrayed as anything but heroes, it was left to the stars of the **campus riot movies**, and films lionizing **draft-dodgers**, to provide role models.

Coming to terms with the war

Only in 1978 did Hollywood finally pluck up enough courage to confront the war head-on, and so aid the nation's healing process – **movies-as-therapy**. In the years since John Wayne's *Green Berets* had battened down the hatches against Communism, America had first lost sight of justification for the war, and then effectively lost the war itself. Movies no longer sought to make sense of past events, but to highlight their futility; for the generation of young Americans unfortunate enough to live through Vietnam, mere survival was seen as triumph enough. As audiences were exposed to their first dramatized glimpses of the war's unpalatable realities, they were confronted by disaffected troops seeking comfort in prostitution and drug abuse, along with far more shocking examples of soldiers' fraying moral fibre.

Such themes were woven through the first of the four movies of note released in 1978, **The Boys in Company C**, which follows a band of young draftees through their basic training stateside, and then into action. In one particularly telling scene, American lives are lost transporting what turns out to be whisky and cigarettes to the front. A similar futility underpins **Go Tell the Spartans**, in which Burt Lancaster's drug- and alcohol-hazed troops take, and then abandon, a camp – an idea reused nine years later in *Hamburger Hill*.

Coming Home (1978), which cast Jane Fonda as a military career-man's wife who falls in love with a wheelchair-bound veteran (Jon Voight), was significant for its sensitive consideration of the emotional and physical tolls exacted by the war, and initiated the trend for more measured and intelligent vet movies.

Similarly concerned with the ramifications of the war, both home and away, was **The Deer Hunter** (1978), in which the conscription of three friends fractures their Russian Orthodox community in Pennsylvania. The friends' "one-shot" code of honour, espoused on a last pre-Vietnam hunting trip, contrasts wildly with the moral vacuum of the war, whose random brutality is embodied in the movie's central scenes of Russian roulette. The picture's ending, with its melancholy rendition of *God Bless America* by the central characters, is only semi-ironic, and alludes to the country's regenerative process. For all its power, *The Deer Hunter* is marred by overt racist stereotyping of the Vietnamese who, according to John Pilger, are dismissed as "sub-human Oriental barbarians and idiots". The Vietnamese we see are grotesque caricatures interested only in getting their kicks from gambling and death, and there's a strong sense that American youths ought never to have been exposed to such primordial evil as existed across the Pacific.

Francis Ford Coppola's hugely indulgent but wildly magnificent **Apocalypse Now** (1979) rounded off the vanguard of postwar Vietnam combat movies. Described by one critic as "Film as opera...it turns Vietnam into a vast trip, into a War of the Imagination", the picture's Dantean snapshots of the war rob Vietnam of all identity other than as a "heart of darkness". Fuelled by his desire to convey the "horror, the madness, the sensuousness, and the moral dilemma of the Vietnam war", Coppola totally mythologizes the conflict, rendering it not so much futile as insane. The usual elements of needless death, casual atrocity, moral decline and spaced-out soldiers leaning heavily on substance abuse are all here, played out against a raunchy soundtrack. However, with its stylized representation of montagnards as generic savages deifying Westerners, and its depiction of the Viet Cong as butchers who happily lop the arms off children who have had "American" inoculations, *Apocalypse Now* is little more enlightened than *The Deer Hunter*. Coppola subsequently compared the creation of the film itself to a war: "We were in the jungle, there were too many of us. We had access to too much money and too much equipment and little by little we went insane" – a process graphically depicted in **Hearts of Darkness: A Filmmaker's Apocalypse** (1991).

Returning home

The precedent set by *Coming Home* of sympathetic consideration for **returning veterans**' mindsets spurred many movies along similar lines in subsequent years. These focused on the disillusionment and disorientation felt by soldiers coming back, not to heroes' welcomes, but to indifference and even disdain.

One of the first of these movies was **First Blood** (1982), which introduced audiences to Sly Stallone's muscle-bound super-vet, John Rambo. As we witness Rambo's torment in small-town America, the picture is more "shoot 'em up" than cerebral. Yet its climax, in which Rambo's former colonel becomes a surrogate father figure to him, underscores the tender ages of the troops who fought the war. Other movies of the genre – among them Alan Parker's **Birdy** (1984) and Oliver Stone's **Born on the 4th of July** (1989) – reiterated the message of stolen youth and innocence by screening idyllic, elegiac scenes of childhood. Stone has his hero (played by Tom Cruise) swallowing the anti-Communist line, and returning to an indifference symbolized by the squalor of the army hospital in which he recuperates and by the breakdown of his relationship with his mother. In *Birdy*, doctors at a loss as to how to treat a catatonic patient turn to a fellow vet for help – this sense of America's inability to relate to returnees subsequently resurfaces in **Jacknife** (1989).

Rewriting history

Not content with squaring up to the war in Vietnam, Hollywood during the 1980s attempted, bizarrely, to rewrite its script, in a series of **revisionist movies**. Richard Gere had made the armed forces hip again in 1982's weepie **An Officer and a Gentleman**; a year later the first of an intriguing sub-genre of films hit cinemas, in which Americans returned to Vietnam, invariably to rescue MIAs, and "won". Given a righteous cause (and what could be more righteous than rescuing fellow soldiers), and freed from the chains of moral degradation that had shackled him in previous movies, the US soldier could now show his true mettle. In stark contrast to the comic-book superhuman Americans of these pictures, are the brainless **Vietnamese**, who appear only as cannon fodder.

Uncommon Valor (1983), a rather silly piece about an MIA rescue starring Gene Hackman, kicked things off, closely followed by **Missing in Action** (1983), in which Chuck Norris, the poor man's Stallone, karate-kicks his way towards the same resolution with sufficient panache to justify a speedy follow-up. The mother of them all, though, was **Rambo: First Blood, Part II** (1985), in which the hero of *First Blood* gets to settle some old scores. "Do we get to win this time?" asks Rambo, at the top of the movie. As he riots through the Vietnamese countryside in order to extricate a band of American PoWs, he answers his own question by slaying Vietnamese foes at an approximate rate of one every two minutes.

"It don't mean nothing"

The backlash to the patent nonsense of the revisionist films came in the form of a series of shockingly realistic movies which attempted, in the words of the director Oliver Stone, to "peel the onion" and reveal the **real Vietnam**, routine atrocities, indiscipline and all. There are no heroes in these GI's-view movies, only fragile, confused-looking young men in fatigues, emphasizing that this was a war that affected a whole generation – not just its most photogenic individuals.

In **Platoon** (1986), Oliver Stone, himself a foot soldier in Vietnam, created the most realistic cinematographic interpretation of the American involvement yet. Filmed on location in the Philippines, this movie reminded audiences that killing gooks wasn't as straightforward as Rambo made it seem. As well as portraying the depths to which humankind can sink, Stone shows the circumstances under which it was feasible for young American boys to become murderers of civilians. Its oppressive sensory overload powerfully conjures the paranoiac near-hysteria spawned by fear, confusion, loss of motivation and inability to discriminate between friend and foe. Inherent in its shadowy, half-seen portrayal of the enemy is a grudging respect for their expertise in jungle warfare.

If *Platoon* portrays a dirty war, in **Hamburger Hill** (1987), which dramatizes the taking of Ap Bia hill during May 1969's battle for the A Shau valley, it has degenerated into a positive mud bath. As troops slither and slide on the flanks of the hill in the highland mists, they become indistinguishable, and the image of an entire generation stumbling towards the maws of death is strengthened by the fact that the cast includes no big-name actors – the men who fall on the hill are neighbours, sons or brothers, not film stars. American losses are taken in order to secure a useless hill, a potent symbol of the futility of America's involvement in the war; as one soldier says, time after time, in a weary mantra, "it don't mean nothing, not a thing." Stanley Kubrick's **Full Metal Jacket** (1987) picks up *Hamburger Hill*'s theme of the war's theft of American youth in its opening scene, as the camp barber strips conscripts of their hair and, by implication, their individuality. A brutal drill-sergeant completes the alienation process by replacing the soldiers' names with nicknames of his choosing, and then sets about expunging their humanity – on the grounds that it will only hamper them when they experience firsthand the insanity of the war. However, as US troops plod wearily through a smouldering Hué in the movie's final scene, the usual macho marching tunes are replaced with a plaintive echo of youth: "Who's the leader of the club that's made for you and me, M-I-C, K-E-Y, M-O-U-S-E".

A different perspective

French cinema only began to tackle the subject of Vietnam in the 1990s. If in **Dien Bien Phu** (1992) it confronted its own ghosts, on the whole its output has been limited to visually captivating colonial whimsies, to which the Vietnamese setting merely adds an exotic tang. For example, **The Lover** (1992) works not because it does justice to Marguerite Duras' poignant rites-of-passage novella, but because its extended interludes of heaving flesh are cloaked with a veneer of Oriental mystique created by location filming in Ho Chi Minh City and Sa Dec. **Indochine** (1993) starts off in similarly rose-tinted fashion amid the seductively rarefied atmosphere of a French colonial rubber plantation, and from there it veers off to take full advantage of the romantic possibilities of Ha Long Bay.

Even **The Scent of Green Papaya** (1993), filmed entirely in Paris by French-Vietnamese director Tran Anh Hung, is a fondly nostalgic period piece in which the East's languorous elegance and beauty are shown, minus its squalor, and nothing of import is said about the war experience. Tran Anh Hung's second film, *Cyclo* (1996), is an altogether different matter, a grimy tale of murder and prostitution set in a bleak rendition of Ho Chi Minh City – so bleak that the film is banned in Vietnam. Nevertheless, Tran Anh Hung obtained permission to shoot his latest offering, **At the Height of Summer** (aka *The Vertical Ray of the Sun*, 2000), on location in Hanoi. It's a gentler film with the same languid, dream-like quality of *Cyclo*, in which three sisters prepare to commemorate their parents' deaths. As they do, the dark secrets lying beneath the mask of middle-class respectability are gradually revealed.

The censors lightened up a little more in allowing Vietnamese director Dang Nhat Minh to make his ground-breaking **The Season of Guavas** (2001), which deals with the extremely sensitive issue of 1950s Communist land reforms – the film, however, has yet to be released in Vietnam. Other **Vietnamese directors** beginning to attract an international audience include Tran Van Thuy (*Sand Life*, 2000), Bui Thac Chuyen (*Course de Nuit*, 2000) and **Le Hoang**, whose stark portrayal of prostitutes in **Bar Girls** (2003) caused a major stir. That the film was made at all is thanks to a radical change of policy at Vietnam's Ministry of Culture, which in 2002 stopped vetting scripts and allowed private film studios to start making films.

In Hollywood's output, Vietnamese people have mostly been noticeable by their absence, or through the filter of blatant stereotyping. **Heaven and Earth** (1993), the final part of Oliver Stone's Vietnam trilogy, went some way towards rectifying this imbalance. Its depiction of a Vietnamese girl's odyssey (based on the life of Le Ly Hayslip; see p.524 & p.527), from idyllic early childhood to the traumas of life as a wife in San Diego, symbolizes the trials and tribulations of the country as a whole, and acts as a timely reminder that not only Americans suffered during the struggle. Almost a decade later, Randall Wallace brings a certain impartiality to **We Were Soldiers** (2002), his adaptation of Lt Col Hall Moore and Joe Galloway's blow-by-blow account of the catastrophic battle of Ia Drang, with Mel Gibson as the caring commander. Not that it met with Vietnamese approval: the government banned the film, saying it distorted Vietnamese history, and branded actor Don Duong a "traitor" for his portrayal of the NVA leader pitting his wits – and his men – against the Americans.

Only in the late 1990s were American movie-makers allowed to shoot on location in Vietnam again. Filmed in Ho Chi Minh City, **Three Seasons** (1999) was directed by Vietnamese-Californian Tony Bui, and features Harvey Keitel at the head of a predominantly local cast. It provides a lyrical and graceful portrayal of a city trying to come to terms with the return of the West – personified by an ex-marine (Keitel) looking for the Amerasian daughter he abandoned decades before. The film doesn't dwell upon the war – the state censors on set during filming made sure of that. Nevertheless, by focusing upon the disenfranchised prostitutes, cyclo drivers and street children of the city, it ensures that the conflict's ravages are implicit. In 2004, Hans Petter Moland broke new ground with **The Beautiful Country**, in which a Vietnamese Amerasian, Binh, flees hatred and abuse to search for his GI father.

It took until the new millennium for a big-budget Hollywood movie to be filmed almost entirely in Vietnam. Philip Noyce's atmospheric remake of **The Quiet American** (2002) sticks much closer to Graham Greene's novel in its indictment of American involvement in Vietnam. This, coupled with its portrayal of the Vietnamese struggle as a patriotic fight against colonial oppression, earned the film official approval, allowing it to be screened widely within Vietnam – a first for a major Hollywood production.

Language

Language

Vietnamese

Linguists are uncertain as to the exact roots of Vietnamese, though the language betrays Thai, Khmer and Chinese influences. A tonal language, it's extremely tricky for Westerners to master, though the phrases below should help you get by. English superseded Russian as *the* language to learn following the sweeping changes of *doi moi*, and you'll generally find that Vietnamese isn't called for. Then again, nothing will endear you to locals as much as showing conversational willingness.

Vietnamese was set down using Chinese characters until the fourteenth century, when an indigenous **script** called *chu nom* was created. This, in turn, was dropped in favour of *quoc ngu*, a Romanized script developed by a French missionary in the seventeenth century, and it's this form that's universally used today – though you'll still occasionally spot lavish *chu nom* characters daubed on the walls of more venerable pagodas and temples.

Three main **dialects** – northern, central and southern – are used in Vietnam today, and although for the most part they are pretty similar, pronunciation can be so wildly variant that some locals have trouble understanding each other; in the words and phrases listed below, we indicate important differences between variants used in the north and south. Bear in mind, too, that Vietnam's minority peoples have their own languages, and may look blankly at you as you gamely try out your Vietnamese on them.

If you want more scope than the expressions below allow, invest in a **phrasebook**. *Vietnamese: A Rough Guide Phrasebook* is the last word in user-friendly phrasebooks, combining everyday phrases and expressions with a dictionary section and menu reader, all with phonetic transliterations. If you're determined to master the basics of spoken Vietnamese, there are a number of **self-teaching packs** on the market, such as *Language '30* produced by Audio-Forum (Ⓦwww.microworld.ndirect.co.uk).

Pronunciation

The Vietnamese language is a **tonal** one, that is, one in which a word's meaning is determined by the pitch at which you deliver it. Six tones are used – the mid-level tone (syllables with no marker), the low falling tone (syllables marked à), the low rising tone (syllables marked ả), the high broken tone (syllables marked ã), the high rising tone (syllables marked á) and the low broken tone (syllables marked ạ) – though you'll probably remain in the dark until you ask a Vietnamese person to give you spoken examples of each of them. Depending upon its tone, the word *ba*, for instance, can mean three, grandmother, poisoned food, waste, aunt or any – leaving ample scope for misunderstandings and diplomatic faux pas.

With tones accomplished, or at least comprehended, there are the many vowel and consonant sounds to take on board. These we've listed below, along with phonetic renderings of how they should be pronounced.

Vowels

a	'a' as in father	i	'i' as in -ing
ă	'u' as in hut (slight 'u' as in unstressed English 'a')	o	'o' as in hot
		ô	'aw' as in awe
â	'uh' sound as above only longer	ơ	'ur' as in fur
		u	'oo' as in boo
e	'e' as in bed	ư	'oo' closest to French 'u'
ê	'ay' as in pay	y	'i' as in -ing

Vowel combinations

ai	'ai' as in Thai	oa	'wa'
ao	'ao' as in Mao	oe	'weh'
au	'a-oo'	ôi	'oy'
âu	'oh' as in oh!	ơi	'uh-i'
ay	'ay' as in hay	ua	'waw'
ây	'ay-i' (as in 'ay' above but longer)	uê	'weh'
		uô	'waw'
eo	'eh-ao'	uy	'wee'
êu	'ay-oo'	ưa	'oo-a'
iu	'ew' as in few	ưu	'er-oo'
iêu	'i-yoh'	ươi	'oo-uh-i'

Consonants

c	'g'	ng/ngh	'ng' as in sing
ch	'j' as in jar	nh	'n-y' as in canyon
d	'y' as in young	ph	'f'
đ	'd' as in day	q	'g' as in goat
g	'g' as in goat	t	'd' as in day
gh	'g' as in goat	th	't'
gi	'y' as in young	tr	'j' as in jar
k	'g' as in goat	x	's'
kh	'k' as in keep		

Useful words and phrases

How you greet and then speak to somebody in Vietnam depends very much on their sex, and on their age and social standing, relative to your own. As a general rule of thumb, if you address a man as *ông*, and a woman as *bà*, you can be sure you aren't being impolite. If you find yourself in conversation, either formally or informally, with someone of your approximate age, you can use *anh* (for a man) and *chi* (for a woman). You can also use the same formula to address someone when you know their name. Vietnamese names are traditionally written with the family name first (Nguyen, Tran, Le and Pham are among the most common) and the given name last and between them a qualifying name, which often indicates a person's sex or the particular branch of the family to which they belong. People are usually referred to by their given name so, for example, you would address an older man called Nguyen Van Hai as Ong Hai.

Greetings and small talk

Hello	chào ông/bà	What's your name?	ông/bà tên gì?
How are you?	ông/bà có khỏe không?	My name is...	tên tôi là...
Fine, thanks	tôi khỏe cám ơn	Where do you come from?	ông/bà ơ đâu đến?
Pleased to meet you	hân hạnh gập ông/bà	I come from...	tôi ơ...
Goodbye	chào, tạm biệt	...England	...nươ'c Anh
Good night	chúc ngủ ngon	...America	...nươ'c Mỹ
Excuse me (to say sorry)	xin lỗi	...Australia	...nươ'c Úc
		What do you do?	ông/bà làm gì?
Excuse me (to get past)	xin ông/bà thứ' lỗi	Do you speak English?	ông/bà biết nói tiếng Anh không?
Please	làm ơn	I don't understand	tôi không hiểu
Thank you	cám ơn ông/bà	Could you repeat that?	xin ông/bà lập lại?
Thank you very much	cám ơn nhiều	Yes	vâng (north); dạ (south)
Don't mention it	không có chi	No	không

Emergencies

Can you help me?	ông/bà có thể giúp tôi không?	Please call a doctor	làm ơn gợi bác sĩ
There's been an accident	có một vụ tai nạn	hospital	bệnh viện
		police station	đồn cong an

Getting around

Where is the...?	ở đâu...?	How long does it take?	phải tốn bao lâu?
How many kilometres is it to...?	bao nhiêu cây số thì đến...?	ticket	vé
How do I get to...?	tôi phải đi...bằng cách nào?	aeroplane	máy bay
		airport	sân bay
We'd like to go to...	chúng tôi muốn đi...	boat	tàu bè
To the airport, please	làm ơn đưa tôi đi sân bay	bus	xe buýt
		bus station	bến xe buýt
Can you take me to the...?	ông/bà có thế đưa tôi đi...?	train station	bến xe lửa
		taxi	tắc xi
Where do we catch the bus to...?	ở đâu đón xe đi...?	car	xe hơi
		filling station	trạm xăng
When does the bus for Hoi An leave?	khi nào xe Hội An chạy?	bicycle	xe đạp
		baggage	hành lý
Can I book a seat?	tôi có thể đặt ghế trươ'c không?	bank	nhà băng
		post office	sở bưu điện

passport	hộ chiếu	left/right	bên trái/bên phải
hotel	khách sạn	north	phía bắc
restaurant	nhà hàng	south	phía nam
Please stop here	xin dừng lại đây	east	phía đông
over there	bên kia	west	phía tây
here	đây		

Accommodation and shopping

Do you have any rooms?	ông/bà có phòng không?	room with a balcony	một phòng có ban công
How much is it per night?	mỗi đêm bao nhiêu?	room with a private bathroom	một phòng tắm riêng
How much is it?	bao nhiêu tiền?	cheap/expensive	rẻ/đắt
How much does it cost?	cái này giá bao nhiêu?	single room	phòng một người
		double room	phòng hai người
Can I have a look?	xem có được không?	single bed	giường một người
Do you have...?	ông/bà có không...?	double bed	giường đôi
I want a...	tôi muốn một...	air–conditioner	máy lạnh
I'd like...	cho tôi xin một...	fan (electric)	quạt máy
How much is this?	cái này bao nhiêu?	mosquito net	cái màn
That's too expensive	đắt quá	toilet paper	giấy vệ sinh
Do you have anything cheaper?	ông/bà còn gì rẻ hơn không?	telephone	điện thoại
		laundry	quần ào dơ
Could I have the bill please?	làm ơn tính tiền?	blanket	chăn (north); mền (south)
		open/closed	mở cửa/đóng cửa

Time

What's the time?	mấy giờ rồi?	tomorrow	mai
noon	buổi trưa	yesterday	hôm qua
midnight	nửa đêm	now	bây giờ
minute	phút	next week	tuần tó'i
hour	giờ	last week	tuần vừa qua
day	ngày	morning	buổi sáng
week	tuần	afternoon	buổi chiều
month	tháng	evening	buổi tời
year	năm	night	ban đêm
today	hôm nay		

Numbers

Note that for numbers ending in 5, from 15 onwards, *nhăm* is used in northern Vietnam and *lăm* in the south, rather than the written form of *năm*. Also, bear in mind that an alternative for numbers that are multiples of ten is *chục* – so, for example ten would be *một chục*, twenty would be *hai chục*, etc.

zero	không	two	hai
one	một	three	ba

four	bốn	seventeen	mười bảy
five	năm	eighteen	mười tám
six	sáu	nineteen	mười chín
seven	bảy	twenty	hai mười
eight	tám	twenty–one	hai mười một
nine	chín	twenty–two	hai mười hai
ten	mười	thirty	ba mười
eleven	mười một	forty	bốn mười
twelve	mười hai	fifty	năm mười
thirteen	mười ba	one hundred	một trăm
fourteen	mười bốn	two hundred	hai trăm
fifteen	mười lăm /nhăm	one thousand	một ngàn
sixteen	mười sáu	ten thousand	mười ngàn

Eating and drinking

Useful phrases

bat (north); chen (south)	bowl
bao nhieu tien?	how much is it?
can chen (north); can ly (south)	cheers!
chuc suc khoe	to your good health
cop	cup
da	ice
dung bo da cam on	no ice, thanks
dua	chopsticks
it duong	a little sugar
lanh	cold
nguoi an chay	vegetarian
toi khong an thit	I don't eat meat or fish
nong	hot
rat ngon	delicious

Rice and noodles

bun	round rice noodles
bun bo	beef with bun noodles
bun bo gio heo	chicken, beef and pork with bun noodles
bun ga	chicken with bun noodles
com	cooked rice
com rang (north); com chien (south)	fried rice
com trang	steamed or boiled rice
chao or xhao	rice porridge
mi xao	fried noodles
pho	flat rice noodles, usually in soup
pho bo tai	noodle soup with rare beef
pho bo chin	with medium-done beef
pho co trung	with eggs

Fish, meat and vegetables

ca	fish
ca ran (north); ca chien (south)	fried fish
cua	crab
luon	eel
muc	squid
tom	shrimp or prawn
tom hum	lobster
thit	meat
bit tet	beefsteak
bo	beef
ga	chicken
lon (north); heo (south)	pork
vit	duck
rau co or rau cac loai	vegetables
cai bap	cabbage
ca chua	tomato
ca tim	aubergine
dau	beans
gia	bean sprouts

543

khoai tay	potato
khoai lang	sweet potato
mang	bamboo shoots
ngo (north); bap (south)	sweetcorn
rau xao cac loai	stir-fried vegetables
sa lat	salad
sa lat ca chua	tomato salad
sa lat rau xanh cac loai	green salad

Desserts and fruit

banh ngot	cakes and pastries
duong	sugar
kem	ice cream or cream
mat ong	honey
sua chua	yoghurt
trai cay	fruit
buoi	pomelo/grapefruit
cam	orange
chanh	lemon/lime
chom chom	rambutan
chuoi	banana
dau tay	strawberry
dua	coconut
dua (north); thom (south)	pineapple
dua hau	watermelon
du du	papaya
khe	star fruit
mang cau (north); qua na (south)	custard apple
mang cut	mangosteen
mit	jackfruit
nhan	longan
qua bo	avocado
sau rieng	durian
xoai	mango
tao tay	apple
thang long	dragon fruit
vai	lychee

Miscellaneous

banh	cake (sweet or savoury)
banh mi	bread

bo	butter
pho mat, fo mat or fromage	cheese
lac (north); dau phong (south)	peanuts (groundnuts)
muoi	salt
mut	jam
ot	chilli
tao pho (north); dau hu (south)	tofu
tieu	pepper
trung	egg
trung om let or op lep	omelette
trung ran or trung op la	fried eggs

Drinks

bia	beer
ca phé	coffee
ca phé da	iced coffee
ca phé den	black coffee
ca phé den khong duong	black coffee without sugar
ca phé nong	hot coffee
ca phé sua	coffee with milk
ca phé sua nong	hot milk coffee
tra	tea
tra voi chanh	tea with lemon
tra sua	tea with milk
khong da	no ice
nuoc	water
nuoc khoang	mineral water
nuoc so da	soda water
nuoc cam	orange juice
nuoc chanh	lime juice
nuoc dua	coconut milk
ruou ran	snake wine
ruou trang or choum	rice alcohol
so da cam	orange soda
so da chanh	lime soda
sua	milk
sua tuoi	fresh milk

Glossaries

Words and abbreviations

Agent Orange Defoliant herbicide used by the Americans during the American War to deprive guerrillas of forest cover.

Annam ("Pacified South") A term coined by the Chinese to refer to their protectorate in northern Vietnam before 939 AD; the French later applied the name to the middle reaches of their protectorate, from the southern central highlands to the edge of the Red River Delta.

ao dai Traditional Vietnamese dress for women, comprising baggy pants and a long, slit tunic.

arhat Ascetic Buddhist saint, whose statues are found in northern pagodas.

ARVN (Army of the Republic of Vietnam) The army of South Vietnam.

ben xe Bus station.

bo doi Northern soldiers.

boat people Ethnic Chinese who fled Vietnam by boat in the late 1970s to escape persecution at the hands of the Communists and, later, Vietnamese escaping poverty (see p.477).

bodhisattva An intermediary who has chosen to forgo Buddhist nirvana to work for the salvation of all humanity.

body count Term coined by the Americans to measure the success of a military operation, determined by the number of dead bodies after a battle.

bonze Buddhist monk.

buu dien Post office.

Cao Dai Indigenous religion, essentially a hybrid of Buddhism, Taoism and Confucianism, but hinged around an attempt at unification of all earthly codes of belief (see p.489).

Champa Indianized Hindu empire that held sway in much of the southern half of Vietnam until the late seventeenth century (see box, p.238).

Charlie Nickname for the VC ("Vietnamese Communists") used by American soldiers.

Cheo Form of classical theatre (see p.512).

cho Market.

chu nom Classic Vietnamese script, based upon Chinese.

chua Pagoda (Buddhist place of worship).

Cochinchina A Portuguese term adopted by the French colonial government for their southern administrative region.

colon French colonial expatriate.

com pho Literally, "rice noodles", often used to indicate restaurant serving basic dishes.

cyclo Three-wheeled bicycle with a carriage on the front.

dao Island.

den Temple (Taoist or other non-Buddhist place of worship).

dinh Communal meeting hall.

DMZ ("dee-em-zee") The Demilitarized Zone along the Seventeenth Parallel, marking the border between North and South Vietnam from 1954 to 1975.

doi moi Vietnam's economic restructuring.

DRV (Democratic Republic of Vietnam) The North Vietnamese state established by Ho Chi Minh following the August Revolution in 1945.

duong Avenue.

FULRO (United Front for the Liberation of Oppressed Races) An opposition movement formed by the ethnic minorities of the central highlands, demanding greater autonomy.

Funan Indianized empire, a forerunner of the great Khmer empires.

GI (General Infantryman) Soldier in the US Army.

gopuram Bank of sculpted deities over the entrance to a Hindu temple.

"grunt" American infantryman.

gui xe Bicycle compound.

hang Cave.

ho Lake.

Ho Chi Minh Trail Trail used first by the Viet Minh and later by the North Vietnamese Army to transport supplies to the South, via Laos and Cambodia.

Hoa Ethnic Chinese people living in Vietnam.

Honda om Literally "Honda embrace" – a motorbike taxi.

"Huey" Nickname given to American helicopter, the HU-1.

Indochina The region of Asia comprising Vietnam, Laos and Cambodia.

kalan Sanctuary in a Cham tower.

khach san Hotel.

Khmer Ethnic Cambodian.

kylin Mythical, dew-drinking animal (often translated as unicorn); a harbinger of peace.

Lien Xo Translating as "Soviet Union", this is also used as a term of abuse – and may very occasionally be hurled at foreigners in more remote regions.

lingam A phallic statue representing Shiva, often seen in Cham towers.

mandapa Meditation hall in Cham temple complex.

MIAs (Missing in Action) Soldiers who fought – on both sides – in the American War, but have still not been accounted for.

montagnards French term for Vietnam's ethnic minority peoples.

mua roi nuoc Water-puppet show.

mui Cape.

mukha lingam Lingam fashioned into the likeness of a deity.

napalm Jellied fuel dropped by US forces during the American War, and capable of causing terrible burns.

ngo Alley.

NGO Non-governmental organization.

nha hang Restaurant.

nha khach Hotel or guesthouse.

nha nghi Guesthouse.

nha tro Basic dormitory accommodation, usually found near stations.

NLF (National Liberation Front) Popular movement formed in South Vietnam in 1960 by opponents of the American-backed Southern regime.

nui Mountain.

nuoc mam Fish sauce.

NVA (North Vietnamese Army) The army of the Democratic Republic of Vietnam.

Oc Eo Ancient seaport of the Funan empire, east of modern-day Rach Gia in the Mekong Delta.

ODP (Orderly Departure Programme) A United Nations-backed scheme enabling legal emigration of Vietnamese refugees.

paddy Unharvested rice.

PoW Prisoner of war.

quan District.

R&R ("Rest and Recreation") Term coined during the American War to describe a soldier's temporary leave of duty.

roi nuoc *see* mua roi nuoc.

rong Communal house of ethnic minorities in the central highlands.

RVN (Republic of Vietnam) The official name for South Vietnam from 1954 to 1976.

sampan Small, flat-bottomed boat.

song River.

SRVN (Socialist Republic of Vietnam) The post-liberation amalgamation of the DRV and RVN, and the official name of modern Vietnam.

tai chi Chinese martial art, commonly performed as early-morning exercise.

Tet Vietnam's lunar New Year.

thung chai Coracle.

Tonkin One of the three administrative regions of French colonial Vietnam, from Ninh Binh northwards.

tunnel rats American soldiers trained for warfare in tunnels such as those at Cu Chi.

VC (Viet Cong) Literally "Vietnamese Communists"; term used by the Americans to describe the guerrilla forces of the NLF.

Viet Kieu Overseas Vietnamese.

Viet Minh Shortened version of **Viet Nam Doc Lap Dong Minh**, the League for the Independence of Vietnam, established by Ho Chi Minh in 1941.

VNQDD Abbreviation for **Viet Nam Quoc Dan Dang**, the Vietnam Nationalist Party, founded in 1927.

xe lam Motorized three-wheeler buggy carrying numerous passengers.

xe om Northern equivalent of the Honda om, a motorbike taxi.

Street names

In travelling around Vietnam, it doesn't take long before you can recite the **street names**, a litany of the principal characters in Vietnamese history. Just a few from this cast list of famous revolutionaries, Party leaders, legendary kings and peasant heroes are given below. Other favoured names commemorate the glorious victories of Bach Dang and Dien Bien Phu, and the momentous date when Saigon was "liberated" in 1975: 30 Thang 4 (30 April).

Hai Ba Trung The two Trung sisters led a popular uprising against the Chinese occupying army in 40 AD and established a short-lived kingdom (see p.520).

Hoang Hoa Tham (or De Tham) Famous pirate with a Robin Hood reputation and anti-French tendencies, assassinated in 1913.

Hung Vuong The semi-mythological Hung kings ruled an embryonic kingdom, Van Lang, around 2000 BC.

Le Duan General Secretary of the Communist Party, 1960–86.

Le Hong Phong Leading Communist and patriot who died from torture in Poulo Condore prison (Con Son Island) in 1942.

Le Loi One of the most revered Vietnamese heroes, Le Loi defeated the Ming Chinese in 1427, and then ruled as King Le Thai To.

Ngo Quyen First ruler of an independent Vietnam following his defeat of the Chinese armies in 938 AD (see p.406).

Nguyen Hué Middle member of the three Nguyen brothers who led the Tay Son rebellion in the 1770s (see p.460), and then ruled briefly as Emperor Quang Trung.

Nguyen Thai Hoc Founding member of the Vietnam Nationalist Party (VNQDD), executed in 1930 following the disastrous Yen Bai uprising.

Nguyen Thi Minh Khai Prominent anti-colonialist revolutionary of the 1930s, the wife of Le Hong Phong (see above) and sister-in-law of General Giap.

Nguyen Trai Brilliant strategist who helped mastermind Le Loi's victories over the Chinese. His ideas on the popular struggle ("it is better to conquer hearts than citadels") were used to good effect by Northern leaders in the French and American wars.

Pham Ngu Lao General in the army of Tran Hung Dao (see below).

Phan Boi Chau Influential leader of the anti-colonial movement in the early twentieth century (see p.465).

Tran Hung Dao Thirteenth-century general who beat the Mongols twice in the space of four years, and reached the ripe old age of 87.

Tran Phu Founding member and first General Secretary of the Indochinese Communist Party (see p.466), he died in prison in 1931 at the age of 27.

Travel
store

Vietnam
The hidden ch...

Your Family in Vietnam

QueenTravel ®

Queen Travel - Smiling Vietnam

TOUR & HOTEL

www.azqueentravel.com   or   www.queenhotel4vip.com
Email: queenaz@fpt.vn   Tel:(844) 3 8260860   Fax: 3 8260300
unique address: 65 Hang Bac street - Hanoi - Vietnam

www.buffalotours.com

Buffalo tours

Inspirational Travel
info@buffalotours.com

Vietnam - Cambodia - Laos
Private Tours and Community-based
Volunteer Group Travel

Hanoi: 94 Ma May St., Hoan Kiem Dist.
Tel: (84-4) 3828 0702 - Fax: (84-4) 3826 9370
HCMC: Satra House, Suite 601, Dist.1
Tel: (84-8) 3827 9170 - Fax: (84-8) 3827 9168

Hop over to the REAL Kangaroo Café

Only at 18 Bao Khanh Str., Ha Noi.
(just around the corner from the ANZ bank)

Since 1994 Griswalds Vietnamese Vacations & our
Kangaroo Café have been the leaders in affordable,
GENUINE small group tours. We're listed in all the
leading guide books & have received great reviews in
The New York Times, The Sydney Morning Herald &
The Boston Globe to name a few.

Unfortunately we're always being copied by any number
of unscrupulous & arrogant dills. Be sure to HOP over
to the REAL Kangaroo Café & you can enjoy our famous
food & drinks whilst deciding on where in Viet nam you
want to go.

18 Bao Khanh Str., Ha Noi
Tel: + 844 828 9931 or you can visit our
website at: www.kangaroocafe.com

ELTA ADVENTURE

Specialists in boat travel in the Mekong Delta

★ Overnight on a boat
★ Home-stay with local family
★ Floating hotel
★ Biking trips
★ Boat trip to Cu Chi tunnels (half day)
★ Cruising through the Mekong Delta
★ Cruising to Phnom Penh on the Mekong River

Add: 267 De Tham St., Dist.1, Ho Chi Minh City, Viet Nam
Tel: 84.8.39 20 2112 - Fax: 84.8.39 20 2107
Website: www.deltaadventuretours.com
Email: sgnkimcafe@deltaadventuretours.com

www.roughguides.com

Small print and
Index

A Rough Guide to Rough Guides

Published in 1982, the first Rough Guide – to Greece – was a student scheme that became a publishing phenomenon. Mark Ellingham, a recent graduate in English from Bristol University, had been travelling in Greece the previous summer and couldn't find the right guidebook. With a small group of friends he wrote his own guide, combining a highly contemporary, journalistic style with a thoroughly practical approach to travellers' needs.

The immediate success of the book spawned a series that rapidly covered dozens of destinations. And, in addition to impecunious backpackers, Rough Guides soon acquired a much broader and older readership that relished the guides' wit and inquisitiveness as much as their enthusiastic, critical approach and value-for-money ethos.

These days, Rough Guides include recommendations from shoestring to luxury and cover more than 200 destinations around the globe, including almost every country in the Americas and Europe, more than half of Africa and most of Asia and Australasia. Our ever-growing team of authors and photographers is spread all over the world, particularly in Europe, the US and Australia.

In the early 1990s, Rough Guides branched out of travel, with the publication of Rough Guides to World Music, Classical Music and the Internet. All three have become benchmark titles in their fields, spearheading the publication of a wide range of books under the Rough Guide name.

Including the travel series, Rough Guides now number more than 350 titles, covering: phrasebooks, waterproof maps, music guides from Opera to Heavy Metal, reference works as diverse as Conspiracy Theories and Shakespeare, and popular culture books from iPods to Poker. Rough Guides also produce a series of more than 120 World Music CDs in partnership with World Music Network.

Visit www.roughguides.com to see our latest publications.

Rough Guide travel images are available for commercial licensing at www.roughguidespictures.com

Rough Guide credits

Text editor: Amanda Tomlin
Layout: Ankur Guha
Cartography: Rajesh Mishra
Picture editor: Emily Taylor
Production: Rebecca Short
Proofreader: Anita Sach
Cover design: Chloë Roberts
Photographer: Tim Draper
Editorial: Ruth Blackmore, Andy Turner, Keith Drew, Edward Aves, Alice Park, Lucy White, Jo Kirby, James Smart, Natasha Foges, Róisín Cameron, Emma Traynor, Emma Gibbs, Kathryn Lane, Christina Valhouli, Monica Woods, Mani Ramaswamy, Harry Wilson, Lucy Cowie, Helen Ochyra, Amanda Howard, Lara Kavanagh, Alison Roberts, Joe Staines, Peter Buckley, Matthew Milton, Tracy Hopkins, Ruth Tidball; **Delhi** Madhavi Singh, Karen D'Souza, Lubna Shaheen
Design & Pictures: **London** Scott Stickland, Dan May, Diana Jarvis, Mark Thomas, Chloë Roberts, Nicole Newman, Sarah Cummins; **Delhi** Umesh Aggarwal, Ajay Verma, Jessica Subramanian, Pradeep Thapliyal, Sachin Tanwar, Anita Singh, Nikhil Agarwal, Sachin Gupta
Production: Vicky Baldwin

Cartography: **London** Maxine Repath, Ed Wright, Katie Lloyd-Jones; **Delhi** Rajesh Chhibber, Ashutosh Bharti, Animesh Pathak, Jasbir Sandhu, Karobi Gogoi, Alakananda Bhattacharya, Swati Handoo, Deshpal Dabas
Online: **London** George Atwell, Faye Hellon, Jeanette Angell, Fergus Day, Justine Bright, Clare Bryson, Aine Fearon, Adrian Low, Ezgi Celebi, Amber Bloomfield; **Delhi** Amit Verma, Rahul Kumar, Narender Kumar, Ravi Yadav, Debojit Borah, Rakesh Kumar, Ganesh Sharma, Shisir Basumatari
Marketing & Publicity: **London** Liz Statham, Niki Hanmer, Louise Maher, Jess Carter, Vanessa Godden, Vivienne Watton, Anna Paynton, Rachel Sprackett, Libby Jellie, Laura Vipond, Vanessa McDonald; **New York** Katy Ball, Judi Powers, Nancy Lambert; **Delhi** Ragini Govind
Manager India: Punita Singh
Reference Director: Andrew Lockett
Operations Manager: Helen Phillips
PA to Publishing Director: Nicola Henderson
Publishing Director: Martin Dunford
Commercial Manager: Gino Magnotta
Managing Director: John Duhigg

Publishing information

This sixth edition published October 2009 by
Rough Guides Ltd,
80 Strand, London WC2R 0RL
14 Local Shopping Centre, Panchsheel Park, New Delhi 110017, India
Distributed by the Penguin Group
Penguin Books Ltd,
80 Strand, London WC2R 0RL
Penguin Group (USA)
375 Hudson Street, NY 10014, USA
Penguin Group (Australia)
250 Camberwell Road, Camberwell, Victoria 3124, Australia
Penguin Group (Canada)
195 Harry Walker Parkway N, Newmarket, ON, L3Y 7B3 Canada
Penguin Group (NZ)
67 Apollo Drive, Mairangi Bay, Auckland 1310, New Zealand
Cover concept by Peter Dyer.

Typeset in Bembo and Helvetica to an original design by Henry Iles.
Printed in Singapore
© Jan Dodd, Ron Emmons, Mark Lewis and Martin Zatko, 2009

No part of this book may be reproduced in any form without permission from the publisher except for the quotation of brief passages in reviews.

568pp includes index
A catalogue record for this book is available from the British Library
ISBN: 978-1-84836-084-6

The publishers and authors have done their best to ensure the accuracy and currency of all the information in **The Rough Guide to Vietnam**, however, they can accept no responsibility for any loss, injury, or inconvenience sustained by any traveller as a result of information or advice contained in the guide.

1 3 5 7 9 8 6 4 2

Help us update

We've gone to a lot of effort to ensure that the sixth edition of **The Rough Guide to Vietnam** is accurate and up-to-date. However, things change – places get "discovered", opening hours are notoriously fickle, restaurants and rooms raise prices or lower standards. If you feel we've got it wrong or left something out, we'd like to know, and if you can remember the address, the price, the hours, the phone number, so much the better.

Please send your comments with the subject line "**Rough Guide Vietnam Update**" to ⓔmail @roughguides.com. We'll credit all contributions and send a copy of the next edition (or any other Rough Guide if you prefer) for the very best emails.
Have your questions answered and tell others about your trip at
ⓦ community.roughguides.com

Acknowledgements

Ron Emmons would like to thank: Dang Duc Thuc in Hanoi and Le Van Sinh in Saigon for helping me dodge the floods during this update, and for sharing their considerable knowledge of this rapidly changing country. Others who gave generously of their time and shared valuable local knowledge are: in Ho Chi Minh City, Madam Cuc and Tim Russell; throughout the Mekong Delta, Do Thanh Phuong and Ngo Thanh Phuong; in Ca Mau, Thuy Tran; in Long Xuyen, Huong Dan Vien; on Phu Quoc, Mike Carden; in Da Lat, Michael Sterling and Tran Xuan Hien; in Plei Ku, Siu Cham; in Kon Tum, Nguyen Do Huynh;

in Vung Tau, Vo Thu Thao; in Mui Ne, Dang Mieu; in Nha Trang, Kieu Nhu Quynh; in Quy Nhon, Barbara Dawson.

Martin Zatko would like to thank: the Backpacker staff for help in Hanoi; Miho for help by the lake; Hanh Ly Truong for the salsa lesson and innumerable coffees; Duc in Hoi An for supplying dragon fruits in a time of need; Laura Hong for keeping me going; Za in Sa Pa; and Slo and Erik for their kindness on Cat Ba. Also thanks to Justin Zucker; Katie Strocel; Katie Hupton; Carl Ellis; Claudia O'Rourke; Isabel Brow; Anna Beatnik Livsey and Micael Guilbert.

Readers' letters

SMALL PRINT

Thanks to all the readers who have taken the time to write in with comments and suggestions (and apologies if we've inadvertently omitted or misspelt anyone's name):

Patrick Bach; Rohan Barker; Frank Bidmann; Sarah Carmichael; Tim Claes; Victoria Clayton; Jeannette Croft; David Crosby; Gary Doherty; John and Pam Doniger; Gisela Duong; Tracey Egan; Diana Engesser; Paul Ferguson; Yvonne Fleming; Svenja Frech; Dave Gartside; Sylvie and Paul Gerrard; Peter Goldie; Chris Goward; Sue Hargadon; Thomas Hirsch; Tanja Hugger; Rhett Hutchence; Geoff Hynam; Helga Immerz; John Kaplan; Jean Kauss; Barry Kidney; Wilhelm Koenigsbuescher; Claudia Kuenstler; Markus Lachmann; Verne Lee;

Sonya Lengweiler; Patricia Liscio; Cormac Little; Nancy Marion; Priska Moosbauer; Kaisa Neff; Paul North; Stefan Nost; John Pam; Andrea Peace; Ros Perry; Yan Plihal; Oliver Pogatsnik; Steve Price-Thomas; Pauline and John Prime; Neville Punch; Kathrin Reinhardt; Sebastian Reischl; Sarah Riches; Karl Wolfgang Rumpf; Mark Sachs; Oliver Schafheitle; Norbert Schell; Jon and Leona Scurr; Jeroen Sol; Diane Tordoff; Michael Torok; Jackie Townsend; Sarah Valencik; Martin Winter; Lesley Woodman.

Photo credits

All photos © Rough Guides except the following:

Introduction
Detail of Quan Am Dragon © Ron Emmons
Bai Truong beach, Phu Quoc Island © Guiziou
  Franck/Photolibrary

Things Not To Miss
04 Musician playing the Vietnamese *dan bau*
  © John Kershaw/Alamy
07 Cu Chi tunnels © Ron Emmons
14 Performers, Tet Festival © David South/Alamy
21 Hon Chong Peninsula © Ron Emmons

Black and whites
p.227 View from The Giant Jesus © Ron Emmons
p.275 Crowd on riverbank, Hoi An © Danielle
  Schneider/PNS/Tips
p.396 Woman squatting at Cat Ba harbour, Ha
  Long Bay © dbimages/Alamy

SMALL PRINT

Selected images from our guidebooks are available for licensing from:

ROUGHGUIDESPICTURES.COM

Index

Map entries are in colour.

INDEX

Map symbols

maps are listed in the full index using coloured text

-----	International boundary		⛩	Pagoda
—— ··	Provincial boundary		☪	Mosque
----	Chapter division boundary		⛳	Golf course
=====	Main road		🗼	Lighthouse
———	Minor road		♥	Museum
- - - -	Path		⚘	Gardens
▬▬▬	Railway		⚓	Swimming area
— —	Ferry route		⛵	Snorkelling
———	River		✈	Airport
———	City wall/battlement		★	Transport stop
⚬	Point of interest		⊠	Post office
⚑	Border crossing		ⓘ	Tourist office
⋀⋀	Mountain range		@	Internet access
▲	Mountain peak		⊞	Hospital
⩯	Pass		◉	Accommodation
⭭	Viewpoint		▪	Restaurant
◖	Cave			Building
𝄞	Waterfall		☐	Market
⛩	Hindu temple		⊟	Church
⬙	Cao Dai temple		▦	Park
⊙	Statue		🌴 ▦	Beach

www.roughguides.com

nformation on over 25,000 destinations around the world

- **Read** Rough Guides' trusted travel info
- **Access** exclusive articles from Rough Guides authors
- **Update** yourself on new books, maps, CDs and other products
- **Enter** our competitions and win travel prizes
- **Share** ideas, journals, photos & travel advice with other users
- **Earn** points every time you contribute to the Rough Guide
  community and get rewards

ROUGH GUIDES

Complete Listing

UK & Ireland
Britain
Devon & Cornwall
Dublin **D**
Edinburgh **D**
England
Ireland
The Lake District
London
London **D**
London Mini Guide
Scotland
Scottish Highlands
& Islands
Wales

Europe
Algarve **D**
Amsterdam
Amsterdam **D**
Andalucía
Athens **D**
Austria
Baltic States
Barcelona
Barcelona **D**
Belgium &
Luxembourg
Berlin
Brittany & Normandy
Bruges **D**
Brussels
Budapest
Bulgaria
Copenhagen
Corsica
Crete
Croatia
Cyprus
Czech & Slovak
Republics
Denmark
Dodecanese & East
Aegean Islands
Dordogne & The Lot
Europe on a Budget
Florence & Siena
Florence **D**
France
Germany
Gran Canaria **D**
Greece
Greek Islands
Hungary

Ibiza & Formentera **D**
Iceland
Ionian Islands
Italy
The Italian Lakes
Languedoc &
Roussillon
Lanzarote &
Fuerteventura **D**
Lisbon **D**
The Loire Valley
Madeira **D**
Madrid **D**
Mallorca **D**
Mallorca & Menorca
Malta & Gozo **D**
Moscow
The Netherlands
Norway
Paris
Paris **D**
Paris Mini Guide
Poland
Portugal
Prague
Prague **D**
Provence
& the Côte D'Azur
Pyrenees
Romania
Rome
Rome **D**
Sardinia
Scandinavia
Sicily
Slovenia
Spain
St Petersburg
Sweden
Switzerland
Tenerife &
La Gomera **D**
Turkey
Tuscany & Umbria
Venice & The Veneto
Venice **D**
Vienna

Asia
Bali & Lombok
Bangkok
Beijing
Cambodia
China

Goa
Hong Kong & Macau
Hong Kong
& Macau **D**
India
Indonesia
Japan
Kerala
Korea
Laos
Malaysia, Singapore
& Brunei
Nepal
The Philippines
Rajasthan, Dehli
& Agra
Shanghai
Singapore
Singapore **D**
South India
Southeast Asia on a
Budget
Sri Lanka
Taiwan
Thailand
Thailand's Beaches
& Islands
Tokyo
Vietnam

Australasia
Australia
East Coast Australia
Fiji
Melbourne
New Zealand
Sydney
Tasmania

North America
Alaska
Baja California
Boston
California
Canada
Chicago
Colorado
Florida
The Grand Canyon
Hawaii
Honolulu **D**
Las Vegas **D**
Los Angeles &
Southern California
Maui **D**

Miami & South Florida
Montréal
New England
New York City
New York City **D**
New York City Mini
Orlando & Walt
Disney World® **D**
Oregon &
Washington
San Francisco
San Francisco **D**
Seattle
Southwest USA
Toronto
USA
Vancouver
Washington DC
Yellowstone & The
Grand Tetons
Yosemite

Caribbean
& Latin America
Antigua & Barbuda **D**
Argentina
Bahamas
Barbados **D**
Belize
Bolivia
Brazil
Buenos Aires
Cancùn & Cozumel **D**
Caribbean
Central America on a
Budget
Chile
Costa Rica
Cuba
Dominican Republic
Ecuador
Guatemala
Jamaica
Mexico
Peru
Puerto Rico
St Lucia **D**
South America on a
Budget
Trinidad & Tobago
Yucatán

D: Rough Guide
DIRECTIONS for
short breaks

Available from all good bookstores

"The most accurate maps in the world"

San Jose Mercury News

ROUGH GUIDE MAP

France

1:1,000,000 · 1 INCH: 15.8 MILES · 1CM: 10KM

CITY MAPS 25 titles
Amsterdam · Athens · Barcelona · Berlin
Boston · Brussels · Chicago · Dublin
Florence & Siena · Frankfurt · Hong Kong
Lisbon · London · Los Angeles · Madrid
Marrakesh · Miami · New York City · Paris
Prague · Rome · San Francisco · Toronto
Venice · Washington DC
US$8.99   Can$13.99   £4.99

COUNTRY & REGIONAL MAPS 48 titles
Algarve · Andalucía · Argentina · Australia
Baja California · Brittany · Crete
Croatia · Cuba · Cyprus · Czech Republic
Dominican Republic · Dubai · Egypt · Greece
Guatemala & Belize · Iceland · Ireland
Kenya · Mexico · Morocco · New Zealand
Northern Spain · Peru · Portugal · Sicily
South Africa · South India · Sri Lanka
Tenerife · Thailand · Trinidad & Tobago
Tuscany · Yucatán Peninsula and more.
US$9.99   Can$13.99   £5.99

Plastic waterproof map
ideal for planning and touring

waterproof • rip-proof • amazing value
BROADEN YOUR HORIZONS

ROUGH GUIDES

Sinh Balo
Adventure Travel

Specializing in cycling trips
Cruise up the Mekong river
   to Angkor temples / Cambodia
Family & study tours throughout Vietnam
Customized / special interest journeys

off the beaten track

Sinhbalo Adventure Travel
283/20 Pham Ngu Lao St.
District 1. HCM City. Vietnam.
Tel: (++84 8) 38376766 (3 lines)
Fax: (++84 8) 38367682

www.sinhbalo.com | www.cyclingvietnam.net